# THE RISE OF Militant

Militant's 30 years
Peter Taaffe

Dedicated to all Militant supporters and all those full-time comrades who have ensured Militant has appeared for thirty years, especially the comrades in the production departments.

cover design by Alan Hardman

# THE RISE OF
# Militant

## Militant's 30 years
## Peter Taaffe

Published by Militant Publications

In writing this book, I have received help from many comrades and friends, too numerous to mention here. However, the following deserve special acknowledgement for their encouragement, work, criticism and advice, without which this book would not have seen the light of day: Manny for his herculean efforts in typing the many manuscripts; Josie Nichols, Rebecca Bennet and Helen Redwood for additional typing; as well as Kevin Parslow for gathering materials, and for his exacting research and famous ability to remember and verify facts; Mike Waddington who has been unflagging in his determination to ensure publication; Lynn Walsh who always encourages through invaluable comments, suggestions and criticism; Martin Milne and Sheena Macdonald for typesetting, Ken Smith and Roger Shrives for proofreading; Jim Blair for his cartoons and Alan Hardman for his cartoons and design.

I would also like to thank all those comrades who have sustained *Militant* over the years. I deeply regret not being able to mention all of them by name. Indeed, I have not been able to mention even all the main participants in the struggle to build *Militant*. I hope they will forgive me. Last but not least a special word of thanks to those comrades whose technical skills and labour ensured that we eventually published this book.

The Rise of Militant - Militant's 30 Years

By Peter Taaffe

© Militant Publications

First Edition November 1995

British Library Cataloguing in Publication Data

ISBN No 0 906582 - 47 - 4

Published by Militant Publications

Typeset by Eastway Offset Ltd (TU)

Printed by Biddles Ltd of Guilford

Distribution by World Socialist Books<br>3/13 Hepscott Road, London. E9 5HB<br>Telephone 0181-533 3311

# Contents

| | |
|---|---|
| PREFACE | 7 |
| 1. MILITANT: ROOTS AND EARLY YEARS | 14 |
| 2. AN INTERNATIONAL OUTLOOK | 23 |
| 3. MILITANT AND WILSON'S GOVERNMENT | 33 |
| 4. NORTHERN IRELAND: THE TROUBLES | 39 |
| 5. TORY GOVERNMENT 1970-74 | 46 |
| 6. INTERNATIONAL EVENTS 1970-74 | 63 |
| 7. THE RISE OF MILITANT | 71 |
| 8. THE WORKING CLASS ON THE MOVE: INTERNATIONAL EVENTS 1974-75 | 85 |
| 9. A LABOUR GOVERNMENT - BUT WHERE'S THE SOCIALISM? | 89 |
| 10. ENTER MILITANT STAGE LEFT | 98 |
| 11. SPAIN, PORTUGAL AND ETHIOPIA | 104 |
| 12. THE SOCIALIST OPPOSITION GROWS | 110 |
| 13. THE CRITICAL POINT | 117 |
| 14. THE WINTER OF DISCONTENT: BEGINNINGS | 129 |
| 15. THE WINTER OF DISCONTENT: HIGH TIDE | 138 |
| 16. GENERAL ELECTION: THATCHER TO POWER | 147 |
| 17. THATCHER'S CHALLENGE TO THE LABOUR MOVEMENT | 159 |
| 18. H-BLOCKS AND SOLIDARNOSC | 170 |
| 19. MILITANT SURGES | 175 |
| 20. THE FALKLANDS/MALVINAS WAR | 189 |
| 21. TOWARDS EXPULSIONS | 196 |
| 22. EXPELLED... INTO THE MOVEMENT | 209 |
| 23. A WORKERS' MP ON A WORKERS' WAGE: LIVERPOOL AND COVENTRY | 214 |
| 24. DARING TO FIGHT | 222 |
| 25. THE MINERS' STRIKE 1984-85 | 228 |
| 26. INTO ILLEGALITY IN LIVERPOOL | 248 |
| 27. SCHOOL STUDENTS' STRIKE | 252 |
| 28. LIVERPOOL: ROUND TWO | 257 |
| 29. WINSTON, WESTLAND & WAPPING | 273 |

| | |
|---|---|
| 30. THE FIGHT AGAINST THE WITCH-HUNT | 279 |
| 31. MILITANT AT HIGH TIDE | 290 |
| 32. 1987 GENERAL ELECTION | 295 |
| 33. THE POLL TAX: EARLY DAYS | 308 |
| 34. RUSSIA, TROTSKY AND THE COLLAPSE OF STALINISM | 323 |
| 35. MILITANT IN TRANSITION | 343 |
| 36. INTO TOP GEAR | 348 |
| 37. THE GATHERING STORM | 360 |
| 38. 31 MARCH 1990 | 366 |
| 39. THE RIOT | 380 |
| 40. DEFENDING NON-PAYERS | 390 |
| 41. INTERNATIONAL CHALLENGES & A HISTORICAL SETBACK | 395 |
| 42. THE GULF WAR | 414 |
| 43. THE POLL TAX IS BEATEN | 426 |
| 44. MILITANT FACES A BREAKAWAY | 433 |
| 45. TWO TRENDS IN MILITANT | 445 |
| 46. SCOTTISH MILITANT LABOUR | 453 |
| 47. 1992 GENERAL ELECTION | 464 |
| 48. NEW WORLD DISORDER | 476 |
| 49. FIGHTING FOR SOCIALISM | 482 |
| 50. MILITANT LABOUR LAUNCHED | 504 |
| 51. FIGHTING FASCISM | 512 |
| 52. THE BALKANS | 521 |
| 53. ON OUR WAY TO WEMBLEY | 528 |
| 54. OUR THIRTIETH YEAR - STRUGGLE, SOLIDARITY, SOCIALISM | 536 |
| CONCLUSION | 552 |

# PREFACE

THE IDEA for this book arose when *Militant* was discussing how best to celebrate its 30th anniversary in October 1994. One suggestion, successfully carried out in October and November of that year, was for a national speaking tour by myself, together with Tommy Sheridan and others. A series of very successful meetings was held in all the main areas of Britain. At the same time it was suggested that I should gather together the main articles from *Militant's* 30-year history, for publication in a small book. However, once I began to investigate the viability of such a project it became clear that the publication of a few "representative" articles would not do justice to the subject. Thus the idea of a book celebrating our 30 years of publication took shape.

However, the very scope of such an undertaking - compressing the events of 30 years into one volume - proved to be a much more formidable task than I anticipated. This book could not be produced at "leisure". As general secretary of Militant Labour, I am in a position which demands intense day-to-day involvement in the activities of this organisation. Therefore the writing of this book had to be "fitted in" alongside the more pressing daily tasks of building Militant Labour and participating in the struggle. This is the main reason for the delay in publishing.

Another reason for delay was the difficulty in editing and selecting for publication those extracts from *Militant's* history which best reflect its political position at each stage in its development, as well as the continuity of thought and approach which determined its political approach. This book is not primarily an "organisational" account of *Militant's* evolution. Some organisational details are included but these are kept to a minimum. This is because the aim of this book is essentially to trace out the ideas which motivated *Militant* and its adherents first to undertake publication of the newspaper and then to sustain it, in good times and bad, over a 30-year period.

Right from its inception, *Militant* has been scrupulously democratic, both in its organisation and in its approach towards its politcal opponents in the labour movement. Decisions, including the one which led to the publication of *Militant*, were determined democratically by committed supporters. Those who paid money regularly to *Militant* and were involved in our local discussion groups determined its policy. Leading "Militants" did not have a vast apparatus or mighty resources compelling obedience to its political line. Decisions were arrived at through discussion and debate. At the outset there were a number of leading supporters, based in London, who constituted the National Editorial Board (NEB), who held positions of authority and respect within *Militant*'s ranks. They were elected and subject to recall at any time. At the time when *Militant* was launched and for a period afterwards these leading members were Ted Grant, Peter Taaffe, Keith Dickinson, Clare Doyle (who joined a little later), Ellis Hillman (who subsequently parted company from *Militant*) and Arthur Deane.

Small forces were involved at the beginning. But decisions were only arrived at after intense discussion and debate. Indeed, the intensity of the debate in the Marxist movement sometimes is in inverse proportion to the number of participants! The most controversial aspect at the beginning was over the name. The choice of *Militant* was not initially favoured by many. But the market place for "revolutionary names" is very crowded, which makes the choice of a name for a new publication very difficult indeed. However, the name *Militant* had an honourable pedigree in the history of the Trotskyist movement. It had been the name of an earlier, very small, Trotskyist group, in Britain. It was also the name of the newspaper of the American Socialist Workers Party, which worked closely with Trotsky in the 1930s. However, by the early 1960s the leadership of the SWP was at variance with the leaders of what became *Militant* in Britain. For this reason, if no other, most of the pioneers of *Militant* were not enthralled by the choice of this name. It was accepted at the time, largely because no other viable alternative was on hand. But in the psychology of human beings, names, both of individuals and organisations, become associated in the mind with what they come to represent. And in one important respect the name *Militant* did stand for what its proponents intended: the aim of winning in the first instance, the most conscious, combative, fighting, i.e. militant, sections of the working class. An incident outside a factory illustrated what *Militant* was all about. A supporter sold the paper outside this factory to a regular group of workers. Over a three-week period he observed that another individual from the factory stood watching, noting those who bought the paper. Fearing that this was a management "nark" or supervisor, the seller approached this individual. Rather than being a management stooge he stated that he was in fact the chief shop steward, i.e. the convenor of the workers in the factory. He was observing those who bought the *Militant*, because he wanted to identify those workers capable of becoming shop stewards! Those who were prepared to stand out, who in turn were those who were prepared to buy *Militant,* were leadership material in the eyes of this convenor.

Like the convenor of this factory, but from a broader point of view, *Militant* set its sights in the first instance on the more conscious, politically aware sections of the working class. The winning of these layers, who we consider are "the salt of the earth", is the key to winning the mass of the working class at a later stage.

*Militant,* through deeds as well as words, became, in time, a substantial force within the British labour movement. In the beginning, however, small forces were ranged behind *Militant*'s banner. But the history of the Trotskyist movement in Britain did not begin with *Militant*. There is a long tradition going right back to the 1930s and Trotsky himself, of Trotskyist groups and organisations which endeavoured to find a base within the labour movement and the working class. Some of those who helped to form *Militant*, such as Ted Grant and the Deanes (Jimmy, Gertie, Brian and Arthur), had been involved in the Trotskyist movement for decades. The author does not subscribe to the view that the struggles of small groupings are of no historical significance. As Trotsky pointed out, the theoretical battles which were fought out amongst small groups of Russian revolutionaries in exile, in the back alleys of Paris, the pubs in London or flea-infested barns in Brussels were part of a necessary process, sharpening the political weapons without which the greatest social overturn in history, the Russian revolution, would not have been possible. Without the struggles of past generations of Marxists, particularly the pioneers of Trotskyism in Britain, the success of *Militant* would not have been possible.

The youthful adherents who joined the ranks of what became

*Militant* in the early 1960s, stood on the shoulders of those who maintained the Trotskyist tradition in the most difficult period. However, it is not the intention, nor is it possible within the scope of this work, to deal with this history. Others will have to fulfil that task. The purpose of this work is to show how *Militant* was able to move from "just another" small group into a force able to weld the ideas of Marxism to mass movements of workers. *Militant*, it is true, did not arise fully formed. A preparatory period of assembling new cadres, particularly in the early 1960s, had been undertaken before the launch of *Militant* was possible. Merseyside was an area where Trotskyism, in the form of those who subsequently supported the formation of *Militant*, had put down firmer roots than elsewhere in the labour movement and the working class. Within the Labour Party the Walton constituency was the only one in which the Marxists were able to achieve any appreciable success. Year after year they argued the case for the general programme of socialism, both at the level of the Liverpool Trades Council and Labour Party, which was then a joint body, and at national Labour Party conference. Walton Labour Party remained a stronghold for the forces of Marxism in the late 1950s.

In 1959 George McCartney, a supporter of *Socialist Fight* (the forerunner of *Militant*), was selected as Labour's prospective parliamentary candidate for Walton. In this battle he easily defeated Woodrow Wyatt, then a supporter of *Tribune* but now a rabid right-winger. Unfortunately the 1959 general election, against all expectations, was a victory for the Tories. Despite a tremendous campaign, Labour failed to win Walton.

Among those who joined Walton Labour Party in 1957, thereby coming into contact with the ideas of Marxism, was Keith Dickinson, one of the five *Militant* Editorial Board members expelled from the Labour Party in 1983. Many others played an important role in the development of the forces of *Socialist Fight*. Pat Wall, who had been secretary of Garston CLP at the age of 16 back in 1952, played an important role, as did Don Hughes, Pauline Knight (who subsequently married Pat Wall) and a group of printers including Reg Lewis and John MacDonald.

I came into contact with *Socialist Fight* in 1960 initially after meeting Don Hughes. Before then, support for CND was combined with a keen interest in the basic ideas of socialism and what

I imagined was "communism". After attending a Labour Party public meeting I was contacted by John MacDonald from *Socialist Fight*. At that time a ferocious battle was taking place within the Labour Party Young Socialists on Merseyside between the adherents of *Socialist Fight* and those who subscribed to the ideas of the Socialist Labour League (who subsequently became the Workers' Revolutionary Party). I was invited to meetings of the Socialist Labour League, and had discussions with their Merseyside organiser. Why was I attracted to the much smaller *Socialist Fight*? With very little experience in the labour movement I was nevertheless repelled by the narrow political sectarianism - not to say authoritarianism - of the SLL. We record later how the supporters of *Socialist Fight* won a majority within the Young Socialists.

However, with the decision to publish *Militant*, it was also decided that I be moved from Merseyside to London to become the paper's full-time Editor. I was promised a £10 weekly wage and secure accommodation. However, the accommodation and the £10 wages remained on the plane of "theory", never actually materialising for years. In the well-worn tradition of Marxists and revolutionaries, I was compelled first of all to sleep on the floor of a supporter in Balham, south London. But when a small factional dispute took place, I found myself locked out of this room, sometimes forced to sleep on other people's floors and once or twice spending sleepless nights in the entrances of subways, before finally a decision was taken that I should sleep "illegally" in an office which *Militant* had rented from the Independent Labour Party (ILP). I was compelled to do this for six months in what became an almost cat-and-mouse existence with the caretaker of the building. Not entirely enamoured of Trotskyists, this individual arrived at the ILP headquarters very early every morning to run the ILP bookshop which was located in the basement. This character spent a large part of his time, between 7 a.m. and 9 a.m., trying to catch me sneaking from the first floor office out of the door to take a wash in the public toilets just over the road. Fortunately, the agility of youth had an advantage over older legs and the cat never actually caught the mouse! This precarious existence, both financial and personal, would not have been possible without the help of committed supporters of *Militant*.

*Militant International Review* (MIR) from 1969 onwards was our main theoretical journal. It was first produced intermittently. In time it became a quarterly, then a bi-monthly. In 1995 the MIR was replaced by a new monthly journal *Socialism Today*, edited by Lynn Walsh.

The articles in these journals contain some of the most detailed and penetrating insights into British and world developments over the last two or three decades.

From 1985 Clive Heemskirk, who gained invaluable experience as Militant student organiser from 1981-85, played an indispensable role alongside different editors in the production of our theoretical journal including our new monthly.

There are many very good comrades who over 30 years have made a big contribution to the building of *Militant* and who I have not been able to mention in this work. My sincere apologies to them; due weight will be given to all of them when a more detailed organisational as well as political history will be written about *Militant* in the future. But I hope they will forgive me for mentioning the contribution of Linda Taaffe. She joined me in London in 1966. Since then, both on a personal level, and politically, she has been steadfast in the cause of socialism and Marxism. To all who know her, and particularly to the author, obviously, she has always been a source of encouragement and love, always demonstrating supreme confidence in the goals which we are struggling for.

The fainthearts and sceptics can ask, "how nearer is the realisation of this goal, socialism, which *Militant* set out to achieve?" Look around at your world consumed by racial hatred, ethnic division, war, poverty and unemployment. The best answer to this was given by Leon Trotsky at the dawn of this century. In a dialogue between a pessimist and an optimist he wrote:

> And now that century has come! What has it brought with it at the outset?
> In France - the poisonous foam of racial hatred; in Austria - nationalist strife... in South Africa - the agony of a tiny people, which is being murdered by a colossus; on the "free" island itself - triumphant hymns to the victorious greed of jingoist jobbers; dramatic "complications" in the east; rebellions of starving popular masses in Italy, Bulgaria, Romania... Hatred and murder, famine and blood...
> It seems as if the new century, this gigantic newcomer, were bent at the very moment of its appearance to drive the optimist into absolute pes-

simism and civic nirvana.

- Death to Utopia! Death to faith! Death to love! Death to hope! thunders the twentieth century in salvos of fire and in the rumbling of guns.

- Surrender, you pathetic dreamer. Here I am, your long awaited twentieth century, your "future".

- No, replies the unhumbled optimist: You - you are only the *present*.[1]

Rotting capitalism is incapable of showing a way forward either for the British or the world working class. Nor can the right-wing Labour leaders show a way out of the impasse.

World socialism is the only way of preventing social and political, as well as environmental disaster, on a monumental scale. Consciousness of what needs to be done lags far behind what Marxists call the "objective conditions" of capitalism in Britain and on a world scale. This contradiction, however, cannot last forever. Consciousness will catch up with these objective conditions. When that happens there will be huge leaps in understanding, particularly by the working class. In the course of such movements the ideas of *Militant*, which have already given a glimpse of what is possible for the British working class, will become the political weapons through which the labour movement and the working class will carve out a new world.

Peter Taaffe, October 1995.

# 1.
# MILITANT: ROOTS AND EARLY YEARS

MILITANT AND its supporters were instrumental in humbling Thatcher in Liverpool in 1984. *Militant* supplied the political and organisational backbone to the mighty anti-poll tax movement which buried this tax and consigned Thatcher to political oblivion. *Militant* supporters played a decisive role in the construction of Youth against Racism in Europe (YRE) which helped to stop the fascist BNP in its tracks. This body also organised 40,000 youth to march through Brussels in October 1994, the biggest all-European anti-fascist march ever.

*Militant*'s involvement in these and many other important struggles of the working class in Britain and internationally have earned it the scorn and hatred of the capitalists, their representatives in the media and their echoes within the labour movement, the right-wing Labour and trade union leaders.

A virtual cottage industry has sprung up, dissecting, commenting on and seeking to explain the "*Militant* phenomenon". Literally thousands of items have appeared in the capitalist press, acres of newsprint have been used up, numerous television and radio programmes have been produced in a vain attempt to explain away the reasons for *Militant*'s success. At least five books, dealing with *Militant*'s role, its history and future have appeared (including one in German).

In Britain also, academia has taken a keen interest in *Militant*. Professors have produced learned treatises. Various departments have organised special seminars (needless to say, without a single *Militant* supporter invited). "Papers" and theses galore have appeared.

And yet in all of this no scientific explanation can be found which even begins to explain why *Militant* became an important factor and, on some occasions, a decisive factor in the battles of the labour movement, particularly in the 1980s and early 1990s. Most commentators scarcely venture beyond a "conspiratorial" view of

*Militant*'s success. This superficial, not to say childish, view is incapable of providing even a clue to how *Militant* rose from seeming obscurity to become a durable and important force within the British working-class movement. What were its origins, policies, views on future developments in Britain and the labour movement which allowed it to capture the imagination of important groups of workers while others failed? The answer to these questions can only be found in an investigation of the objective conditions and the subjective role of *Militant* which at each stage led to its formation and growth. Such an approach will also be able to tell us whether *Militant* can repeat its successes in the future.

*Militant* was launched as a monthly publication in October 1964. It was not, of course, the first Marxist journal to appear in Britain. The history of the labour movement, and of the Marxist movement in particular, is littered with ill-fated attempts to form newspapers and organisations. Indeed, some of the founders of *Militant* had themselves been involved with such attempts in the post-1945 period. *Militant*, however, not only endured but has now became a household name.

The 1950s and 1960s were a period when the right-wing of the Labour Party and trade unions exercised almost an iron grip on the movement. A long economic upswing from 1950 to 1974 strengthened capitalism and, at least in the advanced industrial countries, the idea that working-class people could win some improvements that would build up over time into a substantial change in their lives. Those who advocated these ideas were described by Marxists as "reformists". They argued that by piecemeal reforms the wealth and power of the minority in society, the capitalists, could be gradually transferred to the majority, the working class and its allies the middle class etc. The possessing classes, however, will not voluntarily relinquish their wealth and power. Even a well known right wing Labour reformist, George Brown, deputy prime minister in the Wilson government of 1964-70 admitted: "No privileged group disappears from history without a struggle." In the post-war period, a few crumbs from the very rich table of the capitalists were allowed to fall into the lap of the working class. The real living standards of the working class advanced, and the idea of fundamental change - the possibility of a new socialist society - was regarded as a distant ideal, for some, very distant. The historical task of Marxism in the 1950s and even at the time of the launch of *Militant* was to defend the basic ideas of Marxism against those who claimed that Marxism was no longer relevant. That task, which was admirably fulfilled by the older generation which founded *Militant*, was absolutely essential as a means of maintaining the continuity of ideas and organisation which led back to Trotsky and his followers in the 1930s. Our journal has had a big effect on the labour movement. It gathered support on a greater scale than any other comparable organisation, in Britain or internationally.

## COUNTDOWN TO MILITANT

The early pioneers of *Militant* were joined by a new generation brought into political activity in the late 1950s and the early 1960s as a result of the radicalisation of a layer of youth. The growth of the Campaign for Nuclear Disarmament (CND) and the apprentices' strikes of 1960 and 1964 were symptoms of this. It would be amongst youth that *Militant* would make its most rapid progress.

A number of attempts were made to produce a journal before October 1964. *Socialist Fight*, edited by Ted Grant, appeared very irregularly.

A section of the youth in Liverpool produced a journal called *Youth for Socialism*. This followed the abandonment in 1963 of a futile attempt to work together with fellow Labour Party members, the International Socialists (subsequently the Socialist Workers' Party), in a joint youth paper called *Young Guard*. The Young Socialists (YS), Labour's youth wing, which had been re-established in 1960, was at this stage under the control of the youth supporters of the Socialist Labour League (SLL - subsequently the Workers' Revolutionary Party). They had an overwhelming majority on the YS National Committee, which they used ruthlessly to enhance their position and undermine, usually by denigration, their opponents on the left. This was an organisation using methods more akin to Stalinism, with verbal and even physical intimidation, rather than the open, democratic approach of genuine Trotskyism.

The youthful adherents of *Socialist Fight* were in a very small minority even in what subsequently became a bastion for its ideas. In the Merseyside Federation of Young Socialists, between 1960 and 1963, SLL supporters controlled 23 out of 25 Young Socialist branches, the exceptions being the Bootle branch, in which Ted Mooney, a key supporter of *Militant*, held sway, and the Birkenhead branch. But because we patiently argued for genuine Marxist ideas, the support for the SLL gradually withered. Seeing the writing on the wall, they decided to split from the Labour Party in 1964, sometimes deliberately confronting the 'bureaucracy" as a means of provoking expulsions.

Despite the odds, which could be compared to the task of a climber confronting a sheer cliff face, the adherents of what was to become *Militant* waged a campaign throughout 1964 for the funds to launch a journal.

After much discussion, and without complete unanimity, the prevailing view was that the name of the paper should be *Militant*. Its founders did not want a colourless banner, but something that was going to stand out, which would stand for a radical socialist programme and fighting policies.

## MILITANT LAUNCHED

The first issue appeared in October 1964 and to begin with was eight pages. Colour was even added on the second edition of the paper but within two issues the editors were forced to retreat to a four-page monthly. Its supporters managed to sustain the journal through sales and the collection of donations in that first, very difficult year.

*Militant* recognised that at that stage the Labour Party was the mass party of the working class. Not only did it have the electoral support of millions, it was backed by the trade unions and had thousands of members. It had a political life, with debates and a democracy that the party leadership would often attempt to restrict. It also had a youth section - the Young Socialists.

So *Militant* was for Labour, but with socialist policies. At the same time, it looked to the youth, because young people were naturally more receptive to the ideas of change. So the masthead of the paper read '*Militant*: For Labour and Youth'.

The progress of *Militant* from 1964 onwards justified that approach. In the first instance, however, the number of adherents to

*Militant* was very small, no more than 40 nationally, and some of these were not really active. The main base of *Militant* at this stage was in Merseyside, with small forces in London and in South Wales.

In 1963-64 a group of students at Sussex University, Clare Doyle, Bob Edwards, Roger Silverman, Lynn Walsh, Alan Woods and others, many of whom were to play a key role in the history of *Militant*, also supported the ideas and programme of *Militant*.

## ISSUE NUMBER ONE: LABOUR

Despite its small numbers, the paper struck an optimistic note right from the beginning. The first editorial commented:

> We need to educate and be educated. In the beginning, ours can only be a monthly voice, but within that confine we will endeavour to deal with the main problems that face the movement... The most important thing is that we wish to tell the truth to the working class against the lies and the exaggerations of the capitalist class and the half-truths of Labour's officialdom.[1]

The first issue came out at the same time as the election of the first Labour government for 13 years. It devoted space to an analysis of the problems that would confront that government. *Militant* commented:

> When the long post-war economic upswing falters and the boom gives way to recession, then the employers will try to unload the burden onto the shoulders of the workers... Capitalism is still a treadmill with only short periods of uneasy solace for the workers. It can only offer, in the long run, war or slump, annihilation or penury, to the people of Britain and all other countries.[2]

And then in a warning to the Labour right, we commented:

> The Labour leaders' policy of 'playing it cool', of not launching an offensive against the Tories, has had the opposite effect to that which they expected They are showing themselves as 'safe' and 'responsible' leaders. Not fundamentally different from the Tories, the Labour leaders have played into [Tory Prime Minister] Home and company's hands.[3]

As it happened, Wilson managed to scrape into power with a

tiny majority. Warning of the pitfalls that confronted the Labour government, we wrote: "It is impossible to organise and control the resources of Britain while the octopus of private ownership of the major resources remains."

Militant called for a

> detailed plan of production for the next five years, on the basis of state ownership of all industry employing more than 20 workers, drawing on shop stewards, technicians and even small shopkeepers who despite their conservatism are the next to be axed by the monopolies...
> This is the only 'practical' plan which could guarantee victory for Labour at the polls and ensure a change in society and make a return to Tory reaction impossible. Labour may well win [electorally] without such a programme, but [in the end] it will surely go down to bitter defeat, crushed by big business.[4]

The print run was a modest 2,000 but in the second edition it was reported that:

> Within a fortnight of the first issue rolling off the presses, it was completely sold out, with demands for fresh orders coming in which were unable to be met... Because of this success, we are upping the print order from 2,000 to 3,000.[5]

## ISSUE TWO: THE APPRENTICES' STRIKE

A strike of apprentices broke out on 2 November, 1964, over pay and conditions. This illustrated what was to be an enduring feature of the paper, a serious attitude towards the trade unions and industrial struggle. *Militant* and its supporters were determined to find a base amongst working-class youth in particular.

Other left organisations were larger at this stage, some claiming to be 'Trotskyist', but none was able to capture the imagination of youth or organise it in action. Indeed, some of them, like the International Socialists (subsequently the SWP), were a pole of attraction mainly to students. They had little or no base amongst workers.

The 1964 strike was not the first time that the Marxists, who later launched *Militant* had intervened in such a movement. In

1960, after the apprentices in Clydeside had walked out on strike over their conditions, their example spread to Merseyside and other parts of the country. Upwards of 100,000 youth were involved in action. On Merseyside the chair of the apprentices' strike committee was Ted Mooney, the secretary was Terry Harrison. The latter was already a Marxist and a committed supporter of *Socialist Fight*, while Ted Mooney, through his experiences in the apprentices' committee, joined forces with *Socialist Fight*, subsequently becoming a key *Militant* supporter on Merseyside.

The youth supporters of *Militant* drew on this experience in seeking to organise and mobilise the apprentices. Ted Mooney and I played leading roles, together with Harry Dowling and Dave Galashan, in organising an apprentices' strike in one factory, English Electric, on the East Lancashire Road. It was clear that there was massive dissatisfaction with the rates of pay and conditions of the apprentices, and there was widespread support for a reduction in the five-year term of apprenticeship.

At packed meetings in Liverpool and elsewhere a decision was taken to call out the apprentices in November. In Merseyside, Manchester, Dundee and London, as well as many other centres, apprentices struck. They faced big obstacles. Outright intimidation was resorted to by the employers. There was also a complete refusal from officials of the Amalgamated Engineering Union to give them the slightest help. Bert Rule, the Merseyside district officer, publicly threatened apprentices in the *Liverpool Echo* with serious consequences if they downed tools.

They calculated that inexperienced apprentices would cringe at their threats. Cammell Laird apprentices were told in no uncertain terms what lay in store for them if they walked out. A poster was displayed throughout Merseyside's largest shipyard showing a large boot and the words 'Don't strike'. This had some effect amongst inexperienced apprentices. Even where the apprentices came out on strike, as in Manchester, police dogs were used on the picket lines.

The electricians' trade union, which was the ETU (subsequently EETPU and now merged in the AEEU) under right-wing control, as it still is today, played a particularly pernicious role, circulating a letter warning apprentices of the dire consequences if they should come out on strike.

The strike of apprentices was only partially successful, with about 20,000 out of 70,000 engineering apprentices downing tools. Nevertheless, a partial victory was gained when the union leaders subsequently agreed to take up the most important demand: 'Full negotiation rights for apprentices'. Many of the other demands on pay and conditions were subsequently pressed in negotiations.

The apprentices' strike was significant from a number of points of view. It demonstrated in action the mood amongst engineering apprentices. It also steeled a new generation of Marxists in how to organise workers for struggle, above all, how to relate the general ideas of Marxism to the real movement of the working class.

## KEEPING THE SHOW ON THE ROAD

The first years of *Militant* existence underlined the paucity of resources, both in terms of numbers and finance.

At the first all-London public meeting, then called *Militant Readers' Meetings* held on 15 August, 1965, with myself in the chair, Ted Grant, the political editor, spoke to 50 people. The collection realised the princely sum of £4 12s 6d (£4.63).

In March of that year the paper proudly announced "the editorial board have been forced to rent a room to work from." This 'headquarters' was at 197 Kings Cross Road, near Kings Cross Station, in a building owned by the Independent Labour Party. So poor was *Militant* that it announced:

> we are also able to let the room for meetings, and any Labour, trade union or Co-operative organisation interested in booking the room, especially during the week, will be welcome to make enquiries. There is seating for up to 30 and the charge will be purely nominal, but will help us pay our rent. [6]

In reality, *Militant* did not have even the first month's rent for this room. But its adherents were confident that they would find the resources that would match the boldness of their ideas.

In the first year, *Militant* set its sights on a collection of £500 for the fighting fund. Subsequently, the capitalist press were to scream in horror that *Militant* was generating £1 million income a year. And yet it was only able to do this by a combination of clear perspectives, a well-thought out programme of demands and a meticulous attitude towards collecting the resources needed to produce a newspaper and the growing band of full-timers (the term soon adopted to describe those who worked full-time for *Militant*) that went with it.

Although Keith Dickinson was not a full-timer, he did part-time work, making enormous sacrifices and playing an indispensible role in assisting me in the first period after my move from Liverpool in 1964.

Throughout the Labour government of 1964-66 and following its re-election until 1970, *Militant* argued for a socialist policy for the government and the labour movement. We pointed out that if the government remained within the confines of capitalism, it would be forced to do the bidding of big business. The Wilson government actually went from reforms, very small ones in the first period, to counter-reforms ie cuts in living standards, as *Militant* predicted.

Our ideas found their most receptive audience amongst youth. At the time of the launch of the paper, the Young Socialists, after the departure of *Keep Left*, was relaunched as the Labour Party Young Socialists. Because of the disastrous experience of the SLL control of the YS, the LPYS was heavily policed in the first period by the conservative Labour Party officialdom. It was not allowed to formulate its own policy and documents and resolutions were submitted to its conference by the National Executive Committee. Members of the LPYS National Committee were selected and appointed by the right wing. Nevertheless, at rank-and-file level Marxist ideas began to find an echo. John Ewers, YS representative from the South West, was won over to *Militant*'s ideas. Davy Dick, who represented Scotland, was a committed Marxist before he entered the LPYS National Committee. They formed a two-pronged Marxist attack on right-wing ideas on the LPYS National Committee.

# 2.
# AN INTERNATIONAL OUTLOOK

MILITANT HAS never been at all parochial or limited to just national horizons. Even when *Militant* had very few co-thinkers outside Britain, it always proceeded from an international standpoint. Socialism is international or it is nothing.

The great historical merit of capitalism was to develop the world market which made possible world history for the first time. In linking all countries together in one interdependent whole, it also developed the working class, whose interests transcended national boundaries.

"Imperialism" is used by Marxists to describe the economic domination (and in the past direct military control also) of the advanced industrial countries of Europe, America and Japan over the peoples of Asia, Africa and Latin America. If anything their economic weight compared to the ex-colonial world has grown enormously in the last few decades.

The giant transnationals both exploit the workers in the advanced industrial countries and super-exploit those in the "Third World". In the age of 'globalisation', of the General Agreement on Tariffs and Trade (GATT), of the North American Free Trade Association (NAFTA), of the shifting of capital from one country to another, it is evident that the working class needs to organise: first on a continental and then on a world scale. This is obviously necessary at the level of trade unions. The transnationals close down factories in the advanced industrial countries, shifting them to areas of 'low labour costs'.

Some workers are beginning to see the need to put forward the common claims of workers on a continental basis - in Europe this will be the trend in the next period. A worldwide trade union drive is also necessary. No less is the need to organise politically on a world scale. Right from the outset *Militant*, perhaps more than any other journal in Britain, gave a big part of its pages over to international coverage.

In our second issue we covered the fall of Khrushchev, leader of the Soviet Union. "Stalinism" is a term used by Marxists since the time of Leon Trotsky in the 1930s to describe the political regimes of Russia, Eastern Europe, Cuba, China, etc, which rested on nationalised planned economies. They were one-party totalitarian regimes, where a privileged bureaucratic elite dominated the state and society. The development of these countries, particularly of the USSR, was a big issue for Marxists. *Militant* pointed to the achievements of the USSR:

> On the one side enormous scientific achievements enabling the USSR to challenge, and, in terms of the more modern branches of science, to outstrip the strongest capitalist power. On the other side, a political structure which allows the total removal of the seemingly all-powerful head of state, whilst the masses, including the rank and file of the Communist Party of the Soviet Union, stand by as passive observers.

*Militant* stood by Trotsky's analysis, supporting the gains of the planned economy but calling for an additional political revolution to bring about genuine socialist democracy.

The crisis within the bureaucratic elite, reflected in the removal of Khrushchev, indicated:

> the contradiction between socialised and planned production and the stranglehold of a bureaucratic caste. The new leadership, faced with the same problems, will give the same answers, zig-zagging between the right and left, concessions and repression.[1]

## VIETNAM

In the first formative years of *Militant* the key international issue was the Vietnam war. In the analysis of the causes of the war, as well as the formulation of demands to be taken up by the labour movement, *Militant*'s coverage, while not as comprehensive as other journals, stands out as a shining example of the ability of Marxism to analyse and foresee events. As early as 1967, we pointed out:

> The mightiest war machine the world has ever seen is actually losing the war to an army of poverty-stricken peasants, to the people of South Vietnam.[2]

Lyndon Johnson, the US president who had replaced Kennedy after his assassination in 1963, had found his promise of a 'great society' being wasted away in the paddy fields of Vietnam. Even mighty US imperialism could not pursue a policy of 'guns *and* butter'. Arthur Schlesinger, former special assistant to Kennedy, wrote in 1967:

> The fight for equal opportunity for the negro, the war against poverty, the struggle to save the cities, the improvement of our schools - all must be starved for the sake of Vietnam... The Great Society is now, except for token gestures, dead.[3]

Thus early on, *Militant* pointed to the colossal contradictions in the position of US imperialism. If the US continued the war, it would mean a huge increase in arms expenditure, which in turn would mean a slashing of social expenditure at home, which was bound to lead to a revolt, particularly of the poor in the US. There would inevitably be more and more US fatalities. This would open up huge social divisions which could paralyse the military intervention in Vietnam.

No other political grouping was prepared to make such a bold prediction at a very early stage in the war. The victory of the Vietnamese would be a shattering blow to imperialism, particularly to the US giant, giving enormous impetus to the struggles of the workers and peasants throughout Asia. However, while *Militant* supported the struggle of the workers and peasants in Vietnam for national and social liberation, it did not uncritically support, as others did, the Stalinist leaders in North Vietnam and their counterparts leading the movement in the South.

Because of the social forces involved, predominantly peasant masses struggling for land and freedom from imperialism, any successful regime which would emerge from this struggle would not be a 'socialist' one. It would be a regime on the model of China or the Soviet Union, with a planned economy but ruled by a one-party totalitarian regime.

Others, claiming to be Marxist or even 'Trotskyist', gave uncritical support to the Vietnamese National Liberation Front (NLF). Because of the prevailing mood of uncritical adulation of the NLF leader Ho Chi Minh, on demonstrations the students mindlessly chanted "Ho, Ho, Ho Chi Minh". Some found themselves at the head of big movements of the youth in opposition to the Vietnam war, but they were not capable of substantially increasing their forces because their intervention was based on a false premise. As they were uncritically tail-ending the Stalinist leadership of the NLF, something they would repeat in all movements of a 'national liberationist' type, what point was there in workers or youth involved in that struggle joining them? Far better to identify with the real McCoy, that is Stalinism itself.

*Militant*'s slogans were clear: 'For the withdrawal of US imperialism and all imperialist forces.' The result of this would have been the collapse of the South Vietnamese regime, as subsequent events demonstrated. It was a puppet regime propped up by US bayonets.

## THE WORKING CLASS

Marx did not refer to the organised working class by accident. Only this class, organised and disciplined by large-scale production and industry, could develop the necessary social cohesion and combativity to carry through the tasks of the socialist revolution. The peasantry, by its very nature, is divided into different strata, the upper levels tending to merge with the capitalists. The lower levels of the peasantry are closer to the working class and, through economic ruin, tend to fall into the ranks of the working class. The same holds for the modern middle classes, both of the town and country areas.

Echoing the arguments of the ruling class, many 'Marxists' considered that the working class in the advanced industrial countries had been bought off, become 'bourgeoisified', and was therefore no longer the main agent for socialist change. This led them to seek salvation elsewhere, either in Tito in Yugoslavia, hailed as an 'unconscious' Trotskyist, or Mao Zedong or Fidel Castro. Echoing the false theories of those like Frantz Fanon (who based himself on the experience of the Algerian Revolution), the poor peasantry, the 'Fedayin' and guerrilla armies were seen as the forces to liberate the world from the yoke of landlordism and capitalism. The 'epicentre' of the world struggle for socialism now lay in the colonial and semi-colonial world.

*Militant* explained the significance of the events in the colonial and former-colonial world. The movement for national liberation, involving two-thirds of humankind, in the 1950s, 1960s and 1970s represented one of the most splendid movements in history. Millions of imperialism's slaves in Asia, Africa and Latin America threw off the chains of direct imperialist military domination, stepped onto the scene of history and tried to take their fate into their own hands.

Nevertheless, from a world point of view, the decisive forces for socialist change were still concentrated in the advanced industrial countries. This did not mean that the masses in the colonial and semi-colonial world should 'wait' until the workers of Europe, Japan and North America were ready to move into action. On the contrary, *Militant* gave support to the movement of the colonial peoples, both politically and organisationally, even when it was under the leadership of bourgeois or pro-bourgeois forces. This was done in solidarity with this movement and also because all blows against imperialism in the 'underdeveloped world' would ultimately benefit the struggle for socialism in the advanced industrial countries and on a world scale.

Because these movements were largely based on the peasants they were by their very nature limited. Even at that stage, *Militant* pointed to the future awakening of the working class in the former colonial and semi-colonial world. Decades of industrialisation and urbanisation had developed to the point where the strengthening proletariat was potentially the most powerful movement for change.

Even in the 1960s, *Militant* also pointed to the increased social tension, bordering on civil war, between the classes which had developed in some of the advanced or semi-advanced countries of Europe.

## TURNING POINT: FRANCE 1968

In April 1968, Ernest Mandel, leader of the Trotskyist United Secretariat of the Fourth International, spoke at a meeting in Caxton Hall, London, to his followers. On behalf of *Militant*, I spoke from the floor, questioning Mandel's writing-off of the working class of the industrial countries. Mandel's reply was that the working class of the advanced industrial countries was quiescent, was likely to remain so as long as the US dollar remained stable, and that this situation would not change for at least 20 years. His conclusion was that the 'epicentre' of the world revolution had shifted to the former colonial and semi-colonial world.

One month later, events erupted in Paris which were to culminate in the greatest general strike in history. Ten million workers occupied the factories and even the representatives of the French ruling class believed they faced overthrow.

*Militant* hailed the movement in France with the front-page slogan: "All power to French workers!"

> Ten million workers out! Hundreds of factories occupied and controlled by the workers! Schools taken over by pupils and progressive staff! Capitalist newspaper lies 'censored' by printing workers! TV lies censored by reporters and technicians! Universities taken over! Docks, post offices, ships, taken over! What a mighty demonstration of the invincible power of the working class when it begins to move! What a crushing blow to the cynics, sceptics and apologists for big business who have written off the working class as 'apathetic', 'bought off', etc - and to the professional, orthodox economists none of whose arduous study of the complex mechanics of capitalist economics could enable them to discern the gigantic force beneath the surface of modern society: the creator of the new society to come - the working class. How clear it should be to even the most politically uneducated workers that their French brothers would be in power today, but for the cowardly policies of the French labour and trade union leaders.[4]

The student movement began around relatively minor demands in one area, but after being attacked by the police, rapidly became a national mass campaign which preceded the movement of the working class:

> The *Daily Express* reported that 80 per cent of the population was for the students. The industrial workers and particularly the young ones were emboldened by the success: "The students came first. They acted as a spark. They caused the government to yield... they gave us the feeling that we could go ahead,' said one of them to a *Times* reporter.[5]

*Militant* reported:

> Even the farmers were in revolt at the rapid decrease in their incomes... A gigantic wave swept from one end of France to the other. Not only

the industrial workers but the bank employees, white-collar workers, and the catering workers have responded to the call to strike. While only ten per cent were unionised, over 50 per cent of the labour force is involved which is incontestible proof of the revolutionary energy and determination that has been unleashed. As in all revolutions, from the cracks and depths of society the formerly politically backward workers, the sweated and impoverished, the demoralised and cynical, have been brought to their feet. The poor farmers have set up barricades around the city of Nantes and other cities 'in support of the workers and students' (*The Times*, 21 May,1968). Exemplary order is maintained and, as even the capitalist press has been forced to admit, the workers 'check and grease factory machines that are lying idle.'[6]

Our conclusion was:

All the conditions for a successful overturn are there: the workers are determined to go the whole hog. The middle class, particularly its lower layers, look with profound sympathy on the strike wave and in many cases join in eg on the ships, "even the officers have joined in the sit-ins begun by the crews." (*The Times*, 23 May 1968).
It is the working class which has the effective power in the factories, the ports, the mines, and the streets. A classic revolutionary situation exists. Even the televising of the debate in the National Assembly was only done by permission of the workers' organisations, as even a Gaullist MP was forced to admit. Those instruments of state repression which are still in the hands of the government, the police and the army, are completely unreliable. The police themselves have been touched by the hot flares of revolt. Their union issued a warning to the government that the "police officers thoroughly appreciated the reasons which inspired the striking wage earners and deplored the fact that they could not by law take part in the same way in the present labour movement... the public authorities will not systematically set the police against the present labour struggles." (*The Times*, 24 May 1968) In the event of a clash, many serious matters would arise, in other words, many sections, if not the majority, would go over to the workers. The army also would be split from top to bottom if the officer caste sought to intervene. This is shown by the comments of the national serviceman when he was "asked if he would fire on the students and workers, he replied: 'Never. I think their methods may be a bit rough but I am a worker's son myself'" (*The Times*, 25 May, 1968) If ever there was a time when the working class could take power peacefully, that time is now.[7]

*Militant* called for the organisation of councils of action to be spread in every factory and workplace, to be linked together on a district, regional and national level.

Unfortunately, the French 'communist' and 'socialist' leaders were more terrified of the movement than the government and the French ruling class. After the events, *The Economist* commented:

> They [the Communist Party] acted like Fabians, not like revolutionaries. And ever since they have emphasised that their party is one of law and order. They kept silent when the police occupied the Sorbonne. They dissociated themselves from the 'rabble-rousers and ultra-left provocateurs' and acquiesced in the government's decision to ban all the small left-wing revolutionary movements.[8]

And yet de Gaulle, President of France, in the midst of these events, admitted to the US Ambassador to France at the time, Sargent Shriver: "As for the future, Mr Ambassador, it depends not on us, it depends on God!"[9] He believed that 'communism' was about to triumph in France and accordingly fled to Baden Baden in West Germany. There he conferred with the commander of the French NATO troops, General Massu. In exchange for de Gaulle's promise to free some of the right-wing generals and army officers involved in the military revolts in Algeria in the early 1960s, Massu promised, if necessary, to march his troops on Paris. Massu had himself been implicated in these military revolts and linked to these generals.

But his help was not needed. To the astonishment of the representatives of the ruling class, the Communist Party competed with the Gaullists as the party of law and order. Later their election posters declaimed: "Against disorders, and against anarchy - vote Communist".[10]

## REVOLUTION DERAILED

The movement was derailed by a combination of the cowardice of the workers' leaders and the promise of elections by de Gaulle. The disappointment of the working class, and sections of the middle class, at the failure to capitalise on the revolutionary opportunity which existed in May-June 1968 led to the defeat of the workers' parties in the subsequent election. Nevertheless, as we pointed out:

One thing is certain - the Gaullist 'invincible' regime is finished. Whenever its demise comes, within weeks or months, its position has been irretrievably damaged. The French workers will not only have succeeded in bringing about its downfall, but also in beginning to undermine all the honeycombed theories of 'social peace' which have proliferated in the western labour movement in the last 20 years.[11]

The French revolution - and that is what the May-June events represented the beginning of - was a turning point for the labour movement in France and internationally. It put to the test all trends and groupings. Not just the official leadership of the movement, but all the numerous groupings of various sizes were found wanting. One of the largest, the LCR (Revolutionary Communist League) in France, based its approach on the absolutely false theory that the students were the 'leaders' and detonators of the revolution. They advanced some hare-brained ideas in the course of the May-June events. Ten million workers had spontaneously occupied the factories. And yet this tendency produced a leaflet distributed to the workers of Paris with a quote from Lenin from 1901 alleging that 'socialist consciousness could only be brought to the working class from the outside, that is by the intellectuals.'

This quote, subsequently repudiated by Lenin, has been used by some organisations to try and justify their attempts to impose their own brand of 'leadership' on the labour movement. The history of the working-class movement shows that this idea is absolutely false.

Chartism, the first independent working-class political movement, took shape before Marx had developed the ideas of scientific socialism. The ideas of socialism existed in both the German and French workers' movements before Marx and Engels. The Paris Commune was not an invention of Marx, but arose from the experiences of the French Parisian masses through the Franco-Prussian war and subsequent siege of Paris.

Marx generalised the experience of the working class, as did Lenin and Trotsky. But it was not they who, for instance, invented the idea of 'Soviets' but the workers of St Petersburg in the 1905 Russian revolution. Marxism can sum up the experiences of the working class in the form of a perspective and programme. But genuine Marxism has nothing in common with the those who believe that the working class and the labour movement is merely putty to be moulded at will by 'socialist intellectuals'. The workers of Paris, when they read the LCR leaflet, looked at the LCR members in puzzlement, shrugged their shoulders, and got on with the business of trying to carry the movement forward.

## REVOLUTIONARY WAVE

The events of the 1960s left an indelible impression on the consciousness of all who lived through them. In France it led directly to a movement on the political plane with the reformation and filling out of the Socialist Party in the early 1970s.

It also had a profound effect in Britain. Youthful supporters of *Militant* reported that their rather conservative parents and the older generation in general were enormously revived by the French events. Many dared to hope during May-June 1968 that a new, socialist society was finally within the grasp of the working class. There is little doubt that if the French workers had taken power it would have spread like a prairie fire throughout the whole of Europe. This was shown by the upheavals which were taking place in Italy almost on the level of France. There was also turmoil in Germany, where the student movement initially was, if anything, on a more advanced level than that in France in May-June 1968. There was also the rumbling opposition to the Franco dictatorship in Spain and the Caetano authoritarian regime in Portugal. Both regimes were on their last legs and a new generation of workers inspired by socialist and communist ideas had arisen.

1968 will be forever remembered as a political turning point in the post-1945 period. The outlook of millions of workers throughout the world profoundly changed.

# 3.
# MILITANT AND WILSON'S GOVERNMENT

IN BRITAIN this period saw the beginning of a transformation of the organised labour movement. The Labour government of 1964, with a small majority of four, went back to the polls in March 1966. The result was a decisive victory for Labour with Harold Wilson re-elected as prime minister. But, given the state of British capitalism, recorded in our pages, the Labour government moved from mild reforms in the first period following October 1964 to counter-reforms.

Very quickly after the election victory of 1966, the government introduced a "total freeze on wages and prices for a period of six months". *Militant* predicted that while the right-wing trade union leaders would acquiesce to this policy, it would inevitably break down as workers' resistance grew. The incomes policy brought the government into collision with organised labour, which had supported the re-election of Wilson with high hopes of an improvement in their situation.

**SEAMENS' STRIKE**

In July 1966 a seamens' strike broke out. Wilson darkly hinted at a "communist conspiracy" and declared that the Executive Committee (EC) of the seamens' union (NUS) was under the control of a "tightly-knit group of politically motivated men". One of the members of the EC of the NUS at that time was John Prescott, now deputy leader of the Labour Party.

Starting the strike very tentatively, the seamen became more and more militant as it developed. Even the right-wing dominated NUS leadership began to demand the nationalisation of the industry. They denounced "the shipowners' handling of an industry essential to a maritime country. Subsidy to a group of private and grossly overpowerful magnates is contrary to all the traditions of the labour movement - we say that the shipping industry's crisis should be finally resolved by nationalisation."

The strike, fought over six-and-a-half weeks, showed the magnificent solidarity of the seamen and resulted in some concessions being made. The 40-hour week was granted a year earlier than the owners intended. Nevertheless, a complete victory was prevented because the right-wing union EC refused to carry through the call for a complete strike of all British shipping.

The Trades Union Congress, foreshadowing what happened in the miners' strike in the 1980s, and most other unions, did not offer direct assistance to the seamen. Nevertheless, this time, unlike in previous industrial disputes (as with the dockers, for instance, during the Labour government of 1945-51), Wilson did not dare use troops or the Royal Navy. *Militant* predicted that the NUS would inevitably be transformed by this struggle, and this is subsequently what happened.

## INDUSTRIAL ACTION

During 1968 a series of strikes began to break out in other industries on a local level, the strike of the sewing machinists at Fords and other movements were symptomatic of the emergence of working-class women. *Militant* in October 1968 commented on a "Liverpool strike wave". Building workers came out on strike and marched through Liverpool city centre in September. Municipal busmen had come out for 13 weeks in Liverpool just prior to this. Dockers had struck and there was growing dissatisfaction in the English Electric plants in Liverpool because of a merger between the company and GEC. Correctly, workers feared massive redundancies. This movement was paralleled by strikes in other parts of the country, particularly in the Midlands, which reflected the growing dissatisfaction with the policies, or lack of them, of the trade union and Labour leadership. Subsequent actions by the GEC/AEI/English Electric bosses entirely justified the workers' fears.

In August 1969, they declared that 4,800 men and women would be made redundant nationally, with over 3,000 concentrated in Merseyside. 1,500 were to go in the Netherton, East Lancashire Road, factory. The stewards immediately proposed a one-day strike which was successful at all three Liverpool factories. A mass march also took place on the strike day through the streets of Liverpool. There was overwhelming support for an all-out strike against redundancies. Two "sit-down" strikes had also taken place in the East Lancashire Road factory which indicated the growing resolve of the workers to use whatever means necessary to defend the factory from closure. *Militant* called for the whole of the combine to be called out and demanded nationalisation under workers' control of this firm which had clearly failed the workers.

## WORKERS' CONTROL?

International events, above all in France in the previous year, had popularised the ideas of workers' democracy and workers' control. The idea of a takeover, of an occupation of the factory to prevent redundancies began to grow, particularly amongst the advanced workers and the shop stewards committees. But there was no clear understanding of the ideas of workers' control or workers' management and in particular the difference between the two conceptions.

Under the direction of the Institute for Workers Control, run from Nottingham by Ken Coates, who subsequently became a Labour Member of the European Parliament, the idea of taking over the factory and continuing production was supported by some stewards. *Militant*, on the other hand, was in favour of stopping production and occupying the factory to prevent redundancies. The GEC management and the capitalist press were terrified of this development. Every dirty trick was then used to distort the workers' case and vilify the shop stewards.

The shop stewards, however, did not prepare the workers adequately. They believed it was sufficient to issue a call, to make a case at a mass meeting, and the workers would follow. On the day of a scheduled mass meeting to discuss occupation, members of management led a counter-demonstration along with a right-wing shop steward who spoke admiringly of management "co-operation". They took over the platform at the mass meeting. Loudhailers were supplied by the management to a right-wing shop steward who shouted down and drowned out the voice of the convenor, Wally Brown. The result was confusion and defeat for the idea of a takeover by a vote of two to one. The management then sought to use this to undermine the stewards. Nevertheless, an overwhelming vote of confidence was given to the action committee to continue the fight by other means.

An indication of the mood that developed at this time and furthered by the takeover proposal was that Hugh Scanlon, then president of the engineering union, the AEU, declared in an interview in the *Morning Star* that his union would not tolerate sackings and called for "work or full pay". The election of Scanlon, an avowed Marxist at that time, as president of the engineers' union, of Jack Jones as general secretary of the Transport and General Workers' Union, and of Lawrence Daly as the mineworkers' union general secretary, indicated the swing towards the left which was beginning to take place amongst the more politically conscious sections of the working class. This process was not restricted to the unions. The Labour Party also began to swing leftwards.

## MILITANT'S FIRST THREE MILLION VOTES

This was most clearly reflected at the 1968 Labour Party conference. *Militant* ran a headline in November of that year: "Almost three million votes for alternative socialist policy". A resolution was moved by Liverpool Borough Labour Party and seconded by Bristol North-East Constituency Labour Party (CLP) calling for the

> taking into public ownership [of]... the 300 monopolies, private banks, finance houses and insurance companies now dominating the economy, and... producing a positive national plan anchored to socialist production.[1]

The conference carried by five million votes to one million "the repeal of the anti-trade union legislation" of the Prices and Incomes policy.

The Liverpool resolution was the most striking example of the growing support for *Militant*. It found more and more of an echo amongst leftward moving workers, above all amongst the youth. By 1969 we could report:

> The attendance of more than 150 people at the *Militant* meeting [at the 1969 Labour Party Young Socialists' conference] addressed by Peter Taaffe and of more than 250 at the *Militant* forum with *Tribune*,

where the differences between the two journals were clearly brought out, is an indication that the discussion around the ideas of Marxism will clearly continue and develop within the movement.[2]

## IN PLACE OF STRIFE

A decisive issue in pushing Labour and trade union members to the left was the decision of the Labour government to carry out the bidding of big business and introduce anti-trade union legislation. The misnamed "In Place of Strife" proposed "compulsory strike ballots", "cooling-off periods" and other measures to curtail the power of organised labour.

It was met by an outcry amongst workers, provoking a series of warning strikes at local, regional and national level. This forced the TUC to oppose the government on this issue. This measure, upon which Thatcher and the Tories subsequently based their vicious anti-union laws in the 1980s, was proposed by 'left-winger' Barbara Castle, who was the employment minister at the time. Even Tony Benn, then occupying a 'centre' political position, initially supported Castle's anti-union laws in the Labour cabinet.

But the implacable opposition of the organised Labour and trade union movement resulted in a split in the Cabinet. James Callaghan, reflecting the pressure of the trade union leadership, came out in open opposition to Wilson. Eventually a majority of the Cabinet opposed the Wilson-Castle proposals. If Wilson had not backed down in the teeth of this opposition, he would have been replaced as prime minister.

But the ruling class were furious at this development. These were the minimum measures they required - the shackling of the unions - in order for their programme of cuts in living standards to be carried through. A chorus began to develop about the "chaos" and "anarchy" which allegedly manifested itself in society, at football matches and on the factory floor. A howl went up in favour of the replacement of the Labour government by a "national government" along the lines of Ramsay MacDonald's in 1931. There was even talk of the need for a military coup under Lord Mountbatten, a solution canvassed at the time by the owner of the *Daily Mirror*, Cecil King.

In January 1969, we reported on the

thinly disguised venom [of] *The Times*, main organ of British capitalism, [which] came out on 9 December in a long editorial statement for the formation of a 'National Government'... The owner of *The Times*, Roy Thomson, with his editor William Rees-Mogg, unsuccessful Tory parliamentary candidate, joined up with Cecil King, the *Daily Mirror*, and a motley crew of Tories and ex-Labour renegades in a campaign of slander against the labour movement.[3]

That a section of the capitalists were turning in this direction was an expression of the crisis of British capitalism at that stage. But *Militant* pointed out:

> 1968 is not 1931. The industrial power of the working class has never been greater. Moreover, there has been a significant shift towards the left by the active elements in the unions and the Labour Party in the term of this Labour government.[4]

It was the fear that Labour would be pushed further and irretrievably towards the left which stayed the hands of the capitalists at that stage. However, this theme of a 'national government' was to come back many times in subsequent years when the capitalists felt that Labour was incapable and the Tories too enfeebled to carry out its wishes.

# 4.
# NORTHERN IRELAND: THE TROUBLES

MEANWHILE, A drama was beginning to unfold in Northern Ireland which would rumble on for more than 25 years. Up to the late 1960s *Militant* had no support outside of Britain. Fortunately, Paul Jones from Derry was won to *Militant's* ideas while he was studying in London just before the outbreak of the "Troubles". When he returned to Ireland, this led to an invitation to me to visit Derry in 1969, which was followed by a visit to Dublin to discuss with some old Trotskyists as well as a new layer of youth who had come to the fore within the Irish Labour Party youth section.

Even Northern Ireland was affected by the radical wave which swept the world in 1968. Naturally this affected the younger generation more. The Civil Rights Movement arose from the changed situation in Northern Ireland and was heavily influenced by the movement internationally. And it was Protestant youth, just as much as their Catholic counterparts, who moved in a radicalised direction. Thus only a minority of the students at Queen's University, Belfast, a hotbed of the civil rights movement, came from Catholic backgrounds.

Yet three-quarters of the students supported the Civil Rights Movement. Moreover, Bernadette Devlin, on the basis of an astounding 90 per cent turnout, won a parliamentary by-election in Mid-Ulster in April 1969 with the votes of an estimated 6,000 Protestant workers and farmers. However, sectarian divisions between Catholics and Protestants while they had softened amongst a new generation, were played upon by Ian Paisley and the Unionist leaders. A civil rights movement, which appealed on a class and socialist programme to Protestants as well as to Catholics, could have decisively changed Northern Ireland at that time.

Instead, the newly emerging Catholic middle class, typified by John Hume in Derry, bent all their efforts to direct the civil rights movement to achieving "equality" for the Catholics. On the basis of diseased British capitalism, sharply expressed in the much worse social conditions in Northern Ireland, this could only mean a programme of "sharing out the misery". This in turn would naturally be seen by the Protestant population as taking from them to give to the Catholics. Only by opening up an entirely different economic vista, the socialist transformation of society, and linking this to the day-to-day struggle of all workers, would it have been possible to unify Catholic and Protestants together in the struggle against the Unionist hierarchy and British big business.

Out of this movement *Militant* was able to win some important figures who were to play a leading role in the Irish labour movement, North and South. John Throne was from a Protestant background (his father had been the head of the Orange Order in Donegal) but had become a socialist and was involved, in a prominent position, in the Civil Rights struggle in the Bogside Defence Association and the Northern Ireland Labour Party in Derry, being chair of the Young Socialists. After a process of intensive discussions and working together with *Militant* supporters, he committed himself to *Militant*. He played a key role, in building the influence of *Militant* in the North and later in the South, at one time serving on the Executive Committee of the Southern Irish Labour Party and although no longer in Ireland continues to play an important role today. Peter Hadden, had already committed himself to *Militant* while still a student at Sussex University. When he returned to Northern Ireland in 1971 he played a vital role both theoretically and organisationally in maintaining the thread of Marxist ideas, in some of the most difficult conditions for Marxists anywhere in the world. Others like Gerry Lynch, Bill Webster, Manus Maguire and many others too numerous to mention also made a big contribution to building a powerful Marxist presence around *Militant*, later *Militant Irish Monthly*.

There were determined efforts made in this direction by the small forces of socialism and Marxism that had begun to gather support amongst the youth and more advanced workers. The Derry Labour Party and Young Socialists became a focal point for Protestant and Catholic workers and youth alike looking for a new road in opposition to the dead end of a return to the past. They were to play a crucial role, in particular in the August 1969 confrontations and in the early 1970s.

## MILITANT OPPOSES TROOPS BEING SENT

*Militant*'s analysis of the situation has stood the test of time like no other group. Thus, when British troops intervened in 1969 *Militant* opposed this. These troops had been sent in by the Labour Home Secretary, James Callaghan, encouraged by some like Bernadette Devlin (later McAllisky) who later on opposed the troops and moved to a Republican position. In the September 1969 issue our front-page read:

> Northern Ireland - For a united workers' defence force - Withdraw British troops - Disband B-specials and police thugs - For jobs, schools, homes, take over monopolies - Catholic and Protestant workers fight for a united socialist Ireland.

The article pointed out:

> The electric events in Northern Ireland have shaken to their roots the Unionist Stormont government and shocked out of its sedate calm the British ruling class... the Catholic population is no longer prepared to accept the writ of a government which rules by police and Paisleyite terror. Forced to defend their area of the Bogside the Catholic workers have taken over the running, policing and organisation of the area through the establishment of defence committees. At the same time - and it is this more than anything which will strike terror into the hearts of the capitalists - an increasing section have begun to see their fight not in a religious form but as a class issue...
>
> At bottom, the uprising in Derry was against the system itself, the lengthening dole queues, the worst housing in Britain, and misery on a mass scale. This anger against the capitalist system erupted in the insurrection - and that is what it undoubtedly was - against the attempts of their traditional enemies, the police, to unleash another reign of terror amongst the Bogside workers.[1]

Dealing with the events in Belfast, which were far more vicious and bloody, we commented:

> With sticks and stones in Belfast, the Catholic population confronted an armed mob which bristled with rifles and machine guns. In Derry, the workers had prepared well before the August days, having learned from the bitter experiences of the past year.[2]

Events had blown up in the face of the British ruling class who in the past "by a policy of divide and rule... [had] successfully derailed the social revolution that was developing" at the time of partition.[3]

> [But] such is the irony of history, the very same Unionist party installed as a bulwark against the development of united working-class action, is now, by its refusal to bend to the new pressures, threatening to unleash a process pregnant with dangers for imperialism.[4]

Pointing to the events in Derry, *Militant* explained that

> the Bogside fought with fury against the thuggery of the police. Under heavy siege for over 50 hours, they held off the police attacks. This was despite the indiscriminate use of lethal and heavy CS gas, taken, it is believed, from army stocks.[5]

*Militant* sought to realistically appraise the situation which confronted the Catholic population during the siege:

> It was at this stage that they mobilised the B-specials, the Paisleyites in uniform, hated by the Catholic population. They were laden with .303 rifles, sub-machine guns and automatic weapons. A slaughter would have followed in comparison with which the bloodletting in Belfast would have paled into insignificance, if the Labour government had not intervened with British troops. But it would be fatal to think that the troops were used solely to defend the Catholic population from attack by the Paisleyites and B-specials.[6]

The ruling class feared the political upheavals, destruction of property and the political vacuum which would have been created if civil war had followed:

> Sections of the workers would have learnt in action very quickly, as many Bogside workers have, to put class action first. Thus even faced with sectarian attack, the Derry Labour Party has increasingly found an eager response to the idea of appealing to the Protestant workers... As absolutely necessary as it has been to defend the area against police and Paisleyite attack, an opportunity has existed for appealing to Protestant workers.
> The call made for the entry of British troops will turn to vinegar in the mouths of some of the Civil Rights leaders. The troops have

been sent in to impose a solution in the interest of British and Ulster big business.⁷

## DERRY "BARRICADES BULLETIN"

The extracts printed in the same issue of the paper from the *Barricades Bulletin*, the daily news-sheet of the Derry Labour Party, showed the clear class instincts of the best of the workers.

> The barricades must stay up until we are sure we are all safe from state-controlled terror or victimisation. We are not defending the social conditions of the people in the area, the low wages, unemployment, bad housing, etc. In fact, the greatest part of our fight is the fight against these conditions.
> Just because barricades have to be erected around the Catholic area of Bogside doesn't mean we believe in Catholic power, this would provide no solution to our problems. People in Protestant areas have a perfect right to defend themselves if they feel they are going to be attacked by Catholic bigots... What is needed is to build a party that can defeat the Unionist government, this would need to be a Labour Party with massive trade union backing... Working-class unity in a Labour Party on this programme will provide the only real and lasting solution to the rule of sectarian terror and the terrorist rule of rent, profit and interest.⁸

Pointing to the solution, the Bulletin declared:

> No Unionist government will ever again peacefully send its police force into this area... direct rule from Westminster solves nothing. The incorporation of the six counties into the 26 would only happen via bloodshed, and would at any rate in no way help solve our economic problems - indeed, in many ways, these would get worse.
> The whole system of economic and political organisation will have to be changed - both North and South. We need a movement of solidarity in the South, which fights for us by fighting against the Fianna Fail regime. Only thus can we convince the vast majority of Protestant people we are not asking them to join the Free State [i.e. the Republic] as it stands. The Bulletin ends with a call to "Smash the Unionist government! No trust in Tories! Forward to the workers' republic!"⁹

*Militant* went further in advocating

common action through a joint defence committee (which) can begin to defeat the grip of Tory Unionism. The vehicle for this is the labour movement and trade unions themselves. In the heat of the August battles there were a few small signs of what could have been done if the labour movement would have given a clear class lead. In the Belfast Harland and Wolf shipyards a mass meeting of 9,000 workers, Protestant and Catholic, responded to an appeal to refuse to fall for sectarian slogans and divisions. A Transport and General Workers' Union official commented to *The Sunday Times*: 'The initiative came entirely from the union - none of the credit belongs to the management.'

At the same time, in the Ardoyne area of Belfast, it has been reported that sections of Protestant and Catholic workers came together to form common committees to defend their areas.[10]

In fact, peace committees developed on quite a wide scale in East Belfast in reaction to the sectarian terror that stalked the city. Moreover, the Northern Ireland Labour Party attracted the support of Catholics and Protestants looking for a way out; it got 100,000 votes in the 1970 general election.

It was not just the British capitalists but their Southern Irish counterparts who took fright at the socialist trend which seemed to influence the movement in the North. They bent all their efforts to derail the movement. They were presented with this opportunity by the complete unpreparedness of the IRA in the North to fulfil their role as traditional defenders of the Catholic population. Under the influence of the Communist Party, the leadership of the IRA, Cathal Goulding and co, had decided to move in a more 'political' direction than the IRA traditionalists liked even selling their weapons. Their incapacity to defend the Catholic population of Belfast in particular in August 1969 led to the appearance on Belfast walls of graffiti; "IRA - I Ran Away". This led to a split in Sinn Fein and the IRA, resulting in the formation of the 'Provisionals'.

The character of the new Provisional IRA was made clear in Sinn Fein's journal *An Phoblacht*. It denounced "Cuban-style commune politics" and "doctrinaire socialism".

Even as the Provisionals were in the process of formation, *Militant* criticised its perspective for military action as a means of driving the British army out of Northern Ireland. It pointed out that

British imperialism, unlike in 1920 at the time of partition, would have liked to withdraw from Northern Ireland.

However, to have done so under conditions then existing would almost certainly have resulted in a sectarian civil war. In such a conflict, it was likely the Catholics in the North would be driven out to the South. The Irish army would have been incapable of preventing this, as they were probably materially weaker than a potential armed Protestant force in the North.

All the parallels drawn by the Provisional IRA leadership (let alone the British political groups who clung to their coat-tails) with the struggle in the former colonial and semi-colonial world, were erroneous. In Algeria, for instance, the French settlers or 'colons', accounted for no more than ten per cent of the population. A war of national liberation was successful in forcing the withdrawal of French imperialism. The settlers also fled, most of them to France. In the past, however, even the 'colons' had been open to the ideas of socialism and 'communism'. They could have been won to the struggle for national liberation if it had been conducted on a class and socialist basis, rather than the nationalist approach of the Algerian FLN (National Liberation Front).

In Northern Ireland the so-called 'colons' or 'settlers' were two-thirds of the population! One million people were killed in Algeria. How many would it take before the policies of the Provisionals were shown to be inappropriate?

Twenty-five years later, in the Downing Street declaration of December 1994, British imperialism stated - and the Provisionals have now accepted this - that they have no "strategic or selfish interests" in Northern Ireland. The Provisional leadership now in effect accepts what *Militant* has always argued, that it is not British imperialism but the opposition of the 1.5 million-strong Protestant majority of Northern Ireland which opposes forced incorporation into a capitalist united Ireland.

*Militant*, and later our Irish co-thinkers around what was originally called *Militant Irish Monthly* and now *Militant Labour* (in the North) and *Militant* (in the South), alone argued consistently for this position over the last 25 years. At the same time, *Militant* argued for a class and socialist alternative. In the changed situation, both North and South of the border, a real viable alternative for the working class in both parts of Ireland can emerge.

# 5.
# TORY GOVERNMENT 1970-74

WHILE THE 1969 events were unfolding in Ireland, 10,000 Merseyside dockers went on strike over the refusal of container base employers to take on dockers registered under the Dock Labour Scheme which guaranteed minimum wages and conditions. This was the beginning of a massive rationalisation of the labour force which was subsequently to result in the decimation of the dock labour force. After initial confusion, the whole of the docklands came out in support of workers who had boycotted containers at depots where unregistered labour was employed. This was a foretaste of the battles to come, which would spark one of the greatest postwar industrial struggles in the early 1970s.

The determination of the dockers enabled Jack Jones, who was then the secretary-elect of the Transport and General Workers' Union, to emerge from negotiations with a settlement far better than he had originally put forward. *Militant* had warned:

> Workers in every industry are facing the problems of redundancy. The mines and railways have revealed the end product in concrete terms. Containerisation alone will affect other main employment sources on Merseyside... The Labour Party has committed itself to the nationalisation of the docks. This policy must be carried out as the only lasting solution to this problem.[1]

This was a fitting end to the tumultuous decade of the 1960s, which had started with the events leading to the formation of the Labour government and the establishment of *Militant* and ended against the backdrop of worldwide social and socialist upheavals and growing radicalisation in the British labour movement.

Looking towards the next decade, *Militant*'s editorial in January 1970 was headed: 'Into the '70s - a decade of revolution'. This was an accurate forecast of what was to come in the next ten years. Our editorial declared:

In marked contrast to the beginning of the 1960s, the coming decade of the 70s is looked towards with foreboding by all shades of capitalist opinion. At its outset, the ruling class hailed the 1960s as a 'new age'. The mass unemployment, misery and class battles of the 1930s were no more; 'social harmony' was to be entrenched with only a few remaining social problems to be tidied up and 'the affluent society' would then be consolidated.[2]

## TORIES IN

Only months into the new decade this prognosis was being borne out. The Labour government was defeated in the June 1970 general election 'amidst scenes of wild jubilation at the Stock Exchange, the rocketing of shares in the market by a record £1,500 million (£30 for every man, woman and child in the country).' The Tories had been returned to power with an overall majority of 30 on 18 June.

> Owing to the disillusionment which had set in by the counter-reform policies of the Wilson government, the turnout was the lowest of any election since 1935! In the traditional strongholds of Labour in London, the mass abstention of the workers (a majority in some cases) indicated the deep unease at the campaign conducted by the Labour leaders and their record when in power.[3]

Overall, the Labour vote had dropped by 888,000 with its share of the total vote dropping from 47.9 per cent in 1966 to 43 per cent. Significantly, the drop in the turnout compared to 1966 was four per cent, from 76 per cent to 72 per cent. This almost solely accounted for the overall drop in the Labour vote. Pointing to the lessons of the Labour government, we stated:

> The Marxist wing of the labour movement consistently warned that tinkering with the system, attempting to manage capitalism better than the party of the capitalists themselves would inevitably lead to a setback for Labour.[4]

In trying to draw the lessons of Labour's defeat, Hugh Scanlon, President of the AUEW, declared: "In future, the trade union movement will have to raise the fundamental issues of control and ownership of industry."

*Militant* said:

> The victory of the Tories will result in titanic class battles in Britain, as Jack Jones explained, the like of which has not been seen since the days of the Chartists, if they proceed to translate their reactionary promises into action.[5]

Lodged in the situation which was developing in Britain was the possibility of a general strike. Heath, the new Tory Premier, made more than one veiled warning of such a possibility. In November 1970 *Militant* warned:

> The Tory government, joining battle with the entire labour movement, is staking everything on winning a test case against the local council manual workers. Determined to crush the revolt of the low-paid, it has thrown every available weapon against them: press hysteria, high-paid 'volunteer' strike breakers, gangs of down-and-out blacklegs, and Her Majesty's troops.[6]

*The Times* even went to the lengths when dealing with the dangers of inflation to include in an article an ominous reference to 'some sort of authoritarian regime' if inflation reached the rate of 50 per cent.

> The first thing to do, and the simplest, is to start beating strikes. The local authorities should be given total support in refusing to make any further offer, even if the strike lasts for months. The next stage should be to make it a national rule that any strike is followed by the immediate withdrawal of all offers made before the strike.[7]

The Heath government was to heed this advice.

## INDUSTRIAL RELATIONS BILL

Before the year was out, Heath's Tory government had announced its intention to savagely curb trade union rights with the introduction of its Industrial Relations Bill. Thousands of workers marched in protest on 8 December and *Militant* reported a "huge sale of over 1,000 copies up and down the country."[8]

Early into the new year an immense movement of opposition to the anti-union bill began. We reported:

> The new year saw a wave of strikes throughout the Midlands. On 11 January, 20,000 Wolverhampton workers marched through the streets during working hours... The next day, probably 1.5 million workers were involved in one way or another in action against the 'bosses' charter'... Large sections of trade unionists have demanded national industrial action from the TUC.[9]

*Militant* explained that it was one thing to introduce anti-union legislation and quite another to implement it in the charged situation which existed at the beginning of the 1970s. What is written through working-class strength and organisation cannot be erased by a stroke of the pen, even by the "mighty legislative pen" of Westminster.

## UPPER CLYDE SHIPBUILDERS

The Heath government was to learn a bitter lesson in this regard during the ensuing months and years. *Militant* also reported on the gathering mood of opposition to the plans of the Tory government to close the huge Upper Clyde Shipbuilders (UCS) in Glasgow. In response to this attack, the workers had occupied the shipyards in their famous 'sit-in'. *Militant* reported:

> Clydeside is beginning to take on its previous ruddy hue. The occupation of the yards, the spreading of the strike, these are the immediate tasks of the UCS workers. It is the responsibility of the entire labour movement to take up the cry for nationalisation of the shipbuilding and shipping industry, and for an end to the businessmen's government. No more deals - scrap the system, not the yards.[10]

In our 3 September issue, we featured the UCS struggle on our front page. There had been massive support for the occupation with huge demonstrations in Glasgow on 18 August. But the government and their appointed 'liquidator' were quite happy

> to see ships being built by workers whose wages were being paid by collections amongst workmates and in the labour movement generally... It is necessary to upset the calculations of the ruling class by a policy of action now! Isolated to just one section of the shipbuilding

industry the 'work-in' cannot maintain itself indefinitely.[11]

A call was therefore made for the nationalisation of the yards as the only guarantee against massive redundancies. At the same time, *Militant* was to the fore in giving support to the occupation. This movement had put its stamp not only on the outlook of the Scottish working class but in a sense on the whole of the labour movement. Tony Benn, who participated in the mass demonstrations and spoke to the stewards and the workers, was affected by the rising militancy displayed in the UCS struggle. He had been on the right, or at best in the centre-left, during the Labour government. Now, under the influence of events, he began to evolve towards the left. This represented not just a personal evolution but the big shifts in consciousness which had taken place amongst advanced workers.

There was an almost continuous rise in consciousness and combativity in the period of 1970-74. There was a certain pause after the Labour government of 1974-79 came to power. But in general the movement steadily evolved towards the left, culminating in the battles between 1979 and 1981 over left policies and Benn's challenge for the Deputy Leadership of the Labour Party.

At the time of the UCS struggle, *Militant* came out clearly not just for the nationalisation of UCS "but... Swan Hunter's, which lost £10 million last year, Cammell Laird's, Harland and Wolf, indeed the whole industry is completely unviable on a capitalist basis."

How true these words ring today with the closure of Cammel Laird's and now a death sentence hanging over Swan Hunter and a minimum workforce at Harland and Wolf. *Militant* demanded that the industry

> must be nationalised under workers' control. Occupation of the yards, on the basis of demanding immediate nationalisation through an enabling bill would shake the Tory government to its foundations. The Tories rushed in an enabling bill to nationalise Rolls Royce. The labour movement must press for similar action for shipbuilding.[12]

The bosses, it was declared,

> made shipbuilding a bankrupt industry - make them redundant, with no bonuses for the mess they have left behind. Provide other work, with no reduction in pay, or maintain the men in their present jobs.

[Above all]: If the Tories and their system cannot guarantee the minimum requirement of a worker, the right to a job, then they and their system must be scrapped and a Labour government, based on taking over the 350 major monopolies, must be brought to power.[13]

But UCS was not the only struggle which convulsed industry in 1971. A work-to-rule by power workers had taken place in January. A power worker, writing for *Militant*, stated: "We were hardly a militant section of the trade union movement but the Tories have really hardened us up." The *Evening Standard* had depicted the men as 'animals'. *Militant* also reported that "John Davis, the Minister of Industry, actually called upon individuals to 'harass' electricity workers and their families for their action."[14]

Rolls Royce workers were also threatened with complete closure of their factory in March 1971 and management tried to use the threat of bankruptcy to undermine their resistance to a wage standstill policy.

## THE DEMAND FOR A GENERAL STRIKE

Above all, these battles were taking place against the backcloth of mass opposition to the Industrial Relations Bill. This culminated in February 1971 in a huge 300,000-strong TUC demonstration marching from Hyde Park to Trafalgar Square, where the call for a general strike was taken up, amongst others, by the huge miners' contingent. Heath himself had mentioned in a TV broadcast his preparedness to "face up" to a general strike.

The issue of a general strike became a hotly debated question in the workers' movement at this stage. Some 'theoreticians' came out in favour of an unlimited general strike. *Militant*, on the contrary, echoing Trotsky's warning to examine the issue of a general strike in a 'painstaking' fashion, argued that a 24-hour general strike of the whole of the organised trade union and labour movement was the most effective way of combating the government at that stage.

In a series of articles, we pointed that an all-out general strike "poses the question of power". It is an 'either/or' situation where the working class goes fully towards the seizure of power or can face a defeat, sometimes a crushing defeat. This was the lesson of 1926, and, in a different historical situation, the recent general strike in France in 1968.

It was necessary to elaborate a programme of preparing the working class for such a struggle. Moreover, a 24-hour general strike in Britain would have much greater consequences than the 24-hour strikes which had become quite common in Italy, for instance. Once the full power of the working class had been demonstrated in a one-day stoppage, an entirely unprecedented situation would open up. At a certain stage, the Marxists themselves would launch the slogan of an unlimited general strike, but only after proper preparation and with the working class fully politically armed and understanding what was involved.

## OUR ORGANISATION GROWS

*Militant*, still smaller than rival organisations claiming to be Marxist or Trotskyist, was struggling to leave behind its swaddling clothes to become a significant force within the labour movement. In the changed political and social situation of Britain, confidently looking towards expanding, we declared in October 1970:

> Apart from the increase in circulation, we have produced leaflets on all the major industrial and political issues. Supporters in a number of areas now produce regular local editions and supplements. In the trade unions it has been necessary to produce special pamphlets going more fully into specific problems facing these industries.
> We have seen established under the impetus of the growing militancy of the white-collar workers and our teacher supporters the regular production of *Militant Teacher*, which of course covers the whole spectrum of education... The *Militant International Review* (our magazine) is now produced every three months.

Greater financial and other commitments from our supporters were called for:

> To publish all that needs to appear, it is essential that we have a *Militant* with more pages, and, as a first priority, on a more frequent basis. All of this is linked to the acquisition of our own press, and a move to new premises... The Editorial Board have set the target of a fortnightly *Militant* by the end of the year.[15]

By February 1971, we could report:

This month has seen a big step forward for the supporters of *Militant*. We have moved into our new premises at 375 Cambridge Heath Road, London. This has only been possible by the devoted and strenuous efforts of our supporters in carrying out massive improvements and repairs to the building.[16]

These premises were bought from the Independent Labour Party (ILP), and were in a state of dereliction. In effect *Militant* had bought for £3,500 the shell of a building. To become habitable it had to be completely renovated from top to bottom: drains had to be laid, joists put in, floors completely rebuilt, walls plastered.

The headline over the October 1970 editorial read, "Build the *Militant*!" This acquired a particular practical significance for those pioneers who laboured to construct the first really independent headquarters of *Militant*.

Into a back shed was packed *Militant*'s first precious printing press, acquired through the diligence of *Militant*'s first printer, Alan Hardman. Also stuffed into this shed was a very archaic folding machine. The plates for the press were made elsewhere. Never to be forgotten by those involved at this time was the extremely antiquated "varityper" on which all the articles for the first issue of the fortnightly *Militant* were set. Patrick Craven in particular performed miracles on this machine for the first few issues. The first fortnightly *Militant* was produced and sold with no more than 217 committed supporters throughout the country.

Big financial sacrifices had been made: "In the last month outstanding amongst many donations was a magnificent £60 from two supporters in Bristol." This step could not have been taken at a more opportune moment. "On the 12 January demonstrations against the Tory government's anti-union bill our sellers rapidly exhausted their supplies of papers."[17]

## ONCE A FORTNIGHT

Some supporters mentioned that "as soon as the workers saw the headlines "Down with businessmen's government" they reached for their money!" Only seven months later, in September 1971, the first fortnightly *Militant* was launched:

> With the awakening of the working class to political life, they (the

working class) would move into the unions and from there into the ward and Constituency Labour Parties... But the policies of the Labour leaders are only preparing for an even greater defeat than last time... The only policy which will save the labour movement from disaster is a Marxist one, as argued by *Militant*... Our paper can become a real weapon for the workers if you, the readers, write for it, criticise and, above all, send us cash to ensure we maintain the fortnightly and go to the weekly *Militant* at the beginning of next year.[18]

As 1971 drew to a close the editors predicted that the next year would see

the gathering storm. The British workers in 1971 have not yet thrown out the Tories or their hated system. But they achieved more than in any year since the war: three mass strikes and a gigantic march of 300,000 against the Industrial Relations Act; two token strikes of 150,000 Scottish workers in support of the mass action by UCS workers; the Plessey sit-in; heroic struggles by many sections of workers, notably the postmen and Ford workers; more mass strikes around the TUC lobby on unemployment; and a landslide rout of the Tories in the municipal elections.[19]

## NOW EVERY WEEK

Very soon we were able to take another big step forward. *Militant* went weekly on 28 January 1972. It was a red letter day for all supporters of the paper and for Marxism in Britain. "This is the first issue of the weekly *Militant*. In the short space of three months, we have changed from a fortnightly to a weekly." The number of committed supporters had increased considerably. Between the launch of the fortnightly and the weekly 137 new supporters had been recruited. However, the total number of supporters was still only 354. The weekly could not have been launched at a better time, coming as it did in the midst of a miners' strike. We announced:

The miners' ranks are firm. They are determined to win their full demands... The government is quite prepared to see the mines ruined and the machinery shattered, costing more than the miners' full demands, rather than concede their just demands... The TUC is dillydallying and vacillating; the Tories are cunningly representing their class implacably, behind the scenes, pushing the Coal Board to resist the claim of the miners, as a blow against the whole of the working class.

If the miners are defeated, the entire working class is defeated. Let the TUC show the same resolution as our class enemies! Mobilise the entire organised movement in solidarity with the miners as a warning to the government against unemployment, rising prices and in solidarity with the miners. The TUC must organise a one-day general strike.[20]

## FIGHTING RENT INCREASES

At the same time, the Tories launched a sharp attack on tenants in the Housing Finance Bill. The purpose was to drive councils, in particular Labour ones, to increase rents. The mass opposition to the Housing Finance Bill was, however, undermined by the NEC of the Labour Party which proposed a campaign of "neutralising or lessening" the increases and "delaying" the effects of the Bill. The NEC and their lawyers advised the movement not to take the Bill head on, but to grapple with legal technicalities. *Militant* quoted the statement of the NEC:

> After much heart-searching, the National Executive has decided not to recommend Labour councils to refuse point-blank to carry through the increases. This is because the government could then appoint a housing commissioner with far wider powers than just raising rents.[21]

This anticipated the role of the right wing in all major battles that were to confront the labour movement in the next period. The same attitude by the leadership was shown in the battle in Liverpool in the 1980s. *Militant* counterposed to this an active programme of resistance:

> The only way to break the proposed law is to break it. The NEC must: (1) call on all Labour councils and local government workers not to implement the rent increases imposed by the bill. (2) Mobilise all tenants and the whole of the working class to back Labour councillors and local government workers, with demonstrations against Tory councils and housing commissioners who impose the increases; with full support, including industrial action, for tenants who refuse to pay these increases and for Labour councils who refuse to impose them, espe-

cially in the event of legal action being taken against either tenants or councillors.

An indication of the mood in Labour ranks was the fact that the London Regional Council of the party had called for

> an immediate freeze on all council private rents; taking over of all empty property, including office blocks, to use as at least temporary accommodation; cancellation of all council debts; institution of interest-free loans to local authorities; replacement of rent tribunals with committees of elected representatives of tenants' associations, trade unions and the labour movement; an immediate target of one million new houses per year; the nationalisation under democratic workers' control of the building industry and the land, together with the banks, building societies, insurance companies and finance houses with minimum compensation on the basis of need.[22]

This highlights just how far the 'modern-day' Labour Party has moved in a rightward direction. Such a principled resolution, moved by supporters of *Militant*, was accepted by the London Labour Party. Other regions of the Labour Party followed suit. In the South West, for instance, the same kind of demands for resistance were made.

There was big opposition to the Tories' housing bill from all sections of the labour movement. But only the heroic councillors of Clay Cross were prepared to go to the end in defiance of the government. Like the Liverpool councillors in the 1980s, they were surcharged and banned from office. Their struggle was fully supported and reported in the pages of *Militant* (and some of the Clay Cross Labour Party members became *Militant* supporters). On 8 December, for instance, *Militant* reported:

> Last Sunday, well over 2,000 tenants and members of the Labour Party demonstrated at Clay Cross in Derbyshire, in support of the Labour council's firm refusal to implement the Tory Housing Finance Act... The solid support of the local tenants was indicated by the fact that the march increased in size five times over as it passed through the council estate and people came out to swell the ranks.

Graham Skinner, one of the famous 'Skinner' family (brother Dennis, Labour MP for Bolsover, is the best known), and one of the 11 Clay Cross Labour Party councillors, speaking to *Militant* commented:

> The other Labour councils have caved in because they were afraid of the implications of not implementing the Act. I can't say that I sympathise with them because I feel that if every Labour council had taken the same stand that we had taken, the Housing Finance Act would never have got off the ground.
> A lot of councillors are basically councillors for their own ego, in my opinion. They get elected on promises and then forget what they were put in for. We at Clay Cross don't forget. We carry out every policy that we issue in our election manifesto.[23]

## MINERS' STRIKE 1972 - SALTLEY GATES

*Militant*, although still a small force, nevertheless played an important role in some of the key battles of 1972. The epic miners' strike of that year, the first since 1926, was fully reported in our pages. *Militant* supporters in Birmingham had played a key role in tipping off the NUM pickets in Birmingham that Saltley Gate was being used as a collecting depot for "scab coal". Lorry drivers from all over the country were arriving at Saltley Gate.

On 18 February, an eye-witness report on what became known as the 'Battle of Saltley Gate' began: "At first there were only ten of us, then 20, 50, 500 and finally 10,000." It had been in response to a tip-off by members of the local Labour Party Young Socialists that the NUM moved into Birmingham. 'Cowboy' lorrydrivers from all over Britain

> driving for large back-handers from their employers were arriving at Saltley Gate to collect 'virtual slag' to sell at inflated prices. But by Sunday 6 February the number of pickets grew to over 500 and the real struggle began.

Initially these pickets managed to turn back a number of lorries but eventually the police arrived in numbers.

> It became increasingly clear that only a massive influx of miners or the combined efforts of the local trade unions, would close the depot and defeat the police tactics.[24]

A virtual guerrilla war took place between miners and pickets on the one side and the police on the other, leading to the final confrontation.

> The (police) squads picked out non-miners deliberately, particularly students, so that they could claim that the miners were being incited by others. The chairman of our local LPYS and a local Labour Party ward member were arrested on trumped-up charges. As the police went for long-haired youths, they actually arrested several young miners from South Wales, much to their surprise! They were obviously not aware of the change in working-class fashions.
> They were really out to get me by the Wednesday, but the miners followed me around, staying close to me so that I could not be picked out by the police. Many miners gave evidence to support students and others unfairly arrested. The police could not split the solidarity of the picket line by their tactics.
> Neither could the press. The *Birmingham Mail* carried an article arguing that the trouble at the depot was caused by "anarchists and Maoists"!

Arthur Scargill, who was in Birmingham at that time, acted in a typically bold fashion when car plant stewards came with collections of money to the miners' headquarters. Instead of expressing gratitude, Scargill refused to accept this financial help, demanding instead that the stewards call their members out in solidarity with the miners. We reported:

> The response from the Birmingham working class was magnificent. Deputations from SU Carburettors, Rover car works, local building workers, were the first there. Women from SU marched to the picket, to a tremendously warm response, and women from the Transport and General Workers' Union handed out free sandwiches and soup each day.

Under mass pressure

> the AUEW decided on a one-day strike for the Thursday (10 February). Sections of the TGWU, including lorry drivers, pledged support. The police and Gas Board chiefs said they would keep the gates open, whatever, sure that they would call the bluff of the picket leaders. But when they saw phalanx upon phalanx of banner-waving workers marching on the depot, they were astonished... Men from Dunlops, British Leyland, Rover, Drop Forge, GEC, etc were there. Birmingham industry was at a standstill and 10,000 people flooded the square

outside the depot, stopping the movement of all traffic. The police closed the gates for the day. Victory was ours. I cannot describe to you the feeling of joy, relief and solidarity that descended over all of us there. Leaflets I brought to hand out were taken out of my hand in bundles by total strangers who distributed them for me - it was like what Petrograd 1917 must have been!

The next day an agreement was signed with the Gas Board, that only essential supplies could be moved, supervised by the NUM and driven only by the TGWU members... The struggle was won by workers in action, united by the organised leadership of the trade union movement in Birmingham... It is also concrete proof of our demand on the TUC to take general action to mobilise the unions nationally in support of the miners.[25]

This incident had a decisive effect in shaping the outlook of workers and bosses. It infuriated the Tories who prepared to take revenge later.

## THE PULSE QUICKENS

The year 1972, particularly the first six or seven months, was one of the most tumultuous in the history of the labour movement since 1945. *Militant* still had small forces. But to re-read the pages of the paper, even for those who lived through the events, is to feel the increased pulse of the labour movement and the working class at that time.

One section of the working class after another appeared to be on strike or considering strike action. In April the paper carried the headline: "Tories incite violence against railmen." Sporadic strike action by railworkers, according to the *Daily Express* "infuriated passengers on the 5.24 from Waterloo to Dorking" who then decided to "hijack their train at Epsom when the driver plans to leave them." *Militant* pointed out that "as a result of this vicious sort of propaganda, hundreds of railwaymen have been jostled, hit and spat upon by sections of the 'Bowler Hat Brigade'."[26] We also reported a sit-in by Oxford carworkers at the BLMC (British Leyland) body plant.

## DOCKERS JAILED

But the issue in 1972 which brought Britain to the brink of a general strike, for the first time since 1926, revolved around the battle of the dockers against containerisation. The real purpose of Heath's Industrial Relations Act was demonstrated in this dispute.

Sir John Donaldson, High Court judge and head of the newly established Industrial Relations Court, declared that the union leaders must discipline and even expel their members, area officials and shop stewards, if his court should dictate so. Failure to do so would be met with charges of contempt of court and the unions heavily fined. Refusal to comply resulted in fines of £5,000 and £50,000 on the Transport and General Workers' Union.

The arguments of *Militant* about the nature of the Act and the analysis of class relations were demonstrated in May, June and July, 1972. Through the medium of the government, the capitalists were attempting to bind the unions to the state and convert the leadership into what the American socialist Daniel De Leon (1852-1914) called 'Labour lieutenants of capital'.

Some union leaders in the Technical Administrative and Supervisory Staffs (TASS), declared their intention to pursue a policy of "non-compliance" with the Act. But prominent left trade union leader Jack Jones announced that the TGWU would not undertake any "illegal actions". Under pressure from Jones, the executive committee of the union agreed - but only by the casting vote of the chairman - to pay the court's fines. *Militant* pointed out that if the whole of the trade union movement defied the court, there would not be enough jails to contain those who would defy the act.

Jimmy Symes, chairman of the Liverpool dock shop stewards committee, told *Militant*, "Unions weren't built on funds; they were built on the blood and sweat of their members. The strength of any union depends on its shopfloor."[27]

But the government was using the docks' dispute as a trial of strength with organised labour. In June 35,000 dockworkers, backed by millions of other workers, "in one day of action have reduced the Tory Industrial Relations Act to ashes and humbled the government which tried to use it to dragoon the trade union movement."[28]

However, the dispute on containerisation, centring on Chobham Farm in east London, threatened at one stage to become a fratricidal struggle between different sections of the same union, the Transport and General Workers' Union.

*Militant* suggested a conference of the dockers and workers involved in Chobham Farm and the containerisation issue as a means of working out a common policy in opposition to the employers. The bosses believed they could exploit the divisions between the workers at Chobham Farm and elsewhere. Using Donaldson and the Industrial Relations Court, five dockers' leaders were jailed in July. As soon as the imprisonment took place any 'sectional' conflict evaporated and a mass movement developed from below. This more and more assumed the proportions of a general strike.

## MASS MOVEMENT FROM BELOW

And it was not just token or one-day action which developed. In the most militant areas, workers were talking about coming out for longer. This movement had all the features of a potential '1968'. Even the general council of the TUC came out in favour of a 24-hour general strike, but only after it had become clear that the dockers were about to be released. As soon as the government and the capitalists saw the reaction of the working class as a whole, they suddenly improvised a 'fairy godmother', in the form of the Official Solicitor, who intervened and secured the release of the dockers. This prevented a general strike from taking place.

This movement vindicated the analysis of *Militant*. The paper had argued that lodged in the explosive situation in Britain was the possibility of a general strike.

It was not just the heavy battalions which moved into action. Previously inert sections of society were infected with the general disaffected mood which percolated through industry and society throughout the year of 1972. In May of that year *Militant* reported:

> Last Tuesday (9 May) saw a march of over 3,000 school students from the North London area to protest against conditions in schools. Two young comprehensive schoolgirls stated: "Nine out of ten of us don't stand a chance of getting a proper job when we leave school. We've all had enough; it is our future which is at stake and we plan to do something about it."[29]

This was at a time when unemployment had barely touched a

million. This movement, in which young *Militant* supporters participated, foreshadowed an even bigger movement which developed in the 1980s. The fact that *Militant* could intervene in such movements, with young, fresh forces, was itself a reflection of the growth and support of the Labour Party Young Socialists and within this a huge increase in the support for *Militant*.

## LABOUR PARTY YOUNG SOCIALISTS

*Militant* had gained the majority on the Labour Party Young Socialists National Committee by 1972. This became a powerful weapon for intervening in workers' struggles and the labour movement generally. The paper reported on 23 June, 1972: "Over 100 delegates from tenants associations, trade unions and Labour Party branches attended the London LPYS conference of tenants and Labour."[30] The LPYS was to the fore in the intervention in all the big disputes of 1972 and attracted to its banner the best, most combative, elements amongst the youth.

# 6.
# INTERNATIONAL EVENTS 1970-74

1972 SAW a massive escalation in the conflict in Northern Ireland. At that time it was not at all easy or 'popular', in Northern Ireland or Britain, to point out the facts of the situation in Northern Ireland, even to the most advanced workers.

On Sunday 30 January, at the height of the miners' strike, 13 unarmed demonstraters were shot down in Derry. Our headline was: "Derry - this was murder". We said that the day would "go down in history as the North of Ireland's Bloody Sunday." This edition came out when a rally of striking miners took place in Trafalgar Square. Many miners reacted - and not at all positively - to the brutal facts outlined in the pages of *Militant*. We said that this event was "to be compared to the Croke Park massacre of 1920 when 'black and tans' (the paramilitary police auxiliaries) shot down 12 civilians."[1] We carried eyewitness reports. Brian Docherty, a *Militant* supporter, wrote:

> I was in Chamberlain Street when the Paras attacked. The crowd retreated in panic and I ran into the courtyard at the back of Rossville flats, but I stopped when I saw that we had been outflanked by soldiers, who had taken up positions at the corner of the flats... Suddenly I realised that it was gunfire. I dived behind a wall. I looked up and saw a para who fired his rifle and hit a youth who was only 12 feet away from me. Someone shouted out at me: "Look, he's been wounded," and we rushed over and carried him to the other side of the block and he was taken to hospital. The man was unarmed and he was shot down by a British soldier as he ran for cover.[2]

Paul Jones, another *Militant* supporter, wrote:

> William McKinney, aged 27, was shot dead by troops. When Mrs Collins went to help him, she was told to leave him alone by a paratrooper. When she persisted, she was hit on the head with a rifle. Later, when she was able to reach the boy, along with the 'Knights of Malta' and McKinney's mate, McKinney was dead. Mrs Collins says

that she neither saw nor heard either nail bombs or shooting before the Paras opened up... James Rea, say the residents of the maisonettes opposite Rossville flats, was sheltering for cover, already wounded in the arm, when paratroopers approached him. "Don't shoot. I haven't a gun," he shouted. The paratroopers then demanded that he surrender, which he did, and then he was shot dead.

We said

the responsibility lies not just with the paratroopers, who are candidates for the role of the Praetorian Guard of British imperialism, but the Tory government, finance capital which backs them and the system they represent. The terrible bloodletting in Northern Ireland is the legacy of centuries of domination by the British ruling classes. Their rule has traditionally been one of blood and iron. This massacre is just the latest in a chapter of horrors so far as the Irish people are concerned.[3]

Representing *Militant*, I had been in 'Free Derry' at the invitation of local socialists only a week before this incident. Then it was still possible to find, at least in Derry, enthusiastic support for the ideas of a non-sectarian, class alternative. But in the aftermath of these events, *Militant* reported:

The outraged Catholic youths have flooded towards the Provisional and Official IRA... There will now be a new influx of Catholic youth into the IRA... the rage of the Catholic population is entirely understandable. They feel like striking back, with arms, against those responsible for this massacre. But to propose a new campaign of terror and reprisals is no way to avenge the dead and will only reproduce the bloody events in Derry on a larger scale later. The British ruling class can be made to pay for these events only if a strategy for an attack on the whole capitalist system is worked out by the leaderships of these organisations. A campaign of individual assassinations of British soldiers can only provide an excuse for further repression. Also, it can only reinforce the hostility of the ordinary soldier to the Catholic population.[4]

## WHAT ABOUT THE TROOPS?

With regard to the use of British troops, we stated: "There is no way to bring about the withdrawal of British troops and British imperialist domination except on a class basis."[5] A report (based on my visit before Bloody Sunday) pointed out: "One thing is absolutely certain; the British army... has welded practically the whole Catholic population against them by their methods." I saw at first hand the methods used by the British army in searching a street:

> The tactic is to tear up floorboards, rip down ceilings and wallpaper and wreck furniture. This is done in 98 out of a street of, say, 100 houses. In two houses, the troops will take care to avoid doing any damage and these householders will then be asked to sign dockets to say that no damage has been done.[6]

The level of repression was intense:

> At the rate at which the army is going, over half the Catholic male population will be 'lifted'. And not just the supporters of the Official or the Provisional IRA are subject to this treatment... The sellers of *Militant* or any labour movement paper can be picked up for interrogation.[7]

Following the events of Bloody Sunday, the whole of Ireland was convulsed by protests. A general strike broke out in the South which paralysed the country. The fate of Irish capitalism itself seemed to hang by a thread; the mass of the Irish population were blaming the Irish government for doing nothing to protect their counterparts in the North.

The rage against the British government and British imperialism, who they clearly held responsible for the massacre in the North, culminated in a mass march on the British embassy in Dublin. The Irish government and police were compelled to stand back impotently as the crowd burnt the embassy to the ground.

Because there was no lead from the tops of the workers' organisations, either in the South or the North, this movement inevitably subsided. But the events of Bloody Sunday further deepened the morass which British imperialism found itself in over Northern Ireland. Its campaign of repression acted as a recruiting sergeant for the IRA. *Militant* representatives were to visit Northern Ireland as well as Southern Ireland consistently during the early 1970s.

## MILITARY COUP IN CHILE

Events in Chile also featured heavily in *Militant* between the Allende government's election in 1970 and General Pinochet's coup of September 1973. In 1972 the paper warned that this would be

> a decisive year for the Chilean workers and peasants. Chilean society teeters on the brink of crisis. The question is posed: will the workers and peasants succeed in guaranteeing the gains of Allende's Popular Front (UP) government, by pressing forward to socialist revolution, or will the reaction strike with ferocious vengeance on an even more terrible scale than General Banzer's coup in Bolivia in August 1971?[8]

These proved to be prophetic words. *Militant* warned against the vacillation and dangerously irresponsible reformist illusions of Allende, the 'Marxist' president. He had held the masses back:

> with phrases warning against 'provoking reaction' and thinks he can 'neutralise' the generals - the faithful servants of the capitalists, by flattering them and praising their 'Chilean respect for democracy'.[9]

Despite the claims that Chile was the 'England of Latin America', the Chilean army had organised no less than nine coups since 1920.

Allende was only allowed to take office after promising, in a little publicised document, that the armed forces would remain untouched by his government. This was a guarantee that the reactionary officer caste would retain its reactionary grip. It would be ready to strike at the most appropriate moment. *Militant* pointed out that throughout 1971,

> reaction has been paralysed by the overwhelming enthusiasm of the masses for Allende's government. The CIA has been stumped also. Direct intervention in Chile by US imperialism will provoke an explosion amongst American labour and youth... [10]

*Militant* stated bluntly:

> Only a bold revolutionary programme can guarantee a peaceful transition: (1) Peasant committees should be set up to take over the land... A decree on land nationalisation would legalise the accomplished revolutionary fact. (2) Workers' control of industry... to prevent factory closures. Industry should be nationalised with minimum compensation on the basis of need only. (3) Action committees... should be set up by the trade unions to force landlords and traders to reduce prices and rents. (4) A workers' militia, based on the unions, should be set

up to defend the workers' gains... Allende should appeal to the rank and file (of the army) to set up soldiers' committees. Every effort must be made to draw the workers in uniform closer to their brothers in industry. Faced with a powerful movement in the army, the generals would be suspended in mid-air.[11]

Allende's response to the pressure from the left was: "We must not forget that we are within the framework of a legal bourgeois regime." This was only to encourage the reaction and to increase the impatience of those on the left. In the concrete situation, *Militant* stated:

> Marx explained that the boss-class could not be overwhelmed by using its own state, that it was necessary to raise the workers' organisations - most developed in the form of Soviets [workers' and peasants' committees] - to state power, completely paralysing and dismantling the old state in the process. This is the only road for the Chilean workers and peasants.[12]

A few months later, we warned: 'Generals poised'. The article detailed the attempts at reaction - the shopkeepers' strike in September and the lorry owners' stoppage and lockout throughout Chile in October to undermine the Popular Unity government. These measures were testing the ground for the time when the generals could step forward:

> They are being groomed by the capitalists and landlords as the 'arbiters' of the 'nation'. After a sufficient period of 'anarchy' the generals will be able to step forward as the 'saviours' of the country.[13]

## THE MIDDLE CLASSES COULD BE WON

The other side of the process was also highlighted: "But the reactionaries still live in mortal dread of the Chilean workers." In relation to the protests of the middle class, we stated that

> only the working class, fighting on a clear socialist programme, can really defend the interests of the small proprietors... It would be possible to grant cheap credit to the small farmers, the shopkeepers... to develop their businesses until voluntarily they would agree to form co-operative enterprises, eventually merging with state industry when they

could see that this path would lead to a better standard of life for them.[14]

A clear warning was given:

> In Chile, disaster looms! Time is short! It is an open question whether the elections scheduled for February 1973 will take place or whether the bosses will move before then.

*Militant* called for the Chilean workers to

> Break the coalition with the capitalist parties! Socialists, demand the arming of the workers against the fascist commandos! Appeal to the troops! Link the workers' organisations on a programme of taking power![15]

At this time, the Labour Party Young Socialists sent a letter to their Chilean counterparts, the youth of the Socialist Party of Chile, which found a ready response. In the issue of 15 December *Militant* stated that: "Even Allende pointed out that the country was 'on the brink of civil war'." The denouement was not to come for almost nine months, but it came on 11 September 1973, with terrible consequences for the Chilean workers.

## PINOCHET'S COUP

All of the warnings about a threatened military coup seemed to be borne out. In August *Militant* pointed out that a national stoppage had been organised by the lorry owners' association, openly backed by internal counter-revolutionary forces linking up with the CIA. The July crisis had been "'resolved' by bringing three military commanders into the UP (Popular Unity) government. The UP government ended up granting all the lorry owners' main demands."[16]

The counter-revolution had attempted a coup, prematurely in June. The reason why the coup had failed was because "if so far the Chilean army has held back, the explanation is to be sought not in any peculiar national tradition, but in the formidable strength now acquired by the labour movement." In effect, the ground had not been fully prepared for open reaction and "loyal army units" had rallied to the side of the government.

At the same time, we pointed out that, "As news of the coup spread, thousands of workers struck, occupied their factories and, leaving armed pickets on the gates, marched on the presidential palace." If only this kind of approach had been adopted when the fatal blow was to strike in September.

Allende had

> appealed for a return to work and riot police were sent in to break up the milling crowds. Only this cowardice, this treachery, this total lack of respect, enabled the bosses to gasp for breath once more. Only the blocking of the movement of the masses as a result of this betrayal emboldened the road hauliers enough to raise their heads in defiance of the UP.

It was quite clear that "there is no shortage of courage, or willingness to fight. What is lacking is leadership."[17]

Reports were carried showing that the armed forces had disarmed workers and were conducting vicious and rigorous searches for arms in factories and workers' districts. "Naval officers have taken harsh action against the sailors who had been affected by revolutionary propaganda, conducting searches among them."

In effect, the officer caste in Valparaiso had arrested and were torturing those soldiers and naval ratings who were warning of a coup and urging Allende to arm the working class. *Militant* demanded that "the workers' organisations need to be armed in defence against the fascists." *Militant* appealed to the

> left wing, especially the Socialist youth (who) must fight for committees of action for the defence of the rights of the workers and the defence of the revolution to be set up in every factory, workers' district, armed forces, to be linked locally, in the districts and nationally together with all workers' organisations to provide the necessary invincible framework for pushing forward the revolution and defeating the counter-revolutionary plots of reaction. Arm the workers! Expel the capitalist ministers, civilian and military, from the UP government. For a socialist Chile![18]

Above all, warned *Militant,* "the capitalist class is preparing for civil war." The tragedy was that these words were written in a British newspaper without full access to the genuine forces of Marxism in Chile. The latter did not have a clear understanding or perspectives of how to change the situation. There were undoubtedly many heroic rank-and-file members of the Socialist and Communist Parties who were prepared to fight. There was a significant section of the youth in the Revolutionary Left Movement (MIR) who were armed. But there were no serious attempts to set up broad-based genuine workers' defence organisations. The lack of such organisations, flowing from the false policies of Socialist and Communist leaders, resulted in a catastrophe for the Chilean workers.

Two months later, after Pinochet launched his military coup, *Militant* reported, "Thousands of workers have died defending their occupied factories, or defiantly facing military assassination squads." We stated:

> If socialism itself is not a sentimental dream, then there is only one conclusion: the leadership and programme of the workers' organisations was false. And that is our conviction. The workers were led like lambs to the slaughter by the utterly false programme of their leaders.[19]

Only a few days before the coup, on Sunday 9 September, over a million workers had marched passed Allende on the balcony of the presidential palace in Santiago, the majority demanding arms. The workers tried heroically to defend the gains of 1970-73. However the tactics deployed were not those that could guarantee victory.

# 7.
# THE RISE OF MILITANT

IN BRITAIN, the Labour Party conference in October 1972, reflecting the huge shift towards the left in the trade unions and the Labour Party, passed a *Militant* resolution. By 3.5 million votes to less than 2.5 million, the conference voted for a programme which included the demand for 'an enabling bill to secure the public ownership of the major monopolies'. The conference called on the executive to "formulate a socialist plan of production based on public ownership, with minimum compensation, of the commanding heights of the economy". "This is an answer to those who argue for a slow, gradual, almost imperceptible progress towards nationalisation."[1]

The conference was moved when Pat Wall declared: "No power on earth can stop the organised labour movement!" He concluded by calling for Labour to win the workers to a programme of taking power by taking over the 350 monopolies which controlled 85 per cent of the economy.

Ray Apps seconded the resolution. He was to become almost a permanent fixture at Labour Party conferences, so much so that when the purge of *Militant* took place in the 1980s, *The Times* happily concluded that the conference had become an "Apps-free zone". Ray pointed to the 'excellent reforms' in Labour's programme but observed that "they cannot be carried out". At this conference, Patrick Craven, a well-known *Militant* supporter, received 51,000 votes in the election for the NEC, which reflected the support of between 45 to 50 local parties.

The week before the conference *Militant* recorded the significant growth in its support: "From a four-page monthly to an eight-page weekly in 13 months." Commenting on the progress which had been made it stated:

> The first eight-page *Militant* is out! This is the greatest achievement of our paper in its eight-years' life. In just 13 months it has been trans-

formed from a monthly four-page paper, with excellent articles, but poorly produced and drab looking, to a magnificently produced weekly eight-page paper. Politically we believe that *Militant* has always carried the best reports and clearest analysis of events in the labour movement and the world. The great handicap has been space.[2]

*The Times* had "looked hopefully towards 1972 as an improvement over the previous year". They commented that 1971 "was not a good year for Conservatives".

1972 was even worse. The miners had shattered the government's eight per cent wage norm, winning an increase of 22 per cent. In the miners' strike 65,000 miners out of 280,000 were involved in pickets. In answer to this, Tory Home Secretary Carr promised to set up "mobile squads" of police to counter the actions of the workers. The Heath government did not quite manage to do this but Thatcher, who followed him, learnt the lessons of the 1972 and 1974 miners' strikes and prepared the police in a paramilitary fashion to crush the miners next time they went on strike.

Indicating the power of the labour movement, even Vic Feather, the general secretary of the TUC in 1972, had declared: "No-one can do anything to the unions that the unions don't want done." *Militant* pointed out that

> the relationship of forces between the capitalist class and the working class is overwhelmingly favourable to the latter. But they are bound and gagged by their own leadership.[3]

Even after these tumultuous events, the general council of the TUC were still engaged in talks with the government!

## FROM OUT OF THE SEWER - THE NF

*Militant* warned that the path was not going to be smooth so long as capitalism remained. In December 1972, the National Front, the latest version of a fascist organisation in Britain, polled 12 per cent of the vote in the Uxbridge by-election.

> Northern Ireland is sufficient proof of the fact that lodged in every capitalist society are the psychopaths, sadists and maniacs who could make up the shock battalions of fascism under the 'right conditions'.[4]

*Militant* did not fall for the nonsense peddled by some, that the National Front and its leader, Webster, were on the eve of taking power. Only after a series of defeats of the working class, and after a base had been created amongst the ruined middle class and a section of the declassed workers, could fascism pose a big threat. Even then, it would not take the classical form of Hitler or Mussolini as had been the case pre-war. In the modern epoch, fascism would only act as an auxiliary to a military-police dictatorship.

Indicating the big changes which had taken place in Britain, *Militant*'s last issue of 1972 carried a table of strikes from 1963 to 1972. In 1963, 1,755,000 days had been lost in strike action. This had risen to almost 11 million by 1970. But, in the year 1972 this had doubled to over 22 million days lost in strike action. This was just one indication of the convulsive mood. It was no accident that it was precisely in this period when the working class was moving into action that *Militant* had made such decisive strides forward both in the expansion of the press and in the number of supporters who filled out our ranks. But, if anything, 1973 was to exceed in scope and importance even the events of the previous year.

Then, as now, with the rise of unemployment and the worsening of social conditions, the fascists and neo-fascists also began to gain some support. We reported:

> In the 1970 election, the 'Yorkshire Campaign Against Immigration' as it then was, recorded votes of over 20 per cent in several wards. Significantly, at a time of growing militancy, this vote fell sharply in 1971.

Yorkshire was one of the areas where racism was on the rise. *Militant*, dealing with the conditions in Bradford, stated:

> It is obvious that in these circumstances, pious appeals to brotherhood and racial harmony from the well-heeled do-gooders are worse than useless... It is not Race Relations Boards that are required, but positive action by the labour movement.[5]

Calling for workers to mobilise against the danger of racism in the area, *Militant* declared:

> Many Labour leaders think if they ignore the issue it will go away.

Other local leaders pander to racial prejudice thinking that will prevent 'racial extremists' from gaining support. No greater or more fatal mistake can be made. The movement must be mobilised now, locally and nationally. It must be geared to an anti-Tory, anti-capitalist campaign.[6]

As a result of the pressure of *Militant* supporters within the labour movement, and particularly the Labour Party Young Socialists, the national executive of the Labour Party sanctioned a national demonstration in Bradford, which took place in May 1974. This was the first national mobilisation of any section of the official labour movement against racism.

## GROWTH OF THE LPYS

The Labour Party Young Socialists, as a result of the general radicalisation of working-class youth and the consistent work of the Marxists, grew by leaps and bounds during the period of 1972-73. This was shown at the 1973 conference of the LPYS in Skegness where over a thousand delegates and visitors attended. *Militant* reported:

> The democracy of this conference is a shining example to the labour movement. The minority of the National Committee [non-Marxists and anti-*Militant*s in general] submitted their own documents to the conference for discussion. Differences were dealt with in a comradely way by the majority of delegates. Young Socialists must fight for similar rights for minorities in the trade union and Labour Party conferences.[7]

At the Skegness conference, there was tremendous enthusiasm for the ideas of Marxism underlined by the biggest ever *Militant* public meeting held at an LPYS conference up to then. All the fringe meetings were well attended, as was the week-long rally which followed the conference. *Militant*, however, still only had 397 organised supporters by March 1973 despite its growing influence. By July of the same year it had grown to 464.

It was not just at conferences of their own organisation that the weight of the LPYS was felt. The representative of the LPYS on the NEC of the Labour Party, Peter Doyle, was a key member of the Left who succeeded in getting the NEC to adopt a programme for the public ownership of 25 of Britain's top companies. The day after the NEC, Harold Wilson threatened that the shadow cabinet would veto its inclusion in the next election manifesto. *Militant* commented:

> Is national conference the supreme policy-making body of the Labour Party, or is it just a rally to cheer the politicians at the top? The NEC should be inundated with resolutions of support to strengthen its hand in defending party democracy.
>
> At the same time we must ask why the NEC has not insisted on the full implementation of the Shipley resolution? Which 25 companies, and why only them? Is it the intention to nationalise their assets or as originally proposed only for a state holding company to buy a 51 per cent share in them... If public ownership is the best system, then it applies to the entire economy. We do not want to take over every barbers' or fish and chip shop, but the giant monopolies that dominate the economy, numbering some 250-300.[8]

Interestingly, *Militant* quoted in the same issue the comments of Denis Healey:

> We are all agreed with the need for a massive extension of public ownership... establishing comprehensive planning control over the hundred or so largest companies in Britain... and to extend public ownership in the profitable manufacturing industries.[9]

Roy Hattersley, the leading right winger, also "argued in favour of nationalising North Sea gas and oil, development land and rented property."

This decision to propose the nationalisation of the 25 companies was carried with the decisive vote of Peter Doyle, LPYS representative on the NEC. This indicated the crucial role which the LPYS, and through them the Marxists, played in shaping the policy and the direction of the labour movement at this stage (and later, as *Militant* supporters, Nick Bradley, Tony Saunois, Laurence Coates, Steve Morgan, Frances Curran, Linda Douglas and Hannah Sell did over the next 15 years).

1973 seemed to demonstrate an almost unstoppable movement towards the Left within the labour movement.

In June of that year, *Militant* again reported on the progress of the Clay Cross struggle. John Dunn, a Clay Cross LPYS member and a future Clay Cross councillor, reported:

> Had other authorities built houses at the same rate as Clay Cross, we would have had the figure of one and a half million new houses being built every year. The complete municipalisation of all rented property is rapidly seeing the end of all landlords capitalising on second-rate property... No child in Clay Cross has missed his or her free school milk since 'milk-snatcher Thatcher' tried to take it away.[10]

Meanwhile, the Clay Cross councillors were being dragged before the law courts for refusing to implement the Housing Finance Act. The effective leader of the struggle, councillor David Skinner, appeared before the High Court on Monday 9 July, when judgement was reserved for two weeks. Writing in *Militant*, he declared:

> Our opposition was based on being honest with ourselves and the people who put us there and because, even in local government, it is possible to assist in changing society. To hear most councillors talk one would imagine they are incapable of organising resistance to the impositions of the central government. If all the Labour councils followed the example of Clay Cross it would be impossible to carry out the Housing Finance Act.

He went on:

> By not implementing the Act we have saved the working-class ratepayers £70,000. We do not look after only the tenants but the council employees as well. The unions claimed a one-third increase in wages which we have granted.[11]

Later they were surcharged and banned from office.

## WORKERS' PARTICIPATION OR CONTROL?

At the same time, *Militant* devoted considerable space to dealing with the key political and theoretical questions which had been raised in the ranks of the workers' organisations. Because of the tendency towards sit-ins, big strikes and the question of ownership of industry being raised in the course of this movement, the question of workers' control and workers' management featured very highly on the agenda of the labour movement. Mixed up with this were the ideas of workers' participation pushed by employers' representatives and also by sections of the trade union leadership. On workers' 'participation' *Militant* pointed out:

> If union officials were to rub shoulders more often with the capitalists on joint committees, swig their whiskey, etc, then they may be more disposed to take a 'responsible' attitude towards redundancies, rises in prices while wages are held down, and all the other crimes of capitalism. This is the fond hope of Heath and his crew. When stripped of all the fancy language, this is the real essence of 'participation' as envisaged by the capitalists and their hirelings.

Amongst leftward moving workers, however, there was a keen interest in workers' control. There was confusion over the demands for workers' control and management which was reinforced by some on the left. *Militant* explained:

> Both demands apply to different stages of the class struggle. Workers' control is only possible on a mass scale in the period which immediately precedes or just after the socialist revolution... Workers' control means that the workers exercise control over the capitalists, checking the outgoings and ingoings, having access to all the books and accounts of the capitalists... Workers' management, on the other hand, comes from above and is exercised by the workers' state, that is, the centralised soviets representing the workers as a whole.[12]

Some right-wing Labour leaders at the time sought to discredit the ideas of workers' control and management by denouncing them as 'syndicalism'. *Militant* argued that:

> The ideas of the syndicalists, that after the socialist revolution each industry will be managed and controlled by the workers in that industry, is completely utopian. Its implementation would lead to the complete breakdown of the economy and society, with one industry pitted against another. It would be impossible to implement a national plan, without which industry, science and technique could not develop.[13]

## THE LESSONS OF CHILE

The Chilean events dominated the British and the world labour movement from September onwards. It was a major item of discussion at the October 1973 Labour Party conference. Jack Jones remarked at a fringe meeting, with Tony Benn sitting alongside him, that he could perceive of a situation where a Labour government, led by Benn, could come to power and be faced with the same kind of conspiracy as Allende faced in Chile.

However, the dominating theme of the conference was a discussion around the radical programme adopted by the national executive of the Labour Party.

The pronounced shift towards the left was reflected in the documents of Labour's NEC. In 1972 and 1973 intense discussion took place which was supposed to outline a programme for the following ten years during which, it was assumed by the Labour leadership, they would be in power. The final document, *Labour's Programme 1973*, was one of the most radical left, documents ever accepted by the Labour Party.

It outlined far-reaching reforms to be introduced by a future Labour government. It made some references to partial nationalisation of the 25 biggest manufacturing companies. This represented a huge step forward in the thinking of the labour movement. *Militant*, while welcoming this proposal, nevertheless argued that it was still inadequate, given the crisis which faced British capitalism.

The programme summed up, in the main, the prevailing views of left reformism which dominated the Labour Party and to some extent the trade unions. *Militant* pointed out that to nationalise 25 profitable industries represented a fundamental attack on the very foundations of capitalism. The British ruling class would not roll over and play dead like a playful cat.

Moreover, the conference was debating these ideas precisely one month after the overthrow of the Allende government which had attempted to implement a similar programme. Allende had nationalised, under the pressure of the masses, which intensified after the failed coup of June 1973, 40 per cent of industry. But because he did not go the whole way and take over the 'commanding heights of the economy', Allende did not meet the demands of the masses but nevertheless irritated the ruling class. With their power undermined, but still largely intact, they were given time to prepare their bloody settling of accounts with the working class. *Militant* called for the taking over of the 250 monopolies, the banks and insurance companies, with compensation on the basis of proven need.

A sometimes passionate discussion took place at the 1973 Labour Party conference around these ideas. The conference reflected a dramatic shift towards the left of the politically conscious section of the working class.

The 1973 programme was accepted. *Militant* described it as "the most impressive programme since 1945". It was true, that compared to the Shipley resolution which was adopted in 1972, Labour's programme was not as radical. Moreover, a similar resolution to the Shipley one, moved this time by Brighton, Kemptown and Walton Constituency Labour Parties (composite 34) won only 291,000 votes, with 5.6 million votes against.

At this conference the clear socialist message of *Militant* found a ready response from delegates. But at the 1973 conference, enormous pressure was exerted by the leadership on the delegates, with appeals to unite on the eve of an expected election. The big unions in particular were mobilised to cast their block votes against the democratic decisions of their own conferences.

At the same time, the whole leadership, including those who stood on the right, such as Peter Shore and Denis Healey, supported the NEC's left stance. Yet despite all the pressures, some 250 constituency parties voted for a clear Marxist programme.

## NATIONALISE 25 OR 200?

Crucial in defeating composite resolution 34 was the intervention of the leading left spokesman. Jack Jones of the Transport and General Workers' Union said of our programme: "We don't think the objectives outlined there could be achieved by the next Labour government." More significantly, Tony Benn, while acknowleging that it was "firmly based upon the ideas of Clause IV", said that it "confuses strategy with tactics" and that the party is "not ready for composite 34".

Benn was the ablest and most sincere left spokesperson. But his arguments also revealed the limits of his perspectives, programme and also his understanding of the situation which faced the labour movement. He stood first of all for the takeover of the 25 companies and then 'step by step' moving towards taking over the majority of at least the big companies. His arguments flew in the face both of the experiences of the Chilean workers and the whole history of the British labour movement. We argued that no lasting reform can be achieved by the next Labour government unless it begins by first taking over the 'commanding heights' - the banks, the land and the 250 giant monopolies - into its hands, and that this can only be done by mobilising the movement in support of emergency legislation.[14]

Benn received loud applause at the conference for the statement: "If we do not control or own them (the monopolies), they will control and own us." This was a direct reflection of the pressure of the Marxists, gathered around the *Militant*, on the leading lefts within the labour movement. Yet Benn and the other lefts did not draw all the conclusions from their own statements. Nevertheless, an indication of the mood of the conference was shown in the left rhetoric of those to the right of Benn, the Tribunite left.

## TRIBUNE

The present *Tribune* leadership would undoubtedly cringe in embarrassment when confronted with their statements of 1973. *Tribune* greeted the conference with the exultant headline: "We've kept the red flag flying here." Michael Foot characterised the 1973 programme as "the finest socialist programme that I have ever seen in my lifetime." He was to sing a different tune in the 1980s.

As significant were the votes for *Militant* Ray Apps and close ally David Skinner, who received 81,000 and 144,000 votes respectively in the elections for the Constituency section of the NEC. 150 people attended the *Militant* conference meeting and over 1,000 copies of *Militant* were sold. *The Times* summed up the conference thus:

> The doctrines of class conflict and state ownership are Marxist doctrines, and so long as both are preached at their conference, the Labour Party must not complain at being described as under the influence of Marxist ideas.[15]

For once, this was a truthful account of what had transpired at the conference and what was also taking place in constituency parties and trade union branches.

A month after the conference, however, Labour suffered a defeat in the Glasgow Govan by-election and also recorded low votes in a number of other seats. The ruling class were exultant and blamed Labour's programme for these setbacks. In reality, the opposite was the case. The programme adopted by the conference was never used to organise a bold campaign which clearly set Labour apart from all other parties. This was particularly evident in Govan where at least the Scottish National Party, as *Militant* reported "grasped that there was a basis for a radical sounding campaign." The SNP demanded the setting up of a Scottish Parliament with control over industry. Their slogan "Poor British or Rich Scots", clearly related to the discovery and potential revenue from North Sea oil.

## 1974 MINERS' STRIKE

The Heath government, smarting from the bloody nose which it had received at the hands of the miners in 1972, once more decided to take them on. This was a conscious decision to defeat the British workers by breaking their 'brigade of guards'. The miners' work-to-rule, combined with the electrical power workers refusal to work around the clock, ushered in a 'state of emergency'. Petrol rationing, power cuts and a 13 per cent interest rate were introduced. Through Heath, British capitalism quite clearly believed that this was a fight to the finish.

Echoing the sentiments of the government, *The Times* declared: "We cannot afford the cost of surrender." This mouthpiece of big business raised the spectre of an 'authoritarian solution' to Britain's crisis. It implied that to grant the miners' claims would result in uncontrollable inflation and in this situation

> you do not then only have cranks, or shabby men in Hitler moustaches, advocating an authoritarian solution. The most calm and respectable people come to believe that the only remaining choice is to impose a policy of sound money at the point of a bayonet.[16]

*Militant* declared:

> A victory for the miners will be a body blow to the Tories and a triumph for the whole working class. But to win this bitter fight, the whole movement must be mobilised and the campaign extended onto a political plane for the defeat of the Tory government.[17]

The government in effect declared a lock-out for two days every week against the British working class. As 1974 began *Militant* commented:

> Many bosses had jumped the gun, laying off 554,000 workers by last weekend. One to two million totally unemployed is predicted very soon, as the bosses use the emergency as an excuse for sackings; 100,000 in steel alone has been forecast. 15 million workers will be affected with the drastic cut in wages that implies.[18]

*Militant* demanded: (1) Recall of the TUC conference; (2) Work or full pay; and (3) A one-day general strike. The intimidatory methods of the government did not have the desired effect in splitting the rest of the working class away from the miners. The *Evening Standard* reported on the views of workers forced out of their jobs in the queue on a London employment exchange: "To a man - and woman - they were behind the miners."[19]

Nevertheless, the Heath government persisted with its trial of strength, even resorting to openly publicising the training of the army and the police in riot control techniques. The army displayed its prowess at Heathrow Airport. Tanks and other military hardware, allegedly for use in 'anti-terrorist' and 'anti-subversive' situations, were deployed. This prompted Scottish miners' leader, Mick McGahey to say that if soldiers were asked to break a miners' strike then

> I will appeal for them to assist and aid the miners. Troops are not all anti-working class... Many of them are miners' sons - sons of the working class.[20]

This provoked the fury of the ruling class. The London *Evening Standard* carried the comments of the commanding officer of a British infantry battalion:

> Give me the chance to go and pick up Mr Michael McGahey and if it turns out to be my last assignment in the army I should die happy. The kind of remarks he made about appealing to the troops represents a very sinister trend - not because he made them, but because we are too weak-willed a society nowadays to clap him straight inside for incitement to mutiny.

However, the *Evening Standard*, much more cautiously, summed up the thinking of a section of the ruling class:

> How far could the government rely on the army to do whatever was asked of it in a major industrial emergency? If McGahey and his supporters appealed to British soldiers as fellow workers, would there ever be a chance that they could cause a military unit to break ranks?

One Glasgow soldier declared:

> I wouldn't move coal. It's not my job; if the miners want to strike for more money, good luck to them.[21]

The whole furore around this issue indicated the heightened class tensions which existed in Britain at this stage. *Militant* pointed out:

> Such champions of democracy as the Tories depict themselves today would not think twice at abandoning their democratic veil if they felt it necessary. It would be a fatal mistake to bow down to the army.[22]

Another example of the attempt at intimidation of workers was the arrest, trial and subsequent jailing of two building workers, the Shrewsbury Two; Ricky Tomlinson (who later earned fame by appearing in *Brookside*, and other TV programmes and films) and Des Warren, (Des was sentenced to three years and released after 30 months; Ricky got two years and was released after 18 months).

## GENERAL ELECTION

Faced with a rising tide of discontent, however, the Heath government was panicked into calling a general election on the theme of 'Who rules - Us or the Miners?' The February 1974 general election shaped up to the be the most important and one of the dirtiest since 1945. The miners' action had polarised not just society but the labour movement.

In the general election, the whole movement mobilised behind the miners and in support of Labour. This was the first general election in which *Militant* supporters were able to play a crucial role in a number of key marginal seats, particularly through the intervention of the Labour Party Young Socialists. In the Bristol

South-East constituency, held by Tony Benn, the Tories and Liberals were making a determined effort to defeat Labour.

A defeat for Benn would represent a blow against the whole of the Left. This was the reasoning of the strategists of capitalism. *The Times* had admitted as much: Tony Benn's "defeat... would check the whole left-wing movement in the Labour Party at a particularly important moment." In reply to this we countered:

> over 400 Labour Party Young Socialists poured into Bristol last weekend to help the South-East Constituency Party fight this crucial marginal seat. They came from all parts of the country, in buses, cars, and minibuses: from South Wales, London, Gloucester, Devon, Birmingham, Coventry, Manchester, Medway towns, Harlow, Nottingham and other places.[23]

This intervention was decisive in holding the seat for Labour. *Militant* supporters played a crucial role in ensuring a Labour victory. The paper's opponents also suggested that it was decisive in a number of seats. In view of later charges of "sectarianism" against us, it is important to note that despite the fact that there was no parliamentary candidate clearly supporting *Militant* or Marxism, we nevertheless threw our full weight into ensuring a Labour victory.

Yet *Militant*, and particularly the Labour Party Young Socialists, earned nothing but praise, not just from those lefts like Tony Benn who publicly recognised their role, but also from those on the right like Paul Rose, MP for Blackley in Manchester.

At that time, *Militant* clearly warned that a new Labour government which remained within the framework of capitalism could be frustrated by the serious crisis of British capitalism.

# 8.
# THE WORKING CLASS ON THE MOVE: INTERNATIONAL EVENTS 1974-75

IN APRIL 1974, the Portuguese revolution reduced the 50-year old Caetano dictatorship to dust. *Militant*, which sent Lynn Walsh to Portugal, reported: "All the faces of world reaction are watching with horror the revolutionary storm which is sweeping Portugal."[1] Initiated by the young army officers in revolt against the catastrophic colonial wars in Mozambique and Angola, millions of workers poured out onto the streets of Lisbon and the other towns of Portugal to celebrate a new dawn.

Workers seized the headquarters of the old fascist-controlled trade unions, and discussions took place over whether the factories should be taken over. The workers and the youth fraternised with the army, with ordinary soldiers and sailors in uniform participating in the mass demonstrations in Lisbon and elsewhere. But, as in many revolutions, having overthrown one dictatorship, and without strong conscious leadership and organisation, power was handed over to another potential dictator, General Spinola.

This was a man who had fought for Franco in the Spanish Civil War and served on the Eastern Front with the Nazi army during the second world war. When handing over power, Caetano declared: "General, I surrender to you the government. You must take care because you must keep control. I am frightened by the idea of the power loose in the streets."[2]

We said that with a decisive, clear leadership, the Portuguese workers could have established the foundations of socialism. Nevertheless, we anticipated:

> If, as is almost certain, a popular front government [ie a capitalist government supported by the workers' parties] is formed in Portugal in the immediate future, although it will be enormously popular at first, the realities of class conflict will be manifested. The demands of the workers will not and cannot be met on the basis of capitalism.[3]

In the first flush of enthusiasm, the workers had spontaneously raised red flags and carried slogans such as 'Long live the socialist revolution'.

One indication of the enormous radicalisation was that the Socialist Party, consisting of a mere 50 people in exile and led by a Paris-based lawyer, Mario Soares, in a matter of months became a mass party. Soares, under the pressure of the masses, declared: "The Socialist Party stands on the basis of Marxism." In reality Soares had never developed into a rounded-out Marxist, only mouthing Marxist phrases, but remaining firmly within the framework of capitalism. This was to be tragically demonstrated in the next two to three years.

## GREECE - JUNTA OVERTHROWN

On the heels of the Portuguese events came the revolutionary explosions in Greece of July 1974. This was triggered by the seizure of power in Cyprus by the tiny EOKA B fascist elements and the eviction of President Makarios from office. This in turn led to the Turkish invasion which ended in the partition of Cyprus, with one-third under Turkish control.

These events enormously encouraged the forces of Marxism in Britain and also resulted in new groups looking towards the ideas of *Militant* in those countries which had overthrown dictatorships. In Greece, two groups of Marxists in Athens within weeks of the overthrow of the dictatorship had read about the ideas of *Militant*, agreed with them, and opened up discussions with us.

One group was led by Nicos Remoundos, who fought against the junta in exile and still plays a key role in the Marxist movement and the Left in Greece. Another youth group in Cyprus around the newly formed Socialist Party moved in the direction of *Militant,* later joining the ranks of our international co-thinkers. Of the original group won to *Militant's* ideas Andros Payiatsos and Doros Michael still play a key role in Greece and Cyprus.

In Sweden, through the intervention of *Militant* supporters in the LPYS at the International Union of Socialist Youth (IUSY) conference, Arne Johansson and Anders Hjelm were won to *Militant's* ideas. They played a decisive role in building a powerful Marxist force in Sweden which now rivals *Militant Labour* in Britain in its specific weight in the labour movement.

Roger Silverman made an initial visit to Greece in September and I went in December. This resulted in the winning over of the two groups to *Militant*'s outlook and the idea of organised international collaboration. The Greek Marxists, gathered around the journal *Xekinima* (Beginning), have played an important role in the workers' movement in Greece, particularly in Pasok (the Greek Socialist Party), which was formed in 1974.

Even before Andreas Papandreou, the leader of Pasok, had envisaged the development of such a party, *Militant* had predicted its emergence. A new generation of workers looking for a revolutionary solution, repelled by Stalinism, would look towards the creation of such a party. Pasok was formed in September 1974 and became a mass organisation from its inception.

Moreover, it moved to what Trotsky called a 'centrist' position, oscillating between the ideas of Marxism and reformism. At this stage, Papandreou represented a left expression of centrism. This in turn drew into its ranks some of the best sections of the youth and intellectuals, thereby providing fertile ground for the growth of Marxist ideas. The present organisation of Pasok, led by an ailing Papandreou, is a far cry from the heady, radical, revolutionary days of 1974.

## WATERGATE

Meanwhile, another massive upheaval unfolded in the United States. President Nixon, after a desperate struggle to cling to power, was forced to resign. If he had not done so, he would have been impeached (i.e. prosecuted and removed from office by Congress), which would have been a devastating blow for the whole political system of the US ruling class. As it happened, the 'Watergate scandal', as *Militant* pointed out, provoked a potentially revolutionary crisis in US society. The catastrophe of Vietnam led to the open revolt of the US armed forces, in turn igniting the upheavals in the cities. In 1970 the National Guard had been used against the first national Teamsters' (lorry drivers) strikes. Some of these National Guardsmen were then sent to Kent State University in Ohio to police an anti-Vietnam protest: three students were shot dead by the Guards.

Two-thirds of the population had wanted Nixon out and prosecuted. If a mass socialist party had existed, this political crisis could have become the starting point for the overthrow of the mightiest capitalist power on the globe. These events underlined *Militant's* contention that it was not just economic collapse, slump or recession, which could provoke a revolutionary crisis. The Dreyfus affair in France, in the 1890s (involving the frame-up of Captain Alfred Dreyfus by the French officer caste) was an example of how a political event could lay bare the essence of capitalist society, its state, hypocrisy, etc, and pose the need for the revolutionary overthrow of capitalism. Watergate fell into the same category. The American ruling class saved its bacon by switching from Nixon to Ford and withdrawing from Vietnam.

# 9.
# A LABOUR GOVERNMENT - BUT WHERE'S THE SOCIALISM?

AFTER THE savage attacks on the working class under the Tory government a certain relief was felt by workers with the election of a Labour government. Nevertheless, there was also a determined mood to push for the implementation of radical policies. This was demonstrated at the LPYS conference and rally at Easter 1974. Tony Benn opened the conference and

> praised the work of the LPYS in the election campaign, particularly the decisive intervention of 400 Young Socialists in the key Bristol South-East seat. He conveyed the gratitude of the local party... He said that the Tories were out to neutralise the Labour government and exert pressure for the formation of a national coalition.[1]

At this conference, Nick Bradley, the *Militant* candidate from the Deptford Labour Party Young Socialists, was elected as the LPYS representative on the NEC of the Labour Party by 143 votes with his nearest rival, Rose Digiorgio, receiving only 18 votes. All the meetings and the rallies were full to capacity indicating that the LPYS was the strongest youth organisation, not just in Britain but - certainly politically - in the whole of Western Europe.

In Britain, following the election of Labour, workers were pressing forward in an attempt to ensure the implementation of the reforms which had been promised. In the Health Service, for instance, at Charing Cross Hospital, the NUPE branch moved to ban 'private practice'. This represented an attempt to force Health Minister Barbara Castle's hand but reduced Tory spokesmen to apoplexy. *Militant* reported: "Already 110 hospitals in the North East and many others in Yorkshire and Manchester have been operating a ban on private patients." The article pointed out:

> What has really sent a shiver through their spines has been that these

workers have taken seriously the programme of the Labour government.[2]

In retrospect and in view of the catastrophic position in the Health Service today, with the virtual dismantling of the NHS, these movements were extremely significant. It demonstrates that if Labour had then based itself upon the movement of workers from below, and linked this to a change in society, the present health nightmare which confronts workers could have been entirely avoided.

Ian Burge, a long-standing *Militant* supporter and a leading steward at the London Hospital (who tragically died in 1980), wrote in a characteristically incisive article:

> Ancilliary workers in some hospitals have in fact been operating sanctions against private treatment since the strike campaign on wages in early 1973.

He demanded:

> Take over the drug companies and use this money to pay the health workers a decent wage. Abolish private medicine, give all support to the healthworkers' campaign. Let the health service be run by elected workers in the service, with trade unionist delegates from the district and government representatives.[3]

## SCOTLAND: HOME RULE?

At the same time, in Scotland the future themes played out in full today were developing in outline. In August 1974 *Militant* carried an article headed: "Scottish Parliament: will it answer workers' needs?" It pointed out that the executive committee of the Labour Party in Scotland had voted by six votes to five to recommend "opposition to any form of Assembly"! The Scottish Labour Party in effect said that an Assembly was irrelevent, stating:

> The essential strategy of the Labour Party is to bring about a fundamental and irreversible shift in the balance of power and wealth in favour of working people and their families. In the light of this criteria... constitutional tinkering does not make a meaningful contribution towards achieving our socialist objectives.

*Militant* was only just beginning to formulate a clear analysis and a programme which took account of the growth of national feelings in Scotland. Nevertheless, *Militant* argued:

> If the majority of Scottish people desire a Scottish Parliament, or if there is a majority for complete self-government, this is their right, and Labour would be bound to support it. There can be no question of maintaining the 'United Kingdom' against the will of the people of Scotland.[4]

The national question in Scotland was to come back onto the political agenda again and again. It compelled the Marxists to undertake a re-evaluation of the issue and to work out a programme capable of answering the legitimate national demands of the Scottish people. We did not always have complete agreement within our ranks, even losing some supporters when we argued for a programme for national rights. Subsequent events demonstrated that only *Militant* was capable of working out such a programme. This is one reason why in 1995, Scottish Militant Labour has had a bigger effect on this and other issues than any other organisation in Scotland.

## OCTOBER - OUR TENTH BIRTHDAY AND A GENERAL ELECTION

October saw the tenth anniversary of the founding of *Militant*. A special celebration article in the paper referred to the statements in our first issue. The editors claimed: "*Militant* has lived up to those aims."

> The sunny optimism of the strategists of capital still lingered on in the early 1960s. They had relegated to the pages of history the terms 'slump' and 'mass unemployment', 'poverty' and 'starvation'. They maintained that these denoted an age of barbarism which the 'new capitalism' had put an end to once and for all.[5]

The editorial compared the mood of the capitalists in the 1960s to that which existed in 1974, particularly following the Portuguese, Greek and US upheavals. Reflecting this pessimism, Willy Brandt (leader of the SPD) the West German 'Labour Party', had stated following the Portuguese events that "Communism (meaning in this case the taking of power by the working class) or fascism" was the choice Europe faced in the following 20 years. *Militant* believed:

> the next stage in the struggle in Britain will be a further swing towards the left. However, victory over the Tories and the system which breeds them can only be achieved on the basis of the re-arming of the Labour movement with a socialist - a Marxist - programme.[6]

*Militant*'s support had received a big boost in 1973 and 1974. By July 1974 the number of organised supporters stood at 517.

And this was underlined by the general election, the second in 1974, which was called in October. Labour won a tiny majority. The Tories were massacred in Scotland and Wales; in both areas they were forced into third place behind Labour and the Nationalists. The Tory Party received its lowest ever share of the poll, a mere 35.7 per cent of the vote. An indication of the swing towards Labour was that between February and October 1974 the Tory vote dropped by over 1.5 million votes. At the same time the Liberal shadows of the Tory Party had suffered a crushing rebuff, dropping 700,000 votes while fielding an extra 100 candidates.

## LABOUR WINS: MILITANT WARNS: CAPITAL STRIKES

The result meant that workers extended more time to the Labour leaders to fulfil their promises. The majority would have been greater if an enthusiastic, radical, socialist campaign had been conducted as urged by *Militant*. Despite the victory, Labour leader Wilson announced on TV on the Tuesday following the election (8 October) that he would immediately open talks with the CBI. *Militant* commented:

> Along this road lies disaster for the labour movement. It was not idle speculation when the editor of *The Times* commented two days before the election that the party that won the election would be the party most likely to be destroyed by events!

We continued:

> The top 20 companies are controlled by just 297 men. 85 per cent of production is in the hands of 250 giant monopolies.[7]

The government would either have to capitulate to the monopolies or rest on the labour movement and carry out socialist policies. The Labour leaders advanced the idea of a so-called 'social contract', which was "wage restraint by any other name."

Within weeks, *Militant*'s predictions had been borne out, as sections of the ruling class threatened a 'strike of capital'. Pilkington Glass, for instance, had declared that they would refuse to invest unless the government capitulated to the demands of the CBI. This was followed by similar declarations by the bosses of Hawker Siddeley and Metal Box. We pointed out "What else is this but the most blatant blackmail? They are sending the CBI leaders to 10 Downing Street, with a savage threat to the Labour government: 'Capitulate to us or else'!"

In November, Labour held its rearranged party conference in Central Hall, Westminster, which lasted for only two days. The conference took place just six weeks after the election. Ray Apps, a delegate to the conference, warned of the dangers facing the Labour government if conference decisions were not implemented. He wrote in *Militant*:

> It has to be said that the government has given in to this [the bosses'] blackmail... Handouts of £1,600 million have been made to big business.[8]

A few crumbs had been left over for the working people, 'in the form of family allowances and pensions increases' but these were to be delayed until the spring of the next year.

As an indication of what was to come, the financial editor of *The Times* praised Chancellor Healey's "tough orthodoxy". The conference reflected the outline of the future clashes in the party. Callaghan opened the conference with threats that inflation and unemployment would spiral unless the social contract was upheld. General secretary Ron Hayward, on the other hand, attacked those "who would treat the conference with contempt". He said that ward secretaries were more important to the party than ministers!

The emergence of *Militant* during the election campaign, and our growing strength, clearly reflected at this conference, sent shivers down the spines of the right wing. It set the scene for the witch-hunt which was soon to begin and unfolded over more than a decade, first against *Militant* and then against the rest of the left.

## BIRMINGHAM BOMBED

In November, the horrific Birmingham Pub bombings took place, resulting in the death of 19 people and the injuring, scarring and maiming of nearly 200 predominantly young people. *Militant* declared unequivocally: "Bombings play into the hands of reaction." *Militant* had consistently opposed the oppressive role of British imperialism in Ireland. But at the same time we had opposed the disastrous policies of terrorism of the Provisional IRA. The extension of the campaign to Britain held out potentially disastrous consequences for the British working class. *Militant* pointed out that "whoever planted them, the fact stands out that the Birmingham bombs can only benefit the interests of the enemies of both British and Irish workers." The immediate aftermath resulted in a backlash against Irish workers in Birmingham and other parts of the country. This was undoubtedly whipped up by the small fascist groups who reared their heads after the bombing.

This incident also provided the opportunity for the British ruling class, through the Labour Home Secretary, Roy Jenkins, to rush through repressive legislation. This was the 'Prevention of Terrorism Act' which has been used to harass and intimidate innocent Irish and other workers for over 20 years. Moreover, the bombings led to the arrest of the totally innocent Birmingham Six and their inhuman incarceration in British jails. It also created the hysterical atmosphere which was to later lead to the jailing of innocent people like Judith Ward, the Guildford Four, and others. *Militant* reported:

> At the huge British Leyland Longbridge factory, fights have broken out between British and Irish men who have worked together for years. In 30 leading Birmingham factories workers have struck, demanding action against the IRA.[9]

But the effects were not confined to Britain, as *Militant* commented: "The worst reaction will probably be in Northern Ireland itself, and the brunt will be borne by precisely the people that the IRA claims to protect - the Catholic workers."[10]

The intervention of the fascists, however, could not succeed in channelling the anger at the bombings in a sustained reactionary direction. Far more important in the consciousness of workers in Birmingham and elsewhere was the daily problem of struggling to live and their ability to face up to the offensive that was being conducted by the employers.

## THE RISING TIDE OF INDUSTRIAL STRUGGLE

An intensive struggle was unfolding on the factory floor as the employers sought to take revenge for the defeat of their party in the general election. Reflecting the increased growth of Marxists in the factories, the pages of *Militant* carried many detailed reports of what was taking place.

In September 1974 an article by Bill Mullins, who was a British Leyland senior shop steward representing 10,000 workers, wrote:

> It is difficult for someone who has never worked in a car factory to visualise the destructive nature of the work, destructive to the body because of the pace of the work, destructive to the mind because of the mind-bending repetition of the work.

A ferocious offensive was being conducted by management who were

> saying that the workers of BLMC must take a drop in their standards of living because they will not be able to afford the sort of minimum pay increases that are necessary to remain at the present standard of living.

The article concluded:

> The answer must be that the workers are not prepared to pay for the mismanagement and incompetence of the company. The demands should be: a minimum increase of £15 a week; the books to be opened [for inspection] to the trade unions. The nationalisation under workers' control of British Leyland.[11]

A Sword of Damocles, in the form of threatened closure, was held over the heads of Leyland workers. Even though it was the country's largest private employer (about 160,000 workers at this time) reports circulated in the capitalist press showed that the company was in difficulties and was turning to the Labour government for financial handouts.

Detailed, explanatory articles by *Militant* supporters Bill Mullins and Bob Ashworth, who both worked at Rover Solihull, showed up the state of the company. *Militant* published a resolution from the Rover production workers in Solihull who, among other things, demanded that if BLMC was asking for 'government cash handouts', then the Labour and trade union movement must

> demand that the Labour government nationalises BLMC under workers' control with members of the board of management being elected on the following basis: one-third elected by workers within BLMC; one-third elected by the TUC; one-third appointed by the government.[12]

A meeting in Birmingham of all Leyland convenors nationally passed the resolution from the Rover Solihull plant which demanded workers' control. Some amendments were carried to the resolution but, nevertheless, the fact that a significant group of workers had demanded workers' control of their industry indicated the mood that was developing. Even Labour MPs were affected.

At a meeting organised in Preston by the Labour Party Young Socialists, with 80 in attendance, a Labour MP, George Rodgers, agreed with all the speakers that nationalisation was the only way out. This was in sharp contrast to the Labour government's proposals, to be implemented through the recently formed National Enterprise Board (NEB). *Militant* pointed out that "over half of British manufacturing output is controlled by the top 100 companies". Moreover, the Tories, through 'state intervention' had doled out between 1970 and 1974 £3 billion (£2 million a day) to their friends in big business.

Despite the clamour for the nationalisation of failing capitalist firms, the Labour government, through the NEB, continued the policy of bailing them out. Tony Benn, as Industry Minister, presided over this policy, which was increasingly criticised by both Labour and trade union members.

## THE SHREWSBURY TWO

At the same time, the building bosses and their legal hirelings were refusing to budge in the face of a wave of protests demanding the release of the jailed Shrewsbury pickets. In November the appeal of the pickets was turned down. This was followed by protest strike action by Glasgow shipyard workers, building workers and others who marched on Ucatt headquarters in Glasgow to demand action to free "their jailed brothers". Similar action took place in Liverpool, Edinburgh and other parts of the country.

Demands were sent to the Labour Home Secretary, Roy Jenkins, calling for the pickets to be released. A telegram from over 100 Merseyside building shop stewards to Jenkins declared: "We supported you in your re-election to the government. We ask you now to support us."

The example of the release of the Pentonville dockers because of mass pressure was still fresh in the minds of both building workers and the ten-million-strong trade union movement. However, calls to the TUC and the Ucatt leadership unfortunately fell on deaf ears. The Shrewsbury pickets were to languish in jail. Against the general background of the industrial upsurge in militancy, in the 1970s, the lack of will of the TUC to mobilise the labour movement with all its power to force the release of the Shrewsbury pickets was perhaps the most shameful.

## TEMPERATURE RISES - FIRE AT OUR OFFICE

In the midst of these events, in February 1975, *Militant* suffered a big blow. One of our buildings in Commercial Road, East London, was gutted by fire and some vital printing machinery and most of the upper floors of the building were destroyed. This did not cripple *Militant* because the main headquarters was in a separate building.

Nevertheless, the 14 February issue of *Militant* was produced under exceptionally difficult conditions. An urgent appeal was made to *Militant* supporters, who responded magnificently. For a time the paper had to be produced without colour. As soon as the means to go back to regular production was acquired a two-colour, 16-page paper was back in production.

# 10.
# ENTER MILITANT STAGE LEFT

ORIGINALLY PERCEIVED as someone who would take on the working class, Heath had been knocked off course by the ferocious resistance to his policies by workers between 1970 and 1974. The battles of UCS, the miners' strikes of 1972 and 1974, the defeat of the Tories in the 1974 general election, all signified the colossal potential power of the organised working class and labour movement. Thatcher's rise to the leadership of the Tory Party, backed by her zealous 'guru', Sir Keith Joseph, signified the adoption of the club in place of the velvet glove by the capitalist backers of the Tory Party.

But in 1975 the labour movement was compelled to pay more attention to their own right-wing Tory 'infiltrators'. Arch-rightwing Labour MP Reg Prentice in March criticised the trade unions for allegedly 'welching' on the 'social contract'. It was not the first time, as seen earlier, that Prentice had sided with the enemies of the labour movement. At the height of the confrontation with the Tories in 1972 Prentice spoke out against the Pentonville Five. He had also refused to meet a delegation from the West Ham trades council, in his local area, who were lobbying for the release of the Shrewsbury pickets.

Prentice was not the only one. Roy Jenkins and Shirley Williams were a right-wing wedge within the Cabinet against any attempt to bow to working-class pressure. They had come out full-square in defence of the Common Market, which alienated them from the leftward moving workers within the labour movement.

Prentice's continuous attacks on the trade unions brought him more and more into conflict with his Constituency Labour Party in Newham North East. This led to pressure for his replacement as an MP, which was theoretically allowed under Labour Party rules and in which we played a big role. The merest hint of opposition to Prentice, however, elicited the unprecedented move of 181 MPs, including 13 cabinet ministers, 'backing Prentice'. Ultimately,

Prentice defected to the Tories and became a Tory minister. A newly formed 'Social Democratic Alliance' came into being, allegedly to fight the 'drift to the left'. At the same time, every single left-wing delegate to the Newham North-East Constituency Labour Party was harassed by the press.

*Militant* declared: "If Newham North-East Labour Party sticks to its guns it will have the overwhelming support of the party rank and file. It will mark a big step forward in the struggle to make Labour MPs accountable to the organisations of the labour movement."[1]

## BELOFF ATTACKS MILITANT

The same voices defending Prentice were increasingly raised against *Militant* and others on the left, demanding our exclusion from the Labour Party. This campaign led to a major article splashed across the front page of the *Observer* on 31 August, the first of many press attacks on *Militant*. The author of the article was Nora Beloff. The headline over Beloff's hatchet job read: "Trot conspirators inside Labour Party." This 'in depth' analysis was riddled with inaccuracies: *Militant* was referred to as a 'fortnightly' when it was in fact weekly. Ted Grant, who was referred to by Beloff as the "spiritual leader", Nick Bradley, LPYS representative on Labour's National Executive Committee, and myself, were given a special mention. It was clear that Beloff's 'bombshell' had been prepared in collusion with the Labour right. One indication of this was that Beloff featured an alleged threat to James Callaghan in his Cardiff South-East Constituency Labour Party. This was supposed to be orchestrated by *Militant* supporter Andrew Price, "lecturer at Rumney Technical College, who is the prime mover against Mr Callaghan." Beloff accused *Militant* of being a "party within a party", of having secret sources of funds, of propounding all kinds of 'extremist' policies and of having dubious and sinister connections. We replied in *Militant*:

> It is significant that all these attacks, particularly that of the *Observer*, do not deal with the ideas of *Militant*, openly expressed, which have a great tradition in the labour movement and are the continuation of the ideas of the pioneers of the labour movement and of Marx, Engels, Lenin and Trotsky.[2]

Beloff's broadside was not just an assault on *Militant* but was also calculated to create an atmosphere of hysteria which could lay the basis for an attack on the left as a whole. It was also in expectation of the possible measures to be taken at the coming Labour Party conference, one month after these attacks. But while attempting to rally the left against the attacks of the right, *Militant* never in any way hid its political differences with others.

## DEBATE WITH TRIBUNE

The major left trend within the movement at that stage gathered around the journal *Tribune*. Many articles in *Militant* were devoted to arguing against the deficiencies in *Tribune*'s programme in a comradely fashion. In May an article took up '*Tribune* and the struggle for socialism'. We pointed out that the recent elections, which had been fought on the most radical programme since 1945, was largely inspired by the Tribunite left. The latter had also grown substantially within the Parliamentary Labour Party. One-quarter of the PLP, 83 MPs, counted themselves as part of the *Tribune* group. Moreover, left trade union leaders such as Lawrence Daly of the miners' union, Hugh Scanlon, of the engineering union, Jack Jones of the TGWU and others, adhered to the ideas of *Tribune*. Only within the PLP did the right actually have a majority.

Of course Marxists, alongside others on the left, would fight for every improvement in the conditions of workers, would seek to defend and raise living standards. But they also had a duty to point to the real state of affairs in Britain, to explain that all these reforms were temporary so long as capitalism existed. Even *The Times* carried articles in 1975 pointing out that the "era of full employment is over".

In truth, serious capitalist commentators were more accurate in diagnosing the situation than some of the leading left reformist leaders. Tony Benn represented the most left trend within what was a very broad *Tribune* grouping. In the issue of *Tribune* following the October 1974 election victory, the statement of Tony Benn was approvingly quoted: "We said at our last conference that the crisis we would inherit should be the occasion for making changes, not the excuse for postponing it."[3]

Yet Jack Jones in the very same issue of *Tribune* argued for 'patience'. Labour could not proceed quickly to solve all the problems, he argued. *Tribune*'s criticism of the right amounted to a charge of a lack of 'courage' or 'intellect'. *Militant*, on the other hand, pointed out that

> so long as Denis Healey and the Labour cabinet as a whole have opted for working within the framework of capitalism, so must they bow to the remorseless demands of the system. Profits come from the unpaid labour of the working class. In the final analysis, there is only way to increase the profits of the capitalists, by cutting the share of the wealth, created by the labour of the working class, which goes to them.[4]

It was pointed out that

> we will support all steps towards the left within the labour movement. But we also criticise the flabbiness of the *Tribune* tendency, the inconsistencies in its programme, the lack of any clear perspective for future developments and their empirical reaction to events. It is not excluded, and indeed it is likely, that the *Tribune* or a section of it, under the hammer blows of events, could embrace some of the ideas presently advanced by *Militant*. But the experience of the prewar 'lefts' like John Strachey or the ILP [Independent Labour Party], much further to the left than the present *Tribune* tendency, demonstrates that mere verbal radicalism is not sufficient.[5]

Around this time in 1975, a meeting took place between *Militant* representatives and a delegation from the *Tribune* Group of Labour MPs. It became quite clear that while the MPs were worried at the drift to the right of the Labour government their opposition would not go beyond mere verbal posturing. That is why the *Tribune* group of MPs' invitation to Constituency Labour Parties, trade unions, co-ops and individuals to discuss a special statement with a view to organising a campaign never really got off the ground.

## COMMON MARKET REFERENDUM

The ferocious campaign around the Common Market referendum widened and deepened the splits at all levels of the labour movement. Through the initiative of the Labour Party Young Socialists, together with other independent socialists, an internationalist and class campaign was conducted by the Marxists during the 1975 referendum campaign.

This culminated on 31 May, as *Militant* reported, with "2,000 working class internationalists who marched through the centre of London last Saturday calling for an ongoing campaign to build a socialist Europe."[6] The Young Socialists and many Constituency Labour Parties were represented. Speaking at the Trafalgar Square rally which followed the demonstration were Nick Bradley, the National Executive representative of the LPYS, Eddie Loyden, Labour MP for Garston, and myself.

The 'Noes' were heavily defeated by two to one in the referendum. Those supporting and propping up capitalism were ecstatic. The result was greeted by the capitalist press as a "new D-Day" and predictably as a "rout of the left". The right wing in collaboration with the majority of the Tory and Liberal parties had won largely on the basis of a scare campaign that Britain would face "economic catastrophe" if it was locked out of the Common Market. On the other hand, the anti-market camp, particularly the labour Left, did not even make the slightest hint of a class or socialist approach in opposition to the Common Market. Even worse, some of the left actually linked up with the nationalist right in opposition to 'European unity'. The main apologists for this alliance between Labour anti-marketeers, dissident Tories, Liberals and nationalists was the British 'Communist Party'.

*Militant*'s criticism, in advance, of the programme of the left was entirely borne out. Nevertheless, the results of the referendum emboldened the capitalists to exert even greater pressure on the Labour government for savage cuts in living standards. An open campaign was launched to replace the government with a 'national government', if the Labour leaders proved unwilling or unable to meet the demands of the bosses. Jo Grimond MP, a senior parliamentary leader of the Liberal Party, made a vicious attack on the trade unions:

> One danger needs no introduction. It lies with the bosses of some trade unions. Of course they can be regarded as doing no more than their job. No doubt the medieval barons made the same claim.[7]

He denounced this 'barbarism' and pressed for "a coalition... to form around a determined group of men and women who will use the resources which the government still has to hand."[8] Wilson, bowing to the pressure of big business, removed Tony Benn as industry minister, and consigned him to the equivalent of a 'Siberian power station', the Energy Department. *Militant* launched a counter-campaign, summed up in a front page headline: "No retreat - stop coalition conspiracy."[9]

## ANOTHER RAMSAY MACDONALD?

At the same time *Tribune* MP Stan Thorne revealed that some right-wing Labour MPs had been involved in secret talks with Liberals and Tories on the issue of splitting Labour and forming a new coalition government, as MacDonald had done in 1931. Under pressure, *Tribune* stated that they were against the adoption of 'coalitionist' policies by the Labour government. They declared that they would campaign, "within and outside", parliament, against any retreat of the Labour government on its manifesto commitments.

However, the strategists of capital were not prepared to sanction a coalition government at this stage. On the one side, they feared pushing the labour movement even further towards the left, a process which would inevitably lead to the growth of Marxism. On the other hand, why go for an open coalition when a right-wing dominated Labour government was carrying out coalitionist policies, the programme of the capitalists themselves? This is what the 'social contract' represented. *Militant* pointed out that against a background of rising inflation - some reports said that prices could increase by 53 pence in the pound by the end of 1975:

> [the proposal of the TUC for a] ten per cent 'rise' is a cut! Either ten per cent across the board, or a flat rate increase (about £6). The proposals of the government and the TUC mean a savage cut in working peoples' living standards.[10]

However, the social contract was sold to the unions by the leadership by conjuring up the spectre of a return of rampant Toryism to power. The social contract would hold for a period of years but it broke down in the most dramatic circumstances, with the Marxists playing a decisive role.

# 11.
# SPAIN, PORTUGAL AND ETHIOPIA

WHILE HIGHLIGHTING the turbulence within the British labour movement, *Militant* never hesitated to draw the attention of workers in Britain to the even greater upheavals taking place on a world scale. For instance, at the Labour Party Young Socialists national conference a demonstration of 600 Young Socialists, *Militant* reported, marched "through the streets of Blackpool in the direction of the Norbreck Castle Hotel where an exhibition called 'Spain '75' was being held."[1]

This was part of the Spanish Young Socialists Defence Campaign, which was a big feature of the LPYS's work at that time. Indeed, important industrial workers had been won to the ranks of *Militant* through its internationalist approach on issues such as Spain.

Underpinning this campaign was the perception that Spain stood on the eve of revolution. In 1975 Franco was still alive, just about. No other organisation looked more towards the colossal changes which loomed in Spain. *Militant's* analysis posed the need to prepare for a revolutionary general strike to overthrow the weakened dictatorship. Moreover, basing itself upon the experiences of Greece and Portugal, the paper predicted that following the overthrow of Franco or any successor, new mass organisations of the working class would emerge. A new mass socialist party, for much the same reasons which led to the formation of Pasok in Greece, would inevitably take shape. The Communist Party would also grow.

Interestingly, in opposition to *Militant*, *Tribune* and the majority of left Labour MPs, never mind the Labour right, supported the old exiled leadership, the so-called "Historico" wing of the Spanish Socialist Party (PSOE). They opposed the wing of PSOE led by a young lawyer, Felipe Gonzalez. *Militant* alone predicted that the 'Historicos' represented a dead end and that the internal leadership of the Gonzalez-led wing of PSOE would become a mass formation, attracting significant support from the Spanish workers.

*Militant*'s prediction was borne out. But the very same forces which previously pilloried the paper's positon, and by implication Gonzalez, switched. The Historicos were dropped (eventually merging with PSOE) and Gonzalez was embraced. Gonzalez then claimed to be a 'Marxist' like his counterpart Soares in Portugal. However, once he became the leader of a significant mass force, he sought to root out and expel those Spanish Marxists who were linked to *Militant* in Britain. Thus those who derided the idea that Gonzalez would lead a significant force in Spain became his new 'friends' and those who predicted that PSOE would become the major force of the Spanish working class were rewarded with expulsions. Truly there is no gratitude in politics!

Nevertheless, in 1975 the explosive revolutionary situation unfolding in Spain allowed the rapid crystalisation of a Marxist cadre rooted within what was the outline of a future mass organisation. Spain was considered by *Militant* to be a key country in the unfolding revolutionary wave sweeping through Europe. Therefore a number of attempts had been made to establish a group of co-thinkers in the country. All were unsuccessful until a delegate from the Spanish Young Socialists visited the British LPYS National Conference. This individual was Luis Rodriguez, who because of the repressive regime in Spain, went under the pseudonym of Rati. He had discussions first with myself, then at the LPYS conference with Ted Grant and Alan Woods. The latter played an important role in laying the basis for the creation of what became an important Marxist force within the Spanish Young Socialists and PSOE. Alan Woods went to live in Spain for a number of years, which effectively cut him off from playing any role in the decisive events of the 1970s and 1980s which were to put *Militant* at the centre of events, particularly in the Labour Party. However, the force which he helped to create in Spain was able to play a role in 1975, and 1976 and in the school students' strike in 1986. Tragically, like their counterparts in Britain who split from *Militant* in 1992 (see chapter 36), they have been incapable of facing up to the changed situation resulting from the collapse of Stalinism and the 1980's boom. They have converted the ideas which justified work within PSOE, entirely correct in 1975 and later, into an ossified dogma. They are incapable of adopting the flexible tactics demanded by the new situation. Fortunately, new youthful forces, adhering to the internationalist approach of *Militant Labour*, have begun to develop in Spain to continue the tradition which began in the period 1975-76.

In Portugal, also, 1975 was a decisive year. An attempted coup by Spinola in March 1975 resulted in a counter-movement from below which pushed the Portuguese revolution even further to the left. This development gave the capitalists nightmares. *The Times* concluded that in Portugal "capitalism is dead".

This did in fact appear to be the case. Spinola's coup, with similarities to the counter-revolutionary attempt of Kornilov to derail the Russian Revolution in August 1917, had provoked massive opposition from the workers. Even the conservative paratroopers refused to accept his counter-revolutionary orders. During these events, *Militant* reported:

> Many soldiers handed out guns to the workers. The magnetic pull of a working class determined to defend its liberties was enough to win over the most brutalised section of the armed forces. In embryo, an armed workers' militia already exists.[2]

More than 50 per cent of industry was taken under state control through the decree issued by the 'Supreme Revolutionary Council'. They ordered the state takeover of the finance houses and the banks. And yet capitalism, as subsequent events demonstrated, was not yet dead. Unless the working class organises its own alternative state, sets up workers' and farmers' committees with democratic control and management - in other words, establishes a democratic workers' state - capitalism, as all revolutions have demonstrated, can always make a comeback.

This is precisely what happened in Portugal. But, given the overwhelming relationship of forces in favour of the working class, this could not, as even *Militant* expected at a certain stage, take the form of open reaction. As with the German revolution in 1918, counter-revolution was forced to don the mask of the Social Democracy. Through the medium of the Socialist Party leader Soares, capitalism gradually reassembled its shattered state machine. And then it began to claw back the gains of the revolution which resulted, in the 1980s, in the handing back of industry, the banks, and the land to their former owners.

The twentieth anniversary in 1994, rekindled interest in the Portuguese revolution, showing that an indelible stamp has been left on the consciousness of the people of that country. A revival of the aims of the Portuguese revolution is inevitable in the next period.

# ETHIOPIA

In Ethiopia, on the other hand, 1975 saw a further push towards the left by the Derg, the military government installed in power after the overthrow of Haile Selassie. It was compelled by the pressure of the situation to nationalise the land and commercial assets formerly belonging to the Emperor and to bring under state control the banks and insurance companies. Moreover, it announced it was about to take over 72 foreign and locally controlled companies and a majority shareholding in 29 others. Ethiopia represented an important development for the colonial and semi-colonial world. It was the last example in the post-1945 period of the process which led to the establishment of what *Militant* had characterised as 'proletarian bonapartist regimes', i.e. planned economies but with one-party totalitarian regimes.

Similar tendencies had been evident earlier in other parts of the colonial and semi-colonial world. The most notable development in this respect was the victory of the Chinese revolution in 1944-49. Breaking with capitalism, nationalising the land and beginning to establish a planned economy, the regime of Mao Zedong, however, had nothing in common with the regime of workers' democracy of Lenin and Trotsky in 1917. Mao began where Stalin ended, as a one-party totalitarian regime. Although resting on a planned economy, right from the outset, the Chinese Revolution established a 'deformed' workers' state. Even during the postwar economic boom the former colonial and semi-colonial world faced social and economic catastrophe. A combination of factors (which space does not allow us to fully examine here)[†] pushed Castro, orginally a liberal democrat, into breaking with American imperialism. The armed revolution against the Batista regime, the mistakes of the Eisenhower administration as well as Kennedy, in taking reprisals against Castro, because of his limited action against foreign capital and the pressure of the armed masses, all acted to push Castro into taking over the majority of industry. Faced with an embargo from the US, the Russian bureaucracy stepped in to provide huge

†*see Militant's pamphlet on Cuba.*

financial support. They supplied oil to the Cuban regime, to the value of $2 million a day. Thus right under the nose of American imperialism a 'proletarian bonapartist regime' was established.

*Militant* pointed out that something similar was now unfolding in Ethiopia. Terrible famines, a constant feature of Ethiopia, the callousness and ineptitude of the corrupt previous regime laid the basis for big changes. Mass demonstrations and strikes of the workers of Ethiopia shook the country to its foundations. The lower officer caste, from middle-class economic and social backgrounds, were affected by events around them. Seeing the progress made in the totalitarian states of Russia and China, which also guaranteed the privileges of the elite, they used this as a model for Ethiopia. Tragically, this prediction of *Militant* was borne out.

## TACTICS FOR THE STRUGGLE

In 1975 the seeming success of the Ethiopian regime, the alleged triumph of guerrillaist methods elsewhere, the outbreak of assassinations, kidnapping, and terrorism internationally compelled *Militant* to devote attention to opposing the ideas of terrorism.

Marxists oppose the hypocrisy of the ruling class who denounce 'terror' yet employ terror on a world scale in defence of their system. Terrorism, particularly individual terrorism, was proving to be attractive to a layer of predominantly middle-class youth internationally. *Militant* argued: "In common with liberals the individual terrorist believes that the capitalist system rests on individuals."

The assassinations of the most brutal representatives of a regime do not lead automatically to its downfall. There are more than enough candidates in the ranks of the capitalists to replace those struck down by the assassin's bullets. 'Individual terrorists' - or urban guerrillas - substitute themselves for the masses. They believe that it is their actions and not the conscious organisation of the masses which will effect the necessary change. As Trotsky wrote, they actually "lower the masses in their own consciousness, reconcile them to their impotence and direct their glances to the great avenger and emancipator who will some day come to accomplish his mission."[3] It was not terrorism but the mass mobilisation of an armed working class which carried through the greatest overturn in history, the October 1917 Russian Revolution.

Not only in Ireland, but, even more importantly from an international point of view, also in Argentina, a big layer of the youth were directed towards urban guerrillaism. They were cheered on by some so-called 'Marxists', usually from the sidelines. A tragic example of this was found in Argentina. A section of the Peronist youth, in the ranks of the Montoneros (representing about ten per cent of the Peronists, ie 300,000), had originally deployed terrorist methods against the military dictatorship. Following the overthrow of the Argentine dictatorship and its replacement by Peron, the Montoneros could have become a weapon to help to transform the outlook of Peronist workers in a socialist direction, particularly in the trade unions.

This was the perspective sketched out by *Militant*. But some alleged 'Marxists', some even claiming to be 'Trotskyist', reinforced the guerrillaist and terrorist illusions of the Montoneros and even more so that of the ERP (People's Revolutionary Army). That chapter of guerrillaist and terrorist illusions, so evident in the late 1960s and 1970s, was a symptom of the crisis of world capitalism. At the same time, these false policies led to the elimination and the wastage of the revolutionary energy of a generation who could have become an important lever for transforming the labour movement.

# 12.
# THE SOCIALIST OPPOSITION GROWS

WILSON'S GOVERNMENT lurched even further to the right following the Common Market referendum. This brought it more and more into conflict with the ordinary members of the Labour Party but also with an increasing section of the Parliamentary Labour Party. In the pages of *Militant*, Eddie Loyden, MP for Liverpool Garston, wrote an open letter to Harold Wilson:

> We are returning to the conditions of the 1930s. In the Merseyside development area we have an unemployment rate of 10.6 per cent - twice the national average. This is the result of a system based on anarchy and greed when small groups of wealthy people control vital sectors of the economy and can take decisions affecting the lives of millions of workers. We call for the adoption of radical socialist policies by the Labour government.[1]

The same demands were echoed at the 1975 Labour Party conference. *Militant* reported confidently "Marxist policy gaining support". This was because of the harsh experience of the British working class against the background of a devastating world recession. Some famous giants of British industry were threatening to go to the wall. Faced with the collapse of car giant Chrysler, the Labour government rushed in to give this multinational a 'present' of £162.5 million for the upcoming Christmas holiday. For the workers, Christmas meant 8,000 of them went down the road. At the same time, cuts were being proposed in the railways which provoked massive demonstrations of rail workers; on one demonstration in London in December more than 350 copies of the *Militant* were sold.

Symptomatic of the period was the fact that the year closed with another significant demonstration organised by the LPYS in Liverpool.

As 3,000 marched through the city it was greeted enthusiastically by passers-by on the streets. At the end of the demonstration, a meeting was organised in St. George's Hall addressed by Eric Heffer MP who argued for public ownership to save jobs. He demanded that: "Those wanting to split the labour movement (backed by the Tory press) must be told that we will not allow it to be split, but will unite everyone fighting for socialist policies." Representing *Militant*, I supported Eric's statement and went on to declare that

> the Labour Party Young Socialists and Labour Party members who support *Militant* had been accused of 'infiltration', including comrades who had given years, even decades, to the party. But the real infiltrators were the Liberals and Tories masquerading under the name of socialists.[2]

1975 represented a further increase, both in influence and numbers, for the ideas of *Militant*. The organised supporters of *Militant* increased substantially in 1975 from 517 at the beginning of the year to 775 at the end. This force, still relatively small in numbers but extremely influential, with a much wider layer of general supporters, was the subject of a consistent onslaught from Labour's right-wing. These attacks really began in earnest in 1975 on a national scale.

## THE UNDERHILL REPORT

Foremost in the campaign against *Militant* was Labour's National Agent Reg Underhill. In November 1975 he had submitted the first outline of what became the infamous 'Underhill Report' to Labour's national executive claiming to deal with the origins, policies and activities of *Militant*. This followed the *Observer's* assault on *Militant* in July, which was now followed by 'revelations':

> The Young Socialists and their delegate on the national executive Mr Nick Bradley are closely associated with [*Militant*]; their members write for and sell its newspaper... they [the YS] are unanimous in opposing not only Mr Prentice, but also the whole Parliamentary establishment. Paradoxically, their paper *Left*, edited by Mr Bob Labi, is financed by Transport House.[3]

The linking of *Militant* with the fate of Prentice and other 'threatened' MPs revealed the real purpose of the witch-hunt.

The Newham North-East Party voted by 29 votes to 19 to invite

Prentice to retire as MP at the next General Election. Other MPs, like Frank Tomney in Hammersmith, were facing the same kind of challenge.

The right of the PLP invoked the doctrine of the 'divine right of MPs', conjuring up at the same time the '*Militant* spectre'. Its 'evil hand' seemed to be everywhere.

Saner voices were heard emanating even from the Parliamentary Labour Party. Paul Rose MP, who had sent a letter to *Militant* thanking its supporters for their help in the 1974 General Election campaign, wrote in the *Daily Telegraph*, of all places, arguing that it would be wrong

> to regard them [*Militant*] as sinister and alien... one cannot criticise the '*Militant*' group any more than the Christian Socialists, Owenites, Co-operatives, Fabians and other so-called moderates who still overwhelmingly control the heartland of the party's territory.[4]

## UNDERHILL DOWN BUT NOT OUT

However, Reg Underhill and his supporters were not at all convinced by Rose's arguments. At the NEC Organisation Sub-Committee Underhill called for action to be taken. He was answered by left MPs Ian Mikardo and Eric Heffer. Mikardo declared that there were

> good articles in their paper - good material in *Militant*. Reg's evidence says that they are pretty small in numbers. With 30 full-time organisers; to only have 800 members is not very good.[5]

Eric Heffer declared:

> My party (Walton) in the past was run by the Deane group (who pioneered Marxist work in Liverpool before the establishment of *Militant*) but that was nothing to get upset about... What is wrong with selling *Tribune* or *Militant* in preference to *Labour Weekly*... don't react to pressure from outside for a witch-hunt... don't push youngsters into a corner.[6]

Underhill interjected, saying that "all the denials under the sun were made by the Socialist Labour League when they controlled the Young Socialists". Eric Heffer angrily hit back: "They were a bunch of gangsters. *Militant* are totally different."[7] The sub-committee decided not to proceed with Underhill's enquiries. Mikardo's support for *Militant* and the YS was welcome but extremely tentative.

Within the Labour Party, in industry, and within the Labour government, serious clashes took place between different wings of the movement. In the first issue of *Militant* of 1976 a report of the recent National Organisation of Labour Students (NOLS) conference showed the lengths to which the right-wing Labour officialdom were prepared to go in order to eliminate *Militant*'s influence.

From now on, every manoeuvre, intrigue, and every kind of rule-bending were to be employed to ensure that NOLS did not go the way of the Labour Party Young Socialists, and fall under the decisive influence of the Marxists. Naturally, *Militant*'s opponents did not see it in this way. We opened its columns to them to explain their opposition to the paper's analysis of the conference. Mike Gapes, the newly-elected chair of NOLS, took the opportunity to attack *Militant* in our columns. He claimed that the conference had in effect "adopted left-wing policies on a variety of issues but so far no report of these political decisions has appeared in *Militant* and it has been implied that socialist and Marxist idea were rejected by the conference. This is untrue."[8]

## MILITANT - FORUM FOR DEBATE

He was answered to by Glenys Bithell in the same issue. She pointed out that

> the leaders of the NOLS 'Broad Left' [identified with Gapes and his supporters] never once raised the simple, effective 'left' demand for nationalisation of Chrysler.

She also pointed out:

> *Militant* supporters in NOLS have gone clearly on record with protests of what they feel are the lowest of manoeuvres against them at the NOLS conference - and comrade Gapes will convince no one that such manoeuvres did not take place by arguing such an issue on the basis of the number of votes involved.[9]

Gapes, a bitter opponent of *Militant,* subsequently became an official at Labour Party headquarters and later a Labour MP. But the fact that he could accept an invitation to debate the issue in the pages of *Militant* demonstrated the general mood of thrashing out differences in discussion that existed, at least on the left, at that stage. *Militant* attempted to deal in a firm but scrupulous manner with the arguments of our opponents. The paper was prepared to give space in its columns to any serious opponent or group who opposed its ideas. The same licence was not always extended to *Militant* supporters by our rivals.

At the same time, *Militant* and its supporters were not treated as pariahs but as a vital and important component of the left. Tony Benn freely spoke to and outlined in writing his ideas in the pages of *Militant.* In a long interview, in which was asked what Benn thought about *Militant,* he replied:

> I read the *Militant* every week. I think the left press plays a very significant part among the relatively small number of active people within the party. *Labour Weekly, Tribune, Militant* and a number of local left papers provide some analysis... I think that an awful lot of people who are not directly associated with the *Militant* tendency, and I'm not associated with *Militant* tendency directly, would feel what is written is worthy of attention by the movement.[10]

Emlyn Williams, leader of the South Wales miners, went further than Tony Benn:

> I like the *Militant.* I like it very much. It is refreshing. It reminds me of the way we raised things when we were young. It puts a very coherent case on all aspects of the labour movement. There are one or two articles I may not like but that is obviously something to be discussed in the movement itself.[11]

Significantly, when NUPE organised a lobby of Parliament against Labour's cuts in public spending, the general secretary of NUPE (now merged into UNISON), Alan Fisher wrote a front-page article for *Militant,* under the headline: "End Capitalist Cuts Now!" He pointed out that

> throughout the country, NUPE members are faced with the possibility of heavy cuts in spending by their employers. The effect of these

cutbacks is to threaten the closure of hospitals, old people's homes and even ambulance stations... Only the socialist solutions outlined by my union and other sections of the labour movement can provide a lasting solution to the problems of homelessness, poverty and deprivation...[12]
Along with an extension of public ownership to cover the major monopolies, which are increasingly dominating the economy, we could start to build a socialist society that has been our movement's historic goal... We do not want to see this government rejected like previous Labour governments on the scrap heap of unfulfilled promises. There is time to change course.[13]

These leading figures in the movement were prepared to write for, speak to and defend *Militant* at a time when the right were demanding that the paper and its supporters be driven out of the party. They recognised that the exclusion of *Militant* from the labour movement, particularly from the Labour Party, would considerably weaken the left as a whole. They did not agree with all of *Militant*'s ideas, but recognised the enormous contribution made by its supporters at every level of the labour movement.

## WORKERS' STRUGGLE

It was not at all accidental that *Militant* grew at this stage. The rightward drift of the Labour government was indicated by Harold Wilson at the beginning of the year when he predicted that there was going to be some "pretty bleak months ahead" and it was going to be "a hard 1976".

## AFRICAN REVOLUTION

While the Portuguese revolution was passing through a difficult phase, the effects of that revolution had been directly reflected in Africa. The collapse of the Caetano regime had in turn pushed forward the revolution in Portugal's former colonies of Angola and Mozambique. This in turn had given an enormous impetus to the movement in Zimbabwe, forcing British imperialism to come to terms with Mugabe and Nkomo.

These victories, and the granting of independence to the former Rhodesia, inspired the new generation in South Africa who organised the Soweto uprising in 1976. *Militant* gave full coverage to the inspirational events of June and particularly the Soweto uprising. South African Marxists writing in *Militant* pointed to the emerging power of black South African workers:

> Still the key to developments in South Africa, if not the whole continent, is the increasingly organised black working class. The industrialisation programme of the capitalists themselves has created the black industrial workers, with their numerical strength, their concentration in the enormous rundown townships that surround the big cities, and therefore all the preconditions for the adoption of socialist ideas.[14]

This was at a time when the exiled ANC leadership scorned the idea that the organised workers were the backbone of the liberation struggle.

This perspective was to be fully borne out with the decisive emergence of the black South African workers and the creation of the mighty Congress of South African Trade Unions (Cosatu) in the 1980s. South Africa was to be a constant theme in the analysis and the demands of *Militant* in subsequent years.

# 13.
# THE CRITICAL POINT

THE BIGGEST 'bombshell' in Britain in 1976 was the resignation in March of Labour Prime Minister Harold Wilson. He had been besieged both within his government and in the labour movement. His departure represented the 'end of an era'. All Wilson's high hopes of a new 'white-hot technological revolution' had been dashed by the crisis of British capitalism.

Under Wilson, the power of capital was not broken. In fact, the opposite process had developed with big business compelling the government to do its bidding. Wilson's own memoirs recorded an infamous meeting with the governor of the Bank of England in 1965. The latter demanded prescription charges for medicines and cuts in social services to protect the pound. Wilson asked the governor what would happen if he told the electorate that he was being blackmailed into deviating from the programme of his party by the moneylenders. The governor replied that he would win an election by a landslide. But Wilson did not go to the people with the story. He accepted the policies of the Governor and of the capitalists.

Ex-Prime Minister Heath commented that Wilson's greatest achievement was "in handling and holding the party together". In other words, Wilson had been the best bet for preventing a split in which the left would have undoubtedly emerged as a majority in the Labour Party. Wilson's replacement, Callaghan, was seen partly as a continuation of the Wilson regime, but also expressed a further edging towards the right. His election was certainly seen by big business as being more in favour of them. Subsequent events were to demonstrate that this was indeed the case. All the journals of big business were urging right-wing stalwarts like Denis Healey and Roy Jenkins to be kept at their posts.

But this only served to inflame the ranks of the movement. *Militant* reported that

Newham North-East and Hammersmith North Constituency Labour Parties have recently exercised, strictly according to Labour Party constitutional rules, their democratic right to decide not to reselect their present MPs. These decisions have provoked a torrent of abuse from the bosses' press and television, which of course thoroughly approve of Prentice's and Tomney's right-wing views. Using the old 'reds-under-the-beds' tactics, the media howl about 'the danger to democracy'.[1]

In truth *Militant* supporters, while present in both parties, were not decisive in the moves against these MPs. Nevertheless, as the best organised grouping on the left, our supporters were identified as the main opponents of the right-wing Members of Parliament who believed that they had a 'freehold' on their job.

The attempt to insulate the Parliamentary Labour Party from the pressure of the rank and file of the movement was not accidental. A remorseless campaign to force through further cuts was undertaken by big business. In the run up to the 1976 Labour Party conference, it reached a crescendo and the issue of cuts exploded during the conference itself. *Militant* summed up the conference

> as one of the most important for decades. It marks a watershed in the development of the labour movement and in the life expectancy of the Labour government itself. An atmosphere of crisis permeated the Winter Gardens and the ghost of Ramsay MacDonald haunted the corridors of the Imperial Hotel.[2]

## THE IMF'S POUND OF FLESH

The pound sunk by nine per cent in the first few days of the conference. Chancellor Healey prepared to leave the conference and fly to the International Monetary Fund but turned back at Heathrow Airport. An infamous deal was then struck involving massive government cuts in exchange for an IMF loan. This generated enormous discontent at the conference.

There were open clashes between left and right, and violent altercations between members of the NEC which were leaked to the press. There was great disenchantment with the right within the trade unions. There were also heated discussions in union delegations, sometimes boiling over into angry shouting matches. Rumour and counter-rumour circulated the hall.

The £2,300 million cut in government expenditure came on top of previous cuts. This prompted *The Guardian* to comment:

> A further round of heavy spending coming on previous cuts which all too clearly have failed to deliver dividends in retaining confidence will make it impossible for Mr Jones, leader of the Transport and General Workers' Union, and Mr Foot (Employment Minister) to hold the line.[3]

Indeed the IMF-imposed cuts threatened the Social Contract, but it would take time (more than a year) for this to be reflected in decisive action against this agreement between the Labour government and the trade unions. The conference was also characterised by a frontal attack by the new Prime Minister, Callaghan, on "the Marxists in the movement and supporters of *Militant*, in particular".[4]

At that stage Michael Foot made it clear that he would not support a witch-hunt. "There is room in our party for many different shades of opinion." At the *Tribune* meeting that night, Eric Heffer directly countered Callaghan by saying that this was "no time to return to the witch-hunts of the past".

The refusal of Michael Foot and other 'lefts' in the 1980s to follow their own advice to the labour movement in 1976 resulted in divisions which played directly into the hands of the Tories. At that time, however, the left adopted a radical stance. At a meeting in October organised by Cambridge Labour Party and attended by 500 people, Michael Meacher, under-secretary of State for Trade, declared:

> For too long we have played down the advocacy of socialism... We are at the end of the capitalist road... The economy has moved from one crisis to another. We have tried different remedies... we now have the lowest strike record in Europe, still no solution... we have the lowest unit costs in Europe, still no solution. It's reckoned with even three million unemployed that there will no solution of the economic problems. It's not the fault of the working class, it's the fault of the system. [applause][5]

This speech was then followed by Michael Foot who immediately poured cold water on Meacher's contribution by declaring that "Michael was dealing with long-term objectives." Instead he came out for vague policies which would allow the labour movement to 'save our country'. A constant theme of the Labour leaders was that any move towards more radical socialist ideas would shipwreck the Labour government and allow the Tories to return to power. In reality, the opposite was the case. Right-wing policies were undermining support for Labour. At the same time a ferocious battle was taking place on the factory floor.

## GRUNWICK'S

One of the most notable was the epic battle at Grunwick's. This factory in Willesden, north-west London, processed films and employed largely Asian women workers. The wages paid were an absolute scandal, with some workers receiving £28 (taking home £21) for a 40-hour week. On 23 August 1976, 200 process workers walked out. The management recruited scab labour to replace them from the huge pool of desperate, out-of-work, youngsters in the area. Strikers commented:

> This management is more suited to the eighteenth century than the twentieth century. They treat the workers like children, with no rights as human beings... If you want to go to the toilet you must raise your hand and wait until the manager gives permission. It's like being back at school! Many of the older Asian women are shy about doing this, so they suffer in silence.[6]

Gradually, as the knowledge of the strikers' case spread, the labour movement mobilised in defence of the Grunwick workers. In November the strike took a dramatic turn. We reported:

> In two separate incidents, police arrested nine pickets outside the factory. They included two strikers, five members of Brent East Labour Party GMC, and councillor Cyril Shore, chairman of Brent East Party.[7]

Such was the mood for solidarity that the national executive committee of the postal workers' union decided to instruct all its members not to handle Grunwick's mail. How far removed are such actions from the present timid approach of trade union leaders.

True, solidarity action is made more difficult by the panoply of anti-trade union laws which the Tories have introduced in the last

15 years. But the trade unions were created by breaking such laws. Only in this way, through struggle and solidarity action, was the right to strike won. Such was the magnetic appeal of the Grunwick Asian women strikers that even members of the Parliamentary Labour Party went onto the picket line. Shirley Williams, presently occupying the Liberal Democrat benches in the House of Lords, to her everlasting embarrassment later on, appeared on the picket line with other APEX-sponsored right-wing Labour MPs.

Grunwick's was important because it indicated the change in approach of the ruling class since the miners' strikes of 1972 and 1974. The police began in almost military fashion to deploy their forces against pickets, which comprised all sections of the labour movement including miners. Mounted and riot police were used for the first time and with a certain amount of success. This was because of the failure of the whole Labour and trade union movement to mobilise behind the Grunwick pickets.

This change in approach was also reflected within the Tory Party and particularly at its conference in October 1976. All the right-wing creatures came out of the woodwork. The conference pledged cuts in taxes by reducing 'government spending'. *Militant* pointed out that

> hospitals, schools, old peoples' homes and welfare will be starved of cash. But wasteful spending on defence will be increased.[8]

It was also pointed out that

> a Thatcher government would be even worse than the hated Heath government which was kicked out by the trade unions amid the economic chaos of the three-day week... The Tories want the state to interfere with the unions - outlawing 'flying pickets', breaking the unity of closed shops and imposing their own rules on unions elections as a condition of unions being 'certified' by the government, similar to the 'registration' under the notorious Industrial Relations Act.[9]

*Militant* outlined in advance exactly the programme upon which Thatcher was to be elected in 1979 and explained how she and her Cabinet were likely to act once in power.

Instead of facing up to this threat, Labour's right wing stubbornly pursued its vendetta against the left, particularly against *Militant*, which risked further divisions. If anything, 1976 witnessed a heightening of the campaign with Sir Harold Wilson and James Callaghan in the vanguard. The fact that an ex-Labour Prime Minister and his replacement were forced to take time out from 'affairs of State' to attack *Militant* emphasised in the minds of the media the 'danger' which loomed.

## ANDY BEVAN

The campaign came to a head in October 1976 in and around the Labour Party conference and its aftermath. The confirmation of Andy Bevan, a well-known *Militant* supporter, as the Labour Party's Youth Officer, was one of the catalysts for this campaign. He was elected, on the casting vote of Ron Hayward, Labour's General Secretary, at a meeting where the procedures had been scrupulously and democratically adhered to. The *Daily Express* screeched: "Just five men have Labour on the Trot... *Express* dossier of the unknowns behind the Red challenge to Jim."[10] The five were Nick Bradley, Peter Taaffe, Ted Grant, Roger Silverman and Andy Bevan. Nor was this campaign restricted to the gutter press. *The Times* carried three lengthy articles and an editorial in early December purporting to alert the labour movement to the "danger" of *Militant*, which it, *The Times*, had 'exposed' as wanting to "establish a group of MPs"![11]

A letter to *The Times* from the satirist, the late Peter Cook, was a small antidote to the press poison directed against *Militant*. He wrote: "I am shocked to learn that by the devious strategy of working hard within the rules, 'extremists' are able to have some influence on the Labour Party. It is against our nature to reward industry and enthusiasm. Sir Harold, as usual, is right. Let us change the rules at once."[12]

An indication of just how the issue of Andy Bevan had become a touchstone for the right was indicated by the statements of Callaghan in the run-up to the Labour Party conference. Under a front-page banner headline, "Red Andy Ultimatum", the *Daily Express* reported that Callaghan was ready to veto a plan for the state financing of parties if Andy Bevan's appointment was to go ahead. By dangling this financial carrot the leadership hoped to bounce the Labour Party conference into rejecting his appointment. But it failed in its objective.[13]

At the NEC meeting before the conference Labour Party Chairman Bryan Stanley reported the recommendation of the Organisation Sub-Committee that Andy Bevan be appointed. Tony Benn pointed out later: "Not a single member of the NEC queried the recommendation... and it was accepted without a vote."

In a private session at the conference an attempt was made by right-wing officials to have this decision cancelled. But after a speech by general secretary, Ron Hayward, on behalf of the NEC this was defeated.

Sensing that *Militant* represented something more serious and durable than the picture of it painted by the tabloids, 'quality' journals of capitalism, like *The Observer,* began to examine what *Militant* actually stood for. Another *Observer* journalist, Michael Davie, came to the *Militant* premises in Hackney to interview me. For the first time space was given over for an explanation of *Militant* ideas:

> "No country constitutes a genuinely democratic workers' state," Mr Taaffe said. He spoke of the "monstrous police apparatus" in Russia, and the dictatorships of China and Cuba. Why would not the same thing happen here, if everything was taken over by the state? "Because Britain has a long democratic tradition, and there is no possibility of a socialist society being attained here without the working class, and the middle class, being convinced of the necessity of the change." I left Mr Taaffe thinking that *Militant* and Andy Bevan between them have got Transport House over a barrel.[14]

But at the Yorkshire Regional Labour Party conference also held in December, both Wilson and Callaghan blamed the growing party divide on 'bedsit infiltrators'. *Militant* pointed out that: "James Callaghan considers (*Militant*) similar to 'fascism'".[15]

The right were attacking not so-called 'infiltrators' but "the changing mood within the local parties who were demanding a break with the policies that reduced the working class and its living standards." Right-wing Labour MP, Frank Tomney, faced with deselection by his party, sent a letter to *The Times* in which he attacked Ron Hayward, party general secretary, for taking no action against 'extremists'. He demanded the reintroduction of a list of banned organisations. The Labour Party Young Socialists was singled out for attack. But as *Militant* pointed out:

Where else in the labour movement is it possible for the minority view to have rights of producing separate documents to a conference against the majority? This is a procedure introduced by the Marxists who form the majority of the youth wing of the party.[16]

The combined assault of the capitalist press, led by *The Times*, and the right-wing Parliamentary Labour Party had been whipped up by the appointment of Andy Bevan as Labour's Youth Officer. The right foamed at the mouth at the idea that a Marxist could be democratically selected for such a position.

Following the Labour Party conference the right even organised for party agents and their union, the National Union of Labour Organisers (NULO), to refuse to work with Bevan. They were joined by the majority of the National Organisation of Labour Students. And yet the Annual General Meeting of the *Tribune* Group of MPs, meeting in the House of Commons on 29 November, voted to support the appointment of Andy Bevan.

Callaghan, in an unprecedented move, sent a letter to the national executive committee demanding the cancellation of Andy Bevan's appointment, already made, as National Youth Officer. But such was the support both at rank-and-file level and in the NEC that Andy was confirmed in his position. Over time, the opposition of the Labour organisers and agents evaporated. This did not prevent a campaign of constant harassment of the LPYS or Andy Bevan. Further undemocratic procedures were also employed in the student wing of the movement. But one beneficial effect of the attack on *Militant* and Andy Bevan was the re-examination of Marxist ideas in the labour movement. Tony Benn was one of those in *The Guardian* (13 December) who defended the presence of Marxism in the labour movement.

## OUR 1976 BALANCE SHEET

1976 was a tumultuous year, with the expansion of *Militant* to a 12-page paper, the appointment of Andy Bevan as the National Youth Officer, and the repulsion of witch-hunting attempts against *Militant* led by the very summits of the Labour Party. As important, the organised supporters of *Militant* had reached 1,000 by May 1976. This was rightly seen by the leadership and supporters of *Militant* as a landmark in its development. However, *Militant* supporters were under no illusion that the witch-hunt would be easily called off. Benn had completed his defence of Andy Bevan by stating

> In my judgement, Andy Bevan has much to offer the Labour Party as its National Youth Officer, at a time when we need to bring young people in to assist our stalwarts. Andy Bevan's speeches about socialism have also, in my presence, drawn a response from older members of the party, who recognise in what he said the authentic voice of a political faith they had not heard advocated with such moral force since their own youth, many years ago, at Socialist Sunday Schools and at street corner meetings.[17]

Notwithstanding this defence, the ruling class did not let up. Through the medium of *The Times*, further efforts were made to pressurise Labour into taking action against the 'Marxists/Trotskyists'. But in the teeth of opposition from the right and also some alleged 'lefts', the national executive committee of the Labour Party decided on 19 January 1977 to finally appoint Andy Bevan as National Youth Officer which they declared was "irrevocable". But as *Militant* reported:

> After one of the longest discussions ever held at the national executive committee of the Labour Party, on a motion moved by Michael Foot, it was agreed to set up a sub-committee to consider allegations concerning so-called 'Trotskyist infiltration' in the Labour Party.[18]

Foot's motion replaced an earlier one by Tom Bradley and John Cartwright, MPs, both of whom were subsequently to desert Labour for the Social Democrats. On the basis of this resolution, the Underhill Report investigating *Militant* was published. On the NEC, Nick Bradley, the LPYS representative, pointed out to Michael Foot that the same kind of attacks now being made on *Militant* had been made "against Bevan in the fifties, as pointed out in Foot's own biography of Bevan. Jim Callaghan supported Bevan's expulsion then."

What was even more galling for the left was that Prentice, who was advocating a new party and a coalition with the Tories, was not being investigated by the NEC. Callaghan at one stage in the NEC meeting claimed that there was proof of a conspiracy to destroy the Labour Party and, pointing at Nick Bradley, said that *Militant* supporters were personally rude and offensive, and acted so towards women members in his own constituency.

Tony Benn refuted this declaring: "His experience of *Militant* supporters was totally different from that of Callaghan. He had been politically criticised by *Militant*, but he did not mind debate." But this did not halt the campaign. Shirley Williams said in a speech in Derbyshire that "there was no room for 'Trotskyists' in the Labour Party."[19] But Williams's approach was at least an attempt to be political. *Militant* devoted a series of articles to the issue of 'Marxism and democracy' which refuted the attempt to put *Militant* Trotskyists into some kind of authoritarian camp along with Stalinism and Fascism.

Going on the offensive *Militant* declared that: "The democratic credentials of the right are suspect." An article in February referred to "the CIA-funded right". In particular, Denis Healey collaborated in organisations which were backed by the CIA.[20]

This charge, which *Militant* again repeated when the five members of the *Militant* Editorial Board were dragged before the NEC in 1983, in Healey's presence, was never effectively answered by him. And yet despite the clamour for action to be taken against *Militant*, once Underhill had completed his report, the National Executive Committee decided to take no action. Instead, it decided in June to "circulate to Constituency Labour Parties the contents of the report of the special committee which examined the document *Entrism*."[21]

## MILITANT IN ACTION

Meanwhile, the growth in *Militant*'s support was reflected in a number of ways. In February, the first significant television programme dealt with *Militant*, ITV's *World in Action*, with an estimated audience of 15 million people. Despite the obvious distortions, which were to become a hallmark of the media coverage, *Militant* invited the cameras into an editorial meeting and carried interviews with myself, political editor, Ted Grant, and leading supporter Pat Wall. A ludicrous attempt to distort and discredit *Militant* was made by a university professor, Gavin Kennedy - a leading member of the Scottish National Party! An SNP parliamentary candidate and renegade from the Labour Party, Kennedy resorted to McCarthyite smear tactics. The programme also showed shop stewards selling 100 copies of *Militant* to car workers in the Rover Solihull plant in Birmingham.

## FIGHTING UNEMPLOYMENT

At this time, the Labour Party Young Socialists were to the fore in organising a successful national assembly against unemployment in London in February. 1,450 delegates from trade unions, shop stewards' committees, Labour Parties and Young Socialist branches as well as unemployed workers, filled the Seymour Hall in London. This was followed up by another successful annual conference of the Labour Party Young Socialists in Blackpool over the Easter holiday. The hallmark of this 16th conference was the evident democratic character of the proceedings which were not present in any other part of the labour movement. The Marxists were clearly in a majority and submitted their own documents and resolutions. But there was also a 'minority document', representing the views of 'Clause Four'. Equal time was given to their representative, John Mordecai, to argue Clause Four's case. Recognising the radical character of the delegates he stated: "The labour movement has to get away from the sterile social democratic compromise with capitalism", but then went on to attack *Militant*'s ideas.[22]

Significantly Arthur Scargill also addressed one of the fringe meetings organised by the LPYS's journal *Left*. He stated: "The people who do not agree with Clause IV of the Labour Party constitution do not rightly belong in the Labour Party." Opposing hints of a compromise with the capitalist parties, he also stated: "A Labour government should not consider any form of alliance with 'the traditional class enemy'." Arthur Scargill was referring to the deal, the so-called 'Lib-Lab Pact', which the Labour cabinet had made with the Liberal Party in March. This statement received loud applause from the well-attended meeting.[23]

The infamous pact was, in effect, a disguised coalition with the junior party of big business. Steel, the Liberal leader, had told his supporters that by experimenting with 'coalition politics' the Liberals had put themselves in a position to gain more seats in the general election and then the Liberals "would be in a position to talk of a coalition with either major party." This perspective for the Liberals was not borne out in its entirety. However, the Liberals were able to act as a brake on a Labour government moving to the left under the pressure of the Labour and trade union rank and file.

The ruling class was satisfied with the arrangement because an outright coalition held out the danger of a 'lurch to the left' within the Labour Party. The difference between the situation which led to MacDonald's 'National Government' in 1931 and the 1970s was the existence of a conscious Marxist left, in the form of *Militant*, within the Labour Party. In the event of a split in the Labour Party - inevitable if a coalition was formed - the left as a whole would gain and within this *Militant*'s strength would increase enormously.

Even at that stage, with *Militant* having no more than 1,200 organised supporters, it was already a factor in the calculations of the ruling class. It is for this reason that they pursued, for over a decade or more, a relentless campaign to evict the Marxists and the left in general from the party.

# 14.
# THE WINTER OF DISCONTENT: BEGINNINGS

THE GRUNWICK dispute, which by April 1977 had lasted more than six months, entered a key phase. Efforts were made to ensure that after the Easter holidays a mass turnout of workers on the picket line each day would increase the pressure on the Grunwick management. The TUC had done nothing to mobilise such support. Moreover, the earlier solidarity action by the post office workers (UPW) had been dropped because of the use of the courts by the employers. The TUC did nothing in defiance of this decision or to mobilise the labour movement behind this key dispute. *Militant* pointed out:

> Any attempt to use the law against the UPW would immediately provoke other UPW branches and also the local trade union movement, who have already shown solidarity, to take action in support of the local postal workers and would force the TUC to move.[1]

Nothing had been done by the government to punish Grunwick for breaking company law. On the other hand, one of the leaders of the strike, Jayaben Desai, had been arrested outside the gates of the factory and charged with threatening behaviour after an argument with the managing director, George Ward. Mrs Desai, was only four foot ten inches high and yet she hasd also been charged with assaulting a director of the company.[2]

At the same time, ex-police Inspector Johnson had been taken on as a personnel manager at Grunwick and other former police officials were also employed to conduct 'security'. These developments enraged the active workers in the labour movement and pressure grew in May and June for action. Increased pressure at the factory gates led to over 100 pickets being arrested in early June. London postal workers then applied a total boycott of mail going to the factory. *Militant* reported that on the picket line the police ruthlessly moved in, fists flew in the air, and senior officers made the first arrests. A girl was dragged across the road through mud and puddles, others were pulled by the hair and punched in the ribs... Such was the brutality that many rank-and-file constables were themselves shocked at the tactics of their superiors!

In a lesson which workers today should heed, *Militant* reported:

> The London postmen decided to wait no longer for the go-ahead from their national officials who have refused to take action for fear of the courts. They have said to hell with the bosses' courts when workers' rights are at stake![3]

The ruling class had no doubts as to the importance of the Grunwick dispute. Thatcher's guru, Sir Keith Joseph, declared: "Grunwick could be all our tomorrows... it is a litmus test."[4]

It became clear as the strike progressed that Special Branch officers had mingled with pickets. *Militant* reported: "When challenged the police claimed that plain clothes men were local constables looking for pickpockets and people carrying offensive weapons."[5]

Yet, despite the clear evidence of police intimidation, Labour Home Secretary, Merlyn Rees, attacked pickets for "violent behaviour against the police force".[6]

And in an echo of the 1966 Seamens' dispute under the Labour government of 1964-70, Attorney General Sam Silkin also referred to 'politically motivated' pickets. His statement was greeted with rapture by the Tories in the House of Commons. Moreover, Gorst, the Tory MP for Hendon North, rode in a bus with scabs as an act of 'solidarity' with them.

APEX leader Roy Grantham, an extreme right-wing trade union leader, called for no more than 500 to turn up to the mass pickets. And the demand for a one-day strike of APEX members in London was defeated by 43 votes to 38 with 16 abstentions at the APEX London area conference.

The crunch confrontation during the dispute came with the mass picket. Commenting on the day's events, *Militant*'s editorial stated: "The tremendous 11 July march outside Grunwick's provided just an example of the mighty strength of the working class."[7]

The report of the events was headlined "Workers halt cavalry charge." The cry of "the workers, united, will never be defeated" was "the chant that confronted the phalanx of 36 mounted police brought in to intimidate and break up the picket." In scenes reminiscent of Saltley Gate, the workers confronted both the police and the scabs who were attempting to enter the factory. *Militant*'s reporter described the mood:

> As the chanting changed to "We shall not be moved" so did the police faces, from one where in a few moments they could bash on our heads with their long clubs to one of demoralisation. Their ultimate weapon, the horse, could not be used without enormous bloodshed, or even deaths.
>
> The workers firmly expressed their power and will to the mounted police with the chant of "Cossacks out!" and "Company police". At the same time they calmly offered their hand to those who were sent to do the dirty work of the ruling class by demanding "Police right to strike - now!" In other words, you can't beat us, so why not join us?[8]

Moreover, "when a blue double-decker bus was seen approaching carrying the scabs the cry, "The bus!" went up, with the resulting effect of doubling the pickets' efforts. Eventually the bus backed away and the police called a humiliating retreat." Victory was within the grasp of the Grunwick workers but the APEX leadership bent its efforts as did the TUC to make the movement 'respectable', that is, to disarm it. APEX threatened to disown the strike committee unless they followed the directions of the APEX leadership and the TUC.

But as August approached, the first anniversary of the struggle was prepared for with further mass pickets. However, the police, learning from previous clashes, kept 4,000 demonstrators away from the factory. The APEX leaders together with the postal workers' leaders had also succeeded in forcing the Cricklewood postmen to lift their blacking of Grunwick mail.

The ground was prepared for a defeat of the Grunwick workers. But this was not before further massive clashes on the picket line. In November, we reported:

> 108 arrests, 12 pickets with broken limbs, 243 pickets treated in hospital. These are the shock statistics behind what the Grunwick strike committee described as "utterly sickening" police action last Monday.

> The mass picket was attacked by a gigantic show of police strength, including 4,000 officers, over 200 SPG [Special Patrol Group] officers plus 38 mounted police.[9]

In the teeth of all of this the TUC did nothing. Yet *Militant* commented:

> It would take just the lifting of the TUC's and the Labour government's finger to ensure victory. Meanwhile, they stand aside and let trade unionists get beaten up by the British police force.[10]

The frustration of the pickets was summed up in the slogan on their placards: "We are starving for action, we are sick of promises." And yet the TUC actually threatened to support suspensions from the unions if mass pickets continued.

This emboldened the ruling class and gave Thatcher the idea of pursuing similar tactics in the event of the Tories coming to power. The Grunwick's strike was preparation by the ruling class for the mighty miners' strike of the 1980s. At each stage, *Militant* had put forward a sober, fighting programme which could have ensured victory. Timidity and outright cowardice had been the methods of the right-wing general council of the TUC.

Left leaders, like Arthur Scargill, had attempted to mobilise their members from below. Rank-and-file postal workers and others were prepared to put their own jobs on the line in defence of workers under attack. Their resolve was not matched by the summits of the labour and trade union movement.

Nevertheless, the Grunwick setback did not discourage other workers from coming out on strike for increases in pay and in defence of conditions. The bakers, for instance, came out on strike on 16 September. A *Militant* supporter, Joe Marino, was a member of the bakers' union executive. In the course of time, Joe Marino was to become the general secretary of the union. Writing in *Militant* he commented:

> The bread strike is over. The owners of Britain's big bakeries who took on the workers in an attempt to cow them by force have themselves been dealt a blow. The unity and determination of the bakery workers has forced the bosses to concede most of the workers' claims.[11]

## FIREFIGHTERS

A bitter dispute of the firefighters also broke out. The Labour government was refusing to concede to their demand for gross pay to be ten per cent above the average industrial wage. This had been generally accepted in the past but was being reneged upon by the Labour government. The strike was solid, with about 99 per cent supporting the strike. *Militant* threw all of its resources into supporting the firefighters. It pointed out that despite the claims of the capitalist press that 'they were greedy', in fact; "when a vast majority of firemen have picked up their wages they then have to apply for free school meals for their children, rent and rate rebates, and in some cases supplementary benefit." [12]

During this strike we met Terry Fields, a leading firefighter on Merseyside.

The press once more attempted to play the same sickening game of blaming workers for some people who died in fires. And yet the attempt to blame the firefighters cut no ice with workers. The high regard in which firefighters were held resulted in tremendous support from the mass of the working class. This was despite the fact that the government decided to use the army and the 'Green Goddesses' for 'emergencies'.

Despite this, the strike ended in victory for the firefighters. As a result of our intervention in this dispute, a number of firefighters in all areas of the country came closer to *Militant*. Subsequent experience was to demonstrate that it was necessary for them to join *Militant*'s ranks. 1977 had witnessed the number of strikes increasing three times compared to 1976. This showed that the 'Social Contract' was bursting at the seams. Events, in which *Militant* was to play a decisive role, were to shatter this in the course of the next year.

## FASCISTS ATTACK OUR HQ

In September, an attempt was made by fascists to burn down the offices and factory at Mentmore Terrace in Hackney, where *Militant* was produced. A special article reported: "A wad of rag soaked in some inflammable liquid had been stuffed through our letter box and the remainder of the liquid poured down and around the doors and then set alight."[12] This was not the first time that such methods had been used by the fascists. Attacks had been made on the nearby Bethnal Green Labour Party rooms. The attack on the *Militant* offices was fortunately unsuccessful. But it was a warning of what the fascists were capable of.

The furious opposition to the National Front had manifested itself in big clashes in Lewisham in August. Despite the fact that 4,000 police had been mobilised to assist them to march through the area, the fascists received a bloody nose. The official organisers of the march, the All-Lewisham Campaign Against Racism and Fascism, dominated by Labour lefts and the Communist Party, had opposed any attempt to physically confront the fascists. Fortunately a significant section of the demonstration, with Labour Party Young Socialists and *Militant* supporters like Brian Ingham playing a key role, decided to stop the fascists.

Nick Bradley, on behalf of the LPYS at a meeting before the demonstration, "explained that only the united action by the working class on the lines of Cable Street could defeat the fascists." This is what the demonstrators proceeded to implement, with spectacular results. Police charged the demonstration and this infuriated the anti-fascist marchers. Bricks and other missiles were used against the fascists after the police had deployed horses, batons and riot shields against demonstrators.

Such was the NF's fear that at least a quarter of their supporters refused to march. *Militant* reported:

> The LPYS, in particular, can be proud of the role played by its contingent. Undoubtedly the most disciplined section of the counter-demonstration, positioned where the police charge began, it set a shining example of how to organise effective anti-fascist action.[13]

## MEANWHILE, BACK IN NEWHAM

The Newham Prentice saga continued to unfold. Two right-wing members of the Newham party, Julian Lewis and Paul McCormick, staunch defenders of Prentice, had decided to take the Labour Party to court. It was subsequently admitted by these two that they were 'infiltrators' into the Labour Party on behalf of the Tory Party. *Militant*'s headline on 15 July denouncing their action was entirely accurate: "Infiltrators take Labour to court".

It was not a coincidence that they were using the same solicitors who were acting on behalf of Grunwick management against APEX. When an injunction was served on Andy Bevan, by this time vice-chair of the CLP, at a constituency party meeting, he ripped it up. Yet despite this, when the case came to court in November, *Militant* could report:

> Newham victory... total victory! Complete vindication! All seven members of the Newham North-East Labour Party have had the cases brought against them by the High Court dismissed... Costs, which will probably ammount to between £7,000 and £10,000, were awarded against Milsom (a right-wing member of the CLP), whose expenses have been underwritten by the anonymous backers of Lewis and McCormick. [14]

Meanwhile, Prentice's position became more and more untenable and in October, following the Labour Party conference, Prentice drew the logical conclusion from his position and defected to the Tory Party. The 181 Labour MPs who had supported him were rewarded with the statement: "If I blame myself for anything it is that I did not leave the Labour Party earlier on." Right-winger Neville Sandelson stated: "I am astonished we tried to help him. I am disappointed." [15]

Labour Party conference in October recorded a further significant growth in the support for *Militant* with over 500 delegates buying copies of the *Militant* and more than 200 turning up at the *Militant* Readers' Meeting. Ted Mooney, standing for the Conference Arrangements Committee as a *Militant* supporter, received 424,000 votes. The 1977 conference, however, was a relatively tame affair representing somewhat of a pause between 1976 and 1978. The retreats of the government were being pondered over by the ranks of the movement.

## SIXTEEN PAGES

Only a few months into 1978 *Militant* once more expanded to become a 16-page paper. By this time our organised supporters had increased to 1,140. A number of leading left figures welcomed the expansion of the paper.

> I welcome the enlargement of *Militant* as it is necessary that every view within the labour movement is widely discussed. *Militant* plays an important role, especially among the youth...[16] (Eric Heffer MP).

Sid Bidwell MP stated

> The paper will, I know, concentrate on stripping fact from fiction and presenting these ideas in an unvulgarised way. In this country the Labour press generally is weak. It is therefore good news to hear of your step forward... and perhaps I could contribute from time to time.[17]

From the unions, Walter Cunningham, chair of the Hull Docks Shop Stewards Committee commented:

> I have taken the *Militant* for over four years, because apart from the persistence of your sellers, which is to be admired, the *Militant* has always strived to be honest and responsible in its reporting of local issues and in the docks industry.[18]

Events were to soon demonstrate how important an expanded paper was.

In the early months of the year, despite the massive demonstration at Lewisham, the fascists once more raised their heads, this time in Birmingham. *Militant* reported in February "Young Socialists Rally Thousands" to confront "Birmingham NF meeting". A massive demonstration marched through the streets of Birmingham led by the Labour Party Young Socialists, where "thousands of working-class shoppers, immigrant youth and football fans joined in a magnificent demonstration of revulsion and anger at the National Front youth movement who were meeting in Birmingham last Saturday." [19]

The Birmingham demonstration was followed by an Anti-Nazi League demo of 80,000 followed by a rally and concert in London in May. All of these events combined to finish off the National Front. Their leaders admitted later on that the determined resistance of 1977-78 in effect smashed the attempt of the fascists to gain a foothold in Britain. In general, the lead was given, not by the organised labour and trade union movement from above, but by activists from below, in which the Marxists around *Militant*, along with others, played a key role.

And yet the fascists were not to sink into the background before carrying out murderous attacks on the Bengali community in the Brick Lane area of Tower Hamlets. After the murder of Altab Ali, a factory worker, 20,000 came out in a protest march. The fascists had been responsible for creating the atmosphere where, for instance, Bengali brewery workers in the area had been brutally attacked by car loads of thugs as they left work. With the fascists selling their vile literature - trying to intimidate the local people - at the end of Brick Lane, *Militant* reported: "About 2,000 people occupied the end of Brick Lane in a determined and successful attempt to prevent the National Front from selling their fascist scribblings on this, their traditional site."[20]

These incidents demonstrate that time and again, despite the setbacks for the fascists, they will inevitably return unless the labour movement is vigilant and above all changes society.

But the increased role of *Militant* in these battles once more resulted in an attack on its premises. In July "fascist thugs smashed two windows with bricks that landed in a first-floor office. 'Hackney YNF' and 'NF' were daubed on the walls outside."[21]

The battle against the fascists had rekindled an interest in politics amongst black and Asian youth in Britain. *Militant* was the most successful organisation, then and now, in drawing this layer, particularly working class blacks and Asians, into active involvement. Contrary to the distortions of its opponents, who characterise us as having a 'crude' approach to the battle against racism, and particularly the struggle of blacks, it has always demonstrated a principled but also flexible approach. The need for a common struggle of black and white against racism is obvious. At the same time, and at an early stage, *Militant* recognised the need for specific organisations which could involve black and Asian workers in the struggle at the level that they were at. Under some circumstances, this necessitated special organisations, which black and Asian workers controlled and at the same time also acted as a bridge to the broader struggles of the labour movement. Accordingly, *Militant* supporters were instrumental in setting up a branch of the People's National Party Youth (UK) in Britain in which Bob Lee and Colin DeFreitas played a vital role. The PNP, under Michael Manley, had just won elections in Jamaica on a radical programme. The first conference was held in June 1978 with over 100 young blacks attending.

# 15.
# THE WINTER OF DISCONTENT: HIGH TIDE

IN 1978 it was developments within the Labour Party which stood out, intertwined with events in industry. The issue of Labour Party democracy was once more the key question which emerged in the course of the year. Ray Apps, well known as a *Militant* supporter, was a member of the Labour Party National Executive Committee working party on the issue of the reselection of MPs. The right were fighting a rearguard action with Prime Minister Callaghan, desperately manoeuvring to prevent the principle of election and reselection of MPs being enshrined in the constitution. Writing in *Militant*, Ray Apps declared: "We [the left] consider it vital that, together with the procedure for automatic reselection the local parties should have the right to proceed without reference to the National Executive Committee".[1]

In May we were able to report "Liverpool: Marxist policies win votes." A number of *Militant* supporters were elected to the city council. Derek Hatton, who had been won to *Militant* in 1978, standing for the first time in Tuebrook Ward. He increased the Labour vote by 50 per cent, pushing the Liberals into third place, but was not elected on this occasion. Many commentators then and since seek to explain support for *Militant* in Liverpool as arising from some kind of 'conspiracy' or due to a 'raiding party' tactic. In fact it was patience and consistent work over a period of time, a combination of being the most hard-working members of the party and winning support for our ideas, that allowed *Militant* to become the dominant trend within the Liverpool labour movement.

## 1978 LABOUR PARTY CONFERENCE

We made a magnificent intervention at the 1978 Labour Party conference.

The background to the conference was the growing revolt against the 'five per cent limit' imposed on workers' wages by the Labour government. The Ford strike, which had recently broken out, transformed the mood of the conference and shattered all the plans of the right-wing Labour cabinet. It was a *Militant* supporter, Terry Duffy, delegate from Liverpool Wavertree, who successfully moved the resolution rejecting the five per cent, which in effect shattered the Social Contract and opened the floodgates to the industrial movement. He pointed out that the trade unions had formed the Labour Party and maintained their loyalty to the party, but today the unions had to say: "Enough is enough. Workers will not stand for any more cuts in living standards."[2]

The conference hall also echoed to calls for socialist policies. Re-selection of MPs was a major theme, as it was for the next three conferences until the historical decision in favour was secured in 1981. The rearguard battle of the PLP against reselection was summed up in the speech of Joe Ashton, the right-wing Labour MP, who complained in the conference debate on the issue: "I've got just four minutes to save 300 jobs." *Militant* commented that this showed "his greater attachment to his career than the party workers who gave him the 'job'."[3]

It was not just on this issue but on a whole range of social questions that the conference took a radical stance. NUPE leader, Alan Fisher, spoke at the conference to *Militant,* explaining "why we are fighting for the £60 minimum wage." He stated:

> We know from the views that *Militant* has expressed that they have supported us in the low pay campaign; they've supported my own union in the battle we had during the last two years over the question of cuts in public expenditure.[4]

Summing up the mood of the conference *Militant*'s editorial declared: "How many Labour activists can remember an annual conference which came out so decisively against the main planks of the Labour government's economic policy?"[5]

At the very successful *Militant Readers' Meeting* organised on the Tuesday of the conference, Ray Apps declared:

> The events of yesterday's debate were a historic event for the labour movement and a complete surprise for the right-wing leaders in the

Party and the trade unions... Unless Jim Callaghan is prepared to bend and come to an agreement with the TUC that would give workers a higher rise than five per cent, the government will be heading for disaster.[6]

The conference decisions gave an enormous boost to the Ford workers. The paper carried the slogans of the demonstrators outside the negotiations between the employers and the trade unions: "£20 on the pay; one hour off the day; productivity deals no way."[7]

Because *Militant* had now become a sizeable organisation with a national network of support, it was able, through the work of our supporters, to have the most complete coverage of any newspaper on the dispute. We carried reports showing the colossal support of women in the dispute: "We Ford wives are a hundred per cent with the strikers."[8] This was particularly important given the attempt of the Tory press to whip up an alleged 'wives' revolt' against the strike.

The strike gathered momentum, with the hardening mood of the strikers indicated on Friday 3 November, when 16,000 Dagenham workers rejected the company's so-called 'final offer'. News of this ignited celebrations in the other plants throughout the country.

During the course of the strike the electricians' leader, Frank Chapple, as usual, sought to derail industrial action by refusing to pay his Ford members strike pay. This provoked a movement from the EETPU members: "Ford electricians occupy EETPU headquarters."[9]

After a battle lasting for over a month, agreement was reached with the bosses which smashed the five per cent limit. The workers chalked up an increase of nearly 17 per cent - 9.5 per cent on the basic rate, two per cent on holiday pay and five per cent attendance allowance. This was accompanied by so-called 'penalty clauses' and the 35-hour week was not achieved.

But the strike enormously enhanced the confidence of the working class and boosted other workers ready to take action. One section of workers who were encouraged by the Ford dispute and were featured heavily in the pages of the *Militant* was the bakery workers who came out on strike.

This union had undergone an astonishing transformation. Previously controlled by neanderthal right-wingers the situation had so changed that by 1978 Sam Maddox, the general secretary of the union, was writing in the pages of *Militant* urging support from other workers.[10]

## MILITANT GROWTH IN TRADE UNIONS

*Militant* grew substantially in this period amongst the youth in the Labour Party and in the trade unions. The most significant development was the growth of *Militant*'s support within the unions. In the Post Office Engineering Union (POEU), later to become the National Communication Workers' Union (NCU), *Militant*'s influence and support grew substantially. Post Office engineers were pressing for the immediate implementation of the 35-hour week while the right-wing leaders of the union were dragging their feet.

In the Civil and Public Services Association (CPSA), the opposition to the right-wing leadership went even further. At the CPSA conference in May there were gains for the left. Four *Militant* supporters were elected onto the national executive committee. The run up to this conference had been marked by a vicious political assault on a prominent official, Terry Adams. He was on the right's political hit list for being an alleged 'member/supporter' of *Militant*. But a determined fightback from below had defeated all the attempts of the right wing to carry through sackings of dissident officials.

*Militant* warned in October:

> Sooner or later... the strategists of capital will conclude that the Labour government has served its purpose as far as they are concerned. In any case, if the government continues its present policies into next year, especially if it takes on more and more sections of workers fighting for decent living standards, it will virtually ensure a defeat for Labour.[11]

These prophetic words were unfortunately borne out in the May 1979 general election.

Before then, however, we saw from the depths of society the most oppressed and low paid step onto the scene. The general radicalised mood had politically affected the unions. Much to the fury of Tory MPs and the capitalist press, the National Union of

Railwaymen had taken a decision to expel any member who proved to be a member of the National Front.

Long before the Tories came to power *Militant* warned that Thatcher "would eventually be forced to launch an offensive against the working class and its organisations. Ridley indicates this [Ridley, a Tory MP, had prepared a blueprint for confronting the unions]: 'In the first or second year after the Tories' election, there might be a major challenge from a trade union either over a wage claim or redundancies.'" Ridley foresaw that this would come in the mines and therefore proposed: "(a) build up of maximum coal stocks, particularly at the power stations; (b) make contingency plans to import coal; (c) encourage the recruitment of non-union lorry drivers by haulage companies to help move coal where necessary; (d) introduce dual coal/oil firing in all power stations as quickly as possible."[12]

Right-wing Tory MP Ronald Bell, again indicating the future role of the Tories, stated: "Strike-breaking must become the most honourable profession of all."[13]

## FLOODGATES OPENED

1979 was a decisive year in many respects. No sooner had the year opened than in area by area, lorry drivers began to come out on strike, sick of years of low pay and long hours. Lorry drivers at Tilbury commented to *Militant*: "Well, I've just read your report in *Militant* and there's nothing more to say. That's the best report we've ever seen; it's a good paper".[14]

Discontent was welling up from below. This movement became what the enemies of the labour movement called 'the dirty jobs strike' and 'the winter of discontent'. A movement was developing which had some of the features of a rolling general strike. The London *Evening Standard* once more urged the government to use troops against strikers and pickets. Alongside lorry drivers, train drivers were also drawn into the movement. The mood was shown on the historic 22 January demonstration of public-sector manual workers where 80,000 marched through the streets of London.

Meanwhile, throughout the country an estimated one million public-sector workers took some form of strike action. But then the employers and their kept press began an offensive. Ambulance drivers who had come out on strike were predictably blamed for some deaths that had taken place. Nevertheless, the movement proved to be irresistible. The health service was affected, local authority workers were drawn in. Thatcher declared: "Now we find that the place (Britain) is practically being run by strikers' committees... they are 'allowing' access to food. They are 'allowing' certain lorries to go through."[15]

It was true that, as *Militant* pointed out, nothing moved in parts of the country without the permission of strike committees. This had very little to do with the trade union leaders but arose from an irresistible rank-and-file movement from below. The bitterness of the tops in society was indicated by the fact that a consultant surgeon, Mr Patrick Chesterman based at Reading Hospital, demanded from patients who turned up for treatment to know whether they were trade unionists. If they answered "yes", he then stated "I am not seeing trade unionists today" and they were refused treatment. *Militant* pointed out that "the demand for a living wage is seen as treachery by the capitalists."[16]

The movement of different sections of workers prompted *Militant* to comment in an editorial:

> To ensure [a victory], the unions nationally should give clear direction to workers in key sections - such as water and refuse collection - to become fully involved in the action. This must be backed up by joint shop stewards committees in every local authority, university, area health authority and water authority, planning and co-ordinating activity. Liaision is also essential across these four public-sector industries.[17]

The ruling class attempted to denigrate the strikers by seizing on the refusal of gravediggers in Liverpool to 'bury the dead'. *Militant* supported the action of the low paid, but on all occasions linked this to the maintenance of 'emergency services' in order to cut across the attempt of the capitalists to attack strikers as 'irresponsible'.

The Labour leaders would later attempt to blame the 1979 election defeat on the alleged negative effects of the revolt of the low paid in that year. In reality, it was the government's actions in holding down wages and conditions, bending the knee to capital, that stored up the huge opposition of working people which burst out in the 'winter of discontent'. A socialist fighting leadership of the movement would have based itself upon the demands of working people and linked the struggle for a minimum wage and a cut in the working week to the idea of changing society. But in the immediate period prior to the election, the Labour leaders did everything to play into the hands of the Tories.

## SCOTLAND - MAJORITY FOR DEVOLUTION

They alienated the population of Scotland, for instance, by the way that the referendum on 'devolution' was conducted in March 1979. A majority of those who had voted, 51.6 per cent, were in favour of the setting up of a Scottish assembly as proposed in the Labour government's Scotland Act. *Militant* supported the demand for a Scottish Parliament but with powers to introduce socialist measures.

But opponents of devolution had inserted a clause in the Act stipulating that at least 40 per cent of those eligible must vote in favour before they would acccept the decision. And yet if this 'qualification' had been applied to parliamentary elections, hardly a government since 1945 would have been eligible to assume office. The Labour leaders' double standards in 1979, as well as the general decline of Britain, was to store up future problems for the labour movement in Scotland. Their actions were to give a boost to nationalism over a period of time.

## IRANIAN REVOLUTION

Not neglecting international issues, and not withstanding the huge fermentation in Britain, *Militant* drew attention to important events abroad. Internationally, the Iranian revolution dominated the early months of 1979.

*Militant* considered this development so important that one of its leading supporters, Bob Labi, went to Tehran to witness the mood in the aftermath of the overthrow of the Shah.

His visit was at the suggestion of an Iranian exile group who said they would put us in contact with factory and oil workers. However, the person who was supposed to meet Bob in Tehran did not go back because it was too dangerous and did not tell us of his change of plans. Bob only realised this after a long wait at Tehran airport! So Bob was on his own, not knowing the language and without a translator. This did not stop him discussing with activists or attending demonstrations.

The 1979 Iranian revolution was rich in lessons for the working class on a world scale. It shattered the idea that armed force by a totalitarian 'authoritarian' regime can bridle the masses for ever. But the tragedy was that there was no genuine Marxist movement capable of harnessing the movement which overthrew the Shah and setting up a democratic socialist state.

The opportunist policy of the Communist Party, the Tudeh - sometimes supporting the 'modernising' role of the Shah - had left a vacuum which the radical Islamic fundamentalists were allowed to fill. In the beginning, Khomeini's fundamentalists were compelled, because the masses were armed and determined, to proceed very, very cautiously to derail the revolution. Eventually, however, they ended by concentrating power exclusively in their own hands. Effective power rested in the hands of the Revolutionary Islamic Committee. This body, however, was under enormous pressure from the masses. In the first stages, the Bazargan government strove to preserve capitalism. The real power, however, was in the hands of the committees and the militias, which were politically under the influence of Khomeini. Indeed, Bazargan was actually appointed by Khomeini as prime minister and was in effect forced to rely on Khomeini to carry out the necessary government measures.

With mass demonstrations demanding action against unemployment, and increases in wages, etc., the Khomeini regime announced in July 1979 the nationalisation of all insurance companies, which followed the takeover of the banks. The regime was clearly a bonapartist one, balancing between an aroused working class, the capitalists and the bazaar merchants. The shift towards the left on economic policy was however accompanied with ruthless repression against all opponents of the 'Party of God', the mullahs' party.

In September 26 oppositional newspapers were closed. Khomeini had consistently opposed the left, denouncing those who wanted to continue a general strike as "traitors. We should smash them in the mouth."[18]

Nevertheless, in many factories workers' committees or trade unions were formed and the workers were drawing up a list of social demands. Following his visit to Tehran, Bob Labi wrote:

> Workers have not only been fighting for purely economic demands. Many workers, in particularly the oil workers in Abadan and tractor workers in Tabriz, have been calling for the sacking of the old bosses and the right to elect new managers themselves. Workers at the General Heating and Ventilation factory in Tehran have been given permission by the government to run their factory themselves after the old bosses had fled. At the same time, a struggle has been developing for full trade union rights and the dismissal of the old SAVAK (secret police) appointed "workers' representatives".

He went on to comment:

> All that is preventing the rapid overthrow of capitalism in Iran is the absence of an independent workers' party campaigning on... a Marxist programme.[19]

The original hope of the Iranian revolution for a new chapter of democracy and socialism was to be dashed on the rock of Islamic fundamentalism. Nevertheless, the lessons of the Iranian revolution - how the masses move, how a well-armed capitalist army can disintegrate, the laws of revolution and counter-revolution - were drawn on by *Militant* when analysing other situations in the following years.

# 16.
# GENERAL ELECTION: THATCHER TO POWER

THE MAIN issue in Britain in 1979 was the looming general election. The manifesto which was formulated by the National Executive Committee of the Labour Party in April was a disastrous retreat. The socialist policies repeatedly demanded by Labour Party conferences were completely excluded from the programme: "The few radical reforms included in the draft manifesto have also been dropped."[1]

There was no demand for the immediate implementation of a 35-hour week, nor was there any commitment for the abolition of the House of Lords, repeatedly demanded by Labour Party conferences, nor any promise to implement the long-promised wealth tax. It was the programme of the right-dominated Labour government, rather than the left National Executive Committee.

*Militant* warned what a Tory government would mean for the workers of Britain. Once they were returned to power they would

> immediately cut at least another £700 million off public expenditure... Reductions in company tax and top rates of income tax for the rich... Cuts in government hand-outs to industry, particularly state industry, together with other 'monetarist' policies - which would result in more decrepit capitalist firms going to the wall - would inevitably mean a dramatic increase in unemployment.[2]

The paper urgently called for "all the resources of the labour movement" to be mobilised to keep out the Tories and ensure the return of a Labour government. And yet, on the eve of the election, the right-wing Manifesto Group declared: "The Labour Party must be the party of a permanent incomes' policy."[3]

When the battle lines were drawn, *Militant* supporters throughout the country threw themselves fully into the battle to defeat the Tory enemy. Flying the flag for Marxism as Labour representatives were three candidates, Tony Mulhearn in Crosby, David White in Croydon Central and Cathy Wilson in the Isle of Wight. None were easy seats to win and predictably *Militant*'s enemies attacked the campaigns. Surprisingly, this was led by a 'left', Pete Wilsman, a member of the Campaign for Labour Party Democracy. In a letter to *Militant*, he claimed that *Militant* had done "very badly" in Croydon. He was answered in articles in the paper pointing out that:

> six public meetings were held, including one at which 350 people came to hear Tony Benn at 6pm on a Saturday. Neil Kinnock also spoke at a 100-strong meeting in support of David White.[4]

The meeting on the New Addington estate was a reflection of the enthusiasm locally for the campaign. The election material issued in the constituency also got an excellent response. 1,500 copies of *Militant* were sold and 150 were recruited to the LPYS. Had Croydon Central been fought on the programme of the right wing, it could have been a disastrous result.

Although Crosby was a safe Tory seat, a very effective campaign was launched and Tony Mulhearn received 15,000 votes, an incredible 26 per cent of the poll.

## BLAIR PEACH

In the South-East, excluding London, only seven out of 132 seats were won by Labour. During the election campaign the racists and fascists, with the National Front in the lead, tried to march through Southall, the heart of London's most concentrated Asian Community. However, they got more than they bargained for.

A total stoppage of work took place in the area in response to the Indian Workers' Association's call for a general strike. As the time for the march approached "groups of Asian youth began to collect outside the Town Hall where the NF meeting was scheduled to take place that evening."[5]

The police resorted to heavy-handed tactics against the anti-fascists as they had done previously. This provoked big skirmishes, with the police becoming ever more violent.

Police charges and the use of riot shields, together with the deployment of the Special Patrol Group, resulted in the tragic killing of Blair Peach by the police. Shamefully, Labour Home Secretary Merlyn Rees, declared that there would be no public enquiry, only an internal police investigation into his death. In effect, a police riot in defence of provocative action by the fascists had taken place. Labour Party Young Socialists in Southall and *Militant* supporters were in the thick of the battle. However, as opposed to other groups, this intervention was through a disciplined and organised contingent. In this and in subsequent battles against the racists and fascists what stood out was the organised approach of *Militant* supporters as opposed to the anarchic actions and 'improvisation' of others. Haphazard tactics are completely insufficient when confronting fascists backed by the forces of the capitalist state.

Overall, the 1979 General Election was a disaster for Labour and the working class. Conversely it was a day of jubilation for the rich. On polling day £1,000 million was added to shares and the Stock Exchange closed with the share index at a record high.

The actual vote for Labour was the lowest since 1931. Callaghan attempted to argue that the election was a vote "against last winter". The real responsibility for the disaster was on his shoulders in pursuing the disastrous five per cent limit on wages and other right-wing policies. The consequences of the election internally within the Labour Party would be "in the constituencies, right-wing MPs will be called to account. Re-selection will again become a key issue. The Labour Party will undoubtedly turn further to the left in the next period. Fear of this has already been expressed in the capitalist press." [6]

In Scotland there had been a solid class vote for Labour, with the SNP losing nine of its eleven seats. In the South, however, particularly in London, the South-East and to some extent in the Midlands, "the Tories clearly succeeded in drawing the votes of politically backward workers, including trade unionists, together with the expected middle class votes - thus gaining a significant number of constituencies." [7]

## FIRST TORY BUDGET

*Militant* predicted that a recoil would take place as workers felt the consequences of the Tory victory. This was demonstrated in the reactions to the first budget in June. There were paltry tax cuts for the average wage earner which would be wiped out by inflation in a few months. At the same time, VAT was increased to 15 per cent and the Tories gave notice of further savage attacks on the living standards of working people. *Militant* predicted that

> the working class will now face a period under the most reactionary Tory Government since the 1930s. Thatcher has made it clear that she and her Tory crew intend to repeat all the anti-working class and anti-trade union attacks of the 1970-74 Heath Government - and worse.[8]

## EURO-ELECTIONS

In June 1979, a month after the General Election, there were elections for the European Parliament in which Terry Harrison stood as the Labour candidate for Merseyside. This was the first time that Marxism in Liverpool had an opportunity on the broad electoral front to test its ideas. Terry Harrison fought a very spirited campaign in what was in general a very lacklustre event. In contrast to those on the left who opposed the Common Market (now the EU-European Union) on a nationalist basis, Terry Harrison counterposed to this the Socialist United States of Europe. In this election the idea of a Labour representative receiving no more than the average wage of a skilled worker was first raised.

> I undertake to receive from my salary the average wage of a skilled worker, and donate the rest back to the labour movement. All my expenses, I believe, should be vetted and questioned by the labour movement.[9]

Such was the hate campaign whipped up against Terry Harrison that at one stage someone fired an air rifle at him from a council tower block while he was canvassing in the Lee Park area of the city. The windscreen of his car was shattered by the shot, narrowly missing him. The main purpose of the campaign was not to secure 'victory', as welcome as this would have been, but to reach workers with the ideas of socialism and Marxism and to raise the level of political understanding. However, the mass of the workers on Merseyside were totally indifferent to the outcome of the election. The national result seemed to be a foregone conclusion, with the To-

## General Election: Thatcher to Power

ries and the right wing of the Labour Party, backed up by the media, whipping up the prospect of even greater unemployment and impoverishment if ever Britain came out of the European Union.

In a unique event for an election, in one polling district in Vauxhall Ward not a single vote for any candidate was recorded. However, the defeat of Terry Harrison in this election did not, as our opponents predicted, undermine the support for Marxism amongst the Labour Party rank and file. This was shown at the October 1979 Labour Party conference which carried overwhelmingly on a card vote the historic resolution in favour of mandatory reselection. At the same time, conference also passed the proposal for the NEC to have the final say in the party's election manifesto. The most notable feature of the conference was the swing to the left in the trade union delegations. Historically the left within the Labour Party seemed to develop as a reflex from the defeat of a Labour government, at least in the post-1945 period. It was in the aftermath of the defeat of the Wilson Government in 1970 that a large left reformist wing around Tony Benn began to take shape. During the government of 1974-79 the left still remained as a force within the party, but it took the defeat of Labour in 1979 for a movement of opposition to the right to develop. *Militant* supporters played a key role in this process and this was widely recognised, even in some of the most unlikely quarters.

In a television interview Shirley Williams and Jim Callaghan acknowledged the growing support for *Militant* within the Labour Party. In unusually candid comments Callaghan stated on TV:

> We (the Labour Party) have neglected education. We've allowed it all to fall into the hands of the *Militant* group. They do more education than anybody else.[10]

He also went on to a frontal attack on the main demand of *Militant* for the nationalisation of the 200 top companies:

> You've got to carry the people of this country with you on a basis that they accept that what you are doing is relevant to their problems. Now we mustn't go to the point where we put up some nostrums like, what is it, nationalising 200 companies... there are people in the party who want to nationalise 200 companies. If you were to do that, the country would say, 'This isn't relevant. No, we don't understand what this is about.'

*Militant* commented:

> The fact that Callaghan should go out of his way to mention *Militant* and criticise the call for the nationalisation of 200 major monopolies is eloquent testimony to the widespread support for this demand in Labour's ranks. If it is so 'irrelevant', why is Jim so concerned about it?[11]

At the conference, reponsibility for defeat was placed firmly on the shoulders of the right wing, as shown by the opening remarks of Frank Allaun, the party chair. He pointed out that the TUC had almost unanimously rejected the rigid and inflexible five per cent ceiling of one year previously. But the right-wing Labour cabinet had taken no notice and "that is why Mrs Thatcher is in 10 Downing Street."[12]

Even the party general secretary Ron Hayward lambasted the right in the PLP. At the same time:

> he also warned the trade union leaders that they would call for as many enquiries as they liked, but if it was a purge of left-wingers or Marxists that they had in mind, they should bear in mind that these were the Party's activists and 'they couldn't replace them'.[13]

This was an indication of the relationship of forces within the Labour Party. The left were overwhelmingly in the ascendent. The attempt of Callaghan to assert the 'independence of the parliamentary party' was firmly repudiated at the conference. Speeches from well-known Marxists and *Militant* supporters like Pat Wall, Ray Apps, Jeremy Birch, Chris Huxtable, John Byrne, Derek Hatton, Tony Mulhearn, Terry Pearce, Ian Stowell and Fiona Winders were received with acclamation by the conference.

At this conference the most crucial debate centered around the differences between the *Tribune* programme, left reformism, and the programme of Marxism. Tony Benn in the major debate on the economy had been compelled to answer our arguments.

He opposed a "massive extension of public ownership and national plan of production", counterposing to this a more 'gradual' programme to "take over industry".[14]

Nevertheless, this conference was probably the most left in character since Labour had adopted the 'socialist clause', Clause IV, in 1918. The elections to the NEC had resulted in even greater strength for the left. One of those elected at this conference was Neil Kinnock, then on the 'extreme' left of the party. At the *Tribune* meeting he had commented that Jim Callaghan had congratulated him on his election to the NEC but had then stated: "You know, Neil, there is only one way to go from here - that's down." Kinnock answered: "Well, I said, I'm always willing to learn from someone with experience."[15]

## PRESS ATTACKS

These developments provoked the wrath of the capitalist press. The so-called 'quality' press fired salvos at *Militant*. The gutter journals of capitalism sought to identify *Militant* with 'terrorism'. In answer to a particularly vicious attack from the *News of the World*, under the headline "The Truth about Britain's Red Army" (alongside a story headlined, "a Nude Model's Brush with Sniper")[16], *Militant* was portrayed as sympathising with the IRA and every stripe of terrorist. I replied on behalf of the Editorial Board, stating that the *News of the World*

> clearly gives the impression that *Militant* supports the IRA. This is what Gordon Leak wrote: "Marxist groups have close links with Russia and the IRA"... We opposed the programme and the methods of the Provisional IRA right from its inception. A cursory examination of the pages of our newspaper would show that we have consistently maintained this position... is it not then the height of journalistic irresponsibility, not to say political illiteracy, to give your four-and-a-half million readers the impression that *Militant* supports terrorists?[17]

A similar smear job was undertaken by the *Sunday Express*. Neither the *Express* nor the *News of the World* published our letters. *Militant* stated in an article on the Provos' campaign:

> One of the theoretical foundations of Marx was his opposition to the tactic of individual terror... In 1972 the first copy of the *Militant Irish Monthly* carried a major article headed: "Provisional IRA strategy will not defeat imperialism"... British Imperialism, which is an economic as well as military system, can only be overthrown by the united mass action of the Irish working class.[18]

In lines which stand out in their clarity, particularly when counterposed to the current 'peace negotiations', we also stated:

> It is perfectly true that the Provos could continue some form of operations for a long period of time... But whether imperialism can quickly defeat the IRA is scarcely the main point. For those who support the Provos the real question is not so much whether they can be defeated but whether they can succeed in defeating imperialism. The answer is firmly no. Not in 1979, not in 1980, nor - should they continue - until the year 2000 will they succeed in this. The real legacy of these bombings has been to provide the ruling classes, North, South and in Britain with an excuse to step up repression.[19]

There was real fright in the ranks of the ruling class, echoed by the right within the Labour Party, at the prospect of a massive shift toward the Left. In this situation the ideas of Marxism would become a significant pole of attraction.

The tremendous growth and influence of the Labour Party Young Socialists under the influence Marxist ideas was indicated by the 450 youth who gathered at the 1979 Summer Camp. They were addressed by Tony Benn. Labour's youth had even taken the struggle for socialism to the House of Commons. In a debate in a parliamentary committee room, in which the LPYS wiped the floor with the Young Tories, 200 young people, predominantly young workers, assembled in July to hear Tony Saunois, then the Young Socialists' representative on the NEC of the Labour Party, debate with a boneless wonder from the Tory Party.

## RIGHT THREATEN BREAKAWAY

While still members of the party, Roy Jenkins and his supporters had actually called for the formation of a new 'centre party'. William Rodgers, prominent leader of the misnamed 'Campaign for A Labour Victory', had threatened to split the party. Rodgers had even admitted that if Labour adopted left-wing policies it could win a general election, but went on to complain that such a result would be to place the continuation of capitalism in peril. It would, he said: "impose a heavy burden on our parliamentary system and our mixed economy." This was the clearest statement up to then of the complete abandonment by the right of any idea of changing society in a socialist direction. That is why they directed their fire - and called for purges - against the most steadfast advocates and upholders of the socialist aspirations of the party. Rodgers even demanded that the party be returned to right-wing hands "within a year". The capitalist press, with the *Daily Telegraph* in the vanguard, urged them to "move fast in order to establish such a party" and split Labour.

We argued that notwithstanding any immediate short term success for such a party, boosted by massive press publicity, "there will be no long-term future for Labour's right wing".[20]

Rodgers, the advocate of so-called 'popular' policies, had only 176 members in his moribund Constituency Labour Party in Stockton, in North-East England. The statements of Rodgers and Jenkins were merely the opening shots in a battle which was to stretch over the next year and ultimately result in the right splitting away.

## INDUSTRIAL INTERVENTION

On the industrial front the employers, encouraged by Thatcher's victory, took the offensive against the working class. The year-long bitter battle, which followed the closure of the Western Ship Repairs yard in Birkenhead, was still continuing. *Militant* supporters, particularly Richie Venton and Richie Knights, played an active and key role in this dispute. *Militant* supporters' proposals were adopted by the workers' Action Committee and also by the workers at mass meetings. One such proposal was for a Labour government to nationalise the yard, under workers' control and management, to protect jobs. Many mass meetings were held and two demonstrations were organised through Birkenhead. The right-wing Labour leadership, however, had refused to act over Western's closure when they were in power. Although the yard was not saved, the role played by *Militant* supporters in the dispute, and the taking up of *Militant*'s ideas by the workers in struggle, marked a qualitative development of the intervention of Marxism in industrial disputes on Merseyside.

British Leyland manager, 'wonder kid', Michael Edwardes, was trampling on all the hard-won rights and conditions of the workers. Edwardes, as part of the plan to hammer BL workers, had taken the decision to sack Derek Robinson, prominent CP member, convenor of the Longbridge Stewards and Chairman of the BL Stewards Combine Committee. This was a step towards destroying workers' rights throughout the combine. Commenting on this 16 years later, the *Financial Times* described Robinson's sacking as "the Cuban missile crisis of Britain's carmaking industrial relations... his [Robinson's] ejection put the entire union shop steward movement on the defensive." Yet the sacking of Robinson provoked a spontaneous walkout involving at least 50,000 workers.

The intention of the right-wing trade union leaders was to destroy the momentum of the strike by calling instead for an 'inquiry'. This gave the initiative back to the management and ultimately resulted in the isolation of Robinson. This in turn prepared the ground for further blows against the stewards' organisation. *Militant* pointed out: "Even former AUEW right-wing supporters have been staggered by the blatant refusal to defend a basic trade union principle: defence of a victimised shop steward."[21]

Given the evident rise of workers' anger the question was posed in the pages of *Militant*, 'How long will Thatcher last?' The question of time scale is always the most difficult in politics. We did not always get the timing right but usually correctly indicated the general processes which would lead to certain conclusions. We said:

> Such is the situation of British capitalism, that the ruling class will return again and again in an attempt to weaken and hamstring the unions, and drive down the living standards of the working class. But if Thatcher proved to be too stubborn, the ruthless British capitalists and their representatives in the Tory Party will not hesitate to remove her from office.[22]

This prognosis was not immediately borne out. The Falklands War and the shift towards the right within the Labour Party, together with the economic boom of the 1980s, boosted her position. Nevertheless, it was confirmed when Thatcher was toppled in 1990 as the ruling class concluded that the disaster of the poll tax demonstrated that she had passed her 'shelf life'.

## STEEL STRIKE

1980 was to see a heightened polarisation between the classes in industry and a widening of the gulf between left and right within the Labour movement. Steelworkers were the first into battle. An official national strike was called, the first time that official action had been sanctioned since 1926. The steel bosses had calculated that given the massive rundown in the industry, with job losses seeming to be accepted with minimum resistance, they could get away with a four per cent increase in wages. They were taken aback when out of 700 branches of the Iron and Steel Trade Confederation (ISTC) only 12 voted against strike action. Behind the steel bosses stood the Thatcher government who were looking for every opportunity to take on and crush a decisive section of the working class. But the steelworkers demonstrated magnificent fighting capacities with unprecedented solidarity from other workers. *Militant* distinguished itself in the strike with detailed accounts from steelworkers. The sales of *Militant* soared and the more advanced steelworkers began to enter the ranks of the Marxists.

But once more the official right-wing trade union leaders refused to take measures which would make the strike bite. They refused to extend the strike to the private steelmakers. We commented:

> After ten weeks on the picket line, the steelworkers determination is unshaken. When the ISTC president, speaking at a Scunthorpe rally, called for "an honourable settlement", he was met with a spontaneous chorus of "20 per cent and no strings".[23]

During this strike, and as part of the general debate on economic issues then taking place in the labour movement, the issue of import controls once more surfaced as a key question. Many workers in desperation at the run down of industry were latching on to this seemingly simple panacea. This was reinforced by the rise in unemployment as the recession of 1979-1981 began to bite. More manufacturing industry was lost in Britain than during the slump of 1929-33. On import controls *Militant* argued:

> Aneurin Bevan once described import control as building a wall around chaos. The threat to workers' jobs comes from the workings of the capitalist system, not from foreign competition... import controls would not give a 'breathing space' to reinvest. Without the restraint of foreign competition, the British bosses would merely again raise prices

of their goods. This would not even save jobs, as the extra twist to inflation would cut into workers' real living standards, reducing the market even further, and again unemployment would be threatened.[24]

After an epic battle lasting more than 13 weeks the steel strike was settled in April. However, the negotiating committee of the ISTC only accepted it by 41 votes to 27.

# 17.
# THATCHER'S CHALLENGE TO THE LABOUR MOVEMENT

THE RESISTANCE of the steelworkers considerably enhanced the resolve of other workers to stop the Thatcher juggernaut in its tracks. The mood of the working class was demonstrated in the mighty 140,000-strong TUC demonstration through London in early March. This was called to protest against the government's anti-union laws and its economic policies. It was the biggest union demonstration since the protest against Heath's anti-union act in February 1971. Noticeable was the participation of *Militant* supporters and particularly Labour Party Young Socialists who were "applauded as they entered Trafalgar Square singing the 'Internationale'."[1]

There was a general feeling, percolating the labour movement and the working class, that British workers faced an economic catastrophe unless the leaders of the movement acted. *The Times* was speaking about the "irreversible decline" of British capitalism. With this could come a drastic undermining of all the past gains of workers.

The mood began to grow for the TUC to call a one-day strike - on 14 May, it had been suggested. The TUC called a "day of action" but refused to go the whole way and call for a complete shutdown. Notwithstanding the attitude of the leaders, 14 May was still a massive demonstration of working-class opposition to the Tory government. The key industries, the mines, railways, ports and shipbuilding were paralysed by strike action. Tens of thousands of workers stopped work to take part in the day of action. *Militant* supporters spoke on platforms throughout the country receiving an enthusiastic response. The main reason for the partial success of the day of action lay not with the leaders, the TUC tops, but with the shop stewards and trades councils who took local initiatives. There was no clear call for a campaign to force a general election and bring down the Tories. However, the increased combativity of the working class, shown in the steelworkers' strike, in the magnificent demonstration in March, and also in the day of action on 14 May raised once more the issue of the general strike.

*Militant* devoted space to discussing this issue from a theoretical and practical point of view. Marxists do not play with the slogan of a general strike. In times of heightened class tensions some organisations rush forward with the slogan for an unlimited general strike. On the other hand, right-wing trade union leaders feared the idea of a general strike as the devil fears holy water. In April, Len Murray, general secretary of the TUC, opposed the idea of a general strike in a TV interview on the grounds that if the unions won they would not know what to do with the power they had! He had also denounced as "political illiteracy" the widespread feeling of workers to make the 14 May stoppage a means of mobilising the mass of the working people for a general election to bring down the government.

*Militant* carried a thoroughgoing analysis of the situation in Britain comparing it to the time of the last general strike in 1926. That was a serious defeat for the working class which took decades to recover from. A general strike under modern conditions, particularly in the early 80s, would not necessarily turn out as in 1926. The outcome in 1980 "would be similar to that in France 1968". The 1968 general strike was only called off by the granting of big concessions to the working class in the form of wage increases and cuts in the working week:

> So too in Britain a similar development will undoubtedly mean a partial victory for the working class. But the derailment of a general strike could also result in disillusionment for advanced workers particularly as power would be posed before the working class. For all of these reasons *Militant* opposes the slogan of an unlimited general strike at this stage in Britain. The task is to win the vast majority of the trade union and labour movement to the programme and the perspective of forcing the resignation of this Tory government, and the coming to power of a Labour government on a socialist programme. This can best be achieved by the slogan of a 24-hour general strike, as a warning to the Tories.[2]

*Militant* then went on to show that after a general strike, even one limited to 24 hours, that Britain "would never be the same again. A 24-hour general strike or a series of 24-hour general strikes could prepare the ground for an all-out general strike at a later stage."[3]

While the history of this time tends to concentrate on the battles between right and left within the labour movement it is often overlooked that it was also a period of big demonstrations and huge social convulsions.

For instance, the left-controlled NEC of the Labour Party called a series of magnificent demonstrations on the issue of unemployment. Over 150,000 had gathered in an historic demonstration in Liverpool in November 1980. This was followed by massive demonstrations in Glasgow, Cardiff, Birmingham and London. For the first time in generations the Labour Party had actually taken the initiative in mobilising working people in action.

The relationship of forces was such that the Thatcher government was compelled to step back from its plans for a head-on confrontation with the labour movement. This was shown in the mining industry in early 1981. The threat to begin the closure of the mines was met with the threat of immediate strike action in South Wales. This resulted in panic within the government. Thatcher, for the first time since she came to power, was forced into a

> humiliating retreat... there was not even the faintest hint that the government could have used the Employment Act against the miners or against solidarity action, and it is already clear that the episode has boosted the morale and confidence of other groups of workers such as the civil servants and water workers who are now preparing to take on the Tories over pay.[4]

However *Militant* went on to warn: "The miners showed what could be done by bold and determined action, but if the Tories are allowed to do it, they will come back later with further attacks on workers' rights and living standards."[5]

As in the past (for instance in 1925) when the capitalists face resistance by the labour movement they bide their time, build up their forces, and prepare to strike later. Invariably the tops of the trade unions complacently accept the situation without any serious preparation for future battles. The miners were to pay a very heavy price later after Thatcher and her boot boy Nicholas Ridley had built up coal stocks, beefed up the police and prepared new laws in order to try and smash the miners.

## MILITANT'S 500TH EDITION

This movement coincided with issue 500 of *Militant*. The confidence of the paper's supporters was indicated by the statement celebrating this event: "The newspaper is more than paper and print and photographs. It is an expression of what is now a vibrantly Marxist current inside the working class."[6]

*Militant*'s enemies certainly recognised its significance. In January 1980 the house journal of British capitalism, *The Times*, under the headline, "Time for a Purge", called for action to be taken against *Militant*.[7]

They directly linked the swing towards the left with the increased significance of *Militant* and its supporters within the labour movement: "The growth of the *Militant* tendency is, therefore, linked to the constitutional disputes within the party."[8]

*The Times*'s companion in lies, *The Sun*, carried one of many similar diatribes against *Militant* under the headline "The Danger that Lurks in the Left". The twist this time was "how they [*Militant*] get at the kids".[9]

As usual it was "Dr Death", David Owen, who let the cat out of the bag. He revealed the real intentions behind the attack on *Militant*. At a meeting in Newcastle, organised by the misnamed Campaign for a Labour Victory, Owen singled out *Militant* as the "real enemy" but told the meeting that, "the group that we are after is the [left-wing] NEC".[10]

Owen's speech signified that the right, increasingly isolated within the labour movement, were hysterically attacking the left as a step towards an open split in the Labour Party. In February 1980 the Social Democratic Alliance announced that they would stand their own 'Social Democratic' candidates against left Labour candidates in the next general election. If such a statement would have been made by *Militant* it would have led to immediate expulsions from the party. No such action was taken against the right. Indeed, 'left' leaders like Michael Foot attempted to persuade and plead with them not to split the Labour Party.

But the threats of the right were to no avail. At the Labour Party conference in October

> an historic step forward was taken... when the constitution was amended to provide for the automatic, mandatory reselection of MPs, and when conference voted for the principle of a wider franchise for election of a party leader.[11]

However, the run-up to the conference was punctuated with the rising tide of attacks on *Militant* fuelled by the Underhill Report. Consisting of 522 pages and weighing 5lbs, and at a cost of £35, this report was calculated to cripple *Militant*. But the left national executive committee merely noted the report, refusing to carry out the instructions of the capitalist press and the Tory leadership for a purge of *Militant*.

## THE RIOTS

In April 1980 there were youth explosions and riots in Bristol. This was followed by similar events in April 1981 in Brixton and, in July, in Toxteth, Liverpool. In all three movements *Militant* was present, playing a positive role to win the youth to socialist ideas. The explosions were the result of heavy-handed police patrolling and harassment of the youth, combined with mass unemployment and the worsening of the social conditions of the poor in the inner-city areas. *Militant* quoted from a statement from the LPYS: "Since its formation the Special Patrol Group has been systematically deployed against blacks and trade unionists engaged in action."[12]

*Militant* demanded an end to police harassment, the disbandment of the Special Patrol Group and a job and living wage for all. But as serious as St Paul's was, it was as nothing to the upheaval which took place in Brixton. *Militant* reported:

> It was provoked by a massive police presence on Friday night and, specifically, the fighting was started by one particulary brutal arrest at about 5pm on Saturday. The youth of the area hit back at police.[13]

The spark which led to this explosion was "the feelings of frustration and anger... in the black community over the Deptford fire, in which 13 black people died."[14]

Contrary to the arguments of the press at the time, and legend since then, this was not a 'race riot'. The anger and violence was directed entirely against the police.

> The fighting mostly involved blacks, but that was because it was mostly blacks who lived in the decayed, central area of Brixton. But both black and white youth were involved. White people moving about the area of the fighting, of whom there were a great many, were not attacked, or threatened, or intimidated.[15]

*Militant* supporters intervened to try and give the movement a positive direction. Under their initiative the Labour Committee for the Defence of Brixton was formed, which organised mass meetings and elaborated a fighting programme, the central demands of which were:

> An urgent labour movement enquiry, step up the fight for socialist solutions to the social and economic crisis underlying the explosion [and for an] enquiry into the police.[16]

This committee received widespread support both from the community and the labour and trade union movement. *Militant* supporters, such as Clare Doyle, played a central role in the organising of the Defence Committee. Because of this intervention and a visit to Liverpool at the time of the Toxteth riots she was predictably dubbed "Red Clare" by the media.

These events were the most serious riots in Britain this century. Brixton and Toxteth were just the most visible expression of a widespread uprising that was taking place, certainly amongst the youth, in 1980-81. We pointed out:

> Riots have broken out in nearly all the main cities because the same bleak conditions, the same frustrations, the same hatred of the Tories and the same anger at the police exists everywhere.[17]

The Tory government was stunned by these events with Thatcher herself visiting Liverpool and according to *The Times* visibly "tired and drawn". *Militant* reported the comments of a Liverpool worker: "If we'd have got hold of her, she would have been hung, drawn and quartered!" *Militant* earned the hostility of the capitalist press and the right in the labour movement because it intervened in every movement of the working class, including these events, seeking to give a positive lead. As the Toxteth riots unfolded the LPYS also intervened:

> Our second leaflet on Sunday night pointed out the futility of rioting, and pointed to a political answer to these problems. The response was tremendous. Along Upper Parliament Street and Kingsley Road, amid all the fighting, there was an understanding of the reasons for the rioting that showed the real readiness to fight against capitalism. The fact that this hatred of capitalism was being channelled into a riot is a condemnation of the Labour and trade union movement, which has failed to give a real alternative to those youth, a condemnation of successive Labour governments which have abjectly failed to solve the social problems.[18]

We did not hesitate to show the negative aspects commenting that the mood of sympathy at the outbreak

> changed completely as the night wore on. As we left the main area of the riot, we walked down Lodge Lane. Not a policeman was in sight, yet gangs of youth were breaking into shops, setting fire to buildings and intimidating the local population. Any sympathy that there was rapidly disappeared, as people used the riots to line their own pockets.[19]

We concluded:

> The Young Socialists and the Labour Party can really grow out of the present events. But only if we state clearly our opposition to looting and violence, and stand firm on our socialist programme.[20]

In the aftermath of the riot the Scarman Report, commissioned by the government, revealed in plain language that a section of the police had for years been systematically harassing youth, especially black youth. Also the government conjured up a 'Minister for Liverpool', Michael Heseltine, who promised to eradicate the social conditions which had led to Britain's most serious riot this century. *Militant* pointed out: "Heseltine's visit to Liverpool is a farce! It is designed as a public relations exercise to cover up the fact that the Tories have no answers."[21]

This Tory millionaire had just spent £10,000 on food and drink at a lavish birthday party for his daughter. The net result of Heseltine's and the Tories' intervention in Liverpool was a massive tree planting exercise in Toxteth. Liverpool wags commented it was good for the dogs but the unemployed got little change out of Heseltine. However, one result of the riots was the demand for greater control of the police, particularly of the infamous Liverpool police chief, Kenneth Oxford.

## MORE SUPPORT FOR MILITANT

The increased intervention of *Militant* and the Labour Party Young Socialists both in 1980 and 1981 led to a substantial increase in *Militant*'s support and numbers. The number of *Militant* supporters had leapt to 2,360 by July and increased to 2,500 by the end of the year. The LPYS also grew. This was clearly revealed at the conferences that took place in Llandudno in 1980 and in Bridlington in 1981. The LPYS, under the influence of *Militant* supporters, did not restrict its activities to the committee rooms of the labour movement but was active in all movements affecting the youth; on the street, in the factories, offices and workplaces. They also led an important series of labour movement demonstrations in 1980-81 and sought to intervene in all issues which affected working-class youth.

In the teeth of the obvious widespread support for *Militant* even the capitalist press, at least the most sober of them, were forced to conclude that *Militant* had built up its support on the basis of arguments, ideas and adherence to the democratic traditions of the labour movement. In the *Financial Times*, Margaret van Hattem commented:

> Where it [*Militant*] is strong, its strength derives partly from a high degree of activity and organisation, but equally from the fact that the most active party members do not object.

She debunked the right's charges against *Militant*:

> More important, they appear to be doing nothing dishonest or unconstitutional - there is nothing to stop the right wing from adopting the same tactics, but they are not doing so.[22]

Van Hattem went on to record the comments of an older, non-*Militant* worker in Liverpool: "They're a breath of fresh air." Moreover, membership of the Labour Party had actually increased following the swing towards the left and if the policies of *Militant* had been adopted, the influx of members into the party would have become a flood. One indication of this was the response to the Labour Party Young Socialists' election broadcast, resulting in over 2,000 applications for membership in 1980.

## A LABOUR SPLIT?

On the prospects of a split within the Labour Party, *Militant* commented:

> Where this has been tried by the right-wing social democrats in other countries like Japan, Holland and Australia, however, it has come to grief. With inevitable class polarisation taking place, these right-wing split-offs, after some initial success helped by press backing, have gradually lost support.[23]

One of the concerns of the capitalists, which explained the ferocity directed against *Militant* and the left in general, was what would happen if a new Labour government came to power. Such a government would come under terrific pressure from the working class for radical measures to be taken to solve the economic crisis. We pointed out:

> Therefore, they (the capitalists) will be suggesting that the right wing adopt a division of labour. Behind the scenes they will be advocating that some of the right stay in the Labour Party as an obstacle to socialist measures in the new Labour government.[24]

If Labour had come to power it would probably have split, with the right reflecting the pressure of the capitalists within the cabinet. The disastrous events of the Labour government of 1929-31 could have been repeated. In 1931 the right did employ a division of labour. Herbert Morrison initially wanted to support the National Government. He was dissuaded from doing so by none other than Ramsey MacDonald, who told him in a conversation on Westminster Bridge to stay within the Labour Party "where he was needed".

While Jenkins, Owens, Williams and Rodgers - the 'Gang of Four' - were preparing to split from Labour, others on the right remained within the Labour Party on a mission to save it from the 'left'.

The decision of the right to split from the Labour Party, clearly evident throughout 1980, produced panic within the ranks of the 'official' left. *Tribune*, for instance, launched a vitriolic attack on *Militant* in March 1980.

This emanated from Richard Clements, who was close to Michael Foot, who was elected as party leader in November 1981. Despite *Militant*'s request, *Tribune* refused to give the right to reply. Letters from *Militant* supporters were either edited out of all recognition or were completely suppressed.

The tone of *Tribune*'s attack was illustrated by the following statement:

> If there were a political Trades Descriptions Act, the Militant Tendency would be sued for false pretences for its claim that it is 'Marxist'. Its policies are a mishmash of Lenin's slogans combined with a few selected quotations from some of the most uninspired of Trotsky's thoughts.[25]

Clements even went on to claim that *Militant* had a "Stalinist organisation which makes the British Communist Party look like the Liberal Party in prayer." Stalinism is not simply a term of political abuse, it is an exact term for describing the character and methods of the totalitarian bureaucracy which dominated the planned economy of the Soviet Union.

*Militant* pointed out that the accusation of 'Stalinism' coming from *Tribune* was a little rich in view of the fact that in its 40th anniversary issue *Tribune* had reprinted an obituary of Stalin written by Michael Foot first published at the time of his death in 1953:

> Of course, the achievements of the Stalin era were monumental in scale... who, in the face of these colossal events, will dare to question Stalin's greatness, how superhuman must be the mind which presided over these world shattering developments?[26]

*Militant*, following in the tradition of Trotsky, had always shown that Stalinism was a perversion of the genuine socialist ideas which led to the October Revolution. Never for a moment had *Militant* or its predecessors given credence to the dictatorial role of Stalin or his successors.[27]

The shift of *Tribune* to an openly hostile position towards *Militant* was a foretaste of how it was to develop in the future. From a journal of the left it became increasingly the mouthpiece of those former left MPs like Kinnock and Foot himself. They were evolving toward the right in opposition to Tony Benn and the leftward moving rank and file of the party. However for the time being, these attacks did not prevent the swing toward the left within the party and, with it, the buoyed-up support for *Militant*.

The conflict between right and left came to a head at the Labour Party special conference in January 1981, at Wembley. The conference firmly adopted the electoral college for the election of the party leader and endorsed the decisions of mandatory reselection and the other democratic gains chalked up at the October 1980 Labour Party conference. Wembley was the last straw for the Gang of Four. With the open backing of big business the day after the conference they announced that they were to form a separate Social Democratic Party (SDP).

The right-wing splitters were actually cashing in on the disillusionment of workers with their own past policies. There was disillusionment with the Tories, but many workers and particularly middle-class voters still remembered the retreats of the Labour government of 1974-79. This government had been dominated by the right. While strenuous efforts were made to keep these Labour renegades inside the fold, increasingly brutal attacks were made on *Militant*. Yet the ranks of the movement remained firm. For instance we reported in March 1981:

> At a 2,000-strong Labour rally in Brighton last Saturday, the party's activists and supporters gave their unmistakable answer to Labour's enemies who have been furiously attacking the party's 'swing to the left'.[28]

At this meeting Michael Foot shared a platform with *Militant* supporter Rod Fitch, Labour's new parliamentary candidate for Brighton, Kemptown. Foot's acceptance of *Militant* supporters, lukewarm at best, was not to last long. Once the pressure came from the right he was to the fore in seeking to drive out what he called a "pestilential nuisance".

# 18.
# H-BLOCKS AND SOLIDARNOSC

IN 1980-82 there were other vital issues of concern of which *Militant* took account. In Northern Ireland in 1981 the long-running conflict in the H-Blocks, the dirty protest and hunger strikes, were coming to a head. Much space was devoted by *Militant* to this issue with our Northern Ireland co-thinkers detailing the horrific conditions in the prisons.

The H-Block protests had been provoked by the withdrawal by the Thatcher government of prisoners' 'special status'. We said:

> 'H-Block', like all aspects of repression, is really a class question. But if the labour movement does not take it up it will be championed by bigots who will turn it into a sectarian issue. Opposition to repression, which is a fundamental duty of socialists, is not akin to support for the Provisionals. To oppose the horrific conditions of the 'H-Blocks' and Armagh is in no way to support the false methods of struggle which organisations like the Provisionals have taken up both in Ireland and Britain.[1]

We went on to point out that:

> The labour movement must fight for the scrapping of the entire repressive apparatus. It must also take up the issue of those who have been convicted by the non-jury Diplock courts.[2]

Did this mean that *Militant* was in favour of the release of sectarian bigots? Despite the small forces of *Militant Irish Monthly*, no other organisation had attempted, as they had, to work out a policy in opposition to repression which would also get the support of the organised labour and trade union movement.

> During the 'Troubles' unpardonable atrocities from both sides have been committed by sectarian bigots who are the enemies of class unity. Such would be the 'Shankill butchers', cut-throat assassins of innocent Catholics, or those who gunned down quite mercilessly ten Protestant

# H Blocks and Solidarnosc

workers at Bessbrook, South Armagh, in 1976.[3]

The proposal was therefore made for "a review conducted by the labour movement of the cases of all those convicted on offences arising out of the Troubles. On the basis of such a review, the movement should itself decide who should be designated as a political prisoner, so as to campaign for that person's release." Tony Saunois, on the NEC, won Labour's support for a campaign along these principled lines.

Thatcher, however, remained inflexible in the face of the gathering protests of the prisoners. This resulted in May 1981 in the death of Bobby Sands, followed by the other hunger strikers. This in turn led to an intensification of sectarian divisions. Unfortunately, these came just at a time when the labour movement and working class of Northern Ireland, through strikes, occupations, anti-Tory demonstrations and other activity by the trade unions, had begun to unite Catholic and Protestant workers in action. A number of Northern Ireland trades councils were preparing to challenge the Tories and the bigots in local elections on an independent working-class basis.

*Militant* never shrank from describing conditions as they really were. A very vivid report followed a visit to a blanket protester in Long Kesh was by well-known *Militant* supporter, Bill Webster, who lived in Derry. It showed the horrific conditions at this time. As a result of this kind of intervention by *Militant Irish Monthly* supporters, a dialogue opened up between *Militant* supporters and some of the prisoners in the jails. Only through this kind of stubborn, consistent and heroic work has the ground been prepared for winning the Northern Irish working class to socialist ideas.

## SOLIDARNOSC

The other key development on the international arena was the drama unfolding in Poland. Huge strikes had convulsed Poland in the course of 1980. This compelled the Stalinist regime of Gierek to make some 'democratic' concessions. The workers' protests had mushroomed under the banner of the newly-established 'Solidarity' (Solidarnosc). Such was the movement that Gierek was compelled to cede power to the military leader Jarulzelski. This was one expression of the utter rotting of the Polish 'Communist' Party. *Militant* pointed out in April 1981 that

> despite naked threats of Russian intervention, regardless of the 90-day 'truce' on strikes between the government of Jarulzelski and the independent unions, and in the teeth of the opposition of their own leaders, enormous outbursts of anger, including local general strikes, continue to roll from one end of Poland to the other.[4]

The movement in March 1981 represented the biggest general strike witnessed in the postwar period in Poland or in Eastern Europe. Solidarity mushroomed into an organisation ten-million strong. This compared to the three million members, who formally belonged to the Polish CP. The Stalinist regime hung by a thread. In the conditions then obtaining in Poland it would have been possible to have carried through a political revolution, to have established workers' democracy. However, the 'Russian Bear', the Russian bureaucracy, were threatening a military intervention unless Jarulzelski reined in the movement. The utter demoralisation behind the scenes of the bureaucracy was shown by the comments of a Silesian (south-west Poland) bureaucrat: "We have lost confidence in the Central Committee and our children have lost confidence in us."[5] At the same time we stressed:

> Because the Solidarity leaders... have refused to pose the issue of peaceful political revolution to establish workers' democracy. They must inevitably seek an accommodation with the 'liberal' wing of the bureaucracy. But basic demands for reform raise the need to end the corrupt totalitarian bureaucratic regime.[6]

The movement of 1980-81 in Poland clearly was in the direction of political revolution.

## A RELIGIOUS CLOAK?

It is true that it was cloaked in religion. The Catholic Church was the institution which had, for want of an alternative, played the role over centuries of a kind of guarantor of Polish nationalism. It is also true that there were some pro-capitalist trends within Solidarity. But the overwhelming majority of Solidarity members and supporters at this stage did not look for salvation in a return to capitalism. Capitalism became an alternative only after the crushing of the movement by the military. Together with seeming advantages of capitalism during the 1980s boom this decisively changed the outlook of the Polish workers. At the last Solidarity conference in October 1981, one worker from the Lenin shipyard in Gdansk stated: "Some time ago everything was in our hands, all of Poland was watching."[7]

The crucial question pointed up by this historic conference was the role of the Solidarity leadership. *Militant*'s correspondent who attended it reported that

> the workers feel power slipping away from them. Instinctively, they are reaching out for a new way forward, for an alternative to the compromises of Walesa. They are seeking a road to genuine workers' power.[8]

Unfortunately, time did not permit the emergence of a genuine Marxist current and in December 1981 the counter-revolution struck. Jaruzelski arrested the Solidarity leaders, 'suspended' Solidarity itself and declared strikes illegal "for the time being". He attempted to take back all the gains and democratic rights conquered in the previous 17 months. Russian military intervention risked provoking a national uprising of the Polish people. By choosing to mobilise behind a Polish military figure the counter-revolution took the safest course. Walesa initially was reported to have been allowed to go free while the regime urged him to enter negotiations with Jaruzelski.

While there was considerable latent resistance to the establishment of military rule, at the same time the movement of the workers, because of the deficiencies of the Solidarity leaders, had arrived at a *cul-de-sac*. A certain weariness and exhaustion had set in which led to a temporary defeat. A new movement, which was to rise later in the decade, took an entirely different form from that of 1980-81. The Stalinist military counter-revolution had a big retrogressive effect on the outlook of the Polish workers. Not just the bureaucracy but the very idea of a planned economy received a big blow in the events of December 1981. From now on pro-capitalist tendencies would predominate, even in the workers' movement and in the workers' consciousness. This would be reinforced by the

1980s 'boom', particularly from 1984-85 onwards. It was for this reason that Thatcher received such a raptuous reception in Gdansk in November 1988, from the same workers who had moved to embrace the ideas and programme for workers' democracy in the events in 1980-81. The crushing of that movement and the complete failure of the Stalinist Jaruzelski regime to develop society led to the collapse of support for the ideas of socialism and the planned economy. Infatuation with the 'market' became the norm.

# 19.
# MILITANT SURGES

IN THE early 1980s growing class polarisation and the consequent tendency for the bosses to bolster their repressive apparatus raised the issue of the capitalist state and how the labour movement should approach this issue. *Militant* dealt fully with this in a series of articles. It had long been the hallmark of self-appointed 'Trotskyist', organisations - usually consisting of a handful of 'commentators' - to accuse *Militant* of abandoning the Marxist position on this question.

In order to clear up confusion about the real ideas of *Militant* the editors set out to explain the basic Marxist approach towards the state and how to apply this to the contemporary situation in Britain and the world. In the words of Engels, the state in the final analysis consists of armed bodies of men and their material appendages, prisons, etc. Some on the left argue that this concept no longer applies to the modern state. Yet all the key positions in the civil service, the police and, in particular, the army are in the hands of people who have been specially selected by education, outlook, and conditions of life to loyally serve the capitalists. *Militant* gave detailed figures showing that the officer caste were in the main drawn from the public schools and belonged to the 'AB' socio-economic group, the 'top 12 per cent' in society. There was an intertwining between the tops of the state, the civil service, the army, the police and the government. Indeed

> the monopolies have more and more fused with the state machine in the postwar period. This is perhaps shown most vividly in the movement between the tops of the civil service and the boardrooms of the monopolies.[1]

Many examples were given, among others by Barbara Castle, who detailed how she became in effect the puppet of top civil servants who "control every single ten minutes of a Minister's day and night... Ministers can't even choose who drafts their replies to letters." Tony Benn has also given an example of how, when he was Energy Minister during a strike at the Windscale Nuclear Plant, civil servants informed him that unless troops were used to move nitrogen across a picket line "a critical nuclear explosion would take place". It was subsequently discovered that these warnings were totally unfounded.

Using the example of Chile, *Militant* warned that the British capitalists would emulate Pinochet if they faced a similar situation. The beefing up of the police, the use of Special Patrol Groups, particularly in industrial disputes, the use of the SAS in Ireland, the widespread use of snooping and telephone tapping by the secret service; all indicated the pro-capitalist role of the state. It was not 'neutral' between the capitalists and the labour movement.

At the same time, it was necessary to register the big changes that had taken place in the state and its relationship with society. In Holland for instance, trade union rights had been granted to soldiers. The same rights should be demanded for British squaddies. Moreover, the army, as the events of Iran had demonstrated, always reflects the social balance in society as a whole, in the final analysis. France 1968 showed that a movement of the working class could attract the ordinary soldiers. Any attempt to use the troops in Britain in the early 1980s against the working class would have split it from top to bottom.

To merely repeat the fundamental and basic ideas of Marxism on the state is not sufficient to convince working-class people. At least a minimum amount of skill in presenting these ideas and relating them to the present understanding of working people is required. Having enjoyed democratic rights perhaps longer than any other equivalent working class there are bound to be strong democratic 'illusions', for instance, in Parliament. *Militant* owes its success partly to its ability to explain Marxist ideas on the state in such a way that, firstly, workers will listen to, then on the basis of arguments and experience, accept these ideas.

However, *Militant* has been careful not to foster, as others have done, illusions in the capitalist state. It cannot be peacefully 'reformed' out of existence:

> It would be fatal to pretend, as the Communist Party leaders and the

reformist left of the Labour Party do, that 'the democratization of the state' will be sufficient in itself to guarantee the British working class and the Labour government against the fate which befell their Chilean brothers and sisters. This would above all be the case when attempts are made to 'democratize' their state. The capitalists would take this as a signal - particularly if the army is touched - to prepare to crush the labour movement. Does this then mean that the state must remain untouched by the labour movement, as the right wing of the Labour Party maintain? On the contrary, measures to make the state more accountable to the labour movement must be stepped up. But the limits of such measures must also be understood by the labour movement. The capitalists will never permit their state to be 'gradually' taken away from them.[2]

Experience has shown that only a decisive change in society can eliminate the danger of reaction and allow the 'democratization of the state machine' to be carried through to a conclusion with the establishment of a new state controlled and managed by working people.

These lines in no way contradicted the contention of *Militant*, for instance in France 1968 or in Chile at a certain stage, that theoretically a 'peaceful or relatively peaceful' transformation of society could take place. But the precondition for this would be the organisation of the full power of the Labour movement, consciously organised and prepared, which would only be fully possible on the basis of a far-sighted Marxist leadership and mass party. Measures of a halfway character do not satisfy the working class, yet irritate the ruling class and give it time to prepare to take back any gains which the working class have achieved.

## BENN FOR DEPUTY

Britain was not isolated from the political ferment affecting other countries at this time. It took the form in Britain largely of the continuing struggle between right and left within the labour movement. Dramatically, this was taken a stage further in April 1981 when Tony Benn announced that he had decided to stand for the deputy leadership of the Labour Party. The capitalist press and television went berserk. Not just the right but erstwhile left wingers, like Judith Hart MP and Alex Kitson of the Transport and General Workers' Union, urged Benn to step down in the interests of 'party unity'. Benn replied by stating that what good was it fighting for democratic rights, including the electoral college for elections for the leadership and deputy leadership of the party, if those rights were not to be exercised. He declared that:

> It was in the interest of 'party unity' that we were asked to support the five per cent pay policy, the IMF cuts, a 'Yes' vote to keep Britain in the Common Market, and other departures from the 1974 Labour Party manifesto.[3]

The rest of 1981 was dominated by this issue. The mass of ordinary workers in the constituencies and in the trade unions lined up behind Tony Benn. In an editorial we declared:

> Despite our criticisms of the deficiency of his programme, a victory for Tony Benn in the deputy leadership election would represent an enormous step forward. It would give a further push to the campaign to fully democratise the labour movement and for the adoption of a socialist programme.[4]

The idea that left policies were in some way alienating workers was confounded by the May 1981 local election results. Labour won control of 14 councils and the Tories lost overall control of another eight. All six metropolitan counties, together with the Greater London Council, were now under Labour control. Millions of voters wanted the Tories out. *Militant* pressed for the Labour leaders to campaign to force a general election. However, the right were more concerned to concentrate their fire against the left. There was clearly a rising tide of discontent and an urge for action by the organised labour movement. The 'People's March for Jobs' culminated in a huge demonstration in London. Some of the organisers of the 'People's March', particularly the Communist Party, attempted to make it 'non-political', anti-Thatcher but not clearly anti-Tory, let alone anti-capitalist! Yet at the rally in Trafalgar Square the speeches of Tony Benn, Arthur Scargill and Dennis Skinner calling for bold socialist action were received enthusiastically. *Militant*, despite harassment from stewards under the influence of the Communist Party, made a very successful intervention in this demonstration.

## MILITANT WOMEN

As *Militant* developed so did our influence amongst women, particularly working-class women. More and more women joined our ranks, which in turn helped to transform the approach of the paper and its supporters. From its inception *Militant* had always featured women's issues but as it developed roots amongst women and began to work seriously in this field, our approach and programme became more precise. Many women *Militant* supporters contributed to this. Margaret Creear, who became *Militant*'s Women's Organiser, undoubtedly made an important contribution in ensuring that *Militant* was not only to the fore on women's issues but took a pioneering position on many key questions affecting the lives of women. For instance, at Brights in Rochdale, a campaign was successfully waged to keep the 120-place nursery open. Support was given to the previously most downtrodden workers in the 'sweatshop revolt' that erupted in the aftermath of the Grunwick's dispute. *Militant* was involved in immigration issues, most famously in the successful campaign in support of Anwar Ditta, who had been refused permission to bring her children to Rochdale. All of these aspects brought new Labour Party Women's Sections and Councils into activity, with *Militant* women in the leadership.

This was reflected in a growing profile at the Women's Conference where we were an important factor in the move to the left. Forty delegates attended the *Militant* meeting with over £100 raised for the fighting fund. A special *Militant* pamphlet *Women and the Fight for Socialism* was enthusiastically received, with 166 copies being sold.

Meanwhile, in the midst of increased class polarisation in society, upheavals in the labour movement, and an increasingly beseiged Tory Government the ruling class sought to divert attention with the July Royal Wedding. Di and Charles were the 'social cement' which would bind the nation together. *Militant* did not just concentrate on contrasting the obscene display of wealth of the Royals with the increasingly desperate poverty of millions of other young couples in working-class areas. It also pointed to the possible future role of the monarchy in conditions of sharp, class polarisation.

The monarchy has the power to dissolve parliament, to appoint and even to dismiss the prime minister. In the event of a left Labour government coming to power, the monarchy could be deployed as it had been in Australia, through the governor general, to dismiss Gough Whitlam's Labour government. However, events have moved on since the 'royal bliss' of 1981. The monarchy is now, at best, a flawed weapon. The shenanigans of the royals and their obscene wealth in the face of the deepening poverty of millions has undermined the popularity of the monarchy, even in the South and the Midlands where it was always strongest. It is now an open question as to whether Charles can be used as a symbol of the 'nation' with enough authority to dismiss a government that the capitalists considered dangerous. *Militant* has consistently called for the complete abolition of the monarchy and the House of Lords.

The prospect of a government coming to power pledged to do this seemed, however, to have been dimmed somewhat by the outcome of the Labour Party conference of 1981. Tony Benn lost to Denis Healey, the standard bearer of the right, by 0.8% in the election for the deputy leadership. Healey secured his victory with the votes of MPs who had deliberately stayed in the party to defeat Benn, prior to deserting to the Social Democrats. However, the greatest rank-and-file anger was directed at former lefts, like Kinnock and former members of the parliamentary *Tribune* group, who either abstained or voted for other candidates, thus ensuring a Healey victory. Yet this decision did nothing to dissuade the right, boosted by support from the capitalists, from splitting from the Labour Party. They wanted to inflict as much damage as possible before deserting. Following the party conference demands grew from the right for action to be taken against *Militant*. Yet the right was not strong enough to prevent Constituency Labour Parties in Brighton, Bradford, Coventry and Liverpool from selecting parliamentary candidates who agreed with many of the ideas of *Militant*. Moreover, the national executive committee of the Labour Party was compelled to ratify these decisions, such was the enthusiasm and increased activity which their selections had generated.

In Brighton, for instance, Rod Fitch told a packed rally of 350 people:

> Today we are seeing the rebirth of the Labour Party away from just the election machine of the past, into a campaigning socialist party,

that will fight for working people.[5]

## YOPS

*Militant* supporters were to the fore in seeking to organise the youth against the attempt of the Tory government to put them through the misnamed 'Youth Opportunities Programme' (YOPs), a cover for creating slave-like conditions for young people. *Militant* supporters in the LPYS were instrumental in setting up the 'YOP Trainees Union Rights Campaign'. A founding conference was called in November 1981 with over 300 YOP workers, trade unionists and Young Socialists attending. It was the Marxist[5], particularly in the Labour Party Young Socialists, who were instrumental throughout the 1980s in organising the resistance of the youth, firstly against YOPs and then against the Youth Training Scheme. Thousands, even tens of thousands, of young people were touched by the ideas of Marxism in the course of this campaign. Many joined the trade unions, some joined the Labour Party, and some joined *Militant* itself.

But, irrespective of *Militant*'s contribution to the overall strength of the labour movement, the right were hell-bent, in the aftermath of the defeat of Tony Benn at the October conference, to proceed to a witch-hunt. The fact also that the government was beefing up its policies and personnel in order to deal with the working class was an entirely secondary issue to them. In September Thatcher had sacked her so-called 'wet' Cabinet Ministers. Tebbit had replaced Prior as Employment Minister, heralding an intensified attack upon the trade union movement. Tebbit casually commented on the *Today* programme that he had found that attacks on the trade unions were "attractive"[6]. This marked the beginning of a serious assault on trade union rights. Eleven separate anti-union measures were to follow in the next decade.

But they could have been prevented and the government stopped in its tracks, there and then, if the labour movement would have been fully mobilised on a left programme.

## CND

One symptom of the situation of the radical mood at this stage was the massive turn out of a quarter of a million marchers at the CND demonstration in October 1981. Consisting mainly of young people, the demonstrators cheered Tony Benn most loudly. Yet it was Benn who was coming in for vilification from the right as being 'out of touch'. Undoubtedly tens of thousands of workers and youth were alienated from the labour movement by the attacks of the right on the left, egged on by the capitalist and their press.

There were soothing words from the Labour leadership for the SDP traitors and threats of expulsion against *Militant*. In December 1981 the organisational sub-committee of the national executive committee used its majority, on the casting vote of Michael Foot, to instigate yet another investigation into *Militant*. At the same time, it was decided not to endorse Peter Tatchell as parliamentry candidate for Bermondsey, but this was subsequently overturned.

Tony Benn correctly explained that what the right were proposing was a cleaning up of the Party - to make it fit for the SDP defectors to rejoin. This was at a time when workers were crying out for unity against the common enemy as shown by the massive anti-unemployment demonstrations which the Labour Party continued to organise in different parts of the country. At the 20,000 strong demonstration in Birmingham, Tony Benn received a long ovation, with whole sections of the crowd chanting his name. Similarly YS speaker, Laurence Coates, who followed Denis Healey was cheered when he called for action against the Tories, beginning with a 24-hour general strike. The mood, however, changed when Healey began to speak. Healey made provocative statements, attacking the decisions on extending party democracy of the previous two years. This was despite the fact that there had been an 'unwritten agreement' amongst the leadership not to mention the internal situation in the party. This provoked outrage from ordinary workers who booed Healey. Naturally it was *Militant* supporters who were blamed by the *Sunday Mirror*: "Uproar broke out when about 50 *Militant* supporters of Tony Benn tried to storm the platform in a 'Gag Healey' mood.'[7]

This was totally untrue, as *Militant* made clear: "*Militant* and the Labour Party Young Socialists make it clear that it is not the method of Marxism to barrack the speaker to the point where they cannot carry on."[8]

Originally Michael Foot had totally underestimated the electoral potential for the SDP, backed up as it was by the resources and the publicity machine of big business. Foot had proclaimed that the SDP would not "win a single seat" in Parliament. *Militant* on the contrary, while opposing the policies of the SDP, warned that unless they were

> effectively countered by Labour, the SDP, with the backing of big business and the media, could win 30 or 40 or more seats in the next general election, thus blocking the return of a majority Labour government.[9]

The SDP did not gain this number of seats but attracted enough votes to split the anti-Tory camp and allow Thatcher to return to power in 1983. However, in panicky flight before the success of the SDP, Foot had swung to the opposite extreme, accepting Healey's idea that the SDP could win a 100 seats unless Labour watered down its policies. Callaghan joined in an article in the *Daily Mirror* demanded that *Militant* should be expelled from the party. He also called for the 'disaffiliation' of the Labour Party Young Socialist and a new system for reselecting MPs.[10]

## MILITANT PARLIAMENTARY CANDIDATES

While the witch-hunt was developing, the mood of Labour's rank-and-file was such that the right could not prevent the selection of parliamentary candidates who agreed with many of the ideas of *Militant*. In February Terry Fields was selected as prospective parliamentary candidate for Liverpool Kirkdale. After a reorganisation of electoral boundaries he was selected for the new seat of Broadgreen. A hue and cry then began by Labour's opponents to block the endorsement of Marxist candidates. The Liberals' prospective candidate for Kirkdale demanded that Michael Foot refuse to endorse Terry Fields, allegedly because "he would frighten off businessmen coming to Merseyside".[11]

But the selection of Terry generated enormous enthusiasm, leading to increased members for the party and the Young Socialists. Shortly afterwards Derek Hatton was selected as the parliamentary candidate for Wavertree. At this stage four *Militant* supporters had been selected as parliamentary candidates in Merseyside; Terry Fields in Kirkdale, Tony Mulhearn in Toxteth, Terry

Harrison in Edgehill, as well as Derek Hatton. Alongside of these in the city were also other left candidates; Eddie Loyden in Garston and Bob Wareing, who at this time stood on the left, in West Derby. Together with Eric Heffer and Bob Parry, both prominent left members of the *Tribune* group, Labour on Merseyside had an almost 100 per cent left Labour ticket for the next general election.

In February, both Pat Wall and Terry Fields were endorsed as candidates by the organisational sub-committee of the National Executive Committee. This did not stop the frenzied attempts of the right to drive *Militant* out of the Labour Party.

The mood of the right was reflected in the report of a secret 'Solidarity' meeting in London. Solidarity was the Labour right's own organisation. It was declared: "the Militant Tendency can no longer be allowed to parasite on the party... the Labour Party was a broad church, but that there is no room for athiests". Roy Hattersley made it clear at this meeting that it was not just *Militant* but other left groups who were being targeted by the right. He demanded that the NEC "institute a thorough enquiry into the various anti-democratic and de-stabilising groups that are damaging the party." Reflecting how out of touch they were from the mood of the ordinary party members a Solidarity briefing paper described the policy of "no cuts, no rent or rate increases" as "the politics of Never-Never Land". They declared "Labour councils would not be able to protect all services and all jobs." While they were preparing to drive *Militant* from the party, Solidarity spokesmen such as David Norman of the POEU declared that, if the SDP traitors approach the Labour Party: "we should welcome them back".[12]

Clearly, here was a an organised right wing 'party within a party'. Yet the right on Labour's NEC did not even think of proposing an enquiry as had been done with *Militant*. The gutter level of the right was shown by the statement of a prominent right-winger, Gerald Kaufman:

> It's very boring being in the Labour Party at present, attending General Management Committees where routine resolutions are put forward. I appreciate that we don't want to be bored and would prefer going to the theatre, opera, football, stripshows (some groans), but you'll have to forego these for a time to gain the price of tolerance; you have to sit it out at these terrible meetings to the end.[13]

Meanwhile, *Militant* was heavily involved in the urgent issue of trying to save the youth from mass unemployment and the government's slave labour schemes. On 25 February 1982 thousands of youth were mobilised in the highly succesful YOPs lobby of Parliament. So successful was it that Tebbit railed that Tony Benn, in supporting it, was "encouraging wild expectations... among young people". Benn's rejoinder was "what is your wild expectations, a job - is that a wild expectation?"[14]

A magnificent 3,000 strong rally and meeting in the Festival Hall was held after the lobby. The meeting was addressed by Tony Benn, myself, Dennis Skinner and Shareen Blackhall, who had been on the TUC's recent "March for Jobs".

## PAT WALL AND CIVIL WAR

It was because *Militant* attempted to sink roots in the working class and were not just sitting in Labour committee rooms that the ferocity against it by the capitalist press was so great. No opportunity was lost to vilify and distort our ideas. One of the most blatant examples was the campaign whipped up over a speech by Pat Wall in March. *The Sunday Times*, portrayed Pat Wall as being hell bent on "civil war" and "bloodshed".[15]

Ironically, in a debate against the SWP, Pat Wall repeated over and over again, his belief that it was theoretically possible that "a peaceful transition to a socialist Britain" could take place *if the full power of the Labour and trade union movement were used*. He also warned against the possibility of violence and 'civil war' being organised by the capitalists once their wealth and power was threatened. In an editorial statement on the dirty methods of the press, we declared:

> at the meeting Pat explained that the *Militant* was in favour of a peaceful transformation of society. No supporter of *Militant* would ever advocate or encourage 'bloodshed' or 'civil war', as the press tried to suggest. On the contrary, Pat was explaining that if there was any threat to a peaceful transformation of society, that threat would come from the capitalist class itself... The leader of the Tory Party in 1912 actually supported a mutiny of officers based in Ireland who opposed the policies of the majority of Parliament... Mussolini, Hitler and Franco were at one time praised and supported by leading figures in the Tory

Party. More recently, Ian Gilmour, supposedly a 'liberal' in that party, wrote that "Conservatives do not worship democracy... For them majority rule is a device... for Conservatives, therefore, democracy is a means to an end and not an end in itself."[16]

The harassment of Pat Wall and his family following this speech indicated the lengths to which the press were prepared to go in order to pillory *Militant* and its supporters.

Pat Wall's wife, Pauline, was forced at her own home to stick up the National Union of Journalists 'Code of Professional Conduct', in an unsuccessful attempt to prick the consciences of the Fleet Street hounds who persecuted her, Pat and their family. An example of the methods used is shown by the following questions which were put to her by journalists:

> What do you feel about being married to a violent man?... Does he cuff the children?... Are you digusted with him?... Why does your husband advocate violence?... Why is he calling for blood on the streets?[17]

The press even approached Pat Wall's employers asking them what they thought of his political opinions. Anonymous letters were sent to them suggesting that Pat should be sacked. But the press attack did not work. Pat Wall remained as the parliamentary candidate for Bradford North. He was defeated in the 1983 general election, because votes were syphoned off by Ben Ford the previous MP and defector to the SDP. Labour's right distanced themselves from Pat Wall and his campaign. In 1987 Pat was revenged for this defeat with his triumphal election to Parliament.

The Labour leadership, who were bending the knee to the press campaign against *Militant*, were incapable of mobilising the labour movement to defeat the threat posed by the defection of the SDP traitors. This was shown in the Hillhead by-election which took place in March 1982. Labour lost this seat to SDP leader Jenkins. More important was the massive defection of previous Tory voters, with the Tory vote dropping by 14.5 per cent. This was in a seat that Labour had held since 1919. In a series of by-elections - Crosby, Warrington and now Hillhead - SDP support had grown. Within 24 hours of the vote the right, led by Healey and Hattersley, predictably attempted to unload responsibility for Labour's failure on the shoulders of the left, and in particular of *Militant* supporters.

In reality, support for the SDP was a vote against the policies of the Labour government of 1974-79 led by the right. The irony of the situation was that the SDP leaders were the very authors of those policies which they were now capitalising on as a 'new' party. Moreover, the right-wing Labour leaders remaining in the Labour Party were prevented from effectively attacking their former political bedfellows because they shared the same outlook and approach. While preparing a purge of the left they held out the hand of friendship to Owen and Jenkins, offering an unofficial coalition, if the SDP held the balance of power after the next election.

## ANTI-UNION LAWS

While Labour was 'a house divided against itself' the Tories took the opportunity to introduce a brutal attack on the trade unions. When Tebbit introduced his infamous 1981-82 anti-union Act, *Militant* declared:

> If Tebbit's proposals ever become law the trade unions will be dragged into a legal morass. The trade unions would face the possibility of bankruptcy and individual trade unionists will face the threat of imprisonment.[18]

Tebbit spoke of the need to 'neuter' the unions through this legislation. He proposed that the Tory judges should decide whether or not industrial action was 'lawful'. At the same time, union funds could be taken by companies for compensation for losses incurred through 'illegal' industrial action. Moreover, industrial action was to be declared illegal unless it was 'wholly or mainly' concerned with a British trade dispute and the term 'trade dispute' was further narrowly defined to mean only disputes between workers and their immediate employers. There were also proposals for attacks on the closed shop and the ground was prepared to make it easier for victimisation of strikers to take place. *Militant* pointed out that "unions have the power to smash it [Tebbit's proposals]". We were at one with the statement of Arthur Scargill, newly re-elected as president of the National Union of Miners, who declared:

> Legislation is introduced by Parliament, but we should remember the law on advances of our freedoms and liberties are due to men and women who, when their conscience has compelled them, have been prepared to defy the law... If legislation is introduced which erodes our basic freedom and democracy or threatens our right to combine, we should oppose it with the same vigour and determination of our forefathers. I believe it will be necessary to use all measures, including industrial action, to defy Tebbit's law and defend our movement.[19]

The failure of the right-wing leadership of the general council of the TUC to heed this advice meant that the British workers paid a heavy price over the next decade. Decisive action at the stage when this legislation was introduced would have shattered the government, as it did in 1972, ten years earlier. Weakness invites aggression. Prevarication, hesitation and outright cowardice, the hallmarks of the right of the trade unions, were to embolden the Tories.

# 20.
# THE FALKLANDS/MALVINAS WAR

IN 1982 the Falklands War broke out, seemingly as a bolt from the blue which was to have a decisive effect on events in Britain.

From the outset *Militant* posed the question: "Whose class interest is served by the Argentine invasion and whose class interest is served by the British military expedition?"[1]

The seizure of the Falkland/Malvinas Islands arose from the desperate attempts of the Galtieri dictatorship to ward off the threat of revolution in Argentina. Not for the first time a military dictatorship had engaged in a foreign adventure as a means of reinforcing its grip on power. Prior to the invasion, Argentina had witnessed an upsurge of working-class opposition to a brutal regime which had engaged in kidnappings, assassinations and torture. 20,000 people had 'disappeared'. Only in 1995 was it revealed by a military whistleblower just how this was done. Officers took it in turns to throw naked prisoners out of aircraft over the Atlantic Ocean. This was a military police dictatorship which had used fascist methods against its opponents but was now facing judgement day after a six-year bloody reign of terror. It was for this reason that Galtieri had reactivated the 150-year old claim to the Malvinas.

Just a few days before the invasion on 30 March tens of thousands of youth and workers had defied the military on the streets of Buenos Aires, protesting against impoverishment, unemployment and the suppression of trade union and democratic rights. 1,500 political and trade union opponents of the regime had been arrested just prior to the invasion. A series of general strikes had also broken out. What would the working class in Argentina have gained from the taking of the Falklands/Malvinas? If the junta had succeeded this would have prolonged the life of the military dictatorship and worsened the conditions of the Argentine workers. On the other hand, argued *Militant*, "the real motive for the belligerent attitude of the British capitalists is simply their enormous loss of face."[2]

The British capitalists, like any ruling class, ultimately base their position on their income, but also on their power and prestige. Thatcher on behalf of British capitalism, invoked the rights of the Falkland Islanders. Britain was alledgedly defending democracy against 'fascist' Argentina. Yet, asked *Militant,* why had the Tories been quite happy to sanction massive arms sales to this 'fascist' junta and to remain completely silent about the repression of the Argentine working class?

Moreover, they had very little regard for the Falkland Islanders themselves, refusing to develop the island's services. The *Financial Times* commented when the conflict broke out: "It is precisely because no substantial British interest was involved that the crisis was allowed to arise in such a careless way." Rather than the Falkland Islands being a paragon of democracy, as Thatcher tried to pretend, it was in effect little more than a benevolent dictatorship with its fate being decided by one firm, the Falkland Islands Company. Nevertheless, for British capitalism to simply have allowed the Argentine junta to seize the islands without any response would have struck a massive blow to its already diminished power and prestige.

*Militant* opposed the class collaborationist position of Labour's front bench, which not only supported Thatcher but demanded war against Argentina. In fact Labour support for the Tories was a vital ingredient in the steps leading to the sending of the Task Force. *Militant* declared:

> Workers can give no support whatsoever to the lunatic adventure now being prepared by the Thatcher government... the Labour Party and the trade union movement could stop Thatcher dead in her tracks. The labour movement must declare that it has no confidence whatsoever in the policies or methods of the British government... Labour must demand a general election in order that a Labour government can support and encourage workers' opposition in Argentina.[3]

Notwithstanding this a legend has grown up around *Militant*'s alleged position at the time of the Falklands/Malvinas War. Ultra-left critics give the impression that *Militant* did not oppose the war. The above statement and those in the theoretical journal *Militant International Review* in June 1982 makes the position absolutely clear: "We are against this capitalist war."[4]

But *Militant*'s position was at odds with those lefts like Tony

Benn. There was common ground on opposing the war. Differences arose on just how this was to be done and what slogans to raise within the British Labour and trade union movement. How to appeal to the majority of workers in order to mobilise effective mass oppposition? It was not sufficient merely to denounce the war or just to call for the Task Force to be withdrawn. The capitalists would be impervious to such an appeal and *Militant* estimated that the working class, because of the issues involved, would also remain deaf to such calls. The consciousness of the British workers over the Falklands/Malvinas and, for instance, at the time of the Gulf War were entirely different. The latter was quite clearly seen as a 'war for oil'.

To force the withdrawal of the Task Force would have involved the organisation of a general strike, which itself would have posed the question of the coming to power of a socialist government. Yet at the outset of the war, such a demand would have received no support from the British workers. We pointed out:

> The Falkland Islanders were quite understandably opposed to Argentine sovereignty if that meant the same 'rights' for them that it meant for ordinary workers in Argentina itself.[5]

The democratic rights of the 1,800 Falklanders, including the right to self-determination, if they so desired, was a key question in the consciousness of British workers.

A socialist solution to the problem of the Falklands/Malvinas posed the need for a socialist Argentina, and perhaps a socialist, democratic, federation of Argentina and the Falklands/Malvinas with full automonous rights for the Islanders. However, a forcible annexation by the Argentine dictatorship of the Falkland Islands was an entirely different matter. Although the population of the Falklands had dwindled to 1,800, hardly a nation in the classical sense of the term, they nevertheless have the right to enjoy their own language, culture and if they so desire their own form of government. Marxists could not be indifferent to the fate of the Falklanders, particularly given the consciousness of the British working class as it developed over this issue. *Militant* could not condone the Islands' subjugation by the dictatorship, represented on the Islands by the newly established military government of General Mendes. This creature was a veteran of the Junta's 'dirty war', the extermination campaign against socialists and workers as well as the guerrilla groups, who had taken up arms against the Argentine military regime.

At the same time, socialists and Marxists had no confidence in the Tory government and its attempts to resolve the crisis by arms. The Task Force was sent to the Falkland Islands, not to defend the Islanders' rights and conditions, nor was it a question of British 'democracy' against 'fascist' Argentina. While the capitalists retained their power they would use it to defend their class interest at home and abroad. But the demand for a general strike, particularly at the outset of the war, it was clear, would have recieved no support, even from the advanced section of the working class. Even those who declared in favour of "stopping the war" drew back from calling for a general strike. Nor would the call to stop the war or to withdraw the fleet have provided a basis even for a mass campaign of demonstrations, meetings and agitation. This was because it left unanswered, in the eyes of workers, the vital question of the rights of the Falkland Islanders and the question of opposing the vicious military police dictatorship in Argentina.

The only way to stop the war was to bring down the Tory government. But Thatcher had the support of the Labour Party and trade unions. Without this Thatcher could not have gone to war. Michael Foot supported sending the Task Force but, on the eve of the first engagement, also argued that it should not be used. This was a completely inconsistent and ineffectual stance. As if the Tories had sent the Fleet 8,000 miles across the Atlantic simply as a 'show' of force.

*Militant* argued that the Falklands/Malvinas conflict was not a reason for calling off the struggle against the Tories. On the contrary, the looming conflict would drain the resources of British capitalism. Big business would attempt to make the workers pay. This underlined the urgency of stepping up the struggle to bring down the Tory government.

In contrast to *Militant*, many so-called Marxists in Britain and internationally, gave either tacit or open support to the Argentine dictatorship. This could only play into the hands of the Tories and British imperialism.

These groups reasoned that the only consistent way to oppose the British ruling class was to support the enemy of British capitalism. They ended up by giving support to the Argentine military-police dictatorship. Thus from the correct starting point of opposition to this capitalist war these groups ended in a political *cul-de-sac*.

Their analysis allegedly drew on Lenin and Trotsky's attitude toward the first world war. Lenin's idea of 1914 - 'Revolutionary Defeatism' - was invoked. This was done without bothering to examine the circumstances and without understanding Lenin's method. There were enormous differences between the circumstances of the first world war and the clash almost 70 years later between British imperialism and Argentina over the Falklands/Malvinas.

On an historical point: Lenin himself explained in 1921 that the slogan of "a civil war of revolutionary defeatism" was a slogan for the core of party activists to draw a clear line of distinction between traitors who had supported the war in 1914 and genuine Marxism. It was not a 'slogan' for winning the mass of the workers in Russia or elsewhere.

Trotsky also pointed out on the eve of the second world war that the slogan of "revolutionary defeatism" could not "win the masses", who did not want a "foreign conqueror". He went on to point out that the decisive role in the conquest of power by the working class in Russia in October 1917 was played not by the refusal to defend the "bourgeois fatherland" but by the slogan of "All Power to the Soviets" and only by this revolutionary slogan. The Bolsheviks' criticism of imperialism and militarism could never have won the overwhelmingly majority of the people to the side of the Bolsheviks. The argument that in the Falklands/Malvinas War it was simply a case of 'imperialist' Britain against a colonial country, Argentina, did not hold water.

This was used by some as justification for supporting the Junta. The Argentine regime's invasion was not a war of 'national liberation' against imperialism. On the contrary, in seizing the Falklands/Malvinas the Argentine Junta was pursuing the 'imperialist' aims of Argentine capitalism.

Galtieri had invaded the Islands for political reasons - to head off revolution and to save his regime. Behind Galtieri stood the Argentine financiers and capitalists, eager to get their hands on the economic potential of Antarctic oil and other natural resources in the region. *Militant* pointed out that it was ludicrous to describe Argentine capitalism as a completely dependent, 'comprador' capitalist regime dominated by the agents of foreign capital. Statistics showed that Argentina, despite its neo-colonialist subservience to US imperialism as well as West European and Japanese big business, nevertheless had all the characteristics of a semi-industrialised capitalist economy.

The situation would have been different if British imperialism had decided to invade Argentina itself. This was a scenario which Trotsky clearly had in mind when commenting on a hypothetical situation involving Brazil in the 1930s:

> In Brazil there now reigns a semi-fascist regime that every revolutionary can only view with hatred. Let us assume, however, that on the morrow England enters into a military conflict with Brazil. I ask you on whose side of the conflict will the working class be? I will answer for myself personally - in this case I will be on the side of the 'fascist' Brazil against the 'democratic' Great Britain. Why? Because in the conflict between them it will not be a question of democracy or fascism. If England should be victorious, she will put another fascist in Rio de Janeiro and will place double chains on Brazil. If Brazil on the contrary should be victorious, it will give a mighty impulse to national and democratic consciousness of the country and will lead to the overthrow of the Vargas dictatorship. The defeat of England will at the same time deliver a blow to British imperialism and will give an impulse to the revolutionary movement of the British proletariat.[6]

Merely repeating Trotsky's words, without grasping his method, the sects seized on this as justification for their "critical support".

If there were an Argentine population on the Islands, subject to British rule against their will, the situation would also have been different. Then there would have been a case for a national liberation war to free the Islands. Even then the Marxists would advocate class independence from the Argentine dictatorship. But this was not the case in 1982. Apart from one or two Argentines married to Islanders, there had been no Argentinians on the Islands for 150 years. "Galtieri's war" was a classic case of a crumbling military dictatorship seeking salvation in a foreign adventure.

While *Militant* defended the analysis and main slogans which we put forward in Britain in the course of the conflict, at the same time it recognised that a different emphasis would have been needed to be adopted by Argentine Marxists. While they would be duty bound to oppose the war, pointing to the real aims of the Junta, at the same time once the war had begun the Argentine Marxists would have stood for the full mobilisation of the working class on a clear anti-capitalist, anti-imperialist programme. This would have necessitated calling for the expropriation of all 'imperialist assets' in Argentina, starting with those of British imperialism. At the same time they would have called for the arming of the working class, and by implication the overthrow of the military dictatorship, as a means of winning the war. In contrast to the Junta Argentine Marxism would have offered full automony to the Islanders in the context of a socialist federation with Argentina as a step towards a Socialist United States of Latin America.

British imperialism triumphed over Argentina and in so doing gave an enormous boost to the Thatcher government. However, such an outcome was not at all pre-ordained, as subsequent accounts demonstrated. *Militant* argued at the time that if one of the British aircraft carriers had been sunk in the invasion of the Islands the war would have developed over a much longer period of time. Then, as the body bags began to come home, the earlier support would have begun to evaporate. Thatcher was lucky that in this conflict she came up against a more corrupt and incompetent regime than her own. But as *Militant* had also foreshadowed, the consequences of the defeat of the Argentine Junta was its overthrow and the danger of revolution; one of the reasons why Reagan was a little reluctant to support Thatcher, his number one ally.

In Britain the 'Falklands factor' had a decisive effect in 1982-83. Britain's 'triumph' conjured up shades of a 'glorious imperialist past'. The effect of this was more striking in the South-East and the Midlands which was historically the home of Joseph Chamberlain's 'imperialism'. Boosted by massive support from the press, Thatcher was able to equate, for a time at least, Britain's military triumph with hopes of a return to Britain's past 'economic glory'. In the May 1982 council elections, despite four million unemployed, falling living standards and generally disastrous economic policies, the Tories in fact held on, registering a net overall gain of a handful of seats. The Falklands factor would be part of the explanation for Thatcher's 1983 general election victory.

# 21.
# TOWARDS EXPULSIONS

THE MOST notable Labour success in the 1982 council elections was in Liverpool. Here the Labour Party, heavily influenced by *Militant*, conducted a fighting socialist campaign against the Liberal incumbents. The Tory press and their Liberal acolytes pilloried the 'Militant Tendency'. A typical example of the red scare tactics was a leaflet put out by the Liberals which proclaimed that *Militant* wanted to "ban religion in favour of Militant atheism". It issued a leaflet with a tear-off slip to be sent to Michael Foot calling on him to disassociate himself from the "policies outlined above" and called for an "urgent decision" on the enquiry into '*Militant Tendency*'. This showed how the campaign of the right wing of the Labour Party for a witch-hunt played into the hands of the capitalist parties.

But in the aftermath of the elections the *Liverpool Echo* for once came close to the truth: "The city voters clearly rejected the anti-Marxist campaign."[1] In many wards there were huge orange hoardings on the gable end of houses spelling out the main Liberal slogan "Marxists Out - Liberals in". It wasn't just the Liberals but their allies, the SDP, who took a hammering, earning it the cruel nickname of 'The Sudden Death Party'. The outcome of the election was that Labour was the biggest party with 42 seats but the Liberals and the Tories still had between them 57 seats. Some of the right wing argued for Labour to take minority control. However, the left succesfully defeated this proposal. The Liberals were left holding on to power, the "poisoned chalice". Big cuts loomed, including rent increases and the probable loss of 4,000 jobs. The record of the Tories and Liberals in the next 12 months was to prepare the ground for a massive Labour victory in 1983.

**CPSA**

Meanwhile, on the industrial front the most notable feature of *Mili-*

*tant's* work was the triumph of the left in the CPSA. In fact the 1982 conference was perhaps the most important in the union's 79-year existence. Radical policies were adopted and a fighting leadership was elected to carry them out. Kevin Roddy, a well-known *Militant* supporter, was elected as president. The Broad Left swept the board in the elections to the national executive committee with a majority of 24 to four, among whom were numbered seven *Militant* supporters. The conditions which led to this left victory had been prepared by the complete failure of the right wing. They were weak, vacillating and hesitant. Kevin Roddy was the first left president for over 30 years and when his election was announced a wave of spontaneous enthusiasm swept through the conference hall. Labour Party affiliation was carried for the first time. *Militant* had long campaigned for this, despite the witch-hunt taking place in the party.

However, active workers in the labour movement were preoccupied throughout 1982 with the gathering witch-hunt against *Militant* and the left in general. The press had whipped up the hysteria in the run-up to the National Executive Committee meeting on 23 June. More and more demands were made for the expulsion of *Militant* supporters from the Labour Party. The arguments of the press were echoed, one after another, by right-wing MPs and trade union leaders.

Terry Duffy the right-wing leader of the engineering union (AUEW) sought to blackmail Labour's NEC by hinting that he would refuse to pay a promised £2.5 million towards Labour's election fund. The ostensible reason for this was the adoption of Pat Wall as the Labour candidate for Bradford North. Duffy was threatening to support Ben Ford the 'Independent' Labour candidate. Action was demanded not just against *Militant* but against others on the left. Roy Hattersley wanted action to be taken against the Labour Co-ordinating Committee (LCC). Sid Weighell suggested that Tony Benn should leave the Labour Party and establish his own party. We commented:

> Labour's right wing clearly see the witch-hunt against *Militant* as the beginning of a purge against any who dissent. It is a campaign to destroy all the gains won over the past three years on democracy and policy.[2]

But there was ferocious resistance amongst the socialist rank and file of the Party. Two hundred Constituency Labour Parties protested to the NEC against the witch-hunt. The regional conferences of the Scottish, West Midlands, London, Southern and South West Labour Parties opposed any witch-hunt. In the North West a motion supporting expulsions was contemptuously dealt with; a delegate moved "next business". Numerous protests took place at labour movement meetings throughout the length and breadth of the country. Wales was an arena of ferocious conflict between *Militant*, the real left in the vital heartland of South Wales, and the right-wing parliamentary and council careerists. From this area came some of the finest, most steadfast adherents to *Militant* and Marxism; the late Muriel Browning, indomitable socialist fighter, shop steward and unwavering in her support for working people in struggle; Andrew Price one of the best socialist orators in the ranks of *Militant* and steadfast supporter of Marxism, along with key supporters like Alec Thraves, Roy Davies, Dave Reid and many others. It has been for over 30 years one of the bastions of *Militant* support. In 1982 the South Wales *Evening Post* reported:

> Almost 300 trade unionists and Labour Party members turned up at the '*Militant*' rally. They heard Mr Peter Taaffe, the editor, outline the programme of *Militant* and answer Labour's right-wing allegations of infiltration.[3]

On the other side of Britain, even in an area associated with "champagne socialism", according to the local newspaper, "Moves against *Militant* Tendency have been condemned by Hampstead Labour Party."[4] The *East End News* carried favourable comments from Ian Mikardo, Left MP for Bethnal Green:

> Recalling Labour's national executive committee meeting he says, 'from 1951 onwards there was never a meeting without some violent attack on the left... Michael's (Foot) adjective for them was "gruesome".

The article continued:

> Their [*Militant*'s] policies of a 35-hour week, a £90 minimum wage and the nationalisation of the 200 largest monopolies... may be narrow... but they can hardly be described to fall outside the boundaries

of Labour's own Clause IV part 4, "common ownership of the means of production, distribution and exchange". [5]

The annual conferences of UCATT, GMWU, USDAW, the general secretary of the Transport and General Workers' Union and such bodies as the Glasgow district committee of the AUEW all opposed the witch-hunt.

*Militant*'s warning that the witch-hunt was linked to the attempt to shift Labour Party policy to the right was borne out by the preamble to the publication of Labour's Programme for 1982. It read: "A Labour government could not possibly implement all the policies contained here in its first term of office". The *Financial Times* reported that this had been inserted at the behest of "the Shadow Cabinet which was concerned that the left might have used the programme to commit a Labour government to introducing impractical policies"[6]

The NEC, as widely expected, went ahead in June with measures which could eventually lead to the expulsion of *Militant* supporters. This was taking place against the background of a run-up to a general election. But the right was determined to "seize the time". Denis Healey at the National Executive Committee declared "it's not a witch-hunt - it's a *Militant* hunt".[7]

The Hayward-Hughes report, named after the chief officers of the NEC who had "investigated" *Militant*, was passed by 16 votes to ten, and found former leftwingers Neil Kinnock and Joan Lester in the camp of the right. Former left Alex Kitson from the Transport and General Workers' Union, alongside party leader Michael Foot, also supported the first steps toward a witch-hunt. Yet Foot had outlined in his biography of Nye Bevan that the very same charge of organising a "party within a party", was the right's accusation against Bevan in the 1950s. Kinnock, seeking to justify his support for the right, asserted that *Militant* was "mobilised dishonesty and organised menace".[8] We answered:

> Is it honest to stand for election to the NEC as a left winger and then vote consistently with the right wing on all major issues? Is it honest to maintain, as Neil Kinnock did, that ideas were not the issue and then to vote for the suppression of the LPYS pamphlet *Ideals of October* [about the 1917 Russian revolution and its Stalinist degeneration] because its contents were 'Trotskyist'?[9]

The swing towards the right of former lefts was also indicated in the vote of the *Tribune* group of Labour MPs, by 23 to 20, to accept the Hayward-Hughes report. The *Tribune* newspaper itself, at that stage much more critical of the Labour Party leadership, described the parliamentary *Tribune* group as "dead".

The contradictory position within the Labour Party was underlined by the fact that while *Militant* was being witch-hunted the National Executive Committee of the Labour Party was forced to sanction a Labour Party party political broadcast on the problems of Britain's youth. It featured interviews with LPYS members and brought in a flood of membership applications. Over 600 calls were answered on the night of the broadcast alone. Two-thirds of these were of YS age, proving that, "given the resources to get our message across, the potential for building Labour's youth movement is boundless".[10]

The broadcast also underlined the massive support for socialist policies in the ranks of the party. *Militant*'s growth in support amongst Black and Asian youth was reflected in the LPYS Black Youth conference which took place in July and attracted 130 to the event organised at County Hall in London. No other organisation in Britain was capable of making such gains amongst Black and Asian youth.

In the Women's Sections the ideas of *Militant* also found increasing support. The Labour Party Women's conference in Newcastle was the biggest in history and over 80 attended our *Militant* Readers' meeting.

At the same time, a ferocious battle was developing in industry particularly amongst healthworkers and railworkers. An all-out strike of ASLEF workers had begun in June. The issue of flexible rostering - in effect an attempt to lengthen the working day - was at the heart of British Rail's attacks on the railworkers. *Militant* demanded that: "The TUC pull together all the muscle of the working class to back up health and railworkers with a 24-hour general strike; we can start the real battle and turn BR's execution threats into the death knell of this Tory government."[11]

Healthworkers came out in a series of strikes for a desperately needed increase of 12 per cent in pay. On 23 June a one-day strike was declared in the North East which received enormous support from healthworkers. From 19-21 July, three days of action were organised by healthworkers throughout the country to underline their claims. This received big support and mass demonstrations also took place. Yet when the movement was at its height the TUC stepped in on "Black Sunday" (20 July) to force ASLEF to terminate their strike. We commented:

> It has been reported that the Finance and General Purposes Committee [of the TUC] had, disgracefully, even raised the threat of the expulsion [from the TUC] of ASLEF, [unless the strike was terminated].[12]

We drew a parallel with what was happening in the Labour Party:

> Those TUC leaders who have been the most consistent advocates of a purge of *Militant* from the Labour Party are the same people who have reneged on the interests of ASLEF members in this strike. *Militant* supporters are 'guilty' of fighting for exactly what ASLEF members and workers need - for a bold and determined leadership in the Labour Party and trade unions.[13]

## OFF TO WEMBLEY

Notwithstanding these important developments *Militant* was still compelled to devote considerable space and the efforts of its supporters to mobilising against the attempts to carry through expulsions. The paper decided to call a labour movement conference to be organised in September 1982, this was to demonstrate the strength of feeling against the witch-hunt, prior to the vital Labour Party conference. This conference took place on 11 September at the Wembley Conference Centre. It was without doubt one of the most decisive events in the history of *Militant* both before and since. It was a powerful demonstration of the roots which *Militant* had built up in all sections of the working class and labour movement. Nearly 3,000 delegates and visitors packed out Wembley Conference Centre to express their determined opposition to the proposed register and the threat of expulsions. Tony Saunois, the chair of the event, reported that 1,622 delegates from Constituency Labour Parties, 412 trade union delegates and almost 1,000 visitors were in attendance. The conference had a stunning effect:

> The size of the crowd at the packed Wembley Conference Centre sur-

prised *Militant*'s critics, even on the left, who had said there was not enough support for the group... to fill the place. (*Mail on Sunday*, 12 September 1982.)[14]

Another right-wing rag, the *News of the World*, commented:

> By any yardstick yesterday's rally by supporters of the *Militant* Tendency was menacingly impressive... Almost as big as the Labour Party itself could muster.[15]

Even *Labour Weekly*, then the official journal of the Labour Party, grudgingly admitted:

> The size of the Saturday conference "Fight the Tories not the Socialists", organised by supporters of *Militant*, is a worry to those people hoping for easy expulsions of a few prominent *Militants* from the Labour Party.[16]

This conference received massive TV and press coverage. The statement of myself, speaking in the morning session when I declared "for everyone they expel ten will take their place", was featured in TV and Radio broadcasts.

The conference had been called very quickly by seven Labour parties, with arrangements being made in the summer period of July and August. In view of this the size and mood at the conference was a triumph for the organisers. It was, moreover, a very broad labour movement conference. Les Huckfield won tremendous applause when he said: "We are the Labour Party." Many non-*Militant* supporters who took a principled position against the witch-hunt spoke. Bob Wright, assistant general secretary of the AUEW, blamed the right wing for the "Cold War" that was being waged on the party. Ken Livingstone, then leader of the Greater London Council, declared at the conference:

> The people fighting to get rid of *Militant*, were previously fighting alongside those who deserted to the SDP in London. They were to spread their nets as far as *Tribune* and the GLC to make the Party safe again for traitors. *Militant* supporters had fought for cheap fares, he said, not those attacking *Militant*.[17]

Terry O'Neill, President of the Bakers' Union, declared:

When Pat Wall is the candidate for Bradford North I will go to Bradford and go on the doorsteps to tell people that Pat is a fighter for the working class.[18]

Nevertheless, the right wing were hell bent on introducing the proposed register of "non-affiliated groups" as the first step of the purge. In September the battle lines were drawn between right and left for the upcoming conference in October. The main spokespersons of the right abandoned any pretence that *Militant* was being attacked for its organisational structure and zeal. It was its politics and ideas which they objected to.

That the register was a device for taking action against *Militant* was shown by the fact that we had been given until 21 September to register, while everyone else was given until 31 December. Failure to register, party leader Foot made clear, would result in immediate expulsions. At the same time general secretary, Jim Mortimer had written to constituencies saying the register would not apply to "organisations which include both members of the Labour Party and persons who are not members of the Labour Party." As *Militant* commented:

> This leaves the Labour Party in the ludicrous position of banning groups that consist of long-standing loyal and hard-working party members, yet tolerating party pressure groups that include Tory MPs, businessmen, international tycoons or representatives of the Pentagon.[19]

## LABOUR PARTY CONFERENCE

The Labour Party conference of 1982 was a tumultuous affair. In the conference and outside sharp exchanges took place between the left and the right, both on the issue of the proposed purge and on Party policy. During the conference itself a special live edition of the TV programme *This Week*, with 14 Million viewers, saw myself and Tony Mulhearn debate with right-wing Labour MP, Austin Mitchell and prospective parliamentary candidate, John Spellar, before a live audience of delegates and visitors.

At the *Tribune* fringe meeting Neil Kinnock was given a roasting because of his decision to line up with the right wing. Constantly heckled during the meeting to explain his position on the register, Kinnock kept promising, "I'll come to that", but never actually got round to mentioning the register. Instead, juggling with various definitions of "earnest" and "serious" socialists, he treated the audience to several long quotations from Professor Hobsbawn's book *The Forward March of Labour Halted*. This 'thoughtful' but pessimistic Communist Party academic was claiming that there was a big swing to the right in the country and therefore the left should beat a retreat and compromise with the right. Joan Maynard, implacable leftwinger, from the chair, declared bluntly: "There is only one division that matters within the Labour Party, between socialists and non-socialists." She went on to answer Kinnock's charge of "hitlists", that it was Kinnock himself who had started the hitlists by attacking Tony Benn for standing in the deputy leadership contest. His abstention had been in reality a vote for Denis Healey. The volume of applause left no doubt of the audience's support for this devastating answer to Kinnock.[20]

At the conference itself Jim Mortimer read out the list of the alleged policies of *Militant*, which bore no relationship to the truth. *Militant* were declared to be in opposition to unilateral nuclear disarmament, against rights for women, "soft" on the gay and lesbian issues, etc. The best answer to this diatribe came in the debate on unilateral disarmament which was opened by *Militant* supporter, Sue Beckingham, delegate from Bristol South East, moving a resolution which clearly stated that the next Labour Government should "carry out the unilateral disarmament of nuclear weapons". Sue was cheered when she attacked Callaghan, Healey and other former Cabinet Ministers who had secretly agreed to the updating of Polaris.[21]

Sue Beckingham was one of the most committed and self-sacrificing of *Militant* supporters almost from its inception. Even while she spoke at this conference she was suffering from cancer that was to prematurely and tragically end her life.

The 1982 conference in terms of the voting on the register marked a shift towards the right. The right now had a 19 to 10 majority on the national executive committee. Some "soft lefts" who had gone along with the right, like Joan Lester, were actually knocked off the NEC. This reflected the anger of the rank and file over their desertion to the camp of the right. Pat Wall, twice selected as parliamentary candidate for Bradford North, got 103,000 votes, a substantial increase on the figure that he received the previous year. The register, predictably, was passed by 5.1 million votes to 1.5 million. This did not accurately reflect the mood of the rank and file of either the unions or the Labour Party. Right-wing trade union leaders shamefully and blatantly used the block vote to back up the right-wing purge. But this was at the cost of splits in many union delegations, with some of the biggest unions only voting narrowly in favour of the register. The miners voted 29 to 20 for the register and the Transport and General Workers' Union delegation, contrary to its own executive's position, voted 21 to 13 in favour. Significantly, a number of unions voted against the register and a witch-hunt: NUPE, UCATT, ASLEF, SOGAT 82, the FBU, the Bakers, the Boilermakers, AUEW-TASS, and the Agricultural Workers. Notwithstanding the acceptance of the register, the mood of the rank-and-file was unmistakably towards the left as the conference debates on policy and programme demonstrated. There was big support for Joan Maynard when she declared during a conference debate: "The Tories don't *talk* about class war because they are too busy *practising* it."[22]

## WE TRY TO REGISTER

Following the conference and despite serious objections to the register, *Militant* decided to reply to the questions sent to the Editorial Board as a step toward registering. To the question "what are the aims of the group" we declared:

> We support the basic socialist aim of the Labour Party embodied in Clause IV, Part 4 of the constitution... We are committed to fighting for the return of a Labour government on the basis of a socialist programme. We fully support the implementation of Labour's programme and the radical policies adopted by conference... *Militant* also believes that the struggle for socialism is international. We support the struggle throughout the capitalist countries for the socialist transformation of society. We support the struggle of the workers, peasants and all exploited people of the ex-colonial and semi-colonial countries against imperialism and its puppets, but we believe that national and social liberation can only be carried through on the basis of international socialist perspectives. In the Stalinist states of Russia, Eastern Europe and China which have nationalised, centrally planned economies but are ruled over by totalitarian, one-party dictatorships, we support the

struggle for workers' democracy.[23]

The reply also went on to declare:

> We entirely refute the idea that we breach Clause II(3) of the constitution. We do not have our 'own programme, principles and policy for distinctive and separate propaganda'. *Militant* has always urged support for Labour's duly selected council and parliamentary candidates regardless of their views within the party. We are urging our supporters in the Birmingham area, for instance, to work for John Spellar, Labour's candidate in the Northfield by-election on 28 October, regardless of his vociferous support at Conference for witch-hunting measures against *Militant*... Our position is in marked contrast to that of groups like Solidarity, Manifesto and other right-wing groups which are opposed to the implementation of Clause IV, part 4, and many key elements of Labour's current programme.[24]

The reply gave answers to all the questions asked on the issue of how *Militant* was organised. In answer to the "charge" that *Militant* was guilty of the crime of being organised internationally the Editorial Board replied:

> As internationalists we have contacts with co-thinkers in many countries. We contribute articles to Marxist journals abroad, and we regularly publish articles by socialists active in other countries. The right wing of the Labour Party also has international links. But there is a "small" difference between us and the right. Our contacts are within the international labour movement; the right has links with international organisations and journals which are supported and financed by the enemies of the labour movement, like the Labour Committee for Trans-Atlantic Understanding, the European Movement, the Bilderberg Group, the International Institute of Strategic Studies, and other bodies backed directly or indirectly by the CIA or the US Government. We believe it is high time the Labour Party conducted a thorough investigation into the right's sinister connections.[25]

As to where *Militant* receives its funds:

> *Militant* is entirely financed by its own supporters within the Labour Party and the trade unions... *Militant* supporters are among the most active and energetic in working to build the Labour Party Young Socialists, to increase Labour Party membership, and to develop campaigning activity. Through this activity we help to bring enormous ad-

ditional funds into the party. Our supporters also take their share of collecting subscriptions, organising jumble sales and socials, and other fund-raising work.[26]

The reply contrasted this activity with that of the right wing:

While the total income and expenses of Labour MPs at Westminster and in the European Parliament must be in the region of £5-£6 million (apart from consultancies, directorships, TV appearances, etc.) they are estimated to be contributing a mere £15,000 to the Labour Party annually. A modest levy from Labour's 238 MPs and 17 MEPs would wipe out Labour's current financial deficit at a stroke! *Militant* advocates that Labour MPs should be prepared to represent the labour movement and the working class on the average wage of a skilled worker, plus legitimate expenses. All the rest of their salaries and expenses should be donated back to the labour movement.[27]

The reply also took the opportunity to refute Jim Mortimer's attack on *Militant*'s alleged policies at the 1982 conference.

You [Mortimer] attacked our 'mistaken' views on nuclear disarmament... Yet our recent pamphlet *What We Stand For* restates our consistent position on this: "Massive cuts in arms spending... support for unilateral nuclear disarmament, but with the recognition that only a socialist change in society in Britain and internationally can eliminate the danger of a nuclear holocaust"... we were particularly surprised, moreover, that during your speech you asserted that *Militant* supporters were "the ideological allies of the right wing of the Conservative Party". This was on the grounds that we allegedly opposed 'Detente', that is discussion between the superpowers on arms reductions. We find this incredible. Who in their right mind could oppose negotiations between the powers to reduce nuclear arsenals? We support any attempt to reduce the danger of war and cut the grotesque waste of arms spending. However, we do not believe that talks between the powers will ever really eliminate the danger of war, as all the unsuccessful talks and agreements of the last 30 years show...

In your speech you also implied that we were opposed to the struggle of women and blacks. Again, this a complete distortion of our position. In *What We Stand For*, we call for "Opposition to discrimination on the basis of sex... for equal pay for work of equal value; for a crash programme to build nurseries, schools, etc." *Militant* supporters, moreover, have been prominent in building the Women's Sections of the Labour Party and in bringing working-class women into activity in the Labour Party and trade unions. In *What We Stand For* we also call for 'Opposition to racism and fascism and all racist immigration laws... we also recognise that only by unifying black and white workers in the struggle for socialist change will racism and fascism be effectively abolished." The allegation that we do not support the struggle of blacks is particularly ironic in view of the record of *Militant* supporters in the Labour Party Young Socialists, a section of the labour movement which has an unparalleled record in fighting against racist and fascist organisations and in campaigning for the demands of black and Asian workers and youth.

There were also allegations that *Militant* has attacked trade union leaders and Labour ministers as "renegades" and "traitors" to the working class. We challenge you to substantiate this allegation. Where in all our published material have we used language of this kind in relation to the trade union leadership or past Labour governments? We have always fought for the return of a Labour government. *Militant* has consistently repudiated the ultra-left idea that it "makes no difference" whether there is a Labour or Tory government. We supported all previous Labour governments, and welcomed the reforms they introduced. But we have also repeatedly warned that, on the basis of capitalism, especially today's diseased British capitalism, it is impossible for Labour governments to secure permanent improvements for the working class.[28]

The National Executive Committee of the Labour Party in November had decided, notwithstanding *Militant*'s reply, to begin the proceedings for the expulsion of the five members of *Militant*'s Editorial Board: Ted Grant, Peter Taaffe, Clare Doyle, Lynn Walsh, and Keith Dickinson. Between them they had a collective membership of the Labour Party of 121 years.

The NEC also decided that those prospective parliamentary candidates who "support the ideas of *Militant* will be investigated". This proposal was only carried by 12 votes to 11 and was opposed by Michael Foot, Neil Kinnock, Tony Benn, John Evans, Frank Allaun, Laurence Coates, Judith Hart, Jo Richardson, Tom Sawyer, Dennis Skinner and Audrey Wise. We commented: "The purge will not stop at *Militant*. It will grow to other left groups within the party".[29]

# 22.
# EXPELLED... INTO THE MOVEMENT

AFTER MUCH discussion the *Militant* Editorial Board reluctantly concluded that it was necessary to take legal action against the right wing to secure our democratic rights. This naturally was a controversial decision which earned the ire both of the right-wing and of ultra-left groups. At the outset even within the ranks of *Militant* there was not universal acceptance of this position. However, through debate and discussion, the overwhelming majority of *Militant* supporters supported the proposal for legal action suggested by the Editorial Board.

The right-wing labour and trade union leaders were in no position to complain about legal action. They had never hesitated to go the capitalist courts against *Militant* and its supporters. The left in Britain have on occasions been given no other choice but to take legal action against infringements by the right of the rules of unions. *Militant* gave the example of the Boilermakers' Society, where action had been taken on two occasions. The London Central Branch of the Electricians' Union was currently challenging its leadership in the courts. *Militant* did not believe that this was the main way to fight the witch-hunt. At best it was an auxilliary which could temporarily stay the hand of the right wing and allow time to build up support amongst the ranks to prevent a purge, or at least limit its scope. Michael Foot, party leader, denounced *Militant* for taking this action. But in his biography of Aneurin Bevan he shows that when Bevan was faced with a similar situation, expulsion from the Labour Party, he threatened to go to "the highest court in the land". This was because he considered he was being treated in an unconstitutional manner.

On the day when the *Militant* Editorial Board was hauled before the National Executive Committee of the Labour Party in December, the case for a temporary injunction to restrain the NEC was heard and rejected by Mr Justice Nourse. The judge did not reject *Militant*'s arguments but said that the Editorial Board should have gone to court when the Hayward-Hughes report had first been published in August 1982. He also stated that *Militant* should have gone to court to demand a fair hearing before the party conference at the end of September. The paper's contention that the Editorial Board had not been given the evidence, or sufficient details of the evidence, was accepted by the judge.

## EXPELLED

The meeting with the National Executive Committee in December 1982, was both a farce and a travesty of natural justice. The general secretary, Jim Mortimer, unbelievably refused the request to outline the alleged evidence proving that *Militant* was a separate organisation. The Editorial Board members and the left at the NEC were astonished to discover that no such statement would be forthcoming. NEC members, in the meeting prior to the Editorial Board entering the room, had been told that they were to be prevented from asking questions. This was confirmed by the Chair, Sam McCluskie, in the Editorial Board's presence. The Editorial Board protested about the procedure and it was then decided that the NEC would have to re-discuss the question and therefore we withdrew into another room.

When we returned to the meeting of the NEC we were told that Mortimer would then make a statement. This merely amounted to him reading out extracts from his speech to the Labour Party conference and part of a letter which had been sent to *Militant*'s solicitors five days before. There was absolutely nothing new in this material. At one stage Dennis Skinner burst out that this was merely a "kangaroo court", a claim which was substantiated by the proceedings which followed. Skinner withdrew from the meeting after Lynn Walsh asked McCluskie and Mortimer to state what changes they required *Militant* to make in the alleged structure of the newspaper. He pointed out that discussions had been held with the previous general secretary, Ron Hayward, and we had agreed to consider changes in how *Militant* organised. Objections had been made that *Militant*'s sellers' rally, organised nationally each year, was restricted to supporters of the *Militant*. We subsequently gave an undertaking to open these meetings up to the Labour Party rank and file and to the media. But the request for further clarification was met with a stony silence.

Under protest the five Editorial Board members then proceeded to outline their opposition to the claims made in the NEC motion for them to be excluded from the party.

After this we then withdrew, and the five of us were then summoned to face expulsion at the NEC to take place in February. This was another farce and as expected, the right-wing used their majority to carry through the *Militant* Editorial Board's expulsion from the Labour Party, in the full glare of massive media publicity.

## BERMONDSEY BY-ELECTION

The right wing took this action, in the knowledge that it was bound to split the Party, on the eve of the vital Bermondsey by-election. This was widely seen as a test run for the general election. Bermondsey Labour Party together, with 50 or 60 other Labour Party bodies, had approached Cambridge Heath Press, which printed *Militant*, to print some of their election material. This became the excuse for a further hue and cry against *Militant* and the Left. At the same time, the right pursued a policy of distancing themselves from the Labour candidate Peter Tatchell. This, together with the dirty anti-gay publicity against Tatchell, largely through a Liberal whispering campaign, resulted in the defeat of Labour in what was once a solid Labour seat. During the by-election the press had given their blessing to John O'Grady, the so-called 'Real Labour' candidate. When it became clear that he could not beat Peter Tatchell, there was a decisive and orchestrated switch of O'Grady and his supporters towards Simon Hughes, the Liberal candidate.

It was no secret in the corridors of Westminster that the majority of Labour MPs actually wanted a Labour defeat. Responsibility for this defeat clearly lay on the shoulders of the right. Bermondsey had become a 'rotten Borough' under the rule of the Labour right, typified by the former MP for the area Bob Mellish. He chaired the London Docklands Development Corporation. This body presided over disasters for the inhabitants in the area. This was one reason for the switch of Labour supporters towards the Liberals. One worker commented:

> Some people keep saying it was the press that lost Labour the seat, but

there's more to it than that. We are not stupid here you know, we know whats going on. You've got to see what has happened over the past. I've been Labour all my life. I'm almost ashamed to admit to you that I voted for the Liberals. I know that they are not socialist, but something had to be done. Labour's taken us for granted for too many years. Sixty years they have been in here and look at it! They have let the area run down.[1]

## REINSTATE THE FIVE!

Following the expulsion of the Editorial Board members a massive counter-campaign was launched in late February and March by supporters of the *Militant*. In two weeks more than 3,000 workers came to meetings addressed by EB members and more than £3,500 was raised in collections.

The tone of our paper was to emphasise opposition to capitalism and the Tories. Unlike some journals we did not go in for denunciations of our opponents but attempted to explain issues and to win fresh layers of workers, sometimes criticising, in a positive way, the inadequacies of the left leaders. *Militant* did not close its eyes to the deficiences of left leaders like Tony Benn, Dennis Skinner or even Arthur Scargill. This undoubtedly irritated these leaders, who are more used to uncritical acclaim from those on the left, rather than constructive criticism.

We also took every opportunity to win support for our ideas. One such example of our approach was a meeting held in March 1983 in the mining area of Newbridge, Gwent, South Wales. Tony Benn addressed a mass meeting of 700, which *Militant* supporters along with others had prepared for by going out to the pits and the villages to build support. The battle within the Labour Party was not an end in itself but was to prepare a mass force to back up workers in struggle.

In complete contradiction of what they had argued only a month or so before, the Labour right wing did not hesitate to resort to the "capitalist courts" in an attempt to cripple *Militant*. James White, Labour MP for Glasgow Pollok, took out a libel writ against *Militant* for reporting on a dispute involving workers in a firm jointly owned by him and his wife. For good measure he also took similar action against the *Glasgow Herald*. White's allies in the trade unions, the right-wing general secretary of APEX, Roy Grantham and side-kick Denis Howells MP, used this incident to demand that *Militant* be placed on a "proscribed list". It had "slipped their mind" that this infamous right-wing device for excluding the Left from the Labour Party had been abandoned in 1973!

# 23.
# A WORKERS' MP ON A WORKERS' WAGE: LIVERPOOL AND COVENTRY

FAR WEIGHTIER matters than a Labour Party witch-hunt were, however, on the minds of workers in the first part of 1983. In Liverpool, for instance, the Liberal/Tory controlled city council had decided to turn over refuse collection and street sweeping to private contractors. A mass campaign - "The Campaign against Privatisation" - launched by the manual workers led by Branch 5 of the GMBATU was a model; it both informed the workforce and prepared them for battle.

The stewards decided to call a mass meeting. This was then followed by a decision calling for an all-out strike by all council workers to coincide with the council meeting called to make the decision on privatisation. The majority of the workforce voted in favour of strike action. On 27 April 1983, just before the Council elections, 20,000 city council workers struck in reponse to the Joint Shop Stewards Committee's call for action against privatisation. Thousands lobbied the council's Finance Committee meeting. Their anger was directed at Liberal leader Trevor Jones, who was virtually mobbed. He was only able to enter the meeting after the intervention of shop stewards. Faced with an all-out indefinite strike ten days before the local elections, Trevor Jones backed down.

At the council meeting, when the Tories moved the privatisation proposal, the Liberals voted with Labour to beat the Tories! Trevor Jones's intention was to bide his time, work for victory in the May elections and then to recommence an all-out offensive against the workers. He was severely disappointed. Labour romped to victory on the basis of a radical fighting socialist programme. Jones then declared: "It [the election result] will eventually lead to the overthrow of free society as we know it."[1]

Labour had held on to all its seats and gained eleven others at the expense of the Liberals and the Tories. The Labour vote increased by 40 per cent. Yet the Liberal's election campaign consisted mainly of smear tactics directed against *Militant* supporters in the Labour Party. Following the victory Tony Mulhearn declared: "The nonsense of the Rolls-Royce, gold chain, and coach and horses is not needed in Liverpool... possibly the gold chain will be put in a museum along with the defeated Liberals".[2]

22,000 more Liverpudlians had voted for Labour because of its programme of "no privatisation, a £2 rent cut, no spending cuts, a massive housing repairs programme, 6,000 new council houses, 4,000 new council jobs and no rate rises to compensate for Tory/Liberal cuts". Significantly in Broadgreen, soon to be an area for an historic victory for Marxism and Trotskyism, Labour's vote climbed by 50 per cent.

This result, which gave an enormous boost to supporters of *Militant*, was the ideal dress-rehearsal for the 1983 General Election. Thatcher seized the favourable conjuncture provided by the victory in the Falklands to "go to the country" in June 1983.

A minimum of 200 canvassers were involved in Broadgreen over weekends, with the average being 250. On election day 500 workers from Liverpool and other parts of the country worked in the Broadgreen constituency. Few other campaigns had generated such commitment and enthusiasm. Only those of Pat Wall in Bradford North and Dave Nellist in Coventry South East had brought forth a similar reponse. However, the Labour right systematically sabotaged Pat Wall's campaign. Terry Fields, on the other hand, merely had to contend with the slanders of the Liberals and the Tories. So effective was his campaign that the Liberal candidate confessed that it was "unlike anything he'd seen in the country, even in by-elections".[3]

Terry Fields spoke at more than ten factory gate and canteen meetings. At a bin depot about 200 drivers waited from 6.30 am to 7.30 am for a gate meeting before starting work. 2,000 gathered on 17 May for a North West Regional Labour Party rally at St George's Hall, where Michael Foot spoke alongside seven Labour parliamentary candidates. Foot was compelled to hail the recent local election victory:

> It was tremendous the way Liverpool has set the standard in local elections just before the general election. It was very fitting that just before

we cleared the Tories out of Westminster, we, here in Liverpool, should have such a wonderful success in the council elections.[4]

Labour nationally received its lowest share in the poll since 1935. Nevertheless the 1983 general election was not the overwhelming triumph for Thatcher which historians claim. The popular vote for the Tories fell by nearly two per cent, or 700,000 votes, compared to 1979. At the same time three million fewer workers voted Labour than in 1979. The capitalist inspired scheme for splitting the Labour vote had partially succeeded. Disenchanted Tory voters and some Labour voters also swung over to support the SDP/Liberal Alliance.

The right wing had effectively sabotaged Labour's campaign. Denis Healey and James Callaghan explicitly distanced themselves from the manifesto commitment to unilateral nuclear disarmament.

Labour's radical proposals were undermined when the Labour leadership was incapable of answering the question: "How will it be paid for?" Foot emphasised the need for borrowing, devaluation and reinforced the impression that Labour intervenes to spend its way out of a crisis. This raised the idea of a massive expansion in public expenditure but without the economic base to sustain it.

The election results in Liverpool, however, stood out in marked contrast to most other regions. Completely against the national trend there was a swing to Labour in Liverpool of two per cent. This, we commented, "was due in no small measure to the influence of *Militant* supporters in that city, where Terry Fields was elected as MP in Liverpool Broadgreen".[5]

Alongside Terry Fields in Parliament was Dave Nellist, Labour MP for Coventry South East, who had also chalked up a notable victory in the general election.

## A MODERATE OFF HIS KNEES

In Parliament the working class found no better representatives than Terry Fields and Dave Nellist. The bitterness, the class loathing, which the majority of workers on Merseyside felt for the Tory victors, was voiced in Terry Fields's maiden speech in Parliament. New members of the House of Commons are expected to introduce themselves, heartily congratulate opposition speakers, and wish well to their retiring or defeated constituency rivals. Such pleasantries were cast aside when Terry Fields rose to speak. He made it clear he was there to represent the Liverpool workers. They had elected him to fight on their behalf, not to go around congratulating the Tory enemy. He was there not to appeal to the ruling class, but to express the real feelings of the working class against the Tory government and the system they represented. His full speech was printed in *Militant* and was widely circulated in the labour movement both on Merseyside and nationally.

The general gloom that had descended on the labour movement in Britain in the aftermath of Thatcher's return to power did not affect *Militant* supporters given the success in Liverpool and in Coventry. And within a month of Thatcher's victory *Militant* featured a dispute at "Lady at Lord John" in Liverpool which was to become a landmark in the struggle against sexual harassment at work. This dispute became the basis for Lezli-Anne Barratt's marvellous film *Business as Usual*, starring Glenda Jackson, John Thaw and Cathy Tyson. This dealt powerfully with the issue of the emerging power of working-class women and their refusal to accept the conditions of the past, including sexual harassment. Audrey White had been sacked after protesting about sexual harassment of staff at the Liverpool branch of the firm. Sexual harassment, *Militant* declared, was

> a product of society's attitude that women are only a temporary workforce and that women's real role in society is only in relation to men and that men can treat women as goods and chattels in the home and at work, an attitude that goes back as long as private property has existed, from slavery to capitalism. The "Lady at Lord John" dispute helped a lot of men both in the unions and outside to realise that sexual harassment is a class matter and cannot be fought by individual women.[6]

A very succesful picket was conducted outside the shop which resulted in many women being brought over to trade unionism as a result of this heroic struggle. Audrey White was actually removed from the shop by police when she was dismissed and the company tried to use the law to stop trade union action. The pickets were served with an injunction, accusing them of molesting and conspiring to do damage under the Tories' anti-union laws. But the pressure of public opinion which had built up over the court action resulted in the right to picket being endorsed. The management pulled back from using further legal measures for fear that this would widen the dispute. Despite all the obstacles in their path the strikers forced the company to re-employ Audrey White with back pay and even a discount for union members was won. *Militant* commented: "This dispute has not only been an education to the pickets and the trade union movement but also to the four million unorganised shop and office workers".[7]

## YOUTH

At the same time there was gathering opposition to the Tories' Youth Training Scheme (YTS). Half a million youth were to be subjected to industrial conscription at £25 a week. Dave Nellist in a forceful maiden speech in the House of Commons, highlighted the gathering opposition to the YTS. He ardently championed the rights of youth in the nine years that he was in Parliament. In his speech he pointed out:

> only one in ten of those leaving the fifth form last summer have found work. In a city (Coventry) that was built on engineering, only 243 out of 5,000 who left school this summer found apprenticeships... I speak today as the youngest Labour member elected in last month's general election. That gives me a special responsibility in this place to champion rights, and to give voice to, the hopes and aspirations of millions of young workers.

Pointing to a switch in the attitude of the Tory government towards youth he asked:

> What changed the attitude of the Tory Party during the past four years... the principle answer is the events of the summer of 1981 - the riots on the streets of Liverpool, London, Manchester and other major cities - a desperate action by tens of thousands of teenagers to draw attention to the poverty, despair, demoralisation, harassment and anger of being young and unemployed under a Tory government... Thousands of YOPsters have been recruited by the Labour Party Young Socialists into membership of the Transport and General Workers' Union, the General, Municipal, Boilermakers and Allied Workers' Union and

the National Union of Public Employees and into other non-general trade unions... I issue a warning to the government. Do not be misled by the siren voices of the media into believing that somehow in the 1980s we are witnessing the creation of a right-wing generation of youth or that the labour movement is demoralised or weak when faced with another term of Tory rule... Our labour produces the wealth, which the government's capitalist society squanders on useless weapons of nuclear destruction, on tax cuts to the super-rich, on stockpiles of food at a time of growing poverty and on keeping five million people unemployed. As, in the 1980s, society approaches a crossroads, the socialist programme will gain significant support.[8]

## BACK TO WEMBLEY

In September 1983, just four months after Thatcher's election victory, in organising another rally at Wembley, *Militant* gave a stunning demonstration that despite all attacks it remained a powerful and growing force. Almost 3,000 workers and youth packed the Wembley Conference Centre. In the year that had elapsed between the Labour Movement Conference against the witch-hunt and this event, *Militant* could now claim that "two *Militant* supporters spoke as Labour MPs." Sitting alongside them on the platform was Derek Hatton, soon to be a household name, who declared that now Liverpool would carry out its promises of creating new jobs and building houses. On behalf of the Editorial Board, I reminded the audience that in the previous year the Labour Party right wing had started the process of expelling the five *Militant* Editorial Board members by saying 'cut off the head of *Militant* and the rest would die'. They had noticeably not made the same expulsion threat "to people like Chapple [then leader of the EETPU and also the current chairman of the TUC] for their anti-Labour Party statements." But, the right had "only succeeded in expelling us back into the movement." I called for "all who agreed with our policies to join with *Militant* in transforming the labour movement to a powerful body which could itself change the whole of society."

Other speakers included the inspirational Anton Nilson, the legendary Swedish worker, who had become a pilot with the Red Army during the Russian Revolution. Dave Nellist spoke, as did Terry Fields who joked "that he had thought of turning up in disguise because of the dangers of being associated with *Militant*". Ted Grant, representatives of the youth, and Micky Duffy from the Northern Ireland Public Services Association (NIPSA) also spoke. One of the most outstanding features of the rally was that £40,000 was promised for the *Militant* Fighting Fund.[9]

## LABOUR PARTY CONFERENCE

The very success of *Militant* was itself a reason for the right wing to press ahead with the expulsion of the Editorial Board members at the October 1983 Labour Party Conference at Brighton. Against the background of huge TV and press coverage - which assumed the proportions of a rugby scrum outside the conference hall - the five of us were allowed into a closed session of conference to appeal against the NEC's decision to recommend their expulsion. The right-wing officialdom went to extraordinary and ludicrous lengths in order to prevent the five from receiving any press publicity. They were ushered in through a back door and asked to leave through a back door as well, an offer which we none too politely refused. A Labour Party official rugby tackled a TV cameraman and a well-known commentator in order to prevent us being filmed for the TV News.

Compelled to give the five a hearing because of the threat of transgressing the principles of "natural justice", the Labour Party conference session dealing with the witch-hunt was a farce. No court in the land would have allowed the defence first of all to state its case before the prosecution outlined its charges. But this was precisely the format adopted in dealing with our expulsion. We were allowed five minutes each to make our "appeal".

Predictably the votes, which had already been lined up by rightwing union general secretaries, were heavily in favour of the platform's recommendation for expulsions. But 80 per cent of the delegates from the Constituency Labour Parties and a considerable number of rank-and-file trade union delegates voted against expulsion. This was all the more remarkable given the fact that the conference showed a powerful urge for unity.

The election of Neil Kinnock as the new leader and Roy Hattersley as his deputy seemed to many to point to a more favourable period for Labour. While there was big support for Kinnock, this was tempered with a determination on the part of the delegates not to divide the movement. An extremely sympathetic attitude was shown in the conference sessions and afterwards in private discussion towards the Editorial Board members and other *Militant* supporters. With a mixture of amusement and indignation the press and the Labour Party right wing confronted the spectacle of the five Editorial Board members, the day after their expulsion, sitting in the conference hall as *Militant* representatives.

In the general euphoria surrounding the election of Kinnock, *Militant*, virtually alone, struck a critical note. It warned about the future consequences of a Kinnock leadership. Kinnock was the perfect "left" screen, behind which the right could begin the counter-revolution against the gains on policy and programme registered in the period of 1979 to 1982. A veiled counter-revolution by the right was set in train soon after the election. The reselection of Labour MPs was to be challenged by the right. All the conservative forces in the Labour Party - the place men and women, self seekers, the party's own officialdom, and the union leadership - looked for a figure to front their "counter-revolution". Kinnock had been sounding out this layer in the period before the election and in an energetic campaign for the leadership afterwards. The support he got from the unions came from the right and the nominal "left". Kinnock had all the neccesary attributes required by Labour's conservative, privileged stratum of MPs, councillors and the rest. He still claimed to be on the left, although he had long since distanced himself from Benn and had voted for the expulsion of the *Militant* Editorial Board in February 1983. The election of Roy Hattersley as leader, rather than deputy leader, would have complicated the task of shifting the axis of the labour movement to the right. Hattersley, at the Labour Party conference two years later, publicly recognised this when he said that the party had chosen correctly when they elected Kinnock in 1983! Hattersley is not known for false modesty!

# 24.
# DARING TO FIGHT

**THE PROBLEMS** for the new Labour leadership were that while they wanted to go to the right, within the working class and amongst the conscious, socialist elements within the labour movement, the trend was still clearly toward the left. Developments in Liverpool and a series of industrial movements throughout 1983 in which *Militant* were to the fore, was an unmistakable expression of the mood. Liverpool's epic battle between 1983 and 1987 is fully documented in our book *Liverpool a City That Dared to Fight* .

The mass demonstration of more than 20,000 people which marched through Liverpool in November 1983 reflected the powerful militancy which was sweeping the city at this stage. The turn-out exceeded all expectations. Unlike other demonstrations, thousands had turned up well in advance. Many had travelled to the demonstration on the city's buses which were free, the result of an unofficial gesture of support from the bus drivers. At the Pier Head meeting following the demonstration, Tony Mulhearn declared that it was

> the biggest local demonstration we have seen since the struggle against Heath's Industrial Relations Act - the biggest in fact since the war. And I think that it is a clear indication to the Tory government, to the establishment and to the ruling class that it would be a mistake to take Liverpool on. This is a clear message to Thatcher and her supporters. So far and no further![1]

Tony Benn pointed out that "when the older generation look at the marchers they see the **LPYS** and they see the Labour Party they joined in the 1920s and 1930s". The council in preparation for the day had produced 10,000 bulletins and the District Labour Party also distributed 180,000 copies of their paper, *Not the Liverpool Echo*. Derek Hatton called for a city-wide general strike in support of the Council and Eric Heffer, Labour MP for Walton, called for extra-parliamentary action.

This was taking place while the Tory government was preparing brutal measures to crush the organised power of the working class, and in particular the miners.

This warning was underlined by the decision of Eddie Shah the owner of the *Stockport Messenger*, produced at his Warrington plant, to smash the National Graphical Association (NGA). Under the Tories' 1982 Employment Act the union faced sequestration for defying a court judgement of a £50,000 fine against the NGA. The mass picketing and the brutal attacks of the police angered workers who poured in from all parts of the country to support the printers. Regular clashes unfolded between the massed ranks of workers and the beefed up police who were defending Shah, a friend of Thatcher. In a special issue *Militant* declared:

> The gloves are off. The ruling class are out to destroy the print union, the National Graphical Association. £175,000 of the union's funds has been seized... it has been grabbed on the orders of a well heeled judge... All three print unions: SOGAT 82, NUJ and NGA have legal threats against them... The Tories have declared war. The working class must be the victors.[2]

However, *Militant's* call for a 24-hour general strike to be organised by the TUC went unheeded. Arthur Scargill, virtually alone among leading trade union figures, called for decisive action:

> To stormy applause (at a meeting in Birmingham of 500 miners, rail and steel workers), (he) called on the TUC and Labour Party to show the same dedication and committment to the NGA and our class as the Tories show to their class, including the organisation of the most massive picket ever seen.[3]

He also echoed *Militant's* demand for a 24-hour general strike to defend the NGA.

## TUC - NO ACTION

This strike was the first in a catalogue of major retreats which seriously undermined the powers of resistance of the organised working class through their trade unions. But it could have been a famous victory.

Despite the fact that the Tories, in the usually crude fashion of

Norman Tebbit, had made it clear that they were intending to 'neuter' the trade unions, the TUC did nothing. Shah received open support from the Newspaper Publishers' Association, from the right-wing Institute of Directors, from the police and the whole of 'official' society. Yet right-wing trade union leaders like Bill Sirs of the Iron and Steel Trades Confederation, and Terry Duffy of the AUEW urged the printers to "remain within the law". This emboldened Shah and the forces of the capitalist state to put the boot in. Vicious scenes were played out on the picket line.

The printers were defeated at Warrington and the vital ingredient in this defeat was the role of the right-wing TUC leadership. We declared:

> A defeat is bad enough - but what makes this one all the more bitter is the abject and disgraceful surrender of the TUC right wing and its general secretary, Len Murray, without even token resistance to the Tories' vicious class laws... The NGA had already been fined more than £650,000, including the biggest fine in British legal history, and faced writs for damages in excess of £3 million. Dozens of newspaper publishers were queuing up at the law courts.[4]

*Militant* had argued for an all-out printers' strike in the teeth of such attacks. The majority of print bosses were afraid of such action, as was shown by the secret approaches of Robert Maxwell to Shah during the dispute. When the possibility of an all-out strike loomed Maxwell, the owner of the *Mirror*, could only comment: "God help us all". While criticising the right-wing of the general council, *Militant* also called for the Left to take effective action:

> the TUC general council, with its inbuilt right-wing majority, does not reflect the true balance of industrial power within the movement. The left leaders of the TUC, therefore, those who supported the NGA, must now be prepared to organise outside the framework of the TUC.[5]

## MILITANT ENTERS THE LANGUAGE

Had such advice been heeded then the right's abdication of leadership over Warrington could have led to a strategy for mobilising a left fightback in preparation for the battles to come. Instead, the government, emboldened, decided to illegalise the trade unions at

GCHQ in Cheltenham. Mass walkouts took place but again the general council of the TUC refused to put forward a fighting and active policy for defeating the government. The press and media coverage of *Militant* throughout 1984 was intense. "Militant" and "Militant Tendency" became buzz words and were used sometimes indiscriminately to denote any challenge to accepted authority.

In his novel, *First Among Equals* (published in 1984) even Jeffrey Archer could not resist getting in on the act. Dealing with a "mythical" MP in Edinburgh he writes: "His General Management Committee, which now included five members of Militant Tendency, tabled a motion of no confidence in its member".[6]

The journal of the National Union of Journalists fed the impression that *Militant* was everywhere:

> Central TV were filming the pilot of a new comedy series in the middle of Nottingham. The series called the Tolpuddle Inheritance is about the imaginary goings on in an imaginary union and stars Brian Blessed. A large group of actors holding banners and placards were holding a mock demo in the middle of the street when a bloke turned up and tried to sell them copies of *Militant*.[7]

Even a BBC disc jockey commented: "One of the reasons why Frankie Goes To Hollywood was so successful is the fact that they banned it; rather like the Militant Tendency - you ban it and it gets more popular."[8]

*Militant* supporters were found in the most surprising quarters and came in all ages:

> Neil Kinnock may be just a little embarrassed this morning when he learns the identity of the innocent-looking seven-year-old to whom he recently presented second prize in a competition organised by Labour for children's drawings on the Health Service. The £30 prize went to one Daniel Walsh for his study of children waiting to be X-rayed. But it now turns out that he is the son of Lynn Walsh, who was expelled from the Labour Party at last year's Blackpool conference for his activities as deputy editor of the Trotskyist weekly, *Militant*. Asked what he would like from the prize, Daniel told his mother - though not, thankfully, Mr Kinnock - "A Big Track, a Spirograph and my dad back in the Labour Party."[9]

Even top Tory Virginia Bottomley's brother-in-law Henry

Bottomley expressed a passing sympathy: "Some people might regard me as a bit to the right. But in fact even though *Militant Tendency* has some strange ideas I agree with a number of them - at least it would be nice if it were possible."[10]

But one of the surest indications that *Militant* had 'arrived' was shown by a question in a GCE A Level from June 1984: "Consider the role, policies and significance of the following:" amongst the subjects listed was "the Militant Tendency"[11]

Also, during a miners' lobby of Parliament during the strike the following exchange took place in the Commons:

> Mr John Stokes (Halesowen and Stourbridge): On a point of order, Mr Deputy Speaker. Are you aware that striking miners are on the Terrace of the Houses of Parliament and are selling a newspaper that I believe is called *Militant Tendency*? Is that in order?
> 
> Mr Deputy Speaker (Mr Harold Walker): That is a matter that will be looked into by the appropriate authorities.
> 
> Mr Kaufman: Perhaps the hon. Gentleman should hurry down to the Terrace, as he might learn something that would broaden his point of view.[12]

## BLOC

In these circumstances *Militant*, with a growing and powerful influence in many trade unions, took the initiative with other lefts in organising the Broad Left Organising Committee (BLOC). Some 20 individual 'Broad Lefts' organised on a national scale and some on a regional basis came together in a call for a conference to take place on 24 March 1984. This conference, which attracted more than 2,200 delegates, packed out Sheffield's Oxendon Centre and was the most succesful trade union rank-and-file gathering since the 'Liason Committee for the Defence of Trade Unions' organised by the Communist Party in the 1960s and 1970s. Tony Benn was cheered when he thanked all those "flying canvassers" who had gone to Chesterfield to help to secure his recent by-election victory. He also outlined the attacks on democratic rights by the government and called for the defence of councils such as Liverpool. He said: "The future lies with socialism - as such we must build our forces. In that sense we do not want sectarianism or witch-hunts. In the movement we must argue our case, not denounce it or expel it out".[13]

Such were the numbers and the enthusiasm that two overflow meetings had to be arranged. Nearly 500 people who turned up hoping for last minute tickets had to be turned away; there was just no room. A section of the conference, mostly drawn from ultra-left groups, declared that the ranks of the movement were "demoralised" and that the working class had swung to the right. Some even argued that this therefore meant that it was wrong to build a Broad Left movement in such a period. This was answered by many *Militant* supporters, such as Alistair Tice from NUPE, who explained that certainly trade union membership had fallen, but this was mainly through mass unemployment, unlike in the 1930s when union membership fell by a half through the widespread demoralisation of ordinary workers. The conference had a powerful effect with workers represented from all areas of the country and from most unions.

# 25.
# THE MINERS' STRIKE 1984-85

MEANWHILE, A conflict loomed in the mining industry. Coal Board boss Ian MacGregor had announced plans to close 20 pits and do away with about 25,000 jobs. The closing of Cortonwood provoked a movement of Yorkshire miners which began to spread to all areas of the British coalfield. It became quite clear almost as soon as the strike had begun that the ruling class, and the Thatcher government in particular, had meticulously planned for this battle. They had been given a bloody nose and had been compelled to retreat in the face of the miners' movement of 1981. From the outset *Militant* declared:

> The huge military-style police operation ordered by Home Secretary Leon Brittan against the striking miners, is the biggest such operation since the 1926 general strike. It dispels any lingering illusions there might be that the police are a 'community' based force not directly involved in the implementation of political policy.[1]

At a cost of £500,000 a day 20,000 police were deployed throughout the country to deal with the strike.

The Ridley plan, leaked in 1978, proposed the building up of coal stocks, the beefing up of the police and other state forces, the altering of the law to hamper and restrict strike action and the use of all possible force to smash the miners. The miners were traditionally the British workers 'Brigade of Guards'. A defeat, as humiliating as possible, was the conscious aim of Thatcher. The government provoked strike action in 1984. Thatcher set out to create an 'industrial Falklands'.

The miners, Scargill, the Left, and *Militant* were perceived as the 'enemy within', bracketed together with the 'enemy without', Galtieri, who had been humbled in 1982. Yet any serious and honest analysis of the miners' strike, which can only be touched on here, conclusively demonstrates that in this epic struggle Thatcher's strength lay not so much in herself nor in the forces ranged on her side but in the cowardly 'generals' of the TUC on the other side.

The press revealed that three army barracks had been made available to accommodate the roving vans of police strikebreakers. All the paraphernalia of riot control, special helmets, shields, flameproof suits and police dogs, not to mention spotter aircraft and helicopters, were carefully assembled. From the very first week of the strike *Militant* commented that we had

> always argued that the police, the judiciary and the law in general are not 'neutral', but instruments of the employing class, and nothing better illustrates that than the use of the police in the last week.[2]

The police had assumed legal powers far above anything they had used in the past, stopping cars and buses and turning them back hundreds of miles from their destinations, intimidating bus companies into refusing contracts with miners and even threatening to arrest Kent workers if they strayed outside their home county. One solicitor in Kent, commented to *Militant*:

> There is no such offence as secondary picketing except in the civil law and yet the police are using the criminal law to prevent people from picketing peacefully.[3]

The police were backed up by the Attorney General, Tory MP Sir Michael Havers, who pointed out that the

> police have powers to turn back anyone... if they thought they were attending a picket where there might be a breach of the peace. Failure to comply would make workers liable to arrest for obstruction.[4]

Hammering home the class character of the conflict, we pointed out that "the Tories' explanation and the police action, therefore, merely confirm that law is applied in a class manner". We warned that "it is still not ruled out that steps could be taken to try to sequestrate parts of the NUM assets, as in the case of the NGA." This prediction was to be confirmed before the year was out. We emphasised that:

> there is no road out for the workers on the basis of the present system.

Capitalism is itself creating all the conditions of class conflict and social upheaval.[5]

Once the strike began all the conservatism which weighs down workers in 'normal' periods evaporated. One of the most striking features of the dispute was the magnificent movement of the women from the mining communities, whose organisation of a support network was crucial to enabling the strike to continue as long as it did. They inspired tens of thousands of women everywhere to fight. *Militant Women* played a big role helping to set up support groups, feeding the miners and helping the women's pickets as the dispute went on. Many of these women joined the Labour Party and established Women's Sections. During this period Margaret Creear, a well known Militant, was first elected to the Labour Womens' National Committee.

There was massive enthusiasm for the strike which developed rapidly from below. We declared that:

> there must be a national lead to assure miners in all areas that the action is serious and will have an effect. And there should be a clear demand for no pit closures except for proven exhaustion of resources or genuine safety reasons, and even then only with the guarantee of alternative jobs for miners affected. The rail and steel unions must be approached to build a real fighting Triple Alliance at national level - and in every area in support of the basic industries.[6]

In March 1984, *Militant* warned that "the NCB would aim in South Wales, Kent and areas of North East England to reduce coal mining to a mere memory."[7]

Our pages reflected the growing militancy not just in the traditional heartlands of Yorkshire and South Wales but in Nottingham also. Pickets from other areas arriving at Bevercotes declared:

> If we'd listened to the media yesterday, we'd have been terrified at the resistance they portrayed. We've come here and found it's totally different. The reponse has been marvellous. We just told everyone it was an NUM picket and asked them not to cross. 90 per cent haven't crossed.[8]

## NOTTS AND THE BALLOT

However, the failure of the strike to develop fully in the Nottingham coalfield undoubtedly complicated the battle. Both at the time and since not a little ink has been spilled over the issue of whether it would have been more effective if the miners had called a ballot, even while they were out on strike, to confirm an overwhelmingly majority in favour of strike action.

Right wingers like Hammond, the leader of the electricians' union at the time, declared subsequently that he would have been in favour of bringing out electricians in the power industry if the miners had held a ballot which found in favour of strike action. This was a fig leaf behind which the right-wing attempted to hide their nakedness during the most important industrial struggle since the 1926 general strike. Nevertheless, it would have been better tactically for the NUM leaders to sanction a ballot a few weeks into the strike. This would have resulted in a probable 80 per cent to 90 per cent majority in favour of strike action. Would a successful ballot have guaranteed victory to the miners? If the Nottinghamshire coalfield had voted against then it does not take a great imagination to picture how the leaders of the scab Union of Democratic Mineworkers (UDM) would have reacted. They could have advanced the argument that Nottingham voted against strike action and therefore was 'opting out'. But a majority in favour of action on a national level could have convinced the majority of Nottinghamshire miners to strike.

The Nottinghamshire UDM leaders were secretly, from very early on in the strike, in touch with Thatcher's representative David Hart, who financed and supported their strike-breaking measures. A ballot during the strike action, when a vast majority of British miners were out on strike in any case, could have added to the power of the miners' case.

## MILITANT MINERS

*Militant* pointed out that this was the most important class conflict for decades. Pointing to the example of 1926 the paper showed that:

The TUC leaders [during 1926] became a brake on the movement. From the very first hours of the general strike, the TUC leaders were looking for an excuse to call it off.[9]

Therefore while urging action by the general council in support of the miners' *Militant* also called on the miners to pursue a parallel course of appealing to the ranks:

> Most miners today have already realised that the majority of the present TUC general council are no better than the leaders of 1926. Their policy of 'new realism' has meant little more than abject surrender.[10]

Therefore, at each stage *Militant* urged the miners to adopt the strategy of appealing to the ranks of the movement to put pressure on the tops for solidarity action. At the same time, the paper suggested that the miners take the lead in calling for the left leaders on the general council to pursue an independent strategy to that of the saboteurs on the right.

*The Guardian* commented on a meeting in the Nottinghamshire coalfield, which indicated the mood of miners at the time:

> This was a rally of mainly young men who had been on the picket line most of the week, who feel a sense of bitter injustice, who want a social revolution.[11]

1984 was a year when *Militant* made a decisive intervention and contribution to the struggle in Liverpool. But the paper and its supporters were no less ardent in supporting the miners. Consequently our support significantly increased amongst miners and workers generally. At one stage during the strike 500 miners were recruited as committed supporters of *Militant*. This growing support made it neccessary for the Editorial Board to step up the struggle for greater resources. In April we commented:

> This week *Militant* has had to add four extra pages to its normal 16. One reason is the sheer number of events to cover: May Day, local elections, LPYS Conference, Liverpool council's special meeting, the miners' strike, Labour's national executive on the Blackburn expulsions, the Libyan Bureau Siege, the union conference season and May Day greetings. But another vital reason is to allow space to produce our special appeal and to explain what a crucial stage our paper has

reached. Most weeks now, we have enough material for double the number of pages we can print.[12]

One pointer of the paper's success was our Fighting Fund. In 1978, £66,000 had been collected: in 1979 £80,000; in 1980 £93,000; in 1981 £105,000; in 1982 £148,000 - a total of nearly £500,000 in five years. But now we needed new premises. Therefore an urgent appeal for £35,000 was launched to add to the sum of £140,000 already raised (£30,000 was raised in two weeks). Due to the heroic efforts of our supporters and readers it became possible to buy large premises in Hackney Wick and gather together all the operations involved in the production of *Militant* in one building. Previously they had been scattered over three buildings.

## ORGREAVE

Revenge for the Tories' humiliation at the hands of the miners at Saltley Gate in 1972 and more recently in 1981 was taken by the police on the Orgreave picket line (outside Sheffield). The most brutal methods yet seen in this or any previous dispute were played out in the full view of the world's media. The conflict gave the impression of a virtual civil war in the mining areas of Britain. We prominently featured two photographs which summed up the role of the police: one where a picketing man was beaten by a riot policeman in full protective clothing while a miner was pinned over a car.[13]

Another more famous incident (captured in two photographs) showed a woman from the Sheffield Miners' Support Group calling for an ambulance for an injured miner as a mounted policeman tries to chop her down. We reported:

> The beating continues and she backs away. Afterwards the mounted police were cheered by their infantry ranks, with riot shields banged in appreciation.[14]

Eyewitnesses at an earlier battle reported:

> The baton charge has returned. This brutal police method of attacking pickets, synonomous with the industrial battles of the 1920s, has become a standard tactic of today's police... The idea is to hurt peo-

ple, intimidate people, frighten people.[15]

Even Arthur Scargill was arrested on a trumped-up charge of obstruction. We commented:

> There will be a widespread belief that this arrest was a deliberate, pre-planned move by the police, not just to impose a fine, but, as with other miners, to try and impose stringent bail conditions that would keep him [Scargill] well away from picket line, and therefore stop him carrying out his duties as the president of the National Union of Mineworkers. In the event, the magistrates rejected the police request and granted unconditional bail.[16]

Eyewitness accounts in *Militant* show that by 9.30 am on the day of the first Orgreave battle there were about 7,000 pickets assembled. It was then that

> the real battle began. It was the most terrifying thing I have been through in my life... What made it worse for me was that this was happening in the village where I'd lived most of my life... I saw an elderly miner of about 60 have his head split open by a baton... The riot police would march straight up to you shouting 'one two, one two' and provoking the miners: "Come on then, have a go"... And one snatch squad policeman went too far and got snatched himself! They had to send police horses in to get him back - he was in a far from healthy state when he emerged from the picket.[17]

Ordinary police were too unreliable for this dirty work as shown by *Militant*'s report of the comments of the Yorkshire police as the battle unfolded:

> Some were very bitter at what was happening. One policeman told us his father was a miner and was in the picket somewhere. He said they didn't want anything to do with it - they had to live in the communities; what had happened today would never heal. He'd come into the police force to fight crime, not his family.
> He said he hadn't thought much about a trade union for the police before but this had shown the importance of proper trade union rights for policeman. Another policeman said, pointing to the riot squads: "Those bastards have been brought up from London. They're up here to harm you. They're nothing to do with us."[18]

A group of miners from the North East writing later in *Militant*

## The Miners' Strike 1984-85

about their experiences at the battle at Orgeave commented:

> No matter how hard it gets to stay out something like this makes us feel even more determined to win. We won't give in. When we arrived at 6 am, the police were already lined up - front line riot shields, and behind, the police on horses. Down the hill in the field there, were police with dogs... Their truncheons were drawn from the start, no messing about. When we started shoving, the police started cracking out at the front line, really hard, straight away... The police are definitely not 'a peace keeping force'. They were treating us like animals, chasing us with dogs and horses. Some pickets outside the plant had been shoved into this field - it was completely flattened, concrete lamp posts and walls crushed. Lads were coming away crying, heads bleeding, bruises all over their backs, some having to be carried... A man, his wife and bairn just standing at the bus stop were beaten up by the police. There were some rocks thrown and stakes in the ground to stop the horses coming but what else can you do? You can't outrun a horse, and the police came with truncheons, padding, shields etc, against pickets in jeans and T-shirts.[19]

These brutal scenes at Orgreave, together with similar scenes that were enacted in numerous pit villages throughout the coalfields, laid bare before the miners and working class as a whole the nature of the capitalist state. An army of occupation descended on the coal fields, particularly in the heartland of the strike, the Yorkshire coalfield.

I witnessed one of many brutal scenes in Allerton Bywater. On an early autumn morning, a thousand policemen confronted miners and their families in a bitter conflict in this village. Such actions changed forever the consciousness of workers, particularly the miners. Because of this *Militant*'s ideas found a powerful echo. It shared with and assisted in all the struggles of the miners but at the same time put forward a strategy which it considered was capable of ensuring victory. Following the first battle of Orgreave *Militant* advised that

> at local level, direct approaches should be made, backed up by arguments and mass leafletting, to steelworkers, lorry drivers and power station workers. The leaders of the TGWU and the ISTC should back up this campaign with a national internal drive in support of the miners. Wherever possible mass meetings should be organised and a call for solidarity, addressed by striking miners... Conferences of shop stew-

ards should be organised, specifically to prepare for solidarity action. These conferences should be called either directly by the NUM, by local trades councils or by the Broad Left Organising Committee. This strike also now demands national action and a national co-ordinated drive for solidarity by the Trades Union Congress. It would be naive however to put too much faith in the TUC, given its role recently in the ASLEF dispute, in the battle over the Stockport 6, over GCHQ and, more recently, Murray's (general secretary of the TUC) attempt to sabotage the one-day strike organised by the Yorkshire and Humberside TUC. The left unions should therefore come together independently to organise solidarity.[20]

At the same time *Militant* believed that

> the NUM could lay before such a conference in detail all that was needed in solidarity action, to stop the movement of coal and win this strike. High on the agenda of such a conference would be the calling of a one-day general strike, which, if it was organised, would involve the members not only of the left wing unions, it would inspire the rank and file of every union in Britain. It would result in a magnificent show of strength of the entire labour movement around the miners and prepare the way for an historic victory.[21]

Because *Militant* was capable at each stage of putting forward demands which could take the movement forward it caught the ear of the best and most combatative section of the miners. We were able to organise in June 1984, in Sheffield a successful meeting of miners and supporters of *Militant* to discuss what stage the strike had reached and the way forward. Over 150 miners attended to hear Brian Ingham, *Militant*'s national industrial organiser, and myself. Miners from every part of the British coalfield were present.

The miners began to get greater and greater support from the organised working class. We declared in July:

> A miners' victory is there for the taking. The magnificent show of solidarity by the dockers would now give a huge impetus to the fight to save our jobs and industry. The victory of Liverpool council, forcing the Tories to retreat, is a beacon for the miners and the whole of the labour movement. Even before the dockers struck against the use of scab labour on Humberside, support for the miners among trade unionists has been growing. There is overwhelming support for our fight amongst railway workers... after 18 weeks of a bitter strike, miners will

not settle for anything other than absolute guarantees about their future jobs, livelihoods and communities.[22]

It must not be forgotten that during the course of the miners' strike many workers who struck in solidarity with the miners lost their jobs, some of them permanently. The dockers' action had been provoked by the use of scab labour at Immingham. But one docker at the Immingham picket line told our reporter: "This is solidarity with the miners - we should have been out from the first week of the dispute".[23]

In the light of the solidarity action from the dockers, and indications that others, such as the seafarers, would give support, We once more demanded that the miners step up the action. It pointed out that

> a 24-hour general strike must now be organised to stop the Tories' attacks on workers. If the government uses troops (rumoured at the time) to scab on striking miners or dockers, an all-out strike must be organised... All the struggles of the miners, dockers and seamen have come together. Thatcher has claimed that it is a fight of 'only 200,000' workers against all the rest, but the trade unions must now demonstrate that the miners, dockers and seamen do not stand alone.[24]

*Militant* did not leave it at empty calls but got down to specifics. It pointed out that

> the TUC right wing have shown that they are incapable of putting up a serious fight. If they were a leadership worthy of the name, they would have organised a 24-hour general strike before now. Instead, the National Union of Mineworkers should use its authority to take up the call for a national campaign. The NUM executive should name the day, in a week or two, for a national day of action in which they would invite the other left unions to take part in a 24-hour general strike.[25]

The left unions were pressed, once more, to take the initiative in preparing for a 24-hour general strike. The miners had changed "the entire landscape of British society."

In a balance sheet of the strike at the end of July *Militant* pointed to the preparatory steps which Thatcher and the Tory Cabinet had taken before the strike. Yet such had been the resistance from the miners and the working class generally that, despite all the plans formulated by Thatcher's hatchet man MacGregor, the strike could easily have been won. One indication of the change in outlook was the statement of a young miner at one of our public meetings during the strike that: "Socialism had literally been knocked into his skull."[26]

The powerful effect of the strike on the rest of the trade union movement was detailed. The right-wing trade union leaders faced mounting criticism. 300 motions of censure had appeared on the agenda of the Civil and Public Services Association (CPSA) conference against Alistair Graham, general secretary of the CPSA, and the old right-wing executive. One month before in June he had been removed from the TUC general council. At the USDAW conference the executive was beaten no less than eleven times and the new general secretary of NALGO had to face severe criticism for not supporting the NGA during their dispute.

Almost insurrectionary moods had appeared in areas of Yorkshire. *Militant* had given a detailed account of the 'riots' in Maltby where police had rampaged through the village, and in Fitzwilliam where we had an important base amongst the miners. Not the least of the effects of the miners' strike was the lasting impression made on women, particularly on the miners' wives and girlfriends. *The Times*, organ of big business, had described the emergence of the miners' wives support groups as "the turning point in the strike". One women commented to *Militant*:

> We never used to take any notice of politics and government, but we have to now. We've stopped buying newspapers. *The Star* won't be delivered after they said something like 'Britain doesn't owe the miners a living'. They're so bad we don't even believe the ordinary everyday stories anymore. We can't go back to the old routine after the strike. [27]

In August there was an attempt to sequestrate the resources of the South Wales NUM. About 400 LPYS members, at their camp in Gloucestershire, were bussed down to the blockade at Pontypridd. Brian Ingham, on behalf of *Militant*, addressed the demo from the NUM platform. Ian Isaac, a member of the South Wales NUM executive and *Militant* supporter, also addressed the demo. He played a pivotal role in the strike in South Wales and nationally.

## KINNOCK CONDEMNS NUM

However, right at the crux of the battle came Neil Kinnock's speech at the Trade Union Congress in September when he condemned 'picket violence'. His tirade implicitly denounced miners' pickets. Mealy-mouthed phrases were used as a cover:

> We must put that case without violence... violence distracts attention from the central issues of the dispute... violence has given the government its only bone of excuse to gnaw on... violence... disgusts opinion and divides union attitudes... it provides opportunities to our enemies.[28]

It was Kinnock himself who had provided the main "opportunity to the enemy" by this speech. There were no ringing denunciations of police violence or the curtailment of civil liberties, no pounding on the table over the harassment and intimidation of striking miners. Not suprisingly the capitalist press had a field day. We commented:

> By this kind of speech, Neil Kinnock not only fails to support miners fighting for their jobs and communities, he gives full credence to the vicious press smears against the mineworkers. He unwittingly gives succour to all those newspapers and Tories calling for judicial vengeance in the form of hefty prison sentences and fines on the many miners unjustly arrested in the last six months.[29]

Even before the strike Kinnock's position was underlined by his statement in 1983 to the effect that Arthur Scargill was destroying the coal industry single-handed. A biography, *The Making of Neil Kinnock* by Robert Harris, was published at this time. He gave a detailed account of his evolution from a left firebrand into a staunch defender of the right wing within the Labour Party and the unions.

The press speculated that Kinnock was about to chastise the miners and push through 'one person, one vote' for parliamentary reselection. But they had seriously miscalculated, underestimating the enormous strength of feeling at all levels of the party and the unions for the miners. Colossal support for the miners put its stamp on the proceedings at the Labour Party conference. Commenting on the miners' debate, We reported that it had

> created an electric atmosphere that also put its mark on the police debate which followed in which the platform was defeated twice. The same was true on reselection, which showed the iron determination of the party rank and file not to go back on the gains acheived in the past.[30]

Kinnock received the obligatory standing ovation for his traditional leader's speech but this session of the conference was "a much more polite affair without the spontaneous cheering and football crowd enthusiasm that had greeted Arthur Scargill 24 hours earlier."[31]

Kinnock did not repeat his blunder of the TUC conference, being careful this time to blame the government for the violence of the miners' strike and even making a passing criticism of the police. This did not satisfy many of the delegates who were looking for much bolder support for the miners.

At that conference more than 500 attended the *Militant* Readers' Meeting to listen to Ted Grant, Tony Mulhearn, myself and Terry Fields MP. An impressive collection of £1,500 was taken, serving to underline that despite all attempts to cripple *Militant* by expulsions we continued to go from strength to strength.

## NUM FINED

No sooner had the Labour Party Conference finished than a massive £200,000 fine was imposed on the NUM and Arthur Scargill by the Tory courts. Rubbing salt in the wound the Tory Law Lords demanded that the NUM should pay the court costs of the two Yorkshire scabs who had brought the original action. We commented:

> There is the likelihood that the court will impose an even greater fine - of perhaps £500,000 - if the NUM refuse to "purge their contempt." The Tory Law Lords had been encouraged "by the equivocation of labour and trade union leaders in recent weeks; the failure of the union leaders to properly raise the issue at Labour Party conference, and by the failure of the GMBATU leadership to respond sufficiently to the jailing of the 37 Cammel Laird's workers.[32]

A call was made for a special NUM delegate conference to reaffirm the strike as official. At the same time it was suggested that a special appeal be directed to NACODS, the pit deputies' union, to stand shoulder to shoulder with the NUM given that their jobs were now on the line. As the year closed it was clear, as we pointed out, that

> the working class now faces its most serious challange since 1926. If, as has been reported, the TUC leaders refuse the support requested by the NUM, then the left trade union leaders - and especially the leaders of the mineworkers themselves - must make an independent call for industrial action.[33]

The issue was now not just the fate of the miners and their jobs but the right of the unions to take effective industrial action. We declared:

> Hesitation could have disastrous consequences. The ruling class are waging naked class war. Organised workers must meet fire with fire... The Tories' strength is illusory, based only on the passivity of the trade union leaders.[34]

Summing up the effects of the miners' strike *Militant* declared:

> This struggle has become a beacon to the working class even on an international plane... Striking miners... have taken part in many international speaking tours, collecting tens of thousands of pounds. Workers internationally have been and still are looking towards Britain and holding their breath - hoping for a miners' victory over the detested Thatcher government.
>
> The Tories proclaimed that the miners have no support in Britain, yet the collections of over £1 million a week flatly contradicts this... The political involvement of miners and their families has led even the bishops of the North East to comment on the interest now shown in 'revolutionary ideas'... The ruling class has created a chasm between the classes. British society will never be the same again. The editorials of the capitalist press have talked of 'civil war without bullets', of 'the enemy within' - all of which indicate how seriously they view this class war... 1984 was a year in which the sceptics were confounded and the view of Marxists confirmed - that when they think they are right, working-class people will move heaven and earth to fight for their future. That fight will go on in 1985, and later, and until so-

cialism becomes a reality.[35]

## MILITANT MINERS ON TOUR

The miners' fight did go on in 1985 but without the victory that was there for the taking, because of the pernicious role of the right-wing trade union leaders.

In the first months of 1985 *Militant* chronicled the continuing campaign of the miners both on a national and international level. Many miners, some of them supporters of *Militant*, had travelled to the four corners of the world where there was a clamour from the labour movement to hear first hand accounts of their struggle. Roy Jones, a striking miner and *Militant* supporter from North Staffordshire, spent a month in South Africa at the invitation of the South African National Union of Mineworkers and was accepted as its first white member. His trip "was very succesful in raising finance, £220 immediately with a promise of more from a very poor union."

Roy was as affected by the combativity of the South African miners as they were inspired by the struggles of the British workers. He explained that he was

> convinced at the need for direct links with the South African NUM. It is a fast growing union, expanding from nothing five years ago to 100,000 in the autumn with the aim of 200,000 by the January congress.[36]

Other visits, involving *Militant* supporters, were made to Greece, Spain, the USA, Germany, and many many other countries. But in February as the strike began to approach its eleventh month the resolve of some miners began to crack. A new wave of clashes between pickets and police broke out as the police attempted to protect a few miners who were drifting back to work. We recorded a typical clash in Easington, County Durham:

> "I've never been so frightened in my life. I used to respect the police, but never again" said retired miner, Joss Smith.[37]

He had been arrested in the clashes that resulted from the attempt of the police to escort a handful of scabs who had returned to work. However, in March after more than a year on strike for some miners, the heartbreaking decision was taken to return to work. The miners did so with banners flying and bands playing generating a mixture of emotions amongst working people. Tears were brought to the eyes at the memory of the sacrifice which the miners had made not just for themselves but for the whole of the British working class. This was mixed with anger directed at those who had deserted the miners, stabbed them in the back, and assisted the Tory capitalist enemy to defeat the strike. We commented:

> History has been made by those who returned to work this week. The miners' strike of 1984-85 will never be forgotten, certainly not by those who took part, nor by future generations... Society will never be the same again. The miners have brought class politics back on the agenda. Theirs will be the standard by which all struggles are measured... They have not been humiliated. But vital lessons will have been learned. Above all, this strike has demonstrated the necessity to unite workers together in action if any one section, however strong, is to overcome the combined power of the management, government, press and police, which was unleashed on the miners.[38]

In an extensive review of the miners' strike *Militant* dealt with the arguments of those who believed that Thatcher's 'strategy' had suceeded.

> Nothing could be further from the truth. She wanted an industrial Falklands, a short, sharp victory. She got a strike that lasted a year, cost £7,000million and will have a lasting affect on class relationships.[39]

The role of the trade union leaders was analysed:

> Ned Smith, the now ex-director of labour relations of the NCB commented that the failure of the Trades Union Congress to deliver 'total support' for the miners was the turning point in the attitude of the government. What of the left-wing leaders of the trade unions? Without the pressure of the rank and file, the right-wing leaders of the TUC would have attempted to organise a surrender to the Tories months ago. The left genuinely wished to help the cause of the miners. They simply lacked the most elementary strategy, tactics and methods to do so, and the necessary confidence and faith in their own rank

and file. This strike demonstrates sharply the importance of theory and of an understanding of perspectives for those who have leading positions in the labour movement. The infection of 'new realism' had even spread through most of the left leaders. Despite the example of the miners and their families and all the magificent support, they still simply did not believe their own members would respond if called upon to fight.[40]

Dealing with the mood of the working class towards the strike we wrote:

> Seamen blacked coal throughout. Railway workers in the NUR and ASLEF stood firm despite victimisations of their own members. Even in these two industries, however, little was done by the leaders to link up in action with the miners. Seamen face a range of acute problems. In the course of this strike, privatisation of Sealink went through. A campaign by the leadership for all-out strike action alongside the miners could have saved not only Sealink but would have massively enhanced the struggle of the miners.[41]

The lengths to which Thatcher was prepared to go to isolate the miners was described:

> Thatcher personally intervened in negotiations over railway pay to ensure that the offer from the railways board was sufficient to attract the railway union leaders and avoid a strike of railway workers together with the miners...The Transport and General Workers' Union, the largest left union of all, has the capacity in a whole number of industries to cripple the economic life of British capitalism. Shamefully, the powerful machine of the Transport and General Workers' Union was never decisively turned towards the miners' strike. Dockers refused to handle coal. As a result two disputes flared up. The Tories stumbled into the first. The second was cynically and carefully provoked. When the dockers came out, the worst fears of the capitalist class had been realised; another strong group of workers was fighting side by side with the miners. Frenzied talk of a 'State of Emergency' flared. The Tories were reeling. But instead of openly and boldly fighting to link the dockers and the miners' strike together, the leaders of the TGWU presented the dockers' dispute as an entirely separate affair. They denied that the strikes were political when clearly, as with the miners' strike, they were cynically provoked by the Tory government.[42]

Pointing to decisive stages in the strike, *Militant* commented:

> One moment stands out from all the rest. In November, following the strike at BL (British Leyland), the TGWU was fined £200,000 under the Tories' anti-trade union legislation. The TGWU executive's reaction was opposition, but with folded arms... The leadership refused to pay the money, refused to go to court, then they simply sat back passively while the sequestrator plundered TGWU funds. The lesson is: left-wing leaders are generally closer and far more subject to the pressure of the rank and file. But in fighting to elect left-wing leaders in all the unions, activists should ensure that these leaders are selected on their proven record and on a clear socialist programme which meets the needs of the rank and file. The left must demonstrate a clear willingness to campaign and mobilise the ranks of the union to fight on such decisive issues.[43]

Despite the heroism and tenacity of the NUM leadership, it lacked a clear strategy at decisive moments.

> In the run up to the TUC, *Militant* argued for the NUM to name a date two or three weeks after the TUC. Such a call for general strike action would have set in train an unstoppable process. Activists throughout industry would have begun immediately to organise support. Pressure from below would have forced the left trade union leaders to line up with the NUM. The TUC itself would have been forced to add its authority to this action. Instead, the NUM complied with the idea of more general calls for support. A resolution from the furniture trades union for a day of solidarity action was withdrawn from the agenda. *Militant* continued week after week to argue the case for the NUM to boldly seize the initiative by naming the date for a one-day general strike.[44]

In early 1985 the South Wales NUM did call for a one-day general strike. Militant produced 50,000 leaflets for the NUM to publicise the case, but the tide was already beginning to turn. A key issue in the strike was the question of the Nottinghamshire coalfield and the role of NACODS, the pit deputies' union:

> The rank and file should not be blamed. With different leadership they would have joined this battle. Eighty-one per cent of NACODS members voted for strike action.[45]

The NACODS leaders, with the Tories in dread of a total mining stoppage, negotiated their own separate deal. NACODS members along with NUM members paid for the cowardly actions of their own leadership by the subsequent loss of many of their jobs in the period that followed the strike.

Commenting on the political implication of the strike and the role of the Labour leaders, we said:

> Miners will never forget how this deep, abiding loyalty [to Labour] was repaid during this dispute by Neil Kinnock and the other Labour leaders. Only once did Neil Kinnock find the time to visit a picket line... After negotiations had been broken off by the Coal Board, Neil Kinnock was too busy to attend. When the full weight of the law was being thrown against individual miners, he advised meek compliance with the capitalist courts and the decisions of Tory judges... Kinnock and other leaders lined up with the Tories against a general amnesty, giving credence to the idea that miners were violent criminals who deserved to be sacked and face a lifetime on the dole.[46]

However, the strike, we predicted, would have a lasting effect on British society and above all on the working class:

> This strike has seen the radicalisation of whole communities. Within the NUM, the young lions - as they were dubbed - burst into the strike with incredible courage and energy. They and the youth around them in the pit villages were the vanguard of a social explosion of which the Tories are terrified. They have rekindled the very finest traditions of struggle and solidarity. As long ago as June, *The Times* was to comment that ironically, "the dispute that some politicians hoped would break the power of the NUM has actually created new cadres for the future".[47]

The 1984-85 miners' strike was, and remains, the most important industrial dispute of the last two decades, possibly since 1945. Contained in this drama, with elements of civil war between the classes, were all the ingredients for a future larger battle on a national scale. Cynics and faint-hearts will point to the defeat of the strike and the subsquent slaughtering of the coal industry with the loss of hundreds of thousands of jobs, as proof of the 'futility' of the strike.

Far worse than a defeat after an honourable battle is ignominious retreat without a shot being fired. Nothing is more calculated to demoralise the working class than the sight of a leadership which turns and runs from a battle when it is clear that there is no other way out. Scargill and the NUM leadership were quite aware of the huge build-up of coal stocks in the run-up to the strike. They also understood that the threatened closure of Cortonwood, the trigger for the strike, was a provocation. But to have accepted the closure of one pit, while it still had plentiful supplies of coal, would have been the thin end of the wedge. The course chosen by the NUM leadership and by the miners themselves has laid down a fighting tradition which will be taken up by future generations of workers.

# 26.
# INTO ILLEGALITY IN LIVERPOOL

MARCH 29 1984 was a decisive date in the history of Liverpool. The council was due to meet to discuss Labour's so-called 'illegal budget'. Coinciding with this, the city saw one of the largest city-wide general strikes in Britain's history. Upwards of 50,000 workers and young people packed the city centre. This showed the depth of support for the stand taken by Liverpool's Labour council against Tory cuts. Castle Street facing the town hall was jam packed with demonstrators shouting support for the councillors inside. The crowd sang in football style: "Labour council, Labour council, we support you evermore".

Inside, the council meeting had ended in a tactical victory for Labour. The Tories, the Liberals and right-wing Labour failed to impose a cuts budget. On rising to reply to the Liberals, Labour's deputy leader Derek Hatton was greeted by cheers from the public gallery, and applause punctuated his speech.

> The choice for the people of Liverpool was clear. Either to back Labour's budget or to go back to the Dark Ages of Liberal-Tory alliance. The Council was only asking for £30 million from the Government's contingency funds. In the recent budget, the Tories had given £35 million to 650,000 already earning over £15,000 a year.[1]

Liverpool's stand had not been arrived at by an easy route or without controversies both within the labour movement and also within the ranks of *Militant* itself.

## MILITANT DEBATE

We debated our approach at every stage. This was not uncommon in the labour movement despite the shrieks of the right wing about 'secret caucuses' of the left. The right and the left have always discussed their different approaches. *Militant* was no different. When the right, and an increasing section of the 'careerist left', criticized us for being a 'party-within-a-party', it was because *Militant* supporters were better organised than them.

In January 1984 a National *Militant* Editorial Board had been held in London, with Tony Mulhearn and Derek Hatton attending. The battle in Liverpool, which was now entering a decisive phase, was a main item of discussion. Contrary to the myth of the press that *Militant* was 'monolithic', then and subsequently there were different views on how to approach issues. In the discussion at the NEB it was the opinion of Ted Grant that the unity of the Liverpool Labour Group would fracture under the pressure of the situation. He argued vehemently that enough right-wing councillors would defect to the Tory/Liberal camp in order to prevent the passing of an 'illegal budget'. The contrary view was advanced by Tony Mulhearn and Derek Hatton, supported by myself, Lynn Walsh and others at the meeting. They argued that such was the overwhelming pressure of the labour movement and the working class that even nominal right-wingers could be swayed to support the position of the left. Such views were dismissed by Ted Grant. He argued that we should prepare for right wing defections in Liverpool. Failure to to do this would demoralise *Militant* supporters.

Ted Grant's views that the illegal budget would not be passed proved to be wrong. True, some right-wingers did defect - the 'scabby seven' - but enough rallied to the side of Labour to prevent the Liberal/Tory budget from going through in March.

## 95 PER CENT VICTORY

Following a series of skirmishes with the Tory government, including negotiations with the Environment Secretary, Patrick Jenkin, agreement was reached, which was "a 95 per cent victory". An assortment of opponents of Liverpool and *Militant* - the so-called Communist Party, the varieties of ultra-left sects, together with the Tory government - tried to down play Jenkin's and Thatcher's retreat. In the council chamber a demoralised Trevor Jones in the debate over the package "quoted from *Socialist Worker*" which accused the Labour council of a "sell out".[2]

However, the reaction of the capitalists to the £60 million concessions won by Liverpool said everything about the victory. *The Times* thundered: "Danegeld in Liverpool" (Danegeld was the tribute paid by English kings in the tenth century to buy off Danish invaders). Besides itself with fury, it went on:

> Today in Liverpool, municipal militancy is vindicated... a third rate provincial politician, a self-publicising revolutionary... Mr Derek Hatton has made the government give way... Mr Hatton and his colleagues threatened a course of disruptive action. Their reward is the abrogation of the financial targets which 400 other local authorities have been told are immutable... in order to buy off *Militant*.[3]

These were heady days for *Militant* supporters in Liverpool. The campaign was marked in April with a hugely successful *Militant* public meeting, attended by 500 workers, followed in May with another stunning victory for Labour in council elections. The 9 April meeting at St George's Hall received the platform speeches enthusiastically: the speakers included myself, Steve Sullivan, a miner on strike at Sutton Manor, Tony Mulhearn, newly elected to the city council, Derek Hatton and Terry Fields MP. On the evening of 29 March when the council had taken the first step along the road of threatening an 'illegal budget' the *Militant* premises on Lower Breck Road was crowded with people clammering to join. Committed supporters of *Militant* were excluded from the building so that new 'recruits' could crowd into a meeting addressed by leaders of *Militant*. Over 40 people agreed to join *Militant* on that night alone.

Given the rapid growth of *Militant* it was little wonder that alongside the thousands of daily items in the press 'a more serious', more intensive effort would be made to detail the growth of our support. The first into the field was Michael Crick, a journalist with Channel Four News. His book called *Militant* and the second edition, *The March of Militant*, claimed to show the: "origins, organisation and aims of *Militant*, which is now Britain's fifth strongest political party".[4]

The first edition of Crick's book came out in 1984 but the second edition was produced in 1986 when the witch-hunt was in full swing. In 1984, in his first edition Crick was forced to concede "*Militant* is here to stay", as its ideas and influence continued to grow. His book also brought us recruits in Australia and Canada![5]

## WEMBLEY, THREE YEARS IN A ROW

If there were any doubts that *Militant* was still on a rising curve these were answered by the 3,000 supporters who once more turned up to Wembley for what was now the annual rally of *Militant*. We commented:

> Such was the mood and humour that passers-by could have been forgiven for thinking the crowds were returning from a Wembley Cup Final. Maybe a bit smaller than that at the moment, but we've booked the Albert Hall for next year - (3 November).[6]

Frances Curran, then the LPYS representative on Labour's NEC, was only three when *Militant* was first produced! She addressed the 1984 rally pointing out,

> My parents wouldn't have believed what is happening today to young people. A third of secondary school children have taken drugs, and there are 20-year-olds who have never been able to get a job.

She went on to point out that

> the YS have collected £250,000 to £300,000 that we know of for the miners. They organised the first demo in the Notts area in Mansfield and Steve Morgan, the previous YS representative on the NEC, proposed the 50p levy on all party members.[7]

Tony Benn amongst many others spoke at this rally and eleven Labour MPs sent congratulations. Again the fighting fund collection exceeded all expectations with £12,000 raised.

# 27.
# SCHOOL STUDENTS' STRIKE

THE OUTCOME of the miners' strike undoubtedly had an immediately chastening effect on the consciousness of workers and their preparedness to struggle. But, as we argued at the time, it was not the same as in 1926. That defeat demoralised the miners and undermined the confidence of workers for a decade or more. Following the defeat of 1926 the working class transferred their hopes to the political plane, and the election of a Labour government. More important than the psychological effect of the defeat of the 1984-85 miners' strike was that it coincided with a world economic upswing. This allowed the capitalists a certain leeway, at least in the advanced industrial countries. The number of strikes declined in the 1980s largely because of the Reagan/Thatcher 'boom'. Those fortunate to be employed were able to get wage increases which kept them abreast of the cost of living and in some cases led, through overtime, productivity agreements, etc, to rises above the rate of inflation. The other side of the 1980s boom was the enormous and growing disparity between rich and poor.

Rather than crushing the spirit of revolt the miners' strike had exactly the opposite effect particularly on the new fresh layers of the working class. This was shown in the school strikes which broke out in March 1985, barely weeks after the end of the miners' strike. The first signs of a movement came in mid-March with a number of student strikes and walkouts throughout the country. Of course, the press were quick to blame it on the industrial action by teachers that was taking place at the time. They blew up small incidents, trying to present a picture of 'rampaging children' let loose by 'irresponsible' teachers. The real reasons for young people's discontent lay in their frustration, with no prospect of a real job when they left school; the dole or conscription onto YTS was the only future for them. Faced with this movement of school students the police were deployed. In Middlesbrough mounted police patrolled daily. *Militant* detailed a series of strikes in the Portsmouth area.

# School Students' Strike 253

These strikes

> were initially a confused action against the teachers, because they feared a potential "threat to examination chances". [But] the LPYS immediately took the initiative. At one of the schools involved there are eight LPYS members. In an emergency leaflet the teachers' campaign for better pay was forcibly explained... The YS received support from the majority of students for opposing the mindless violence of a small minority. [The strike began to gain support and] later spread to the Bridgemary School in Gosport, from its outset the action was in support of the teachers.[1]

But these were just small movements before the explosion which detonated in Glasgow one week later. Organised by the Labour Party Young Socialists, with *Militant* supporters in the lead, "a general strike swept through Clydeside schools, bringing 20,000 pupils out... They gave Thatcher a defiant message - 'We're not having YTS job conscription'." One fourth year student from Sacred Hearts School commented to *Militant*: "The rally was tremendous. If we had more like it we'd really get somewhere. This will be like the miners. I think YTS is slave labour."[2]

More than 10,000 students poured into Glasgow city centre in what Glasgow's *Daily Record* called the "biggest show of pupil power ever in Britain". Speakers were amazed when schools with improvised banners marched to the rally to be greeted with thunderous applause and roars of "Here we go". Many made home made banners with slogans like "No Slave Labour" and "What About a Future". Red flags flew all around the indoor rally. An old man approached the organisers and said:

> You know, after the battle of George Square in 1919, my father said we would rise again. I always believed him and I have seen it today.[3]

Predictably, this magnificent display of working-class youth's opposition to the slave labour YTS scheme was condemned by the right-wing leaders of the Labour Party in Scotland. Previously they had condemned, at the Labour Party Scottish conference, the "narrow sectarian nature" of the LPYS in Scotland. But as we explained:

> Now the LPYS is condemned for leading mass demonstrations... They expected between 1,000 to 1,500 people, which would be a reasonable

return on 10,000 leaflets in normal circumstances. The organisers can hardly be blamed for the initiatives of the Thatcher-hating school students who built the movement themselves. In fact the organisers deserve credit for the way in which the demonstration was channelled into acceptable forms of protest when the numbers could have overwhelmed them.[4]

This new 'Revolt on the Clyde' led to an even bigger movement of school students throughout Britain two months later. The LPYS consciously prepared for and championed this movement. They used their Easter conference attended by over 2,000 young people as a platform to launch a campaign for a national stoppage of youth. 200 gathered at a fringe meeting, chaired by Frances Curran, to hear Colin Baird from Glasgow and Nancy Taaffe from London, who set the turmoil in the schools against the background of the miners' strike, Tory attacks on youth and past school strikes. A School Students' Action Committee was formed, a steering committee elected and a decision to call a national half-day school strike (except in Scotland because of earlier exams) on 25 April.

Additionally, Jackie Galbraith, one of the main organisers, together with Colin Fox, of the Strathclyde strike, spoke at the *Militant* Readers' Meeting. This conference also elected Linda Douglas to the NEC, the first black person on Labour's executive. But the success of the 25 April school student strike exceeded all expectations:

> A quarter of a million school students have given a crushing answer to the Tories, the press and the cynics in the labour movement... Thatcher condemned it. So did the Liberals. Unfortunately too the TUC and Labour leadership condemned it.[5]

Kinnock condemned the organisers as "dafties" but in Kinnock's own constituency 500 joined the strike. We declared:

> The Marxists in the labour movement make no apology for backing the school students to the hilt. It is essential that the despair, the frustration and anger of youth is channelled in a positive direction, linking up with the labour movement. The students themselves understand it - in Pontypridd the thousand-strong school student demonstration called on the leader of the South Wales miners to lead them into the town, which he proudly did.[6]

Every area of the country seemed to be touched by the strike. Even in Northern Ireland 3,000 had come out with only a week's notice and completely cut across the sectarian divide. In London

> thousands joined the strike... in Brent school students sent out flying pickets to build the strike... in Southampton prefects and teachers at one Catholic girl's school linked arms across the gateway to prevent students leaving. Similarly at Portsmouth Grammar School, students were beaten back from the gates. In Plymouth four LPYS members have been threatened with expulsion from the Labour Party for supporting the strike.[7]

But all the threats came to nothing:

> 10,000 school students marched through Liverpool. The mood was electric.[8]

The Labour leadership denounced the strike, but they were also aware that one of the keys to the future success of Labour would be the mobilisation of youth. The strike had convinced them of the enormous discontent existing among all layers of the youth. So, at the same time as they evicted the Youth Trade Union Rights Campaign (YTURC), which had been behind the strike, from Labour Party national headquarters they also rushed out a 'Youth Charter'. The printing trade union SOGAT immediately stepped in and offered alternative premises to YTURC. The government also learned from the events of 25 April. Recognising the angry mood amongst school students they made some concessions. They had reacted in a similar fashion in 1981 when the Labour Party Young Socialists had organised a massive campaign on the issue of rights, training, conditions and wages against the forerunner of the YTS, the Youth Opportunities Programme. As soon as they saw this movement developing the government increased the YOP allowance. Now they took note of the mood of youth as shown by the 25 April strike. Tory spokespersons withdrew the idea of conscripting youth, by withdrawing unemployment or social security pay, for those who refused to go on YTS. The school student strike was a landmark. It served to underline the enormous impact which the miners' strike had made on youth.

## INTERNATIONALLY

While *Militant*'s coverage in 1985 was heavily concentrated on domestic issues the unique international reports still brought alive to a British audience events and stories which were found nowhere else. In May the paper reported on the expulsion from Zimbabwe of a group of Marxists, led by David Hemson, associated with the South African journal *Inqaba*. The prime minister of Zimbabwe, Robert Mugabe, had used his May Day speech to denounce the Militant Tendency! David told us:

> Throughout interrogation, the Central Intelligence Organisation (CIO) (they were given this name by Ian Smith, by the way) defended Zimbabwe's corrupt union leadership and showed hostility to socialism, to the British trade unions and to Arthur Scargill in particular, and the left of the Labour Party...[9]

Showing the connection between the arrests of these Marxists and events in Britain David commented:

> By the Thursday, 7 March, we realised a lot of their information came from Britain directly. They were relaying information on the Labour left, including details of leading left wingers' private lives and even details of tensions within the Labour Party. They said we were not really Labour Party we were *Militant*.[10]

# 28.
# LIVERPOOL: ROUND TWO

WITH THE ending of the miners' strike Thatcher was free to concentrate on isolating and defeating Liverpool's Labour council. Michael Parkinson in his book *Liverpool on the Brink* states:

> By the mid-1980s, the Conservatives saw Liverpool as the power base of the *Militant* Tendency and they wanted to defeat it. The scene was set for a political confrontation... the government recognised that it had lost the propaganda battle in 1984 and had failed to get its arguments across to the electorate. The government now decided to shift the ground of the argument and attacked the Labour council in future directly, portraying the conflict as not a technical dispute about money and the grant system, but as a *Militant* plot against the government.[1]

The government was soon preparing its next round of measures against local councils.

Many councils were compelled by force of circumstances to consider taking the 'Liverpool road' and illegal defiance of the government. The common position of a number of councils led to a united front in late 1984 between Liverpool and other authorities which had been ratecapped. A debate opened up among the leaders of the ratecapped councils as to which tactic for fixing the annual rate, due to be set in March 1985, could best mobilise the undoubted opposition which existed to the government's policies.

Liverpool's method of setting a rate that left the deficit in the budget, presenting a clear demand on the government to give more resources to the council to make up the difference, had shown in practice that it was an excellent means of mobilising the mass of the working class for battle as it was clear what the aims of the fight were.

The 'trendy left' of Ken Livingstone from the Greater London Council, David Blunkett in Sheffield and Margaret Hodge, leader of Islington council, counterposed to this their own tactic of the 'no rate' policy: the idea being that the council would refuse to set the local property tax, known then as the rates. This would eventually lead to the position of each council being different, making it virtually impossible to harmonise the precise date when all councils were to face bankruptcy. Moreover, the 'no rate' policy was a negative one, leaving the initiative in the government's hands.

There was also another profound difference between Liverpool's approach and that of the other 'left' councils. Liverpool completely opposed the idea of off-setting government grant cuts by massively increasing rates. The advocates of the 'no rate' policy were not. Despite the misgivings and warnings of *Militant*, Liverpool went ahead with the 'no rate' policy in the interests of a common front against the government. Twenty-five councils had decided to make a common stand against the government.

In the run-up to budget day plans were laid for the mobilisation of workers in Liverpool to coincide with a stoppage of local government workers nationally on 7 March. Once more, a mass demonstration of 50,000 marched on the Town Hall, "one of the biggest in a hundred years", declared Tony Mulhearn. At the Inner London Education Authority (ILEA) meeting some Labour members joined with the Tories and the SDP to push through a legal rate after eight hours of debate.

Then the GLC, headed by Ken Livingstone, led the retreat of other councils. Despite all his heroic words and gestures he led the majority of London Labour councillors into the position of "remaining within the law" by setting a rate and budget which would mean cuts. This represented a turninig point in the struggle of Labour authorities against the government.

The GLC's opposition was merely verbal and was a repetition of the climbdown in 1982 when the Law Lords ruled against the 'Fares Fair' cheap transport policy. *Militant* subjected the GLC leadership to severe criticism:

> Ken Livingstone, in a report to the Greater London Labour Party Executive, attacked the "posturing of some borough leaders" who adopted a policy which allowed them to "duck the issue of illegality" at the 7 March budget meetings but "left the GLC and ILEA out on their own" because of the legal requirements for the upper-tier authorities (like the GLC and ILEA) to set a rate by 10 March.[2]

But he totally ignored the fact that three days before the GLC finally set a rate, one council, Hackney, had already gone 'illegal' by refusing to set a rate in defiance of a court order to do so. Moreover, the GLC manifesto for the 1981 election had declared: "Mass opposition to Tory policies led by a Labour GLC could become the focal point of a national campaign, involving other Labour councils, against the cuts." This section of the manifesto had been written by *Militant* supporters but was supported by the London Labour movement as a whole.

## MILITANT MPS UNDER ATTACK

Terry Fields was earning the well-merited hatred of the Tories and the ruling class. By the same token, his standing and that of Dave Nellist also rose enormously amongst the working class. They used Parliament in a way that Labour should always seek to do, as a platform to organise and mobilise working people in struggle. Taking alarm at the growing popularity of these two MPs, and particularly their decision to live on no more than the average wage of a skilled worker, the right-wing Labour Party leadership actually tried to stop them giving money back to the party out of their parliamentary salaries. Their stand, along with that of NUM-sponsored MP Dennis Skinner who gave all of his salary to the miners for the duration of the strike, had earned them enormous popularity.

This incident showed the fear of the right wing of the demand for a worker's MP on a worker's wage. Their attacks on Dave Nellist and Terry Fields were made against the background of a serious financial crisis for the Labour Party. But it was all part of the campaign of the press, TV and radio, backed by the right within the party, to break the leftward movement in the Labour Party, typified by the battle which now revolved around Liverpool. The NEC also conducted an investigation into Coventry South-East in 1984, centred around Dave Nellist's victory! We warned the labour movement about the coming offensive:

> A series of attacks on *Militant* supporters suggests that the right-wing leaders of the Labour Party and some trade unions may be starting a war within the party... in a frank admission of their intentions, a delegate to the 1984 NUPE conference called for "a purge that would make Stalin look like a social worker".[3]

In July the Welsh executive of the Labour Party expelled Tony Wedlake, an LPYS representative, and Chris Peace, who had actually topped the poll at the Welsh Labour Party conference in elections to the executive committee.

## LIVERPOOL - DEADLINE APPROACHES

Despite this, Liverpool, where *Militant* still had its strongest base, was set on a collision course with the government. Right up to the day that the council was supposed to set a 'legal' rate, the government had been confident that Liverpool would come to heel in the wake of the capitulation of the other councils. On 13 May, Patrick Jenkin repeated his early refusal to talk to the council. John Hamilton, leader of the Labour group, angrily declared: "If he came to Liverpool to try and explain his policies, then his ideas would be slaughtered."[4] By the end of May four councils were holding out on the 'no rate' policy: Southwark, Camden, Liverpool and Lambeth. On 22 May the District Auditor threatened the Liverpool councillors with heavy fines and banishment from office unless they set a rate within nine days.

As crunch time approached, both the government and the *Liverpool Echo* expected the council to capitulate. There was of course serious discussion amongst *Militant* supporters at local and national level and within the local labour movement as to what course of action should be pursued. At the end of these debates, with the collapse of the 'no rate' front, it was concluded that the only course of action was to confront the government. At the eleventh hour, on 11 June, the city council once more appealed for discussions with Jenkin. He refused, hoping to see Labour eat dirt and relishing the prospect that this time round he would be "dancing on Derek Hatton's grave." In an editorial *Militant* urged Liverpool to stand firm and at its historic meeting on 13 June the District Labour Party unanimously agreed to set a nine per cent rate - no higher than the real rate of inflation and with no cuts.

Nearly all the Labour councillors were there, and there was not one dissenting voice at the meeting when this policy was advocated. Moreover, any last minute hesitations were dispelled the next day when Thomas MacMahon, the District Auditor, sent a letter saying: "A crime had already been committed" and he was going to act against them (the councillors) for losses incurred between 1 April and June. Thus any potential defectors were dissuaded from such a course by the fact that even if they betrayed Labour, they could still be surcharged.

Rarely had the Liverpool labour movement been so united. With a nine per cent rate and with a government refusal to give further grants, it was quite clear the city would run out of money at a certain stage. Labour was not setting out to deliberately bankrupt the city but intended to use the time available to mobilise the population and to appeal nationally to local authority workers to exert pressure on the government. Initially stunned by the decision of Liverpool to stand and fight, once they understood what had happened, the government and the press then launched a furious offensive against the Liverpool labour movement. The air was thick with denunciations of Liverpool and threats to send in the government agents, government commissioners. The District Auditor, with semi-dictatorial powers, also decided to surcharge the 49 Labour councillors £106,000 for "wilful misconduct". This only served to galvanise support behind the Labour council.

The mass support for the council was linked to the fact that the people of the city could see the effects around them of what a fighting Labour council meant. Sometimes even the *Echo* would carry a letter, from unusual sources, recording the progress that had been made:

> As a visitor from Portsmouth to your city, I have been most impressed by the housebuilding programme of your city council. In Portsmouth, with a Conservative council, no houses are to be built in the next five years, yet Hampshire faces an extra 250,000 people needing accomodation in the same period. Does it really matter if the *Militant* is behind the city council if they are the only people in the country standing up against a mad policy of turning Britain's major cities into slums? I would support the 'man from Mars' if he built 2,000 houses in our city.[5]

## SCOTTISH PROGRESS

The paper and its supporters enjoyed strong support in Scotland, particularly in Glasgow and Edinburgh. In fact, prominent Scottish

*Militant* supporters came close to winning positions as Labour Parliamentary candidates. In Provan constituency Ronnie Stevenson, stalwart of *Militant* for over 20 years, stood for selection against Hugh Brown the sitting MP in 1982 but was defeated by 31 votes to 24. In 1985 Jim Cameron, one of the ablest representatives of *Militant*'s views and a prominent trade unionist, stood for the vacant seat following Brown's retirement. He was defeated by just one vote by Jimmy Wray at the selection conference. Other *Militant* supporters came close to selection in a number of constituencies in London, Gateshead East, Swansea, Southampton and Greenwich.

## THE REDUNDANCY NOTICES

Some of these former lefts were to play a baleful role in the Liverpool drama which came to a head in September and at the Labour Party conference soon after. One of the issues which was seized on by all the enemies of Liverpool council and *Militant* was that of the so-called 'redundancy notices'. (We have fully dealt with this issue in *Liverpool - a City That Dared to Fight*.) Faced with resources running out, the Labour Group had made contingency plans after legal and financial experts had advised that under the 1978 Employment Protection Act, once the money ran out, they would have been forced to terminate the contracts of all council employees. Failure to do so could have left the councillors personally liable for the £23 million 'redundancy pay' to which the 30,000 local authority workers were entitled. Under local government law, a council cannot lay off workers but has to terminate their contracts, which in affect is redundancy.

Moreover, the City Treasurer advised that failure to act 'legally' by issuing the redundancy notices would have resulted in the Public Works Loan Board refusing permission for Liverpool to raise loans on the money market to pay for day-to-day expenditure. This in turn would have meant that the council would have run out of money within a few weeks. Therefore workers would receive no wages after this period. The 'legal' device of redundancy notices would at least allow wages to be paid until the end of 1985. This would have allowed time to build a campaign to force the government to pay back the cash stolen from the city. The ruling class has deliberately framed local government law in order to entangle councils in such legal niceties. If the Liverpool council had been made up entirely of *Militant* supporters, which it was not, this course of action would not have been adopted as the Marxists would have gone the whole way.

But the councillors felt let down, particularly by the refusal of the white-collar union leaders to fully back them. The Labour Group decided to use the 'tactic' of issuing 90-day notices to the 30,000-strong workforce to ensure a breathing space in order to build the campaign. It was absurd to suggest, as the press did, and to their shame the national trade union leaders, that 30,000 workers were to be sacked. The whole point of this exercise was to defend jobs. However, the issuing of redundancy notices turned out to be a major tactical error.

The great military strategist Clausewitz once said: "Military warfare needs the kind of mathematics of a Euclid or a Newton." More simply, political algebra is necessary. For anybody leading a major political struggle, it is necessary to visualise, not just how the active workers will view the problem, but how your enemies can exploit your statements, strategy and tactics.

When this tactic was explained to those workers who could be reached there was support and understanding. This was the case amongst the great majority of manual workers. For the wider population of Liverpool and on a national plane and even the majority of the 30,000 local authority workforce they got their information from the fragments of news snatched from the television and the press. As soon as the issue of 'redundancy notices' was raised a massive hue and cry was set up by the national press. The 'redundancy notices' issue split the leaders of the council workforce.

Many white-collar workers were genuinely concerned that if their contracts were terminated, and in the meantime the threat of surcharge brought a Liberal/Tory Coalition to power, many would not be re-employed. The tactic of 'redundancy notices' was taken without the prior knowledge and support either from the local *Militant* or national leadership. In Merseyside, as well, the majority of *Militant* supporters were opposed to this tactic. Although *Militant* exercised a powerful influence on the Liverpool struggle it was by no means automatic for our viewpoint to be accepted. As soon as we heard, via radio and television, that this 'tactic' had been resorted to we expressed our opposition. However, this did not take the form of a 'public denunciation' but of seeking to explain why the councillors thought that they had been compelled to take this action.After a series of debates the Joint Shop Stewards Committee on the 7 September rejected the 'redundancy plan'. It was now clear that the council could run out of money not in December but in a matter of weeks.

## LIVERPOOL'S ACTUAL RECORD

The most disgraceful feature of the 'redundancy notices' issue was the completely disloyal backstabbing methods of the right-wing Labour and trade union leaders, led by Kinnock at the Labour Party conference a few weeks later. It remains an incontestable historical fact that Liverpool's socialist council did not carry through one single redundancy. Indeed, it created more than 2,000 jobs, built 4,000 council houses with front and back gardens, sports centres and even a park.

The same claims could not be made by those who denounced *Militant* and Liverpool city council over the 'redundancy notices' tactic. In Sheffield, for instance, those like David Blunkett who subsequently pilloried *Militant* carried through a retrenchment programme which eliminated many thousands of local government jobs. The same story was repeated elsewhere.

Once the option of the 'redundancy notices' was defeated the Joint Shop Stewards Committee met and proposed an all-out strike to force the government to aid the council. We commented:

> The confrontation looming between Liverpool and the government is entirely due to Tory policy... What makes Liverpool special, apart from the fact that it is a city with exceptionally poor housing and high unemployment, is the fact that it has a council which is determined to stand up to the Tories' policy.[6]

Pointing to the frenzied headlines in the capitalist press, we warned:

> It is not even ruled out that the Tories would be stupid enough to use troops to run some council services, although this would only harden the council workforce and strengthen solidarity action elsewhere.[7]

The *Daily Mail* even painted a lurid picture of those in council care and 'approved schools' being evacuated "to the Isle of Man". Kenneth Baker, the Environment Secretary who had replaced the hapless Jenkin, denied the government were considering the possible use of troops in the event of council services collapsing, but admitted:

> The government has general contingency plans for the maintenance of essential services throughout the country. It is up to the council to put things right.[8]

## ALL OUT?

The decision to go for all-out strike action initiated a period of unprecedented and widespread political debate that spread far beyond the council workforce to all corners of the city. The pioneers of Trotskyism in the city in the 1930s had wistfully looked towards the day when a mass meeting under their influence would take place in the Liverpool boxing stadium. Now the outline of this scenario was beginning to take shape. One section of the workforce after another trooped toward the stadium to discuss and debate the merits and demerits of an all-out strike. Local cafe owners and pubs ran out of food and beer as workers poured into and out of the stadium.

Unfortunately, the teachers voted narrowly not to come out on strike. This caused great bitterness amongst other workers and was a considerable boost to the government and the opponents of the council.

The leadership of the teachers at this stage, was typified by Jim Ferguson, a member of the Communist Party. GMBATU members however, in a series of mass meetings, voted by 4345 to 2934 in favour of all-out strike action. UCATT's shop stewards voted by 54 to four to recommend strike action which was upheld at mass meetings. The TGWU also voted by a massive majority in favour. The majority of manual workers had now voted in favour of strike action. 58 per cent of GMBATU members voted for strike action. UCATT members voted by three to one and the TGWU also voted by a majority to come out on strike. Of the manual unions only the EETPU, had voted against. Therefore, the decision as to whether the council workforce would undertake an all-out struggle lay in the balance pending a decision of the leaders of NUPE and NALGO. 'Ultra-democrat' Jane Kennedy of NUPE refused even to sanction a vote on the issue amongst the 2,700 NUPE members. Her behaviour was not lost on low-paid NUPE members whose jobs were at stake in this battle.

In the aftermath of the 25 September strike these workers, many of them very low-paid women workers, almost mobbed Jane Kennedy at an unprecedented NUPE branch meeting. Hundreds turned out, blocking Dale Street and forcing the NUPE leadership to abandon the meeting. It was NALGO leaders Graham Burgess and Peter Creswell who played a crucial role in relation to a call for a strike on 25 September. They were on record in favour of strike action but did absolutely nothing to campaign in favour. On the contrary they expressed negative feelings about the effectiveness of strike action. At the mass meeting in the stadium, the NALGO leaders formerly put the motion for strike action, but were heavily defeated by 3,891 to 1,455.

## 7,200 MAKE A STAND

*Militant* commented:

> The 7,200 workers who voted for an indefinite strike took a conscious decision to make an enormous sacrifice in order to defend their livelihood.[9]

However, in view of the split in the labour force the councillors, heavily influenced by the arguments of *Militant*, had to take a fateful decision on the early evening of 24 September. The question was posed: should the manual workers, despite being in a minority, unilaterally take strike action? The manual workers had voted solidly in favour of strike action and would have been able to 'tie up' the city if they had come out. The caretakers alone could have closed all the schools in Liverpool. The only branch of the GMBATU which had voted against strike action was in the Education Department, which was led by Convenor Peter Lennard who was not a *Militant* supporter. Indeed he was later to become an opponent of *Militant.*, for a mixture of personal and political reasons. Amongst those sections of the workforce where *Militant* supporters were in strength or had a decisive influence, the case was put firmly and the majority of the workers, in a secret ballot, voted for strike action.

The total vote of all workers was 7,284 for strike action and 8,152 against. In this situation to have gone ahead with all-out strike action would have resulted in a split between the trade unions, with the possibility of conflicts on the picket lines, which would have been exploited by the press and all the opponents of the council. Therefore, while saluting the workers who voted in favour of strike action, particularly the manual workers, the stewards recommended that the all-out strike be called off. Acquiescence to this decision was achieved with some difficulty. Many council workers, such as members of the security force and cleansing workers who had most to lose if the council was defeated, congregated at the Town Hall to await the decision of the stewards. It also seemed as if the world's media were gathered outside the Municipal Annexe that evening. The press at one stage had to be protected from the anger of these workers, and only the intervention of *Militant* supporters from amongst the stewards, prevented a violent assault on the press corps. Frustrated in the call for all-out strike action the stewards of the manual workers then decided to recommend that a one-day strike go ahead the following day, 25 September. We commented:

> Tens of thousands of workers demonstrated their defiance of the Tory government in Liverpool on Wednesday. Hundreds of banners from trade unions, Labour Party and LPYS branches from all parts of Merseyside and all over the country were held aloft by the mass of marchers. There was not a hint of resignation or defeat.[10]

The Labour and trade union leaders were determined to crush Liverpool and the dangerous example which showed that 'militancy pays'. While in Liverpool, on the evening of 24 September, Anthony Bevins, *The Times* political correspondent, confided to a *Militant* supporter that Kinnock was planning a "bombshell" against us. Kinnock was confident that this would effectively eliminate the influence of Marxism in the city.

Fifteen months later, after Kinnock had tried every measure to undermine support for *Militant* the same Bevins, having shifted his journalistic allegiance, was to write: "He [Kinnock] had not broken the Trotskyists and never will". [11]

## LABOUR PARTY CONFERENCE

The issue of *Militant* dominated not just the Labour Party conference, but the Liberal, Tory and the SDP conferences. David Alton, Liberal Chief Whip, demanded that Neil Kinnock "expel Militant leaders of the council." Four cabinet ministers at the Conservative Party conference, led by Tebbit and Thatcher, denounced *Militant* and Liverpool City Council. They also demanded that Neil Kinnock carry through the expulsion of *Militant* from the Labour Party. Indeed, Thatcher took it on herself in the House of Commons to taunt the Labour leadership and demand that they take action against the Marxists.Thatcher, on behalf of the capitalists was the real instigator of the witch-hunt against *Militant*.

Yet an opinion poll carried in the *Sunday Times* on 29 September showed that the electors of Liverpool would vote Labour by an overwhelming majority. 55 per cent said they would vote Labour, 34 per cent SDP/Liberal Alliance, and eleven per cent for the Tories. This represented an incredible nine per cent increase in Labour's share of the vote since the 1984 elections.

## KINNOCK'S GROTESQUE SPEECH

But all of this was of secondary importance to Kinnock as he prepared to send a signal to the ruling class. Not one syllable of Kinnock's tirade will be accorded any importance by history, save for his venomous assault on the heroic Liverpool city councillors which outdid even the Tories in its viciousness. Not a word of support was uttered for the struggles of Liverpool council in defence of the workers of the city and yet not a word of criticism was made either about those Labour councils such as Rhondda, Newcastle or Wakefield, which had provoked strikes by privatisation, closure of nurseries and other cut backs. His infamous statement about the alleged "grotesque chaos of Labour councils hiring taxis to scuttle around the city handing out redundancy notices to its own workforce", produced pandemonium in the Conference Hall.

Eric Heffer, National Executive Committee member, and MP

for Liverpool Walton, stormed off the platform. Boos and catcalls greeted Kinnock's statement. While the Liverpool councillors were in power, from 1983 to 1987 not one worker was made redundant. Unfortunately, the same could not be said of Neil Kinnock. In the autumn of 1987, he pushed for 40 real redundancies amongst staff at the Labour Party's Walworth Road headquarters.

Kinnock's attack provoked widespread indignation throughout Liverpool. The council telephone exchange was jammed with calls of protest. It was interpreted by the great majority of Liverpudlians as yet another attack on the city. The whole Labour Group was united in its condemnation of Kinnock's attack. Even right wingers like Roy Gladden and Joe Devaney, prospective parliamentary candidate for Mossley Hill, were at one with *Militant* supporters in repudiating Kinnock's speech. The Liverpool Labour MPs were unanimous in their condemnation. Bob Parry, the Riverside MP, denounced Kinnock as the "biggest class traitor since Ramsey MacDonald".[12]

The capitalist press greeted Kinnock's speech with hosannahs. The press were demanding not just action against Liverpool councillors and *Militant* but also against Bernie Grant: "Give Bernie Grant the boot", declared the *Daily Express*.[13]

At the Tory Party conference the following week Tebbit declared:

> Nothing could have really changed until extremists and the *Militant* were thrown out of the [Labour] Party altogether. The Labour Party is not going to be able to hide Mr Scargill, Mr Hatton and Bernie Grant under the cloak of moderation. We must not let Mr Kinnock rest until he moves those people from positions of power in his Party.[14]

At the beginning of 1985 Labour stood at 38 per cent in the opinion polls. Two years later, after the assault on *Militant*, which went hand in hand with the jettisoning of left policies and the attack on the reselection of MPs, Labour's popularity remained at the same level. It subsequently sank to 31 per cent in the June 1987 general election. The immediate effect of Kinnock's speech was that it guaranteed *Militant* had the biggest and most successful meeting ever at a Labour Party conference:

> Around 700 delegates and visitors made the *Militant* Readers' meeting the biggest and liveliest ever. The meeting was on Tuesday night,

just after Kinnock's attack on Liverpool council, and this gave an added edge and spirit to the meeting. The contributions and discussion, and the magnificent collection of over £2,100 for the *Militant* fighting fund - the highest ever - was the best reply to Kinnock's slurs and mudslinging.[15]

The meeting was broadcast live on *Channel Four News* at 7 o'clock.

## KINNOCK ATTACKS THE MINERS

Kinnock followed up his attack on Liverpool with a dirty speech, which brought tears to the eyes of miners and their wives present in the conference hall, when he refused to support indemnification of the fines incurred by the miners' union by a future Labour government. He also opposed the future lifting of the surcharge on the councillors in Liverpool and Lambeth. He claimed that no other government had ever acted in this fashion. Yet in 1975 the Labour Government had passed the Housing Finance (Special Provisions) Act to indemnify councillors fined and disqualified for failing to obey the Heath government's Housing Finance Act obliging them to put up council rents. Because of a rebellion by the Labour right in the Commons, this legislation did not protect the Clay Cross councillors who had taken the lead in the rent struggle that year.

Despite Kinnock's intervention, the conference passed a motion calling on a Labour government to recompense the miners and reinstate sacked miners. It also upheld an NEC resolution which promised indemnification for councillors. But the right wing and the capitalist press corps who were present in force were eagerly looking for the defeat of the motion supporting the Liverpool struggle.

The debate at the conference was one of the most rigged in the recent history of the labour movement. A number of right-wing speakers were lined up to lambast the council and *Militant* supporters. The only supporters of Liverpool allowed to speak in the debate were Derek Hatton and Tony Mulhearn. The right wing could not prevent this since they were moving and seconding the motion.

Kinnock was not rewarded for his assault on Liverpool. On the contrary, more blood was demanded from him. Tebbit, in a debate in the House of Commons on 12 December noted:

> We Conservatives wish the leader of the opposition well - it is always good when he pops in to listen to the debate - in his forthcoming purge of Militant Tendency supporters... in Liverpool and in other cities.
> A furious Kinnock retorted: "Forget it."
> But Tebbit would have none of it: "Can we forget the purge so soon? Will there be a purge in Birmingham and Manchester?"

And when the Labour leadership (energetically and verbally) protested at Tebbit's tactics, he linked Kinnock with Liverpool's 'desperadoes': "We have seen the attitudes and tactics of *Militant* Tendency tonight.'[16]

## MILITANT RALLY AT THE ALBERT HALL

If the attack on Liverpool and Militant was meant to cower us it had the opposite affect. For the first time *Militant* had organised its National Rally at the Albert Hall. Reporting on the event *Militant* stated: "5,000 people cheering for socialism in the Albert Hall. £26,587 raised in the fighting fund collection. Last Sunday's *Militant* Rally broke all records." Alongside myself and Ted Grant spoke Harry De Boer, veteran of the workers' struggle in the USA, one of the pioneers of the flying pickets in the Minneapolis general strike of 1934 when he was shot in the leg. He had also met Leon Trotsky in Mexico in 1940 and was imprisoned for his opposition to the second world war. At the age of 80 Harry De Boer had not lost any of his socialist and revolutionary commitment, telling the rally:

> Trotsky told me, a trade union movement alone cannot solve the problems of workers. You need a Labour Party controlled by a democratic trade union movement. Lots of people are elected to office and then forget who put them there and why. Our slogans in 1934 were "every member an organiser" and "make Minneapolis a union town". The labour movement's slogans internationally should be "Organise the world's workers" and "workers of the world unite".

Alongside him spoke Terry Fields who declared:

> The gloves are off. The people of Liverpool are fighting back as never before under the banner of Liverpool city council. They are resisting the lies, filth and distortion of the press.

Jack Collins, the general secretary of the Kent NUM, declared: "We have got to project what socialism means... if we are to protect the interest of the working class."[17]

This rally, which "broke all records", was the best answer to the venomous press campaign and that of the right wing of the Labour and trade union movement.

# 29.
# WINSTON, WESTLAND & WAPPING

APART FROM the Liverpool drama the most important events in the closing months of 1985 were the "inner-city explosions". A black woman, Cherry Groce, was shot in the back in the presence of her children by police in Brixton. The protests led to clashes between youth and police in the area. We commented:

> For most of the youth involved it was a spontaneous expression of frustration and anger. At the same time, as in all such situations, a minority can use the spontaneous lashing out at all the local symbols of authority and wealth as a cover for assaults on local people, thefts from homes, and even rape.[1]

A week later Cynthia Jarrett of Tottenham, north London, died during a police raid. This led to the Tottenham riots in which one policeman, PC Blakelock, was killed. We commented:

> No one, least of all socialists, can condone rioting. But on an estate where more than half of the 16 to 18-year-olds are unemployed, where police automatically treat blacks as 'suspects', it is understandable that the brutal use of the police force can easily spark off rioting where any available weapon is used.[2]

Winston Silcott was jailed for this murder, but after a big campaign over years, the conviction was overturned. Winston, however, remained in prison as a result of an earlier conviction, which is also being challenged. The campaign, led by his brother George, has continued to seek Winston's release. George has spoken at many of our meetings, including the rally that launched *Militant Labour*, and our first conference.

## WESTLANDS

At the beginning of 1986, just at the time when Thatcher appeared to be safely ensconced in power, having seen out Galtieri and the miners, the Westland crisis detonated. We commented:

> The public strife within the Tory Party over the Westland affair has given workers a revealing glimpse of the greed, deceit and hypocrisy of the ruling class. Behind their facade of respectability, and statesmanship lies the reality of businessmen, politicians and top civil servants motivated by their own self interest. Only their greater interest in protecting their wealth and power from the workers forces them to patch together a public face of unity and common purpose.[3]

Heseltine, who at the time of the Westland affair was denouncing back-stabbing practices largely because it was carried out by Thatcher, was himself prepared to use precisely those methods when it suited him. It was Heseltine who insisted on the prosecution of Sarah Tisdall and Ponting, under the Official Secrets Act for daring to reveal what was going on within his department over cruise missiles.

The fate of the Westland workers was secondary in this cynical battle for money, power and prestige by a handful of tycoon's and their political friends. Dave Nellist in Parliament called for the nationalisation of Westland and its incorporation into a renationalised British Aerospace. Exposing the complete hypocrisy of the Tory government and the split in the ranks of the capitalists, he said:

> In February 1971 the Prime Minister Heath took one night of parliamentary time to push through a bill to take Rolls Royce into public ownership. A year ago Lawson, through the Bank of England, bought and effectively nationalised Johnson Matthey Bank for a nominal £1.[4]

He demanded the nationalisation under workers' control and management of Westland and the aircraft industry of Britain.

Thatcher survived the crisis over Westland. But she subsequently admitted that she, and her entourage, were fully expecting that she would be forced to resign. She had reckoned without the ineptitude of Neil Kinnock. He also subsequently admitted that his lamentable parliamentary performance had thrown a lifeline to Thatcher.

Not just Thatcher's fate but that of the whole Tory cabinet was at stake. Two cabinet ministers had been forced to resign, Heseltine and Brittan, and another, the Solicitor-General Mayhew, almost followed them. Thatcher hung on because of the complete ineptitude of Kinnock.

## WAPPING

It was working people who were to pay dearly for the dereliction of their elementary duties by the Labour leadership. They were looking for deliverence from rapacious Thatcher capitalism with the election of a Labour government. None more so than the printers in Fleet Street. Rupert Murdoch had declared war on them. He had sacked all his Fleet Street workers and was printing his papers in a new plant at Wapping. He had thrown down

> a challenge to the entire trade union movement. If he wins, one of the best organised battalions of the working class will have been vanquished.[5]

Murdoch had exploited every opportunity provided by his friends in the Tory government to use the laws which they had introduced against the unions. The print workers had a proud record of union organisation which had improved wages by which all workers had benefited. The government was in complete disarray over the Westland scandal and they had still not dared to proceed with the sacking of GCHQ workers for fear of the massive industrial action which this would provoke. It was clear that Thatcher and the print bosses could have been forced to back down if there was solid united action.

> As a first step the TUC has no alternative but to expel the EETPU for its strike-breaking activities at Wapping. At a time of industrial war, there is no place within the ranks of organised labour for a body which not only does nothing to support the struggle to defend trade unionism but actively mans the barricades for the enemy.[6]

The EETPU leadership had collaborated with Murdoch in supplying the scabs who had taken the jobs of Fleet Street workers at Wapping. Right from the outset, we had demanded all-out strike action throughout Fleet Street and the newspaper industry generally. The paper also went further and said that action would not be effective until printworkers come out on "all-out industrial action". Printworkers should absorb the lessons of Warrington and the miners' strike. Pressure should be exerted on the general council of the TUC for effective action, a one-day general strike of all workers in support of the printers. But:

> activists at every level have to take the responsibility for convening mass meetings of the membership in the workplaces and the union branches, to explain the issues at stake and to generate action from below to achieve a national mobilisation.[7]

As the dispute intensified so also did the repressive methods of Murdoch's protectors, the police. In mid-February we reported the comments of a 17-year-old girl who was amongst 5,000 demonstrators on the regular Saturday night picket which was attacked by the police:

> Police snatch squads attacked after a section of us were forced into a barricaded street. I was pushed in the face and was grabbed by my hair... Another girl and myself were caught by surprise and knocked to the ground. My head hit the pavement... The police fought as if it was an all-out class war.[8]

And the answer to Murdoch's all-out war?:

> The only possible course of action is to deepen and extend the dispute... Already the *Express* wants a 50 per cent cut in their workforce. *The Guardian* wants a massive job cut. The fate of every print worker depends on the outcome of this struggle. The print bosses are out to smash the pre-entry closed shop, the bedrock of our strength.[9]

## ANGLO-IRISH AGREEMENT

While class war had broken out on the streets of Britain, once more in Northern Ireland a dramatic escalation in religious sectarianism had taken place. This had been provoked by the Anglo-Irish agreement between the British and Southern Irish governments. Massive Loyalist protest demonstrations had taken place with the threat of an all-out Loyalist stoppage looming and a whole series of sectarian incidents taking place.

*Militant* pointed out:

> The agreement has changed nothing for the working class. Poverty remains, 22 per cent of the workforce are unemployed. A quarter of total household incomes comes from social security benefits, as opposed to 14 per cent in Britain as a whole. The real solution of the Tories is cuts and more cuts. A drastic cut in the Housing Executive budget will mean that in the financial year of 1986-87 a grand total of 15 new 'Executive' homes will be built in the western half of the province.[10]

At the same time, the repression continued unabated, as was shown by the shooting of a 20-year-old Catholic youth, Francis Bradley. He was killed by army undercover units in South Derry. The "shoot to kill" policy was clearly in operation.
*Militant* concluded:

> For the working class, both Catholic and Protestant the agreement, far from leading to a solution, will make things much worse. It means a continuation of poverty, added repression, and a huge increase in sectarianism... Only the Labour and Trade Union Group has been alert to the dangers. They have demanded a special rank-and-file conference of the trade union movement to discuss how to prevent the further division of the working class, and also to present a socialist alternative to the Anglo-Irish deal.[11]

The most tragic fall out of Thatcher's blunder in proceeding with this deal was the escalation of sectarian murders. *Militant* supporters in Northern Ireland also suffered in July 1986. Colm McCallan, a prominent and courageous member of *Militant Irish Monthly* and the Labour and Trade Union Group, Colm McCallan,

> was shot by Loyalist assassins outside his home in North Belfast in the early hours of the morning. Colm was only 25 years old, was an ex-production worker and a member of the Amalgamated Transport and General Workers' Union, who had become a *Militant* supporter in 1981. He was extremely proud of his socialist ideas, once remarking that joining *Militant* was the most important decision he had ever made.

We reported:

> His killers are almost certainly the same UVF gang which murdered

Catholic building worker Brian Lennard, on Belfast's Shankill Road a few days earlier. Like him, Colm was shot because he was assumed to be a Catholic.[12]

He was one of a number of martyrs who had laid down his life for socialism, workers' unity, and the ideas of *Militant* and *Militant Irish Monthly* .

# 30.
# THE FIGHT AGAINST THE WITCH-HUNT

IN BRITAIN political martyrs were being created by the actions of the right wing of the Labour Party who were continuing a relentless campaign against the leaders of the Liverpool council struggle. The right wing of the Labour Party prepared to expel them from the party, while the District Auditor prepared the ground to drive them from office. The months of December 1985 and January 1986 was the time of the "Great Slander", as the attacks on Liverpool reached a peak. The Liverpool struggle, like the miners' strike, illuminated the gross bias of the capitalist-controlled media in the modern epoch. Every single leader of *Militant* at local and national level was singled out in a campaign of unprecedented personal vilification. The TV programme *World in Action* was perhaps the worst example, with a vicious character assassination of Derek Hatton undertaken by so-called "investigative journalists". Any attempt by Derek Hatton to reply on the programme to the accusations made were either edited out or he was shouted down. Even the *Sunday Times*, not noted for its sympathies with *Militant*, admitted: "This was not an interview, this was an interrogation."[1]

The unprecedented media barrage was grist to the mill of the right wing. They dropped any pretence of fairness or that an unbiased approach would be adopted. This was summed up by Tom Sawyer, who, speaking at the national executive committee of the Labour Party in February, 1986 said, "I defy anyone to tell me how you can go to Liverpool and defeat *Militant* by argument." [2]

It was clear that brutal organisational measures, a mass purge, was on the agenda irrespective of any outcome of the inquiry. Kinnock, demonstrating clear personal spite - fatal for any political leader - was carried away by his 'war' against *Militant*.

One of his aides said on *Granada* Television, "Kinnock hates *Militant* more than he hates the Tories."[3]

The NEC inquiry was to drag on for almost a year and was to bedevil and split the labour movement throughout this period. The capitalist media had a field day in creating the impression of a Labour Party divided and riddled with "loony lefts" and "crooks". The dispiriting, not to say demoralising, effect of these developments on the labour movement was expressed in the Tynebridge parliamentary by-election on 5 December 1985. Labour won but with a turnout of only 38 per cent.

*The Times* demanded a far wider purge. Its editorial comment singled out Diane Abbott and Bernie Grant for expulsion. We correctly warned that "the attempt to purge the Labour Party of Marxism could cause Labour to lose the next general election."[4]

While the NEC Turnock enquiry was taking place *Militant* supporters did not sit on their hands waiting for the blow to fall. On the contrary, an enormous fight back campaign was launched throughout the country. This kicked off with an enthusiastic meeting of 800 people who poured into the Manchester Free Trade Hall to hear Derek Hatton and myself, together with John Tocher, Broad Left candidate for the AUEW presidential elections.

This was followed by meetings of more than 1,000 in London, 1,300 in Glasgow, 1,300 in Edinburgh, 1,000 in Newcastle and one of the biggest meetings of the labour movement in Sheffield, of 700. Even in Neil Kinnock's constituency of Islwyn, 500 workers turned out to greet enthusiastically the speeches of Derek Hatton and myself at a meeting in a local school hall. The mean minded local right-wing supporters of Kinnock on the local council took their revenge later by prosecuting me, as editor of the *Militant*, for posters which had been put up advertising the rally, for which we were fined £400.

These meetings were attended by more than 50,000 workers and comprised the biggest meetings since the miners' strike, in some areas the biggest for 40 years.

These events prepared *Militant* to face up to the witch-hunt that was under way in Liverpool. Despite the fact that at least 100 Constituency Labour Parties, four District Labour Parties, 65 trade union organisations, 15 Women's Sections, over 100 branch Labour Parties, 107 LPYS branches and nine Labour Clubs had passed resolutions against the witch-hunt and the Liverpool enquiry, the right wing and the "soft left" were hell-bent on expelling the Liverpool *Militant*s. After 60 hours of questioning 120 Labour Party members, tens of thousands of pounds wasted on wages, hotel bills, fares, including air flights to Liverpool and Scotland, the investigation team did not produce a single shred of evidence to back up the dirty allegations of "physical abuse" or "literal corruption" made against Liverpool *Militant* supporters. Moreover, the inquiry team where sharply divided. Two members, Audrey Wise and Margaret Beckett, rejected the witch-hunting measures of the right-wing majority and produced a minority report.

The report of the majority repeated some allegations, but in a roundabout, vague and nit-picking way. Tucked away in it was the admission:

> The investigation team do not take seriously all allegations of *Militant* activities in Liverpool... However, there are undoubtedly a large number of supporters of the broad line taken by the *Militant* in Liverpool, and others who are prepared to go along with most of the policies, particularly whilst *Militant* has appeared to be the only credible focus of left-wing activity within the party in Merseyside.[5]

The majority report concluded that 16 party members be re-invited to answer questions, with the clear implication that expulsions would follow. The DLP was suspended and two full-time officers were appointed to police the party. In place of the DLP was appointed a "Temporary Co-ordinating Committee". In place of the democracy of the DLP, with massive attendances of 700 or more, deliberate steps were taken to restrict attendances. So much for the argument that *Militant* and the left supported the idea of "small unrepresentative caucuses" and that the right wing of the party stand for "mass involvement". Indeed, the subsequent history of the Labour Party from 1986 onwards demonstrates irrefutably that while the right wing would like a "mass" paper membership, like the devil fearing holy water, they are opposed to the mass involvement of ordinary members in the running and control of the party.

The minority report of Beckett and Wise, while making a number of proposals about the reorganisation and efficient running of the DLP, completely opposed the main recommendations of the majority. It warned of the "terrible dangers" of expulsions based on unprovable assertions. The right-wing majority on the NEC however were impervious to such warnings. The capitalists, through their press and media, had made it clear that the litmus test for Labour's "fitness to govern" was the expulsion of *Militant* and the neutering of the left.

At this time George Robertson MP, leading light of the right-wing Solidarity group, had called for an investigation into Tony Benn because of his opposition to NATO. The Labour Party's head of information, Peter Mandelson, even approached the BBC's *Question Time* programme to try and get Tony Benn taken off the panel in the week when the expulsion issue was coming up at the NEC.[6]

## 1,000 LOBBY NEC

On the morning of 26 February, the day when the NEC was to meet to consider the DLP enquiry reports more than 1,000 workers, *Militants* and non-*Militants*, gathered in a massive display of opposition to the NEC outside the Labour Party headquarters in Walworth Road.

Someone blundered: Derek Hatton and Tony Mulhearn were waiting in a room at the front of the building. Not ones to miss an opportunity, they opened the window and waved to the crowds - a scene transmitted by all television channels.

At the NEC Eric Heffer spoke for virtually all Labour Party members at that time in Liverpool when he said to Kinnock: "I shall never forgive you for what you've done to my party and Liverpool."[7]

The right wing throughout the enquiry had promised a proper opportunity for any "defendant" to challenge any spiteful smears and allegations made against him. One of the charges against Derek Hatton was that he was a "full-time or part-time worker for the *Militant* Tendency". Yet everybody knew that he worked for Knowsley Borough Council.

It was quite clear that the show trial being prepared by the right-wing majority on the NEC would not conform to natural justice.

While at the same time conducting a massive campaign within the ranks of the movement in opposition to expulsions the "Liverpool 12", the most prominent "defendants" decided to seek an injunction in the High Court to prevent the NEC from proceeding. Those charged had not been allowed to see the evidence, they would not be allowed witnesses in their defence and moreover the nine members of the enquiry team would not be able to vote impartially at the NEC meeting because it was they that had drawn up the charges against the accused.

Just 24 hours before the NEC were due to meet, a High Court Judge had likened the NEC proceedings as similar to those of a "supergrass" system. This judgement threw the leadership into turmoil. A sensible leadership would have cancelled the proceedings in order to ponder the implications of the judgement. Not so Kinnock and the right-wing majority of the NEC. Kinnock's attempt to proceed resulted in the most open, public and visible split in the NEC of the Labour Party ever seen. Frances Curran, Tony Benn, Eric Heffer, Eric Clarke, Jo Richardson, Joan Maynard and Dennis Skinner dramatically walked out of the meeting making it inquorate. The left members of the NEC who had walked out of this "Star Chamber" received the same kind of vilification which the Liverpool *Militants* had been subjected to over months and years.

The *Financial Times* gave a hint at why *Militant* had been successful:

> Tireless dedication and hard work for the party and potential voters was a principal means through which *Militant* deservedly accrued a moral basis for its power in Liverpool. Will the less politically zealous be able to find the same energy? Constitutional battles still have to be fought at a practical level.[6]

The NEC in effect was forced to drop the majority report and completely changed tack. They would no longer be relying on the majority report as evidence. They also altered the charges in pursuing the 12 members of the Liverpool labour movement. The evidence that the NEC would now use consisted of advertisements and leaflets for *Militant* meetings, and press reports of these meetings and rallies. The pretence of the 12 being expelled for "malpractices" in the running of the DLP, "intimidation" and "reprehensible trade union nomination rights" was exposed. The main criteria for carrying through expulsions was that people like Derek Hatton and Tony Mulhearn had spoken at "*Militant* meetings".

And yet it had been revealed that Kinnock himself had spoken on a platform at a meeting organised by *Militant* supporters at Swansea University in October 1980! At that meeting attended by

150 people Neil Kinnock had even given £5 to the *Militant* Fighting Fund.

In a witch-hunting atmosphere the NEC met on the 21 May to consider for the tenth time the first of the cases, that of Tony Mulhearn. Despite his effective rebuttal of all the charges he was duly expelled at 1 o'clock in the morning. The next day Ian Lowes was expelled.

In an attempt to create a smoke screen of 'fairness' they dropped the charges against Harry Smith. On going into the NEC he introduced the "friend" he was allowed to have with him: "This is George Knibb: it's a pen name." A Liverpool *Militant* with a sense of humour! This impression was reinforced when Larry Whitty said to Harry, "I suppose you know everyone here?" Harry replied: "Yes, I watch *Spitting Image*!" Afterwards the right tried to give the impression that Harry Smith had given "assurances" to the meeting, but when he left the NEC he made it absolutely clear that he would continue to support *Militant* and appear at *Militant* meetings in exactly the same way as before.[8]

## £35,000 PER EXPULSION

The majority report had cost the NEC in total £100,000, £35,000 per expulsion. Derek Hatton was finally expelled in his absence (while on council business) in late June. Back in Liverpool the party refused to accept the expulsions. Tony Mulhearn's constituency Garston voted by 46 votes to two not to recognise, "this insane action of the right-wing dominated NEC."

## PAT WALL WINS AGAIN

Pat Wall had been selected once more as the parliamentary candidate for Bradford North by the June NEC and he was endorsed when expulsions of other *Militant* supporters were taking place. This contradiction arose from the fact that we still enjoyed colossal support amongst the ranks of the Labour Party and the unions. The right wing were prepared to go against the views of the members of their own party in the case of Derek Hatton and Tony Mulhearn because of the ferocious pressure exerted by Thatcher, the Tories and their media. But in the case of Pat Wall his popularity was so widespread, built up over years of campaigning for Labour, a marvellous speaker at Labour Party conferences, that an attempt to block his nomination or even expel him would have provoked an even greater uproar than in other cases. Even these considerations were to be swept aside later on when Terry Fields and Dave Nellist were drummed out of the party despite their immense popularity. Pat Wall did not live to see these events. Having been selected in 1986 and elected in 1987, he would have met the same fate as Dave and Terry in 1991-1992.

An example of the great popularity of leading *Militant* spokespeople was shown at the Durham Miners gala in July. Derek Hatton had been invited to march with the Wearmouth Lodge, despite the fact that he had suffered a broken leg playing football. He hobbled on crutches at the head of their contingent. A local paper reported:

> Derek Hatton, expelled from the Labour Party for supporting the Militant Tendency, got one of the biggest cheers of the day at the Durham Miners' Gala yesterday. When he marched past the guests standing on the balcony of the Royal County Hotel, Neil Kinnock prominent amongst them, he waved his crutches, and shouted, "You won't get rid of me that easy, lad." He was applauded not just by the crowd but by almost all the guests on the balcony. Neil Kinnock looked acutely embarrassed and retreated into the Hotel.[10]

*Militant* appeared to be everywhere. Even the sports pages unearthed "Militant activity", this time in relation to cricket. The *Daily Telegraph* wrote:

> About 100 anti-apartheid protesters chanted slogans and waved banners as England drew their match with Trinidad yesterday... the demonstration [was] against the England side, which includes five players who have been to South Africa... Among the protesters outside the Queen's Park Oval in Port of Spain was a Militant Tendency supporter, Mr Mark Sarll, 22, an unemployed graduate from Chatham, Kent. "I wanted to show my support for the anti-Apartheid movement here", he said.[11]

## LIVERPOOL LOCAL ELECTIONS

An even more powerful demonstration of *Militant*'s popularity was shown in the May local elections in Liverpool. We declared:

> The election results last week were a disaster for the Tories and a triumph for Labour. But they were also a vindication of *Militant* and its supporters.[12]

We quoted an editorial in the *Liverpool Echo*:

> However experts may analyse the votes, there is not a shadow of doubt that Liverpool's Town Hall election results were a success for *Militant*... Nowhere else were the local issues more sharply defined and more important than in Liverpool... No Scouser could have been under any illusion that a vote for Labour in this city yesterday was a vote for *Militant*.[13]

The Tories ended the election with only seven seats on the council. But the election also represented a bitter defeat for the Liberals. Of the seven seats the Liberals gained, only one was taken from Labour, in Dingle Ward. Even there Labour only lost by 31 votes with a Communist Party candidate taking 44 votes. *Militant* commented:

> After the defeat of the council's budget campaign in November last year, with the impending disqualification of 48 Labour councillors, the threatened expulsion of leading party members and two years of unparalleled vilification, Labour's vote is little short of marvellous... In Speke, Felicity Dowling, one of those threatened with expulsion, romped home with a majority of 1,800, "Everyone knew exactly who I was and what I stood for", she commented, "I've been identified by the party leadership as undesirable, and 71 per cent disagreed."[14]

Other councillors identified with *Militant* also did spectacularly well. Moreover, in other parts of the country *Militant* supporters were elected to a number of councils. Particularly encouraging were the results in Glasgow, where the victor in the Pollokshields/Shawlands ward was Margaret Dick, "self-confessed *Militant* supporter". In Musselburgh, in Edinburgh, *Militant* supporter, Keith Simpson, was elected to the Lothian Regional Council. In Brighton a *Militant* supporter was elected to the council as were supporters in North Tyne, the Wirral, Coventry and London.

The right must have been extremely disappointed, as the Labour Party Young Socialists Conference at Easter once more demonstrated the high morale and fighting spirit of our supporters.

The highlight of the conference was the Saturday night "Labour Unity" Rally. As Derek Hatton and other speakers entered the room the audience rose to its feet as one, clapping, whistling and roaring its welcome. When Derek Hatton rose, he was unable to speak for several minutes due to the deafening applause. He challenged Neil Kinnock to a public debate with the time, venue and chair of Kinnock's choice:

> Then the rank and file can decide what they want. Intimidation has become a new word for democracy. If the right win a vote, it's democracy, if they lose it's intimidation.[15]

Although *Militant*, as a consequence of the spread of the witch-hunt, was prevented from holding its traditional readers' meeting, visitors and delegates still contributed a magnificent £5,341 to the fighting fund in the course of the weekend.

Notwithstanding all of this support Derek Hatton, Tony Mulhearn, Ian Lowes, Tony Aitman, Richie Venton, Cheryl Varly, Roger Bannister and Terry Harrison were expelled. They were allowed to appeal to the 1986 Labour Party Conference in Blackpool.

They demanded the NEC should allow the media, particularly television and radio, to carry the debate live. When the eight arrived at the conference on the morning of 28 September, they repeated their request. This was refused by the NEC. Derek Hatton and Tony Mulhearn then led a walk-out of the eight from the Conference Hall. They were met by the world's press, mingling with many Liverpool *Militant* supporters cheering them to the echo.

Derek Hatton's statement was carried in all the papers and on the television that evening:

> We are not prepared to give credibility to a farce. We're not prepared to see a British labour movement that is more akin to Stalinist Russia.[16]

The union block votes were mobilised to crush the Liverpool *Militant*s; but 263 constituencies, nearly half of the total, plus the bakers' and the furniture workers' unions still voted against expulsions. The capitalist press the next day outdid themselves in the vitriol directed against the Liverpool *Militants*. Having exhausted all suitable adjectives to describe *Militant* supporters - maggots, corrupt, termites, intimidators - the *Daily Mirror* editor decided that *Militant* supporters must come from outer space! Its headline read "Defeat of the Aliens".[17]

In Liverpool, however, the Labour Group still continued to recognise Derek Hatton and Tony Mulhearn as members. This enraged Kinnock who threatened a wider purge if the expulsions were not accepted. After some discussion and debate and with great reluctance it was agreed amongst *Militant* supporters to recommend to the broad labour movement that Derek Hatton and Tony Mulhearn should not attend Labour Party meetings. This was done in order to prevent the closure of Labour Parties and other expulsions of comrades.

Repression against the Liverpool *Militants* through the Labour Party's national executive committee enquiry went hand in hand with an open assault by the forces of the capitalist state. We have detailed (in Chapter 21 of *Liverpool - a City that Dared to Fight*) the spiteful and systematic pursuit of the Liverpool councillors for defending the working class and hard-won rights and services of the city. On 8 September the District Auditor McMahon imposed a £106,000 surcharge against the Liverpool councillors, dismissed them from office, and banned them from holding any office for five years. On the same day, the Lambeth councillors received a surcharge of £126,947 from the Metropolitan District Auditor, Skinner.

The legal appeals of the councillors, although ably presented, were nevertheless turned down by the capitalist courts. The High Court's decision to uphold the District Auditor's surcharge and disqualification of the councillors was met with complete silence by the leadership of the Labour Party. We commented on the attitude of the Labour leaders:

> While the Tories are using the courts to crucify councillors, Kinnock is mis-using the Labour Party's constitution to do the same. On the same day that this judgement was made, a Tory minister announced the diversion of £500 million from the cash starved inner cities to the Tory shires. What were the Labour Party and trade union leaders

doing? The general secretary of the Labour Party was busy cooking up charges to expel some of these councillors from the Labour Party.[18]

One of the most outstanding aspects of the Liverpool struggle was that following the fining and banning, ordinary workers rallied in support of the councillors with bucket collections in the city centre. Cash also flowed in from trade unions and Labour Parties all over the country in a massive collection to pay the fine. Upwards of £600,000 pounds was collected over a period to pay off the fines of the Liverpool councillors. The campaign to raise money was largely undertaken by *Militant* supporters, who collected mainly from workers.

# 31.
# MILITANT AT HIGH TIDE

IN EARLY May *Militant* reported from Wapping:

> Last Saturday, in some of the worst scenes of violence ever seen in this country, the police unleashed a vicious attack on print workers, women and children. Demands were immediately raised to stop Fleet Street. SOGAT London Machine Branch members agreed there and then to push for this... Now should be the time to widen the action and advance to victory.[1]

The trade union leaders, in confining the dispute to News International, were isolating the strike and limiting the strike's effectiveness. The boycott campaign of Murdoch's papers was not enough. As the News International bosses felt that they were getting the upper hand, punitive action was taken against those who were in the front line of defending the print workers.

There were numerous arrests on the picket line, including many of our supporters. But the police went beyond the picket line:

> On 13 August two police officers arrived at the home of Peter Jarvis, London NGA member and *Militant* supporter, and arrested him and his baby daughter, who he was minding at the time. Peter was held in custody for ten hours. This was an act of gross political victimisation.[2]

Peter had been named in an injunction by TNT, the firm used by Murdoch for his scabbing operations, alongside five other print union members. This restrained them from "encouraging", "participating in" or in any way "facilitating" any unlawful gathering outside the TNT premises. There was a very quick and effective campaign to get Peter released because there was not the slightest shred of evidence that he had been responsible for actions in any way unlawful. The police attempted to put Peter in a line-up where he would stand out like a sore thumb: "I was in an old pair of jeans and an old sweater. All the others had neat trousers and white shirts."[3]

As a result of mass pressure he was released by the police. The role of *Militant* supporters was shown in incidents like this. By the beginning of 1987 the Wapping battle had been going on for a year. If anything, the tempo had been stepped up, particularly on the side of the police, who at the end of January once more mercilessly beat demonstrators.

While this was happening the general council of the TUC had in effect abandoned the printworkers and allowed the scab union, the EETPU, who were in collusion with News International at Wapping, to escape scot free. The NUJ leadership had also been hesitant about taking disciplinary action against the Wapping chapels who had repeatedly crossed the picket lines. Because the Fleet Street NUJ members made up the bulk of finances for the unions the NUJ leadership trod carefully. In February the union leaders threw in the towel. The year-long fight put up by 5,500 sacked printers had shown the combativity of the working class. It had also shown the lengths to which the bosses' state would go to defend their interests. More than 120,000 police days were given over to the struggle to defend "law and order". £14 million had been spent on the policing bill - £4.6 million of it on overtime. There had been 1,462 arrests on the picket line and one death, Michael Delany, aged 19, who had slipped under the wheels of a Murdoch truck on his way home from a party. He was not connected with the dispute.

Murdoch in effect doubled his profits to £2 million a week by the use of scabs. Once more an employer had carefully prepared the ground to take on the unions. He had been bolstered by the anti-trade union laws introduced by his friends in Parliament. The union leaders had been warned early on that a battle loomed. There is no doubt that if decisive action had been taken earlier, the whole strike could have been avoided. We commented:

> Murdoch's forces had been concentrated into Wapping. His weakness was elsewhere. The whole News International empire should have been put under siege. But the threats of sequestration hemmed the union in around the confines of Wapping... *Militant* had constantly urged the use of the one asset the courts couldn't sequestrate - the solidarity of the print workers. To win a victory the strike had to be extended to the other sections. The most vulnerable were the Fleet Street workers,

who should have taken solidarity action. The union leaders ran scared, conceding to the demands of other proprietors many of which were similar to Murdoch's. This has resulted in the loss of over 10,000 jobs in Fleet Street... It should be remembered that two print workers Mike Hicks and Bob Shirfield, are still in jail.[4]

Above all, the general council of the TUC backed up the EETPU collusion with management by refusing to expel them from the TUC.

## JOHN MACREADIE ELECTED

The growing importance of *Militant* in industry was underlined by developments in the CPSA. The election of John Macreadie as the new general secretary of the union had sent a frisson of fear through the ranks of the right wing, throughout the trade unions generally as well as in government circles. When the results were announced John Ellis, the right wing candidate, commented: "I took a short break because I thought it was the last chance I would get for a holiday for some time. I thought I would be general secretary."[5]

On the most flimsy pretext, the right wing moved to invalidate the results. John Macreadie, nevertheless, declared on national lunch-time TV: "I'm the new general secretary of the CPSA."[6]

The right trotted out the usual accusations of "ballot rigging", despite the fact that John Macreadie had been elected in probably the fairest election in the history of the CPSA. The right then proceeded to move heaven and earth to have his election blocked. We reported: "Right wing hijack CPSA":

> The right wing have decided to overturn the democratic wishes of the membership... The members voted for a new leadership, but the right wing have declared no confidence in the membership. They have hijacked the union, putting in the defeated candidate.[7]

A ferocious campaign by the left then opened up in the unions. Legal action was also taken in an attempt to stop the coup of the right wing against the democratic wishes of the members.

However, with the help of the judiciary, the right frustrated the members' democratic decision in electing John Macreadie. The courts sanctioned the re-run of the election for the general secretary. All the stops were then pulled out in support of John Ellis, the right's candidate. He won with 42,000 votes to John MacCreadie's 31,000. He was helped into power by the splitting tactics of Broad Left 84, dominated by the Communist Party, who put up its own candidate, Geoff Lewtas, who received 13,000 votes. In the House of Commons a right-wing Tory MP, Peter Bruinvels and two other Tory MPs welcomed "the victory of John Ellis in the ballot".[8] There was a tremendous sense of disappointment amongst left activists in the union. But rather than undermining *Militant* support it strengthened it for the battles to come.

Indeed, John Macreadie was soon elected onto the general council of the TUC, the first ever *Militant* supporter to hold this position. At the TUC Congress in September 1987 he emerged as a significant figure, standing for the fighting traditions of trade unionism and opposing the policies of despair summed up in the "New Realism" of the right-wing general council. This aroused the ire of the capitalist press. Even before the TUC Congress had finished the London *Evening Standard* carried the statement of John Ellis CPSA General Secretary under the headline "*Militant* hounding me out". He complained that "a campaign of vilification and victimisation" had been taken against him; the union had decided that his Opel Senator car was not his and if he wanted a car he should buy one. The new left-wing controlled National Executive Committee of the union had also linked his pay to that of a Senior Principal Secretary in Whitehall and awarded him a £5 per week pay increase. Moreover, his American Express card, to pay for "official union business" was also withdrawn. He received £26,000 per year while many CPSA members were on as little as a £110 per week after tax.[9]

## ALBERT HALL ROCKED

The by now traditional *Militant* rally,

> was a magnificent success and a sharp rebuff to those who thought that support for the paper was in decline. But more than anything else it was a triumph for political ideas.[10]

For the first time lasers were used at a mass rally in Britain. There was grudging recognition that *Militant* was here to stay:

The Tendency determined to show that the past year's setbacks had left it bloodied but unbowed, joined rock-and-roll effects with political rhetoric in a slick and seamless display.[11]

Even the *Daily Telegraph* commented: "Militant Tendency demonstrate its defiance with a glossy high-tech rally at the Albert Hall."[12] The *Daily Mail* followed suit: "It was *Militant* with lasers, cabaret and amplified music which came to London to prove it was not beaten yet."[13] While the *Financial Times* commented: "*Militant* organised a defiant, full hearted gathering... it remains very much alive and totally unrepentant."[14]

The fighting fund collection exceeded even the previous year's incredible target, reaching a final total of almost £35,000. Surprisingly even arch right-winger Frank Chapple in the *Daily Mail* commented: "The spectacular 5,000-strong Militant Tendency rally in London's Albert Hall was an impressive show of strength."[15] Michael Cassell in the *Financial Times* reported:

> About 5,000 *Militant* supporters gathered to participate in a rally which, with its dramatic laser light show and video review of 1986, displayed a professionalism and passion that easily challenged Labour's conference at Blackpool.[16]

This journal, one of the main organs of big business, commented on the speeches:

> The cheers were reserved for people such as Mr Tony Mulhearn, for 23 years a Labour Party member until his expulsion by Labour's national executive committee. Mr Mulhearn defiantly holding on to his post as President of Liverpool District Labour Party, recited its achievements in Liverpool, including creating 10,000 jobs in the construction industry and building 4,500 new homes... Mr Peter Taaffe, Editor of *Militant* and another expelled party member, stated that: "It was a devastating indictment that, after a seven year-long nightmare' the Tories stood any chance of re-election. If the Labour leadership opened a door to another five years of Thatcherism, it would never be forgiven by the working class." The undisputed hero of the day, however, was Derek Hatton, who said he still spoke, despite the Labour purge, as deputy leader of Liverpool city council.[17]

*Militant number one (above) and Peter Taaffe Editor 1964-92 (right)*

*Editorial board: left to Right Clare Doyle, Peter Taaffe, Lynn Walsh, Ted Grant and Keith Dickinson*

*Militant on the march (above) 1971 and (below) 1981*

*Militant Rally- Albert Hall 1985 (above)*

*Militant Rally- Ally Pally 1988 (below) left Bob Wylie, Ronnie Stevenson, Claire Murray, far right Pauline Wall*

*Clare Doyle (above)- For many years Militant's national treasurer, (now an international worker for the CWI)*

*Bellow the 1985 Rally collection , almost £30,000 - three years later a record breaking collection of £52,000*

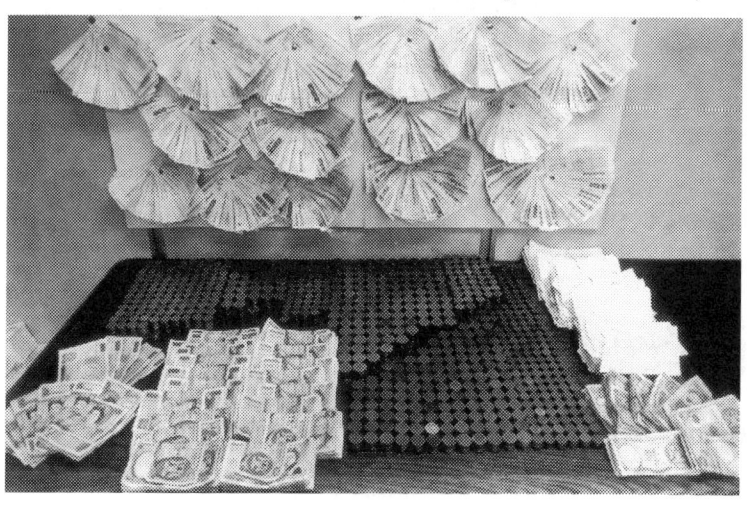

Pat Wall

Ray Apps

Just before Terry Field's first speech in Parliment (left to right) Tony Saunois, Clare Doyle, John Pickard, Terry Fields MP, Peter Taaffe, Dave Nellist MP, Ted Grant, Brian Ingham, Laurance Coates

*Lobby against expulsions in Islwyn - fifth from right Alec Thraves*

*1984- Miners demo - Terry Fields(left) with LPYS contingent*

*Hannah Sell*

*Paul Jones (centre), Gerry Lynch (right) in Derry 1972 - return to find the army had blown up their parked car!*

*Derek Hatton addresses one of the Liverpool City Council Demos flanked by Bob Wareing MP (left) and Tony Mulhearn (right)*

*Andrea Enisuoh, a Militant supporter and first black women elected to the NUS NEC*

*Below- Lesley Mahmood- on right, speaking at our meeting at 1991 Labour Party conference, with Julie Donovan, left, and Martin Smith*

*Peter Hadden, Secretary of Northern Ireland Militant Labour*

*Derek Hatton at the Durham Miners Gala*

*Alan Hardman cartoonist, designer, printer, engineer - one man production army!*

Margaret Creear

Lois Austin

Militant contingent on Demo against domestic violence - far right Jose Tierney (Terry Field's agent) and Lesley Mahmood (then a councillor)

*Battle of Turnbull Street- October 1991 - back left George McNeilage*

*Christine McVicar*

*Alan McCombes*

Alan Hardman's cartoons have appeared in Militant for over twenty years. On the following pages are just some of his outstanding work.

The final three cartoons are from Jim Blair, a Scottish firefighter, who's work of the last few years has added to our campaigns.

# VIETNAM PEACE!

"...To robbery, butchery and rapine, they give the lying name 'government', they create a desolation and call it peace..." TACITUS in 98 AD, on the Roman Emporers

"THERE IS NOTHING TO STOP ANY CITIZEN CROSSING A PICKET LINE IF HE BELIEVED IT RIGHT TO DO SO, I WOULD NOT HESITATE TO DO SO MYSELF" James Callaghan, House of Commons, January 23rd

DO NOT ADJUST YOUR SET - THE DISTORTION IS DELIBERATE.

WILL WE BE ABLE TO BUY IT BACK AGAIN WHEN I LEAVE SCHOOL DAD?
REDUNDANCY PAYMENT
CLOSED

# CHILE 'DEMOCRACY' RESTORED

Militant 14 September 1973

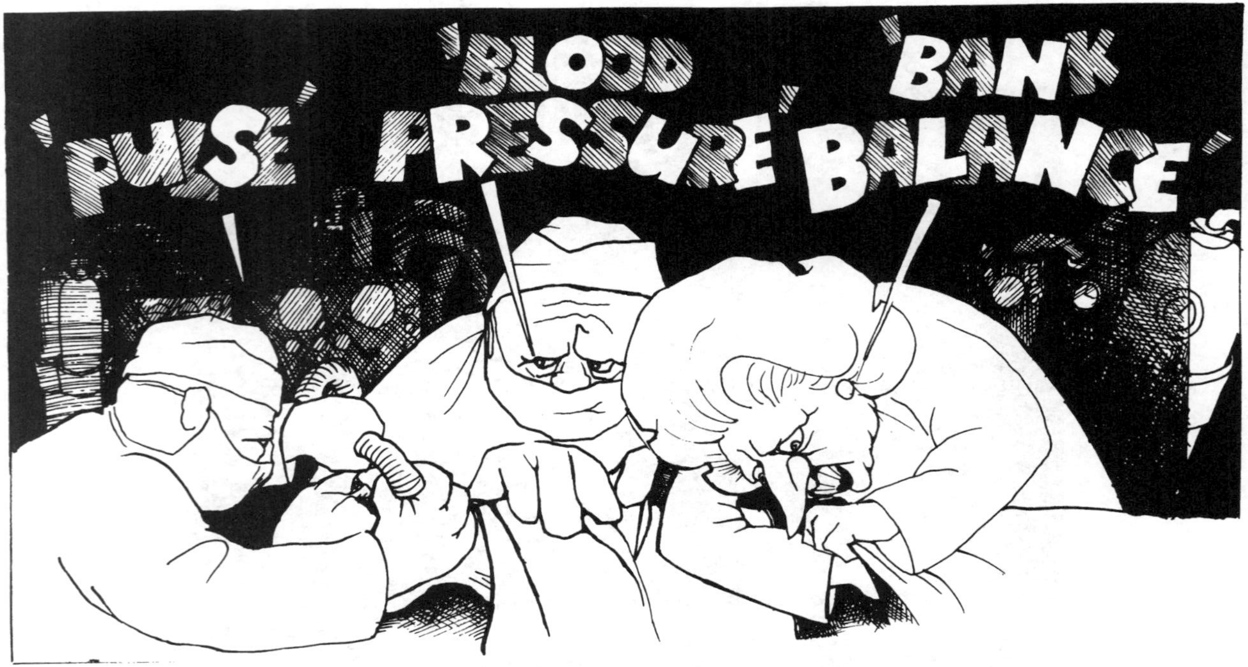
'PULSE'
'BLOOD PRESSURE'
'BANK BALANCE'

NO-TO THATCHER'S NUCLEAR CRUISE

HOLY GHOST MY BACK SIDE!!
THAT'S AN OBVIOUS CASE OF CO-HABITATION
AND IF I'M NOT MISTAKEN
THREE ILLEGAL IMMIGRANTS AS WELL

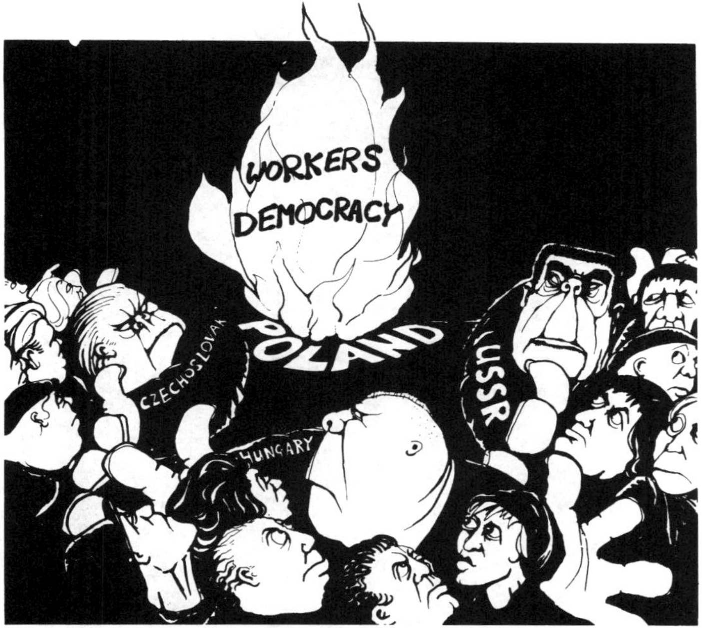


'MOVE ALONG COMRADES.. WE'LL MAKE SURE IT DOESN'T SPREAD'

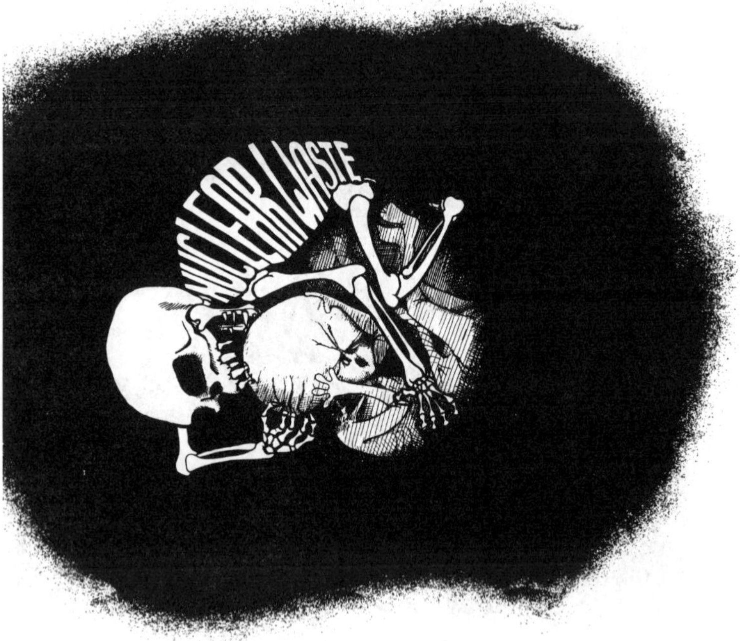
NUCLEAR WASTE

## The Role of the State

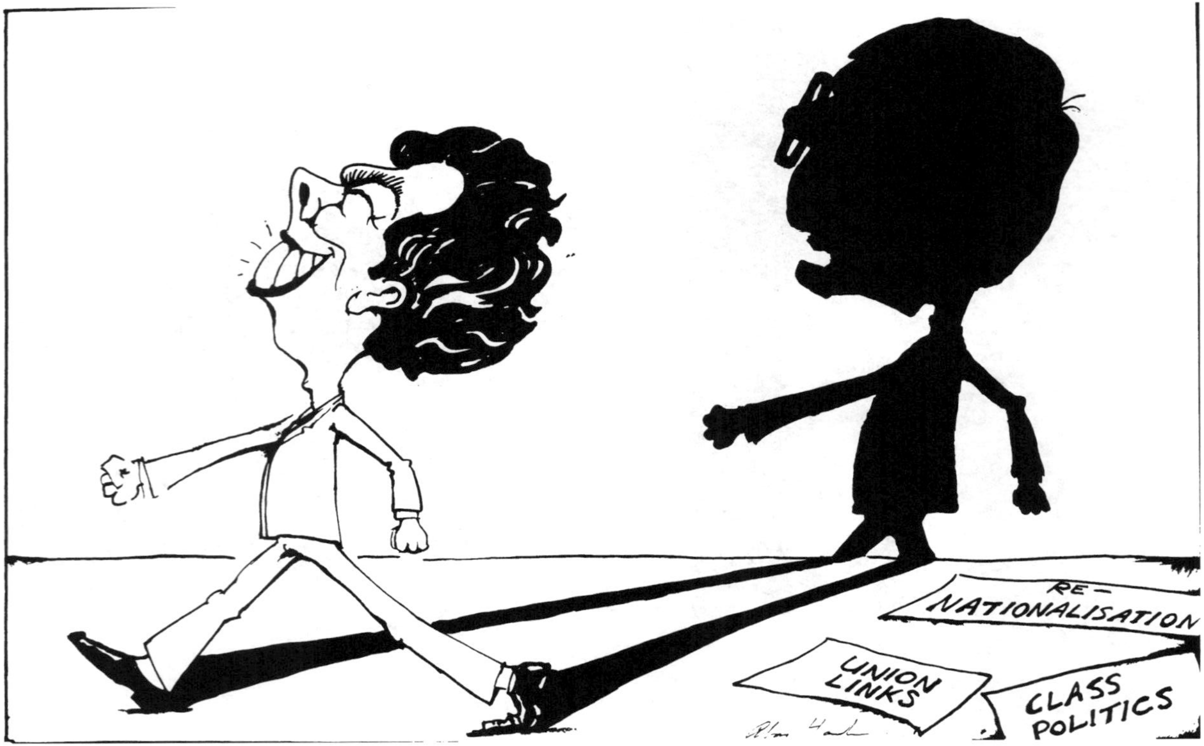
RE-
NATIONALISATION
UNION
LINKS
CLASS
POLITICS

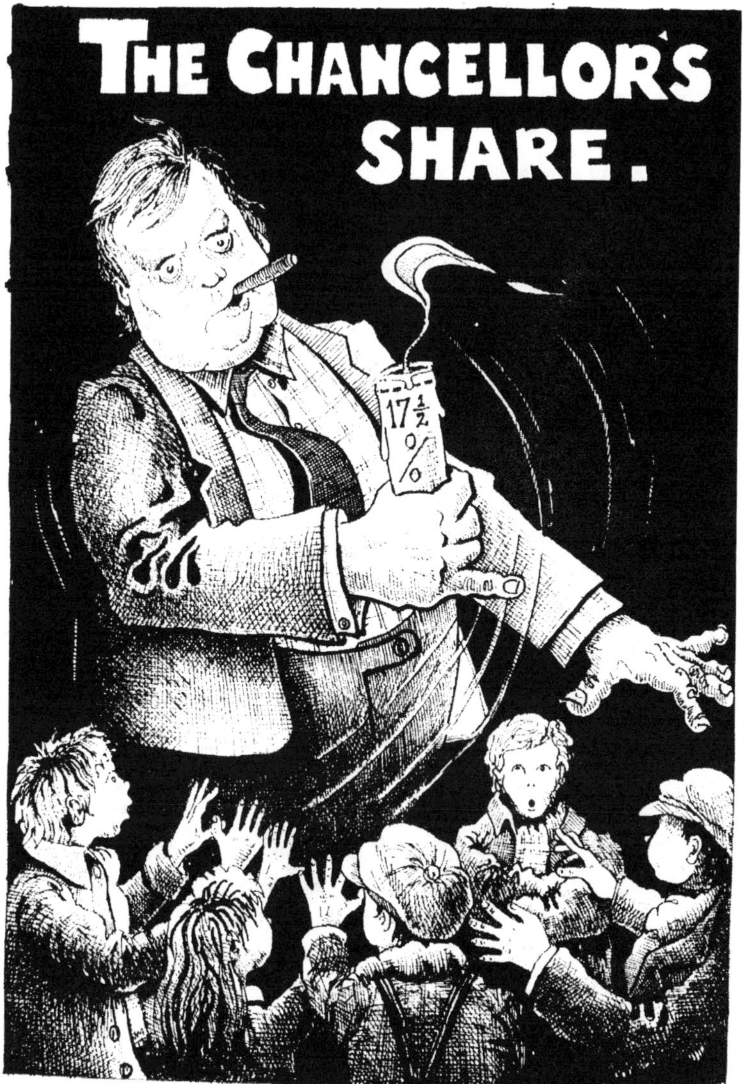
THE CHANCELLOR'S SHARE.
17½ %

He used to be a Bailiff but he wanted a job that was easier than collecting Poll Tax!
BLAIR.

PROFITS
BLAIR

# 32.
# 1987 GENERAL ELECTION

THE 1980s have been pictured in some quarters as grim years for the labour movement, with little combativity and preparedness to struggle on the part of the working class, reflected in a diminishing number of strikes. In truth the early part of the decade was characterised by the bitterest class conflicts Britain had witnessed since the 1926 general strike. Even during the latter part of the decade, as the Reagan/Thatcher "boom" took hold, the preparedness of working people to struggle was evident. However, cowed by the anti-trade union laws and the defeat of the miners and the printers, the national trade union leadership invariably raised the white flag. All these ingredients were present during the battle to save Caterpillar in Scotland in 1987. This was a struggle to save one of the last remaining elements of the manufacturing base of the Scottish economy. Faced with closure, the Caterpillar workers at the plant at Tanochside decided to occupy. They became a beacon to workers throughout the redundancy ravaged West of Scotland. A big solidarity movement began to develop, shown particularly with cash donations. *Militant* recorded the magnificent response of workers to the Caterpillar workers' action. We also outlined a strategy for victory. The stewards' approach was to "politically pressurize Caterpillar management into reversing its closure".[1] However, after meeting the Scottish Office the management killed off any prospect of withdrawing their closure.

In a series of articles we pointed out that the argument of the management that closure was due to "overcapacity" was false: "The demand for tractors in the Third World is enormous. A publicly owned factory could sell them at non-profit levels to satisfy the demand."[2]

The solution,

> which all socialists must push for, involves continuing the occupation

to build a campaign for the nationalisation of the plant. If Thatcher and the Tories can nationalise Johnson-Matthey Bank for £1 and immediately write off hundreds of millions in debt, how can a profit-making factory and its workforce be sacrificed?[3]

In the months that followed the occupation there were huge demonstrations in support of the workers' occupation. An estimated 8,000 marched through Uddingston just outside Glasgow. Bystanders cheered the demonstration and the LPYS contingent, as ever the most vocal, received tumultuous applause to shouts and songs; "Fight for jobs - Save the Cat" and "We want nationalisation". The Caterpillar workers' inspiring action provoked sympathy worldwide, with the first steps taken toward an international Caterpillar workers' combine committee. A mass demonstration of 5,000 in Glasgow at the end of March was followed by the Caterpillar workers voting by a small majority to continue their action. But they had not reckoned with the national Labour and trade union leaders. Disgracefully, Neil Kinnock, who had visited the West of Scotland on 30 January, was unable to fit "into his schedule" a visit to the Caterpillar workers. He had actually been at a Labour Party Scottish Executive meeting and then a "Burns supper" in nearby Motherwell.

But the decisive action in ending the occupation came from the leaders of the engineering union, the AEU. In agreement with the Advisory, Conciliation and Arbitration Service (ACAS), they had forced the Joint Occupation Committee to accept an agreement which gave them very little. As the workers went back they declared: "We've been sold down the river Jordan" (Bill Jordan was president of the AEU).[4]

In fact the key role in ending the occupation came from Jimmy Airlie, AEU official and then a member of the Communist Party, who threatened to wrest control of the dispute from the JOC and conduct a secret ballot or mass meeting himself. He threatened the workers that unless they accepted the agreement the union would isolate them and remove all financial support.

The role of the right-wing trade union and Labour leaders in battles such as this, and later on the issue of the poll tax, was to undermine the confidence of a section of the Scottish working class in Labour. It also played into the hands of the nationalists. *Mili-*

*tant*, by taking a principled position, backed up by energetic support for workers in struggle, increasingly took on the role which the Communist Party in the past had done; mobilising class fighters who also have an idea of how workers' struggles can be succesfully concluded.

## HERALD OF FREE ENTERPRISE

March 1987 witnessed the sinking of the *Herald of Free Enterprise*, at Zeebrugge. Adding to *Militant*'s feelings of outrage over the tragedy - entirely due to the employers' lust for profits - was the knowledge that Geoff Haney, a *Militant* supporter had been killed. In honouring Geoff, a "Marxist fighter", we commented:

> We should be in no doubt that the real tragedy lies in the fact that those business magnates of P&O Lines who Geoff fought against were responsible for his and over 130 other deaths.[5]

He had been a National Union of Seamen representative, for which he had been continually victimised. He had been to Chile where he witnessed the horrific conditions facing the workers. He had risked his job to protect three Chilean Socialist Party stowaways who were caught on board the ship and locked in the hold. He wrote an article vividly exposing the harsh barbaric tortures of these youth and the cruelty of the shipping company. In lines that are as relevant now, we commented:

> some local seamen have said that "it was a matter of 'when?' not 'why?'"... the boat was top-heavy for profit. The danger of water in the car deck is well known. Why else would notices "Not to be opened at sea", relating to tank covers, be welded to the car deck floor in full view of all employees?[6]

## TOWARDS THE ELECTION

Faced with an approaching general election the attention of the working class and the labour movement was transferred from the industrial to the political plane. The right-wing NEC of the Labour Party were preparing for the election by dealing further blows at the left and particularly against the youth wing of the Labour Party, the Labour Party Young Socialists. The right proposed a series of measures which they calculated would undermine our influence within the LPYS.

All of this was taking place when it was clear that the election of a Labour government could depend on the 6.2 million 18-25 year-olds. Sixty per cent of these had declared that they would not vote, with only 1.1 million intending to vote Labour. One of the reasons for this was the failure of the Labour leadership to adopt a fighting youth programme, as suggested by the LPYS: grants for young people, full-time education for those over 16 and the demand for a minimum wage. However, the attacks of the right could not prevent another succesful LPYS conference at Easter with more than 2,000 young delegates and visitors pouring into Blackpool.

Ron Todd, general secretary of the Transport and General Workers' Union, declared at the conference that the unions should not run away from taking on the Tories; weakness only encourages people like Thatcher. The *Militant* Readers' Meeting was banned from the Conference Hall, but although it was held four miles away and 1,600 came on buses, it was another successful event as shown by the £7,000 fighting fund collection. The conference had become a magnet for all workers seeking assistance in struggles. Strikers from Caterpillar, Moat House, HFW Plastics, Salford Plastics, Ardbride, Keetons, Derby Trader, Hangers and a large delegation from the civil service dispute, all attended the conference.

## ELECTIONS - MILITANT VINDICATED

Soon after came the test of the local elections and general election. Between May 1986 and May 1987 Kinnock and his advisers were obsessed with the need to "root out" and destroy the Liverpool *Militants*. But it took the Tory House of Lords, which banned Labour councillors from office, to put control of Liverpool city council temporarily in the hands of a Tory/Liberal junta. Some unions voted not to collaborate with an unelected administration. The Liberal-dominated regime went ahead with the restoration of the Mayor's office, with Lady Doreen Jones, the wife of Liberal leader, Trevor Jones, receiving the chain of office.

Ribald jokes about "jobs for the family" were widespread in the city. The Marxists christened her "Doreen the Brief". Despite the claims that the "*Militant* era was buried" the local government election results showed exactly the opposite. In Liverpool, the "loony left" tag would not stick. The council had consistently concentrated on those issues close to the working class of the city: jobs, local council services, education, and the marvellous house building programme.

The real question in the 7 May election: would Labour, with its Marxist leaders, be vindicated for its historic stand in the city? All commentators, without exception, were convinced that Labour was heading for a resounding defeat but Labour with *Militant* supporters in a prominent position, threw themselves into the campaign and the result on 7 May was a magnificent victory for Labour. In some respects, it eclipsed Labour's victories in the previous four years. We reported:

> Last Friday the phones of Liverpool socialists were buzzing with calls from throughout Britain: What a result! Congratulations, you've given us all a real boost in our area. "Last laugh for Labour", was the *Daily Post* headline.[7]

"An amazing bounce back after the disqualification of 47 Labour councillors by the House of Lords," was the dumbfounded admission of the rabidly anti-socialist *Liverpool Echo*.[8] Even Norman Tebbit commented: "Quite extraordinary. It's going to take quite a lot of thinking about for all of us."[9]

On a night when Labour lost seats to the Tories in Manchester, Blackburn, Crewe and the Midlands, Labour was spectacularly successful in Liverpool. Election pundit Anthony King, speaking on BBC's *Newsnight*, remarked: "Liverpool has declared political UDI."[10]

The turnout was 50.2 per cent, five per cent up on the previous year and only just below that of 1984, when the elections were held in the middle of the dramatic struggle and on the eve of a famous victory. In some wards the turnout was 59 or 60 per cent, something which was unique at that stage to Liverpool council elections. The most spectacular results were in those wards in which well known *Militant* supporters were candidates. A significant body of workers had consciously differentiated not only between Labour, and the Liberals and Tories, but also between right-wing Labour and those who stood on the left. It was not uncommon on the doorstep for Labour councillors to be met with the statement: "I am Labour, but I'm *Militant* Labour." Others demanded to know where the Labour candidate stood on the issue of the defence of the debarred Councillors. Many commented that they were reluctant to vote for imposed candidates.

The "Liberal counter-revolution" had lasted only six weeks in Liverpool. That was enough. The right wing of the Labour Party tried to cover up the role of *Militant* and pretend that it had nothing to do with this splendid victory. But not so the bosses' press. *The Economist* commented:

> Liverpool produced the most paradoxical result. The Alliance had a lead of 0.1 per cent over Labour, but Labour regained control of the city council by a majority of three seats. The three point rise in Labour's share of the votes since last year suggest that most of Liverpool's working-class voters have accepted *Militant*'s explanation of Liverpool's financial crisis. The continuing collapse of the Tory vote - only 9.5 per cent of Liverpudlians now vote Tory - shows that the government's version has been rejected by Liverpool's middle class too. Liverpool's present bewildered local mood deserves much more attention than it has received. It cannot comfort Mr Kinnock.[11]

Once the 1987 general election had been declared and the battle lines had been drawn *Militant* supporters threw themselves into the fray together with the rest of the labour movement. There were four Labour parliamentary candidates subscribing to our ideas standing in this election. Terry Fields was fighting to hold on to Broadgreen in Liverpool as was Dave Nellist in Coventry South East. Pat Wall was once more standing as the Labour candidate for Bradford North, but this time with a much better chance of success. Alongside of them was John Bryan, selected as Labour candidate in Bermondsey. *The Independent's* conclusion was shared by most of the press:

> Richard Pine (Liberal candidate for Broadgreen), 34, is virtually certain to defeat Terry Fields, *Militant*-supported Labour MP at Liverpool Broadgreen.[12]

But they had not taken into account the huge effect of the mighty struggles between 1983 and 1987 on all strata of the population.

This was the main factor in the sweeping victory for Labour in Liverpool and indeed the Merseyside area as a whole when the general election took place on 11 June.

It is true that Labour appeared to have an uphill task in Broadgreen where, unlike in 1983, the Alliance partners fought a united campaign. Moreover, the Liberals were starting from a position of holding 13 out of 15 council seats in the constituency. It would require an election campaign on a much higher plane than even in 1983 to guarantee victory for Labour. Broadgreen Constituency Labour Party had been suspended for more than 12 months before the election, and its officers were under threat of expulsion, yet there could not have been a greater contrast between the campaign in Broadgreen and Labour's disastrous national campaign.

The leadership of the Labour Party relied predominantly on the media and photo opportunities. The Broadgreen campaign was a model, both in political content and organisation. In all seats where *Militant* supporters stood as candidates mass canvassing covered every part of the constituency, with detailed discussions on policy taking place on the doorsteps. All four constituencies were canvassed many times before election day. In general there was no "poster war" because the opposition parties were simply crushed by the sheer numbers of Labour posters displayed throughout each of the constituencies (with the exception perhaps of Bermondsey).

A no less impressive campaign was conducted in support of Dave Nellist. In one weekend 344 copies of *Militant* were sold by door-to-door canvassers in Coventry South East.

In Bradford workers poured in from the whole of Yorkshire and much further afield to support Pat Wall. There was a determination this time to prevent the split in the Labour vote which kept him out of the House of Commons in 1983. During the campaign an eight foot by twelve foot cartoon by Alan Hardman, depicting Thatcher's demolition of industry in Bradford North, was fixed onto the side of a Labour Party member's house. When Kenneth Baker visited Bradford and tried to do a walkabout, a demonstration of teachers and lecturers from NATFHE (the lecturers' union), the National Union of Teachers (NUT) and the LPYS forced him to cut it short. He showed his real views of teachers by calling the demonstrators "a rabble". A council street cleaner working nearby came over to see what the commotion was. When he saw Baker he started waving his fist and shouting "Maggie out". The Women's Section held an election rally aimed at Asian women, with an all-female platform; 20 local working-class Asian women and three other local women attended.

## BERMONDSEY

In Bermondsey where John Bryan had the most difficult task in overcoming Hughes's majority he acquitted himself brilliantly in debates with Hughes and at public meetings. As John Bryan became more and more successful the "nice" Liberal Simon Hughes began a red scare campaign. He put out a leaflet condemning Labour's John Bryan as a "hard and dangerous revolutionary".

There was no clue as to its source other than the name of Simon Hughes's election agent at the bottom. This only served to strengthen support for John Bryan as Labour in turn indicted the Liberals for their shameful record and racist policies in Tower Hamlets.

During the election 72 Bengalis were being evicted by Tower Hamlets council. When Hughes was canvassing a council estate in Bermondsey, an area with many black families, local Labour Party and LPYS activists asked him through a megaphone about the racist policies of his counterparts in Tower Hamlets. An impromptu street meeting ensued, in support of John Bryan. Speeches were made to loud applause from the residents. Hughes looked more and more dejected.

John Bryan halved the Liberal majority with a 2.6 per cent swing towards Labour. Even the humiliated Tory candidate congratulated John on a "professional campaign, easily outstripping the other parties". It was not just "professionalism" which led to such a spirited campaign but the fact that Bermondsey Labour Party, under the influence of our supporters, had rekindled the spirit of real socialism in the minds of the local people. The Bermondsey result was in complete contrast to those in the rest of London. Labour lost Walthamstow, where the local Labour council had increased the rates by over 60 per cent (following the national leadership's strategy). Labour also lost Battersea and Fulham, where a moderate candidate, Nick Raynsford, had received so much praise for winning the by-election the previous year.

Over 200 new members joined Bermondsey Labour Party during the campaign. On the final weekend of the election campaign over 700 took part in a mass canvass. One of the most outstanding successes were the street meetings. Dozens of them were held throughout the constituency. Estates were leafleted beforehand then, at the appointed time, the Young Socialists' "Battlebus" would pull up in the middle of the estate blasting out Labour's theme music: *Rocky IV*.

One indication of the colossal effect of the mass campaigns conducted in constituencies where *Militant* supporters were the candidates was the reception given to Arthur Scargill in Liverpool and Tony Benn in Coventry South East. A thousand people crammed into one Broadgreen election meeting to hear NUM President Scargill speak on behalf of Terry Fields.

Nine days earlier a similar mass meeting in Broadgreen had taken place addressed by Tony Benn.

700 People had also flocked into a public meeting organised in Coventry South East to hear Benn speak on behalf of Dave Nellist. Dave denounced the "millionaire tendency" and its government and called for a Labour victory. At the end of the meeting a pensioner remarked to a steward, "That's what all meetings should be like. A thousand meetings like that up and down the country and Labour will romp home, with or without TV."[13] But Labour did not "romp home". The Tories won again.

Responsibility for this defeat lay squarely at the feet of Kinnock and his cohorts. Labour had only increased its share of the vote by a miserly few per cent. Unbelievably, Kinnock's speech attacking *Militant* and the heroic Liverpool councillors at the infamous 1985 Labour Party conference set to Brahms and broadcast on television, was perceived as the "master stroke" which would ensure a Labour victory. All the capitalist commentators hailed his "brilliant" 1987 election broadcast. Naturally they were quite happy to see Kinnock attacking his own side rather than the Tory enemy. There were of course some bright spots for Labour. Foremost amongst these were the victories of Labour at Liverpool Broadgreen, Coventry South East and Bradford North. Also, as we commented:

John Bryan's splendid campaign in Bermondsey also gave a glimpse at what Labour could have achieved on the basis of a mass campaign fought on socialist policies. Liberal luminary Simon Hughes, despite using every device from the Liberals' dirty tricks department, saw his majority halved.[14]

Terry Fields increased his majority by 60 per cent with an almost 13 per cent swing from the Tories to Labour. Massive swings towards Labour were recorded in all the Liverpool seats. It was not an accident that the five Liverpool Labour MPs - although Bob Wareing wavered and opposed them later on - had remained unshakable in defence of their council comrades.

The victories of the left provoked officials at Walworth Road to comment to the press: "It's been a good night for the nutters."[15]

The architects of Labour's defeat were the leadership of the Labour Party. No real alternative had been spelt out by Labour nationally. Hattersley, the shadow chancellor, had fought on the insane programme of: "Vote for us and we'll increase your taxes." Labour's campaign, designed to win the middle class, had exactly the opposite affect. The skilled workers and home owners were alienated. The number of skilled workers voting Tory increased from 38 per cent in 1983 to 42 per cent in 1987. Labour's performance nationally was abysmal.

During the election ruthless control was exercised from the top. There was very little canvassing, with few election leaflets and public meetings were ticket-only affairs with audiences that were meticulously vetted by Labour Party officials. A media campaign, little different from those conducted in America by the Democratic Party, was supposed to usher in a Labour victory.

## PAT WALL

Soon after entering Parliament Pat Wall, continuing the tradition set by Terry Fields and Dave Nellist, made a fiery maiden speech. He commented on the efforts which the Tories had made in an effort to prevent him from entering Parliament. Indicting the government and British capitalism for the collapse of the former industrial areas of the North he commented:

> When I arrived in Bradford 18 years ago, it was at the time of the

building of the M62... which was to bring renewed prosperity to industrial areas of Lancashire, west, north and south Yorkshire. Now it runs from redundant Liverpool, through de-industrialised Lancashire and West Yorkshire. It bisects north and south Yorkshire, with the closed steel mills and empty pit villages of two eras of MacGregor. It ends in the port of unemployed Hull, where today there are not even any fishing boats.[16]

Looking to the 1990s Pat Wall went on to state:

> I have to tell the good people of East Anglia and the Thames Valley, the majority of whom voted for the Conservative Party in the last two elections, that a further crisis will hit the South more than the rest of the country. It will hit the service and financial sectors. The good people of those areas might find that their dreams will turn to ashes tomorrow, like the dreams of Bradford, Liverpool, Manchester, Newcastle and other workers over the past ten years. I believe that we shall not see the death and abolition of socialism. The people in the southeast and the more prosperous areas will learn, like those in Bradford... that socialism is more relevant than ever.[17]

Pat was to make a huge impact, particularly on the working class of Bradford and Yorkshire in general, which was tragically terminated by his untimely death in 1990.

Shortly after he had been elected Pat Wall came under attack, along with other supporters in his own constituency.

But for the Labour leadership socialist principles were going out of the window, as the Labour Party conference in October demonstrated. There was an inquest into Labour's failure in the general election. The right ascribed their defeat to the fact that the working class, seduced by council house sales and "wider share ownership", had become welded to Thatcher's capitalism. They were completely silent on the socialist victories in Broadgreen, Coventry South East and Bradford North. Eric Heffer reminded the conference that he was an MP with a 23,000 majority in what had been a Tory seat in 1964. He attacked those like Bryan Gould, who peddled so-called new theories of share ownership and moderation. Former Tory voters, "quite a few of them yuppies", came straight over to Labour in Liverpool.

We can win the next general election if we do what we did in Liverpool... We built 5,000 houses, sports centre and put 10,000 workers into employment. That's the way to beat the Tories.[18]

Tom Sawyer denied that there were purges in the party which was met with a groan of disbelief from the conference. Their reactions were understandable given the fact that surcharged Liverpool councillor, Felicity Dowling, lost her appeal against expulsion by five million to 750,000 votes later in the week.

Virtually all the constituencies voted for her, particularly when she challenged Kinnock to "debate our differences in front of the workers of Liverpool and if they vote for my expulsion only then will I accept it". [19] Afterwards, Eric Heffer went up to embrace her in front of the whole conference. He was followed by delegates lining up to shake her hand.

The bureaucratic officialdom which strengthened its domination of the Labour Party in the mid-1980s, was utterly incapable of attracting significant layers of youth into its ranks. A significant section of youth, particularly because the poll tax resulted in a massive refusal to register, had actually dropped out of the political process, big sections even refusing to vote. By the time of the 1992 general election 45 per cent of 18-25-year-olds did not vote.

## THATCHER'S THIRD TERM - HER DEMISE PREDICTED

*Militant*'s main job in the aftermath of the Tories' third successive election victory was to present a balanced picture of the future. All the fainthearts were once more either weeping in their beer or ready to slash their wrists. We commented:

> In the light of her 106 majority, Thatcher thinks that she now has an unassailable position from which she can continue her crusade against socialism and Marxism and finally extinguish "the enemy within". But, important as the election is as a barometer of the mood of the working class, it is for Marxism just 'a moment in history'.[20]

Reality always has two sides, as Karl Marx pointed out. Checked on the parliamentary plane the mass of workers would inevitably seek solutions to their problems outside of Parliament in the period after the election. It tended to be forgotten that Thatcher, just nine months after her 1983 triumph, faced the miners' strike. In

France the Chirac government had not been in power for more than eight months when a movement of millions of students and workers came out onto the streets and routed it. We predicted:

> If Thatcher had retired after two terms, she may have been able to bask in the illusion of her 'success'. Now, like Wellington, she will learn that "nothing except a battle lost can be half so melancholy as a battle won".

The economic, political and social scenario which was likely to open up in Britain, would make it:

> extremely unlikely that she will finish this term. Long before then the Tory Party will be riven with splits and divisions which will make the Westland Affair look like a little local difficulty. She will be forced to go to Dulwich (her private home) before 1992.[21]

Alone amongst non-Marxist as well as 'Marxist' journals, *Militant* correctly predicted the downfall of Thatcher. Moreover it was able to play a crucial role, through the poll tax struggle, in bringing this about.

# 33.
# THE POLL TAX: EARLY DAYS

> "For the first time a government had declared that anyone who could reasonably afford to do so should at least pay something towards the upkeep of the facilities and the provision of the services from which they benefited. A whole class of people - an 'underclass' if you will - had been dragged back into the ranks of responsible society and asked to become not just dependants but citizens. The violent riots of 31 March in and around Trafalgar Square was their and the Left's response. And the eventual abandonment of the charge represented one of the greatest victories for these people ever conceded by a Conservative Government."
>
> (Margaret Thatcher: The Downing Street Years: page 661)

JUST ONE month after the Tory victory, on 17 July, *Militant* carried the front-page headline "Tory Poll Tax Robbery". One result of the general election was to reduce the Scottish Tory representation at Westminster to such an extent that they could now get into two taxis. Thatcher planned to take revenge by first of all introducing the poll tax in Scotland. We pointed out: "the Thatcher family in Dulwich will save £2,300 per year... an average family in Suffolk will pay an extra £640." Addressing the Labour leaders, *Militant* stated:

> We don't just want concessions or amendments, we want this legislation chucked out. The labour movement throughout Britain must campaign around this issue. It is just the kind of extra-parliamentary campaign that can build the Labour Party and the unions... the movement must mobilise and fight back, drawing up plans for non-co-operation and non-implementation of this legislation.[1]

We prepared very early on for a fightback against this measure, above all in Scotland where the poll tax was first introduced. The Scots had voted massively against the Tories but because of the votes of England the Tories were once more in power in Westminster. This stoked up national indignation at the prospect of a further period of Tory arrogance towards Scotland.

Support began to grow for a Scottish assembly: "Opinion Polls show that four out of every five Scots are in favour of some sort of devolution."[2]

As shown earlier, we had long favoured the establishment of a Scottish Assembly. But now given the enormous support amongst the Scottish people for an Assembly, Labour had began, for the first time since the 1970s, to take the national question in Scotland seriously. However, this was accompanied by the bending of the knee to the Tories on other issues. After initially adopting a policy of "non-compliance", i.e. non-co-operation or non-implementation with the poll tax, the Convention of Scottish Local Authorities (COSLA), in September 1987, decided to resume talks with the Scottish Office. Moreover, some Labour authorities, like Strathclyde and Lothian region, were agreeing to massive cut-backs totalling £10 million under the pressure of the government.

*Militant* pointed out that one of the fears of the government of an Assembly was precisely how it could be used, particularly by the left, and the Marxists:

> A left-wing administration in Edinburgh coming into conflict with a Tory government in London would pose a potentially more explosive situation than in Liverpool in 1984/85... the possibility of a left-wing Scottish Assembly, perhaps influenced by the ideas of Marxism, sends shock waves through the ranks of the British establishment.[3]

## LESSONS OF LIVERPOOL

While the lessons of the Liverpool struggle were still fresh, *Militant* decided to produce a book *Liverpool, a City That Dared to Fight*, written by myself and Tony Mulhearn, chronicling the main events between 1983 and 1987.

One of the most welcome reviews appeared in *Militant* itself from Eric Heffer, Labour MP for Liverpool Walton. The very fact that Eric wrote this after the expulsions of the main Liverpool *Militants* had taken place was both an indication of his principled stand and also that it was not possible even then for the right to just trample on the left. Eric correctly saw the Liverpool struggle as an inspiration for future generations of socialists, which will be studied and followed as was the popular struggle of the early 1920s when George Lansbury, one time Labour leader, was the leader of Poplar council...

Whilst not agreeing with all that is said, I do feel it is an important book. Peter Taaffe and Tony Mulhearn have produced a document that all future writers about the struggle will need to delve into for basic source material... The Liverpool struggle, like the miners' strike of 1984-85, was an important part of the class struggle taking place against the Thatcher government. It was 'politics put to the test' and contrary to what some would say, it was a test that the Liverpool councillors and party members passed. Yes, they made mistakes, but only those who do nothing and sit back in their armchairs pontificating about those who do, never make mistakes.[4]

## FIGHTING THE POLL TAX

As one chapter closed on an epic struggle in which *Militant* supporters played a key role, another one opened up. The poll tax was a key issue, in a sense the most decisive, which faced the labour movement in Thatcher's third term of office. Many sections of the movement opposed the poll tax, mostly verbally, but *Militant* gave it prominence and at an early stage pointing to the consequences for the government and Thatcher herself if the poll tax was introduced. At the London launch of the Liverpool book, attended by all the main newspapers, radio and television, I commented:

> The vast majority are opposed to this tax, but the Labour leaders have made it clear that the struggle is to be restricted to Parliament. But the history of this government is that they do not listen to parliamentary speeches. Only when a mass struggle is mobilised, as it was in Liverpool, can the labour movement force the 'Iron Lady' to retreat. Scottish councils have the same choice as in Liverpool. Either they can get the odium of implementing the poll tax or, like Liverpool, say no, refuse to collect it and call a one-day general strike. Otherwise they might as well resign their positions. There is an explosive situation developing on the housing estates. The government has made a big error. The poll tax will involve tenants and owner-occupiers, old and young. The whole position of the government could become untenable if Labour takes a stand on this issue.[5]

Later in the year we drew some general conclusions, which we to underline *Militant*'s approach in the next five years of intense struggle on this issue. The paper commented:

> In the afterglow of her re-election in 1987, Thatcher confidently declared that the poll tax was to be the 'flagship' of her government. The Titanic was the flagship of the British Merchant Navy and considered unsinkable until it hit an Atlantic iceberg! Now the Tories are on a collision course with a far more formidable obstacle - the embittered and mobilised Scottish working class, and only just behind them their English and Welsh counterparts! With clear leadership the labour movement can sink the Tory flagship without trace. When the flagship goes down, the Admiral either goes down with it or is sacked.[6]

Through the poll tax Thatcher achieved what the Labour and trade union leaders had failed to do in the previous nine years - she had united and generalised the struggles of the working class against her government. Previously, she had been very careful not to take on the whole of the working class or to open up an offensive on two fronts. But the poll tax affected young and old, employed and unemployed, the sick and disabled, council tenants and house owners, as well as the black and Asian populations. Thus all except the upper middle class and rich were to be hit by the poll tax.

The fatal error which she and her ministers made was to mistake the stand of the Labour leaders as an accurate reflection of the mood on the ground.

## SCOTLAND

A labour movement campaign against the poll tax was launched in Edinburgh in December 1987, initiated by *Militant* supporters. Soon after this, steps were taken in the West of Scotland, particularly in areas like Pollok, to organise anti-poll tax unions. This led to the idea, promoted by *Militant*, for a West of Scotland Anti-Poll Tax Federation. But before this step had been taken there had been serious discussion both in Scotland and nationally in Militant's ranks, about the programme and the organisational steps to be taken to maximise the greatest possible mass resistance to this measure.

In April 1988 I visited Glasgow for a one-day conference with delegates from every area of Scotland where *Militant* had support and influence. This meeting clarified important tactical issues and gave the green light to *Militant* supporters in Scotland to concentrate on the poll tax as the key issue and to link the struggle with the battle that was likely to develop on an all-British scale later. *Militant*'s attitude was summed up in a centre-page article of the paper:

> This is the biggest single general attack on the living standards of the working class not just from this Tory government, but probably this century... The Thatcher juggernaut is at the gates of Glasgow and Edinburgh. She intends to roll it over the 'whitened bones' of the Scottish labour movement and then trample over the English and Welsh working class.[7]

The April Scottish conference of *Militant* took the decision to organise anti-poll tax unions throughout Scotland and to systematically press for the adoption of a programme whose central demand would be "non-payment" of the tax. At each stage, the fighting approach of *Militant* contrasted sharply with that of the leadership of the Scottish labour movement.

At the Labour Party Scottish conference in March 1988 the delegates had responded enthusiastically to a parade of speakers, including *Militant* supporters, who passionately argued the case for defiance of the poll tax. Dick Douglas, then a Labour MP and who stood on the right of the party, declared: "There is an army waiting to be led down the road of non-payment." He compared Neil Kinnock to "a general leading his troops into battle carrying a white flag." [8]

On the day that the conference had opened, a poll showed that 42 per cent in Scotland favoured an illegal non-payment campaign against the poll tax. Amongst Labour voters the figure was as high as 57 per cent. Yet the speech to the conference by Neil Kinnock was so poor that the Labour loyalist *Glasgow Herald* wrote that it was "universally rated as a disaster".[9]

The conference voted by two to one for a resolution opposing "illegality". It was at total variance with the mood of the vast majority of delegates, particularly from the constituencies. But the trade union tops cast their block votes in favour of the Labour Party's Scottish leadership. Nevertheless it was decided to reconvene the conference in the autumn to reconsider the non-payment option. This gave an opportunity to the advocates of non-payment to mobilise working people in action in favour of this demand. We reported in April that massive meetings on Scottish housing estates had shown that workers expected the Labour leaders to take a lead. In Pollok, Glasgow,

> 400 people packed into a public meeting to establish an anti-poll tax union in the area. "What are we going to do? How can we fight this?" they asked. A shop steward from Govan shipbuilders asked the local Labour regional councillor, "If the regional council is so against this tax then why have they got people running around harassing tenants and intimidating old age pensioners with post cards and registration forms?"

Tommy Sheridan, then a little known *Militant* supporter, declared to thunderous applause:

> We need councillors who are prepared to fight, to stand up now against this tax and lead us into battle. Seventy-five per cent of Scots oppose the tax. One-and-a-half million are willing to defy the law. We need Labour representatives who are also willing to defy the law.

He was elected secretary of the anti-poll tax union in Pollok and

> reminded the meeting of the 47 Liverpool councillors who were prepared to stand firm and defy Tory law. "We need them here in Pollok", was the audience's response.[10]

In July 350 delegates representing thousands of workers in 105 anti-poll tax groups, mostly from community councils and tenants' associations, agreed to set up the Strathclyde Anti-Poll Tax Federation. This conference called unanimously for a mass campaign of non-payment and for Labour councillors to refuse to pursue non-payers. It also called for the Scottish TUC to step up their campaign and organise a 24-hour general strike. Tommy Sheridan was elected unopposed as secretary of the Federation and promised vigorous leadership from the newly elected committee.

## HOW TO FIGHT THE POLL TAX

Just before this conference *Militant* had produced a pamphlet *How to Fight the Poll Tax,* written by Alan McCombes. It pointed out:

> already, a full year before the poll tax is due to be collected, a huge groundswell of resistance is developing in towns and cities throughout Scotland.

But it was "still fragmented and lacking in co-ordination". Alan called for the mobilisation of the widest layers of the working class and for

> public meetings in every town and village, and housing scheme; and above all by a mass campaign of door-to-door canvassing in every locality with the aim of achieving at least a million pledges to refuse to pay the poll tax.[11]

We also reported that at

> a meeting of 180 at Cowglen, a comrade of the late Red Clydesider, Harry McShane, summed up the stage we have now reached; "these Labour councillors don't seem to know anything about our history. We have always had to struggle... The only why to break the poll tax is to break the law."[12]

Speeches like this and written material disseminated through hundreds and thousands of working-class channels, familiarising working people with the reality and the details of the poll tax, created the basis for the greatest mass movement of civil disobedience seen this century. Even at the national Labour Party conference in October, to the horror of the leadership, *Militant* supporters called for defiance of the poll tax. Glasgow councillor Jim McVicar was cheered when he called for the party to back non-payment.

> We can't just wait for a Labour government. A mass campaign is the only way to guarantee a Labour victory. The choice is between the red flag of socialism and the white flag of surrender.[13]

Alec Thraves, a delegate from Swansea, recalling Neil Kinnock's

1985 conference attack on Liverpool councillors, said that if Labour did not organise a successful campaign of non-payment "we will see the grotesque chaos of Labour councils, yes Labour councils, scuttling round in taxis handing out eviction notices to people who can't afford the poll tax." Donald Dewar shadow Scottish secretary condemned non-payment as "tactically naive and wrong in principle".

The advice of one Labour right winger to a woman who could not afford to pay the tax was: "If you can't pay I am sure the courts will be lenient with you!"[14] The Labour leadership at this stage were putting forward as an alternative to the poll tax the idea of "two taxes". The cowardly refusal to support non-payment was a gift to the Scottish National Party (SNP), which, under the impact of the radicalisation of the Scottish population, had evolved from "Tartan Tories" into an increasingly radical nationalist party. At Labour's special Scottish conference, *Militant* warned:

> The SNP are praying that Neil Kinnock's policy of blind subservience to Thatcher's law will prevail at the conference. This would give the nationalists the biggest boost since the discovery of North Sea oil.[15]

Predictably, the conference rejected the "non-payment option". And retribution was not long in coming: on 10 November Labour lost the Govan by-election. At the general election there had been a Labour majority of 19,500 in the 15th safest Labour seat in Britain. Jim Sillars, the SNP candidate, won the by-election with a 33 per cent swing from Labour. Sillars, who had formerly been a left Labour MP, consistently outflanked Labour in radicalism: "I concentrated on the fact that Donald Dewar is telling people to pay the poll tax while the SNP is organising a campaign against it."[16]

Some of the areas with the most oppressed workers, were festooned with SNP posters during the election. There was a noticeable lack of enthusiasm for Labour. The dispirited comment of one worker seemed to sum up the mood in the Labour ranks: "The SNP have got the Proclaimers; we have Wet Wet Wet."[17] We commented:

> Govan was a test bed for the filofax-Kinnockite Labour Party. The headquarters had more computers than the Starship Enterprise! An

army of full-time organisers were drafted in to operate them, run the campaign and ensure victory. The new moderate image secured the blessing of the *Daily Record* and *Evening Times*. So everything seemed set fair. Except that no computer or newspaper editor knocked on a door.[18]

Following this debacle the Labour establishment tried to blame Bob Gillespie, the defeated Labour candidate. He had been imprisoned in a political straitjacket, with MPs Donald Dewar and Brian Wilson writing his speeches and watching his every word. The right had preferred Anne McGuire, a long-standing anti-devolutionist and advocate of paying the poll tax, as their candidate.[19]

There was no question that a fighting socialist campaign would have cut across the rise of the SNP. Yet the right wing and the press actually hinted that *Militant* was to blame for Bob Gillespie's defeat. We answered:

> On the contrary, if *Militant*'s socialist policies had been adopted and fought for by the Labour Party in Scotland, there would have been as spectacular a victory in Govan as in Liverpool in the 1987 general election.[20]

Two months before, at the special Labour Party conference, one delegate had warned:

> If we go into Govan and tell people they are to go without essential food and clothing to pay the poll tax, we will not receive a warm welcome.[21]

The Govan result sent shock waves through the labour movement in Scotland. It indicated the danger posed to Labour by the SNP and more important, in a sense, the anger that existed at the denial of the Scottish people's national aspirations.

## NHS

Already in 1988 it was clear that the poll tax was the key issue confronting the Scottish working class. But in the rest of Britain it did not loom as large as in Scotland at that stage. The attack on the National Health Service was more to the fore. The vulnerability of the government on this issue was shown by Thatcher's statement during the 1987 general election that "the National Health Service is safe in the hands of the Tories". This was sheer hypocrisy, as was demonstrated soon after the election. The resources devoted to the NHS and particularly the conditions of health workers were undermined. In the first months of 1988 the anger of health workers exploded. The trigger for what became a powerful national movement did not come from the tops of the health service unions. The strike by 38 nurses at North Manchester General Hospital and the threatened action of the blood transfusion workers brought into the open all the accumulated anger and resentment of NHS staff. It was not the TUC general council, with nine million workers behind them, nor the leadership of NUPE or COHSE, the health unions, who forced the Thatcher government into a humiliating reverse, but 38 nurses. Twice in two days the "unbending" Tory government was forced to give way to striking health workers. It first capitulated when the Manchester nurses struck over their unsocial hours payments. It then gave in to the blood transfusion workers over meal allowances.

One of the leaders of the Manchester nurses, Joan Foster, revealed why they had not told the NUPE and other health union leaders, let alone the Labour Party leaders, that they were to go on strike: "We didn't want to be told that we couldn't go out on strike."[22]

There was as much suspicion of the 'left' NUPE leaders as of those on the right. Even *The Independent* had a headline: "Strikes by health workers have Cabinet on the run"[23]: The movement completely confounded the advocates of the 'New Realism', which held such sway over the trade union leadership. In the wake of the 1987 general election they had become obsessed with the idea that strikes and the unions were "unpopular". We declared:

> Health workers have every right to strike, but they need the full, active support of other trade unionists... At the moment nurses' action has been limited to 24-hour strikes, and correctly with carefully organised emergency cover.[24]

We favoured 24-hour strikes in areas where the nurses had moved into action, for regional strikes as a step towards national action. But the trade union leaders were singing a different song. We reported:

> at the London co-ordinating committee of COHSE, the general secretary, Hector McKenzie, told assembled stewards from striking hospitals that they did not have the open backing of the national union.[25]

Contrast this with the stand of John Macreadie, at the 27 January 1988, TUC general council meeting. He called for a one-day general strike in defence of the NHS. This was referred to the TUC Health Services Committee, because the "health unions themselves had still not met to formulate any form of action."[26] Yet there is no doubt that John Macreadie reflected the mood from below. Such was the pressure that the TUC health committee was compelled to call a national demonstration on 5 March. Immediately this was announced a head of steam in favour of action began to build up. Workers in different regions took part in demonstrations and called on the union leaders to take action. In the midst of this movement Arthur Scargill was re-elected as the President of the National Union of Mineworkers with 54 per cent of the votes cast, a clear eight points ahead of right-wing candidate, John Walsh.

As the battle lines were drawn in the health service, our supporters threw themselves squarely behind the health workers. John Macreadie pointed out:

> At the recent general council meetings [of the TUC], just five minutes was spent discussing the health dispute. I warned that without a co-ordinated lead, individual groups of workers taking solidarity action could be singled out for victimisation. Now civil servants have also been threatened. If any workers are picked on for striking for the NHS, the trade unions must organise the fullest action to defend them.[27]

In answer to the foot-dragging of the national leaders, we devoted two pages to outline the case for a one-day strike. Rodney Bickerstaffe, leader of the National Union of Public Employers (NUPE) had been approached on a demonstration to sign a petition organised by BLOC calling for a one-day general strike. His answer was "never"! His deputy, Tom Sawyer, who with Kinnock had been as much responsible as anyone for the 1987 general election debacle, also pitched in:

In the NHS unions we have got the power of patient care, the power of love and the power of compassion. This power is bigger than the power of force. The people selling papers on the demo calling for a one-day general strike are wrong. There are many ways to win. The power of restraint is better than the power of force. With the power of restraint we will win... A one-day general strike would lose support. It is a battle between the forces of good - the health workers and the public - and the forces of evil - Moore (the then Health Secretary), Currie and Thatcher.[28]

*Militant* responded that it would take more than "love" to shift Thatcher, her government and their implacable hostility to the nurses and the health service.

There was overwhelming support for the nurses, as shown by the strikes of Merseyside Vauxhall workers and Frickley miners who came out in solidarity action. Yet, the Thatcher government was prepared to ride out any movement unless the full power of the labour movement was mobilised. Even the *Daily Telegraph*, which kneeled at the shrine of Thatcher, pointed out that 80 per cent of the population supported the nurses, and, more significantly, 66 per cent of Tories polled supported them. In its stand against Thatcher Liverpool city council reaped huge political dividends for Labour in the 1987 general election: 57 per cent supported Labour. At the end of the miners' strike Labour's support had risen by more than ten per cent compared to the previous general election in 1983. Kinnock had dissipated this support with witch-hunts and his move towards the right.

For the tops of the trade union movement limited action and demonstrations were merely a means of workers letting off steam. However, for workers in Britain a one-day general strike would be seen entirely differently. It would fuse working people together and trigger a political earthquake.

Demands, slogans for struggle, must take into account the real level of the workers' movement, including that of the leadership.

Recognising the changes which had taken place in the upper echelons of the trade unions, *Militant* declared:

> only when the movement reaches fever-pitch will the TUC general council ratify a 24-hour general strike. The workers movement, not just in Britain but internationally, must develop from below before the

trade union and labour leaders give support. Even then it will usually be lukewarm, with the purpose of derailing the movement at the first opportunity.[29]

Many workers asked *Militant* supporters whether a 24-hour general strike would be sufficient to force the government to retreat. After all in Italy, Spain and France 24-hour general strikes were quite common. But in Britain the situation was different. If properly prepared it would completely undermine the Tory government. "It could be an occasion not just for parades, but for mass meetings to reach to every corner of British society."[30]

Once having felt their power, the working class would be eager to show it again. A number of one-day general strikes could unfold. This would mobilise and rouse new layers of the working class, particularly those outside the trade unions who had not been affected by previous action. However:

> the Marxists would oppose general strikes on the pattern of Italy over the past 15 years. There the one-day general strike has been used as a safety valve to dissipate the anger and opposition of the working class to the various capitalist coalitions... At a certain stage, even an all-out general strike will be posed in Britain. However we are not at that stage. A general strike is an 'either/or' situation. Two forces, two states, are established which vie for supremacy, as the 1926 general strike indicated.[31]

The call for decisive action was vindicated in the massive TUC health march through London on 5 March, which was a "marvellous confirmation of the undiminished strength of organised labour".[32]

Even the general secretary of TUC, Norman Willis, said that the march of 100,000 to Hyde Park was: "one of the biggest marches in the history of this country".

A call for a one-day general strike on 14 March, Budget Day, was taken up by the demonstrators.

However, the great enthusiasm on the march was dissipated at what was probably the most uninspiring rally ever staged at the end of a mass demonstration of British workers. There were just four speakers: Norman Willis, pensioners' leader Jack Jones, "Agony Aunt" Clare Rayner, and Archbishop Trevor Huddlestone. Willis was the only union speaker -actually *singer*, as he did a Karaoke! - and incredibly there were no speakers from the health workers' unions.

However, following this massive display of working-class power there was determination to support the action planned for the eve of the Budget. Miners, dockers, bus crews, shipyard and aircraft workers joined thousands of health workers on that day. In London in relentless drizzle, 3,000 health workers and other workers marched from the South Bank to a rally in Friends' Meeting House. The meeting prior to the demo was everything the rally and march on the 5th was not, with chants, cheering and the singing of "We're going to strike for the NHS".

*Militant* supporters played a key role, particularly in areas like Sheffield in organising a movement which resulted in 5,000 marching in a lively and enthusiastic demonstration to defend the health service. The movement of health workers in the months of January, February and March 1988 - if built on - could have stopped the Thatcher government in its tracks. However the contrast between the attitude of ordinary health workers and the trade union leaders was evident at each stage. The fact that Thatcher as well as Major were given the opportunity to systematically dismantle the health service is in no small measure down to the inaction of the national trade union leaders.

## P&O

At the same time another bitter conflict with all the same ingredients as in the health dispute, broke out between seafarers and shipping line P&O. This company attempted to sack all its Dover ferry workers because of their refusal to accept a cut in manning levels which, apart from anything else, were a threat to passenger safety. The sacking of the 2,300 seafarers at Dover was an attack on all seafarers and a mood for national action developed.

Early indications showed that there was likely to be a decisive two to one majority for action. But then the ferry owners scurried to the court and the judges obliged by declaring that the dispute only affected P&O Dover workers. Yet it was quite clear that if P&O got away with significant reductions in the workforce others would follow. Therefore, all seafarers were keen to come to the assistance of the Dover workers. But once again the union leaders trembled before the Tory judges. A ballot for national action was called off midway through the procedure which angered the mass of seafarers, particularly the P&O workers, who were left isolated.

*Militant* supporters made an impressive intervention in the strike, with Tony Mulhearn speaking in Dover to a packed meeting of P&O workers. *Militant* supporters clashed even with those "on the left" of the NUS executive. The latter had decided that the best strategy was to restrict the Dover dispute to a local level. Some of them argued that if other ferry workers, such as Sealink workers, came out on strike, "this strike would be lost". However, support for our ideas on how to conduct the strike grew with the strike itself. All initiatives in effect came from below with the rank-and-file seafarers raising the cash, organising support groups and mounting a campaign for national industrial action.

What added to the bitterness of the seafarers was that their employers P&O had given a £100,000 hand-out to the Tories. Pressure from below had compelled the NUS leadership to sanction national action, which then had resulted in sequestration of union assets. Following sequestration the union leaders backed away.

In February they wound down the national strike, which was gaining momentum in solidarity with the Isle of Man Steam Packet workers. Decisive leadership then would have struck a blow for all NUS members. After weeks of fighting alone, a minority of seafarers began to loose heart. Small breaches in the strike were then utilised by P&O and some sailings were restarted. McCluskie, leader of the NUS and so effective in expelling Liverpool *Militant*s from the Labour Party, was totally incapable of giving a decisive lead to seafarers at a critical hour. The consequence was that the P&O workers in Dover were isolated and ultimately defeated.

Out of this dispute were won some key workers to *Militant* who played an important role both in the industry and the wider struggles of the labour movement in Dover and other areas.

# 34.
# RUSSIA, TROTSKY AND THE COLLAPSE OF STALINISM

MEANWHILE, INTERNATIONALLY big events in the USSR were shaking the Stalinist regime of Gorbachev. Events in Armenia indicated that "never before, at least in its own backyard, has the bureaucratic elite which dominates Russian society faced a challenge on such a scale."[1]

The mass movement in the Armenian capital of Yerevan compelled a 'liberal' Gorbachev immediately to put Glasnost (openness) into cold storage. Foreign correspondents were prevented from visiting the area, in a desperate attempt to suppress all reports. Gorbachev represented that wing of the bureaucracy which saw the need to liberalise and carry through reforms from above in order to prevent revolution from below. But *Militant* had predicted that such methods invariably produce the results they were designed to avoid. In a totalitarian system, the slightest concessions can open the floodgates to revolution.

In his book *Perestroika*, published only six months before the Armenian events, Gorbachev had boldly claimed:

> The revolution and socialism have done away with national oppression and inequality and ensured economic, intellectual and cultural progress for all nations and nationalities.[2]

However, the bloody conflict between Armenians and Azerbaijanis over the issue of Nogorno-Karabakh (the Armenian enclave in Azerbaijan) had given the lie to this claim. Indeed the bureaucratic elite which dominated Russia and the Soviet Union had failed not only to solve the national question but had actually guaranteed through their totalitarian grip its re-emergence in an aggravated form.

The bureaucracy's approach to the national question flew in the face of Lenin's bold and sensitive position on this issue. This was demonstrated by the events in Armenia in early 1988. *Militant* stated that "The events in Armenia show that national protests will fuse with and be fuelled by the resistance to the bureaucracy's rule."[3]

The upheavals in 1988 were prepared by demonstrations and meetings in October of the previous year. They were initially over the issue of Nagorno-Karabakh but coalesced with a movement demanding the shutting down of dangerous chemical plants and a nuclear power station.

The Armenian revolt was the first indications since the upheavals in Poland of a process which eventually led to the complete overthrow of Stalinism. As the movement developed the Russian bureaucracy was riven with divisions. This was personified by Gorbachev himself who actually stood for greater but "legal" privileges for the elite that dominated Russian society. We commented:

> seventy years after the Russian revolution, and moreover with capitalism on the eve of a new recession, one wing of the bureaucracy now looks towards the 'market' as a solution. One of Gorbachev's political advisors had condemned "the concept of state socialism" as a "Stalinist error".[4]

Gorbachev himself, at the beginning, was a representative of the bureaucracy looking to widen its popular base. However, events in the next year were to see the situation spin out of control ending up with the shattering of Stalinism in 1989-90.

## ALLY PALLY RALLY

In 1988 the beginning of change in the Stalinist states formed the centre-piece of the *Militant* National Rally, which this time was held at Alexandra Palace. Reflecting the huge growth in support for *Militant*, this was the biggest rally, with almost 8,000, participating. *Militant* supporters had exceeded 10,000 in number, with thousands more counted as sympathisers:

"A deafening counterblast to rumours that Labour's Marxists are in retreat. Here was an army on the march for socialism".[5] For nearly two hours the crowd poured into the vast hall. The speakers appeared on the platform to music, pyrotechnics, the waving of red flags and a huge portrait of Leon Trotsky which was unfurled behind the stage. An important theme was the struggle to defend the socialist cause to which Trotsky devoted his life. The size of the rally was shown in the 506 children in the crèche, bigger than many schools. The confidence and enthusiasm of those present was again shown in the gigantic collection of £51,725.

Speaking at the rally alongside myself, Ted Grant, John Macreadie, left MP Ron Brown, Janice Glennon (for the youth), was Veronika Volkov, the great grand-daughter of Leon Trotsky. She had arrived at the rally in place of her father Esteban Volkov, Trotsky's grandson, who was not able to be present because of his wife's illness.

## ESTEBAN SPEAKS

However, in a satellite phone link-up from Mexico, Esteban Volkov spoke to the rally:

> Leon Trotsky was a man of inexhaustible generosity, always well-disposed to share sparse resources with comrades with economic problems. He maintained a close interest in them and in all his close friends... Even in his last moments of consciousness (following the assasin's blow)... he was able to make a joke about his hair that was being cut, trying to mitigate the deep suffering of his courageous inseparable wife, Natalya, who stood beside him until the last moment. A great Marxist theoretician and dauntless revolutionary, his dedication to working-class interests and his faith in the communist future of mankind made him one of the most indomitable heroic revolutionaries in history... In the ebb of the revolutionary tide, he kept the beacon of Marxism-Leninism brightly lit. Trotsky left an invaluable contribution to the arsenal of Marxist theory and methodology to the working class.

Esteban Volkov quoted his grandfather's testament: "Life is beautiful, let the future generations cleanse it of all evil, oppression and violence and enjoy it to the full."[6]

The impact of the rally was, once more, recorded widely in the capitalist press.

1989 was a decisive year in world developments. It will be associated with the collapse of Stalinism, which Militant, as the biggest Trotskyist tendency in Britain and one of the largest on a world scale, had confidently predicted.

## SUPER-POWERS

After the Second World War two super-powers bestrode the world arena, Stalinist Russia and US imperialism. The Soviet bureaucracy and Western capitalism rested on mutually antagonistic social systems but also leaned on each other against the threat of revolution from the working class. The military encirclement of the Soviet Union (imperialism's nuclear arsenals were undoubtedly used by the Russian bureaucracy to stay the hand of the working class), was a factor in preventing a movement of working people to overthrow the bureaucracy; the workers feared opening the floodgates to imperialist intervention.

In this period the prospect of capitalist counter-revolution was "virtually ruled out". The development of the planned economies, even during the boom of 1950 to 1975, exceeded the growth of world capitalism. The bureaucracy played a certain role in borrowing technique from the capitalist west and developing the infrastructure of a modern economy, but with enormous overheads.

Stalinism in this period did play a relatively progressive role, fulfilling the tasks which historically capitalism proved it was incapable of carrying through in Russia; developing industry science and technique, but at two or three times the cost of capitalism. Capitalism does have the check of the market, of competition, on a national and international scale. But the uncontrolled caste which dominated the planned economies swallowed up an enormous amount of the surplus and thereby undermined the advantages of the plan even when it was developing at a much faster rate than under capitalism. But once society in the USSR developed a certain level of production and technique, ie became a modern economy, the old bureaucratic method of rule from the centre was incapable of working. From becoming a *relative* fetter the bureaucracy became more and more of an *absolute* fetter on any further progress of these societies. The tendency of Stalinism to resort to zigzags, veering from left to right, from one expedient to another, did not free it from its historical impasse.

Periodic eruptions of mass discontent were an expression of its inherent instability. As we have seen, all the movements prior to the 1980s in the Stalinist states showed some of the features of what Trotsky perceived would be the political revolution - Hungary 1956 being the classical form. The masses demanded democracy, the elimination of the privileges of the bureaucracy, an end to one-party totalitarian regimes and a defence of the planned economy. Even in the movement in Poland 1980-81, while there were pronounced pro-capitalist features, this movement in general still saw itself as one pitted against the bureaucracy, but preserving the gains of the planned economy.

## POLAND

The crushing of the Solidarity movement in December 1981 by Jaruzelski had a decisive effect on the consciousness of the Polish working class. So discredited was the "Communist" Party, the party of the privileged elite, that the Stalinist counter-revolution took place through the military elite, personified by Jaruzelski. Together with the 1980s boom this completely undermined the idea that the ills of Polish society could be cured on the basis of a movement against the bureaucracy alone. Pro-capitalist ideas, occupied a minority position in the Polish movement of 1980-81. But on the basis of the crushing of the movement, the imprisonment of Solidarity workers, a further period of stagnation and regression of the Polish economy, led to pro-capitalist ideas becoming the predominant trend both within the ranks of the intelligentsia and also within the working class. There seemed to be no way forward on the basis of Stalinism, even the "reformed" version. The upswing of the 1980s, particularly the period of 1985-1990, contrasted favourably in the minds of the masses with the dire situation in the Stalinist states.

The processes at work in Poland existed, to a lesser or greater extent, in all the Stalinist states of Eastern Europe and the Soviet Union. However, illusions in the "market" were more pronounced in Poland and at an earlier stage this became clearer to us, after some comrades had visited the country. The most visible expression of this was approval given to Thatcher on her visit to Poland in 1988. Open support for the ideological fountain-head of capitalist reaction, particularly by the Gdansk workers, came somewhat as a shock to those, such as *Militant*, who looked towards a political revolution as the most likely outcome of any movement against the regime.

One of the difficulties for Marxists in correctly assessing the mood in the Stalinist states was the totalitarian character of these regimes. The assembling of a sizeable force, able to gauge the mood of the masses, was difficult, if not impossible, because of the pervasive grip of the police and severe repression. This was the case even in those regimes, like Poland and to some extent Hungary, where the hold of the Stalinists had been considerably loosened. Even then it would not have been possible to have easily corrected what subsequently proved to be an inaccurate assessment of the mood of the masses in these states as it was developing in the 1980s. Indeed, the consciousness was very confused, particularly in countries such as East Germany and the Soviet Union.

The movement against the regime in these countries initially contained elements of political revolution. In the first instance, the mood of the masses was to look for democratic change but on the basis of the planned economy. However, once the grip of Stalinism had been lifted and the masses were able to gauge the situation fully, the extent of the obscene privileges of the elite were revealed. This had a decisive effect on consciousness. These societies were not just standing still but going backwards. The "fireworks" of the world capitalist boom and with it the living standards of the 1980s contrasted favourably in the minds of the masses with the stagnation and decay of Stalinism. These regimes had stood still or even gone backwards for a large part of the 1970s and the 1980s.

## FACING UP TO A NEW SITUATION

Following the events in Poland *Militant*, at least the majority of its leadership, attempted belatedly, but honestly, to face up to this situation. Rather tentatively the "theoretical possibility of a bourgeois counter-revolution" unfolding in the Stalinist states was posed.

At an international gathering in Belgium in December 1988 of the co-thinkers of *Militant*, myself, in agreement with what subsequently became the majority of the *Militant* leadership, Lynn Walsh, Tony Saunois, Bob Labi, Clare Doyle and Peter Hadden, from Northern Ireland, raised the possibility of bourgeois counter-revolution. Neither Ted Grant nor Alan Woods spoke in that discussion but Ted Grant privately complained that he disagreed with my analysis.

We were the only Trotskyist tendency internationally that had begun in the late 1980s to pose the theoretical possibility of a bourgeois counter-revolution. Following the collapse of Stalinism and the moves towards the "market", *Militant* is also the only tendency to have fully and correctly analysed and foreshadowed how events developed and to show the limited possibilities for capitalism in these countries.

## WHAT WE SAID

A perusal of the columns of *Militant* in the crucial year of 1989 attests to this. Hungary was further down the road to capitalist restoration and developments there were fully analysed. The statement of Pozgay, representing the Hungarian bureaucracy, showed the way in which it was moving: "The socialist model chosen or enforced in 1948-49... has proved to be false in its entirety."[7]

Despite this, the conclusion which we drew at this stage was that capitalist restoration was the most unlikely scenario either in Hungary or in the rest of the Stalinist states. Events in Russia had shown that the elements of the political counter-revolution were maturing. This was shown in particular in the elections to the "Soviets". These elections revealed the hatred of the bureaucracy:

> Posters made clear the general mood: "Not the people for socialism but socialism for the people"; "Do away with the special privileges for politicians and bureaucrats"; "Servants of the people should have to stand in queues".

At this stage, one opinion poll we quoted showed that "only three per cent would vote for a capitalist party in multi-party elections".[8] This is an answer to those who argued at the time and since that a return to capitalism, certainly in the Soviet Union, was pre-ordained. In the mid-1980s not just the working class but the mass of the intelligentsia looked towards reforms, the removal of the privileges of the bureaucracy, but the retention of the planned economy. On the outcome of the elections, We argued that they demonstrated a

> yearning to return to a system of workers' democracy as it existed after the 1917 revolution under Lenin and Trotsky, before it was brutally suppressed by the bureaucratic counter-revolution.[9]

Gorbachev had originally come to power as a representative of the "reforming" wing of the bureaucracy, not as a conscious agent of imperialism. Yeltsin, as subsequent events demonstrated, was a more open and conscious representative of that layer of the bureaucracy which believed that its privileged positions could only be maintained on the basis of the dismantling of the already weakened planned economy and a movement towards capitalism, disguised as "democracy".

Such was the rapid development of events in the Stalinist states that throughout 1989 *Militant* was compelled to constantly re-examine and re-evaluate its analysis. In July the paper posed the question: "Can capitalism be restored in Poland?"[10] Following Thatcher's visit, US President Bush also staged what in effect became a triumphal procession through the streets of Gdansk. The crowd had chanted "Stay with us, Stay with us!" Solidarity leader Lech Walesa declared: "We will build America here in Eastern Europe." Jaruzelski, utterly demoralised at the ineffectiveness of his military Stalinist counter-revolution, actually admitted in a book the failure of "socialism": Capitalism, according to him, was the only road for Poland. He spoke in glowing terms about Thatcher's defeat of the British miners. In view of these developments *Militant*, the majority of the leadership, frankly stated that:

> Stalinism in Poland, Eastern Europe and the USSR has exhausted all possibilities for real development of the productive forces. Complete stagnation and even regression in some fields (even in comparison with the palsied capitalism in the West) is evident. Under capitalism the limits to the development of the productive forces are private ownership on the one side and the limitations of the nation-state on the other. Industry, through the big monopolies, has outstripped the narrow limits of the 'home market' and looks to the world market as its base of operations. In the Stalinist states private ownership has been abolished. But the vast scale of waste, mismanagement and squandermania, which is inevitable under a totalitarian regime within the confines of the nation-state, limits the utilisation of the full capacity of a planned economy. Both capitalism and Stalinism face the greatest crisis in their history. But compared to the decay and stagnation in Eastern Europe the economies of Western Europe, Japan and America through the present eight-and-a-half-year boomlet appear to be far more successful. In all the Stalinist states a wing of the bureaucracy is blinded by the seeming "economic fireworks", as Trotsky put it, of capitalism.

> Undoubtedly if world capitalism experienced another boom on the level of 1950-1975 the theoretical possibility of a return to capitalism in Eastern Europe and the USSR could not be ruled out. Even then capitalist restoration would come up against the resistance of the working class... A savage austerity programme would also be the starting point of a triumphant capitalist counter-revolution. But the workers resistance would be even greater.[11]

The only thing wrong with this analysis is its excessive caution as to the processes developing in the Stalinist states. Such was the decay of Stalinism that it took not a structural world economic boom but the "hollow" boom of the 1980s to act as a magnet to the workers of these states. However, even in late 1989 the signals from the former Soviet Union were mixed.

Terry Fields had made a very successful visit to the USSR particularly to the mining areas. The leaders of the miners in Siberia had written in August to Terry Fields, Pat Wall and Dave Nellist explaining that they "share the principles which Lenin proposed for a creation of the democratic workers' state". This was in reply to a letter sent by the MPs to the workers when they were on strike in July.[12]

## CHINA - CENTRE STAGE

The imminence of a political revolution, or the perception of this, in the Stalinist states had been reinforced by the earth-shaking events in China in April, May and June. Chinese leader Deng Xiaoping justified the Chinese elite's reforms - decentralisation and a greater reliance on market mechanisms - by proclaiming: "To get rich is glorious."[13]

Initially, the reforms had produced spectacular results in agriculture and industry. But the success was short lived as the growth in agriculture slowed down and a certain overheating began to develop in the economy in the late 1980s. Workers had been hit by the negative effect of the reforms. Living standards improved for a while but rapid growth, mainly in the rural and private sectors, brought with it a big rise in inflation, shortages and unemployment. Over 50 million "wandering people" desperately searched for work. We showed that

Even in their most dynamic periods the bureaucratically planned economies have always suffered from the problem of imbalances... According to Deng, "there are no fundamental contradictions between a socialist system and a market economy". But markets are essentially unplanned, attracting resources to the most profitable fields regardless of the overall needs of the economy and undermining the effectiveness of central planning.[14]

Faced with setbacks to his reform programme Deng began to falter. The hard-line defenders of bureaucratic centralism, such as Li Peng, went on to the offensive against leaders like Zhao Ziyang, the Communist Party's general secretary. The inevitable corruption and nepotism associated with the partial restoration of the market aroused the discontent of the masses. This was initially reflected in the movement amongst the students. The middle layers in society, particularly the students, are always a weather vane of deeper processes at work in society. The discontent of the students had resulted in demonstrations in January 1988, which led to the resignation of general secretary Zhao Ziyang, in June of the same year. The students denounced corruption, demanded human rights, and called for the release of jailed dissidents. The hardliners, fearing that the student movement would spill over into workers' protests, denounced Zhao and the reformist wing. This factional struggle within the ranks of the Chinese leadership opened the door to a movement of the students, to the beginnings of a political revolution and the subsequent massacre in Tiananmen Square.

The students gathered behind the Zhao wing of the bureaucracy as a means of democratising the regime. In April and early May, Beijing was convulsed with three mighty demonstrations of over 100,000, the last one in time for the anniversary of the historic student demonstrations of 4 May 1919. The students demonstrated great initiative

> in building their own campus co-ordinating committee, embracing 30 colleges and universities in Beijing. They turned their back on the tame, officially recognised student unions, which branded the new committees 'illegal'.[15]

Their target was the nepotism, particularly of the "gilded youth", the children of the top bureaucracy. For instance Deng's son headed a "charity" that was surrounded by the stench of corruption. His sons-in-law occupied important positions in the profitable state arms procurement agency. The sons of premier Li Peng and the party secretary Zhao had prominent positions in one of the special economic zones. This contrasted with the squalor of the students' living conditions, mainly living on campus, four or six bunks cramped into small rooms.

When they marched in their thousands they sang the *Internationale*. It is true that alongside of this was an imitation "Statue of Liberty" in Tiananmen Square. This undoubtedly showed the confused consciousness, which was inevitable in the first period after the emergence from the dark night of totalitarianism. But their slogans showed that the students were searching in the direction of a political revolution: "Long live freedom, long live democracy... Down with tyranny and dictatorship."[16]

Moreover, they indicated a sure instinct in seeking to link up with the workers who in turn greeted them as they marched past factories, offices and building sites: "Long live the workers!" shouted the students "Long live the students!" came back the workers' reply.

Faced with this mass movement the hard-line wing of the bureaucracy, which Deng had now in terror joined, sought to gain time in order to prepare the forces to crush the movement. However, each movement of the students was bigger than the last and undoubtedly provoked a revolutionary wave throughout China. By the time Gorbachev visited China on 15 May a million, perhaps two million, workers were out on the streets of Beijing. The movement swept from one end of China to the other, Guangzhou, Shanghai and many other areas being caught up. Workers and even the army openly fraternised with the students.

After Gorbachev had departed large detachments of troops, with tanks began to move on Beijing. Millions of students and workers swarmed out to meet them, halting their advance. On 20 May one squad of riot police attacked a barricade but were repulsed. Other policemen went over to the side of the demonstrators:

> Despite Li Peng's declaration of martial law, key army units turned back after coming face to face with the masses. The commander of the 38th Army, who had a student daughter with the protesters in the

square, announced that he would not implement orders to intervene.[17]

The army chief declared that the army would not move against the students and the workers in Tiananmen Square. All the conditions were there for the overthrow of the bureaucracy. The leadership was suspended in mid-air, with the bureaucracy itself and the army split from top to bottom. It was even reported that six of the seven military regional commanders had refused on 20 April to attend a meeting called in Beijing to plan a strategy of attack against the protesters. But what was missing in the situation was a leadership with clear aims and demands which could link up the movement of the students with that of the workers. Timing in a revolution is of the essence. Failure to seize an opportunity when the time is ripe can mean that a revolutionary opportunity can slip easily through the fingers. Engels summed up the essence of the situation when he said that there are periods of years, sometimes 20 or more, which appear just like one day in the life of society. On the other hand, there are days in which the events of 20 years can be compressed. Woe betide the revolutionary party that fails to seize the opporturnity which is presented in such a period.

The Russian working class probably had the opportunity in 1917 in September, October and November to take power. With the democratic vote of the soviets (workers' councils) behind them the Bolsheviks took power on 25 October. An inordinate delay on their part could have meant that the opportunity would have been missed and may not have occured again without the counter-revolution first raising its head and crushing the revolution. A similar situation, with the same opportunities, existed in China, in April, May and June 1989. What was involved was not a social revolution to alter the character of the economy or change the ownership of the means of production, but a political revolution to change the "superstructure", to replace a one-party totalitarian regime with workers' democracy.

Gradually the hard-line wing of the bureaucracy represented by Li, and then Deng, assembled the forces to crush the movement of the students. The lengths to which the elite were prepared to go was shown by Deng who brutally hinted at future casualties: "In China a million people is still only a small number."[18]

The first moves against the students and workers in Tiananmen

Square came on Saturday, 3 June. At dawn, 10,000 young, unarmed soldiers marched down Changan Boulevard toward the Square. They were rapidly blocked and surrounded by the crowd of over 20,000 people, who began to form barricades. "Go home! The people's army should love the people!" shouted the crowds. Many of the soldiers turned and fled, while students and workers fraternised with others. But Li and Deng began to build up a force of 100,000 troops around Beijing. On Sunday, 4 June they were deployed to carry through the infamous Tiananmen Square massacre.

Steve Jolly, based in Australia, had been asked by *Militant* and our co-thinkers internationally to go to Beijing to cover these historic events and to convey the solidarity of *Militant* supporters. He spoke to a mass meeting in Tiananmen Square where he put forward a programme for workers' democracy which received enthusiastic support from the mass of the students gathered there. He was a witness to the Tiananmen Square massacre; his account was more vivid than anything which appeared in the bourgeois press:

> The day after the massacre on Tiananmen Square the call for a general strike was written in blood on the walls and windows around the city. Before the bloodletting everyone knew that the army was about to attack. Students and workers stopped buses and trucks. Lorry drivers set up barricades.
> On the south side of the city I saw a convoy of about 40 army trucks which had stopped. Workers and youth pleaded with the soldiers inside. Others were brought in for the attack. Students I was with told me to go, as the troops were likely to attack. I marched forward with them. One worker I spoke to told me he was wearing a lucky coat. He kept it on. After the attack the four friends he was with were all dead. I saw one tank crush 20 people on the ground... I spoke to groups of workers and youth, explaining Lenin's four demands for a workers' democracy, elections of all officials subject to recall, no official to receive more than the average wage of a skilled worker, an armed people and not a standing army... After the attack they enthusiastically backed them. Some shouted: "The people must be armed for insurrection." [19]

As the Chinese students were gunned down by the "socialist" Peoples Liberation Army they sang the *Internationale*. Six students, one after another, advanced toward the army, each picking up and raising the red flag that had fallen from the murdered comrades hand. Throughout the world there was a massive wave of solidarity for the heroic students and workers of Beijing.

## SOLIDARITY

In Britain a demonstration of thousands assembled in London's Chinatown. The only speakers from the British labour movement were MPs Tony Benn and Dave Nellist who were enthusiastically received. Dave Nellist hailed the magnificent movement of Chinese workers, students and peasants as "a beacon to workers across the world... Deng and Li Peng will not succeed in repressing the demands for socialist democracy."[20]

He also called for the implementation of Lenin's four demands for workers' democracy. The demonstration, which reached 5,000 at its height sang the *Internationale* as it marched to the Chinese Embassy.

The world capitalists, their press and media, had given extensive coverage to the Tiananmen events. However their real feelings were expressed on the television programme *Newsnight* by Ted Heath, former Tory prime minister and Henry Kissinger, Nixon's right-hand man in Vietnam.
Heath stated:

> The Chinese students and workers aren't after the sort of democracy we advocate... They were singing the *Internationale*. [21]

Kissinger complained that it was unfortunate that the mass movement had sullied the end of Deng's career. For the record, both opposed the spilling of blood. But more important for them was the maintenance of the trade and other relations with the Chinese bureaucracy. Perhaps the most sickening contribution came from Gerald Kaufman, Labour's foreign affairs spokesperson, who declared that "one could understand the Chinese government wanting to get control of the square, although they had gone immeasurably too far in retrieving control."[22]

The crushing of the Tiananmen movement had a profound affect internationally and within China itself. The Stalinist counterrevolution did not lead to a lengthy period of consolidation of the regime. Given the social overturn that was imminent in Eastern

Europe and the Soviet Union, China also was destined to move towards the market.

The Chinese privileged elite had been careful to avoid the "mistakes" of Gorbachev. They had fully accepted the need to move towards the restoration of capitalism but had also set their faces against democratisation. They correctly feared that democratic concessions would open up the floodgates to a new Tiananmen which would sweep them away. Despite the big growth of the economy and the existence of pure capitalist sectors, such as Guandong province, new "Tiananmens" are being prepared. In the first instance it will probably not take the form of the 1989 movement with demands for a political revolution prominent from the outset. The crushing of the movement in 1989 and other events have temporarily dimmed the attraction of socialism for a broad layer of the Chinese working class and peasantry. The masses in areas such as Guandong, have already experienced the barbarism, inevitable when capitalism is restored. Moves have already been made towards the establishment of "Solidarity" type unions.

## OVERVIEW

There were two sides to the movement which swept Eastern Europe in 1989. On the one side, the planned economy began to be liquidated. This strengthened capitalism above all in the ideological sphere. It allowed the possessing classes internationally to conduct a campaign extolling the virtues of their system. But on the other side it also provided a living example of mass movements of "the people" which could reduce to dust regimes that appeared to be impregnable.

1989 also saw the disintegration of Stalinism not just in its "home base" but in its outposts as well. One expression of this were developments in Afghanistan.

Internationally, the Russian bureaucracy had moved from a position of supporting the establishment of Stalinist (that is, deformed workers' states) in Cuba, Ethiopia etc, right up to the mid-1970s, to an opposite standpoint when it came to the issue of Nicaragua. The Sandinista regime could have undoubtedly pushed in the direction of a workers' state, following the overthrow of Somoza in 1980. But it was actively discouraged from doing so both by the

Russian bureaucracy and also by Castro on behalf of the Cuban elite. The latter had himself established a deformed workers' state in 1960 without first receiving the blessing and prior ratification of the Russian bureaucracy. The existence of a Cuban deformed workers' state, on the doorstep of American imperialism, strengthened the Russian bureaucracy under Khrushchev. They were quite happy to financially underwrite the Cuban regime.

But the increased economic difficulties of Russian Stalinism, together with other factors, had produced a change in approach by the time of the Nicaraguan revolution: "One Cuba is enough", was their watch word.

They had originally intervened in Afghanistan for strategic and other reasons. They wished to establish a friendly "buffer" state on their borders, one that would rest on the same social foundations as their own. But the outlook of the bureaucracy had undergone a change in the course of the 1980s, particularly with the coming to power of Gorbachev. American imperialism had poured in arms and resources to back up the rag-tag and bobtail "Mujaheddin". Given the preparedness of the Russian bureaucracy to defend the gains of the Afghanistan "revolution" *Militant* originally discounted the possibility that the Mujaheddin could win. However, it was clear that given the *rapprochement* of the Russian bureaucracy with US imperialism plus the rising cost of underwriting the Kabul regime, Gorbachev reassessed the position. The collapse of the Kabul regime and an ensuing period of chaos became a distinct possibility.

## AFGHANISTAN - DISAGREEMENTS IN MILITANT

An estimation of what was likely to happen was a source of friction between the majority of the Editorial Board, led by myself and Lynn Walsh, and Ted Grant and Alan Woods. The perception of Woods and Grant that the Najibullah regime was firmly ensconced in power and would not be dislodged, flew in the face of the evidence on TV screens and in the press every day. While the Mujaheddin could not "win" in the sense of taking over and ruling Afghanistan in a stable fashion, nevertheless the withdrawal of the Russian bureaucracy and a period of ensuing chaos was on the cards. Lynn Walsh and myself insisted that *Militant* deal with this in their analysis of the situation in Afghanistan.

This was resisted by Ted Grant. The majority's views prevailed and was reflected in the material that appeared in the *Militant*. In February 1989 *Militant* commented: "Much to the surprise of Western capitalist governments, all Russian forces will be withdrawn from Afghanistan before 15 February." It went on:

> Exaggerated propaganda stories have always been a feature of reporting from Afghanistan, and this undoubtedly continues. Nevertheless, the picture of chaos and deepening collapse which emerges from television reports and from serious capitalist journals is too consistent to ignore.

Najibullah, in a desperate attempt to conciliate imperialism, now that the Russian bureaucracy was pulling the rug from underneath him, was forced to abandon the "Marxist" label. Commenting on this we stated:

> The Russian withdrawal, under these circumstances, is a defeat for the bureaucracy. This has been admitted, implicitly, in recent statements by Gorbachev and foreign minister Shevardnadze. Rank-and-file Russian soldiers are leaving without any sense of 'revolutionary achievement'.[23]

Gorbachev had clearly decided that given the wider global political objectives of the Russian elite, it was not worthwhile holding onto Afghanistan. However, *Militant* did not draw from this the conclusion that the ragbag of religious and tribal groups which made up the "Afghan resistance" were capable of unifying themselves into a coherent national movement with common objectives. We warned that a period of chaos and civil war between the different Moslem groups would ensure that the country would sink back into the traditional feuding between different religious and national groupings. The conclusion drawn was that

> Whatever happens, it now seems unavoidable that the revolutionary changes inaugurated in 1978-79 will be rolled back in a large area of Afghanistan. Responsibility for this setback lies with Stalinism which has nothing in common with genuine Marxism or internationalism.[24]

This analysis was vehemently objected to by the Grant/Woods trend. They demonstrated an atrophy of thought in refusing to face up to the new problems which had been posed by the rotting of Stalinism and its effects both within the Stalinist states and on a world scale.

## CONSEQUENCES IN SOUTHERN AFRICA

Their incapacity was also revealed in another conflict which broke out in *Militant*'s ranks of the issue of events in Southern Africa. Ted Grant refused to admit that the apartheid regime could withdraw from Namibia. Unfortunately he had persuaded the leaders of *Congress Militant* (our South African counterparts) to adopt a similar standpoint. He was opposed on this once more by myself, Lynn Walsh, Dave Cotterill and others. At the December 1988 international gathering in Belgium, Dave Cotterill argued that the apartheid regime would withdraw from Namibia because of a number of important changes that had taken place. Above all, the changes which had taken place within the Russian bureaucracy presented the de Klerk regime with "a window of opportunity" to execute a strategic retreat without endangering the position of the South African ruling class or the interest of imperialism.

In the past, the South African regime had used ruthless military repression in Namibia. As with their intervention in Angola and Mozambique this arose from a fear that a series of deformed workers' states were being established on its doorstep. If they were allowed to succeed and stabilise themselves this would have inevitably reinforced the oppositional movements of the South African working class. Even when they were forced to withdraw from Angola, South Africa, with the connivance and financial support of imperialism, bolstered the counter-revolutionary Unita forces. They also pursued a ruthless policy of destabilisation in Mozambique, with disastrous economic and social consequences for that country, felt right up to the present. Faced with a similar threat in Namibia, the de Klerk regime would have continued its policy of repression.

But the crucial new factor in the situation was the change in the position of the Russian bureaucratic elite. They were more concerned with their own power, prestige and income than the interests of the oppressed masses of the third world. Given its economic weakness, the Gorbachev bureaucracy was cutting its losses internationally and was pressurising former "allies" into accepting the continuation of capitalism. This was the pre-requisite for the Namibian agreement.

The "socialist" policies of SWAPO, the guerrilla movement, were dispensed with in favour of a "mixed economy", that is capitalism. Since coming to power in November 1989 SWAPO has entirely justified the hopes placed in it by imperialism and de Klerk. Rather than carrying through a radical programme of nationalisation and reforms, to benefit the masses, they have pursued the opposite policy of maintaining "private property". The investments of imperialism has been guaranteed and repression has been used against movements of the working class (such as the miners), to defend and improve their situation.

The failure to recognise the new element in the situation led Ted Grant and Alan Woods to make mistakes on perspectives both in relation to Namibia and more seriously on South Africa. If their views had persisted it would have seriously disorientated *Militant* members and supporters both in Britain and on an international scale.

All the factors which made for the Namibian settlement were present in South Africa, only more so. Repression was not working in the changed situation of South Africa. By the end of the century or shortly afterwards it was estimated that there would be 50 million blacks in South Africa and five million whites. All the policies of apartheid were breaking down as blacks moved into the major cities completely ignoring and cancelling out the "pass laws" and the vicious "Group Areas Act". At the same time, the changes in the Soviet Union had a similar, if not greater effect, on the ANC leadership as it had on the SWAPO leadership. Fearing a revolution from below, in time-honoured fashion the de Klerk regime was looking for reforms from above. In secret negotiations with Mandela, even before he left prison, De Klerk had arrived at an agreement to initiate negotiations leading to elections on the basis of "one person, one vote", but not genuine "majority rule".

Irrespective of the changes that were taking place, Ted Grant completely discounted such a possibility. He stubbornly argued *Militant*'s previous position. He maintained that there was no possibility of elections, of universal suffrage, of a dismantling of apartheid within the confines of capitalism. The march of events, particularly following the release of Mandela, completely bore out the position of those who opposed him. The majority had theoretically and ideologically rearmed *Militant* on these issues. Failure to do so would have undermined the forces of Marxism in the complicated situation which developed in the late 1980s and early 1990s.

# 35.
# MILITANT IN TRANSITION

WITH THE attacks on the LPYS by the right and its consequent decline, *Militant* supporters had to supplement work in the YS with building up the Youth Trade Union Rights Campaign (YTURC). While launching further attacks on the Labour Party Young Socialists the right-wing national executive committee confidentially conceded, "YTURC is picking up the ground very successfully." The *Sunday Times* commented: "Labour is losing its musical battle for the soul of the party's youth and *Militant* is holding its own."[1]

The conclusion of the right was to attack YTURC and further undermine the rights of the LPYS! Yet the YTURC national conference in April 1988 had attracted 1,000 young workers, students and trainees, the biggest gathering of working-class youth in Britain at that time. Once more the *Militant* meeting was packed out, despite all attempts to undermine our support by the right.

## BENN CHALLENGES KINNOCK

So unbridled were the right in their attacks on the left, and so open were they in abandoning the socialist ideas of the movement, that Tony Benn decided to challenge Kinnock for the leadership of the Labour Party and Eric Heffer stood for the deputy leadership. The capitalist press were squarely behind Kinnock in his attempt to create a sanitised, tame, Labour Party. The job completed they were then as equally ruthless in denigrating Kinnock himself.

John Prescott, who also entered the election fray stated: "I have no time for fainthearts who would seek to deny the Labour Party's trade union link and see it as a political liability."[2] We urged Benn and Heffer to "run a mass active campaign of meetings at every union conference and big rallies in each city.'[3]

The problem was that their troops were rather thin on the ground. The "trendy left" had deserted in droves to the right. Other workers, disheartened at the lurch to the right of the Labour leadership were abandoning the Labour Party or, in many cases, passing over to us. The 1988 leadership challenge of Benn and Heffer was in reality the last spasm of an organised left within the Labour Party. In the next five years and beyond the left were to be than no more than a faint echo of the powerful force it had been in the early 1980s, as workers looked outside of the Labour Party and increasingly to organisations like *Militant* for answers to their problems. The party conference made clear to all that the Labour leadership had concluded that electoral succes lay in falling on their knees before "the market".

## WHAT CONCLUSION TO DRAW?

*Militant* was slow to draw all the necessary conclusions from these developments. It still defended, and did so for a number of years, the perspective of mass movements feeding into the Labour Party and transforming it. However, the experience of mass struggles outside the Labour Party, above all in the poll tax, were to convince the majority of *Militant*'s supporters and leaders that the old tactic of concentrating most of its forces in the Labour Party had been overtaken by events.

## POLLOK

In Pollok a truly mass campaign in favour of non-payment had been led by the anti-poll tax unions with *Militant* supporters like Tommy Sheridan in the vanguard. Their efforts were rewarded with vicious attacks by the local MP. Yet, they had been instrumental in recruiting 128 new members to the Labour Party in one week. Instead of congratulating *Militant* supporters the Pollok MP, James Dunnochie, publicly attacked Tommy Sheridan and called for the party's National Constitutional Committee to investigate *Militant*'s activities in the constituency.

Labour Party members responded with a meeting on 7 August in the Pollok ward with more than 100 local people in attendance. The meeting pledged that they would fight to the finish to "keep the socialist banner flying in the area." The meeting passed a resolution criticising the enquiry call and censured the local MP. This meeting then decided to support Tommy Sheridan in a challenge to the sitting MP during the next re-selection process. The ward party also put out 5,000 leaflets answering the attacks of the MP and printing extracts of his secret letter to Labour's NEC for all to see. The hard core of the right wing on Strathclyde regional council then made it clear they were going for mass expulsions of *Militant* supporters and anti-poll tax activists in Glasgow. They drew up a list of 20 in Pollok and ten in Cathcart, singling out anti-poll tax leader Tommy Sheridan for disciplinary action.

Earlier in the year a member of the press corps in London had been told "off the record" by a senior Labour Party official in Walworth Road that, "Yes there is going to be a mass witch-hunt in Glasgow."[4]

But nothing could stop the head of steam that was building up behind the anti-poll tax struggle. The Scottish TUC (STUC) were compelled to call a demonstration on 10 September but no call was made for effective action. Campbell Christie, general secretary of the STUC did, however, declare: "People in Scotland will stand with us and say no."[5]

But when the question was asked what would happen when the bills arrived in the following April his reply was: "Let's get to April and then decide what to do." The STUC's "broad-based" strategy - involving all classes and all parties - completely failed. Moreover, the possibility for any effective campaign by Labour or the STUC was killed off at the Scottish conference in April 1989. The debate was stormy and impassioned. Speakers were cheered and booed and constituency delegates overwhelmingly showed they favoured mass non-payment of the tax. Dewar, the party spokesman, while ostensibly attacking the Scottish National Party in effect attacked *Militant* for advocating non-payment.

Notwithstanding this, and with the support of the block votes of union leaders, opposition to non-payment was carried.

## WHERE NOW?

The decision at this conference undoubtedly had a demoralising affect on many workers and initially on some of those who were in the forefront of the campaign. How was it possible to conduct a successful campaign against the government in the teeth of the open resistance of the Labour Party in Scotland and the mere acquiescence of the STUC? During the Liverpool struggle such was the pressure from below that the Labour leadership, including the right, were compelled to either give verbal support or remain silent at the height of the movement.

Special meetings of *Militant* supporters were therefore necessary to explain that there were more powerful forces at work in the poll tax battle than Thatcher, or union general secretaries wielding block votes. The poll tax represented such an assault on the living standards of the working class that resistance was inevitable. Even without our involvement and the anti-poll tax unions there would just be too many people, particularly the poor, who could not and would not pay. The question was whether the resistance to the poll tax would be scattered and incohate or be given an organised expression.

From the outset, we were confident that in Scotland more than a million could be persuaded and organised to resist and refuse to pay the poll tax. This was perceived by opponents as utopian and an indication that we were "out of touch". On the contrary, it was the summits of the labour movement as well as the Thatcher government who were incapable of envisaging the forces that would be conjured up by the poll tax and the campaign of mass resistance which we would help to organise.

As the year drew to an end the second conference of the Strathclyde Anti-Poll Tax Federation was held. It agreed to hold a big "poll tax non-payment" demonstration on Saturday 18 March and called on workers and youth throughout Scotland and the rest of Britain to come to Glasgow on that day in a mass show of defiance.

## MAHMOUD MASARWA

Internationally, Mahmoud Masarwa, a Palestinian socialist and trade union activist, and also a prominent co-thinker of *Militant* in the Middle East had been arrested by the brutal Israeli security forces. Arrested in July 1988, without charges, he was denied access to a lawyer or visits from his family. Defence Minister Yitzhak Rabin (now the Israeli prime minister) had personally intervened to deny Mahmoud the right to be represented by his lawyer. Mahmoud was framed and after a beating was forced to "confess" his alleged "crimes". In the months and years that followed *Militant* conducted an international campaign for his release. Dave Nellist and Paddy Hill (of the Birmingham Six) attended his trials and appeals. This persecution of Mahmoud was itself a testimony to the growth of support for *Militant* and its ideas on a world scale.

# 36.
# INTO TOP GEAR

**MILITANT'S VIEW** view of the future was expressed in the first issue of 1990. The main headline: "Revolution in Eastern Europe", and next to the masthead: "1990 - The year we'll beat the poll tax".[1]

The previous year had witnessed the gathering storm on this issue. At the beginning of 1989 the words of Glasgow councillor Chic Stevenson, Vice-Chair of the Strathclyde Anti-Poll Tax Federation, became the watchword for the struggle in Scotland in the next year.

> I'm having nothing to do with Thatcher's poll tax. I am voting against Glasgow district council setting its part of the tax at £92 per person, along with five other councillors... A mass non-payment campaign will still have to be organised. It has the support of local Labour Parties and the mass of people in the housing schemes. With that support, Labour councils could make the poll tax inoperable if they called on people to refuse to pay. It is not the job of Labour councils to do the Tories' dirty work. I was elected to fight Thatcher, not to bow the knee to her poll tax.[2]

Backing words with action plans proceeded for the March mass demonstration in Glasgow against the poll tax. The demonstration had to be built for without the involvement of the official labour and trade union leadership, indeed in the face of their open and bitter attempts to scupper it. But they had discounted the depth of feeling throughout Britain on this issue. Workers outside of Scotland were determined that the maximum assistance would be given to Scottish workers in this crucial battle.

## RED TRAIN - POLL TAX EXPRESS

In London they raised the finances for a "Red Train" to speed to the "front-line". We described the atmosphere:

> "The Anti-Poll Tax Express", said Euston Station's huge illuminated

train information board... All 600 seats are taken - the train is packed. Many are school students, a good number of black youth; three women from an estate in Deptford who had decided to go just the night before; trade unionists and Young Socialists... singing and chanting lasts the whole journey: no chance of any sleep!... I can hear bagpipes. What's the time? 4.20 am - we're there! The piper passes the window flanked by two comrades with red flags. It's our early morning call!... The Scottish comrades welcome us - we're having a rally right here in the station.[3]

There was a phenomenal turn out from Merseyside as 1,000 travelled from the area to this demonstration.

20,000 took to the streets of Glasgow against Thatcher's iniquitous tax. The determination to defeat the poll tax was shown by a Welsh worker who gave up two tickets for the Wales v England rugby match: "The match is only for 80 minutes but the poll tax could last the rest of my life."[4] Weather-wise, it was a terrible day in Glasgow, with the rain lashing down from early morning till well after the demonstration finished. But with banners waving the spirit was greater than on a blisteringly hot sunny day. Rallying in Alexandra Park, Tommy Sheridan, chair of the Scottish Anti-Poll Tax Federation, told thousands:

A lot of people said we couldn't deliver this demonstration...we've proved them a thousand times wrong. We have caused a tremor which will turn into an earthquake of mass non-payment... But it will be not enough to go to demos. We need you to go back to your housing schemes and unions and get active. If every trade unionist puts pressure on their leaders, then Maggie Thatcher will not be able to collect any poll tax because the unions will stop it being implemented... We are building a new Red Clydeside in Scotland that will not pay the poll tax.

Ron Brown, Labour MP for Edinburgh Leith, declared:

We cannot afford to wait for three years for the next Labour government, because we need a mass campaign against the poll tax to make sure we get that Labour government.

Hannah Sell, who was still the youth representative on Labour's NEC, declared:

I'll make sure the NEC hear about it. They want a million new party members. We must ensure that they are a million working-class people prepared to fight against the poll tax.[5]

Terry Fields, brought solidarity on behalf of the workers of Liverpool. His courageous stand on the poll tax, including his preparedness to go to prison, was to earn him the abiding hatred of the right wing of the labour movement and a deep regard and affection by ordinary workers.

## TO REGISTER OR NOT

In the period running up to 1 April, the issue of whether people should register or not was a hotly debated issue both within the ranks of *Militant* and in the anti-poll tax movement. Registration was due to take place for the poll tax in England and Wales in May, but had been a big issue in Scotland in the whole preceding period. There were those like Tommy Sheriden who consistently refused to register and there were many others who joined him. However, we considered that

> non-registration is not an effective way of fighting the poll tax. Whether people register or not, they will still be put on the registers. Yet anyone deliberately refusing to register will be liable to a £50 fine. We therefore do not advocate a policy of non-registration. But that does not mean that we just sit back while registration takes place. The issuing of the forms should be the signal to step up the campaign against the poll tax and lay the basis for a mass movement of non-payment - the only policy which can effectively defeat it.[6]

Militant sought to emulate what was done in Scotland. We advocated that in the rest of Britain a campaign should be adopted involving sending back the forms demanding more information before filling them in, lobbies, demonstrations and mass gathering-in of forms and collectively sending them back.

There was considerable feeling against Labour councillors who were complying with the poll tax and energetically pursuing the issue of registration. In the Labour-controlled Central Region of Scotland the bank accounts of those not registering were frozen and the £50 fines deducted. We recognised that resistance would continue but that to go the whole way on non-registration would be ineffective and would rebound on the movement. At the same time the anti-poll tax unions were pledged to defend all of those who refused to register and to fight the fines or any other victimisation imposed by councils.

On the issue of the alternatives to the poll tax we demanded the restoration of government grants stolen from local councils by the Tories. In 1989 this had accumulated to over £29 billion. With this cash restored it would then be possible to improve services and even lower rates. The alternative of the Labour leaders, which very few could understand, of a local income tax, which would raise about 20 per cent of the councils' revenue, and a property tax alongside of it, was completely inoperable and was soon dropped.

## 24 JUNE GLASGOW DEMO

The introduction of the tax in Scotland widened the circle of protest. The March and April Scottish demonstrations were followed by a confident, lively, and a youthful, demonstration on 24 June in Glasgow. Hillhead MP George Galloway called it a "great river of a demonstration".

Thousands of people gathered, a sea of red and gold and red and white banners, flags and placards. Neighbours at their windows waved happily at the march, banners hanging from the windows. Galloway declared: "This is indeed part of the army of one million people who have refused to pay." He was followed by Dick Douglas, one of the few MPs still supporting mass non-payment who declared: "This is a remarkable grass roots rally. It's a disgrace that the leaders of the labour movement aren't here."[7]

## ON THE MARCH IN JULY

That second front was opened in July in the mass TUC demonstration in Manchester and in Walthamstow, the first London demonstration against the poll tax took place. In Manchester 30,000 rank-and-file trade unionists from every part of Britain showed their hostility to the poll tax. It had been officially called by the TUC but no real preparation had been undertaken. The most that any national union did was to send out one leaflet to shop stewards. It was a sea of banners and demonstrators with *Militant* supporters finding a great response in the demonstration.

The only discordant note struck on this day was from a carefully selected "shop steward" from Scotland who opened the rally with an attack on the poll tax but then went down like a lead balloon when she declared that "non-payment was not an option". There was uproar which did not abate when Norman Willis, general secretary of the TUC spoke. He restricted himself to appeals to family values and decent standards. David Blunkett, MP, and others attacked non-payment or avoided any mention of how to fight the tax. When the Manchester Red Choir came on to close the rally they announced that they had been forbidden to sing one of their songs because a line in it called for non-payment. The audience clamoured for them to sing it but the TUC effectively censored them by pulling the plugs on the PA.

However, by this time the crowd had dwindled to about 200 as a significant section of the march streamed towards a special *Militant* meeting that was packed out to hear Tommy Sheridan and others who called for the campaign in Scotland to be spread to the rest of Britain. The temper of the opposition to the poll tax was shown by a magnificent turn-out on the demonstration by Alum Rock (in Birmingham) Anti-Poll Tax Union, made up predominantly of Asian workers who chanted, "no poll tax, no poll tax".[8]

The Walthamstow demonstration, although only 200 strong, was typical of the hundreds of such events organised and was significant in attracting workers and youth who "normally" would never participate on a demonstration. There was even a contingent of Leyton Orient football fans. A man actually came up to the anti-poll tax stall and asked: "Are you prepared to break the law?" Before anyone could reply he added, "My grandfather went to prison rather than comply with Tory laws." He was the grandson of one of the Poplar councillors whose slogan: "Better to break the law, than break the poor" was carried on the placards of the march.[9]

At the begining of the resistance in England and Wales there was a certain scepticism as to whether non-payment could be successful. However, in this battle the struggle in Scotland and its growing success was a priceless weapon. Anti-poll tax activists were able to point to the million or more who were refusing to pay the tax. Not a whisper of this campaign appeared in the press outside of Scotland. But by a thousand different channels the information seeped through, particularly through the leaflets and information supplied by the anti-poll tax unions. This played a crucial role in building up and increasing the confidence of workers in the rest of Britain to resist the introduction of the tax.

## DAVE NELLIST SUPPORTS NON-PAYMENT

Lone voices in Parliament, like those of Dave Nellist and Terry Fields, sought to warn the government of what was coming. Together with a number of other MPs just before the Commons rose in July Dave Nellist declared,

> I give a clear warning to the Secretary of State that millions of people in England and Wales will not be able to pay the poll tax and that millions more will be unwilling to... Just under two years ago the Tory Reform Group described the poll tax as 'fair only in the sense that the Black Death was fair, striking at young and old, rich and poor, employed and unemployed alike.'... That description was wrong in one basic respect. At least the rich catch the plague - the rich will not catch the poll tax.

As to Scotland he declared that *"Scotland on Sunday* had estimated that 800,000 Scots are not paying out of 3.9 million who should."[10]

## DISCIPLINED DIRECT ACTION

Even in the summer months of July, August and September the campaign against the poll tax was relentless. The third Strathclyde Anti-Poll Tax Federation conference took place in August on a high note as mass resistance to the implementation of the tax was detailed. Even in far-flung Orkney the number of non-payers was estimated at 43 per cent and in the Shetlands 48 per cent. A highlight of the conference was a speech by Janette McGinn, widow of legendary Scottish songwriter Matt McGinn, who refused to register and had been fined £50. On 4 July some of her possessions were to be poinded (valued) as a first step to a warrant sale. Within hours of contacting the Federation thousands of people were preparing to descend on her home. In the face of this mass hostility the council postponed the poinding. Janette McGinn declared: "the

Federation has shown in action what the words 'unity is strength' really mean".[11]

At this conference the Strathclyde Federation newspaper *Pay No Poll Tax News* was launched.

## THE LOTHIANS

A no less intense conflict was taking place in the East of Scotland where the first anti-poll tax unions had been set up. The Lothian regional council met on 29 August. The usual council business was disrupted by the eruption of fury against Labour councillors who were implementing the poll tax. Councillors sheltered under a bombardment of poll tax payment books thrown from every available part of the public gallery by the angry protesters. The clear message was "return to sender". But the Labour council leader, John Mulvey, refused to issue a clear statement that the council would not prosecute non-payers, who now totalled 160,000 in the Lothians.

## THE FED

Capitalising on the success of Scotland it was decided, with *Militant* supporters giving the lead, to prepare for the coming battle by launching the all-British campaign. A call was therefore made for a conference in the Manchester Free Trade Hall on 25 November. In preparation for this Tommy Sheridan declared: "We believe that we will create such a political crisis for Mrs Thatcher's government that the poll tax will be repealed."[12]

Fifteen Labour MPs backed the new campaign and representatives of 20 regional anti-poll tax federations met to set up the steering committee of the all-British campaign. Tommy Sheridan was elected as Chair.

One of the most vital tasks of the Federation was to counter the misinformation campaign of the government about how many were refusing to pay.

The poll tax struggle undoubtedly redounded to the electoral benefit of Labour. Its position in the polls soared as the battle against the poll tax, to which Labour contributed little or nothing, systemically undermined support for the government. The Labour leaders repaid those who were responsible for this, the anti-poll tax leaders, with persecution.

## LABOUR EXPELS SHERIDAN

After a protracted struggle Tommy Sheridan was eventually expelled from the Labour Party in September. 250 supporters gathered at a lobby of the meeting of the National Constitutional Committee (NCC) which had been convened by the national executive committee of the Labour Party to consider his expulsion. It was more like a Star Chamber. The only connection with socialism on the day of the hearing was the singing of the *Red Flag* and the *Internationale* by *Militant* supporters, anti-poll tax activists and others outside the enquiry. Tommy Sheridan declared defiantly to the crowd, from a second-floor window, that no matter what happened on that day a mass non-payment campaign would continue throughout the length and breath of Scotland.

Tommy Sheridan was expelled for being a member of *Militant* at the very same time that Labour's NEC were re-admitting members of the Social Democratic Party.

## FED ESTABLISHED

On 25 November at Manchester Free Trade Hall Tommy greeted 2,000 delegates, from every region of Britain, as "an army on the march".[13] This conference established the powerful All-Britain Anti-Poll Tax Federation. This body was to play a decisive role in the history of the working-class movement and indeed in British history as events in 1990 were to demonstrate. The officers elected were: Tommy Sheridan as the chair, Maureen Reynolds (from Manchester) as Treasurer, and Steve Nally (from Lambeth) as Secretary, (with Kevin Miles from Wallsend becoming "communications officer" the following year).

Much discussion had taken place in our ranks on what proposals it would put forward at the conference on the structure of the Federation and the composition of the national committee. Such was the decisive influence of *Militant* in the anti-poll tax unions that it would have been entirely possible for us to gain a "clean sweep", and take all positions on the national committee. We decided against this, in order to give the movement as broad a base as possible, to facilitate the drawing in of all genuine forces who were prepared to struggle in action against the tax. Therefore in some areas it was agreed that we would not oppose these non-*Militants*. This was the case in Yorkshire, London and in the South West. Within months of its formation this body was to be catapulted to national prominence as the resistance to Thatcher's tax grew to hurricane proportions.

## ID CARDS AND HILLSBOROUGH

But it was not the only policy of Thatcher which aroused ferocious opposition at this time. She had proposed at the beginning of the year a system of identity cards for football supporters, with the aim allegedly of stamping out football hooliganism. Simon Donovan, a young supporter, suggested we organise a campaign on the issue.

The campaign was very successful, involving fans and players alike. Mike Suter - a supporter of ours - was one of the leaders of the campaign, appearing on **BBC** *Breakfast Time* to argue our case. Leading professional footballers, such as Paul Davis of Arsenal, publicly backed the campaign. This culminated in a rally of 300 fans at Westminster's Central Hall in May, chaired by Dave Webb and addressed by Terry Fields. The Hillsborough tragedy had taken place only a few weeks before. This gave added weight to the campaign because, as Terry Fields commented:

> I had two sons and a nephew at Hillsborough. I shudder to think what would have happened if my sons went having to produce ID cards. We need a workers' inquiry into Hillsborough. People are saying: "We won't get anything out of this police inquiry. What has happened since the *Herald of Free Enterprise* or the Kings Cross fire?"

Criticising conditions at football grounds, he commented: "Sanitation is non-existent, refreshment is unobtainable - then you look up and see directors in their box sipping champagne."[14]

50,000 signatures on petitions were delivered by Terry Fields and others from Liverpool to Downing Street protesting against *The Sun*'s vile reporting of the Hillsborough disaster. The gutter reporting of *The Sun* led to a boycott in Liverpool, and to this day its sales have still not recovered. The city of Liverpool was traumatised by the dreadful Hillsborough disaster. Commenting on the numbers who perished, *Militant* said:

> They died because of a system that puts greed before safety. The working class of Liverpool and Britain demand: "Never again". There must be no cover up. Those responsible must be made to take the blame. Tory minsters try to deflect criticism by hypocritically joining the mourning. Disgustingly, an anonymous police officer tried to blame the fans... Football is a profitable business. Millions are being taken out by the big clubs and pools companies. Now that money must be put back in to bring every ground up to a safe standard. Football clubs should be taken over by local authorities and run for the benefit of the local community. The supporters, the players and the local working-class movement should be in charge. They would ensure safety and comfort and the fullest use of sporting facilities.[15]

## RECLAIM THE GAME

One of our best selling pamphlets - *Reclaim the Game* - written by John Reid was produced at this time. It has gone into three editions and has won support from fans home and abroad.

## MI5

At the same time a television programme *First Tuesday*, confirmed what everyone had suspected, that the Secret Service, in the form of MI5, had systemically spied on *Militant*. This programme revealed that a freelance spy was used to bug our Liverpool offices. Some of the dirty methods of military dictatorships were used by Thatcher and her government against those who dared to oppose them, particularly during the Liverpool battle

Bugging, which is officially banned in many countries, was still taking place in "democratic Britain". It was reported that a certain Coghlan was hired by MI5 to carry out this work. He claimed that MI5 had tried but failed, to infiltrate agents into our meetings, so they had turned to him. At night he installed a spike mike in the wall and window frames of Liverpool *Militant*'s offices. This transmitted discussions in the office to an MI5 agent parked 300 yards away. According to Coghlan, MI5 were "worried at *Militant*'s growth and influence over the city council."[16]

Showing their bile against us, the *Liverpool Echo,* in an outragous editorial supported, the MI5 bugging of *Militant*:

> If the avowed aims of an organisation are to overthrow the democracy in which it operates, then that democracy has the right to keep it under surveillance. *Militant* MP Terry Fields is to ask the government if the bugging is still going on. *The Echo* could add another question: if not, why not?[17]

We replied to the Echo:

> *Militant* defends the democratic freedom to meet, speak and vote - freedoms threatened by Thatcher. It has nothing to hide. If the government wanted to know what we were saying, they should buy *Militant* or listen to our socialist policies at open democratic meetings.[18]

It was noticeable that we were not given the opportunity, on the programme or in the press which featured these revelations, to rebut allegations made against us. There were further revelations concerning spying on *Militant* later. Brian Crozier, right-wing activist and former speech writer for Thatcher, produced a book, in 1994, called *Free Agent*. In this book he admits to "infiltrating" a mole into our ranks in 1979. He concluded we were very effective!

## AMBULANCE STRIKE

In October the ambulance workers came out on strike. The Tories had once more conducted a desperate lying campaign in an attempt to discredit these workers. They even tried to frame workers with lies about "unanswered calls". But this failed once more as the workers remained united and won massive public support. The usual response to ambulance workers collecting on the streets was "you are fighting for all of us". Ninety per cent of the public were backing the ambulance workers' pay claim, with massive collections on the streets; well over £100,000 was collected in Liverpool alone. But such was the frustration of ambulance workers that some, such as in Glasgow, decided to strike even without "emergency cover".

The feeling also grew for all-out strike action in other areas. Under pressure the general council of the TUC decided to call a national demonstration in support of ambulance workers on Saturday 13 January. Their perception of a demonstration was to merely "let off steam". We noted how the 1988 dispute had been "left directionless and fizzled out; history must not repeat itself".[19]

What incensed ambulance workers and others was that while Tory MPs had awarded themselves a ten per cent increase in salary they were standing firm against ambulance workers who demanded a 6.5 per cent increase. Moreover, the government were using troops in a deliberate provocation against the unions.

This dispute dragged on for six months, one of the longest since 1945. But victory was there for the taking, if effective action had been organised.

The ambulance workers' union convened just one national stewards' conference, and that in the last weeks of the dispute. This conference did have an immediate impact, resulting in the army being drafted as crews were suspended. The critical issue, as in other previous major disputes since Thatcher had come to power, was the question of serious solidarity action. The TUC were never requested to organise solidarity action, other than the 15-minute protest on 30 January, 1990. However, that showed the potential. 20,000 workers marched through the centre of Liverpool on that day. 30,000 took to the streets in Glasgow; millions of workers were with the ambulance workers on that day. In its aftermath Tommy McLaughlin, Merseyside Ambulance shop steward declared: "Let's have a nationwide stoppage for a day, not just the official 15 minutes."[20] Unfortunately the unions' leaders were once more running scared.

The deal agreed in March 1990 gave 17.6 per cent over two years but in cash terms was only worth about 13 per cent because of the way it had been phased in. Roger Poole, the chief union negotiator, claimed that the union had driven a coach and horses through the government's pay policy. However, the majority of ambulance workers did not believe it was a good deal. They had a greater awareness of the government's difficulties, with the poll tax and other pressing issues, and believed that effective action would have shattered the government. Eighty-one per cent voted for the deal but only because they saw no way forward after six months of struggle. Nevertheless this battle served to steel and harden a section of the working class who had not been involved in action of this character in the past.

# 37.
# THE GATHERING STORM

IN 1989 all the signs pointed to the weakening of Thatcher and the falling apart of her government. This was revealed in the dramatic resignation of Lawson in October 1989. We commented:

> Thatcher faces the deepest crisis in her decade of power. She can boast of being the most unpopular prime minister since polls began. Her Chancellor has resigned and even her favourite TV interviewer, Brian Walden, persists in asking awkward questions about his departure.[1]

The real reason for Lawson's resignation was that he could see the consequences of his and Thatcher's policies and the economic catastrophe which loomed. We had drawn attention to this well in advance of Lawson's clash with Thatcher.

Lawson jumped ship because he understood that a recession was coming and probably also that Thatcher's days were numbered. Later he commented that the poll tax had also been an important factor in his considerations for resigning. He had, he claimed, always been opposed to the poll tax but kept his own counsel despite the suffering it was inflicting on millions of working people in Britain. One thing was clear; the resignation of Lawson was greeted enthusiastically by workers who saw it as an opportunity to ditch the whole government.

However, the leadership of the Labour Party was incapable of understanding the approaching crisis of world capitalism and with it the shattering of the grip of Thatcher. In 1989 they turned even more decisively towards the right. Neil Kinnock in a meeting of the NEC brazenly declared:

> It (capitalism) is the system we live in and we have got to make it work more efficiently, more fairly and more successfully in the world market place. That is what the policy review is about and we shall reject any sort of naive shopping-list socialism.[2]

The Labour Party conference in October 1989 gave its stamp to Kinnock's ideas, which have been built on first by John Smith and now by Blair. The GMB actually submitted a resolution to conference which gave the national executive (NEC) the go-ahead to reduce the union block vote and to take even more decision making powers out of the conference's hands. This was opposed by us - we were still then able to be represented at Labour Party conferences in significant numbers.

One incident showed how far removed was the rightward moving Labour Party conference from the mass of ordinary working people outside. Christine McVicar from Glasgow Shettleston Labour Party was seen by millions on TV news bulletins when she tore up her poll tax payment book at the conference rostrum. This was not just an individual gesture. She was moving a resolution calling for Labour to back the mass campaign of non-payment. She defiantly declared to the conference:

> Without the Tolpuddle trade unionists and the Suffragettes breaking the law, we wouldn't be here at this conference... I'm ripping up my poll tax book not as an individual but as part of a mass campaign of non-payment.[3]

She was met with cheers from the socialist elements in the conference, and by jeers from right-wing Labour MPs and others. At this conference *Militant* was still able to attract 200 delegates and visitors to its traditional public meeting where £1,723 was collected for the fighting fund. However, the right consolidated its hold in November with the removal of Hannah Sell from the national executive of the Labour Party.

## LPYS SMOTHERED

This in effect marked the winding up of the Labour Party Young Socialists. The "youth" conference which took place in 1989 was a stage-managed and rigged conference under tight right-wing domination and control. 132 voting delegates and 46 non-voting delegates attended. The LPYS had regularly attracted over 2,000 young party members to their conference. The right's plans nearly fell apart when it was discovered at the last moment that their favoured candidate, Hayley Sadler, was not even a Labour Party member!

Through blatant manoeuvres Hannah Sell was replaced by Alan Parry from Knowsley South Labour Party. The themes of the conference were: You must pay the poll tax, taking part in the mass non-payment campaign is irresponsible; You cannot build direct links with youth in the townships of South Africa; and The market can offer a lot to young people. Future movements of the youth would be channelled outside of the Labour Party. This was the consequence of the sabotage of the LPYS by the spiteful right.

## MILITANT REACHES TWENTY-FIVE

In October, the continued resilience and indeed strengthening of *Militant* resulted in the production of a special 47 minute video marking the first 25 years of *Militant*. This was a highly successful venture and has been used numerous times as source material by other film makers in documentaries and programmes about *Militant*.

1990 was the beginning not just of a new year but of a new decade. Buoyed up by the Reagan boom of the 1980s and reinforced by the collapse of the Stalinist regimes in Eastern Europe the spokesmen of capitalism trumpeted "the final triumph" of their system. *The Independent* declared that the new year stock exchange rallies denoted "confidence that - as a system - capitalism is a winner"[5]. Six months earlier the organ of American finance capital, the *Wall Street Journal*, commenting on the competition between capitalism and the "communist" regimes of Eastern Europe, declared simply: "We've won".

Thatcher joined in: "The lesson of the 1980s is that socialism has failed." *Militant*, on the contrary, contended that "notwithstanding this orgy of capitalist triumphalism, the decade now beginning will be one of the most convulsive periods in human history."[6]

This was not blind faith. Marxism is the science of perspectives, rooted in a sober and objective analysis of society, which allows its adherents to trace out the rough outline of how events are likely to develop. The Marxists around *Militant*, basing themselves on Trotsky's analysis, fully anticipated the revolt of the peoples of Eastern Europe which unfolded in late 1989. The perspective raised in the summer of 1989 in the *Militant International Review* was that: "East Germany could very well be the first to trigger upheavals throughout the Stalinist states."[7]

Contrast this with one of the most perceptive writers, John Lloyd, in the *Financial Times*:

> East Germany has no mass movement on the horizon... Czechoslovakia's leadership cannot allow the questioning of the source of its legitimacy in the Soviet invasion of 1968... Hungary faces dissidents, but not yet a proletariat aroused. Bulgaria will introduce Soviet-style reforms, without yet Soviet-style chaos or fledgling democracy. Romania and Albania are clamped in iron.[8]

This was not written at the beginning of the 1980s but three months before the end of 1989! The revolt of the peoples of these states was inevitable. What was difficult to foretell was the exact form it would take and what its likely outcome would be.

At an international conference in the autumn of 1989, *Militant* also drew attention to the gathering war clouds in the Middle East. The Iraqi dictator, Saddam Hussain, had built up a powerful military regime but was also faced with colossal internal contradictions. This would not be the first time in history that a military dictatorship would seek an outlet externally in war. The most likely flashpoint for this, we estimated, was probably a military clash with Israel, the client state of imperialism. Instead of this, Saddam turned his attention towards Kuwait. Nevertheless we anticipated the broad outline of likely developments.

## PERSPECTIVES FOR CAPITALISM

The great majority of economic soothsayers looked forward to a continuation of the boom as the world entered 1990. Yet, despite "Reaganomics" and the superficial froth of Thatcherism, capitalism, as Marx had demonstrated more than a hundred years previously, was incapable of overcoming its inherent contradictions. The fundamental reason why crisis is inevitable is that the working class can never buy back the full product of their labour because their wages represent only a proportion of what they produce. That part of the product which goes to cover the workers' own subsistence is called by Marx "the necessary product". What the worker produces over and above this is the "surplus product".

Capitalism maintains its momentum by ploughing back this surplus into production, into factories, raw materials, etc. But the capitalists' profits come from the unpaid labour of the working class. When profits increase and are invested in new capital equipment, at a certain stage this must be used to produce more consumer goods. Yet workers once again do not receive enough wages to buy them back. This results in "overproduction", that is recession or slump, which in the modern epoch is expressed through "excess capacity".

One of the expressions of the parasitism of world capitalism is that "excess capacity" was a feature of all the advanced industrial countries even during the boom of the 1980s. Completely blind to the workings of their system the economic "experts" of the ruling class, such as the *Financial Times*, were almost euphoric at the beginning of the new decade: "The death of communism means that the whole of Europe will become the world's powerhouse with a united Germany as its engine."

*Militant* on the contrary pointed out:

> There is no possibility of a 'Marshall Plan' for Eastern Europe which could help to sustain world capitalism for another two or three decades... more serious capitalist economists already look towards a recession. Most pray it will be a 'soft landing'. But it cannot be excluded that a 'hard landing' - with serious effects on living standards and conditions for the mass of the working class - could develop early in this decade. It is unlikely we will immediately see a drastic crisis along the lines of 1929-33, more likely a slowing down in the rate of growth or a small recession.[9]

Thus it was *Militant*, proponents of "outdated" Marxism, which was able to correctly foresee the trends in world capitalism. Precise timing in predicting economic processes is difficult, if not impossible, but clearly at the beginning of 1990 we foresaw a world economic recession. It came much earlier than either we, or the few bourgeois economists who anticipated it, expected.

What was the effect of recent tumultuous events on the working class? we answered:

> The effect of the events of Eastern Europe on the outlook and consciousness of the working class is two-sided. The illusions in capitalism of the Eastern European workers, and to some extent those in the

USSR (could result)... in a return to capitalism in Poland and Hungary. In East Germany... there is now widespread support for 'reunification', even if this means a return to capitalism.[10]

But, we argued, the other side of this process was the example it would give to working people throughout the world of what mass movements are capable of. At the Berlin Wall at the turn of the year a banner was held aloft: "Listen world, the people are coming." We commented:

> The idea will be fermenting in the minds of workers of the West - if they, the workers of Prague, Bucharest and Berlin could bring down the tyrants there, perhaps we can topple our government of the rich here.[11]

We did not have to go very far into the new year to see this prognosis vindicated in Britain. The poll tax was the trigger which would alter the political landscape of Britain and establish a benchmark by which all future forms of struggle will be measured. Very few people outside outside our ranks held this opinion at the beginning of 1990.

# 38.
# 31 MARCH 1990

WITH 1990 only weeks old, *Militant* carried a front-page headline "Smash the poll tax" with the call of the All Britain Anti-Poll Tax Federation for, "a mass demo on 31 March"[1]. Thirty-five million people were to receive their poll tax bills in England and Wales on 1 April. The campaign was given a big boost by the Tory *Economist* magazine which stated: "Imagine a country where more than one in ten of the adult population is refusing to pay a tax. Welcome to Scotland 1990." In fact this organ of big business grossly underestimated the true level of non-payment in Scotland which was as high as one in three in Glasgow alone. The *Economist* went on: "Today's drama in Glasgow may be repeated tomorrow in Liverpool. How long before the Tories start to pine nostalgically for the much derided rates?"[2]

Threatened by a mass revolt Tory "unity" began to crack as a backbench revolt seemed imminent. While the Tory poll tax minister Chris Patten had declared that bills would on average be no more than £278 per person, in many areas the bills were £400 or more, and in the London Borough of Haringey the average bill was £579! Pointing to Scotland Tommy Sheridan declared:

> In Scotland the size of the rebellion has exceeded all our expectations. Strathclyde Region has just sent out 250,000 summary warrants against people who haven't paid. 107,000 of these are in Glasgow alone. How can a handful of sheriff officers - the Scottish bailiffs - possibly deal with this number of cases?

He went on:

> We wrote to the TUC suggesting they call an anti-poll tax demonstration on 1 April - but they refused. So we are appealing to trade unionists from every factory and workplace to join the demonstration.[3]

## SHIRES REVOLT

In Tory Berkshire also, in the town of Maidenhead, on a freezing cold Saturday night in January, 2,000 people attended a meeting on the poll tax. The local Tory MP was denounced as the "Ceausescu of Maidenhead". The local Labour representative did not distinguish himself either as he called for people at the meeting to pay the poll tax and was roundly jeered. The majority of the meeting were in favour of a mass campaign of non-payment and the secretary of the Reading Anti-Poll Tax Federation was cheered when he called for a campaign along the lines of Scotland. These were just two of the seismic tremors of the poll tax earthquake that would shake the government to its foundations and topple Thatcher before the year was out. Even the *Daily Telegraph*, staunchly pro-Thatcher, was compelled to write in February: "To say that preparations for the poll tax are in a shambolic state would be unfair to shambles and the honest slaughtermen who work in them."[4] Debbie Clark and John Ewers wrote in *Militant* on 2 March:

> A huge crowd of 1,000 had gathered outside under the floodlights. A massive police and security operation costing £10,000 allowed only ticket holders to get inside. It was like a scene from the Romanian Revolution - except this was taking place in the Gloucestershire town of Stroud. And what had sparked this mass protest? Stroud council was meeting to set its poll tax, eventually agreed at £380 for each adult. 500 tickets for the 'hottest show in town' had been snapped up. Even badly forged tickets were on sale.

The meeting had to be held in the town's leisure centre because the council chambers could only hold 60 members. Steve Nally, secretary of the All-Britain Anti-Poll Tax Federation, congratulated the crowd: "This lobby is the biggest yet in Britain. What is happening in Stroud in an indication of the mood at grassroots level."[5] A big roar went up. Inside the chamber a huge roar errupted when the council voted by 40 to eight to campaign against the poll tax to get it scrapped as soon as possible and to organise a lobby of Parliament. The council leader, an independent, had declared that she wanted to take "the whole town with me" to lobby Parliament.

This meeting and mass pressure on the council arose from the work of the anti-poll tax federation in the town. Moreover, the anger and hatred towards the poll tax was as evident in Windsor, and other Tory heartlands in the area. This was followed by a massive demonstration of 15,500 in Plymouth. It had been initiated by a housewife, Hilda Biles, who told *Militant*: "I've never done anything like this before but somebody's got to do it."[6]

Demonstrations and meetings of thousands were beginning to sweep England and Wales as councils began to meet to set their poll tax rates. The biggest were in the South, with ex-Tory voters declaring that they had been "betrayed". In West Oxfordshire Tory district councillors resigned in protest at their own party's tax and rent increases. Carlisle council refused to set a poll tax rate.

## WALTON - FIRST MOVES

Meanwhile, in Walton in Liverpool a drama was being played out which was to have important consequences for the labour movement in Liverpool and was to lead to a decisive event in the history of *Militant*. The Labour right's hitman, Peter Kilfoyle, full-time party 'disorganiser' and hatchetman, had been selected as Labour Party candidate for Liverpool Walton at the next general election. The MP for the area, Eric Heffer, was seriously ill and had therefore announced his retirement.

The main opponent of Kilfoyle was Lesley Mahmoud, who received majority support, 92 delegates out of 140 present at the selection conference. But Kilfoyle received 19.9 per cent of the union votes to Mahmoud's 17.4 per cent. Many of the branches who voted for Kilfoyle had never met and had ballot papers completed by full-time officials or branch secretaries. Moreover, GMB branch 48 and T&G branch 6/523, both of which had nominated Lesley Mahmoud, found in the shortlisting meetings that the delegates were being ruled out from the ballot. The Ford branch of the Transport and General Workers' Union had four per cent of the electoral college vote. But at a meeting where the left had a clear majority delegates were told that the branch committee had already posted the ballot paper, with the branch votes cast for the right-wing union official, Mike Carr, and with second preference for Kilfoyle.

Eric Heffer, from his hospital bed, demanded a National Executive Committee ban to stop Kilfoyle from standing. He pointed out that as a former regional official in the same region, Kilfoyle had an unfair advantage, with access to membership records of party members and affiliated organisations. There were also many complaints about the way the supporters of Kilfoyle had been selected. Desperate to capture the seat, Kilfoyle sought to ingratiate himself with the left, by attempting to dress himself in *Militant* colours. In his election address he declared:

> This constituency proclaimed (over 35 years ago) the need to take over the commanding heights of the economy and called for the nationalisation, at that time, of over 500 monopolies. In my youth I was always impressed by the material produced by Walton and circulated throughout the party.[7]

His selection outraged the majority of activists within the Labour Party and unions on Merseyside, not all of them on the left. Thus the ground was laid for a bruising battle between right and left in Walton in the near future.

## POLL TAX REBELLION RUMBLES ON

More immediately, the month of March witnessed a dramatic escalation in the struggle against the poll tax. In one month, Stroud was joined by Maidenhead, Bath, Taunton, Oxfordshire and Brighton, areas across the South, not previously touched, for decades, by demonstrations or protests. One after another the populations in these towns rose to denounce the poll tax. Alongside of them were thousands who besieged town halls in London: in Hackney, 2,000 gathered outside the town hall. Hundreds lobbied Southwark council. 2,000 gathered outside Lambeth Town Hall, hundreds outside Waltham Forest and Haringey councils. Practically every area of the South was affected in one way or another by poll tax demonstrations and protests in February and March.

In some areas, the mood turned ugly when protestors were excluded from town halls. In some places, the police turned on protesters. In Southampton the police started attacking 400 demonstrators outside the town hall, and dragged young men and women downstairs by the hair and arms. Twenty-seven people were arrested in Southampton.

In Lambeth, BBC *Newsnight* showed people being arrested. One person was arrested by two plain-clothed policemen, one of whom had a copy of *Militant* in his back pocket. "What was his role on the lobby? Was he carrying *Militant* so demonstrators would not suspect him in their midst?"[8] These were questions asked by TV commentators and protesters alike.

Faced with these convulsions, the Tories' and their newspapers' only reply was to drag up the hoary old myth of "outside troublemakers". A ferocious barrage of slander and lies once more rained down on us in the first two weeks of March. Every Tory minister and every gutter newspaper, seized on *Militant* as the "enemy within". Murdoch's *Times* and *Sun* really plumbed the depths. The *Sun* compared us to football hooligans: "The Militant tendency is Labour's own Inter-City Firm."[9]

To his eternal shame, Neil Kinnock repeated some of the wilder Tory claims. Tony Benn concluded: "The Labour Party is more frightened of the anti-poll tax campaign than of the poll tax itself."[10] The Tory press conjured up the ludicrous spectacle of an itinerant band of professional protestors moving around Britain: in one night they were present in Bristol, Norwich, Maidenhead, Weston-Super-Mare, Exeter, Gillingham and Birmingham, to whip up poll tax protests. In Bath, the council meeting which set the poll tax was delayed for three hours by angry protesters. According to local Tory dignitaries, including the local MP, poll tax minister Chris Patten, they were all "rent-a-crowd outsiders, bussed in from *Militant* places like Stroud!"[11]

How to explain then, that in Bridgewater, 450 had met and agreed to set up an anti-poll tax union. The same in Glastonbury, where 350 assembled, with 200 people at Gatcombe Park (an abode of the royals). In fact the capitalist press was prepared to slander and throw mud at any organisation or individual who was prepared to organise resistance to Tory measures.

## ATTACKS ON ARTHUR SCARGILL

At the same time as we were once more being pilloried, the gutter press also turned its fire on Arthur Scargill. He was attacked by the *Sun*, *Mirror* and the rest of Fleet Street. Following the defeat of the miners they still set out to rubbish the idea of struggle and were determined to rub the miners' noses in it. They insinuated that Scargill and other NUM leaders used hardship money for themselves when the miners went hungry during the strike. The self-proclaimed "socialist", multi-millionaire Maxwell, had talked in one interview about the *Mirror*'s role in defeating the NUM strike. The NUM was "accused of getting money from Russia". But Russian miners willingly gave up a days pay to show their solidarity. The most nauseating aspect of this attack was that former lefts jumped on the bandwagon, attacking Scargill as a means of attacking the idea of militant class struggle.

Thus Scottish NUM president George Bolton (a member of the Communist Party) said that he would oppose the union paying for any legal action, claiming that financial transactions under question were nothing to do with the union. we asked: "How can measures to protect the union's assets from Tory sequestrators be of no concern to the union?" [12]

## PRESS FAIL TO STOP POLL TAX REVOLT

In March and afterwards, the cry of "violence from the left" was to become a constant and overworked theme. It had been seen before in the Liverpool and miners' struggles. The same tactic had been resorted to in the Wapping and Warrington disputes. The ruling class have enormous means in their hands to mould "pubic opinion". A campaign of slander can have an effect in temporarily disorientating workers. However, when great social issues are at stake, their effect is at best peripheral and very temporary, sometimes as ineffective as a snowdrop on a hot stove.

The Tory strongholds of the South were rising up against their "own" government. And it was not just in the South. The Morecambe Conservative Club threatened to disaffiliate from the Tory Party in protest against the poll tax.

A quarter of backbenchers had indicated that they wanted "her" to step down before the next general election. One of her closest confidantes, Ian Gow, who pioneered Thatcher's rise to the party leadership warned her: "There is a clear need to do something." Tory MP, Tony Marlow told a shell-shocked Tory 1922 Committee:

There is a risk that we will be seen to have declared war on the people and, with the levels of the community charge now being fixed, we risk being confronted by a massive and unchallengeable campaign of civil disobedience.[13]

## BAKER ATTACKS MILITANT

Tory Party Chairman, Kenneth Baker, attempting to cover up the cracks, put the boot into *Militant* for allegedly "orchestrating violence", using "bully-boy" tactics and manipulating the All-Britain Anti-Poll Tax Federation. The *Times* echoed him, in an attempt to divert attention from the huge wave of protests that was sweeping from one end of Britain to the other. A desperate, and duly appreciative Thatcher congratulated The *Times* in Parliament for its "excellent article which blamed the 'militant left' for organising 'violence' and 'intimidatory demonstrations'."[14]

On 9 March, it printed a blatant lie: "Mrs Hilda Biles from Plymouth was angry about a front-page interview in this week's *Militant* newspaper which she says she never gave. 'It looks as if they have lifted an interview from one of the local papers in Plymouth'."[15] Mrs Biles had actually given the interview to *Militant* and she subsequently confirmed this. With her agreement, it was recorded and we had possession of the tape. The *Times* had not phoned us to check out the serious allegations that we had concocted an interview, nor did it publish the correction we had requested. On 10 March, the smears continued with wild allegations that

> Trotskyist agitators... closely associated with the All-Britain Anti-Poll Tax Federation... may already have planted computer viruses to disrupt the software of two Scottish boroughs.[16]

However, the ineffectiveness of this "black propaganda" was highlighted in the sister paper of The *Times*, the *Sunday Times*, with columnist Robert Harris commenting:

> I doubt whether the ordinary voter, watching the violence on television, says: 'Look at those horrible communists, Mabel. We must vote for Mrs Thatcher as the only person who can deliver us from these ruffians.' The voter is more likely to say: 'Look at the latest bloody mess that woman has landed us in.'[17]

## FANS AGAINST THE POLL TAX

Even at football matches, fans on opposite sides chanted together: "We're not paying the poll tax." Credit for this initiative must go to John Viner of the Acton anti-poll tax union, who wrote:

> I was going to the Arsenal v Forest match and on the 'spur' of the moment decided to take a few hundred national demo leaflets to give out. When Arsenal ran out on to the pitch I hurled them all into the air and watched them rain down on to the fans around me. I started singing 'We're not paying the poll tax!' and several hundred joined in. Try it at your next game![18]

This example was emulated at Portsmouth, Spurs, Southampton, Newcastle and Watford.

The campaign of vilification had no effect on preparations for the 31 March demonstration. But the press outdid itself with "bullying, intimidatory tactics" in pursuing Federation spokespersons, like Steve Nally. He was hounded and persecuted by the jackals of Fleet Street. His family, neighbours, friends and past acquaintances were all approached for information on his personal life, where his mother used to work, where his father worked, etc. The neighbours rallied around Steve Nally and turned a deaf ear to the approaches of the press. Some articles were complete fabrications, as Steve Nally recounted:

> The worst was the *Independent on Sunday*. They had a photograph with the caption: "Steve Nally, *Militant* supporter who says that it is not the group's policy to incite violence, at the Hackney protest that turned into a riot." That is an absolute lie. That very morning I gave an *Independent* reporter my itinerary for the week. I made it quite clear that I wasn't going to Hackney but speaking at a lobby in Hillingdon that evening and going on to Sky TV. I never went to Hackney.[19]

## KINNOCK WEIGHS IN

However, it was not just the Tories and their hirelings who were putting the knife in. The Labour leadership could not resist joining in. Kinnock condemned the advocates of mass non-payment of the poll tax as "Toytown revolutionaries", a phrase inspired by the *Sun*.

In contrast, Tony Benn put himself behind the campaign against the poll tax: "If enough people stand firm against the poll tax we can compel the government to withdraw it."[20] He demanded that the next Labour government grant an amnesty to all who had refused to pay.

This was roundly condemned by Kinnock and John Cunningham as condoning "law breaking". The implication was quite clear - Kinnock, the Labour leadership and Labour councils would be urged not only not to support mass non-payment but to pursue non-payers through the courts. Even some ostensibly on the left, like Diane Abbott and Brian Sedgemore, Hackney's two Labour MPs, were less than resolute. While declaring how necessary a united campaign was, at the same time they were not prepared to support thousands who could not afford to pay by not paying the poll tax themselves. The audience at a meeting in Hackney interupted the two MPs to ask why they were not supporting the campaign. A heckler shouted at Brian Sedgemore: "We elected you and we can unelect you, unless you stand with us who are not paying." A show of hands was called for and everyone in the room voted that they would not be paying with the exception of the two MPs on the platform.[21]

As the tide of opposition grew, there were many, including the majority of Labour MPs, who began to distance themselves from our programme of mass non-payment.

## WOBBLES AT WESTMINSTER

One of these was Harry Barnes, Labour MP for North-East Derbyshire, who at least tried to argue a case against non-payment. In a letter to Labour MPs, which called for support for a mass Labour Party and TUC organised demonstration against the poll tax in London on May Day, he also attacked the policy of mass non-payment:

> Anger against the tax has started to take off. But much of it is disorganised and directionless and prey to the mis-leadership of groups such as *Militant*... They have moved into the vacuum and assumed, often with the worse sort of manipulation, the political leadership of the campaign... If Labour were to take a more vigorous stance on the poll tax it could help shift debate away from the debilitating notion

that the only effective way to oppose the poll tax is through mass non-payment. [22]

I wrote to Harry Barnes and invited him to elaborate his views in our pages. He responded, explaining his differences:

> Given that non-payment isn't the official programme of the labour movement and following a whole series of industrial and political defeats of the working class during the Thatcher years, I can't see a supposed mass non-payment campaign fulfilling *Militant*'s dreams... Non-payment can, however, be a legitimate part of the campaign, providing those who embark on it are made aware of the draconian measures that can be used against them, plus the limits of the financial back-up that is available to them. Those who go down this road deserve whatever moral and political support we can give them. It will be pursued by a good number of people, including myself. But I won't encourage people to place themselves in personal danger.[23]

He was replied to in the same by Kath Dunn and Rachel McRoy, secretary and chair respectively of the Clay Cross Anti-Poll Tax Union in his constituency. They wrote that Harry had

> criticised the lack of fight from the Labour leaders but unfortunately he has no real strategy himself. Harry is suggesting that the campaign should include non-payers and those who will pay and he refers to the All-Britain Anti-poll Tax Federation as a narrow campaign. This is the opposite of the truth. The mass non-payment campaign has drawn more people into action than any other struggle against the Tory government. For instance in Clay Cross, part of Harry's own constituency, our anti-poll tax union has drawn hundreds of people into activity.[24]

On this issue, right-wing Labour MPs, as well as some on the left, shared common ground. The SWP, for instance, had moved from a lukewarm and passive support for the anti-poll tax campaign to opposition to the strategy of "non-payment". Just prior to the 31 March demonstration, they declared in *Socialist Worker*:

> The government calculates that a passive non-payment campaign can be whittled down eventually to a level it can manage... Activists should recognise a majority of workers are likely to feel they have no choice but to pay. Many will fear the consequences of court proceedings and

falling into debt. Some will fear the loss of their jobs if they are fined.[25]

Some capitalist commentators, like *Guardian* writer Victor Keegan, were to the left of the SWP on this issue:

> Judging by experience of Scotland and opinion polls in England and Wales the number refusing to pay will run into millions. Since enforcement on such a scale is impossible, this will not only bring the law into disrepute, but will generate a fresh backlash against the tax by those who are currently paying up. [26]

*Socialist Worker* was reinforcing the arguments of Labour's right-wing. They had disparaged the non-payment campaign in Scotland, downplaying its significance, and consistently underestimated the numbers who were not paying. They claimed that: "A similar pattern is likely in England and Wales." At the 4 March Scottish Unity conference, where all the regions of the anti-poll tax campaign came together, the SWP opposed mass non-payment and argued that without the backing of the trade union leadership the campaign could not succeed!

The attacks on the movement and on *Militant* were mere pin pricks as the build up to the 31 March demonstration took shape. In the weeks leading up to this event there was much speculation in the ranks of the Federation and also in our national offices as to the expected size of the London demonstration.

Estimates of those attending ranged from 20,000 to 50,000. No one, even those on the ground who were predicting a big turnout, fully anticipated the scale and size of the demonstration which assembled on 31 March.

## ANTI-POLL TAX ARMY

The front page of the *Militant* for the demonstration declared: "Join the anti-poll tax army" and "Don't pay, drive the Tories out".[27] In the same issue, sold widely on the demonstration, details were given of how the sheriff officers were being defeated in Scotland. A report also appeared showing how the National Union of Journalists (NUJ) had voted overwhelmingly for a resolution in favour of mass non-payment of the poll tax.

In a by-election in Mid-Staffordshire held just before the demonstration, a Tory majority of 14,654 in 1987, had been turned into a 9,449 Labour majority. One phrase was heard again and again during the campaign: "She's gone too far!" This was the feeling in particular about the poll tax. A TV company asked voters who deserted the Tories, in a special poll, why they did it. All of them except one said that it was the poll tax which was responsible. Pundits found that people were more interested in the poll tax than in the by-election itself. Two huge anti-poll tax federation public meetings were held in Mid-Staffordshire on consecutive evenings, attended by 350 in Lichfield, and 450 in Rugeley.

These were easily the biggest of the election campaign. Many more would have attended but for the Tory scare stories and the police horses gathered outside the meetings implying that anybody who attended was walking into a riot. Over 20 newspapers and four TV stations attended the Lichfield anti-poll tax meeting. The Labour Party wrote all its members urging them to stay away. Yet, the opinion poll carried in the *Independent on Sunday*, which put Labour 28 points ahead was conducted on the two mornings after these anti-poll tax meetings. They obviously had a profound effect. Yet the response by the Labour officialdom to those who had organised them, which had clearly boosted Labour's support was greater attacks and more repression.

In Liverpool, Labour's regional policeman, Peter Kilfoyle, and national organiser, Joyce Gould, attended the Labour group meeting to make sure that they didn't vote the "wrong way" on the poll tax issue. 27 right-wingers voted for a £448 poll tax, with 21 Broad Left councillors opposed.

The anti-poll tax movement in fact had electorally rebounded to the benefit of Labour. Even Tories like John Biffen recognised this: "The poll tax has been a lightning conductor for the discontent and it explains much of the Mid-Staffordshire debacle."[33]

This discontent was prepared, in the main, and organised by the anti-poll tax federation, with *Militant* supporters and members playing the decisive role.

## THE DEMO

Their reward was the magnificent sight of 200,000 mass demonstrations in London and 50,000 in Glasgow on the 31 March. The

London march, said Tony Benn, was the biggest demonstration since those of the Chartists, 150 years ago. Wave after wave of protesters flooded from buses, cars, coaches, and trains into Kennington Park, the starting point. Many people were forced to get out of buses and walk the last mile as the drivers tried to escape from traffic jams. The vast majority of those who attended had never been involved in a demonstration before. The old, the young, disillusioned ex-Tories, even a retired and bemedalled old soldier from Bournemouth, assembled for this mighty demonstration of working-class power.

In the park, speakers invoked the traditions of the past to vindicate what was being proposed today. Phil Maxwell, then leader of Tower Hamlets Labour group, said that they would not prosecute non-payers if a Labour council were elected in May. He reminded the crowd of the Poplar councillors in the 1920s:

> They did not say 'We would like to give this money to the poor but we would be breaking the law and Ramsay MacDonald would turn around and call us Toytown revolutionaries'... Our struggle is greater than any Tory law. We base ourselves on the struggles of the miners and ambulance workers and all the others who have resisted Tory laws. I have already had my poll tax bill from the council.[28]

He then proceeded to rip it up, to great acclaim and scattered it into the crowd. Margi Clarke, star of *Letter to Brezhnev*, told us that the poll tax was an evil privatisation of the vote.

> I'm fortunate enough to be able to pay the poll tax but I'm here on behalf of everyone who can't. It is brilliant that *Militant* has organised this. I've supported many causes, like Greenpeace. But this campaign needs a cutting edge and that is *Militant*.[29]

Forty Kent anti-poll tax protesters retraced the route of the peasant revolt, beginning in Faversham and marching 75 miles through Sittingbourne, Maidstone and Gillingham. They participated on the march as did demonstrators who had marched all the way from Tory Maidenhead to Trafalgar Square. A packed train arrived from Cornwall. *Militant* sellers did a roaring trade on the day, with 8,000 papers sold in London and a further 1,500 in Glasgow. Such was the anticipation of the organisers of the demonstration that they had requested from the Environment Department permission for the final rally to be diverted from Trafalgar Square to Hyde Park. Also, on the eve of the demonstration, the Federation had issued a call for a peaceful demonstration. And the great bulk of the marchers adhered to this advice. Ian Aitken, of the *Guardian,* no friend of the left, described the march as "one of the biggest peaceful demonstrations ever staged in the nation's capital". It represented a triumph for the anti-poll tax movement, above all the All-Britain Anti-Poll Tax Federation.

In Glasgow, 50,000 marched in scenes reminiscent of the days of Red Clydeside. There was participation from all sections of the working class and it seemed from all areas of Scotland. Tommy Sheridan declared to the crowd, prior to catching a plane to address the Trafalgar Square demonstration:

> Over one million haven't paid. There hasn't been one warrant sale. Over ten million in England and Wales are joining us now. We're on our way to victory![30]

# 39.
# THE RIOT

SCOTLAND'S DEMONSTRATION passed off peacefully, which was not the case in London. The responsibility for this has to be placed firmly on the shoulders of the government and the police. This demonstration had attracted all of those who felt victimised by Thatcher's rule. The homeless, unemployed youth, the oppressed and destitute, miners, as well as printers and others who had felt Thatcher's boot in their back - all were thirsting for revenge against the government and this was an occasion to take it.

However, the march was completely peaceful, like a carnival at the outset. By the time the head of the march had reached Trafalgar Square, there had only been one arrest. The Square was soon full to its capacity of 70,000. This was at a time when the bulk of the march had not yet left Kennington Park. In Whitehall, a group had gathered around the barriers opposite Downing Street. About 150 to 200 of what stewards believed were anarchists and Socialist Workers' Party members were hurling abuse at the police and also at the stewards. Some of the anarchists were drunk and abusive. Many of the stewards believed that the march had been infiltrated by a handful of agent provocateurs as well as unorganised youth who were just looking to take their revenge on the nearest symbol of authority.

## DOWNING STREET

For almost an hour, the stewards had attempted to make sure that the rest of the march just passed by the 100 or so who had sat down opposite Downing Street. Some people, especially those with children, decided to sit on the grass and have a rest. One of the stewards, Colin Fox, reported that as the stewards got to Downing Street, about 40 anarchists were sitting in the road and

as their numbers grew they were obviously intent on causing trouble.

They began throwing placards, cans of lager and even crowd barriers about. They were aimed at the police but most fell short, on people on the march. I shouted at them to stop throwing but it had no effect. By this time they considered the stewards fair game. As some idiot shouted: "Get the stewards first!" I was hit on the head by a full can of lager, causing me to drop my megaphone. As I bent down to pick it up I was kicked three times in the back and legs. Just then, a hail of missiles rained down, the police burst through and started flailing out at anyone they could hit, even though they had stood idly by for a good 40 minutes and watched... What on earth were the police commanders thinking of, charging the 300-400 trouble makers in Whitehall up into the crowd gathered in the Square? It was like throwing a lighted match into a petrol tank.[1]

## CHIEF STEWARD

In effect, this was the beginning of a police riot. Steve Glennon, the Federation's chief steward, takes up the story:

> We diverted the march at Parliament Square along Bridge Street and down the Embankment then up along Northumberland Avenue, as pre-arranged with Scotland Yard. But while this was happening, snatch squads had come in opposite Downing Street. It was bystanders who took the brunt. Then police horses followed going up onto the grass outside the Ministry of Defence where families were sitting down watching the demonstration... Stewards were coming under organised physical attack. People with loud hailers were calling on marchers to attack them as 'police collaborators'... The police had stopped the march entering Trafalgar Square, despite the sheer pressure of marchers still coming in at the bottom of Northumberland Avenue. The scuffles started at the top. This turned into a battle... The riot police then made charges and police vehicles drove at speed into peaceful sections of the crowd... Running battles took place... I appealed to a very senior police officer who was on the [Trafalgar Square] plinth at the time to get through to control and withdraw the horses and riot police. I even said that my stewards would go in and try to restore order. This would have been at great risk to ourselves. By this time, nutters up in the scaffolding were dropping objects down indiscriminately.[2]

There was no doubt that small groups were acting as provocateurs, whether consciously or unconsciously it was not possible to say. But the overwhelming majority wanted to have a peaceful demonstration, as is indicated by the account of Martin Davis, a steward who was sent into Whitehall when the demonstration was diverted:

> We managed to organise a few small meetings in Whitehall, trying to get the demonstrators together and appealed to them to move on, keep the march moving and rejoin the main march on the Embankment. We said that although people were angry, they should save their anger for the bailiffs. The majority agreed with me. We took a vote on it in several meetings and moved on. Obviously the sectarians were very annoyed with what I'd done but weren't prepared to listen to people and take part in a debate.[3]

Following the demonstration and the scenes of chaos and "disorder" which flashed around the world, a colossal propaganda campaign was launched by the Tories and their kept press. The purpose was to smear the organisers of the magnificent demonstration. Yet 99.9 per cent of those who had participated in the march accepted the decision of the Federation for a huge, but peaceful and democratic demonstration of support for mass non-payment. They had actually voted in favour of this before the march left Kennington Park. We pointed out that "a tiny handful of anarchists, egged on, usually from the back, by members of fringe groups... tried to provoke a conflict with the police in Downing Street. These groups had done nothing to build the anti-poll tax movement."[4] The main responsibility for the violence lay on the shoulders of Thatcher and her government.

## 70,000 HOMELESS IN LONDON

There were at that time 70,000 homeless in London alone. There was burning resentment at the systematic harassment of youth by the police in London. "The violence witnessed on Saturday," we said, "is rooted in capitalist society and the brutal class measures of the Tory government over the last decade." We went on to say:

> Does this then justify unprovoked attacks on the police and looting, as the anarchists and some quasi-Marxist sects truly believe? No! It is one thing to understand the causes of... violent behaviour of a big layer of youth and it is another thing to justify it as some of these irresponsible groupings believe.[5]

The 31 March demonstration and "riot" was one of the most important events in labour movement history this century. By itself it did not finish off the poll tax or Thatcher. The honour for fulfilling this belongs to the eventual 18 million-strong army of non-payers and those who welded them into an unbeatable force. But these mighty demonstrations were a visible and dramatic expression both to the British ruling class and to the world of the scale of opposition to the poll tax and the burning hatred of the Thatcher government and the system upon which it rested. It marked the begining of the end of Thatcher. She herself testifies to this in her memoirs:

> ... the most public opposition to the community charge came not from the respectable Tory lower-middle classes for whom I felt so deeply, but rather from the Left... They found little sympathy from the law-abiding mass of Labour supporters. But there were enough people ready to take the lead in organizing violent resistance. On Saturday 31 March, the day before the introduction of the community charge in England and Wales, a demonstration against the charge degenerated into rioting in and around Trafalgar Square. There was good evidence that a group of troublemakers had deliberately fomented the violence. Scaffolding on a building site in the square was dismantled and used as missiles; fires were started and cars destroyed. Almost 400 policemen were injured and 339 people were arrested. It was a mercy that no one was killed. I was appalled at such wickedness.
> For the first time a government had declared that anyone who could reasonably afford to do so should at least pay something towards the upkeep of facilities and the provision of the services from which they benefitted. A whole class of people - an 'underclass' if you will - had been dragged back into the ranks of responsible society and asked to become not just dependants but citizens. The violent riots of 31 March in and around Trafalgar Square was their and the Left's response. And the eventual abandonment of the charge represented one of the greatest victories for these people ever conceded by a Conservative Government.[6]

## REAL THREATS TO DEMOCRACY

Thatcher had pictured the organisers of the campaign as a "threat to democracy". This was from a government which had sought to emasculate the trade unions, including eliminating the right to belong to a union for GCHQ workers, attacking journalists in the press and the media, and driving 17 million people into poverty. The Labour leaders had reacted to the poll tax demonstration and riot with a call, in the words of Roy Hattersley, for "exemplary punishment" for those tried and convicted for participating in disorders. We replied:

> In the light of the frame-up of the Guildford Four, of the Birmingham Six and many others... we do not share Hattersley's touching faith in capitalist justice. [We continued]: It is impermissible to collaborate with the capitalist state, even against those whose methods and actions we implacably disagree with. Disrupters and disorganisers of Saturday's demonstration should be dealt with by the forces of the labour movement and not by the capitalist state.[7]

It was necessary to make this statement because, quite shamefully, Steve Nally and Tommy Sheridan had been accused after the demonstration by the some small groups of threatening to 'name names' of those who deliberately set out to disrupt the demonstration. The implication, repeated *ad nauseum* in the months that followed, was that *Militant* supporters would collaborate with the police and supply to the state names of their opponents who they believed were involved in 'violence'." This was totally false. Steve Nally and Tommy Sheridan were both overwhelmingly re-elected as national officers of the Fed despite these unscrupulous allegations.

In a separate demonstration in Cheltenham, formerly a sleepy backwater, 48 demonstrators were arrested at the same time as the events in London.

## THE AFTERMATH

In the aftermath of the demonstration, *Militant* was full of letters from those who overwhelmingly blamed the police. One account showed that in the Strand, two policemen, when they saw the police vehicles and mounted police being deployed, stated: "Oh, no. They're sending the tanks in!"[8]

One vehicle reversed at 50 miles per hour down the road as people scattered and as a woman with a toddler in a pushchair came running into Charing Cross Station declaring that she had never been so frightened in her life. In Trafalgar Square the organisers had appealed to the crowd to disperse. However, many people, particularly young people had gathered outside South Africa House. But instead of waiting for them to disperse, as they were beginning to, a police commander must have given the order for vans to be driven into the crowd. Dispossessed youth with nothing to lose, many of them homeless, weren't prepared to take this. The decision was then taken to send in the mounted police, many of whom had smiles on their faces as they charged the crowd. The crowd fought back and forced the horses into retreat. But then the police called up the reserves. The overwhelming conclusion was that the police deliberately provoked the confrontation, seizing on the actions of an irresponsible unrepresentative group who were just looking for trouble.

## VIVA THE FED!

However, none of this dampened the mood of elation and the sense of impending victory as the great majority of anti-poll tax marchers left to prepare to continue the battle. Ironically, a South African draft-dodger who was temporarily settled in Britain, was at the Trafalgar Square demonstration and claimed that he had

> learnt an important lesson. I was under the rather naive impression that British policemen are somehow different from their South African counterparts. How wrong I was. It seems that policemen the world over are the tools (in most cases willing) of the ruling class. Certainly, in my part of the crowd the police were incredibly provocative. They sped through the crowd in their riot control vehicles with no regard for those less agile or for those simply unable to move because of the sheer size of the crowd... As the speaker from Romania [Radu Stephanescu, who had been brought over from Romania by *Militant*] pointed out, and as we have learned from countries the world over, people power is a reality which can be obtained by mass united action even when the ruling class and their bully-boys attack the working-class movements. Viva the All-Britain Anti-Poll Tax Federation! Viva![9]

Expressing the awe at the size of the demonstration, were those like a 19-year-old who had gone on a demonstration for the first time on 31 March:

I hope that in 20 years time I can look back and be proud to have been the child of world revolution and tell my children: 'I was there, I saw it all happen, I saw Thatcher fall!' The tail-end of my childhood, my entire teenage years have been intimidated by Thatcherism. I hope that the 1990s and my 20s are free of Thatcherism, as so many in this country do. Then maybe it would be fair. I don't know what the next ten years hold but I do know it's better to die on your feet than live on your knees.[10]

## MEANWHILE AT THE TUC

This was not, however, the view of the right-wing group dominating the general council of the TUC. They had spent so much time on their knees they did not know the difference. Four days after this epic mass demonstration, outside Central Hall, Westminster, an old worker commented to those who had participated:

> You people should be proud of yourselves, organising a march of a quarter of a million. What these people have organised today is pathetic.[11]

"These people" were the TUC, whose rally against the poll tax was about to start. In a hall holding 3,000 people, 800 were admitted, mostly union officials. This was the long-awaited TUC protest which was supposed to have started at 10.30am that day with a march from Euston organised by the Camden trades council and backed by the Greater London Association of trades councils. The police were worried. If the unofficial Federation's march could pull 200,000 on to the streets, how many would turn out on this "official" occasion? The answer soon became clear - about ten: Tony Benn (the speaker), a few union officials and four from the Federation. The march was therefore called off. This fiasco was a product of the puerile, quietist attitude of the TUC towards struggle. At the Central Hall rally, Norman Willis argued that the best way to fight the poll tax was to wait for 1992 and the general election. He then attacked the "violent scenes" in Trafalgar Square. This was too much for postal workers who came to their feet denouncing the violence by the police. One said: "I can't afford to pay my poll tax," to which Norman Willis shrieked: "You are the best allies the government has got!" He ended his contribution with a ranting denunciation of non-payment. An USDAW official tried the same tack, attempting to frighten workers with dire warnings of what would happen to them if they didn't pay.[12]

Campbell Christie, Scottish TUC leader, contrasted the violence in London with the peaceful march in Glasgow on the same day - forgetting to mention that the Federation had organised both. The difference between the two demonstrations was that the police had run riot in London, whereas they had not in Glasgow. In the aftermath of the demonstration police swooped on the headquarters of Islington Against the Poll Tax "and harassment took place of anti-poll tax campaigners in Norwich and other areas". An Old Bailey judge actually ordered 25 newspapers and TV companies to hand over film and photographs of the demonstration to help the police "investigation" into the riot. This was just a legal go-ahead for a police rampage over the next few weeks.

The local elections in May represented a severe defeat for the Tories. They attempted to cover this up, with the aid of their kept press, highlighting the "victories" achieved in Wandsworth and Westminster. We revealed that: "In Wandsworth and Westminster there was open, legal buying of votes.'[13]

A few years later, the District Auditor came to the same conclusion. But at the time of writing he has not been able to act with the same "vigour" that his counterpart in Liverpool and Lambeth did in debarring the councillors in these areas. Nationwide, there was an eleven per cent swing against the Tories, enough if a general election had been called at that stage for a parliamentary majority of 80 for Labour. Bradford, the northern "jewel" in Thatcher's municipal crown, was won back to Labour. In Liverpool, entirely due to the magnificent struggle in the 1980s and the legacy of the 49, the Tories were virtually reduced to a political sect, with just seven per cent of the vote and two councillors. In Scotland, they came third behind Labour and the SNP and there was a massive swing to Labour in the Midlands. Their only crumb of comfort was in London, and even here there was a 6.5 per cent swing to Labour. It was undoubtedly the poll tax and the mass opposition which had been built up that benefited Labour. Despite the disquiet, and the outright hatred felt by many workers at the shameful position of the leadership on the issue of fighting the poll tax, the party was nevertheless seen by the mass of working people as the only viable alternative on the electoral front.

Significantly, outstanding anti-poll tax fighters, like Anne Hollifield in Lambeth and Wally Kennedy in Hillingdon, were elected to local councils.

In Tower Hamlets, on the other hand, the Liberals were helped back into power by stepping into the gutter and openly resorting to racist propaganda. Only later on, when he could no longer avoid it, did Paddy Ashdown and the Liberals at national level ineffectually distance themselves from the racists who had infested the Tower Hamlets party. In the aftermath of these elections, the right staged a coup in Liverpool against Keva Coombes, the leader of the Labour group and a non-*Militant* left-winger. They were only able to do this because Labour's national executive committee had suspended 15 left-wing councillors who had voted against implementing the poll tax. This was just two weeks after Labour had taken a further ten seats from the Liberals.

The events of February and March had shaken the Tory government, particularly the 31 March demonstration. But Thatcher was determined that there would be no turning back. In May she even misquoted Heseltine and declared he was: "right when he said this morning that this Conservative government will fight and win the next general election with the Community Charge in place."[14]

It was clear that Thatcher had retreated into her bunker and was determined not to give an inch. Chris Patten, the Environment Minister had actually charge-capped 21 local authorities - all Labour. Buoyed up by the massive response of the previous two months, the non-payment army was, however, realistic enough to understand that it would take further action, possibly the removal of Thatcher herself, before the tax would be broken. Therefore, a strategy and programme was mapped out for the following months. A number of new initiatives were launched in May, including a meeting of Labour councillors in June, which would pledge not to pay the poll tax. They would plan how to put pressure on local councils not to implement the tax. It was also agreed to hold a trade union conference on 23 June to build support for non-payment in the workplaces. It was also proposed to organise a "long march" from Glasgow to London in early September in order to publicise the non-payment campaign.

In May, Tommy Sheridan travelled to London to address a hushed press conference at the House of Commons. He gave the figures for non-payment in England and Wales which had risen dramatically. Even the Association of Metropolitan Authorities (AMA) had said there was "a massive non-payment rate of around 50 per cent".[15] On the other hand, mass summonses were being prepared of non-payers by some councils. First in line was likely to be Medina Council on the Isle of Wight. *Militant* gave, together with the Federation, very effective advice, both of a legal and non-legal character, on how to fight the poll tax.

# 40.
# DEFENDING NON-PAYERS

INEXPERIENCED AND somewhat naive at the beginning of the struggle, anti-poll tax activists became experts in the task of fighting the bailiffs and in England and Wales (where the enforcement law was different from Scotland) in appearing and defeating council representatives in courts. Legal precedents were set, creating mayhem in courts throughout Britain and reinforcing the clamour for the repeal of the poll tax. Some councils had made block bookings in the courts, indicating the massive strength of the non-payment movement. We advised early on:

> The more non-payers go to court, the more chaos the system will be thrown into. If one out of every 37 people eligible to pay did this, the courts would be clogged up for 17 years.[1]

At the same time, an appeal for industrial action, particularly by those asked to collect the tax, was made by the Federation. There was a reponse to this call in May from workers in Glasgow and London.

At Glasgow's Cranston Hill Social Security office, civil servants struck for a day against deducting the tax from benefits. The strike followed an occupation of the Provan DSS office by the anti-poll tax federation . The Federation had won an assurance that claimants would have the right to appeal against any action taken against them. In Greenwich, strikers in the council's housing department told us: "We don't want to pay it, we don't want to collect it and we wouldn't be having this dispute if it wasn't for it."[2]

The first serious flashpoint in the poll tax courts came in the Isle of Wight. Medina council was the first in England and Wales to issue summonses. In response to this, two meetings were organised by the anti-poll tax federation, with Steve Nally and Alan Murdie (a barrister from the Poll Tax Legal Group) speaking. Hundreds who received summonses came to the court. This did not just happen happen "spontaneously". As soon as summonses were issued, the anti-poll tax union hit the press. This emboldened workers to turn up to court. The huge anti-poll tax meetings prior to the court appearance also had their effect.

The anti-poll tax union had drawn in legal experts who were invaluable in convincing people to appear and represent themselves. Inside the court, booing and hissing at the council's witnesses, only met with mild rebukes so people became bolder. The first batch, which were expected to be dealt with summarily, took one and a half hours. The delaying tactics completely clogged up the courts and people became bolder with more elaborate speeches, points of legal procedure, etc. Eventually, the council accepted that insufficient time had been given between the final reminder and the summonses. All summonses were dismissed and therefore the proceedings were abandoned for the day. Commenting on these events, Steve Nally stated:

> I felt like we had scored at a Wembley Cup Final when the court on the Isle of Wight threw out the 1,800 summonses for non-payment of the poll tax.[3]

A vivid account of these events by Alison Hill concluded:

> based on this experience, I cannot see how successful court hearings can be held anywhere, particularly in the major cities. Such is the angry mood that completely unmanageable situations would arise. The granting of liability orders is not a foregone conclusion if we fight tooth and nail in the courts.[4]

Events similar to those in the Isle of Wight were played out in hundreds of councils throughout Britain. In some areas, the magistrates were forced to concede the right of defendants to challenge the council on procedural grounds in quite an extensive way. In other areas, "hanging judges", stipendary magistrates, ruled with an iron fist and stamped on the democratic rights of non-payers and the principles of "natural justice" which are supposed to apply in the courts.

Graham Lewis from Lambeth, with no legal experience became a local hero and legal whizz-kid. He holds the "world record"; responsible for something like five thousand summonses being overturned.

## NON-PAYMENT CLIMBS

By mid-June, *Militant* was reporting that the *Guardian* had admitted that non-payment was "running at 40-50 per cent in several large towns and cities".[5]

In London, it was quite clear that it was much higher than this and in Birmingham, 300,000 warning letters were sent out to non-payers. A correspondent commented: "I knew Thatcher was done for when I read that according to official figures a third of the people of Tunbridge Wells aren't paying!"[6] Jeffrey Archer ruminated in public: "If we could go back I don't suppose many of us would have brought in the Community Charge. It was a bad mistake."[7]

## TRADE UNIONS AGAINST THE POLL TAX

The conference for trade union action against the poll tax took place in Liverpool on 23 June. It had been held in the teeth of the union leaders' opposition but had assembled 1,287 delegates, from 651 organisations, representing 870,000 workers. The conference was extremely successful and showed the degree of support for the struggle at the base of the trade unions. However, effective trade union action did not take off, mainly because of the sabotage of the union tops, but also because of the successful non-payment campaign which proved in time to be the most effective means of shattering the poll tax.

At the National Union of Teachers (NUT) conference, a *Militant* supporter recounted that he "was only allowed to speak to one harmless sentence of my poll tax resolution - the NEC ruled the rest out of order because it called for non-payment."[8]

The fact that *Militant* was the backbone of the non-payment campaign was of course an additional reason for opposing this motion. The conference had actually voted in favour of strike action against redundancies. Jobs were threatened by the implementation of the local management of schools policy (LMS) and by poll tax capping. The NUT right-wing general secretary, Doug McAvoy, had been trying to make the union give up the strike weapon. He therefore reacted to the resolution by trying to frighten delegates and the membership at large by claiming that the resolution for strike action was "a *Militant* plot". Anita Dickinson, NEC member-elect, answered McAvoy's charges point by point. At the same time, the Federation announced: "Their biggest venture yet - a peoples' march against the poll tax, from Glasgow, the capital city of non-payment, to London."[9]

## POLICE RAIDS

The police, through "Operation Carnaby", initiated after the 31 March demonstration, began to arrest and initmidate those they thought were responsible for the "riot" on that day. In Hackney in June, 60 police officers smashed down doors with sledgehammers, destroyed furniture and fittings, let off a gas cylinder and arrested eleven people on "suspicion". The use of sledgehammers was invoked because of a police claim that they were dealing with barricades, which was nonsense. This raid on the homes of ordinary people took place at six o'clock in the morning. It was a blatant attempt to intimidate anti-poll tax activists. It did not succeed.

## YOUTH RIGHTS CAMPAIGN

While resistance to the poll tax grew, the right-wing NEC of the Labour Party busied itself by disassociating the party from the campaign and then took steps to disassociate itself from the newly-formed Youth Rights Campaign (YRC). With the paralysis and effective closing down of the LPYS this organisation had been formed to harness the energy of the youth who were now by-passing the Labour Party. It held a national conference on 15 April in York Hall, London, usually associated with boxing matches, rather than labour movement conferences. The platform was actually in the middle of the boxing ring. A young Tory councillor, Martin Callaghan ventured into the 'ring' to 'spar' with Paula Hanford of the YRC on the record of the Tory government. The 400 'judges' present considered that he was knocked out in the first round! This contrasted with the attitude of the increasingly rightward moving Labour Party leadership who were more concerned with expulsions than winning the youth who had been raised to their feet by the anti-poll tax campaign.

## IN MEMORY: PAT WALL

The right were also strengthened by the untimely and tragic death of Pat Wall, a lifelong fighter for socialism, a revolutionary, a founder of *Militant,* and a firm friend of all militants. He had been the youngest ever councillor in Liverpool in the 1950s, an executive member of the united Trades Council and Labour Party in which he helped to lead the fight of the left against the old established right wing. Through his job he was able to travel abroad and once canvassed for a socialist parliamentary candidate in Sri Lanka. He championed the cause of a persecuted black youth in the USA and made a lasting impression on the Bradford labour movement.Under his leadership, the Bradford trades council became renowned for its consistent effort to combat racism and to unite all workers against their common oppressors. He was a brilliant speaker, one of the greatest populisers of socialist ideas the labour movement has ever seen:

> A buzz of anticipation would fill a room when Pat was about to speak. He had a gift for relating the general ideas of Marxism to the day-to-day experiences of ordinary workers and for bringing out the essential humanity of Marxism.[10]

His warm personality and his refusal to descend to personal abuse was acknowledged even by his opponents. However, this had not prevented an avalanche of venom and personal attacks against Pat once he was selected to fight as the Labour candidate in the Bradford North constituency. In 1983, at the height of the election campaign, in an unprecedented outburst he was denounced in Bradford's St George's Hall by the then leader of the Labour Party, Michael Foot.

On Friday, 10 August, 700 attended a memorial meeting, chaired by Clare Doyle of the from our Editorial Board. From far and wide they had come to pay tribute to Pat Wall - labour movement leaders like Arthur Scargill and Dennis Skinner MP but also the rank-and-file activists. Terry Fields MP said: "We mourn his passing and we celebrate his life. Sleep well, comrade, in the knowledge you gave your best. No one could give more."[11] Not only was Pat Wall's death a sad personal loss to many comrades, but it was also a blow to the left. His replacement as an MP stood on the right.

# 41.
# INTERNATIONAL CHALLENGES & A HISTORICAL SETBACK

IN BRITAIN 1990 will forever be associated with the poll tax and how it determined Thatcher's fate. But on an international scale it will also go down in history as the year of decisive changes in South Africa, further convulsions in the Stalinist world, and the Gulf War.

The revolution in South Africa, for that is what it was, entered a new phase with the announcement that Nelson Mandela was to be freed. F W de Klerk announced this to the white parliament on 2 February. The African National Congress (ANC) and other banned organisations were to be legalised, a moratorium on hangings was introduced, and talks and negotiations were about to begin. We declared that this was

> a victory above all for the black working class and youth whose tireless organisation and struggle over many years have forced the retreat of the regime.[1]

His release resulted in an outpouring of joy and relief that swept from one end of South Africa to the other and reverberated around the world. The slogans of the masses were "Dissolve parliament now!", "Let the people govern now!" This was a popular way of expressing the demand for majority rule as a means of abolishing poverty wages, inferior schooling, segregated ghettoes and all the panoply of apartheid repression. In Cape Town, the celebrating crowds were confronted with police and dogs, whereas in Johannesburg, crowds of joyful demonstrators poured onto the streets as the news broke. The Cape Town police, as one black student put it, behaved "like a pack of wolves."

Despite these scenes of wild euphoria, we and *Congress Militant* warned: "The ruling class in South Africa and internationally... view negotiations with the ANC leadership as a device for curbing the movement of the masses."[2]

Some discussions took place in *Militant*'s ranks over the appropriate slogans to put forward in the changed situation confronting South Africa. Given the attitude of South African capitalism, backed up by imperialism, there was naturally a suspicion on the part of many workers that negotiations were a device for derailing the mass movement for majority rule. There was a tendency from the outset to reject the idea of negotiations. But it is not possible, particularly after a prolonged struggle with countless sacrifices by the masses, for a serious Marxist tendency to ignore calls for negotiations.

## NEGOTIATED SETTLEMENT?

Sometimes negotiations can be seen as an "easier" and less bloody means of achieving the objects of the mass movement. In Algeria, for instance, in 1960 the FLN (Front National Liberation, the Algerian liberation movement) entered negotiations with the representative of French capitalism, de Gaulle. The latter had originally come to power on the basis "Algerie Francais". But it became clear to de Gaulle - a consummate and brutal representative of French capitalism - that it was impossible to hold down a whole nation in chains. Determined to extricate French imperialism from the impasse he soon entered negotiations with the FLN. In this situation it would have been false to have opposed negotiations given that a million Algerian people had already been killed in the war. There was a craving for peace, both of the French people but particulary on the part of the Algerian masses. Drawing on this experience the leaders of *Militant* and *Congress Militant* put forward the slogan of "negotiations for majority rule".

Explaining its position in the pages of *Militant*, the leadership of *Congress Militant* stated:

> Socialists do not oppose negotiations in principle. It is a question of negotiations over what, and on which terms. But, as the military theorist Clausewitz explained, you cannot get more at the negotiating table than you have won on the battlefield. The first demand of the black masses is for one person one vote in an undivided South Africa. How can de Klerk - or any capitalist leader - concede this? The independent, revolutionary movement of the working class and youth has forced the regime into making the present concessions. But the regime has not yet been defeated. That is why majority rule is not on offer.[3]

De Klerk's concessions arose from a combination of factors; the partial lull in the mass movement following the state of emergency imposed in 1986, the Namibian settlement, but above all the disorientation of the ANC and "Communist" Party leadership in exile, increasingly thrown off balance by Gorbachev's policy changes. Gorbachev's detente with imperialism and the emergence of pro-capitalist forces in the Soviet Union was bound to have a huge effect on an ANC leadership which had for decades in any case based themselves on the programme of "two stages" - the idea that 'democracy' can first of all be established within the framework of capitalism, in co-operation with the 'democratic capitalists'. Walter Sisulu, a top leader of the ANC, had recently stated: "Socialism is merely an ideal, and the ANC is not promoting it at present." Our analysis has stood the test of time. Events between 1990 and 1994 have evolved in their broad outline in the way that was anticipated by these two journals. The South African ruling class gave concessions, the right to vote, "universal suffrage", but because of the various blocking mechanisms agreed to by Mandela and the ANC leadership, this did not result in 'majority rule'.

However, even in the teeth of all the evidence to the contrary Ted Grant stubbornly adhered to the idea that the apartheid regime would make no concessions which would fundamentally alter the basis of that regime. It was just one of many examples of a failure on his part to recognise the profound changes which had been wrought in the world situation. This undermined all the "certainties" of the past. Ted Grant occupied a minority position, which was not reflected in the public position put forward by *Militant*.

## MANDELA'S RELEASE

The actual release of Mandela saw a quarter of a million rally in Cape Town for his first speech after 27 years of imprisonment. In Soweto, AK47s were fired in the air and thousands flocked to Mandela's home in Orlando West. Workers in Durban "toyi-toyied" throughtout the night and thousands marched in Inanda, which had been the centre of fighting between Inkatha and the ANC in the previous months. Among black youth in Inanda Mandela's release triggered massive euphoria, with many thinking that 'liberation' was close at hand. There was even a feeling in the town that the release of Mandela would allow the youth to finish off Inkatha. These hopes were to be cruelly dashed with the savage counter-revolution unleashed by Inkatha vigilantes, which over a few days following the release of Mandela left 50 people dead. Among industrial workers there was a more cautious response, with great mistrust of de Klerk, the bosses and even of some of the ANC leaders.

One metalworker shop steward told us that workers thought: "Nelson Mandela has been released by de Klerk to disarm us", while a hospital worker said, "The capitalists are not interested in how we live. That is why we need socialism."[4]

Nevertheless, Mandela's release was celebrated worldwide with traffic around Trafalgar Square brought to a halt by a jubilant crowd. In London schools children and teachers celebrated. A million had toyi-toyied in Soweto and were emulated by others, particularly the youth, on an international scale. The trust in Mandela in general seemed limitless as he declared to the thousands in Soweto and Cape Town that he stood by the principles that he had been imprisoned for. He supported the guerilla wing of the ANC and "armed struggle". He also called for the nationalisation of the mines and monopolies. He called for "decisive mass action to end apartheid." He called for sanctions to continue. But on the basis of the next three years of negotiations, and the backdrop of savage civil war against the best of the youth and the working class, Mandela was to moderate his demands. Nevertheless, his release and the unbanning of the ANC ushered in a completely changed situation which would inevitably result in a complete dismantling of apartheid and a new era for South Africa.

## EAST GERMANY

At the beginning of the year, following the collapse of the Berlin Wall, the most critical issue was to appraise events in East Germany and likely perspectives. The flood gates had been opened by the collapse of the Wall. The headquarters of the secret police (Stasi) was stormed on Monday, 15 January, in East Berlin. The "Peoples' Police" (VoPo) actually allowed demonstrators into the building, in fact three buildings formerly housing the Stasi. Those who entered were stunned by the sheer size of the complex and the fact that the Stasi had their own shops, stocked with western goods unavailable to ordinary people.

Some looting began to take place, but, as in Russia in 1917, committees were formed spontaneously on the stairs to stop them. Searches took place to ensure that nothing was taken out of the building.

The new prime minister, Modrow, arrived to speak to the crowd. The mood was very hostile to the SED ("Communist" Party). However, the general line of the SPD in the East was to allow the government to rule until elections on 6 May. Supporters of *Was Tun!*, the new Marxist paper of *Militant*'s sister organisation in East Germany, were handing out leaflets, calling for "council democracy". It also called for a campaign for the immediate removal of the government, the breaking off of roundtable talks between the opposition and the government and the formation of councils of action as a basis for workers' democracy. One worker asked our German correspondent:

> "Are you in favour of a market economy?" I replied no. He said he was in favour of a market economy - but one controlled by a strong state! This shows the confusion of ideas in the movement.[5]

This confusion provided the basis for the complete transformation of the situation in East Germany. An opinion poll in December 1989 showed 71% of easterners wanting East Germany to remain a "sovereign state" and only 27% in favour of East and West Germany building a "common state". But the lack of an alternative way forward, the growing feeling that the East German economy could not develop without outside help and hostility to the bureaucratic elite's attempts to remain in power, all came together to fuel the desire for rapid unification with West Germany.

At first the West German capitalists were reluctant to take over the East. But fearing the increasing unrest would start to destabilise West Germany and seeing an opportunity to rid themselves of some of the remaining effects of losing the Second World War, they changed their position.

By February events had moved so quickly that the question of unification of East and West Germany was now posed. Even a few weeks before, we commented, "unification seemed a remote possibility. Now it appears quite possible within a few months."⁶

The SPD played a key role in pushing this process along. In mid-January they were the first to raise the idea of monetary union, something which Kohl only supported in early February. But once the West German government decided to take over the East they moved ruthlessly. Kohl played a leading role in the March East German election, securing 48.1% of the vote for the CDU led alliance when only three months before the CDU was getting only 4% in opinion polls.

It had become quite clear that without the "Wall" the East German Stalinist regime could not sustain itself. The SED had lost over half its members, the economy was in chaos and droves of young people and specialists were threatening to leave for the West. Industrial production had already begun to suffer with a drop of five per cent in the previous year. While recognising the direction in which the movement was going, we still argued:

> Had there been a real Marxist party in the East capable of arming the workers with a programme for the overthrow of the bureaucracy and the establishment of workers' democracy, the political revolution could have easily been carried through. The establishment of a healthy workers' state in East Germany would have had a magnetic effect on the workers of both Eastern Europe and Western Europe, including West Germany (FRG).

The article concluded:

> Unification is now taking the form of a counter-revolution, welcomed by many East German workers at the moment - but which they will come to regret as the full consequences of capitalist rule are brought home to them. The nationalised, planned economy will be rapidly dismantled by the West German capitalists, and the East German workers will experience ruthless exploitation by the big monopolies - who will arrogantly take their revenge for the loss of the eastern zone after the defeat of the Nazis in 1945.⁷

The attempt of Modrow to bargain with the West German Chancellor, Kohl, had come to nothing. Because they wanted to take over the East, the West German government had steadfastly refused to come up with the DM15 billion (£5.3 billion) "solidarity aid". The situation had reached the stage where workers in East

Germany now saw the West as an almost automatic source of higher living standards. We commented:

> They [the working class] will soon find out that everything in the capitalist garden is not so lovely. They will experience intense exploitation - unemployment for many - and cuts in the social wage. Today's illusions will give way to bitter disappointment, and they will move into struggle against their new capitalist bosses.[8]

## COUNTER-REVOLUTION

However, unlike others, some claiming to be Marxists, we faced up squarely to the likely development of events in East Germany and the rest of the Stalinist world:

> The collapse of a nationalised planned economy, even though misdirected by a bureaucracy, is an historic setback for the working class. The bureaucracy has also opened the door to counter-revolution in Poland, Hungary, and possibly other states in Eastern Europe.[9]

We predicted that these countries would face social revolution, "new Octobers", particularly if the planned economies were liquidated, and in some countries where the process was stuck half-way, a mixture of a social revolution and a political revolution would be posed in the future.

In the case of East Germany, we warned about the consequences of a capitalist counter-revolution for the East German workers. In June it became clear that

> employment will fall dramatically. For instance, Opel is planning to employ 3,500 workers producing 150,000 cars a year - in a plant which at present employs 9,200 producing 75,000 cars a year... at the beginning of May the East German Unemployed Association reported that 600,000 workers had been sent 'blue letters' (warnings of redundancy) to take effect on 2 July. With two million unemployed in West Germany already, a capitalist united Germany could rapidly find itself with four million unemployed.[10]

At the same time, West German capitalism, with a trade surplus of DM140 billion in 1989 and overseas assets worth DM500 billion, had significant reserves with which to finance investment in the East. But this was at the cost of enormously burdening West German capitalism. The takeover of the East would have big consequences in Europe in the following years. We said:

> While this state-financed spending could prolong German capitalism's current boom, it will not give East Germans the same living standards as West Germans. A united capitalist Germany could resemble Italy but with a west-east rather than a north-south divide.[11]

East German workers were looking towards unification in the expectation of a rapid improvement in their conditions but the prize that they would reap would be unemployment, rising rents, social cuts and increased prices which in turn would provoke movements of opposition which will have an effect in the whole of a united Germany.

West German capitalism was using the "fast route" of Article 23 of the West German constitution to absorb East Germany as rapidly as possible. In effect "unification" was equivalent to one big monopoly taking over a smaller, dilapidated firm; West German capitalism taking over another "country". Moreover, the West German capitalists had only been able to pursue this policy with the open acquiescence, even assistance, of the East and West German Social Democratic leaders. In the East, the SPD were co-operating in a CDU-led coalition government, an essential step for ensuring a smooth development of capitalist restoration. Because of the consequences for the East German workers and also because it meant the liquidation of the planned economy, the German Marxists, now present in both the East and West German workers' organisations, called for a break with the policy of supporting capitalist unification. They stood for the defence of the nationalised economy in the East and for the unification of Germany on the basis of workers' democracy and socialism.

## GORBACHEV

At that time the social counter-revolution in East Germany had gone much further than elsewhere. In the Soviet Union, however, Gorbachev had also been compelled in February to abolish Article Six of the constitution which guaranteed the political monopoly of the Communist Party. The events in Romania, with the overthrow of Ceausescu, the collapse of ruling "Communist" Parties in several Eastern European states, and above all the growing discontent in the Soviet Union, pushed Gorbachev to take this step. At the plenum of the "Communist" Party where this had been proposed, Gorbachev was confronted by a crowd of 100,000, the first time a mass demonstration for democracy had taken place in the USSR. They demanded the abolition of Article Six, Gorbachev admitted:

> We hoped to mount the peak of the crisis in 1989, but recent events have shown that there has been no change for the better... yes, there are shortages of resources and technology.[12]

Official figures for 1989 claimed that there had been a drop of three per cent in gross national product, but the reality for the masses was that shortages were growing. Significantly, the number of working days lost through strikes and disputes had grown dramatically since the movement of the miners in 1989. Strikes and demonstrations in fact had taken place in many cities throughout the USSR.

## NATIONAL REVOLT

Alongside of this, was the growing nationalist revolt in the Baltic states and the civil war in Armenia and Azerbaijan. Faced with this mass turmoil, the "reformists", the pro-capitalist wing of the bureaucracy, posed the need for an "intermediary authoritarian period". One of them admitted:

> It would have been much better if Gorbachev had strengthened his power in an administrative way, as took place in Hungary under Janos Kadar, or as in China under Deng Xiaoping.

In answer to the question whether the market could be introduced, this individual replied in the negative:

> Obviously not, since 80 per cent of the population would not accept it. The market, after all, denotes stratification, differentiation according to income. One has to work very hard in order to live well.[13]

Echoing this, Professor Norman Stone, the High Priest of Toryism, when asked in a television interview whether he thought a market economy could be introduced in the Soviet Union, replied: "We haven't managed it yet in Liverpool, and what we have in the USSR is Liverpool to a power of 100."[14]

However, *Militant* did not discount the possibility of capitalist counter-revolution in the Soviet Union, particularly in the light of the events in East Germany and the growing revulsion of the masses at the shortages and corruption of the bureaucracy:

> The pro-capitalist reform wing, on the other hand, favour policies which would impose appalling conditions on the working class, threaten the underlying gains of the planned economy, and plunge the economy into chaos.[15]

## PRESS PRAISE FOR GORBY

The abolition of Article 6 was a confession of bankruptcy on the part of the bureaucracy. The ignorant scribes in Fleet Street interpreted this as a blow against "Marxism". We commented:

> The CPSU Central Committee has just agreed to amend the notorious Article 6, which wrote the "leading role of the party" into the constitution. This was written by Brezhnev in 1977. In 1917, the only party to be banned was the Black Hundreds, the fascist party responisble for organising vicious pogroms against the Jewish population. The party of 'liberal' capitalism, the Cadets, was untouched until at the end of that year, it colluded in a violent uprising.[16]

It was an abomination to compare the actions of the Russian elite with the workers' democracy of the Bolsheviks in the immediate aftermath of the Russian revolution.

## TERRY IN SIBERIA

There were still some voices in the Soviet Union seeking to invoke the example of Lenin and Trotsky as an alternative to the market. This was shown at the gathering of 600 delegates and visitors at the independent workers' organisations from all over the Soviet Union, meeting in the Siberian city of Novokuznetsk which proposed to set up a "Confederation of Labour of the USSR".

Terry Fields, MP, was invited to the conference as the only international speaker. It soon became clear to Terry and other British visitors that in the town the workers had begun to develop their control over society:

> Only the most hardened cynic could doubt that the workers can run society after experiencing the efficiency with which the congress was organised - and which contrasted so greatly with the incompetence of the ruling bureaucracy... Members of the workers' committee, which represents all sections of the workforce, are held fully to account. One of them, a miner, explained that he was part of a brigade of five miners. The other four covered his work and released him to do 'their work' on the workers' committee. In return for getting his wages, he had to see them regularly and account for what he had done.[17]

One worker explained to Terry Fields how the bureaucracy in the Soviet Union had been rooted in

> "the backward conditions of society at that time, the low cultural level of the Russian workers, the predominance of the peasantry." Terry Fields addressed the conference, expressing the solidarity of the international working class, but when he turned to the question of the market, with the aim of dispelling illusions, murmurings of discussion was interspersed with applause. A heckler who would simply not accept that there could be problems in a market economy shouted out: "We've had enough!" Other workers countered: "Let him carry on! We want to hear what he has to say!"[18]

Terry finished with an appeal for workers East and West to link up in common struggle for workers' democracy and socialism. Following the official conference session 100 delegates and visitors attended a meeting where a video on the British miners' strike was shown, followed by two hours in which workers eagerly fired questions at Terry Fields to answer. The conference showed the confusion which existed amongst the working class but also the possibilities for putting forward the ideas of workers' democracy if a sufficient Marxist force would have existed at that stage. Commenting on his visit, in an interview with *Militant*, Terry Fields stated:

> I've been very lucky in my life, representing trade unionists and working people in Liverpool. But I never thought, when we viewed from afar the workers' struggles developing in Eastern Europe, that I'd have

the privilege of addressing the first congress of the independent trade union movement of the USSR.[19]

## ROMANIA

In Romania, the movement had features somewhat different to the rest of Eastern Europe. The old regime had been overthrown by an uprising of the workers and the youth, arms in hand. This put its stamp on the movement. Workers in the factories were refusing to return to work until the old managers had been removed. At the same time, independent unions were being hastily improvised and all that remained to do to effect a relatively peaceful transfer of power would be to link up the democratically elected committees on a local, regional and national basis and then proceed to take over the functions of the state. But the absence of a far-sighted Marxist leadership with a mass base produced an extremely unstable equilibrium. On the one side were armed workers with the elements of independent organisation and alongside them the remnants of the old bureaucratic state apparatus. The contradiction between these was to result in sharp turns in the situation before the year was out.

In the first election in June, the pro-capitalist parties suffered a serious setback with a landslide victory for the National Salvation Front (NSF). This was also a body blow to those capitalist politicians in the West who salivated at the prospect of a seemingly unstoppable advance towards capitalism in Eastern Europe. However, an article that appeared in *Militant* in June, somewhat overstated the case,

> The election result shows that the social base of pro-capitalist restorationist trends at this moment in time are extremely weak in Romania. Even the mass of the peasants voted for Iliescu - a fact which cannot be explained away by coercion alone.[20]

In truth, the National Salvation Front also had a programme for a return to the "market", albeit at a slower pace than the open pro-capitalist formations. Soon after its election, it was confronted by violent protests by anti-government student demonstrators in Bucharest which was followed by a counter attack of miners, which was widely commented upon in the capitalist press in the West. To a man, Tory politicians and their press condemned them as "rent-a-mob miners" (William Waldegrave) or "dirty-faced runts" (The *Observer*).

The stand that *Militant* took on these events provoked controversy even within its ranks, which was reflected the paper:

> In Romania at present the workers are clearly opposed to dismantling state ownership. Their revolution was a mass, armed insurrection. That left its mark in the working class's outlook. The working class responded to Iliescu's call because they saw the students' demands for the immediate restoration of the market as a counter-revolution. This is one reason for the vast international propaganda campaign.[21]

It became clear, as information filtered out of Romania, that the students who had gathered in University Square, proclaiming "Down with Iliescu, down with the fraudulent elections!" were completely out of tune with the mass of the working class and the peasantry. This demand was raised only weeks after Iliescu had won with over 85 per cent of the vote, in an election which even foreign observers considered reasonably fair. The arrogance of some of the leaders of the anti-government movement were shown by the poet Doina Cornea, a dissident under Ceausescu, who had linked herself to the right-wing Peasants' Party. She stated:

> I have come to the conclusion that universal suffrage - at least when you are moving from a dark night into daylight - is not fair. It's not the majority who are right. There are a few people... who see we are threatened with another night, the rest don't see it.[22]

This elitist arrogance repelled them from the mass of the working class. We gave critical support at that stage to the National Salvation Front's defence of "state property", but called for an independent mobilisation of workers to defend these gains. It came out for a workers' militia, controlled by committees democratically elected from the factories and workplaces, linking up with the committees of rank and file soldiers in the army.

## DEBATE ON THE MINERS

Such was the controversy around this issue that a page of the paper carried letters which both agreed and disagreed with the line of the editorial board. One from Stoke-on-Trent disputed the contention that the miners were defending "the gains of the December revolution".[23] Another argued that the miners were "putting ordinary workers down".[24] While conceding that there were many excesses in the miners' movement, others, such as a letter from Fife, argued:

> You are right to point out that the students are out of touch with the workers. Having been in Romania in March, when I spoke to the most radical students, I can testify to their confusion and contempt for the working class who they see as ignorant and 'bought-off thugs'.[25]

Another from Blackpool entirely supported the line adopted by the paper:

> The attitude of Marxists to the NSF should be critical support, but combined with a vigorous campaign for workers' democracy and the building of genuine independent workers' organisations.[26]

Another, disputing the earlier letter from Stoke, argued

> I believe only critical support can be given [to the miners]. But I must correct the person who wrote that they were a Praetorian guard putting down ordinary workers. This is not true. They didn't attack workers. They targeted the students whose ideas were counter-revolutionary.[27]

The open debate on this issue in the paper, in which the pros and cons were forcefully argued, gave the lie to those critics of *Militant* who contend that its supporters "receive" worked-out positions which are then just blindly adhered to. Nothing could be further from the truth. On this and on other key questions the widest and most democratic discussion - much more open than under right-wing domination of the labour movement - took place within our ranks.

This was not just because "democracy" is a "good thing". The oxygen of debate, discussion and democracy is vital in a Marxist organisation which is looking for clarification of ideas. So long as it is conducted in a comradely and open fashion nothing but good can come from discussion and debate within the workers' organisations.

## DEBATE ON EASTERN EUROPE

And in a world which was in political and ideological turmoil there were many issues to be debated. One issue was what did the events in Eastern Europe signify for the working class. In April *Militant* received a letter from a reader, Kathleen Jones, in Shropshire. She wrote asking if we were "quite convinced that what is happening in Eastern Europe is revolution, not reaction". She went on:

> In Romania, the crowds yelling for the banning of the Communist Party and the reintroduction of the death penalty do not sound very revolutionary... Visitors to Hungary have reported that too many people there think that Western democracy is ideal. Marxists know that the real choice facing the world is not between dictatorship and democracy but between capitalism and communism... Following the failure of two revolutions - the Russian and the Chinese - I am afraid we may be faced with world reaction.[28]

We fully replied to this important letter. In the revolutions in Eastern Europe, there had been moves towards a revolution - a political revolution to overthrow the bureaucratic Stalinist totalitarian elite - and alongside it a counter-revolution to eliminate the planned economy and restore capitalism. In Eastern Europe revolutions, had leapt, from one country to another as in 1848. Kathleen Jones was implying: "Yes, revolution has taken place, but look how they have ended up." But the mass of the working class, let alone the peasantry, do not go into a revolution with a prepared plan of social reconstruction but mainly with a sharp feeling that they cannot endure the old regime. This is particularly the case in a movement against a totalitarian one-party regime, where the working class are denied full access to information and the media or the right to exchange ideas.

What was unmistakeable in all the movements in Eastern Europe and even in the Soviet Union was that there were, at first, elements of a programme for a political revolution, this was shown in the demands for free elections, independent trade unions, a free press, and above all, the elimination of the bureaucracy's bloated privileges. *Militant* did not dodge the implications of its analysis and pointed to the capitalist restoration in East Germany and the possibility of this being repeated elsewhere in the Stalinist states.

At the same time, because of the unbridled denunciation of all that was associated with the Russian revolution, above all the planned economy, we pointed to the advantages of a plan of production and what this had meant for the Soviet Union:

> Between 1929-1935, industrial production in the USA fell by 25 per cent and in France by 30 per cent. In Britain, it rose by 3-4 per cent. But in the USSR, it rocketed by 250 per cent!

Pointing to the situation that was developing in Poland, we also declared that

> the working class has already had to pay a terrible price for attempts at capitalist restoration. In January (1990) living standards plummeted by 30 per cent and unemployment has spiralled to 250,000 already. 1,500 companies have been marked out for privatisation but only 12 targeted for immediate sale.

As to the future we declared:

> One thing is clear, a stable capitalist democracy is impossible for the countries of Eastern Europe. A fledgling capitalist class, if it manages to survive a very difficult birth, will be forced to take refuge from the anger of the masses by seeking to establish military police dictatorships.[29]

## A BALANCE SHEET

*Militant* presented a balanced picture of the very complex processes unfolding in the Soviet Union. Drawing on history, it showed that

> the seeds of counter-revolution are always to be found in even the greatest revolutions. Whether or not these seeds grow and become full-blown, and thereby inevitably smother and crush the revolution, depends on a number of factors. Not least is the role of a mass party and clear leadership capable of guiding the working class in completing the revolution. If power is not transferred from the ruling class, or caste, either through the absence of this leadership, or because it is

faulty, then the revolution stops half way and the masses become disappointed and indifferent. This creates the conditions for the growth of counter-revolutionary forces and with them the danger of the defeat or derailment of the revolution.[30]

## HISTORIC SETBACK

This general theoretical analysis was vital in consolidating the forces of Marxism in the face of the historic setback, which the liquidation of the planned economies represented. In 1990 it was not at all clear how far this process would go. *Militant* carried many on the spot reports from special correspondents in Russia, which at each stage showed the difficulties facing the bureaucracy in moving along the road to the establishment of a "market". In fact, the difficulties were so great that by mid-November some influential voices in Russia were calling for the establishment of a "Committee of National Salvation" which would replace the rule of Gorbachev and would find no room for Yeltsin either. One of the proponents of this idea was Colonel Alksnis, an advocate of a return to the market but without "democracy". His reasons for advocating this, he expressed in the Congress of Peoples' Deputies: "Most frightening is that the people will come out on the streets."[31]

## NATIONALISM

One of the consequences of the weakening of the rule of the bureaucracy was the unleashing of centrifugal national forces in the Soviet Union. In the course of the year the long-predicted resurgence of Russian nationalism had also materialised. It was expressed in the election of Boris Yeltsin as president of the Russian Federation by its newly created "parliament". Yeltsin used this position as a counterweight to the "national" president Gorbachev. The Russian Federation constituted 148 million people, 52 per cent of the USSR's 290 million. Its land mass covered eleven time zones and Moscow alone had ten million people, more than all the Baltic states combined. In the Russian parliament naked appeals to Russian nationalism were made: "Russia for the Russians". Both the Yeltsin wing of the bureaucracy and the Stalinist "conservatives" complained about the sacrifices of "benevolent Mother Russia" which had been repaid with black ingratitude by the 14 other republics.

It is true that the Russian workers had made huge sacrifices, not only for future generations of Russians, but for the great idea of a democratic, socialist federation which would eventually encompass the globe. We pointed out that

> even in a healthy, democratic workers' state, the national question would have to be approached with great care and sensitivity. In the transitional period from capitalism to socialism, the needs of the economy and an international division of labour would have to be balanced against the needs and wishes of each nation.[32]

However, this would only be possible through a regime of workers' democracy which could both fully exploit the potential of a planned economy and also satisfy the national and cultural demands of each nationality or ethnic grouping. The greatest condemnation of the Stalinist bureaucracy was that at that stage the nations which made up the USSR were at each other's throats.

Gorbachev, it was predicted, would also be incapable of satisfying the demands of the aroused nationalities. Even if the USSR was to break up, we believed, this would not be the end of the matter.

> Even if there were a capitalist counter-revolution, a new emerging capitalist class would have the same voracious appetite as under the Tsar. It would seek to dominate the peoples to the East and the West. It would have the same tendencies as American imperialism, the West European capitalist classes or Japan to defend, if necessary, arms in hand, its 'spheres of influence', markets or potential markets, power, prestige and income.[33]

Is this not what has developed since 1990 with Yeltsin's doctrine of "the near abroad" and the re-establishment of a very loose "rouble zone", whereby former "independent" nationalities have once more come under the benediction of "Mother Russia"?

Stalinism was not capable of solving the national problems of the Soviet Union. On the contrary, it has enormously aggravated them and invented 'new' national problems where they did not exist before. On a capitalist basis, the national problem cannot be solved.

A democratic workers' state would immediately grant the right of self-determination, up to and including the right to secession, to all the peoples. But Marxism does not stand for the Balkanisation of the Soviet Union. The organisation of industry through a democratic plan of production and a division of labour on a continental scale can give immeasurable advantages for rapidly raising living conditions and satisfying the cultural aspirations of the mass of the people. Once peoples are freed from forcible retention within the state and see the advantages of co-operation, to paraphrase Lenin, they would not cut away but voluntarily co-operate in taking all the peoples of the Soviet Union forward. Workers' democracy is the weapon with which the working people of the Soviet Union will carve out a future free from the bureaucratic nightmare of Stalinism on the one side and the horror of mass unemployment, poverty and national divisions of capitalism on the other.[34]

# 42.
# THE GULF WAR

WHILE THE capitalists could rub their hands in glee over events in the former Stalinist states, their perspective for a "New World Order" was abruptly and rather rudely shattered when in August the tanks of the Iraqi military dictator Saddam Hussein rolled into Kuwait. US imperialism, with a little delay, responded by dispatching troops to Saudi Arabia. The events in the Stalinist world had an important effect on US imperialism's decision to intervene. They could not have acted so brazenly or so precipitately without first of all receiving the benediction of Gorbachev. For the first time in the history of the United Nations, there was unanimity in the Security Council which resulted in the US being able to carry a resolution for a total embargo of Iraq: oil would not be exported from Iraq and imports (except food) would not be allowed in. Even the Chinese bureaucracy, eager to arrive at an agreement with imperialism, voted for the resolution. The British gutter press reacted in a predictable fashion with the *Daily Star* wanting the government to drop a "very big bomb" on Baghdad - never mind the fact that British nationals in Kuwait had just been taken hostage.

## AGAINST THE WAR

From the outset, we made it clear where we stood:

> We are not prepared to support any war aims of Bush or Thatcher, they can't be trusted at home or abroad. They only defend the needs of the bosses.[1]

The paper also pointed to the hypocrisy of those who were calling for Saddam's blood and yet backed him to the hilt in the bloody war between Iraq and Iran:

> We won't forget it was Thatcher, along with the French and American governments and the Soviet bureaucracy too, who financed the Iraqi

military build-up. They armed Saddam to the teeth, creating the fifth largest army in the world.[2]

There was no widespread opposition from these governments when the Iraqi regime was pursuing its monstrous genocide against the Kurdish people, with the wiping out of whole villages through gas attacks. This was a war for oil in which workers

> will pay the price. The big petrol companies haven't wasted a second in pushing up prices by as much as 10p a gallon. But they have got 30 days' stocks bought before the Iraqi invasion and the oil price rise.[3]

Clearly, in the past Saddam had been America's man, armed to the hilt during the war with Iran. Saddam undoubtedly believed that he had the silent acquiescence of US imperialism in invading Kuwait. He had actually signalled his intention to invade. Glaspie, US Ambassador to Iraq, met Saddam Hussein on 25 July, just a few days before the invasion of Kuwait, and the transcript of that meeting showed that she turned a blind eye to Iraq's claim to Kuwait. Glaspie had stated in that meeting: "The US has no opinion on an Arab/Arab dispute like your border disagreement with Kuwait."[4] The clear implication was that Saddam was free to invade.

But by invading Kuwait Saddam gained control of 20 per cent of OPEC oil production, which gave him "at least a finger-hold on the lifeline of Western capitalism".[5]

Because of this, Saddam undoubtedly evoked enormous sympathy from the masses in the Arab world, even those who viewed his dictatorship with distaste. At the same time, we did not hesitate to explain the bloody role of the Saddam dictatorship in suppressing the workers, peasants and national minorities within Iraq. We implacably opposed the pro-capitalist, role of the Labour leaders:

> Even before the US had gone into Saudi Arabia or hostages had been taken, Kaufman [Labour spokesperson on foreign affairs] was calling for "unprecedented measures", including a naval blockade of the Gulf and the UN intercepting tankers.[6]

Where the foreign policy of British imperialism was concerned, Neil Kinnock had become a tame pet. He assured the British people that as far as the Tory government was concerned "everything that can be done is being done". And yet these "dedicated democrats" had not even recalled Parliament, nor had the Labour leaders requested this, for fear that the Labour left would embarrass them by opposing the war. Even the right-wing Tory, Rhodes Boyson, asked for Parliament to be recalled.

In fact it took months of mobilisation, reinforcements and the gathering together of the biggest concentration of fire power ever before imperialism felt confident to make its move.

The Gulf War and the important political and theoretical questions which it threw up for Marxists provoked intense discussion within our ranks.

## READERS' QUESTIONS

In the meantime, the readers of *Militant* inundated the editorial board with questions about what position Marxists should take on the war. *Militant* replied to some important letters in its pages in order to open a dialogue with our readers. One letter was from Clive Jones in Oxford:

> I believe that this is a completely different situation to the Falklands and that most people are aware that both the USA and Iraq are pursuing the interests of their own ruling classes but are fearful that Iraq's military action could, if unchallenged, provoke a world war... Many workers have said: "I agree with what you say but how do we stop this madman?"[7]

The Editorial Board agreed that the situation in the Gulf was entirely different to that of the Falklands (see Chapter 20). In 1958, the Tory government had considered ousting the Emir of Kuwait and taking over the country in order to guarantee control of its oil supplies. This fact was sufficient to explode Bush and Thatcher's defence of "poor Kuwait".

The assembling of a massive war machine in the Gulf was not in defence of democracy or the peoples of the Middle East, but to uphold and reinforce the power of the US ruling class and that of Britain, France, West Germany and the rest. We argued that

> if imperialism's combined military might succeeds in crushing Iraq, not only Saddam or the Iraqi people will suffer. Imperialism and its

stooges in the Middle East will use this victory to push back the Arab revolution and to cow, with the implied threat of similar military action, revolutionary movements of the impoverished masses in Africa, Latin America or Asia.

We therefore concluded that,

> for the working class in Britain and throughout the advanced industrial countries, there should be implacable opposition to imperialist intervention.[8]

And yet it was indisputable that there were many workers who were repelled by the Iraqi dictatorship. Taking account of this, we declared that:

> [We do] not give the slightest support to the Saddam dictatorship. We would support the Iraqi workers and peasants in fighting for a socialist and democratic Iraq. If imperialism was to succeed in overthrowing Saddam... the regime that such a defeat would usher in would be a new dictatorship utterly dependent on the imperialist powers... an imperialist victory would also reinforce the hold of reactionary feudal sheiks in the Gulf states.[9]

The conclusion was that opposition to imperialist intervention was necessary:

> Let the peoples of the region, including Iraq, decide their own fate. Democracy will not be established in Iraq or Kuwait with imperialist bayonets. Only a socialist federation of the whole of the Middle East will allow the peoples of the region to really determine their own future.[10]

As to the rights of the Kuwaitis, the position of *Militant* was outlined in the paper.

> Iraqis consider Kuwait to be historically part of Iraq but a socialist federation of the Middle East would give the Kuwaiti people the right to determine their fate in a democratic referendum. They could decide whether they remained separate or linked with Iraq, possibly with some form of autonomy.[11]

## WITHDRAW IRAQI TROOPS?

Another question which was posed was whether *Militant* stood for the withdrawal of Iraqi as well as US forces from the Gulf? The criteria for Marxists on this, as with all other questions, is what would enhance the position of the workers and peasants of Iraq, the peoples of Kuwait and the Middle East as a whole? Clearly, if US imperialism was successful in evicting Saddam from Kuwait then the consequences of this would be the return of Kuwait to the reactionary rule of the feudal sheiks. Its consequences for Iraq, as explained earlier, would be to replace one dictatorship by another, resting on imperialist bayonets. We therefore did not favour this option. On the other hand, a movement of the working class, mobilising behind the peasant masses of Iraq to overthrow Saddam and establish a democratic and socialist Iraq would undoubtedly lead to the withdrawal of Iraqi troops and the right of the Kuwaiti as well as the Kurdish people to determine their own fate.

Meanwhile, the Gulf conflict was coming to a head. The looming prospect of bloody carnage had resulted in early January in British public opinion swinging against the war. The idea that this was a war to protect oil and profits had taken firm root. We called on our supporters to

> involve themselves as fully as possible in the Stop The War protests. Where local committees exist they should participate, putting forward the Marxist programme on this war. Where no committees exist they should set them up. Try to turn the campaign towards the working class movement in the workplaces, unions and Labour parties. Reach out to the youth in the colleges and schools.

We went on to declare:

> *Militant* supporters are not pacifists. We would fight alongside the rest of our class against a threat from anyone to our democratic rights... We will agitate amongst the youth of Britain to oppose the Gulf War and oppose any idea of conscription. We will work to create such mass resistance that the Tories could not contemplate conscripting our young people for this dirty war.[12]

The anti-war movement in Britain did not reach the proportions that it did in other countries. Before the outbreak of conflict there was big opposition to the war, reflected in opinion polls and also in many comments in our pages. One correspondent wrote:

> It reminds me of the Boer war. That was over gold; this is over liquid gold... We're not fighting for democracy. Kuwait has never been a democracy... If you did a census of everybody in the country, no-one would have voted for war in the Middle East. But they would have voted for millions of homes for the homeless and hospital beds for those awaiting emergency operations.[13]

Another correspondent commented:

> An oldish bloke at work said today that people he knew had gone to war to stop the Nazis taking over this country but this time it's not to prevent something like that; it's just for the oil companies. There's no-one except for a few headbangers at work supporting the war. Even these people, once you say to them: "Are you prepared to fight in that sort of war?" soon shut up.[14]

## OPPOSITION TO THE WAR

However, opposition to the war was hedged around with concern for the soldiers in the Gulf. This was a factor in the swing of public opinion in favour of the government once battle commenced. Nevertheless, there was significant and growing opposition to the war. This was reflected in our pages and also in the speeches of left MPs in Parliament. On Monday 21 January, Dave Nellist, speaking in the House of Commons, said:

> Those of us who vote against the war do not do so because we are against British troops... I have stayed up until the early hours to see what has been happening. I have seen American generals treating events as though they were a cross between an American football match and a video arcade. The Scuds versus the Patriots. One almost feels that the next thing to come on will be the 'Bomb of the day' competition... The *Sunday Times* quotes Pentagon experts saying that, within the first 36 hours, about 20,000 tonnes of high explosive were dropped on Baghdad and other towns and that it is estimated that between 100,000 and 250,000 people will lose their lives or be severely injured, suffering internal bleeding as a result of concussive forces.

Pointing to the hypocrisy of the government, he went on:

We do not support the Iraqi regime. But Iraqi pilots were trained in Britain. Perhaps the Republican Guards division is feared because its officers were trained at Sandhurst... This is supposed to be a war for democracy. The government talk of having the government of Kuwait restored. Last week the *New York Times* quoted someone saying that the Emir of Kuwait, once back in his palace, would still be a dictator. Who had that insight? It was Richard Nixon. He should know all about dictators - he propped up so many of them.[15]

## YOUTH STRIKE AGAINST THE WAR IN SPAIN

Throughout Europe, *Militant*'s sister organisations were to the fore in the anti-war movement. In Spain, for instance, the Spanish Students Union (SE) had organised and led a general strike of three million young people on Tuesday 15 January. *Militant* reported:

> Young people in Spain responded marvellously. 90 per cent of secondary school students (1,700,000) and 70 per cent of university students (700,000) answered our call for a 48-hour strike.[16]

There were demonstrations in over 100 regions and cities of Spain.

## DIFFERENCES ON THE MILITANT EDITORIAL BOARD

However, during the Gulf War differences within the *Militant* leadership over the war, which had been simmering behind the scenes, broke out into the open.

*Militant* had called a special conference to discuss the Gulf War in January 1991 (held at the London School of Economics). In the months leading up to this, a veiled 'war' of an ideological and political character was taking place within our ranks. On the one side, was the approach of the minority, typified by Ted Grant, wanting to predict exact time scales. Opposed to him was the majority, led by myself, Lynn Walsh, Bob Labi, Tony Saunois and others who proposed a more conditional approach. The changed world situation, dealt with earlier, demanded a changed approach on the part of the Marxists.

Ted Grant, at one meeting after another, said that if the war was to break out, it would last for a minimum of six months and probably for two years. In Spain, those gathered around *El Militante*, merely repeated this statement:

> A war against Iraq cannot be brief or easy... Once it starts, a war would necessarily be a prolonged and bloody affair. It could last for months or even a couple of years.[17]

*Militant* in Britain, however, never once carried a statement of this character. There was no other member of the National Editorial Board who adopted this approach, apart from Ted Grant himself.

## CONSCRIPTION

Nothing demonstrated Ted Grant's false approach more clearly than his position on conscription. At the rally in the LSE which preceded *Militant's* special conference, a Scottish comrade who was making the financial appeal stated quite correctly, that as an ex-soldier on the reserve list, if he was called up to fight in the Gulf, he would not go. This was denounced by Ted Grant. During his speech, he made the astounding statement:

> If conscription is introduced, let us be clear, the youth must go into the army. Of course (directly addressing the youth in the audience) some of you will be killed. But for everyone killed, ten will take your place![18]

This statement was greeted with stunned disbelief and anger. It was made despite the fact that a clear majority in the leading bodies of *Militant* disagreed with Ted Grant's proposals and had attempted to dissuade him from making these ideas public. Ted was besieged by the youth in the pub after the meeting. Yet despite this, at the conference the next day, he made exactly the same points in the course of introducing the discussion on the Gulf War. This produced a near revolt from the floor with the majority clearly opposed to his statement.

I intervened in the discussion, pointing out that in the event of conscription being introduced, then *Militant's* leadership would call a special conference to determine its attitude towards the issue. It was wrong to merely repeat Trotsky's position at the time of the second world war, as Ted Grant and Alan Woods did. At that time the outlook of the mass of the working class was determined by the threat of invasion from a foreign fascist power, with all which that implied: the destruction of democratic rights and the workers' organisations. In 1990-91 the Marxists were faced with a colonial war of intervention by imperialism in the Gulf. If Ted Grant's position of, in effect, accepting the idea of conscription had become the public position of *Militant*, it would have made it virtually impossible for *Militant* supporters to participate in the growing anti-war movement. Such movements initially were bound to have pacifist overtones. Marxists are not pacifists. But at all times Marxists distinguish between the false hypocritical "pacifism" of the capitalists and their reformist shadows within the labour movement, which invariably acts as a cover for war, and the genuine anti-war mood of the youth.

In the course of the debate at the special conference, I argued that if conscription was introduced (highly unlikely in any case in Britain) it would not mean that young people would passively go into a conscripted army. A situation could well arise where half, if not more, of the youth, would refuse to be drafted.
A similar situation developed in the US at the time of the Vietnam War when thousands of youth refused to do the dirty work of imperialism in Vietnam. On this issue, Ted Grant found no support within the ranks of *Militant*.

This dispute was a skirmish between the growing divergent tendencies within the ranks of *Militant*, which was to break out into open divisions just a few months later (see Chapter 44). It did not, however, prevent a serious intervention in the anti-war movement both in Britain and internationally. In Germany, for instance, the forces of *Voran* carried out an enormously successful anti-war campaign with very limited resources.

## VICTORY FOR BUSH?

The overwhelming superiority of the imperialist forces resulted in a rout of the Iraqi army. A hundred thousand Iraqis were killed or injured in the 100 hours of the land war - 1,000 casualties an hour. The US-led coalition suffered just 300 fatalities. We reported:

In the sands of northern Kuwait, packs of wild dogs tore at the raw carcasses that were once Iraqi soldiers. Iraqi troops had been mercilessly bombed as they retreated, obeying Saddam Hussein's final instruction to comply with UN resolution 660 and withdraw from Kuwait... Many of their officers had already got away, leaving the troops to fend for themselves... Tied down by Western forces and air assaults, they were stuck bumper to bumper in a ghastly traffic jam, 20 vehicles wide. There they perished in their thousands, defenceless, unable to resist. US bombers hardly had time to reload before they went back to join the "turkey shoot".[19]

The collapse of Saddam's resistance was itself a reflection of the internal weakness of his regime. This was something that we had not fully taken into account in our analysis of the situation leading up to the land war. Not only was Saddam confronted with the opposition of the Kurds, but the Shias also constituted a powerful force, demanding democratic reforms and the overthrow of his regime.

The Gulf War, imperialist ideologists argued, expressed perfectly Bush's New World Order. The brutal treatment meted out to the Iraqis was intended to keep the masses in the colonial and semicolonial world in a position of complete prostration before the economic and military might of imperialism.

To have entered the cities of Iraq could have embroiled US imperialism in a long drawn-out conflict resulting in high numbers of casualties. Not only would the coalition, painfully assembled, crumble but so too would the domestic support built up by US imperialism to justify its intervention in the Gulf. Moreover, US imperialism preferred Saddam in power to the alternatives which could follow his rule. This was clearly demonstrated when just a few weeks after the formal ending of the Gulf War Saddam's tanks were unleashed in the south and also against the Kurdish north.

We quoted the statement of a US official who told Western journalists privately: "It's easier to deal with a tame Saddam, than with an unknown quantity."[20] US imperialism's actions following the Gulf War revealed, particularly to the Arab peoples, its real purposes in intervening. It had allowed the Republican Guard of Saddam through US lines to crush the city of Basra, where the Shia population predominated, and assured Saddam that they would not intervene in the Kurdish north. Thus US imperialism gave tacit support to Saddam's bloody repression.

## ON TROTSKY IN RUSSIA

In Russia "the first ever meeting on Trotsky"[21] since the early days of the revolution had taken place, organised by *Workers' Democracy*, the sister organisation of *Militant*. The small but growing forces of Trotskyism in Russia had been instrumental in getting Trotsky's major work *Revolution Betrayed* published in the USSR. One hundred thousand copies went on sale, with an introduction by Elizabeth Clarke.

To launch these two publications *Militant* Editorial Board member Lynn Walsh travelled to Leningrad and Moscow to speak at public meetings about the importance of Trotsky's ideas today.

In Leningrad 50 people gathered in the building from whose balcony Lenin addressed the city's workers in April 1917. This tour took place at a time of further disintegration of the former USSR and with it the collapse in industry and the conditions of the people. A similar picture was evident in the states of Eastern Europe, formerly under the heel of Stalinism. The collapse of Stalinism had also led to a re-evaluation of the history of the regime and the suffering of millions of innocent people. Most accounts in the capitalist press concentrated on "dissidents", largely involving the middle-class intelligentsia, but hardly ever touched on the original "dissidents", the Trotskyists and Marxists who had opposed the Stalinist regime from the standpoint of defending the gains of the October revolution.

We sought to counter this in February with an interview with Alexander Tami, chairperson of Justice, a Russian organisation campaigning for the rehabilitation of victims of Stalin's repression and supplying help for those still alive. At 84 he still retained his "boyish enthusiasm" when talking about the revolution and its leaders Lenin and Trotsky. Though he was not a supporter of Trotsky or the Left Opposition, he was arrested, spending 17 years in the camps and mines of Siberia. This did not destroy his faith in the revolution. Instead he and the other prisoners kept "the image of Lenin before us. We knew some of us would not survive but believed we'd get socialism in the end." Tami went on

It was not a coup in 1917. Even historians today don't understand that. The people were with the Bolsheviks. They were a small party but had authority. There was an armed uprising but no killing. In the February revolution people were killed but in October only six or seven died. People regarded Lenin and Trotsky as equals but thought Lenin was more theoretically developed. He was a lawyer by education and very logical. But Trotsky was next to him, so it was wrong that Trotsky's name was deleted under Stalin.

He recounted a remarkable incident when Trotsky had spoken:

During the civil war I was part of a Komsomol [Communist Youth League] guard for deserters. Some were put in a barracks in Petrograd. Trotsky came to address them in the barracks square. When the chairman of the meeting introduced "Trotsky, the Commissar for War" there was a lot of shouting and swearing: "He's a Jew, a Yid. What's he doing here?" But Trotsky got up and said: "Yes, I'm a Jew. But what kind of Jew am I? One that gives land to the landlords? No, we give land to the peasants. One that gives factories to the big capitalists? No, we gave the factories to the workers". They stopped shouting and started to listen. He was a real orator. When he finished the chairman asked: "Right, who's for the front?" and all those deserters put their hands up! That was the kind of speaker Trotsky was. He could turn a whole meeting around.

He also recounted an incident involving Krupskaya, Lenin's widow, who Stalin had brow-beaten into submission.

She said: "You talk a lot but you should work as Lenin did. Yes, he was a simple, mortal person. You mustn't make some sort of god out of him. It makes me ill how you smear his name." Then she said: "You have to work. I'm afraid you'll talk Lenin to death and not get down to work." Of course she didn't get on with Stalin. When he came into the hall we stood up and started to applaud. She said: "Idiots, idiots! They're making a god out of him. Idiots!" She didn't say it to me. I just heard and saw how she sat there modestly, simply dressed, not with all the pomp of Stalin. I even thought to myself: "How is it that the wife of Lenin is not up there on the presidium?"[22]

# 43.
# THE POLL TAX IS BEATEN

ANOTHER "WAR" of kinds was taking place in Britain, within the labour movement. On 13 August, only a few days after Pat Wall's funeral, two right-wing councillors had entered the constituency office of Pat Wall. They insisted that the two assistants of Pat Wall gather their personal belongings and leave. This was just one example of the mean-spirited and petty approach of the right wing which was developing on a national scale.

In Basildon, three *Militant* supporters, John McKay, Eleanor Donne and Dave Murray were referred to Labour's National Constitutional Committee. Amongst the charges laid against them was that they were on a rally in support of the ambulance workers on 30 January, 1990.

Even in Dover and Folkestone, sacked P&O workers Sue Haynes and Andre Bradford, who joined Labour during the 1988-89 strike, were amongst seven party members under "investigation" along with Eric and Robbie Segal, both members of the Labour Party for 15 years. They were being accused of being "full-time Militants". One of the complaints against them came from an ex-Tory councillor who had joined Labour in the previous year. At the same time, *Socialist Organiser*, had been banned by the leadership. *Militant* defended the right of *Socialist Organiser* to put forward its ideas and sell its journal in the Labour Party, despite the many sharp differences of opinion with them and their supporters.

## LIVERPOOL

In Liverpool, the right-wing Labour Group was putting through rent increases of £4 a week with more and more Labour Party wards coming into opposition. There was opposition even from wards that had not supported the left in the past. The council acted in an unprecedented fashion in serving an injunction on Nalgo strikers. This injunction failed to stop a half-day strike supported by up to 6,000 Nalgo members. The strikers assembled at the town hall and cheered the 29 Broad Left councillors suspended from the Labour Group for opposing the poll tax and rent rises.

## PEOPLE'S MARCH

In contrast to the slavish tail-ending of the Tories, the People's March Against the Poll Tax was about to descend on London on 20 October. The marchers had taken the non-payment message to every part of the country. The incredible effect of this march was chronicled in a pamphlet *Diary of a People's Marcher* by Sally Brown. The highlight of the march, according to most marchers, were the events in Northampton around Cyril Mundin, a 75-year-old pensioner who had been taken to court and threatened with imprisonment for non-payment. The marchers occupied the council treasurer's offices and barricaded the reception area. The police outside were in force all around the building with dogs but phoned the occupiers to negotiate. The marchers explained:

> We demanded to see a council official to get Cyril Mundin's case dropped. The police said the council were terrified - they aren't used to getting their offices occupied. Well, they'd better get used to it.

Eventually, several marchers were arrested. Cyril Mundin still refused to pay the poll tax. He actually marched with the people's marchers out of Northampton and "wished he was young enough to come with us to London but he'll be down for the demonstration on 20 October."[1] Cyril was eventually taken out of the firing line when the *News of the World's* 'Captain Cash' paid his poll tax!

## LONDON DEMO GREETS MARCHERS

There was a tremendous welcome for the marchers on 20 October, 1990, with tens of thousands from London and thousands of others from as far afield as Glasgow and Liverpool. 35,000 in total greeted the marchers in London. A union representative from Beta, the entertainment union, declared:

> I've never been so proud of my union membership as when I saw our banner carried on the 31 March demonstration. I saw I wasn't alone,

that other Beta members were committed to ending the poll tax and fighting for socialism. I feel supported in not paying, knowing my union is backing me. That is what a union should be.[2]

Tony Benn declared at the rally that a *Channel 4* film about *The Battle of Trafalgar Square* demonstration which had recently been broadcast "showed there was a police attack on marchers to try to intimidate people into stopping the campaign."

## BRIXTON PRISON

The demonstration, while being enormously successful in highlighting the level of resistance to the poll tax, nevertheless ended with clashes when a separate demonstration organised by the "Trafalgar Square Defendants' Campaign" decided to march out of the park and picket Brixton Prison. Prior to this, the anarchist 'Class War' group had behaved in a fashion that was totally alien to all the traditions of the working-class movement. They had taken up positions at the front of the rally at the end of the march and began organised barracking of virtually every speaker. They tried to shout down Tony Benn and a couple of them followed Terry Fields MP as he left the rostrum, throwing insults at him. They had shouted at the elected leaders of the anti-poll tax federation and even those stalwarts who had marched all the way on the peoples' march. They threw beer cans at Federation secretary Steve Nally and filthy racist abuse was shouted at a black South African BTR striker who spoke at the rally. There were even chants on the demonstration of "Better dead than red," particularly aimed at the march organisers. We declared:

> Small groups like *Class War* and those they attract are an open door for provocateurs to enter. If the state forces wanted a group to use to incite trouble they would not have to look much further.[3]

We conceded that there were some young people totally alienated from society who could be won to a fighting socialist programme and the class outlook that *Militant* is based on. But at the same time, we pointed out that

> No-one has the right to abuse the democracy of the working class. All

demonstrations must be well stewarded and disciplined. Deliberately provocative actions must be kept in check and attempts to disrupt meetings prevented.[4]

An interesting event occurred at the rally when

> one Scottish lad lost his temper with the heckling and pulled at a heckler's long black mane. The hair came off, exposing a short-cropped scalp, its owner too shocked to do anything. Who was he? Who was he working with? And what, apart from short hair, was he trying to hide?[5]

The march to Brixton Prison was peaceful and largely composed of young people "shouting impolite references to Thatcher". But when it reached the prison, the police would not let the demonstrators cross the road to stand outside the prison gates. As the demonstration arrived, *Militant* described the situation:

> We were getting crushed at the front. There were some minor incidents - a policeman tried to grab a banner and got some abuse. A few empty beer cans were thrown. Then somebody threw a traffic cone. It hit a car. The situation rapidly became violent when a squad of police charged into the crowd to arrest people. This provoked a hail of sticks and bottles into the police lines. The police charged again. People at the front were being indescriminantly hit by police even though they hadn't thrown anything... A man was shouting "calm down!" to both demonstrators and police - he got a baton over the head.[6]

A Federation activist commenting on the actions of the Trafalgar Square Defendants' Campaign (TSDC), wrote: "In the weeks running up to the demos we repeatedly heard rumours of policemen talking of a 'rematch' for 31 March."

Some police chiefs had even told stewards that this was the attitude of some police. And undoubtedly some police saw the march to Brixton Prison as an opportunity to take revenge. At the meetings with the TSDC and Federation stewards the police chief in charge had warned that he would not permit demonstrators to assemble in large numbers outside the prison. The writer went on:

> The demonstrators arrested after the 31 March demo need an active

campaign of defence, so the Federation has always co-operated with the TSDC. But the TSDC ignored the feelings of the Federation that their feeder march would complicate matters, overstretch our resources and deprive the Federation of finances.

At a meeting, just before the demonstration, a Federation organiser warned the TSDC: "If I were you I'd be having a sleepless night about Brixton. You're in a very vulnerable position. I hope you've got your act together."[7]

The only response was a smile and a shrug of the shoulders. There was no stewarding of the picket and there was no clear line of communication of what should happen in the event of trouble breaking out. The actions of the TSDC were just one example of the splitting methods employed by groups with little real support on the ground.

## OPERATION CHEETAH

At the same time, the bourgeois press launched another smear campaign against *Militant*. The *Sunday Times* alleged that we were receiving funds from secret land deals in Liverpool. They had dredged the backstreets of Liverpool, vainly searching for one shred of evidence to link *Militant* with corruption. They had been given the opportunity to launch another vile slander campaign by "Operation Cheetah" involving an army of 280 police officers and the expenditure of millions of pounds. This was aimed against Derek Hatton who after years of persecution was found completely innocent of all the charges laid against him.

## THATCHER OUT!

These events took place on the eve of dramatic developments within the Tory Party. Following the humiliation of the Eastbourne by-election and after coming third in Bradford North, Tory MPs were terrified that even the safest of seats would be lost if Thatcher remained as leader. "The Iron Lady must go" became a behind-the-scenes theme. The crucial shots in the Tory anti-Thatcher campaign were delivered by Geoffrey Howe in the House of Commons in November which led to Michael Heseltine challenging Thatcher for the Tory leadership.

Our banner headline on the 23 November issue said: "Get out! - General election now!" The first part of this demand was fulfilled within hours; Thatcher had failed to get a decisive majority in the leadership elections in the Tory parliamentary party. She resigned on Thursday morning and *Militant* changed its front page to reflect this. The mood was ecstatic amongst working people. A supporter walking through London Bridge railway station said that when the announcement came over the tannoy "they were dancing down the escalators! There was spontaneous cheering, women screaming, and nearly a party on the platform."[8]

Glasgow students walked out at dinner time to hold a party outside the local Tory Party HQ. Press commentators speculated that it was Europe and any other number of issues which toppled Thatcher. But Thatcher and her entourage were clear: It was the poll tax in the main which led to her downfall. In her account of her years in power, she writes:

> Cranley Onslow then gave his assessment. He... did not believe that Europe was the main [issue]: it would not be crucial in a general election. Most people were worried about the community charge and he hoped that something substantial could be done about that. I intervened to say that I could not pull rabbits out of a hat in five days. John MacGregor supported me: I could not now credibly promise a radical overhaul of the community charge, no matter how convenient it seemed.[9]

It was the 18 million non-payers of the poll tax who were decisive in her downfall. Facing electoral massacre if she remained, Tory MPs brought her down after eleven years in power.

The Youth Rights Campaign had organised a champagne party outside Tory HQ the day after Thatcher resigned. And in the week that she resigned, the All-Britain Anti-Poll Tax Federation held their third annual conference with 2,000 in attendance. The Federation conference addressed the crucial issue of how to defeat the bailiffs if they were used in England and Wales as the Sheriff officers had been used in Scotland. Naturally there was rejoicing at the end of Thatcher and of Thatcherism, but a determination to continue the fight until the poll tax was dead and buried.

## BRYAN WRIGHT JAILED

This vigilant approach was vindicated when on Friday 7 December the first non-payer was jailed. This was the first person in 600 years, since the Middle Ages, to be jailed for not paying his poll tax. In prison, Bryan Wright, from Grantham, the poll tax prisoner, was given royal treatment by the inmates: "He's a hero to the lads in prison, even the warders. The prisoners say: "Good for you, Bryan, good on you. You stick it out." [10]

After vigorous protests he was released 14 days later. The implacable mass oppostion to the poll tax and the determination to see the struggle through to the end contrasted sharply with the mood of the Labour leadership. Kinnock was reputed to have been "down in the dumps" because his best bet for winning the next general election, Thatcher, had been removed from power!

In an open letter printed in *Militant* over the headline "Force Tories out", the Editorial Board addressed Kinnock:

> You have moved a vote of no confidence in the government and called for a general election, as *Militant* has done over the last few weeks. If you are serious about this demand, however, it is not enough just to raise it in Parliament... If you need advice on how to organise a mass demonstration, speak to the All-Britain Anti-Poll Tax Federation. In spring, they organised the biggest march since the Chartists.

It went on:

> You are so obsessed about opposing non-payment of the poll tax that you hardly mention it at all. You are still planning to expel Liverpool councillors who voted against implementing this hated tax. Instead you should be proclaiming that it will be abolished as soon as Labour is elected and promising an amnesty from the courts and bailiffs for all those who haven't paid.[11]

We did not, in truth, expect a reply from Neil Kinnock. And in the 'no confidence' debate, in the House of Commons, he was quite pathetic. He actually paid tribute to Thatcher, which must have gone down really well with the 900,000 people waiting for operations or the millions out on the stones who believed that Thatcher and the system she represented was responsible.

# 44.
# MILITANT FACES A BREAKAWAY

THE MONTH of April 1991 proved to be a decisive one in the evolution of *Militant*. The national leadership unanimously decided to support the setting up of an independent organisation in Scotland to take account of the extremely favourable situation which had developed for us there. In view of the fact that a minority, led by Ted Grant and Rob Sewell, subsequently used this decision as the main reason to split away from *Militant*, it is important to record that both Ted Grant and Rob Sewell voted in favour of this decision.

## EXECUTIVE COMMITTEE 10/4/91

At a meeting of the executive committee of the National Editorial Board held on the 10 April 1991 those present were Mike Waddington, Brian Ingham, Ted Grant, Rob Sewell, Jeremy Birch, Nick Wrack, Lynn Walsh, Peter Taaffe, Keith Dickinson, and Frances Curran. The minute dealing with this question reads:

> Peter Taaffe reported that in the discussion with the Scottish comrades, it had been agreed that there would be a big advantage in us establishing some independent organisation which could appeal to the thousands who had been pulled around us during the campaign against the Poll Tax. After some discussion, it was agreed that this be put to the National Editorial Board meeting in view of the urgency and the changes taking place in the Poll Tax campaign at the moment. The name and launching details would have to be worked out with them, but generally, we should first get the approval of the National Editorial Board.

Not one member of the Executive Committee voted against the proposal. At the National Editorial Board meeting which took place on the same day Ted Grant enthusiastically endorsed the proposal despite the opposition from other NEB members. Rob Sewell, lacking a sense of proportion, broadcast his view that a "revolutionary party" should be immediately launched not just in Scotland but throughout the whole of Britain! *Militant* took this decision against the background of the ending of the poll tax.

During the course of the Editorial Board meeting and in my discussions with the comrades from Scotland it emerged that without some kind of independent organisation those who were close to us through the poll tax campaign would not be drawn into the ranks our ranks. There was a real danger that a whole layer who were entirely sympathetic to our strategic aims, programme and our organisation could be siphoned off to the Scottish National Party. Therefore, the common position which arose from this consultation was to make the recommendation to the Executive Committee for a radical departure, particularly in Scotland, from the way in which *Militant* had traditionally organised. It was as a result of this meeting that the proposal at the Executive Committee was made to the full National Editorial Board.

At the Editorial Board meeting on 10 April, the minute dealing with this reads: "Independent candidates: the discussion was on whether or not *Militant* would support independent Broad Left candidates in Liverpool standing against the official Labour Party. Peter Taaffe introduced the discussion. Contributions from Helen Redwood, Ronnie Stevenson, Richard Venton, Alan McCombes, Ted Grant, Ray Apps, Peter Jarvis, Dave Cotterill, Tommy Sheridan and Bill Mullins. Peter Taaffe replied.

The report and proposals of the Executive Committee were agreed with one abstention (Ray Apps) and no votes against. At the subsequent Executive Committee under the title of *NEB Review*, the minute reads:

> Rob Sewell introduced the discussion, referring to the historic decision over the work in Liverpool and Scotland;... we should aim to produce special material on the turn in Scotland, for discussion at the June National Editorial Board. It was agreed that the Executive Committee should meet the Scottish NEB members before then.

It was also quite clear that two of the most prominent opponents of what subsequently came to be known as the "Scottish Turn" of *Militant*, that is Ted Grant and Rob Sewell, enthusiastically spoke in favour of this proposal and voted for it. If they subsequently changed their minds it was not for principled political reasons, as they sought to argue, but because Ted Grant in particular and Alan Woods had come into collision on largely secondary organisational, personal questions, with myself and those in the majority in *Militant*. They did attempt to foster the legend that this decision on the Scottish Turn was "rushed through the NEB and through the EC of *Militant*." If this was the case how was it that two experienced and allegedly "wily" operators such as Ted Grant and Rob Sewell could be rushed into taking such an important decision which subsequently they claimed was a departure from "40 years of work"? The truth of the matter is that this decision was so readily agreed to by the national leadership of *Militant*, and following them the great majority of the ranks, because it flowed from the objective situation confronting us.

## THE BACKGROUND

For months and years before this decision, from many quarters the question had been posed that, given the complete emptying out of the Labour Party, should not we take the step of launching an independent organisation? It was clear that such an initiative would find an echo amongst the advanced workers in Britain, repelled by the increasingly right-wing Labour and trade union leadership.

Our decision to support unofficial local Labour candidates in Liverpool was itself an anticipation of the decision to set up *Scottish Militant Labour* later on. We explained why this decision was taken;

> The right-wing clique who have hijacked Liverpool council have dramatically stepped up their attacks on council workers. Right-wing Labour councillors Frank Anderson and Frances Kidd (both GMB-sponsored) have threatened to send in private contractors to remove rubbish "If our binmen won't do it, we'll find people who will"... Selective strike action has begun... involving 310 NALGO members and 170 GMB Branch 5 workers. More are set to join the action.[1]

Kilfoyle was supporting the sacking of workers. The election in May resulted in a stunning defeat for "official" Labour. Wherever right-wing Labour candidates stood the official Labour vote collapsed. Mass abstentions and increased votes for the Liberals prevented Labour winning marginal seats. Yet these seats had massive Labour majorities when the Liverpool party fought on a socialist programme in the 1980s. In the final days before the polls the official Labour Party placed big adverts in the local press to appeal to Labour voters. The *Liverpool Echo* editorial urged support for Rimmer, the new Labour leader of the council. Neil Kinnock sent a personal message. All this lost votes for the "moderates". The five Broad Left candidates supported by *Militant* triumphed against official Labour, completely vindicating the stand of the *Militant* national and local leadership in supporting the decision to stand independently.

## WALTON BY-ELECTION

This was followed by the Walton by-election in which Lesley Mahmood was the candidate of "Real Labour". *Militant* entirely supported the decision of the advanced workers in the Walton constituency and throughout Liverpool to support a candidate standing in the best left traditions, a hallmark of this constituency. Walton had always been a bulwark of Marxism on Merseyside. The seat had been held by Eric Heffer who had been steadfast in his support of the Liverpool city council and of the heroic 49.

Eric died in May 1991 and his popularity was demonstrated by the thousand people who attended his funeral. The churchyard was lined with banners from the trade unions, anti-poll tax unions and Liverpool's suspended and surcharged councillors. The streets outside were lined with local people to say farewell to a working-class hero. Tony Benn spoke at the service and said that the press had tried to portray Eric Heffer as an old time socialist, a voice of the past: "But this is quite untrue. Eric was the voice of the future of socialist ideas."[2]

However, Neil Kinnock was moving mountains to impose a yes-man on the Walton Labour Party, in the form of Peter Kilfoyle. Kinnock had never forgiven Eric Heffer for his stand at the 1985 Labour Party conference and had not even turned up at his funeral. This was despite the fact that Eric had held high office in the party and fought for socialism all his life. The revulsion felt at the prospect of Kilfoyle stepping into Eric Heffer's shoes provoked his widow Doris into declaring, in an interview with *The Observer*, that Kilfoyle's selection "could be seen as disloyal to Eric's memory" and that "he is not the candidate that Eric would have wanted." Kilfoyle was selected as a replacement for Eric Heffer only because the right resorted to massive organisational manoeuvres during the selection procedure. Complaints of a stitch-up from candidates, scrutineers, door stewards, branch secretaries and other party members were completely ignored by the national executive committee of the Labour Party as they proceeded to endorse Kilfoyle.

In the light of this, the Broad Left convened a meeting on 9 June where a decision was taken for Lesley Mahmood to stand as the candidate of "Real Labour". *Militant* endorsed this decision, with only Ted Grant, Rob Sewell on the NEB and a handful of others in *Militant*'s ranks, opposing the decision.

This was, however, the signal for Fleet Street's hired liars to descend on Liverpool to regurgitate all the vicious anti-*Militant* propaganda of the past. Lesley Mahmood, her agent Mike Morris, and *Militant* were called, "Fascist thugs... more like Hitler's Brownshirts... barbarians... The Beast is *Militant*, the political mutant that has rampaged through Liverpool for a decade."[3]

Killroy-Silk in *The Express* called *Militant*: "A tin of maggots, the stench of which will be around for a long time."[4]

A magnificent campaign was conducted by the supporters of Lesley Mahmood, but the desperation of working people to see the end of the Tory government meant that while thousands agreed with and sympathised with the arguments and the programme of Lesley Mahmood, the majority, many holding their noses, voted Labour. Lesley Mahmood received 2,613 votes and beat the Tory candidate, a commendable achievement in the circumstances. Of course, Kinnock, Kilfoyle and Labour's right were triumphant. However, they had managed to reduce Eric Heffer's majority of 23,000 to 7,000! Alastair Campbell, at that stage a *Sunday Mirror* columnist, and now chief press spokesman for Tony Blair, demonstrated his "neutrality": "M stands for Mahmood, *Militant* and maggots". He had urged the people of Walton to vote "Kilfoyle to help kill off the maggots".[5] Of course, in subsequent comments by Campbell and his like there was no mention of the fact that in the Walton by-election there was a 13 per cent swing against the official Labour candidate, Kilfoyle. The Liberal vote had risen by 11 per cent. However, in the welter of anti-*Militant* propaganda even Kilfoyle was compelled to admit that the right would have difficulties in defeating *Militant* in Liverpool, "militancy... is part and parcel of the beliefs people have in this city."⁶

## LESLEY MAHMOOD

The stand of Lesley Mahmood was entirely justified given all the circumstances in which this by-election had taken place. Superficial commentators, once more wrote off *Militant*, dismissing the votes of 2,613 for socialism as "irrelevant". Surprisingly, praise and a more sober assessment of Lesley Mahmood's performance came from a source, usually prone to criticise *Militant*. Paul Foot wrote in *Socialist Worker*:

> I read everywhere that Lesley Mahmood was 'humiliated' in the Walton by-election, but I can write from long experience of humiliations at by-elections. In March 1977 I stood for the newly formed Socialist Workers Party in the by-election in the 'safe' Labour seat of Stechford, Birmingham. The Tories took the seat, which caused quite a stir. My vote caused no stir at all. I got 377 votes. That was substantially worst than the 550 votes which Jimmy McCallum notched up for the SWP at the Walsall by-election. Spurred on, perhaps, by these triumphs, the SWP put up three more candidates for parliament in the ensuing months: at Grimsby, Ashfield (Notts) and Glasgow, Garscadden. I won't print the exact figures for each constituency for fear of humiliating comrades - but I can say that *the total votes for all five candidates was less than the 2,600 which Lesley Mahmood won at Walton...* I think that's a good vote in the circumstances. It's a reasonable base on which to continue the fight for jobs in Liverpool.⁷

The verdict on Lesley Mahmood's campaign could not be measured merely by the number of votes for her. The campaign had reached to all parts of the constituency and all sections of the Walton community. It had taken the case for socialism to workers and evoked an enthusiastic response.

## IN DUBLIN

In Ireland at this time, *Militant* supporter Joe Higgins, standing as an Independent Labour candidate, scored a spectacular victory in the Dublin county council elections on 27 June. In Mulhuddart, one of three "new" towns on the outskirts of Dublin, he topped the poll with 1,281 votes. The next candidate was 400 votes behind. Joe, like Lesley Mahmood, had been expelled from the Labour Party after being democratically selected by his local party. These developments provoked the ire of Labour's "traditionalists". They also led to the most serious internal debate and discussion for 30 years in the ranks of *Militant*. The argument of Ted Grant and his supporters was that the decision to stand candidates "independently" in Liverpool or Dublin, and setting up an independent organisation in Scotland threatened "40 years work".

## A "THREAT TO 40 YEARS WORK"?

They summed up their arguments in a lengthy document submitted for discussion within the ranks of *Militant*. They argued " Our work in the mass organisations of the British working class was of a long term character", and should be continued.[7] It was our view that Ted Grant and Co. failed to consider the changes that had taken place in the outlook of significant sections of the working class towards what we had always considered to be the "traditional organisations" of the working class.

The 1980s had seen important changes take place within the working class. A certain stratification had developed both economically and politically. Those with jobs had in general managed to keep their heads above water, on the basis of overtime, pay rises in excess of the cost of living, etc. At the same time, a vast army of poor had resulted from Thatcher's ruinous policies. This layer was made up of unemployed, impoverished workers on low wages, the homeless, a big section of alienated youth, and black and Asian workers, etc. They were not only alienated from capitalism but looked with distaste on the official leaders of the labour movement who had moved increasingly towards the right. The bonds between the mass of the working class and its "traditional" organisation, the Labour Party, had been considerably loosened. Within the Labour Party there was no scope to project socialist ideas or, equally important, to intervene in movements on behalf of the working class, like the poll tax. Advocacy of "non-payment" of the poll tax was itself sufficient reason for expulsion from the party.

The minority led by Ted Grant had argued that

> in the 1950s, the internal regime was marked by witch-hunts against the Bevanite left, bans and proscriptions, the repeated closure of the Labour Youth organisation.[8]

But the majority showed that the Labour Party of the 1990s was far to the right of that of the 1950s. While attacks had been made on the left in this period the right had never succeeded in completely destroying the left within the constituencies. Indeed, in the period from 1952 to 1956 the Bevanite left dominated the majority of the Constituency Labour Party seats on Labour's national executive committee. In 1956, the left actually won all the seats in this section and in 1957 Aneurin Bevan won the party treasurer's seat with the support of a number of trade unions, including the National Union of Mineworkers, the Shopworkers, the Railwaymen, the Electricians and the National Union of Public Employees etc. The right moreover had failed to expel Bevan in 1955 because of the resistance from below.

The period of the 1950s was entirely different to that which confronted Marxism in the 1990s. First, through Kinnock, then under Smith and now with Blair, the Labour Party's internal democracy, particularly of the local parties, has been well-nigh destroyed. Peter Hain, in *Labour Party News* in October 1990, described the Labour Party as being dominated by "middle-aged males, working in a professional occupation, in the public sector of the economy."

The membership of the party was increasingly aged; its average being 46-years old. The youth have deserted the Labour Party in droves, attracted to more radical causes such as the anti-poll tax movement, the anti-racist movement, and the more recent struggle against the Criminal Justice Bill. The 'respectable' Labour leadership of Kinnock, Smith or Blair ran a mile from these issues, particularly when it came to action. Ted Grant and co, on the other hand, argued that

> with the most likely approach of a Labour government[!], our task is not to turn away from the Labour Party, but on the contrary, to begin to strengthen our Labour Party work in preparation for the battles that will take place in the unions and be reflected in the Party. This in no way means to bury ourselves in the Labour Party. That would be a

fundamental mistake. But we must urgently correct the drift of comrades out of the party in failing to renew their cards. Why do the work of the right wing and expel ourselves?[9]

This did not match up to the real position.

## LABOUR PARTY LOSING MEMBERS

Not *Militant* supporters, but thousands of workers were voting with their feet and leaving the Labour Party throughout the 1990s. The election of Blair to the party leadership moreover, has only served to accentuate this process. On the electoral plane of course the only viable alternative in the main for workers who want to get rid of the Tories is to vote for Labour. But many will do so "holding their noses", because of their implacable opposition to the policies of the Labour right. On the other hand, there is a significant layer of workers and youth looking for a new radical, socialist and revolutionary alternative. A survey in 1993 commissioned by *Red Pepper* showed that there were three to four million people who consider themselves socialists and "to the left" of the Labour Party.

One of the purposes of setting up Scottish Militant Labour (and Militant Labour at a later stage), was to tap into this socialist, radical mood. Irrespective of time, place or circumstance the task, said Ted Grant was for Marxists to merely sit in the Labour Party waiting for support to materialise when "objective" conditions had sufficiently matured. Anything which threatened ownership of a "precious" Labour Party card was seen as a "sectarian deviation". On this and other issues, Ted Grant and his supporters were prepared to split and break away from the most successful Trotskyist organisation since the collapse of the Left Opposition.

A full and democratic debate unfolded within the ranks of *Militant* in which the views of the majority were overwhelmingly endorsed. At a special *Militant* conference in November 1991 the views of the minority received only seven per cent of the votes.

Defeated on this and other issues, the minority withdrew all financial support from *Militant*, started to collect funds to set up their own press and publishing facilities, and a separate organisation.

## TERRY FIELDS GOES TO JAIL

Both Terry Fields and Dave Nellist had behaved in an exemplary fashion in Parliament. They had been to the fore in the poll tax non-payment campaign. Eventually they were faced with the choice, which many others before them and after had confronted, of either succumbing, paying the poll tax or, on an important issue of principle, standing with those who could not and would not pay. The majority of *Militant* supporters entirely endorsed the stand of Terry Fields and also of Dave Nellist at a later stage. This was done in the knowledge that Terry's jailing, which took place in July, would be seized on by Kinnock as an excuse to remove him as a Labour MP and drive him out of the Labour Party. Kinnock scandalously declared:

> The Labour Party does not and never will support breaking the law. Mr Fields has chosen to break the law and he must take the consequences. He is on his own.[10]

In making this statement Kinnock not only distanced himself from Terry Fields but from the history of the labour movement which is one of defying unjust laws. Four years previously at a party conference Kinnock had presented Labour's merit award to a 102-year-old Suffragette who "was jailed for a day for breaking into the House of Lords". At that conference this heroic "gesture" received "applause and cheers". Now Kinnock was pouring scorn on the heads of those like Terry Fields who were standing up for their class. We asked: What about the Chartists and the Tolpuddle Martyrs, or the dockers who went to jail in defiance of Heath's anti-Union acts in the early 1970s? "Would Kinnock have told them they were on their own?"[11]

He would have found it difficult in 1972 as millions of rank-and-file trade unionists were on the side of the dockers and were threatening a general strike. The day after Terry Fields was jailed the *Daily Mail* wrote:

> The campaign against paying was inspired by *Militant* and became a popular, national drive which contributed to killing the tax and its replacement by the new council tax.[12]

Kinnock's stab-in-the-back for Terry Fields was one of the most shameful incidents in Kinnock's time as party leader. Terry Fields received huge support from all over the country for his stand. One worker from the Old Swan area of Liverpool wrote to him: "We are not members or supporters of *Militant* but we would vote for you as a principled and caring man."[13] Another worker from Tuebrook declared bluntly:

> History will prove the Kinnock gang wrong and traitors, and the few with principles and integrity like yourselves and Eric Heffer and Tony Benn will be remembered with affection and respect long after the other gang have faded into obscurity.[14]

Over 1,000 marched to a "Free Terry Fields" rally outside Walton jail. Arthur Scargill was the main speaker. Terry was freed in September after serving 60 days. But less than two weeks after his release he faced another "trial" set up by Labour's national executive committee, which interrogated him on 25 September in the first steps to remove him as a Labour MP. On that same day the national executive committee of the Labour Party took a similar step against Dave Nellist. Their suspension from party membership on the eve of the Labour Party conference was a step towards expulsion and a gagging measure to prevent them from appealing to the conference and using it as a platform to oppose the policies of the leadership.

## NEC MOVES AGAINST TERRY AND DAVE

The 'evidence' against Terry Fields was that he had made a call for Labour to "nationalise the commanding heights of the economy". However, the real reason for Kinnock's rushed measures against the two was blurted out by Ray Powell, the right-wing Labour whip, who stated that the: "prospect of the two MPs holding the balance of power if Labour is elected with a small majority, filled the leadership with dread."[15]

The national executive committee wanted Dave Nellist to repudiate *Militant* as the price of remaining in the Labour Party. This he refused to do. At the Labour Party conference in October, 350 trade unionists and socialists led by Dave Nellist and Terry Fields marched against the witch-hunt. At the end of the demonstration a successful meeting was held in a local school with raptuous receptions for both Dave and Terry. Tony Benn declared:

> We need a Marxist current in the Labour Party. Karl Marx was no more responsible for what was happening in Russia than Jesus Christ was for the Spanish Inquisition.[16]

Dennis Skinner, anticipating general secretary Larry Whitty's speech the next day, said Terry Fields had been attacked for not supporting Peter Kilfoyle in Walton! But what about the 130 MPs who did not go to Walton? he asked. Skinner also pointed out that at the NEC which took action against Dave Nellist, Clare Short had "harassed Dave" demanding, "we want an answer, yes or no," when they wanted him to renege on his ideas. Before the year was out Terry Fields had been expelled from the Labour Party, the first Labour MP for 50 years to be axed in this way by the party leaders. We commented: "This won't win one extra Labour vote. On the contrary, it will disappoint thousands."[17]

## BACKBENCHER OF THE YEAR

The decision to expel was delayed in the case of Dave Nellist partly because the leadership were embarassed because he had been awarded the "Backbencher of the Year" prize by the *Spectator* magazine. Dave Nellist paid a rare visit to the Savoy Hotel in London to collect his prize. Only a few days later, as he pointed out at the reception at the Savoy, he faced a hearing at the Labour Party in which the charge was been made that he was guilty of "a sustained course of conduct bringing the party into disrepute."[18] At the *Spectator* lunch Dave said: "There are probably quite a few back home who thought I'd done that today coming to this place and sitting down with all you bloated capitalists!"[19]

# 45.
# TWO TRENDS IN MILITANT

DIFFERENCES IN approach toward strategy and tactics are common in the Marxist movement. Everybody puts forward erroneous points at some time, particularly when not all the facts are known. But Ted Grant's approach was distinguished by a dogmatic and stubborn adherence to a point of view when it was clear that he did not have the necessary feel of how a struggle was developing on the ground. Moreover, he attempted to exercise a political veto over differing views and more accurate assessments of a situation.

In the past he had made a big contribution in terms of Marxist theory, particularly in defending the ideas of Marx, Engels, Lenin and Trotsky, both against opportunism and ultra-leftism. But a correct theory in itself is not enough. It is necessary to translate this into programme, strategy and tactics, and relate these to the real movement of the working class. It is this which distinguished *Militant* from all other "Marxist" groups, during the course of the Liverpool struggle and also in the poll tax battle. Despite his past achievements, Ted Grant was sometimes found wanting, particularly in the rapidly changing situation of the 1980s. His lack of tactical awareness and flair was a source of irritation and conflict with some of the main figures in the Liverpool drama.

While Ted Grant was respected by the supporters and leadership of *Militant* it had been evident for some time that his best days, particularly on the public platform, were behind him. It was not the first time in the history of the Marxist movement that a leader can play a key pioneering role at one stage but prove to be lacking once the situation changes. The tragic example of Plekhanov, "Father of Russian Marxism" comes to mind. His role was decisive in the period when the task was to put down roots, to stubbornly defend Marxism against opportunism and ultra-leftism. But the same Plekhanov proved to be utterly helpless in the face of great events, when the rhythm of the class struggle and history changed. Entirely fresh layers had been drawn to the banner of *Militant*, particularly to the mass public meetings that took place in early 1986. It is not possible to take a horse, particularly a young one, out over the Grand National course first time out. It was necessary to present *Militant*'s ideas in the most popular and accessible form, without watering them down or hiding what we stand for. Other, younger speakers and leaders of *Militant* were more able to fulfil this task than someone who was already in his late 70's. This in no way devalued his past contribution nor the continued role he could make. Ted Grant failed to recognise the limitations age placed on everyone. Experience and continuity of ideas and organisation is essential in any Marxist organisation. But it must never become a barrier to a new generation of leaders who are the inheritors of the future and who must inevitably carry the main burden of the day to day work of building a viable Marxist organisation.

Unfortunately, Ted Grant did not recognise this and in 1986 stirred up a fuss within the leadership of *Militant* by accusing others of not putting him up to speak at the mass meetings that were being organised. Most requests from the ranks were for other national leaders of *Militant* to speak at these meetings. At the same time there was a differing approach increasingly evident between Ted Grant and the majority of the Editorial Board. To begin with this was largely one of approach, emphasis and sometimes on tactics. But in the changed situation which had been brought about by the 1980s a series of important differences arose.

## BLACK MONDAY

Just weeks after the 1987 Labour Party conference, where the Labour leaders strained to adapt ideologically to "booming capitalism", came the worldwide and unprecedented fall in share prices. 21 October, "Black Monday" as it came to be known, was triggered by the collapse on Wall Street on the previous Friday. This was the biggest drop in share prices in one day; more than ten per cent of share values were wiped out. In London, Tokyo, Hong Kong, Paris and Frankfurt share prices nose dived. The prices of stocks and shares can become almost divorced from the real values of profits and production in industry, particularly during a frantic boom. In Japan, share prices in 1987 had reached levels equivalent to 150 years' annual profits. However, like a piece of elastic that is stretched to breaking point, at a certain stage the real economy asserts itself and yanks financial markets back in, causing a collapse in share prices. This crisis had been triggered by the attack of James Baker, US Treasury Secretary, on the policies of German capitalism and its central bank, the Bundesbank. But the underlying reason for the crisis was the big disproportion between share prices and the real state of capitalism on a world scale. Ultimately shares, particularly when they collapse, are an indicator of problems to come.

What did the October share crash signify? The answer to this question was hotly disputed within the ranks of *Militant*. On the very day of the collapse Ted Grant argued that this was a precursor to a new 1929-type slump. His thinking was unfortunately reflected in the pages of *Militant*. In its initial comments on these developments it stated: "A major slump in production and trade is assured, perhaps even before the summer of 1988."[1]

Michael Roberts, who shared his view, stated that the October crash

> is a barometer predicting the impending storm that will exceed anything experienced by capitalism in the post-war period, possibly matching the great slump of the 1930s.[2]

The morning after the crash, capitalist journals, like *The Economist*, for instance, were predicting that an economic slump would follow in the wake of "Black Monday". However, it soon became evident that the central banks of Europe, Japan and the US would use their resources to bail out world capitalism. Yet Ted Grant continued with his crude interpretation of the 1987 crash and dogmatically asserted his views at every turn.

He was supported by Roberts and Woods but was opposed by myself, Lynn Walsh, Bob Labi and others. The discussion around this issue within the *Militant* National Editorial Board and the working Editorial Board was searching and at times very sharp. The opponents of Ted Grant rejected the perspective of an immediate slump. This, unbelievably, was pictured by Grant as taking place within a year. Such an approach could completely disorientate supporters. If it should not come to pass, as was likely, we argued, a mood of disappointment, if not dejection, could set in amongst *Militant* supporters. It was necessary to approach these events in a balanced way. The collapse in share prices did indicate growing difficulties for world capitalism. At a certain stage the 1980s boom would give way to a recession, but it was very unlikely that it would be along the lines of 1929-33. World capitalism still possessed huge layers of fat which it could eat into in order to stave off an immediate crisis. There would of course be limits to this; short-term measures could be taken which would only have the effect of piling up problems and aggravating the crisis at a later stage. The Taaffe, Walsh and Labi grouping on the NEB argued that it was possible for Japanese and German capitalism, with their enormous surpluses, to step in to underwrite the dollar and support financial markets, thereby temporarily staving off an industrial crisis.

Contrary to the analysis of Ted Grant this is exactly what happened. A revival of world capitalism took place in the aftermath of the October 1987 crisis. Indeed, the huge injection of credit fuelled a growth of world capitalism at a greater rate than in the period prior to the crash. It was agreed that the underlying crisis of world capitalism would assert itself at a certain stage. This it did in the recession of the early 1990s. But timing in politics, and it should be added in the art of political economy, is important. Ultra-left sects, like a clock permanently stuck at one minute to midnight, have predicted a 1929 type slump for four or five decades. They play into the hands of the capitalist ideologists, who picture Marxists as being incapable of analysing real processes in a balanced fashion.

We have already referred to international developments - Namibia, South Africa and the Gulf War where differences emerged. Just at the time of the debate about the future of *Militant* a bigger drama began to unfold in Russia.

## COUP IN RUSSIA

On 19 and 20 August the old guard "conservative" wing of the bureaucracy organised a coup against Gorbachev. This development, in itself of world importance, precipitated an even greater ideological breach than over Walton or the formation of SML between the majority and the minority within *Militant*'s ranks.

The minority leaned towards "critical support" for the organisers of the coup! They subsequently denied this because of the embarrassment of seeming to side with the pro-Stalinist wing of the bureaucracy. But in a document they put forward as part of the internal discussion within *Militant*, they stated:

> If, as was entirely possible, the regime had been compelled to carry out a policy based on recentralisation and the planned economy, accompanied by terror, this would also give a certain impetus to the productive forces for a period of time.[3]

Their perspective was for the re-establishment of a Stalinist regime, resting on the planned economy, if the coup organisers had succeeded. Moreover, they had argued that this was the most likely outcome of the coup. The previous December, Alan Woods had argued in a discussion on Stalinism:

> Let us be clear, even if there is a struggle between rival wings of the bureaucracy, one wing openly pro-capitalist and another wing - for their own purposes - trying to defend the basis of the nationalised economy, it would be a fundamental mistake to think that we'd be neutral in that situation, even if you had a situation where sections of workers were supporting the other wing.

He went on:

> Trotsky said that in principle you couldn't rule out in advance the possibility of a united front, a temporary and partial united front, between the Trotskyists and the Stalinist bureaucracy, if it came to an open civil war and an attempt to restore capitalism in the USSR.[4]

The majority, on the other hand, argued that there was a fundamental difference between the situation in the Soviet Union in 1991 and the period when Trotsky had envisaged a position of "critical support" for a section of the bureaucracy. The bureaucracy had completely degenerated, with the great majority abandoning support for central planning and the old system. They had embraced capitalism as a way forward. There was no significant wing of the bureaucracy in the period leading up to 1991 which still adhered to the planned economy.

Ted Grant was so convinced that the coup would succeed that as the TV reports came through on the collapse of the coup on Wednesday 21 August he denounced them as "lies" and "bourgeois propaganda". He, Alan Woods and the rest of the minority, had failed to grasp that even if the coup had succeeded this would not have led to a complete restoration of the Stalinist regime.

Jarulzelski in Poland in 1981 had carried through a Stalinist counter-revolution to establish on Polish soil precisely the old regime. But faced with a complete economic, social and political impasse Jarulzelski himself abandoned this task admitting later: "our greatest mistake was to keep the party's monopoly on power, defend nationalised industry and the class struggle."[5]

He accordingly moved towards an openly pro-capitalist position, paving the way for the coming to power of Solidarity and Walesa. And yet the minority, in their document *The Truth about the Coup* argued:

> What would have happened for example if Yanayev and co had seized power? Is it a foregone conclusion that they would have carried out their stated aims of moving towards a 'market economy' albeit at a more gradual pace? For the majority this is a simple question to answer: 'In today's situation, "objectively"... yes.' But does that exhaust the question?[6]

They then postulate the idea that the coup organisers would have been compelled to re-establish the elements of the planned economy, completely ignoring the experience of Jarulzelski and the evolution of the Chinese Stalinists in the aftermath of Tiananmen Square.

Attempting to cover their tracks the minority accused the majority of tail-ending Yeltsin in the August days. This was despite the fact that *Militant* publicly distanced itself from the pro-capitalist Yeltsinites, some of whom flooded towards the defence of their hero at the White House in Moscow.

## RUSSIAN WORKERS OPPOSE THE COUP

What was true, however, was that the mass of population in the Soviet Union was opposed to the coup. Some had illusions in Yeltsin, the majority were opposed because of a fear that the elementary democratic rights they had gained since 1989 would be snuffed out if the coup succeeded. That is why a series of strikes took place in Moscow, the Ukraine and elsewhere. More important than this was the immanent mass support of the working class, more important than those who manned the barricades in opposition to the coup. In the beginning, because of the disillusionment with Gorbachev, there was a certain hesitation in openly expressing opposition to the coup. We summed up this mood on 30 August as follows:

> When the Soviet workers awoke to find the hardliners in power and Gorbachev under house arrest there was a hesitant response. But as the youth began to protest, the working class stirred. The call for a general strike began to get a response.[7]

Even bourgeois journalists remarked on this process. *The Times* reported:

> So far, there has been a mixed response from Russian factories. This is partly a matter of organisational delays; strike committees are being formed and meetings held.[8]

There was a marked difference between the general opposition to the coup in August 1991 and the position taken by the mass of the workers later in 1993. In 1993 the struggle was perceived by the mass of the population, now thoroughly disillusioned with Yeltsin's capitalist "reforms", as between two mafias struggling for control over the heads of the mass of the population. Following the defeat of the coup, our co-thinkers in Russia organised around their newspaper, *Workers' Democracy*, held a public meeting in defence of the ideas of Lenin and Trotsky. This was commented on by Russian television. Over 100 people attended the meeting, the majority industrial workers. Sixty expressed a desire to co-operate in forming a genuine mass workers' party and five agreed to join and participate fully in the activity of *Workers' Democracy*.

The position taken by the minority on the August events in Russia alienated them from the great majority of our supporters. The breach became wider as the practical consequences of *Militant*'s decision to launch an independent organisation in Scotland became even clearer.

After our special national conference in October 1991, the national leadership of *Militant* had pledged that the discussion on perspectives for the Labour Party in particular, and on the strategy and tactics required in the new situation in Britain and internationally, would continue. Ted Grant and his supporters refused to accept this. *Militant* explained in a statement, on 24 January, that the minority had decided to split away:

> Instead of continuing the debate within our ranks, as they had claimed they would, they took steps to set up their own rival publication. They have plans to launch a monthly magazine, moving, as soon as possible, to a fortnightly and a weekly. They now have their own small premises and their own staff and are raising their own funds.[9]

This was clearly a pre-determined decision to split from *Militant*.

## FOR THE RECORD

There was no denunciation of former comrades but a sober assessment of Ted Grant's previous role. At the same time, *Militant* made a forceful criticism of his current mistaken policies:

> We regret that Ted Grant has split in this way. He made a vital contribution in upholding the genuine ideas of Marxism and developing the theoretical legacy of Leon Trotsky in the hostile political climate of the post-war period. He played a key role in formulating the ideas and policies on which *Militant* was built from 1964. Those especially who worked closely with him for over three decades regret that he has now turned his back on *Militant*, on our great achievements in struggle and on the powerful following we have built up in Britain and internationally. It is lamentable that he has allowed his political authority to be used by people whose main concern is not to clarify ideas but to cause the maximum damage to *Militant*. One unfortunate feature of political life is the spiteful urge of former activists to justify their defection by hurling allegation of heinous political crimes at their former comrades. They are wasting their time. This mini-exodus will not deflect us in the slightest from the course we have mapped out.[10]

# 46.
# SCOTTISH MILITANT LABOUR

A RADICAL mood was developing in Scotland which, we warned, would be harnessed by the SNP unless an alternative, socialist, pole of attraction was constructed. In the past, even in the early 1980s, the Scottish National Party was marooned in its rural outpost of northern Scotland and the Western Isles. The left held a majority on the leading bodies of the labour movement both at British and at a Scottish level. The Labour Party organised a mass demonstrations against unemployment, including one in Glasgow of a hundred thousand. As a result of this, Labour offered a genuine alternative to Scottish workers, unemployed youth and students.

At that time, unable to make a breakthrough, the SNP tore itself apart in a three-year civil war. The present leader of the SNP, Alec Salmond, was expelled in 1982 along with others for his membership of the left-wing 79 Group. However, the degeneration of the Labour Party under Kinnock allowed the SNP to recapture ground it had lost in the early 1980s. The SNP accordingly moved towards the left demanding renationalisation of industries privatised by the Tories, the wiping out of Scottish local authority housing debt, the building of brand new council houses, to replace every house which had been sold in the Tories' "right to buy" legislation, the promise of a minimum wage and an increase in the state pension, the abolition of prescription charges, etc. Tory minister Douglas Hurd had accused the SNP of standing for "East European style state socialism". Some commentators even accused the SNP of being "Scotland's Militant tendency".

Facing up to the clear danger posed by nationalism which threatened to infect a layer of the working class, particularly the youth, in the West of Scotland, we declared:

> Scottish *Militant* supporters showed in the anti-poll tax struggle how nationalism can be cut across by vigorously campaigning on the class issues. We must do everything we can to draw the best workers and

young people away from the SNP's empty radicalism to a socialist programme.[1]

## BATTLE OF TURNBULL STREET

Militants in Scotland had prevented any warrant sales taking place. Mass demos combined with disciplined direct action - including occupations - had kept the Sheriffs at bay. In October 1991, ironically during a very right-wing Labour Party conference, Scottish *Militant* supporters, led by Tommy Sheridan, demonstrated precisely why they had built such a powerful position of support in Scotland. October 1 was the date when Scotland's first "warrant sale" was due to take place. Tension had been building for days with council officials and Tory ministers believing this would mark the end of resistance to the poll tax. Press from all over Britain assembled at a police detention centre in the East End of Glasgow, where a sale was scheduled for 11am. It had been turned into a fortress, with masses of police inside. The anti-poll tax protesters massed at the Federation's premises a few hundred yards away. Five hundred people, with Tommy Sheridan in the lead, marched the short distance to the detention centre. The day before Tommy Sheridan had been served with an interdict (an injunction) warning him that if he ventured within 200 of the warrant sale he would be arrested immediately.

The marching column arrived at the building and was confronted by huge iron gates, but proceeded to tear them down and pour into the courtyard behind. Inside stood a hired van, two sheriff officers in front and a stack of poinded (legally stolen) furniture in the back. Immediately this van came under siege. Then within seconds, scores of police came from inside and a mighty struggle erupted between the police and protesters. Completely unable to remove the 500 from the courtyard and with the prospect of hundreds more assembling outside, the police formed cordons in front of the van to protect the sheriff officers and the furniture. Stalemate ensued for an hour as both sides confronted one another. The police were clearly unhappy at the role which had been allotted to them. Ten minutes before the warrant sale was due, as police reinforcements built up outside, Tommy Sheridan was helped up on to a crash barrier. Tearing up his injunction and throwing the pieces of paper into the air, he said the Federation did not want to see any trouble but warned:

> I am not prepared to stand back and watch this barbarism take place. We are warning the police now that as soon as these goods are released from the back of the van, then I, and I believe I am speaking for everyone here, will do everything in my power to prevent this sale taking place.[2]

The rest was drowned out in thunderous applause. The 500 demonstrators stood rock-solid in defiance of the police and actually advanced on the police lines. The police then had to choose, face another "Orgreave" in the centre of Glasgow or back down and abandon the warrant sale. Panic consultations took place between the police, sheriff officers and council officials, and a council official emerged from behind the police lines with a megaphone and stated: "The warrant sale scheduled to take place at 11am today has now been cancelled."[3]

Wild scenes of jubilation swept through the protesters - as if Scotland had just won the World Cup. This spread to the streets outside as word began to filter through. But Tommy Sheridan insisted that the crowd would not move until the van had left the premises, and this was adhered to by the police. This incident was a landmark in the struggle against the poll tax and in the development of *Militant* in Scotland. It also was the incident which led to Tommy Sheridan later appearing in court and receiving a six month jail sentence. It was a fitting backdrop to the formation of Scottish Militant Labour in early December. (This story is told more fully in Tommy's own book, *A Time to Rage*). We outlined the reasons for taking this initiative:

> Twelve years after the inconclusive devolution referendum in 1979 the mood in Scotland has changed dramatically... As leading Scottish Tory ideologist Alan Massie admitted in the *Daily Telegraph*: "Scotland continues to see itself as socialist... many people in Scotland see the Tories as quislings."

Pointing to the desparate social conditions in Scotland, we drew the conclusion:

As a result of the biggest campaign of civil disobedience in Britain this century - in which Scottish *Militant* supporters played a deciding role - the hated poll tax was destroyed, along with the equally hated prime minister, Margaret Thatcher.

At the same time, we pointed out that

> in all the big cities *Militant* supporters and sympathisers are barred from standing as councillors by an undemocratic panel system which gives local party bureaucrats the power to vet every candidate. The party's youth section, the Labour Party Young Socialists, has now been effectively closed down by the party leadership in retribution for its support for *Militant* policies. The witch-hunt has even extended into parliament, with MPs Dave Nellist and Terry Fields now in line for expulsion and Ron Brown [from Leith] and John Hughes [from Coventry North-West] deselected.[4]

Even Tories, one writing in the *Glasgow Herald,* were able to score points at the Labour leader's expense:

> The present-day Labour Party would not allow a free vote on when to take a lunch break. I don't know, nor little care, for Dave Nellist or Terry Fields. Yet I am astonished that two MPs who have served their constituents diligently can be tried and toppled by a kangaroo court. You couldn't throw someone out of a bowling club that easily.[5]

At the same time, once powerful organisations such as the Communist Party had declined drastically. Yet there was a greater need than ever before for a fighting socialist organisation in Scotland, on the three points of John MacLean and the Red Clydesiders - educate, agitate, organise! However, it was made clear that Scottish Militant Labour was not intended as a conventional political organisation, immersed solely in fighting elections:

> While electoral tactics may be necessary in certain circumstances, Militant Labour will devote most of its energies to the daily struggles of ordinary people in the workplaces and communities.[6]

## MILITANTS JAILED

The formation of Scottish Militant Labour was greeted enthusiastically not just in Scotland but throughout Britain. One of its most important battles was still against the poll tax, which although officially declared dead had not yet been buried completely. Indeed, eight months after the end of the poll tax, the persuance of non-payers for arrears continued. The All-Britain Anti-Poll Tax Federation estimated that by November 1991, 117 people had been jailed by 46 councils. Shamefully, 26 of these councils were Labour controlled, including Burnley, which actually imprisoned 23 people. Thirty of those who had been jailed were unemployed and three of those were on invalidity benefit. At least ten pensioners had received sentences totalling 366 days and ten women had been jailed. Amongst these was Janet Gibson from Hull who refused to pay her poll tax and went to jail for two weeks. Other *Militant*s who were jailed included Eric Segal, Ruby and Jim Haddow and Anne Ursell (Kent); Mike O'Connell and Mark Winter (London); John McKay (Basildon); Jim Bates (Milton Keynes); Andy Walsh and Pete Boyle (Manchester); Ian Thompson (Jarrow); Debbie Clark (Stonehouse); Mick Quinn (Caerphilly).

The courts were being clogged up on poll tax cases. 19,556 hours of court time had been used up by the end of 1991 on poll tax cases with 152,275 people turning up to oppose the granting of liability orders against them. A total of 4,258 people had been summoned for committal hearings and well over four million liability orders had been issued. While 2,000 warrants had been issued for the arrest of non-payers, three-quarters of the police forces of England and Wales were refusing to carry them out.

*Militant* accordingly launched a campaign for amnesty for the non-payers. Something like £5 billion was owed by the end of 1991 to local councils in accumulated poll tax arrears. And yet there was still one more year of the poll tax to go. The ending of the poll tax had actually led to more people refusing to pay. Therefore, 1991, a most eventful year in the history of *Militant*, ended against the background of tumultuous scenes in Glasgow in opposition to the poll tax, growing opposition on a British scale, shown in increased numbers refusing to pay this iniquitous tax, and the formation of Scottish Militant Labour as a rallying point to which all those looking for a fighting socialist lead could turn.

## SWEDEN

Meanwhile, in Sweden, our sister organisation, *Offensiv*, won three seats on the local council of Umea. In the course of the election campaign, 15,000 doors were canvassed:

> Workers want a socialist alternative to the pro-capitalist policies being pursued by the present leadership of the social democrats. The election has established *Offensiv* as the major force in the Umea labour movement prepared to fight for such an alternative.[7]

Clearly, Marxism faced an entirely different situation in 1991, not just in Britain, but on an international scale.

## PREPARING FOR A GENERAL ELECTION

In 1992 the Tories were bound to face the judgement of the electorate. A general election could not be postponed and the signs looked ominous for Major and his government. With 80,000 homes repossessed in 1991, 48,000 companies failing and a job loss rate of at least 60,000 a month, claims that "recovery" was on the way sounded hollow.

Tory Chancellor Lamont's claim of just two months previously that the economy would grow by 2.25 per cent in 1992 had been scaled down to a likely 1.25 per cent growth rate. This followed an actual decline of two per cent in 1991. The whole of the capitalist world was now in the grip of recession, as Germany and Japan joined America and Britain in an economic trough. The recession in the early 1990s was the payment for the excesses of the Reagan/Thatcher boom of the 1980s. Recoiling from the inflationary hangover, capitalist governments had resorted to high interest rates and tight controls of the currency printing presses.

We predicted: "The trend of policy over the next few years will be deflationary and the result will be low growth." Lamont, as if confirming our analysis, admitted: "Recessions... are an inescapable feature of market economies."[8]

Yet the Labour leadership had fully embraced the "market" when it was patently obvious it was failing to deliver the goods. Kinnock's "do nothing, say nothing" tactics as a means of winning the general election proved to be disastrous. This election, when it came, would take place in circumstances entirely different to any other which *Militant* had faced before. *Scottish Militant* had decided, with the enthusiastic support of the national *Militant* Editorial Board and a national conference of supporters, to stand Tommy Sheridan, the leader of the Scottish anti-poll tax movement, as a candidate in Glasgow Pollok.

A meeting was called in Glasgow to show opposition to the six-months jail sentence which had been meted out to Tommy for his breach of an interdict banning him from attending the Turnbull Street warrant sale. However, the Labour finance convenor for Strathclyde region, John Mullen, greeted the original sentence with the cry: "Justice has been done".

## POLL TAX HALTED - LEGAL CHAOS

Precisely when Tommy Sheridan was accused of breaking the law it had been revealed that the government had systematically broken their own laws in the way that they had sought to collect the poll tax. They tried to use the 1938 Evidence Act which covered magistrates courts. But this Act treats computer evidence as "hearsay" and does not allow its admission. The 1968 Civil Evidence Act, which sometimes allows computer evidence, was never extended to magistrates courts. We commented:

> The Tories bent the law. When they got found out they changed it. Councils at present have two years after the date the poll tax became due to start applying for liability orders against non-payers. Now they're going to make it six years. But they would never deal with 18 million non-payers or recover £1 billion lost revenue if they gave themselves 100 years.[9]

Tory Minister Heseltine had actually stated that he was going to amend the council tax legislation going through the unelected House of Lords to cover future cases. On this issue alone, if the Labour leadership had adopted a principled position, it would have been able to shatter the Tories in the run-up to the general election.

## DAVE NELLIST GOES INDEPENDENT

Dave Nellist, meanwhile declared at the end of January that he was going to stand as a "Labour Independent" in the Coventry South-East constituency. Members of his constituency endorsed the decision by a five-to-one majority. A broad coalition of workers in Coventry was assembled in support of him. Representatives of the UCATT West Midlands regional council, MSF and APEX convenors at the local engineering works, the branch secretary of UCW Telecom, a pensioners' trade union leader, the trades council vice-chairman, and the secretary of the Rolls-Royce Joint Shop Stewards Committee all expressed support. Moreover, 10,000 electors had been canvassed and 42 per cent of them expressed support for Dave Nellist. Seventy per cent of Labour voters were prepared to back him.

## GEORGE MCNEILAGE JAILED

In Glasgow, George McNeilage, another prominent anti-poll tax leader in Scotland, was jailed for supposedly obstructing and assaulting the sheriffs. He gave a graphic explanation in our pages of his previous very difficult life, but also showed how he had been rescued:

> When I got out [of prison] it was just like before - no job, no money and no light at the end of the tunnel, until I came across *Militant*, which gave me a goal in life.

In prison, George

> went round discussing everything I knew: the poll tax, Liverpool council's struggle, South Africa, Ireland, Scottish nationalism, Russian revolution, the rise of Stalinism, Historical Materialism, Drugs, Red Clydeside... in the billet at night I read Trotsky's *History of the Russian Revolution* and debated politics... it was great having a TV in the billet. We watched sheriff officers being chased out of Glasgow's East End, saw Tommy Sheridan say he'd stand for Parliament and announce the formation of Scottish *Militant* Labour. Great publicity! Next morning people shouted: "Free big George! Smash the sherriff officers! No warrant sales!"[10]

## SML'S FOUNDING CONFERENCE

On 29 February 1992, Scottish Militant Labour held its founding conference generating great enthusiasm amongst those present. A Scottish edition of *Militant* was launched with Alan McCombes as Editor. Within a short period of its launch it was to have a decisive effect on Scottish politics, particularly in the west of Scotland. But in early March, Tommy Sheridan lost his appeal and started his prison sentence. Minutes before he was sentenced, he defiantly declared,

> I do not accept that a crime has been committed. However, you and I know that justice will not be dispensed in this court. What will be dispensed is class law and class bias against working-class people because it is a crime to stand up for the poor. [11]

Lords Ross, King-Murray and Marnoch then proceeded to uphold the six-month sentence for the "crime" of preventing a warrant sale. Two hundred ordinary working class people had crowded into the courts and showed their disgust at the treatment meted out to one who was defending them and their like. They cheered Tommy as he was led away to jail and a chorus went up: "No warrant sales". One woman who lived opposite the prison came up and declared: "Tell his friends and supporters they can call in for a cup of tea whenever they're visiting."[12]

On 7 March, on the electronic scoreboard at Celtic Park, during the Celtic and Morton game, a message flashed up: "Happy Birthday, Tommy Sheridan, from three million friends and supporters. You'll never walk alone." Strathclyde Council Labour leader Charlie Gray was horrified: "I think Celtic should think again about accepting that kind of political advertisement, since it is extremely one-sided."[13]

However, outside the ground fans donated a total of £145 towards the campaign in favour of Tommy's release.

## CAMPAIGN AGAINST DOMESTIC VIOLENCE

In early March the Campaign Against Domestic Violence (CADV) assembled over 500 delegates and visitors at a highly successful conference in Queen Mary College, London.

The organising of this conference, initiated by *Militant* supporters as a campaign to secure the release of women like Sara Thornton, jailed for murdering her violent partner, answered those who have argued that *Militant* ignored the problems of women. It has been claimed by some opponents that, while *Militant* recognised there are special problems and conditions affecting women, the solution to these must be "postponed" until after "socialism had been achieved". No organisation has fought harder to defend and extend the living and working conditions of women, while at the same time explaining the need for a socialist society to complete the liberation of women. The initiative taken on domestic violence was just one expression of this.

At the conference, Julie Donovan, who was the secretary of the campaign, spoke about the medieval laws that sent women to prison for the crime of self-defence. Judges, she said, were unwilling and incapable of understanding the position facing women in violent relationships:

> The home is the single most dangerous place for a woman. The most likely place for a woman to meet her death is in her own bedroom at the hands of her partner. We reject the idea that women get a thrill out of domestic violence. They don't enjoy being beaten, punched, kicked and raped. Many have nowhere to go. We need a political campaign to get the resources, refuges and childcare that we need.[14]

Many moving accounts were given of the harrowing experiences of women who suffered and survived domestic violence. A Liverpool delegate said:

> I'm the mother of seven children and had a drunken, violent husband who regularly beat me up and smashed up our home. The violence was regular. I've been beat up umpteen times and I've brought the police to him umpteen times. They came in and gave a bit of lip service: "It'll be OK. You'll be alright now." As soon as they went, he'd kick off again. I knew this and I tried to tell the police but they just left. Once, three policemen came. The sergeant in charge was a man of about 50 and he actually smelt of drink himself. He went and spoke to my husband and they were like mates. I could hear them from the lobby. He was saying: "Oh you're alright, Stan. F...ing women. They're all the same!"[15]

Naturally, a few delegates, particularly those who had suffered at the hands of brutal men, disputed whether domestic violence occurred as a result of class society. They were answered by delegates, expressing the views of a majority present, who thought that although violence occurred across the classes, nevertheless, the roots of domestic violence lay in capitalist society and the resulting attitudes of men towards women. The working class can begin to change all this.

Fiona O'Loughlin, from Ireland, reported on the case of the 14-year-old young woman who was refused an abortion after being raped: "The judges are totally out of touch. Two-thirds of people in Ireland say that there should be abortion facilities."[16]

She spoke of the fight against the influence of the church on abortion law in Ireland. The conference concluded with a pledge to take the issue of domestic violence to every parliamentary seat in Britain with debates organised by local groups. Campaign organiser, Razina Boston, told *Militant*:

> Our task is to change for good the conditions facing men, women and children. We'll take personal relationships out of the gutter and raise them to the level of mutual co-operation, to create a society without domestic violence.[17]

The CADV also launched a campaign against Tory proposals for what became the Child Support Act (in 1993).

# 47.
# 1992 GENERAL ELECTION

THE MAIN issue confronting us in early 1992 was the general election. Tommy Sheridan would fight the election from his prison cell. In a letter from prison he declared:

> I'm standing in Glasgow Pollok to offer a radical and principled alternative to the run-and-hide Labour candidate and the empty rhetoric of the Nationalists.[1]

Dave Nellist had also declared his candidature for Coventry South East on a fighting socialist ticket. Within four days of the campaign beginning 1,000 window posters went up in the streets of Dave's constituency. In the key Willenhall ward the imposed Labour candidate had only four posters compared to 400 for Nellist. Even the *Coventry Evening Telegraph* was forced to admit, through gritted teeth that "at least he truly believes in what he proposes".[2] The imposed official Labour candidate, Jim Cunningham, had to rely on outside support as local Labour Party members as well as hundreds from outside flooded into the Nellist campaign.

The Terry Fields campaign, on the other hand, combined traditional campaigning on the door step with the latest word in high tech. Hundreds of copies of a video of Terry and local supporters explaining why they were voting for him was another "first" for a political campaign in Britain.

Most of *Militant*'s coverage concentrated on the campaigns of Sheridan, Nellist and Fields. Tommy Sheridan's campaign was unique. Quite apart from the mass meetings within the constituency, there were regular press conferences held inside the prison. These were held in Edinburgh Saughton prison where "prisoner 2/92" held audience with the Scottish and world press. Ronnie Stevenson described the scene:

> Tommy was led in, dressed in the regulation prison uniform of blue serge trousers and a stripped shirt. Although a far cry from a room in

the City Halls in Glasgow, it was good for those of us from outside to see Tommy again and we greeted him in solidarity. It was an emotional moment. We managed to attract more than twice as many journalists as there had been at the press conference of Tory Scottish Secretary of State, Ian Lang, earlier in the day... Tommy finished with a straightforward message. It's simple truth was ringing round the conference room of Saughton prison as we left: "We are not for compromise. Our manifesto is unashamedly for socialism. It is a manifesto to change the way our class lives. Prison walls cannot alter that reality."[3]

A detailed account of the incredible campaign conducted is to be found in Tommy Sheridan's excellent book, *A Time to Rage*.

Equally impressive was the campaign in Broadgreen. The support for Terry Fields was visible, particularly when Liberal leader Paddy Ashdown decided to make a visit in support of his candidate, Rosemary Cooper. He "dropped in" at the St Oswalds Garden flats in Old Swan, one of the most run-down tenement blocks in Liverpool. He was confronted with an estate awash with "Vote Terry Fields" posters. The only local representative to take up the conditions of the tenants, which were abominable, was Terry. Women from the tenants' association shouted at Rosemary Cooper: "What are you doing here? After our vote, are you, Love? or have you come back to vote for more rent rises and redundancies?"[4]

Dave Nellist also evoked tremendous sympathy and loyalty from the workers in his constituency, typified by the comment of one woman who pressed £5 into his hand while he was out canvassing:

> I'm so proud of what Dave has done for this town. If Labour MPs are coming here, tell them to stay away or go to somewhere else where Labour needs a hand in beating the Tories.[5]

## BELFAST

A less publicised, but nevertheless important aspect of the 1992 elections for us, was the candidature of Peter Hadden. He stood for the Labour and Trade Union Group in Belfast South. He campaigned on a programme for class unity between Catholic and Protestant workers against the capitalist common enemy. One Protestant worker stated, "Labour? No problem. You've got me. I lost four friends. I'm voting Labour this time".[6] As demanding as the campaign was in Britain, it could not compare to the situation in Northern Ireland where it was extremely dangerous just to stand in elections, never mind to go out canvassing. Peter Hadden and his family narrowly escaped injury from a terrorist bomb during the campaign. In the middle of the night Peter, his partner and their two week-old child were given ten minutes to get out of the house when a bomb was planted in a nearby RUC police station.

## ELECTION DAY

None of the candidates, standing either as independent socialist alternatives to Labour or under the banner of *Militant* won seats in this general election. Nevertheless, they reached more workers with the genuine ideas of socialism and Marxism than had been possible under the label of the Labour Party. The colossal efforts for the re-election of Terry Fields in Broadgreen was the centre-piece of an hour long *Cutting Edge* programme on *Channel Four* following the election. Entitled *Comrades*, it allowed ordinary supporters, as well as Terry Fields himself, to explain what motivated them and how they related to the struggles to solve the problems of ordinary working people. The programme had a considerable effect, in both attracting new supporters and reviving lapsed supporters.

According to Butler and Kavanagh's authoritative report on the 1992 general election, Tommy Sheridan achieved the finest result of any independent candidate, other than a sitting independent MP, since 1945.

The morning after the election, Ken Livingstone attacked the Labour leadership's "tax disaster". Everyone can be wise after the event. But apart from *Militant*, the left was silent during the election. Above all, Labour massively failed to mobilise the youth, amongst whom were included the most dispossessed, angry and bitter. Neil Kinnock had declared during the election "our policies are extremely prudent". The result was that 44 per cent of those between 18 and 35 years old did not vote in the 1992 General Election. Many were not registered, because of the poll tax, and others consciously decided not to vote.

Dave Nellist had come tantalisingly close to victory in Coventry South East. The imposed Labour candidate had received 11,902 votes, the Tory 10,591 and Dave Nellist 10,551. Trailing way behind were the Liberal Democrats with 3,318 and National Front with 173. Dave Nellist and his supporters knew that if the election was seen as close nationally then people would be more inclined to vote for Cunningham, the imposed Labour candidate. There was a desperation to get rid of the Tories. Cunningham's victory was not an endorsement of his policies. He was hardly seen during the election. Many people who voted Cunningham were subsequently bitterly disappointed that they had lost a socialist MP and Labour was still in opposition. One worker phoned Dave Nellist and apologised to Dave: "If he'd known his support, and that the Tories would win nationally, he'd have voted for Dave. Many loyal Labour voters now feel like this."[7]

In fact when it was clear that Labour had lost the election nationally, disappointment turned to disgust and anger in Coventry South-East as many realised that they had lost a brilliant MP, while next door the Tories had held the marginal Coventry South-West. Local Labour Party members were furious that scores of party members had been drafted in to South-East to fight Dave Nellist and not the Tories: "Three officials had the time to photograph our tellers on polling day but no time to get out votes in South-West seat." On election night the remark was heard from Labour Party members, more than once: "I'll rip up this card and have one of your *Militant* ones."[8]

Despite the result, *Militant* supporters were encouraged by what had been achieved in the election campaign. Opponents had claimed that Dave Nellist would get no more than 1,000 votes. There was even a conscious campaign to hide the Labour candidate from the media and debate. Cynically using electoral law to deny Dave Nellist a voice they made no local attacks on him that would have given him a right to reply. Instead Labour managers used a series of outside bigwigs to attack him. Dave Nellist was allegedly a "splitter" and "a thug".

*The Guardian* reported that "the bitter truth, though, is that Labour's national strategists would not worry that much even if [the Tory] won. It would be a price worth paying."[9]

And yet the morale in the imposed Labour camp sunk lower and lower during the campaign. Their professional poster team for Labour was in a local cafe one day when Dave Nellist entered. They were so taken aback at the greetings to him and his popularity that they commented on it and had their photos taken with him. Workers changed the habit of a lifetime by not voting Labour. 10,551 voted for Dave Nellist despite the fear of letting in the Tory candidate. Politics professor Anthony King had said in the aftermath of the Tory victory:

> Thatcher's impact on voters' views about most subjects was minimal. Her success was with the nation's elite. Even Labour now espouses, if somewhat grudgingly, free markets and private enterprise. The British may hanker after something called socialism. It is no longer on offer.[10]

He was wrong; it was on offer in Coventry South-East and Liverpool Broadgreen, as well as in Glasgow Pollok.

The 5,952 votes for Terry Fields in Broadgreen was as remarkable as that for Dave Nellist. No other candidate was the subject of such naked class hatred and vile abuse as Terry Fields. Far more than the numbers who actually voted for Terry Fields agreed with him on the need for socialism and also that he was the best candidate. But the powerful desire to get rid of the Tories, particularly in a Liverpool blitzed by economic recession, was the most prominent feeling in the minds of workers. Even then many hesitated before reluctantly voting for the official Labour candidate. Tellers remarked that many ballot papers showed a cross for Terry scribbled out and replaced with a cross for the right-wing official Labour candidate Jane Kennedy. But there was much regret once the results became known. They had ditched "one of their own", a fighting socialist MP, and yet a Labour government had not materialised. When, on the Saturday following the election, Terry Fields and Broadgreen Socialist Labour took to the streets to thank people for their support, "many couldn't look Terry in the eye. In three months you probably won't find anyone except for ex-Liberals who'll admit to having voted for Kennedy. The rule-or-ruin policy of Labour's right wing has brought about a total disaster."[11]

In order to unseat Terry Fields, the right diverted canvassers from Alton's Liberal Democrat held marginal in Mossley Hill. Alton kept his seat. Throughout Liverpool, the Labour vote was down in absolute terms. Some of this was due to the fall in the electoral register but Labour's right-wing policies had disenchanted whole layers of the working class. Tommy Sheridan was jubilant. From his prison cell he declared:

> It's an incredible result - we have made history. I'm overjoyed despite being a candidate who's locked up 60 miles away from my constituency. The political 'experts' in Scotland said we wouldn't get over 2,000 votes. We were labelled the fringe party by Labour from the start. But we have won second place, beating the Tories, beating the Nationalists and achieved 6,200 votes for radical socialist policies. The SNP has been routed in Pollok, marginalised in the housing schemes, even though Pollok was identified as the SNP's second target seat after neighbouring Govan... We declare after this result that SML is born.[12]

Not since the legendary Red Clydesiders' veteran Willie Gallacher stood for the Communist Party in the mining stronghold of West Fife, more then 30 years before, had any candidate standing against Labour on a left-wing socialist programme received over 6,000 votes in a general election in Scotland. Moreover, this vote was achieved despite the exclusion from the electoral register in Pollok as a result of the poll tax of over 5,000 potential SML voters. There had been dire warnings by some, standing on the sidelines, that SML would be dismissed by voters as an irrelevant sect completely out of touch with the popular mood. Yet the vote for Tommy Sheridan was 60 times larger than the 106 votes for the Communist Party of Great Britain in Glasgow Central and almost 90 times larger than the 73 votes for the Revolutionary Communist Party in Glasgow Hillhead.

Even the media were forced to recognise the scale of SML's achievement as the "biggest shock in Scotland". ITN the day after the election reported:

> A stunning 6,287... knocking the Conservatives into third place... not a bad result for a candidate who conducted his campaign from cell block H.[13]

The 1992 general election, the fourth Tory victory in a row, was seen as a severe defeat for the working class and labour movement. Young comrades, supporters of *Militant*, as well as hundreds and thousands of Labour workers throughout the country, were in tears as it dawned on them that the Tories had squeezed back in. We asked how was it possible, in the teeth of the worst economic recession for 60 years, that the Tories had crept back in? The Labour right, as always, deflected responsibility from themselves onto the shoulders of ordinary working people. The arguments of the capitalist ideologists, that there had been a fundamental shift towards the right in Britain, became their theme tune. Martin Jacques, ex-editor of *Marxism Today*, reflected this

> We have now entered a world where the Conservative Party has become the permanent party of government, just like the Liberal Democrats in Japan and the Christian Democrats in Italy.[14]

Within a year the Liberal Democrats in Japan and the Christian Democrats in Italy lay fractured and virtually broken under a mountain of corruption scandals. The Christian Democrats disappeared. The Tory Party have followed in their footsteps, split from top to bottom and facing electoral annihilation. Virtually alone, even on the left, *Militant* kept its head, explaining that the election, as important as it was, reflected merely one stage in the consciousness of society and working class, which under the impact of events could change rapidly.

The Tories had a 21-seat majority but this was no crushing victory. They got less than 42 per cent of the votes and if just 2,477 Tory voters, spread evenly across their 11 most marginal seats, had voted against them, John Major would have failed to get an overall majority. Labour's vote went from 28 per cent in 1983 and 31 per cent in 1987 to 34 per cent in 1992. Every part of England and Wales saw a swing to Labour, from 2.5 per cent in the South East to six per cent in the North and Yorkshire/Humberside. But it had become clear in the last few days of the election campaign that Tory waverers who had been thinking of voting for the Liberal Democrats or abstaining, drifted back to the fold. The Tories had successfully whipped up the fear that unless these people voted Tory, Labour could get in. The turnout rose to 77.7 per cent (from 73.2 per cent in 1987) and the Liberal share of the vote dropped from 22.5 per cent to 19 per cent. That was enough to give the Tories the extra votes that clinched their victory.

## LABOUR SQUANDERED POLL TAX LEAD

Nevertheless, this did not sufficiently explain how Labour could have failed to defeat a government which had been so unpopular 18 months before that they were 25 per cent behind Labour in the opinion polls. This, of course, was in the middle of the historic battle against the poll tax. At its height 18 million people were not paying this tax. Seven million more had refused to pay the tax than had actually voted for Labour in the election. Five years before Labour had also achieved a similar lead in the middle of the miner's strike. But each time this lead evaporated. If the Labour leadership had backed these struggles instead of being embarrassed by them, and moreover expelling those who led this battle, then the attitude of the non-payers may have been different. They actually said it would lose votes to defy the government. They therefore capitulated to the Tories - and still lost! We had consistently warned that the opinion polls, right up to polling day itself, reflected more of an anti-Tory mood, than a positive move to Labour. In order to guarantee victory, Labour had to offer a positive alternative, and yet unbelievably the leadership made the same blunder as in 1987, giving the impression that they were likely to increase taxes on sections of the middle class and upper layers of skilled workers. In fact 48 per cent of skilled workers and young voters interviewed on an exit poll reckoned they would be worse off under Labour.

One Birmingham car worker, commenting to *Militant* on the day after the election, pointed out:

> it was very hard to convince people to vote Labour particularly where I work at Leyland Daf. They're fairly well-paid car workers and tax was an issue with them. They thought: "If we vote Kinnock our taxes are going to go straight back up, we're going to be out of pocket". The thing is, Labour's tax plans would not have affected them because they did not earn enough, but it still came across as a issue that might, and it lost votes.[15]

The Labour leaders presented themselves as the alternative board of directors capable of running British Capitalism PLC. Voters, however, plumped for the real party of capitalism. Robert Harris of the *Sunday Times* remarked: "When the point of decision is reached they [the voters] will decide that a capitalist economy is best run by a capitalist party."[16]

The "race card" also played a part. This was highlighted by the *Sun's* "nightmare on Kinnock Street" which asserted that "Labour's luke-warm stance on immigration will weaken European resistence to the threat of massive immigration."[17]

## BNP VOTE IN GENERAL ELECTION

The vote for the BNP in Tower Hamlets was a warning of the underlying danger of a growth in racism. Edmonds, the BNP candidate in Bethnal Green and Stepney, received 1,310 votes. Tyndall, the BNP leader, got 1,100 in Bow and Poplar. Both the Tories and the Liberals were to blame for the BNP's strong showing. The Liberal candidate in Bethnal Green took the opportunity of a trip to Bangladesh to say that there was no room in Tower Hamlets for their countrymen. The Tory candidate put out a leaflet in the election calling for compulsory fingerprinting of Muslims. Both fostered the racism which the BNP fed off. This vote and subsequent actions of the BNP, together with the growth of racism and fascism in Europe, were to lead to huge confrontations the following year. *Militant* was to play a prominent role in combatting this.

## KINNOCK RESIGNS

In the wake of the electoral debacle Kinnock was compelled to resign. The feelings of many were summed up by *Militant* supporter Andrew Price:

> Socialists should always look forwards rather than backwards. But as I sat and watched Neil Kinnock's resignation speech I thought back over my 25 years of political activity in South Wales and what I had seen of Kinnock. Back to the 1960s and the earnest young man desperately trying to make a name for himself as an aspiring MP. Back to his election to Parliament in 1970 and his eloquent speech denouncing capitalism, advocating real socialism condemning the timidity of the Labour leadership... We asked him to speak at meetings organised by *Militant* and he said how delighted he would be to share a platform with those who were making such a positive contribution to the labour movement. Back to 1980 when he and I shared a platform at Cardiff University Labour Club. A trade unionist asked us about how a Labour government would confront the capitalist state... I replied by arguing for the abolition of the monarchy and the House of Lords. Kinnock's response was to stand up and tell a dirty joke about the Duke of York... as I watched him on 13 April denounce the attacks of

the Tory press I remembered 1985, the year that so many of us (including myself) were expelled from the Labour Party and how those same tabloids cheered Kinnock loudly then. No, I did not join Peter Mandelson in shedding a tear at Kinnock's resignation. Yet another careerist has entered the annals of Labour Party history... Kinnock may have succeeded in temporarily separating us from the Labour Party. But we will find a way of getting the message of real socialism to the people who really matter in Britain.[18]

## SCOTLAND

Scotland was to be the testing ground for *Militant*'s independent turn. The formation of Scottish Militant Labour was an attempt to provide a socialist alternative to the free market policies of the Labour and SNP's leaderships. In the general election the SNP had made a significant advance, with a 50 per cent increase in the share of the vote compared to 1987, although it was not as successful as the SNP leaders expected. The desire to see the back of the Tories meant a final rallying behind Labour. Nevertheless, the SNP had made gains among the working class and particularly amongst the 18-24-year-olds, 35 per cent of whom had voted for the SNP, as had 33 per cent of the unemployed. In Glasgow the SNP vote had risen by 38,000 while Labour's had fallen by 50,000 - a 20 per cent slump compared to 1987. While inscribing on its banner the legitimate national demands of the Scottish people, Scottish Militant Labour sought to innoculate the working class, particularly in the heartlands of the West of Scotland, against the virus of capitalist nationalism which seeks to divide one worker against another. It set it sights on the youth and the working class. We predicted that this new Tory government:

> won't be a government of stability or tranquility... A period of intense struggle will begin to open up. *Militant* will be to the fore in all these battles, in the trade unions and through community organisations.[19]

A few weeks after the general election came the local government elections. The results of those elections, particularly in Scotland, showed that all the political obituaries for *Militant* were once again premature. Across Britain, Labour council seats toppled on 7 May. The victory of the Tories in the general election and the dismal record of right-wing Labour councils resulted in thousands of traditional Labour voters staying at home. However, in Glasgow the picture was different. There, as we reported: "The red flame of socialism was burning brightly as the votes were announced."[20]

The main story in every Scottish newspaper the next day was the stunning success of Scottish Militant Labour candidates. The *Glasgow Herald* reported: "There was a deep sense of hurt and outrage among Labour councillors in Glasgow as the full impact of *Militant* successes sunk in."[21]

The *Daily Record* led its front page with "Jailhouse shock! - Labour takes a tanking - poll tax rebel Sheridan is in."[22] *The Scotsman* said: "Sheridan takes Pollok in dramatic victory", describing it as "the night Scottish *Militant* showed it could no longer be ignored in Glasgow." [23]

Even the Scottish edition of the *Sunday Times* proclaimed: "Why Labour lost in Sheridan country." It went on: "Sheridan's campaign was about poverty... He has given hope for the first time... The people of this estate have found a champion and a leader in Sheridan." [24]

Tommy Sheridan and SML made history with a councillor being elected from his prison cell for the first time in Scottish history. The result was that SML now had a group of four councillors in the city, just one less than the Tories and one more then the SNP and Liberals combined. Moreover, only a slender 46-vote defeat in one ward prevented SML having to toss a coin with the Tories to become the official opposition. The mood of desperation after the general election had now been visibly transformed to one of confidence and even elation, especially in Pollok. One woman told the *Sunday Times*: "Tommy understands about damp houses and dole money. He lives in similar conditions to us and he'll do something about it."[25]

SML shattered the views of the sceptics, some of whom had recently departed from our ranks, who claimed that the launch of an independent socialist organisation in Scotland would "fail to cause a ripple on the Clyde". Highlighting the remarkable success of SML was the knowledge that even the Communist Party, once a sizeable force in Glasgow, had never succeeded in gaining council seats in the city.

On 7 May two Communist candidates - both well known local

figures - received just 81 and 99 votes. In contrast to this the seven SML members polled an average of almost 900 votes. Their total vote was greater then the total vote for Scotland's 77 Green Party candidates! More to the point, the SNP was left licking its wounds in Glasgow as a result of the intervention of SML. In Scotland as a whole the SNP won 24 per cent of the vote, pushing the Tories back into third place. At the last local elections in 1988 the SNP vote had lagged behind Labour by 21 per cent. On 7 May however, Labour's lead over the SNP was ten per cent, but in every single seat where SML stood there was a significant slump in the SNP vote.

In six out of seven seats, the SNP was defeated by *Militant* candidates.

SML in Scotland and *Militant* in the rest of Britain intended to be a lever for such a movement.

## LIVERPOOL

In Liverpool, for the first time in years, local elections followed national trends. Five years previously, the Labour Party, standing in the traditions of the 49 surcharged councillors, had produced record turnouts and record Labour votes. Even as late as 1990 Labour polled 91,801 votes, yet by 1992 just 36,677 voted for official Labour. This was the consequence of expelling *Militant* and ditching socialist policies. The Liberals had a made a comeback, regaining ten seats as a result of the disastrous policies of the right. In 1992 the Broad Left and the Independent Labour Party (ILP) had fought in 12 and eight seats respectively. In these seats they had won 17.7 per cent of all votes cast, although only one candidate was victorious, in Everton, where Broad Left councillor George Knibb was returned. Overall in the 20 seats they contested the Left had taken 30 per cent of the total Labour vote. In the Valley ward, Broad Left candidate, Sylvia Sharpey-Schaefer beat official Labour but was pipped by the Liberals. In Netherley, Lesley Mahmood, with 29 per cent of the vote, came second to official Labour. A hung council now existed with Labour having 40 seats, the Liberals 38, and the Left holding 18. The Tories only had two seats. The purge had gone so far that the Liverpool Labour Party relied upon a handful of activists, in some cases on telephone canvassing.

# 48.
# NEW WORLD DISORDER

THE TRIUMPHALISM with which the spokepersons of capitalism had greeted the collapse of the Berlin Wall and the demise of Stalinism gave way to doubts and pessimism. The dazzling future held out for the ex-Stalinist states had become a nightmare, particularly for the peoples of the former Soviet Union. By February 1992 it was clear that "price rises and poverty are the bitter fruit of the attempt to introduce capitalism into the former Soviet Union."[1]

Ninety per cent of Moscow's and Murmansk's populations, for instance, were now on the poverty line because of the massive increases in prices in January, 1992. Food riots and strikes had flared up amongst workers and a big confrontation between students and police took place in Tashkent. This resulted in two dead and many wounded. Previously privileged layers under Stalinism had been thrown into the abyss of poverty. Workers in the former prestige area of space research, including astronauts, had threatened strike action in late January as economic catastrophe and food shortages gripped large parts of the former USSR. However, mass opposition, either in the form of strikes or the creation of a separate mass party of the working class, had not yet materialised. But the situation was so tense that ex-President Gorbachev had warned that Russia was a "lake of petrol".[2] One accidentally dropped match could ignite an explosion. Why had there not been a mass uprising of the workers of the former USSR? An explanation was to be found in the unprecedented drop in production, comparable only with the USA during the 1929-33 slump. We pointed out:

> Neither boom nor slump in and of themselves evoke movements of the working class. It is the change from one period to another that radicalises working people. Trotsky pointed out that the defeat of the first Russian revolution of 1905-1907 coincided with an economic downswing. This served merely to deepen the Russian masses' demoralisation and disappointment. On the other hand, an economic revival, boosting workers' confidence, led to an upswing in strikes and other

forms of struggle. A sudden collapse in the productive forces, and with it mass unemployment, can stun workers for a period, rather than immediately radicalising them.[3]

In the case of the former Soviet Union this demoralisation was further deepened by the lack of a mass workers' party capable of explaining the nature of the economic catastrophe and of putting forward a programme to show a way out. The situation had been compounded by the throwing back of the political consciousness of the working class under Stalinism. However, in opposition to some pseudo-Marxists, we had argued that, despite all the efforts of dictatorships, including the Stalinist variety, society and the working class does not go back to its starting point. The embers of the October revolution remained in the workers' consciousness, especially in Russia.

> These will be fanned into flames, and eventually a roaring fire, once they [the working classs] realise that there is no way forward on the basis of capitalism. The masses would draw this conclusion far quicker if they had at their head a workers' party capable of explaining the process unfolding.[4]

## WORKERS' DEMOCRACY

The small forces of genuine Marxism attempted to take this message to as many workers as possible throughout the former Soviet Union. We reported in March 1992:

> people from Crimea, Ukraine, Belarus, St Petersburg and Moscow met on the 14 and 15 March to pull together support for *Rabochaya Demokratlya (Workers' Democracy)*.[5]

The *Itar-Tass* news agency reported on the meeting as an attempt to organise a "new party". This was not quite accurate, as the 15 people who were present were hardly the basis for a mass workers' party. However, the organisers of the meeting believed that such a mass party could be formed by linking up the various workers' commitees which existed. Those present at the meeting only represented as yet a small movement but nevertheless were quite influential. A representative from Crimea present at the meeting had organised an open-air meeting in the previous week, of 500, on the national question. Reports had begun to appear of

> some students complaining about not having access to sources, for example Trotsky's historic critique of Stalinism. "I'm glad you raised that; look at what I'm working on with my students at the moment!"[6]

explained Valentina Chichkina (vice-president of the philosophy faculty at Lomonosov University, Moscow). The French paper *Liberation* published a report which stated:

> *The Revolution Betrayed* was published in Russia for the first time last year by *Rabochaya Demokrakya*.[7]

The opposition to the new emerging capitalist class was growing but was, and is still, quite small.

## UPRISING IN LOS ANGELES

However, on a world scale capitalism's New World Order looked more like a new world catastrophe, with riots in America and a huge strike wave convulsing Europe. The Los Angeles uprising had shattered the complacency of the US ruling class. This revolt was clearly a turning point in American society as anger exploded at racism and racist policing. The riots were triggered by the acquital of the policemen responsible for the beating meted out to Rodney King by the notoriously racist Los Angeles Police. Despite the fact that the police had used 5,000 volt stun guns, had kicked and clubbed King with an estimated total of 56 blows - all caught on video tape - the Los Angeles Police were nevertheless "declared innocent". This ignited the anger which had been accumlating in all the major cities of the US. The army of poor, deprived and dispossessed, had grown during Reagan's 1980s' boom. The resulting riots were the biggest since the upheavals of the 1960s and left 58 dead, 1,900 injured, 5,200 arrested and a total of 5,000 buildings destroyed. Three-quarters of the dead were black, many of them shot by the police. Millions of TV viewers, worldwide, were horrified by the attack on a white lorry driver. However, this was not typical. It was one of the very few attacks on whites and four blacks actually stepped in to save him from what appeared to be certain death.

US President Bush hypocritically declared: "The scenes in California and elsewhere are so violent it is hard to watch."[8]

With the deaths of thousands of Iraqi workers on his hands his adminstration was clearly responsible for the conditions in Los Angeles, because of the axing of many reforms associated with the Civil Rights movement of the 1960s. However, the marchers and rioters included whites and Hispanics as well as blacks. In Oakland school students and a number of schools walked out in protest. The racial composition was mixed and the mood for unity strong. In the workplaces, *Militant* reported:

> There was a strong mood for unity. *Labor Militant* supporters - *Militant*'s co-thinkers and their paper in the USA - put out a petition condemning the verdict and calling on the local labour movement to organise mass protests.[9]

## SOUTH AFRICA

In its death-agony the apartheid regime was inflicting terrible retribution on the African working class. *Militant* detailed the massacres at Boipatong and the counter-revolutionary violence of Inkatha. Following the Boipatong massacre Mandela spoke at a mass rally of 20,000 where he was confronted with placards demanding "Mandela, give us guns!" At this time the South African socialist Philemon Mauku was imprisoned. Like Nelson Mandela 20 years previously, he was jailed for taking up arms to defend his people. The 24-year-old Philemon was sentenced to three years' jail for having two AK47s. He was helping to defend his community in Alexandra township against the continuing attacks by chief Buthelezi's right-wing Inkatha movement, backed by the police. Philemon was a member of *Congress Militant* and had been visited in prison by 22 comrades from Alexandra in the first fortnight after his jailing. He was released in 1994. The Boipatong massacres pushed the ANC into breaking off negotiations with the government. This was an important turning point in the struggle against de Klerk's disintegrating apartheid regime.

This was followed by an even worse massacre on 7 September, in Bisho the capital of the "state" of Ciskei. 28 people were killed and 200 were wounded. This followed the 70,000 demonstration against Ciskei's dictator, Brigadier Oupa Gqozo. The stooge nature of Ciskei was shown by the use of South African troops by de Klerk. Following the Bisho massacre these troops were deployed to protect South African-owned industrial property. The general strikes following the Boipatong and Bisho massacres, together with those which followed the assassination of Chris Hani, an ANC leader most associated with the "armed struggle", played a decisive role in the phase of "negotiations". The purpose of the counter-revolutionary terror, organised by Inkatha and the South African police and army, was to force concessions from the ANC. But, as we pointed out, the work of the counter-revolution only gave a further spur to the movement of the South African workers. It was this movement which compelled the ANC leadership to stiffen their demands against any white veto. The general strikes had also demonstrated that the working class was the most powerful political force in South Africa. This put its stamp on all future developments. It was this factor that forced the ANC leaders to oppose de Klerk's demands for a significant white veto in a future coalition government.

In October the first visit to South Africa by some of the British *Militant* leaders, Lynn Walsh and Tony Saunois, took place. This was to discuss with our co-thinkers, gathered around *Congress Militant*, and to witness the situation in the country. Tony Saunois, in an eyewitness account, confirmed the overwhelming power of the black working class and the impossiblity of the ruling class seeking to govern in the old way. He commented that it was

> clear that what is intended is a new constitution, which involves the black population in government but leaves real power with the white ruling class. The elected assembly will be bound within the limits of an agreed schedule which will be decided before hand. Into this will be written restrictions and limitations... The ANC leaders are in the process of embracing the ruling class and delivering working-class blacks to capitalism. Though they enjoy massive - but not an unquestioning - support, they are increasingly separating themselves from the working class. The two general strikes in August - amongst the biggest in South African history - were planned in the headquarters of Liberty Life, one of South Africa's top ten monopolies. The same company also supplies ANC leaders with a fleet of limousines.[10]

The death agony of apartheid was inflicting a terrible price on the African majority. De Klerk's careful scheme, of reforms from the top in order to prevent revolution from below, was almost unhinged following the assassination of Chris Hani in April. Hani was probably only second to Nelson Mandela in popularity amongst the masses. More than any other ANC leader he was regarded in the African townships and villages as a man of the people.

He had become a legendary leader of MK, the armed wing of the ANC. On his return from exile in 1990 he had maintained hes reputation amongst ANC militants, saying at one time that a seizure of power by the African majority could not be ruled out if the government refused to concede to the majority. He had also warned of the possibility of a workers' party developing out of the ANC in the future, although he perceived this as a social democratic party rather than as a revolutionary party. The assassination of Hani, by a crazed Polish immigrant, was obviously instigated by the right as a means of disrupting negotiations aimed at a political settlement. Extreme right-wing figure Derby-Lewis and his wife were indicted as being the organisers of this assassination. Hani's murder led on Wednesday 14 April to the biggest "stay away" that South Africa had ever seen. Never before in South Africa's history had so many people joined mass demonstrations as in the 12 days following Hani's murder. 100,000 marched in Durban, 80,000 marched through the Inkatha-controlled area known as "Beirut". At Chris Hani's funeral vigil, 100,000 filed into a soccer stadium near Soweto, with thousands more outside. On the day of the funeral over 90 per cent of workers stayed away from work. However, they didn't stay at home but went onto the streets. At the mass meeting in the Soweto soccer stadium Nelson Mandela received applause. But when Harry Gwala, the ANC leader from Natal Midlands arrived the whole stadium chanted, "Gwala, Gwala, Gwala". He had a militant reputation because of his opposition to power sharing. His defiant speech received greater applause than Mandela's. An indication of the readiness of workers to embrace the ideas of the Marxist Workers' Tendency of the ANC was shown by the sale of more than 500 *Congress Militants* at demonstrations in Johannesburg, Durban and Cape Town.

# 49.
# FIGHTING FOR SOCIALISM

IN THE aftermath of the 1992 general election *Militant* prepared the ground, together with others on the Left, for effective resistance to the Tories. One of the battle lines was in the civil service. *Militant* enjoyed considerable support, particularly in the CPSA. The 1992 CPSA conference, held in late May, had seen the Left decisively defeat the Right on all the key issues raised at the conference. The right wing had retained power but they had left Brighton battered, as the conference had overturned and defeated them on every single policy issue. In one vote, on reducing the size of the standing orders committee, their proposals gained the support of only five or six delegates out of 800. The right wing, described as 'moderates', were in effect the voice of the Tories within the union. The pay deal negotiated by the right was overwhelmingly rejected by the conference. The elections were a disappointment for the Left but they did not give a great deal of comfort to the right either. This was particularly the case in relation to John Macreadie's defeat in the election for general secretary. His vote (10,561 with 13,649 for Reamsbottom) and those for other Broad Left candidates had shattered the right. The ballot papers sent out had resembled football coupons with over 90 candidates' names. Moreover, the postal ballot meant papers were sent to members homes, away from the discussions in the offices. Even then the right wing won by only 3,000 votes and the combined Broad Left and Broad Left 84 vote (who split the vote, polling 3,918) exceeded the right's vote. We concluded: "There is no natural majority for the right in the CPSA."[1]

## YOUTH AGAINST RACISM IN EUROPE

Another key issue on which *Militant* concentrated its energies was that of racism. Racist attacks had swept through many countries in Europe. In one year there had been a thousand in Germany alone.

In France more than 200 North African men had been killed by racists over the previous decade and in Britain there were racist attacks every day, including murders. The success of the National Front in France and the Republicans in Germany had sent a wave of horror through the labour movement, above all amongst the youth. In response to this *Militant* and its co-thinkers in Europe had initiated the Youth Against Racism in Europe (YRE) Campaign. The YRE decided to call for a mass European-wide demonstration against racism in Brussels, hosted by the highly successful anti-fascist organisation Blokbusters. Highlighting the importance which we attached to this campaign, our front-page article declared:

> We in the Youth Rights Campaign want to see an end to racism once and for all. To do that, we need to go rid of the system that breeds it - capitalism.[2]

There was a call for a massive turnout on 24 October from all the countries in Europe, in which the YRE had already taken successful initiatives.

## 24 OCTOBER 1992 - BRUSSELS

After four months of campaigning a marvellous demonstration of over 40,000 marched through the streets of Brussels. The YRE had assembled the biggest anti-racist, anti-fascist, all-European demonstration ever. At 2pm the demonstrators moved off led by the Blokbusters with stewards, supplied with sticks, linking arms and spreading along the front of the march. We reported:

> Despite the pouring rain it was a moment that brought a lump to the throat... The banners told you where they came from - Germany, Ireland, Sweden, Britain, Belgium, Czechoslovakia, Poland, Norway, Austria, Holland and France... Hundreds, perhaps thousands, of Blokbuster placards rolled into view. The unmistakeable clenched fist symbol was everywhere. As the German contingent filed pass, the start of the demonstration was already out of sight a mile up the road. There were stickers, flags and banners everywhere you looked.[3]

The youth of Europe had shown that they would not tolerate the rise of the racists and fascists, and in this fight there was unity behind the banner of the YRE. The demonstration became front-page news with photos in eight out of eleven Belgium daily newspapers. Massive pictures, many of them in colour, showed thousands of marchers filling the streets of Brussels. News of the demo reached the United States thanks to a short report on ABC television news. The media could not agree on the turnout. A Belgian TV station said there was 25,000 while the left-wing German daily newspaper *TAZ* estimated that 45,000 people attended. Confronted by a well-organised, disciplined demonstration, with stewards dressed in the Anti-Poll Tax Federation bibs from Britain, and carrying precautionary sticks the Belgian fascists complained to the government about a display of "paramilitary" force!

The YRE burst onto the scene in this mighty demonstration and was to become even better known in the battles which unfolded in 1993.

## TOMMY SHERIDAN RELEASED

In Britain the continued incarceration of Tommy Sheridan, as with hundreds of other anti-poll tax protesters, showed the brutal face of British capitalism, once its power is challenged. After five months in prison he was released to a tumultuous reception in Glasgow in July. He was greeted by a crowd of 700 at Glasgow's Queen Street Station. The crowd waiting for him was swelled by Post Office workers in their uniforms, oil workers and teachers. Red flags, union banners and SML branch banners mingled together. To a huge roar Tommy declared: "There have been no warrant sales in three years and I re-affirm now there'll be no warrant sales in Scotland."[4]

As a pipe band struck up the crowd marched across George Square so that councillor Sheridan could take his place in the City Chambers. An even greater reception took place in the evening with over 500 people gathering to greet his release from prison. Shortly after this the well known left-wing investigative journalist, John Pilger, wrote:

> I was cheered by the release the other day of Tommy Sheridan after five months in Edinburgh's Saughton jail. Sheridan was imprisoned last January for breaching a court order and forcing the cancellation of a poll tax warrant sale. From his cell, he successfully campaigned for a seat on Glasgow district council. He stood again in the general election as a Scottish Militant Labour in Glasgow Pollok and, for one who

was denied the hustings, he didn't do badly... His greatest victory of course was as leader of the All-Britain Anti-Poll Tax Federation. In Scotland more than half the population still have not paid the poll tax. Long ago Tommy Sheridan would have embodied everything that inspired the Labour Party. He is young and... lives among and fights for the working-class community where he grew up... The term "it makes me so angry" is odd to hear coming from one so young and erudite as Sheridan. It is not difficult to understand his popularity in Glasgow where people talk about their living conditions with anger. Compare his speaking up for people with Labour's current waffle about 'image' and 'electable strategies' and 'socialism empowering the individual'... The legacies of Labour's witch-hunt are the very authoritarianism of which Labour accuses *Militant* and a widespread grassroots belief that socialism itself is now tantamount to 'entryism' in the party. Tommy Sheridan is credited with recruiting some 100 new members to Labour's branch in Pollok... And yet Labour witch-hunted about 40 people from this branch, including Tommy and a young lad he helped to get off drugs by introducing him to Labour politics... And in his principled stand, he shames the party that expelled him as do Terry Fields and Dave Nellist.[5]

Pilger's unfashionable defence of Tommy Sheridan and *Militant* in the pages of the *New Statesman* led to him being accused by the "left" *Tribune* of "being taken in" and "going totally over the top in praise".

Previously, *Tribune* had praised Pilger to the skies for his investigative reporting of the war in Cambodia, and the West's silence over the atrocities committed by the Khmer Rouge. But when he was prepared to write about genuine struggles of workers in Britain, particularly when they featured *Militant* members, he was considered suspect by the ex-Lefts around *Tribune*.

## CHRISTINE MCVICAR WINS EASTERHOUSE

SML in particular went from strength to strength. In September Christine McVicar won a landslide victory for SML in Easterhouse/ Garthamlock capturing twice as many votes as her Labour opponent with the Tories and the SNP well behind. The Glasgow press could not ignore her victory. The *Glasgow Evening Times* called it a "shattering, humiliating defeat for Labour".[6] *The Scotsman* declared the result "another indication of how much of Labour's grassroots support in the poorest areas is defecting to *Militant*."[7] The *Glasgow Herald* simply cried: "Labour routed."[8]

Even SML supporters were stunned but delighted at the scale of the victory. This surpassed even those in the May city council elections. Before the election the seat appeared to be rock solid for Labour. At the regional council elections two years previously Labour had won 71 per cent of the vote. Now SML had captured 54 per cent, despite the fact it did not have the same base of support as in other areas of Glasgow, especially in Pollok on the opposite side of the city. Moreover, Labour had fought hard to hold the seat. It had deployed seven MPs, including two shadow cabinet ministers and a posse of councillors in the campaign. Easterhouse typified decades of social deprivation and neglect. Capitalism and its Tory agents were primarily responsible for these conditions. But Labour, ensconced in the City Chambers for decades, had failed to lead a struggle to change the quite horrific conditions. People in the schemes had a 40 per cent greater chance of dying before the age of 60 than elsewhere in Scotland. More than 70 per cent of children received school clothing grants.

Following Christine McVicar's victory, *Scotland on Sunday* carried the headline: "*Militant* return from dead scares Labour." They commented: "*Militant* drove home the message last week that it is electable under its own colours."[9]

Christine McVicar summed up the significance of the election. "This is a triumph for the red flag over the pink rose, for traditional working-class socialism over the designer yuppies who have hijacked Labour."[10] Many of the uncommitted agreed with her. A young worker interviewed in Easterhouse by *Scottish Television* the day after the election said:

> *Militant* are the only people that have done anything for Glasgow. It's *Militant*s like Tam Sheridan and that lassie McVicar that have stood up and fought for the Scottish people.[11]

Another, a caller to a Radio Clyde phone-in, declared:

> I'm not a member or supporter of *Militant*. But after Thursday I'm a lot more confident that water privatisation will be stopped. If *Militant* stood in Dunoon I'd vote for them.[12]

A pensioner also stated: "That's the first time in 40 years of voting that I didn't vote Labour. But I'm never voting for them again. I'm *Militant* now."[13]

The significance of these remarks were not lost on Labour representatives. Ann McGuire, chair of the Labour Party in Scotland, commented on radio: "The problem that Labour has in Scotland is that we're sandwiched in the middle between the Tories and Militant Labour."[14]

## SML VINDICATED

The election results for SML completely confirmed the reasons for setting up an independent organisation in Scotland. A certain layering, a differentiation, had taken place within the ranks of the working class. This led to a loosening of the bonds between the mass of workers and Labour, the "traditional organisation" of the British workers. The shift towards the right of the Labour leaders had further weakened these links.

A layer of workers, a majority of the more advanced and combative, began to look towards Militant Labour as the only organisation who could effectively lead a fightback against Tory attacks. *Militant*, and Scottish Militant Labour were under no illusion that SML could automatically replace Labour, or that progress would be in a straight line. SML drew its electoral support from two sources. There was an element of a "protest" vote by traditional Labour supporters against the Labour right. Other votes came from a section of workers who had rejected Labour and were looking for a socialist alternative. *Militant* fully recognised that at times the mood of workers, which could assume a desperate yearning to see the back of the Tories, would lead to a rallying behind Labour, and consequently a weakening in support for SML. But a core of workers, reflected first in Scotland, had taken a conscious decision to support us. Their support meant that SML could make important breakthroughs on the electoral front, in the most difficult arena for Marxism. Moreover, this success contrasted favourably with the performance of Left parties in Europe. In most European countries a vote for Left parties of between eight and 20 per cent was seen as respectable. Even the Reformed Communists (RC) in Italy, which had split away from the Party of Democratic Socialism (PDS), the former Communist Party of Italy, was only able to capture 6.6 per cent of the vote in national elections. Therefore, the electoral performance of SML was significant and was recognised as such by a growing body of commentators. It succeeded precisely because it was not primarily an electoral organisation. Elections were an extension of important class battles such as the anti-poll tax movement, the struggle against water privatisation, and later the Criminal Justice Bill.

Inevitably electoral support would wax and wane. There would be occasions when electoral support would decline. British workers will test and retest an organisation before they consider fully embracing it. However, the dogmatic assertion made by some of *Militant*'s opponents that the "unique" character of the British labour movement means that workers will cling, through thick and thin, to their "traditional organisations" ignores the profound changes which have taken place in the last decade and a half.

This "uniqueness" has evaporated as the character of the British labour movement has more and more come to resemble that of its European counterparts. The march to the right of the Labour and Socialist leaders is an international phenomena, as is the alienation of big layers, particularly of the youth. The "bourgeoisification" of the social democratic parties has left a space for the emergence of new left, radical, revolutionary formations. In Britain the ditching of Clause IV, the distancing and possible complete rupture with the unions, the unprecedented apeing of the Tories by the Blair leadership, has already led to the detachment of a significant layer from the Labour Party. Blair is shifting the Labour Party towards a version of the US Democratic Party. Under Kinnock, followed by Smith, and now Blair, the shift towards the right has gone further than in the past. A complete break with the trade unions and the abandonment of Clause IV can significantly alter the character of the British Labour Party. The process can go a lot further. At the very least, this will leave a significant space to be occupied by a party which relates the ideas of socialism to the day-to-day problems of ordinary working people. Scottish Militant Labour and Militant Labour in the course of 1992-94 demonstrated the potential for such an organisation, which could develop by leaps and bounds, once a right-wing Labour government comes to power.

At the Labour Party conference in October, Smith allowed the word "socialism" to pass his lips just once in a 50-minute conference speech. Dennis Skinner was voted off the national executive (NEC). Even Bryan Gould, Smith's opponent for leader and not really on the left of the party, was defeated in the NEC elections. Tony Benn remained as the lone left on that body. This conference also revealed that the Labour Party had spent £700,000 in expelling 40 people from party membership. *Militant* held a public meeting addressed by myself and Tommy Sheridan, with 60 people participating. The mood of the conference was flat with no real debate on most issues.

## PANTHER UK

In contrast, and in the same week as the conference, in Brixton and audience of 2,000, mostly young, blacks packed into a public meeting to hear Bobby Seale, co-founder of the US Black Panthers in the 1960s. This was the biggest indoor public meeting of its kind ever held in Britain. It was hosted by Panther UK, an organisation which *Militant* supporters had participated in founding. During his speech Bobby Seale referred to Panther UK as "this group of young black revolutionaries".[15] Panther UK was an independent black organisation, the launch of which was entirely supported by us. Black Militant Labour members, working in conjunction with others, could relate through this organisation to a significant section of black youth who were alienated from the system, and who were looking towards organised resistance. This naturally provoked the opposition of the professional "race relations industry" who perceive that all matters relating to ethnic minorities are within their ambit. Woe betide anyone who tries to trespass into their "constituency", particularly if they approach race from a class standpoint.

## KIRANJIT AHLUWALIA RELEASED

The victims or survivors of domestic violence were very appreciative of what the organisers of the CADV were able to do. The CADV had conducted a long campaign for the freedom of Kiranjit Ahluwalia. Kiranjit, who was freed in early October 1992, just before a national demo of 2,000 organised by the CADV in central London, Kiranjit had suffered a terrible ordeal at the hands of a brutal husband. She had been jailed for killing him. Kiranjit described the unspeakable indignities she had suffered for more than a decade:

> In ten years the police never helped me once whilst I was suffering but when my husband was dead they couldn't wait to pin everything on me to make their case look good.

Commenting on her time in prison she said:

> For three and a half years my family suffered more than me. Every evening the woman in the next-door cell used to cry for her children. Women like her shouldn't be in prison... I would walk around the exercise yard by myself with my Walkman. Some women came to me. They heard about my case. They said not to worry, that I had done no wrong. Then one of them pulled down her jumper to show me the white scars she had across her neck, chest and arms. Her husband had thrown acid over her... Women need government money to help us and our children. Some people say: "Why don't women leave? Why don't they tell the man to leave the house?" Well, where can the woman go with her children? The woman is faced with the problem of the children's school, the problem of changing her job. [16]

## PIT CLOSURE CRISIS

At the same time, the most serious crisis since the re-election of the Major government erupted in October over Heseltine's announcement of the mass closure of pits. An estimated 30,000 miners, if Heseltine had his way, would now swell the dole queues and 70,000 jobs in related industries would be lost. Attacks on the working class had become so common under the Tory government that the initial reaction, amongst miners and even many supporters of *Militant* in the coalfields, was at first muted. However, once the scale of the jobs slaughter became clear it ignited a massive public backlash against the government. Black Wednesday in September had been a dark day for the ruling class in Britain. "Black Tuesday", the day when Heseltine made his announcement, would mean suffering for the miners and their families if the government was allowed to get away with it. *Militant* made the call for the immediate occupation of the pits. Even British Coal chief Neil Clarke stated that Heseltine's proposals were "the economics of the madhouse". They were a brutal example of the class spite which motivated the government. The Tories had never forgiven the NUM for bringing down their government 18 years before. This was an opportunity to finally humiliate the miners and their families, and in this way further demoralise the working class. We called for

> an immediate strike... Pits on the hit list must be occupied so miners can carry out the maintenance needed to keep them alive. Rail and transport workers must pledge that not a ton will move. Transport workers' leader Bill Morris is promising support. That must mean boycotting coal. He's called for an emergency meeting of the TUC general council. That must organise solidarity action. Words are not enough. This government won't listen to argument, they want the blood of the mining families and of our class. The only language the Tories understand is action. An alliance of rail, power and public-sector workers must be forged and they must prepare for industrial action. The TUC must call a one-day general strike in support of the miners.[17]

If the labour movement were to stand up to Major now they could force the government to drop the massacre of the mines and even force the whole Tory cabinet out of office through a general election.

In making this call, we pointed to the lessons of history. The year-long struggle of 1984-85 was not lost because the miners had lacked determination but because of the cowardly role of the labour and trade union leaders. Neil Kinnock saw the strike as a diversion, a lost year for Labour electorally. Yet Labour stood at its highest point in the opinion polls at the end of the strike. Two years later it had lost another general election. The TUC leaders had refused to call sympathetic action, even when the NUM funds were seized for fighting to save its members' jobs.

The feeling was so great that the miners called, together with the TUC, for a mass demonstration on Sunday 25 October. The lightning change in mood resulting from these events had generated a heightened interest in politics, reflected in the activity of *Militant*, and its supporters. At the demonstrations throughout the country papers were literally snatched out of the hands of sellers as workers eagerly sought information on the way forward for the miners and the labour movement as a whole. For the 25 October demonstration our front page called for a 24-hour general strike: "Mass action for the miners!"[18]

Over 100,000 workers marched in a huge display of working-class power. It was noticeable that the miners' cause had generated support amongst the middle class and many who normally look with disdain on workers' demonstrations through the streets of London. At the rally in Hyde Park the call from Arthur Scargill for the TUC to organise a day of action evoked massive cheering. However, the TUC leaders, it was evident, once more wanted to limit the campaign to appeals to the Tories' "better nature". The need for action was urgent as the government was proposing the closure of the ten most threatened pits in less than 90 days. If the TUC were not prepared to call for action *Militant* urged that "the NUM should". Above all it urged that:

> Arthur Scargill should set the date for that day of action and from below other trade union activists would turn it into a successful one-day stoppage. Miners should go to other workers and appeal to them to join it.[19]

We also urged individual groups of miners to take such an initiative from below.

Although the 25 October demonstration was smaller than the 1990 mass march against the poll tax, the presence of union banners and colliery bands which filled the streets of the West End of London signified the emergence of the organised working class for the first time, on such a big scale, since the 1984-85 miners' strike. The presence of many middle-class people on the demonstration expressed the fact that small business owners and shopkeepers were drawn behind the labour movement. This invariably happens once the mass of workers move into struggle. Yet it was with disgust that many listened in Hyde Park to a representative of the Confederation of British Industry (CBI) and the Liberal Democrat leader Paddy Ashdown. What did the many public-sector workers who marched in support of the miners think of the union leaders standing alongside a CBI boss who believed that their pay should be frozen? These representatives of capitalism received a very rude welcome from workers.

## ANALYSIS CONFIRMED

*Militant*, virtually alone, had said the day after Major's triumph on 9 April that his was not a strong government but one as weak as the British economy it was trying to uphold. The right-wing Labour and trade union leaders were battening down the hatches for a long haul. In contrast the post-election issue of *Militant International Review* stated:

> Notwithstanding the tame opposition served up by Labour's front bench, the social earthquakes which are coming can splinter the government.[20]

Just six months later and this government was on its knees. One big push and it could have been flattened - forced out of office, taking its job-destroying policies with it.

But victory could only have been achieved by a worked-out strategy and clear demands for action. While helping the miners in every way possible *Militant* also argued for a 24-hour general strike. Two mighty demonstrations, on 21 and 25 October, had actually brought the issue of the general strike back onto the agenda.

Bold action was needed if the government was to be forced to retreat. The idea of an all-out general strike was too far ahead of the movement. This idea was once more put forward by some. One such organisation was the Socialist Workers' Party, whose leader Cliff claimed that if the SWP had been double its claimed 6,000 members it would have had sufficient weight to turn the miners' demonstrations into a march on Downing Street which would have resulted in the overthrow of the government!

The irresponsible playing with the idea of an all-out general strike has nothing in common with genuine Marxism. In a general strike the working class develops its own local bodies to organise the strike, to decide what essential products - like food and medicines - should continue to be produced and distributed and what essential workers should be allowed to work. In the 1926 general strike these organisations developed around the trades councils - the councils of action. These grew in power and strength and indeed the strike was gaining even greater momentum when the right-wing trade union leaders called off the strike. In a general strike two alternative centres of power face each other. The official government authorities, whose instructions are ignored by the mass of the population, and the new workers' power, which is taking the decisions about what is produced and what moves. In this situation all that is needed is for the workers' committees to be linked up on a national level and a new potential government power - a democratic workers' state - would exist to challenge the rule of capital. An indefinite general strike is an "either/or" situation. It cannot last forever; at some stage exhaustion of the working class would take over unless the workers firmly take power. Either this happens and the working class reorganises society on socialist lines, or capitalism is let off the hook.

A unique opportunity existed in October 1992 to call for a decisive 24-hour General Strike which would have shut British capitalism down and demonstrated the power of the working class. Timing is of the essence in politics. A favourable opportunity must be seized by a far-sighted leadership. Arthur Scargill had gained greatly in prestige because his warnings about the proposed pit massacre had been vindicated by Heseltine's announcement. He had also called for a national day of action if the Tories would not budge on their pit closure programme. Even in November when the issue of the ten pits under immediate sentence of closure after the 90-day moratorium was up the urge for action was evident. It all came down to the question of what kind of action.

Our call for the 24-hour general strike had received widespread support. At the same time we also called for the NUM to "name the day" if the TUC continued to prevaricate. The issue of pit occupations also came onto the agenda as a means of harnessing the massive support gathered behind the miners. *Militant* urged: "Organise for action! Prepare to occupy the pits! NUM - name the day for a one-day general strike!"[21]

As the year drew to a close the issues generated by these slogans were hotly debated amongst miners and workers generally. However, October 1992 must be seen as a great opportunity which was unfortunately lost because of lack of clarity and decisive action. The miners could have completely shattered the Tory government, possibly leading to its downfall. But the British ruling class, through its institutions and parties, has learnt how to bend with the wind. The government gave way, set up commissions and turned the issue over to a special parliamentary enquiry; they prevaricated until the mood generated by the original pit closures had evaporated and they could then safely close the pits.

## 3,570 VOTES FOR SML

In the midst of these developments Scottish Militant Labour once more stunned opponents by making further headway in Strathclyde regional council by-elections. In the Govan and Barlanark regional by-elections held on the same day in November, we won 3,570 votes - 38 per cent of the total. Labour trailed in second place with 3,217 votes - 34 per cent, followed by the SNP with just 2,415 (26 per cent). In Barlanark and Queenslie, Willie Griffin on behalf of SML scored a magnificent 1,799 votes to Labour's 1,279 to take the seat. SML came a creditable third in the more difficult area for SML of Govan and Drumoyne. The SNP won with 2,076 votes, Labour came second, with 1,939. Our candidate Alan McCombes polled a very creditable 1,771 votes, the Communist Party just 50 votes! The elections meant that two-thirds of the Glasgow Provan constituency, one of the safest Labour seats in Britain was now represented by SML councillors. Before the election our opponents had argued that its support was restricted to the peripheral housing schemes. But the Govan/Drumoyne result, although Alan McCombes did not win, shattered this myth with almost 2,000 workers' voting for SML. The *Daily Record* once more recorded

> Labour's night of misery at the polls. [It went on] Labour were left in a state of shock last night after shattering defeats in two of their Glasgow strongholds. Jubilant *Militant* dealt the first body-blow when they romped home to victory in Queenslie/Barlanark... SML's bandwagon rolled on with a stunning win.[22]

The *Evening Times* editorial commented:

> People have lost faith in Labour as champions of the poor. The loss of two Glasgow constituencies... might not be particularly serious but what should worry Labour is that it is the continuation of a trend. If Labour finds defections to *Militant* spreading to Lanarkshire and the Ayrshire heartlands the party has a big problem on its hands.[23]

*The Herald* went further:

> Increasingly the party locally has acquired the unenviable reputation as a launching pad for career politicians rather than an instrument for improving the lot of the working class. Many Labour councillors slip too easily into the political power games losing sight of the despairing, angry faces that put them there.[24]

The SNP, however, could not take much comfort from having narrowly scraped home in Govan. SNP leader Alex Salmond admitted to the *Sunday Times*, "*Militant* is a threat to the SNP as well as to Labour."[25]

## KEN LOACH INTERVIEW

Ken Loach is probably considered to be the most outstanding film director over the last 30 years able to capture many aspects of working class life. Famous for *Cathy Come Home* in 1966 and *Kes* in 1969 as well as *Hidden Agenda*, he directed a film, at the beginning of 1993 *Raining Stones. Riff-Raff*, was the story of a building site which, apart from *Business As Usual*, contained probably the only favourable reference to Liverpool city council during the 1983-87 period ever to appear in a film. Explaining in an interview with *Militant* why he took a clear political stance, he said:

> it's unavoidable I guess. In the end you can only make films about things that get you wound up and I suppose that's what I've found winds me up.

Explaining why many others avoid any political commentary Loach stated:

> film is a commodity, particularly cinema films. In the cinema each film has to show a return and the whole tradition of cinema culture is built about a good night out, about escapism, there isn't a cinema culture of political engagement. In television it's rather different because there is more range of television output. There's clearly a place for engaged films and documentaries dealing with political subjects.

Asked about *Militant*, Ken Loach declared,

I'm not in a position to give a detailed analysis because I haven't read the paper recently. But I absolutely defend the right of *Militant* and every other left paper to be a contributing part of the labour movement. The left only flourishes on open argument where one analysis is set against another. That's how a radical ideology is formed, it has to be argued out and we all have to make separate contributions to that from a basic Marxist position. I think the negative side of that is sectarianism. None of us admit to being sectarian but nonetheless sectarianism exists and that's a great pity.[26]

## JOHN PILGER

John Pilger also gave an interview. Asked why he had come out against expulsions, he said: "I looked at the way Terry Fields and Dave Nellist were treated. I tried to pick up a representative national picture of how the purge was conducted. And it was clear that in many areas people who have absolutely nothing to do with *Militant* were being expelled."

Did that mean it was OK to get rid of us, but not other lefts, our reporter asked:

No not at all, I don't want that suggested. I believe that people who support *Militant* follow a tradition of dissent within an organisation and have as much right to their views as anybody.

He compared the Labour leader's strategy to that of the *Daily Mirror's* attempts to fight the *Sun* by copying it - destroying its own identity while only creating a bad imitation. He also recognised the impressive achievements of Scottish Militant Labour, which he saw as having moved out of "siege politics - merely defending itself from other people's attacks - and into the community."[27]

## HANDS OFF OUR WATER

Refusing to rest on their laurels, SML also took the initiative in the campaign to prevent the privatisation of Scottish water. No issue, not even the poll tax, had aroused such outrage throughout Scotland as this Tory threat. Opinion polls had shown that 90 per cent of the Scottish population were aghast at the Tory plans to sell off to private interests the one commodity which Scotland has in abundance. However, Scottish television had led with the story, "Tommy says don't pay."[28] Scottish Militant Labour had taken the initiative in setting up the, "Hands Off our Water" (HOW) and a founding conference had been held with 160 delegates from all over Scotland. Representatives of many other parties attended but only Christine McVicar for Scottish Militant Labour put forward a clear campaign involving organised civil disobedience, linked to working-class communities and the trade union movement. She promised SML would not back down when the going got tough and pointed to the electoral success of SML as proof of the popularity of the whole campaign.

## DUNDEE

The electoral battle was extended beyond Glasgow and the West of Scotland, the main base of SML, with the decision to stand in a by-election in the Blackshade ward in Dundee. In the three-week campaign SML notched up 300 votes, 35 per cent of the vote in the Ardler housing schemes. Labour mobilised MPs, MEPs, councillors and full-time officials as they were unable to find a candidate, never mind a single activist, from Ardler who would campaign for them. In four weeks 500 copies of *Militant* were sold in a ward with a registered electorate of just over 2,000. At one public meeting with 50 attending SML's candidate, Liz McBain, spoke together with Tommy Sheridan. Seventeen new members were recruited to SML. Labour's share of the vote was cut from 60 to 45 per cent; the lowest they had ever received in Ardler.

## WE STAND IN LAMBETH

Seeking to emulate the achievements of their Scottish counterparts, London *Militant* supporters decided to put up a candidate in the Bishop's ward by-election in the London Borough of Lambeth. The candidate was Steve Nally, who achieved national prominence as secretary of the All-Britain Anti-Poll Tax Federation. Lambeth is one of the most deprived boroughs in London if not in the whole of Britain. One in four of its people were unemployed, 50 per cent were dependent on some form of benefit and 75 per cent were living below the European decency threshold. The council, from being one of the beacons in the struggle against the Tory government during the 1980s, had, under right-wing Labour in the nineties passed on Tory cuts to local people. By 1993 right wing Labour councillors had already cut £9 million off the budget and were proposing another £15 million cut. This would mean at least 1,000 people being made redundant out of a workforce of 7,000, the price of meals-on-wheels going up by 15 per cent, school dinners increasing by ten pence a day, rents put up by £6-£8 a week and six out of eight play centres being closed. Moreover the two sitting Labour councillors in the ward had said that they would vote for the cuts. Steve Nally was amongst a number of *Militant's* members in the area, including Labour councillor Anne Hollifield, who had been expelled from the Labour Party for standing up for working people. Much debate and soul searching had taken place amongst *Militant* supporters in London before the decision was taken to stand. There was a natural hesitation to plunge into an electoral struggle in an area where *Militant* did not have the same roots, as for instance in Liverpool or in Glasgow. Moreover, Lambeth, like Liverpool, had been the target of vitriolic denunciations of the so-called "looney left" by the Tories and their hirelings in the press. Nevertheless, it was decided to take the plunge and the reward was a successful campaign which established Militant Labour as a powerful force in the area.

As in Scotland, one of the features of the campaign in Bishop's ward was the involvement of working-class people who had previously remained impervious to the message of the "politicians". One of these was Jacquie Lloyd who lived just over the river from the House of Commons but felt as though she lived a million miles removed from MPs who were supposed to be representing her: "I've only voted once since I've lived here because I'm so disgusted with them."[29]

Her experience of politicians, both local and national, was of cuts and insults. Typical of many residents of the inner-city areas of London she was able to reel off a catalogue of problems, a gross shortage of teachers in schools, increased rents and poll tax demands. The £7 rent increase imposed by the council was a real shocker and this had led her to consider voting for the *Militant* candidate. Naturally, people would ask what difference would one councillor make in the local council chamber. Anne Hollifield, a Labour councillor since 1990, answered:

> Well, I've been able to do a fair bit. Lambeth people won't go to jail for not paying their poll tax - I got that through the council. I fought for 18 months and got a hardship committee to look into all poll tax cases. I've helped stop the closure of youth and further education services.[30]

Militant Labour election campaigns were unique. There the usual canvassing on the doorstep went alongside action with local people to change their conditions. During the campaign 250 local women council workers lobbied Lambeth council against the threatened closure of nurseries and play centres and the sacking of workers. Julie Donovan reported:

> We'd organised a meeting to set up a Childcare Defence Campaign but somebody had rung every nursery and playcentre in Lambeth pretending the meeting had been cancelled. But that sabotage didn't stop us organising.[31]

Pressure from *Militant* and others did force the council to retreat on the sacking of six carers.

*Militant* did not expect to win first time out. However, Steve Nally in a short three-week campaign came from nowhere to beat the Tories into fourth place. He received 336 votes, 12 per cent of those who voted. This was only five votes less than the Liberals had polled in 1990 and now they had won the seat from Labour. It was a disgraceful result from the point of view of Labour. To lose a seat like this to the Liberals was a condemnation of the right-wing policies of Lambeth council: a rent rise of £6 - £10 per week, £12 million-worth of cuts and the sacking of workers. *Militant* in its first electoral test in London had beaten the Tory, the representative of the governing party of Britain and the ruling class. The votes for Steve Nally did not tell the whole picture. 600 people had bought our paper. Our stall, out every day during the campaign, as well as our barnstorming electoral methods, had aroused enormous interest in the campaign. 41.6 per cent of the ward turned out to vote, far in excess of the 28 per cent who had turned out in a neighbouring by-election just three weeks previously. Twelve people agreed to join *Militant* and 20 more filled in cards expressing a interest in our ideas. To a Labour Party, increasingly de-gutted of socialism by the right wing, our electoral methods were from another planet. The Labour Party increasingly relied on a handful of activists, and a telephone and media campaign. The only time that the Labour Party advanced out onto Lambeth Walk was to tell *Militant* canvassers: "Ordinary people are just not interested in politics" or to yell "F... off" at two women who made the 'mistake' of asking a local Labour councillor what her policies were.[32]

## TIMEX BATTLE

In Scotland, meanwhile, the Timex battle had begun. This developed into one of the epic industrial struggles of the 1990s. The announcement of lay-offs for half of the workforce led to strike action in defence of jobs and conditions. This amounted to a lockout and mass sackings. One woman, who worked at Timex for 15 years, commented to us:

> We had a one-day strike for the nurses. During the miners' strike we collected and made up food parcels for the pit villages. The women did knitting for the miners' children.[33]

Their support for other workers in struggle in the past was rewarded with huge support from the Scottish working class and labour movement. Within a month support came from the whole of Britain. The strike had blown away the idea that trade union militancy "no longer applies". Timex workers were fighting for many others facing de-unionisation and worsening conditions. In the months that followed, the scenes outside the gates of Timex were of mass opposition, mass pickets of workers from Dundee, throughout Scotland and the whole of Britain. *Militant* urged the Scottish Trade Union Congress to call an immediate one-day protest strike in Scotland. The STUC had at least taken the intiative of calling an all-Scotland demonstration in Dundee on 20 March.

## DEREK HATTON CLEARED

In March the outcome of the two-and-a-half year enquiry, Operation Cheetah, was announced. Derek Hatton and four other defendants were cleared of conspiracy to defraud Liverpool city council over two car park sites that had lain derelict since Hitler bombed them in 1942. The police admitted: "There was no special reason for beginning Cheetah, just the rumours." We commented:

> This trial had nothing to do with land sales. It was politically inspired, designed to attack Derek Hatton and destroy the reputation of 47 surcharged Liverpool Labour councillors and *Militant*. [34]

The Tories had never forgiven or forgotten, as with the miners, the humiliating defeat they suffered at the hands of the '*Militant* council'. Their press, their state and their judiciary had pursued a vendetta against *Militant* and the left and they were assisted in this by Labour's right wing. Even the *Independent* pointed out:

> Many lawyers, including implacable opponents of Mr Hatton, had written off Operation Cheetah as a disaster before the trial opened up... The evidence was so ambiguous that prosecution was scarcely justified. [35]

In pursuing Derek Hatton they did not just want to totally discredit him but the ideas he represented from 1983-1987. Derek Hatton had separated himself from *Militant* in 1988 and explained at the time that his business interests meant he could not be seen as a spokesperson for *Militant*. Yet, if he had been convicted there would have been acres of coverage about Derek Hatton and *Militant*:

> Before the verdict was announced one TV researcher even told Liverpool *Militant* Lesley Mahmood that they would use all their footage of Derek if he was convicted and if not they would just cover the story. [36]

Right-wing Liverpool Labour MPs Peter Kilfoyle and Jane Kennedy had the effrontery to issue statements condemning the Crown Prosecution Service and demanding to know why the trial even went ahead! The actions of the right wing, particularly Neil Kinnock and Roy Hattersley, who had denounced the councillors as "corrupt", had paved the way for the police enquiries. Commenting on the results of the enquiry, we said:

The police have now dropped Operation Cheetah. Even they have realised that £20 million is a lot to spend for nothing. This sum is equivalent to that won back by the 47 councillors from the Tory government, which helped to build houses and create jobs. Had £20 million been given to the council in 1992, 1,000 compulsory redundancies would not have been necessary and the families of those workers would not have been 'existing' on the dole.[37]

The results of Operation Cheetah were not only a repudiation of the police but also of those vicious capitalist organs like Rupert Murdoch's *Sunday Times* which had orchestrated the campaign against Derek Hatton and *Militant*. They had actually linked alleged land deals with money which was supposed to have gone to *Militant*. They carried headlines like: "Fraud fills *Militant* coffers - say police." [38] Detective Superintendent Bill Coady, head of the Cheetah enquiry, fed this mood of suspicion by stating: "There is now a strong suggestion that funds from land deals may have helped to finance *Militant*."[39]

*Militant* rebutted every one of these allegations made by the *Sunday Times* and its reporters. The press, of course, never printed any of this. After the collapse of Operation Cheetah not a word retracting earlier lies appeared in the *Sunday Times* or in any of Murdoch's press.

# 50.
# MILITANT LABOUR LAUNCHED

AFTER MUCH deliberation and debate within the ranks of *Militant*, and after weighing up the effects of SML in Scotland, *Militant* decided to launch, Militant Labour, an independent fighting socialist organisation on an all-Britain scale.

The new organisation made its first appearance at a press conference in the unusual surroundings of the St Ermins Hotel, within shouting distance of the Houses of Parliament. Opening the press launch, campaigns organiser Frances Curran explained the irony of the venue: "It was in this hotel that right-wing trade union leaders discussed how to expel *Militant* from the Labour Party." Dave Nellist, Hannah Sell and Tommy Sheridan, and myself as general secretary represented the new organisation. We declared:

> The Tory government is besieged by mass opposition from the people of Britain but the only hope held out by the Labour leaders for working people is to wait for a Labour government. We intend to provide a fighting alternative in all the areas where working people are involved in struggle.
> We were tolerated when our support was small. But as we became a significant force in the party with the backing of councillors and MPs, the right-wing leadership moved against us. There's no room for dissent in John Smith's grey Labour party. After much discussion and a democratic debate in our ranks we have decided that it is necessary to put our programme and our slogans for real action before working people and to urge them to join Militant Labour.[1]

The leaders of the Labour Party had been reduced to the policies of "Me-tooism". The Tories float a policy; the Labour leaders' reply is: "Me too". At a time when 100,000 jobs were threatened in the public sector in the following year, Labour's chiefs had raised the white flag. Larry Whitty, general secretary of the Labour Party, had instructed local council Labour groups to pass on Tory cuts, including "compulsory redundancies". Moreover, a secret Labour Party report which had been leaked to the *Observer* admitted that there were no more than 90,000 individual members of the Labour Party compared to a million in 1952.

Starting with the expulsion of the *Militant* Editorial Board in 1983, the aim of the Labour right was to cancel out all the gains made in party democracy and socialist commitment during the period 1979-82.

> We launched Scottish Militant Labour (SML) just over a year ago and it has achieved spectacular results. We launched SML for a number of reasons. The crisis of British capitalism is expressed in a sharpened form in Scotland and above all in the major urban areas... Labour was identified as part of the 'establishment' by a large number of workers. This is even recognised by Tom Clarke, Labour's shadow secretary for Scotland. He recently commented in *Tribune*: "One of Labour's problems is that it is seen as the establishment in much of Scotland." By providing a fighting example to working people in struggle, we knew SML would become a powerful force. We were also confident that it would encourage the best socialist workers still in the Labour Party to pressurise their leaders into action.[2]

Indeed this pressure had enabled SML to have a greater effect on the Labour Party in Scotland than when *Militant* supporters still operated within the party. Recognising the success of SML, Michael Dyer, Professor of Politics at Aberdeen University, commented:

> Undoubtedly the most dramatic feature of recent Scottish politics has been the rise of Militant Labour: the only party with reason to be greatly impressed with its own efforts. In such places (Dundee) the SNP is losing support to *Militant* amongst the sub-culture of disaffected and marginalised young unemployed and single parents. With *Militant* emerging as the dominant party of working-class protest in Glasgow, the character of dissent had become less nationalist and more socialist.[3]

Here was a crushing refutation of those who disparaged our efforts to cut across the influence of the nationalists, particularly in the urban heartlands of the West of Scotland. SML had become the main organising force in the campaign to resist the privatisation of Scottish water and was also preparing for a mass non-payment campaign of water bills if the legislation was pushed through. Under the pressure of SML, the Scottish Labour leadership were compelled to organise a demonstration against water privatisation - the first Labour demonstration for 12 years.

Many areas in the rest of Britain had the same conditions that led to the launch of SML. Social conditions in Birmingham, London, Manchester, Newcastle, Cardiff and Swansea as well as many areas in the South were on a par with those in Scotland. English and Welsh councils, dominated by right-wing Labour, were as much a part of "the establishment", in the eyes of those who suffer at their hands as was the case in Scotland. *Militant* had a proud record of struggle and sacrifice on behalf of workers.

## STRUGGLE, SOLIDARITY, SOCIALISM

On behalf of *Militant*'s Executive Committee I declared:

> We have launched Militant Labour with very simple and clear aims. They are to staunchly defend the basic principles of the labour movement: Struggle, solidarity and socialism. Militant Labour will be where all workers are prepared to struggle. We will be prepared to organise and provide the necessary leadership. Wherever workers go on strike, we will do everything we can to build wider solidarity action. We will forcefully argue the case for socialist planning, for democratic nationalisation of the 150 monopolies which control 80-85 per cent of the British economy with compensation on the basis of proven need.
> We intend to carry the battle to all corners of the working class and all parts of the labour movement. The situation of the working class is so urgent, the mood of desperation amongst many working people is so pronounced, that *Militant* must boldly intervene under our own banner. At the same time we support all efforts to fight the rightward lurch of the Labour and trade union leaders. We also support those Labour Party members who strive to transform the party into a fighting organisation for the working class.[4]

But the time was right to offer a clear socialist alternative. If the opportunity presented itself *Militant* would also offer an electoral alternative as well. Militant Labour pledged to stand in elections not for the sake of council or parliamentary positions, but to use election campaigns as a platform to mobilise the resistance of ordinary working people and to broaden our support.

## JAMIE BULGER

The killing of Jamie Bulger in Bootle horrified the nation. However, quite unscrupulously the Tories and their press used this terrible incident as an opportunity to demand harsher punishment and longer sentences and latched onto the feelings generated to demand "secure units" for young offenders. It was quite clear that the Tory press did not have an ounce of genuine concern for the families of the victims. This incident was used as a stick with which to beat the workers of Liverpool. It was also used as a means to persecute single parents and sing the praises of the Tories' model of the nuclear, two-parent family. *Militant* hit back with accounts from workers on the ground, furious at the latest example of gross bias against the people of Bootle and Merseyside as a whole. Above all, Militant Labour led a campaign, ultimately successful, for proper childcare facilities and a creche in the shopping centre where Jamie Bulger was kidnapped.

## GUY'S CAMPAIGN

This was the case, for instance, in the campaign to keep London's Guy's Hospital open. The infamous Tomlinson Report had argued that London had too many hospital beds and yet 300,000 Londoners were waiting for operations. As one patient was discharged another fills the bed. We declared:

> If the Tories think that Londoners will sit back and take this they're wrong. Bermondsey people put up with the closure of St Olave's because we knew we had Guy's in our borough. There is no way we'll allow our only hospital to close. We'll fight for Guy's and St Thomas's too. If Tommy's closes it'll mean twice the amount of people trying to use Guy's. Both hospitals must stay.[5]

A demonstration in Bermondsey was called on 27 February along Long Lane, the site of the battle against the fascists in 1937, when thousands of workers built barricades to stop Mosley's Blackshirts marching. Women flung their eggs and oranges at the fascist scum. As Julie Donovan commented: "That Bermondsey spirit lives on today. The Tories are not on. Guys will stay."[6]

## NEW STAGE AT TIMEX

The battle at Timex also moved into a higher gear and on Monday 11 April the biggest ever mass picket at the gates was followed by a 6,000-strong demonstration of workers in support of the sacked workforce. From early morning over a thousand had thronged the gates, travelling from all over Scotland, and as far away as London, Sheffield and Newcastle. It was also the biggest mobilisation of the police and the conflicts on the picket line saw Scottish Militant Labour (SML) members breaking through the police lines in an attempt to try and bar the buses' path. But they were contained by the police. Two SML members, amongst others, were arrested. Most of Scotland, except Dundee, was on holiday and the STUC leaders had put little effort into building for the demonstration but the turnout was still massive. Significantly thousands of Dundee workers took part, in effect taking industrial action to march to Timex. Some were given time off from work to attend to avoid a walkout. Effectively, a partial one-day local general strike had taken place, without any such call from the STUC leadership. We commented:

> For nearly four months a great national drama has unfolded at Timex. If any dispute shows the charged political and industrial situation in Britain, it's this one... Police, including Special Branch and plainclothes police, are being mobilised throughout Scotland to break the picket line and bus in scabs... It's all part of the Timex dispute.[7]

Unfortunately, but not surprisingly, the trade union officials, with one exception, had tried to dampen down the struggle by threatening to expel pickets from the union and gagging the most outspoken trade union rank-and-file leader, John Kydd. While the attention of Dundee workers was on the Timex dispute and important by-election was called in the city.

## WHITFIELD BY-ELECTION

SML achieved an excellent 307 votes (21 per cent) in the Whitfield by-election on 29 April. Once more the Tories had been reduced to fourth behind the victorious SNP candidate, then Labour and then SML. Sixty-nine people voted for the Tories in the Whitfield ward. Yet in this election the Tories had heralded Whitfield as a triumph of government policy and regeneration. It was supposed to be good territory for them because only 35 per cent lived in council housing. SML candidate Harvey Duke explained that low wages, poverty and the threat of water privatisation would mean that a fighting socialist alternative would gain an excellent response in Whitfield. The vote was even more significant than previous efforts because not a single member of SML lived in Whitfield. As a result of the campaign a new branch of 15 members was set up. Over a dozen street meetings had been held and the case for socialism taken to workers who had not heard it before. SML had exposed the Scottish National Party's (SNP) shady deals with the Tories. As a result the SNP vote fell from 55 per cent in the previous May's district elections to 35 per cent this time round. The SNP's candidate declared: "If SML hadn't stood we would have won by a landslide."[8]

The backdrop to this election was the battle at Timex which had entered a decisive stage in May. On Monday 17 May the statutory 90-day sacking notice was due to expire and the sacked workers could then be offered jobs back. It was clear that the company management was attempting to break the unity of the strikers by offering some their jobs back but permanently excluding others. However, Timex workers had made clear there would be no going back until all sacked employees had their jobs back at the same wages and conditions and the scabs were out of the factory. Militant Labour had called for a one-day stoppage in Dundee for 17 May. The potential undoubtedly existed for shutting down the factories and workplaces and for a mass turnout on the picket line. Workers had indicated that they were prepared to turnout and Arthur Scargill had said that he was attending the 17 May mass picket. The leaders of the engineering union (AEEU) and the STUC leaders feared losing control of the dispute. The Timex management had actually stated publicly that they preferred dealing with the national trade union leaders rather than the local strike leaders.

On 17 May a magnificent mass picket, probably one of the biggest if not the biggest that Scotland has witnessed, took place. There were 5,000 people from every corner of Britain who had assembled to demand the reinstatement of 343 strikers sacked by the

Timex bosses. Despite the largest police operation ever seen in Dundee, production inside the factory had been brought to a virtual halt by the mass picket. Timex management in collaboration with the Tayside police had organised for scab buses to arrive at 6.30 in the morning - an hour and a half early. By then 2,000 demonstrators had assembled at the gates, with hundreds more arriving every few minutes. As the police tried to channel the buses into the factory a ferocious conflict broke out with demonstrators at times succeeding in blocking the road. A 20-minute battle took place at one stage with police fighting ferociously to clear a path for the scab buses. By the time the buses had broken through thousands of more protesters had arrived. Shaken by the size of the demo and fearful of further eruptions of anger, the police were forced to turn away dozens of delivery vehicles and private cars bringing white-collar staff to the factory. Scotland's *Daily Record* characterised the picket as "mob demo terror".[9] But most of the arrests had taken place when the Timex strikers and the mass picket moved in front of the factory gates in an attempt to blockade the buses carrying scabs into the factory. It was the police who fought frantically to clear the road for the buses. SML members were among those arrested during the confrontation.
We asked:

> How much public money was spent on this mammoth police operation? When vital services in Tayside are being run down for lack of cash, Tayside chief constable Jack Bowman can spend hundreds of thousands of pounds in a single day to protect the profits of Timex... Why were two demonstrators charged initially with attempted murder for allegedly blocking one of the back gates of Timex with a mini-bus? Why was this information then released to selected sections of the media, while defence lawyers were kept completely in the dark about the charges?[10]

Why after lurid headlines had appeared in every newspaper in Scotland and across national TV news, were the charges then dropped without explanation?

Despite the mass picket it was clear that only decisive action by the working class as a whole could bring the Timex management to their knees. Arthur Scargill at the rally in a nearby park had declared on 17 May, to rapturous applause, that it was necessary to call a 24-hour general strike to save the mines, reinstate Timex workers and stop privatisation of British Rail

Following the success of 17 May, *Militant* called for an escalation of the dispute through a shop stewards' conference of all Dundee workers which could prepare the way for a 24-hour general strike in the city. One Dundee boss told a shop steward on the 17 May: "I can't let you go to the Timex demo because if I do I can't guarantee that that lot [meaning the workforce] won't follow you out."[11]

If a one-day stoppage was not enough, *Militant* argued, this could prepare the way for workers across Scotland to pressurise the STUC into calling a Scottish one-day general strike.

# 51.
# FIGHTING FASCISM

THE MURDER of Stephen Lawrence in April in south-east London was the fourth such racial murder in the area in three years. This was the area where the fascist British National Party (BNP) had their headquarters. Stephen's murder in Eltham - he was stabbed twice: once through the shoulder and then through the heart - was completely unprovoked. In 1992, 16-year old Rohit Duggal was stabbed to death by a gang of white youths in the same road where Stephen Lawrence was killed. Between August 1990, and May 1991, 863 incidents of racist attacks and harassment were reported to the Greenwich Action Committee Against Racist Attacks. Youth against Racism in Europe (YRE) demanded the closure of the BNP's "bookshop", effectively its headquarters. The emphasis which Militant gave to the YRE came from below, with John Bulaitus, London Militant organiser, particularly in favour of this initiative. The YRE initiated the call for a mass demonstration on 8 May, the aim of which was to close the fascist headquarters. This demand was aimed in particular at the Tory Bexley council which had refused to accede to the pressure that had been exerted against them prior to Lawrence's murder.

The 8 May demonstration was the largest anti-racist mobilisation for a decade - more than 8,000 marched. Significantly, it mobilised a wide layer of black youth who marched together with white workers and youth against the fascist headquarters. The police assaulted the demonstrators, attempting to create the impression of a riotous, uncontrolled "mob". The demonstration was, however, very well disciplined and effectively stewarded by the YRE. It was this which prevented serious injuries, possibly including death, being inflicted by the police who ran riot. This was a ploy to prevent big demonstrations against the BNP.

The Anti-Racist Alliance (ARA) refused to participate in a joint demonstration in Welling, preferring to march on the same day, totally ineffectively, through central London. The Anti-Nazi League, controlled by the SWP, also refused to join in a united non-sectarian demonstration. They held a demonstration one week after the massive and successful 8 May demonstration. It attracted no more than 2,000 people with just a sprinkling of blacks.

Militant Labour was also to the fore in the campaign for the release of Winston Silcott, falsely convicted following the Tottenham riots. It was estimated that up to 700 people may be locked away for crimes they did not commit.

One of these was 22-year old Oliver Campbell was serving a life sentence for a murder he did not commit. This was one of the most blatant examples of the perversion of so-called "British justice". Others included the M25 Three, who were serving life sentences for murders that they did not, and could not have committed. In all three cases, the victims were black. This was just one of the aspects of racism in Britain which had assumed heightened importance in the course of 1993.

Despite the magnificent 8,000 strong demonstration on 8 May outside the BNP's headquarters in Welling, it had not yet closed. An unprecedented degree of pressure had been exerted on councillors - a Liberal councillor reported receiving 100 letters and phone calls from local people who wanted to get rid of the BNP. The Bexley Tory council, however, remained unmoved. Therefore, the idea of another demonstration to be organised late in 1993 had begun to gain support. To discuss the next steps all the anti-racist organisations - the YRE, ARA, the ANL, together with organisations like the Indian Workers' Association (IWA) - had been brought together under the banner of the Stephen Lawrence family to discuss the next stage of the campaign. At the first meeting of this committee, the YRE representatives proposed a national unity demo to pass the BNP headquarters on 16 October. In response to this ARA representatives proposed a march through central London instead, which was later supported by the ANL representative. The YRE had no intention of organising a demo in competition to one organised by ARA and Stephen Lawrence's family. In the interests of unity, the YRE proposed organising a Bexley demo at a later date to avoid conflict with ARA's central London initiative. This was despite the fact that the YRE believed that a demonstration through central London would be seen as missing the target. However, at the campaign's next meeting, the ANL did a complete somersault. Without any discussion or consultation, their representatives announced they would be marching to the BNP HQ on the 16 October. Leaflets and posters had been produced and transport already booked. The YRE argued for unity. They asked ARA to reconsider and met with the ANL and tried to persuade them to change the date of their demo. Both groups refused to change their minds. We declared:

> In announcing its demo as a virtual *fait accompli*, the ANL and its Socialist Workers' Party backers have yet again acted in their own interests and not for the unity of the anti-racist movement. Faced with the flat refusal to reorganise their demo on a later date and given that the key task is to close down the BNP, Militant Labour believes anti-racists and anti-fascists should mobilise for a mass turnout on the Bexley demo.[1]

## BEACKON ELECTED IN MILLWALL

In September the fascist British National Party (BNP) secured a by-election victory in the Millwall ward in Tower Hamlets. This acted like a crack of thunder to waken youth and workers into action. Even Transport and General Workers' Union leader Bill Morris called for the TUC to organise a demonstration against racism and fascism. The victory of the BNP resulted from years of neglect by right-wing Labour in the area, a refusal to follow the Liverpool and Lambeth road and not carry out Tory cuts. Racism had then been fuelled by the scandalous actions of the Liberal-dominated Tower Hamlets council, which had blatantly issued racist leaflets as a means of holding on to control in the area. A few days before Beackon's election there was the cowardly racist attack on a young Asian, Quddus Ali, in Tower Hamlets. He was left critically ill and with brain damage. This naturally triggered outrage. A vigil was called outside London Hospital where Quddus was fighting for his life. It was attended by over 1,000 predominantly Asian youth. Unprovoked, the police attacked the demonstration, with one observer commenting:

> I have been on picket lines at Wapping, the miners' strike and the YRE demo in Welling this year, but I have never seen the police 'wade

in' in such an indiscriminate way.[2]

Unfortunately, there had not been effective stewarding on the vigil. It was not the YRE but the ANL which had called this vigil. Council workers immediately walked out when the BNP victory was announced. Two hundred out of a total staff of 600 attended an emergency meeting convened by stewards the day after the election result.

Phil Maxwell, a Tower Hamlets Labour councillor, called for a complete boycott of Beackon, the new BNP councillor. The election results also galvanised the YRE into organising the youth against BNP paper sellers in Brick Lane. On Sunday 19 September, 100 YRE members occupied the space in Bethnal Green Road where the BNP usually sold. At about nine o'clock some six or seven fascists turned up and started baiting the anti-fascists. They waved a Union Jack and shouted fascist chants. The police protected the Nazis, letting them take photos of anti-Nazis. The fascists attempted to provoke a confrontation. After about an hour 200-300 anti-fascists from the YRE, the ANL and other local people assembled. Then the so-called "toughs" of Combat 18 ran for their lives as the anti-fascists and anti-racists tore through the police lines to get at them. In a diversionary movement, YRE members took action:

> to infiltrate the BNP... [we] started singing *Rule Britannia* and walked into their contingent of about 30. As we came in one fascist in a green shirt said: "Hello lads, well done." The anti-racists across the road were chanting "Nazi scum" at us! We were now in the middle of the contingent. We just screamed "yes" and only one Nazi stood his ground. Edmonds [the fascists' deputy leader, subsequently jailed for "bottling" a young black worker] ran for his life, his lip quivering. His minder, a fat skinhead with tattoos on his forehead was running as well.[3]

## BRICK LANE

The victory in Brick Lane gave a further spur to the campaign against the BNP. Over 1,000 demonstrators turned up on 26 September and the BNP never arrived in Brick Lane for their usual paper sale. It was subsequently revealed that 50 Nazis were arrested on the way to the sale. The fact that the police intervened in this way was itself a reflection of the highly successful campaign launched by the anti-racists and anti-fascists. This campaign was reaching out to all layers of the community, including football supporters. After a Leyton Orient match, for instance, a Militant Labour member was threatened by a group of BNP fascists in a pub. Determined action by the YRE locally, alongside other football clubs in London, put the racists and fascists on the defensive. On 3 October a 3,000 strong anti-racist anti-fascist demonstration, with a large and very vocal contingent from the local Asian community, marched through London's East End. The demonstration had been initiated by Youth Connection representing Asian youth. The YRE took the issues of racism and fascism into all those arenas in which youth were active. In October an album, *By Any Means Necessary*, was produced with a number of top bands donating tracks. The record had been initiated by YRE sympathisers and members in Liverpool where some of the top bands had played at a successful anti-racist festival on August Bank Holiday, attended by 20,000 young people.

## 16 OCTOBER IN WELLING

All of this culminated, on 16 October, in the magnificent anti-racist demonstration of 50,000 which streamed through the streets of Welling in a determined attempt to shut down the Nazi headquarters. This action ranks alongside some of the great anti-fascist, anti-racist demonstrations of the past such as Cable Street, the march through Deptford in the 1970s and the earlier 8 May demonstration.

The demonstration was called under the banner of "Unity", symbolising unified action by the main anti-racist, anti-fascist organisations. The demo was led by the "Unity" banner and behind it Leon Greenman, survivor of the Holocaust together with relatives of those murdered by the racists and fascists. But as the 50,000 demonstrators were assembling, the outline of future trouble was symbolised by the horses and riot police who lined the hills, "like a scene from a modern-day cowboy film. At every side road barriers, police vans and riot police fill the streets."[4]

There had been intense discussion about the route between the organisers of the demonstration and the police in the days leading up to the demo. The YRE members in the meetings of stewards and the organising committee beforehand had warned that the police were likely to wade in. Therefore, measures had to be taken to safeguard the demonstration. The YRE argued for proper stewarding, with organised and identifiable stewards and for a system of communications so that stewards could be in radio contact. The ANL/SWP leaders ridiculed this idea as a "Dad's Army" tactic. Incredibly, they even argued that the stewards' bibs and walkie-talkies looked militaristic and "intimidating". In opposition to police armed to the teeth, with riot shields and on horses, they argued for a sit-down and a policy of allowing the demo to "defend itself". But for the enormous courage of the stewards, led by the YRE and joined by ordinary demonstrators and some courageous rank-and-file members of the SWP/ANL, disaster could have followed the predictable police attack.

## THE POLICE

The police's tactics in the run-up to the demonstration were quite simple: "Predict trouble in advance and we'll get away with anything on the day."[5] They claimed that 2,000 hardened "extremists" were hell-bent on violence. Stories about a small minority ready to attack the BNP headquarters and burn it down were disseminated by Condon, chief of police for the Met. As the march continued to the junction of Upper Wickham Lane and Lodge Hill, the marchers were confronted with an amazing situation. Every road was blocked by police, riot police with shields and batons. No attempt was made to direct the march up Lodge Hill (the police's preferred route). Instead, horses and police lined up facing the demo across the entrance to Lodge Hill. The road to the BNP bunker was full of riot police but unlike every other road there were no barriers. It was clear that this was because the riot police on horseback would be able to charge the demonstrators without having to move steel barriers. As the demonstration halted, riot police charged into the crowd. One steward from Glasgow commented:

> I came face to face with the police and many of them had ripped off the identification numbers on their arms. I soon saw why. The police charged the demonstration and many people were crushed up against the railings. People were running in panic away from the blows of the police. One person fell, then another on top of them, then another.

Soon there were piles of bodies on the floor. People were shouting: "Get us out" and "We can't breathe". I shouted at the police: "Get back. People are going to get killed here." They just waded in. We were pulling people out and passing them on to safety. Some of them were really close to asphyxiation - our stewards saved lives. While all this was going on, the police were still charging, batoning people, climbing over bodies to get to the people behind us.[6]

It was clear the police were following the script written by their Tory masters whose aim was to simply portray the march as "violent left-wing fascists".

## STEWARDING

Eventually, YRE chief stewards managed to negotiate with the chief of the riot police to withdraw his troops 30-40 yards away to stop any more conflict. All the stewards then linked arms to ensure the demo was defended. Many ANL members worked hand in hand with YRE stewards. Julie Waterson, the demo's chief steward, was on the front line with YRE stewards until she got battoned by the police, but there were no ANL leaders to be seen after this. It was left to the YRE stewards to attempt to defend the demonstration and negotiate with the police to withdraw their forces. The bulk of the demonstration was looking for a lead and it was only the YRE stewards who had any idea of how to diffuse the situation and to ensure the safety of those marching. Only the heroism of the stewards, with the YRE giving the main lead, women as well as men, made it possible through tight organisational discipline to stop the police from going on a full-scale rampage. At the end of the demonstration, when the marchers were dispersed, then the police, particularly the riot police, attacked in a cowardly fashion from behind. Many lessons were learnt on that day. It was clear that Militant Labour and YRE members were the only ones who had any serious idea of how to steward such demos. Socialist Workers' Party members had ridiculed their serious approach to stewarding and on the day stewards were harangued by SWP members because they were asked to take the "lollipops" (ANL placards) to the back by the Bengali youth who resented the approach of the ANL/SWP. Nevertheless in the wake of the demonstration *Militant* called for a "united front of all anti-racist organisations with the trade union and labour movement involved." This "would push the fascists back into the sewers." At the same time anti-fascist activity needed to be linked with a programme on jobs, homes, education, etc.[7]

The 16 October demonstration represented a turning point. I was in South Africa at this time, in the house of an African worker in Soweto, when the scenes flashed onto the TV. The courage of the youth and the workers on the demonstration combatting racism had a powerful effect on the African workers engaged in a similar struggle to overthrow the last vestiges of the vicious, racist South African apartheid regime. The truth about the "police riot" of 16 October inevitably came out, even in the heavily censored reports that appeared in the capitalist press.

It also drove home to the ruling class the determination of the anti-racist forces to crush the BNP. It brought out into the public domain the real character of the BNP and prepared the ground for the discrediting and subsequent defeat of Beackon in 1994 and the successful closure of the BNP's HQ in July 1995.

However, none of this would have been possible without the determined action and leadership provided by organisations like the YRE which, avoiding the sectarian pitfalls of the ANL/SWP, sought to build the widest possible movement of youth and workers against the racist and fascist threat. This is clear, from both this movement and others, such as the struggle against the Criminal Justice Bill. The SWP's method was to construct organisations which could initially attract those who were prepared to fight, but they made no serious attempt to build effective structures with full democracy and the right of members to control these organisations. Their main concern was not how best to push forward the struggle on a particular issue but how to recruit, in the most rapid fashion possible, new members to their organisation. This "raiding party" tactic inevitably brought them into collision with those who wanted to pursue a more effective campaign and to build more durable forms of organisation.

Militant Labour supported the most effective tactic to take forward the struggles of workers. Of course, it was interested in building its own organisation as the means of carrying working-class movements through to a conclusion. Without *Militant*, the struggle in Liverpool or the battle against the poll tax would not have been as successful as they were. But to counterpose the need to build your own organisation to the general interests of workers in struggle would be false and counter-productive. This was, however, the approach of the SWP and continues to be so. Hence its "grasshopper" approach to issues. Despite the accumulated prejudice of the "left intelligentsia" against *Militant* even some of them were compelled to favourably compare the flexible and unifying approach of the YRE, under Militant Labour influence, to the narrow sectarian approach of the SWP/ANL.

# 52.
# THE BALKANS

OPPOSITION TO racism in Britain was undoubtedly reinforced by the rise of racist and fascist groups in Europe. The Bosnian nightmare, with its "ethnic cleansing", mass rape and brutal massacres, also fed a mood, particularly amongst youth, that everything must be done to prevent such a scenario opening up in Britain. By 1993 two million people had been driven from their homes in Bosnia and 130,000 had been killed. From Thatcher to David Owen, including those who claimed to stand on the 'left' of the Labour Party, a clamour began for military action against the Bosnian Serbs. Heart-rending pictures, broadcast into every front room, of broken Muslim bodies fed the mood that "something must be done". We conceded:

> Certainly it's true that the Bosnian Serbs, with the hardware of the former Yugoslav army at their disposal, have been responsible for the most extensive ethnic cleansing. But right now Bosnian Croats (supplied by the government of Croatia) and Muslims are both trying to ethnically purify the area around Vitez in central Bosnia.

But we made it clear:

> *Militant* opposes any military interference by the capitalist powers in Bosnia. We don't have any faith in Major or Thatcher to protect mining communities or racial minorities at home, nor do we put trust in them to protect the suffering and oppressed abroad. All they will ever defend are the profits and strategic interests of capitalism. The fate of the Balkan people can only be determined by the working class of the area. And at the beginning of the last two fateful years, the working class was emerging as a force in its own right... In Sarajevo there were unity demonstrations against the nationalist bigots. Serbian gunmen deliberately shot down some of those involved to inject the ethnic poison. A clear call for workers' unity then and for the establishment of workers' defence committees could have held the line against bloodshed in Sarajevo. That could have changed the course of events in Bosnia.[1]

## ARM THE MUSLIMS?

One of the issues which *Militant* was challenged on was its refusal to support the slogan of "arm the Muslims". *Militant* supported the right of all communities, particularly oppressed minorities, to defend themselves against attack, if necessary with arms. We pointed out: "The Bosnian Muslims have this right but so also do the Serbs and Croats where they are in a minority and are attacked."[2]

*Militant* always linked this demand to the idea of establishing democratic defence committees. It was true that Bosnia's Serb and Croat populations had received an ample supply of arms, particularly heavy weapons, from powerful neighbouring states. In the beginning this option was not open to the besieged Muslim population. But the Bosnian Muslims had in effect broken the arms embargo and received quite a plentiful supply of heavy weapons. It is true that vicious persecution of the Muslim population has been carried out, both by Serb and Croat groups. But massacres and persecutions have also taken place against all three ethnic groups which made up Bosnia. *The Independent* in 1993 reported the opening of a "mass grave" containing 17 Serbs, massacred in a wave of revenge attacks on Serbian villages in Fakovici. A similar mass grave of Serbs killed by Muslims was opened in Bosanski Brod, in nothern Bosnia on 2 May 1993. Mutual slaughter, usually provoked by uncontrolled nationalist militias, is inevitable in an ethnic civil war.

The comparison, drawn by some on the left, with the Spanish civil war is completely erroneous. The overwhelming majority of workers and peasants fought against Franco's fascist takeover. This earned the moral and political support of the world working class and the call for arms and volunteers for Spain found a powerful echo in the international labour movement. Things stand differently in Bosnia. The dominant political and military forces on all sides are pro-capitalist nationalists. It is these ethnic warlords, including the Muslim warlords, who at present receive the benefit of arms. We pointed out:

> It will be their class interests, the drive to carve out as much territory and influence as possible no matter the suffering, that predominates over the interests of the ordinary Muslim, Serb and Croat workers and

peasants of Bosnia. This applies as much to the main Muslim leader Izetbegovic as to the main Bosnian Serb leader Radovan Karadzic and the Bosnian Croat creatures of Franjo Tudjman, president of Croatia.[3]

Izetbegovic had, according to *The Independent*,

> put his cards on the table in his 1990 Islamic Declaration. He envisages a pure Muslim state with religious, political and social dimensions wholly integrated. He regards Islam as timeless and above consideration of reform.[4]

A sectarian religious stand like this could not fail to arouse Serbian hostility and suspicion. This was ruthlessly played upon by the Serbian nationalists who warned the Bosnian Serbs that an Islamic state was to be formed in which they would be discriminated against.

The aims of the Serbian and Croatian nationalist forces towards Bosnia were clearly spelt out in a meeting between Karadzic and the Croat representative Boban in the Austrian town of Graz early in 1992. There, as if they were dividing up a cream cake, a plan was devised to carve up Bosnia. Part of the region was to be drawn into a Greater Serbia, part into a Greater Croatia, with a buffer Muslim state in between. The Muslim nationalist/pro-capitalist forces, on the other hand, would not hesitate to repress other national groupings in order to enhance its power and prestige. Even a British officer serving with UN forces in 1993 in the beleaguered town of Vitez believed that any new arms supplies to the Muslim forces would not be used to counter-attack against the Serbs but would be "more likely to go for the weakest target, the Croat towns in central Bosnia."[5]

For all these reasons *Militant* could not put forward the slogan of "arming the Muslims". The principal demand for socialists and Marxists in the very complicated situation of Bosnia would be for a united workers' defence force to repel all attacks on the community. The cynical manoeuvres of each national capitalist grouping is shown by the recent alliance of Croat and Muslim forces in attacks on the Serbs. This is despite the fact that the Croat forces mercilessly attacked Muslims in Mostar in 1993. There have also been many other examples of Muslims brutally repressing Croats. The priorities for the working class and the international labour movement in conflicts such as this should be at the outset to develop independent class action of the organisations of the working class.

## RUSSIA

One of the factors staying the hands of the European capitalist powers was the fear of open Russian intervention on the side of the Serbs, "fellow Slavs". Up to now Russia had had little influence in this area. Yeltsin, in April, had won his referendum with 62 per cent saying they trusted him as president, and 56 per cent approving his "pro-market economic policies". At the same time, there was a vote against any early presidential or parliamentary elections. The outcome of the elections was, in effect, that the Russian workers opted for what they saw as the "least bad" alternative. So lacking was faith in the recently established "democracy" that the polling stations played music and sold cut-price snacks to attract voters. The mood was one of discontent with a large degree of cynicism and apathy. And how could it be anything else, given the catastrophic state of the country with Russian workers' wages now able to buy just half of what they could 16 months before? Moreover, in the course of the campaign Yeltsin had promised everything to anybody in order to garner votes. Kuzbas miners "could have the state's 38 per cent share when their pits were privatised." Student grants, pensions and soldiers' pay would go up, petrol and other prices would go down. In Yeltsin's baggage train were bundles of roubles with which to bribe individual groups of workers. Unfortunately, the alternative to Yeltsin's pro-market disasters was equally unattractive. Alongside extreme Russian nationalists were the former Stalinist politicians in congress, whose dictatorial methods, flaunted privileges, waste and mismanagement were not going to be quickly forgotten. We predicted:

> The referendum will not solve Russia's problems. The bloody conflict in former Yugoslavia haunts Yeltsin. Conflicts around Russia's borders, in Georgia, Armenia/Azerbaijan etc could be mirrored now within the huge Russian federation... Yeltsin's triumph - and that of capitalism - will end up in a hollow victory.[6]

In October 1993, the simmering conflict between the increasingly dictatorial Yeltsin and his opponents in the Russian parliament, led by Alexander Rutskoi and Khasbalatov, reached a bloody denouement. Yeltsin, after a stand off, sent tanks against his opponents. The Russian parliament was consumed by flames after days of gun battles. Militant Labour stood neither for Yeltsin nor Rutskoi. Yeltsin offered nothing to workers. His "fast track" to capitalism was based on a tight monetarist programme dictated by the International Monetary Fund. It demanded a cut in inflation by slashing state spending, lifting all safeguards on workers' rights and rapid privatisation of factories. Rutskoi, on the other hand, argued for a slower transition to the market. He also argued for keeping up state subsidies to industry, privatisation through 'management buy-outs', and state regulation of labour conditions (that is no trade union defence for the workers).

The main problem in Russia is the weakness of independent trade union organisations and the absence of genuine socialist, labour or workers' parties. The indifference of the mass of the population of Russia, particularly in Moscow where the 'drama' unfolded, was shown by the fact that Muscovites, while out walking their dog, would calmly and indifferently observe the conflict between the two sides. We commented:

> Stable capitalist democracy is a pipe dream [in Russia]. The army have saved Yeltsin's skin and they will want an even greater say in the direction of the economy and foreign policy. Even before this crisis, measures had been taken to set up a professional army loyal to the president. As Russia's crisis deepens, Yeltsin's credibility will be undermined and outright military rule could be on the cards for a period, before a renewed movement of the working class.[7]

Events in other parts of the globe also shattered the sunny optimism of 1989-90.

## MIDDLE EAST PEACE?

The bourgeois internationally were deeply pessimistic about the prospects for Russia. However, following the new Palestinian/Israeli deal in the Middle East they were euphoric. The *Daily Mirror* enthused "miracle in the Holy Land." The desperate gamble of Yasser Arafat to shore up his declining support in the occupied territories would, *Militant* argued, be undermined by this deal. It was a betrayal of the national aspirations of the Palestinian people for a separate Palestinian state. Indeed Rabin, the Israeli prime minister, was insisting as the deal was agreed that a fully fledged Palestinian state was not on offer. There was no commitment for the withdrawal of the Israeli settlements in the West Bank and no right to return in particular for those exiled from Israel/Palestine since 1948. Only those who had left since 1967 would be allowed back in. Israeli and world capitalism was no longer fearful of a Palestinian entity under the PLO, which in the past had tended towards the establishment of a nationalised economy (albeit on a bureaucratic Soviet model). Such a development in the past would have acted as a potential rallying point for the Arab revolution. But the collapse of Stalinism and the move to the right of Arafat and the PLO leadership left a vacuum which Hamas and other fundamentalist groups had filled. Despite the promises of massive aid from Saudi Arabia and elsewhere, which *Militant* conceded could for a period mollify the Palestinian population, the national problem would not be solved. Therefore inevitable flare-ups would take place in the future and the fragile peace would be broken. *Militant* predicted that, if not outright civil war, elements of a civil war between the PLO, who became the new police power in Gaza and Jericho, and those who followed Hamas and Islamic Jihad were inevitable. By tying themselves to negotiations with the Israeli, Arab and US capitalist oppressors of the Arabs, the PLO had ended up with a rotten compromise. Only by linking themselves to the struggles of the working class throughout the Middle East and advancing a programme for the overthrow of capitalism, Jewish and Arab, would it be possible to guarantee the rights of all national groups within a socialist federation of the Middle East.

## VISIT TO SOUTH AFRICA

*Militant* also devoted considerable coverage to the unfolding drama in South Africa in 1993. A visit by myself to South Africa in September and October meant that a detailed first-hand account could be given of the mood of African and Coloured workers on the ground.

In a series of articles, the mood of workers in Johannesburg,

Cape Town and Durban was charted. The gist of these articles appeared subsequently in a pamphlet (*South Africa - From Slavery to the Smashing of Apartheid*), which was produced following the victory of the ANC in the general election in 1994. In November, however, former jailers and their ex-prisoners,

> drank and boogied the night away to the strains of Michael Jackson at Johannesburg's World Trade Centre on 18 November. The revellers were inundated with congratulations from around the world.[8]

The cause of the celebration was the adoption of the new South African constitution by representatives of 21 parties. This constitution effectively ended the long night of apartheid and the 350 years of slavery for the African and Coloured people. They were due to get the vote for the first time in the elections scheduled for 27 April 1994. The question was posed by *Militant*:

> But will this usher in the 'new dawn' promised by the constitution's authors? Will it transform the lives of South Africa's 46 per cent unemployed or the occupiers of the seven million shacks?[9]

De Klerk and the National Party had been defeated on a 60 per cent blocking mechanism for the white minority. He may have got away with this a year earlier but the mass movement of African workers had effectively prevented this. "Majority rule", at least in the cabinet, was now a fact where decisions would be adopted if 50 per cent voted for a proposal. Nevertheless, "real majority rule will still be blocked by the ANC leaders' acceptance of a voluntary five-year coalition with the capitalist parties."

We concluded: The drive to elections is now unstoppable. Any attempt to postpone them would trigger off an explosive revolutionary upheaval which the negotiations were precisely designed to avoid.[10]

# 53.
# ON OUR WAY TO WEMBLEY

IN THE the May elections in England *Militant* had done exceptionally well in a number of areas where it stood for the first time. In East Hull, for instance, Keith Ellis gained 771 votes in the county council elections - 34 per cent of the votes cast. He stood as a sitting councillor, having been expelled from the Labour group for voting against a cuts package of £25 million. Nevertheless, this was a tremendous result and followed a very successful campaign of street meetings, house meetings and leaflets on all the important issues affecting workers. His 34 per cent of the vote contrasted favourably with the 44 per cent for the victorious Labour candidate. Labour had received a real fright with all the three constituency parties in Hull putting in time to try and counter the support we were getting. Even East Hull MP John Prescott was brought in. In Bulwell, in Nottingham, Gary Freeman, standing for Militant Labour, got 656 votes, 22.2 per cent of the total. The local Labour organiser had declared that Gary Freeman "doesn't stand a chance". However, in the course of the election he was forced to change his tune. The local press had presented everyone's manifesto but that of Militant Labour. Even the Greens were allowed their own say on policy and were tipped as an organisation with local roots "who may do well". The campaign for Gary Freeman mobilised workers who had been politically apathetic in the past. Thousands of leaflets were distributed, 1,575 copies of *Militant* were sold and four very successful public meetings were held. Crucially, 21 people agreed to pay subs and become members. This laid the basis for a new branch in the Bulwell area.

In Coventry the Tories got a hammering in the Longford by-election. The "party of government" got only five per cent more of the vote than Militant Labour. Rob Windsor, Militant Labour's candidate, received 423 votes, eleven per cent of the vote.

In the North East, in the Hardwick ward of Cleveland county council, Patrick Graham received 341 votes, 24.9 per cent of the vote. One Labour councillor accepted that "Militant Labour won the youth because we no longer campaign or do anything." [1]

The struggle of the Timex workers was one of the centre-pieces of the June national rally called to launch, on an all-Britain scale, Militant Labour as an independent socialist organisation. 1,200 workers, youth, black and Asian workers and working women were mobilised at the Wembley Conference Centre to get the organisation off to a flying start. An impressive array of speakers was assembled, among whom was Sandra Walker, a Timex striker, who got two standing ovations during her contribution. She declared:

> Women are at the forefront of this struggle and have changed from lambs to lions... We need national trade union support. If our forefathers had listened to talk about legality we'd have no trade unions and no Labour Party. There are lots of Timex disputes about. Unity is strength, it's about time we showed that unity and that strength.[2]

I said:

> Labour's leaders practice me-tooism. The Tories decide their policies in the morning, Labour follows in the afternoon. But Militant *Labour* is still fighting. Who can compare with us? How many obituaries and funeral dirges have been said over the bones of *Militant* and then weeks later, as if by magic, we 're-emerge' as the *Sunday Times* claimed recently! Siren voices accuse us of splitting the movement. I was a Labour Party member for 23 years until I was expelled in 1983. We were tolerated when we were small but not now. We are fighting for socialism. In Britain this will not be the one-party prison state of Stalinism but a planned economy based on the ideas of Marx, Engels, Lenin and Trotsky. Militant Labour's best days are ahead of us. Join our fight.[3]

Tommy Sheridan welcomed the launching of Militant Labour throughout Britain:

> We are taking politics out of the smoke-filled rooms and onto the streets of Britain... Scottish Militant Labour's electoral success has proven that radical socialism can grab attention. Elections are an important means to communicate ideas but never a substitute for the class struggle - the everyday struggle in the lives of working-class people.[4]

There were youth speakers, like Lois Austin from Youth Against Racism in Europe, and international speakers, such as Sam, a member of the ANC from South Africa. Raymond De Bord was warmly welcomed as a speaker from the JCR (Revolutionary Communist Youth of France). He declared

> We are a small organisation but we are building an important position amongst French youth. After the YRE demo on 24 October (in Brussels), we set about forming a YRE in France. We met Militant Labour for the first time around the YRE demo and we hope for even closer contact. A victory for Militant Labour in Britain is a victory for socialism in France.[5]

The JCR subsequently joined the Committee for a Workers' International (CWI), the international organisation of which Militant Labour is the British component, and have grown in influence and numbers as a result of its intervention in the workers' and youth resurgence which has taken place in France.

One of the best receptions of the day was for Julie Donovan who graphically described the conditions of working-class women:

> Depression has nothing to do with personality but with conditions. Social Security pay £25 a week less than the government admits is needed for adequate nourishment to stop ill health and sleeplessness. The Tories blame single parents for society's problems and squeezes them with the Child Support Act (CSA). We're no longer putting up with it. Women are getting organised. Fighting alongside DSS trade unionists who have to operate the CSA, we can make it unworkable. Three years ago domestic violence, which hits one in three women, was considered an individual issue and not for the trade unions. Now five unions have taken up CADV's demands. The government wants to turn the clock back but women are getting organised.[6]

Other speakers included Tony Mulhearn, Dave Nellist, Janet Gibson, George Silcott, brother of the jailed Winston Silcott and Larlan Davis from the M25 campaign.

## FIGHTING FUND APPEAL

The appreciation of the speeches was shown in the impressive fighting fund appeal which raised £33,800. There was a gasp throughout the conference centre as the first donation was made. Alec Thraves, who made the financial appeal, had asked if anyone could give a donation of £5,000 - but the first cheque was for £10,000 from a Bristol worker. International visitors also gave impressive sums, £70 from two visitors from Vancouver, £20 from a visitor from Michigan and a £500 pledge from a European visitor.

*Militant's* ability to generate financial resources assumed legendary, if not mythical proportions in the eyes of our opponents. Michael Crick quotes an "ex-member" about her experiences of attending *Militant* events.

> "if your pockets aren't empty... somebody's bound to tip you upside-down to make sure your coffers are bare when you leave. I know people who used to hide their last 30p so they could get home on the bus". (The March of Militant p143).

We did not believe in squeezing our supporters, who were largely workers with limited means, until "the pips squeaked". But *Militant's* ideas did inspire a great spirit of self sacrifice, without which it is not possible to change history. This spirit however needed to be organised. Clare Doyle, as National Treasurer, pioneered the financial methods which became the hallmark of *Militant*. Nick Wrack ably stepped into her shoes and in 1994 became the editor of *Militant*. When he moved on, Judy Beishon, a tireless and tenacious member of *Militant's* financial team over many years, became the National Treasurer of *Militant Labour,* a position which she still holds today.

For Marxists ideas are primary. But good ideas are nothing unless the means of demonstrating those ideas are acquired. A serious attitude towards ideas and a meticulous approach to organisation, particularly to collecting money, was one of the reasons for *Militant's* success.

No wonder an observer at the rally, from the Green Party of Australia, could subsequently write,

> The atmosphere was of angry indignation at capitalism - a sentiment sadly lacking at many other left conferences - and a committment to action... although the SWP claims 8,000 members... its impact on British politics is negligible. Militant, with its base in working-class

communities, has earned a national prominence for its hands-on approach to politics.[7]

Even the *New Statesman*, not exactly to the fore in praise of *Militant* in the past, conceded that the rally was extremely impressive,

> ... there was an energy and enthusiasm at the rally... A clear demand from at least two speakers was for an end to the era of "grey men in grey suits", prompting the one grey man in a grey suit on the platform to remove his jacket. The speeches inclined towards the inspirational... On the way home, I chatted to a fresh-faced young man, who had clearly enjoyed himself. He thought the beginning with the laser show and the music was really good. I remarked on the dual message of using the theme tune... "I didn't know it was from *Jaws*," he said.[8]

But perhaps the best testament to the success of the rally was the Timex strikers' report back to their mates of their impressions: "Every speaker was excellent, a very enjoyable and worthwhile event."[9]

Timex management had, however, declared that the factory would close by Christmas in an attempt to blackmail 150 trained workers back to work on reduced wages. This plan was rejected by 341 votes to two. It showed that the struggle was now a fight to the finish between Timex management and the workers. However, strikers were encouraged by the forced resignation of Peter Hall. But they were still outraged at the prospect of the closure of the factory. When the mass picket on 19 June closed the Timex factory, even the security guards on the site had to find another way in.

At the rally at the factory gates Tommy Sheridan received huge support when he spoke of the need for a 24-hour strike across Scotland. Referring to the threat to remove machinery he declared:

> As far as I'm concerned the machinery and techniques in that factory belong to the people and we should do everything necessary to ensure that the machinery stays there and is not taken abroad to some other multinational.[10]

10,000 people assembled for the march.

At a successful Scottish Militant Labour meeting after the rally SML was thanked by a member of the strike committee for the provision of stewards and for the picket line coverage during the 21-week long dispute. These sentiments were not shared by the *Sunday Times* or *Scotland on Sunday*. A barrage of media abuse had been unleashed against the unions, the workers themselves and SML. The 'quality press' described the struggle over Timex as one between "dinosaurs". The *Sunday Times* in an editorial screamed that the factory had been, "destroyed by dinosaurs".[11] *Scotland on Sunday's* cartoon was of two dinosaurs, one *Militant* and the other of management, fighting it out with the Timex factory in between. "Who is to blame they ask, Peter Hall, Tommy Sheridan or John Kydd junior, the sacked AEEU convenor at Timex?"[12] The women at Timex were described as the "witches of Dundee". However, the *Sunday Times* also indicated the fears of the bosses:

> Timex might be of itself a minor Scottish affair but that's what they said about the poll tax and look what happened to that. Heaven help us if Timex becomes a platform for a rejuvenated crusade against government union legislation.[13]

We asked John Kydd junior for an honest assesment of SML's role in the dispute:

> "The role of SML in the Timex dispute enhanced the class emphasis of the dispute. Their solidarity, support and encouragement helped to bolster the morale of the pickets at every stage of the dispute. Their direct action approach made sure of national recognition and raised the dispute to greater heights. Those who condemned the support of SML failed to recognise the class nature of the dispute and by their actions aided and abetted the Engineering Employers Federation and the company.[14]

## MORE TROUBLE FOR MAJOR

The only thing which was sustaining Major's government in power was the lack of any real challenge from the Labour front bench. The Tories were floundering but Labour's support in the polls had actually dropped by two per cent as general disillusionment with politics had set in. We commented: "The weakest government in living memory couldn't possibly withstand sustained, organised opposition."[15]

Throughout 1993 and most of 1994 the crucial factor sustaining Major in power was the weakness of Labour's front bench allied to a completely impotent union leadership. The roots of this were primarily ideological; the right-wing Labour leaders had gone over to pro-market policies and their differences with the Tory front bench were primarily presentational, or shadings of disagreement. And this at a time of the most devastating recession in Britain for 60 years. It was one of the reasons why Militant Labour again decided to stand in a by-election in Lambeth for the Oval ward on 22 July. The concern which this provoked in the ranks of right-wing Labour was shown by the fact that Scotland Yard's Company Fraud section had arrested Militant Labour councillor Anne Hollifield for voting and presenting a budget during the council's 12 hour marathon budget meeting earlier in the year. This was because she had not paid her poll tax. She was said to have contravened section 106 of the Local Government Finance Act, which forbids councillors with poll tax arrears from voting on matters concerning council tax. The real crime of Anne Hollifield was that she had led the anti-poll tax movement in Lambeth and since becoming a councillor in 1990 had pledged not to pay her poll tax in solidarity with the poorest people in the borough. The election campaign once more went into parts of Lambeth which no other party was able or prepared to go. One incident summed up the effect of the campaign: "Buy that woman a double scotch", [16] shouted three former Liberal voters at Lynne Kelly. She had just single handedly converted them to Militant Labour on their way to the polling station. The Tory agent on election night had declared out loud: "Well at least the *Militant* won't come third; what a relief."[17] But as Steve Nally commented:

> Some relief! Minutes later the blood drains from his face as he realises that in the second Lambeth by-election running we have beaten the Tories.[18]

246 had voted for Militant Labour and hundreds more were enthused and inspired by the campaign. 550 copies of *Militant* were sold and £250 raised for the fighting fund, new members had been

won and 40 had indicated by signing cards that they wanted to join Militant Labour. The effect of the campaign was felt after the result when on the following Saturday an older black worker held up the traffic on Brixton Road as he jumped out of his car and vigorously shook Steve Nally's hands. When Steve told him the result he said: "Well done young man, you tell your people they're on their way."[19]

# 54.
# OUR THIRTIETH YEAR - STRUGGLE, SOLIDARITY, SOCIALISM

IN SEPTEMBER the campaign of Alan Brown in the Dennistoun by-election was a minor triumph. SML came from nowhere to get 22 per cent in a three-week campaign. Up to then the majority of the press had written off SML as an organisation of the "underclass", restricted to the peripheral schemes on the outskirts of the major conurbations. It was a seat where Labour and the SNP expected to squeeze SML out of the picture. Indeed their predictions were for a single figure percentage for SML. Yet SML scored 718 votes, came in third, and once more beat the Tories into fourth position. Michael Martin, MP for the Springburn constituency, in which Dennistoun was situated, had boasted that his constituency was a: "*Militant* free-zone." We commented: "With results like this we'll be knocking on the door of a victory in every seat in Glasgow."[1]

## SPLAT THE VAT

The key issue featured in this campaign and others was opposition to VAT on fuel which had aroused particular anger from the 700,000 pensioners who were at risk of dying from cold. 249 people had died of hypothermia in 1991, 205 of them pensioners. In a letter to a Labour MP, one pensioner told how if he was too cold he would "just make a hot water bottle and retire to bed", because "I must work within the limits of what I can afford to pay for my fuel bills."[2]

Such was the opposition that the question was raised within the ranks of *Militant* of whether it would be possible to lead a campaign for non-payment of VAT along the lines of the poll tax campaign. Recognising the danger, the gas and electricity industries made all kinds of concessions, including temporarily absorbing the cost of VAT; in order to prevent such a movement. The very threat of a non-payment campaign, given Militant Labour's record on the poll tax, water privatisation in Scotland etc, was, together with other factors, an important issue which made up the minds of the electricity and gas chiefs to temporarily beat a retreat. *Militant* expected that in the event of Tory Chancellor Clarke going ahead with the second increase in VAT to 17.5 per cent in 1994 the issue of non-payment could come back onto the agenda. But the Tories were defeated on the second hike in VAT.

## GREENOCK

In late October SML also had a good result in the Greenock by-election. 284 voted for SML, 31 per cent of the vote. David Landells, the SML candidate, was second only to Labour with 404 votes. The issue of water privatisation as well as opposition to VAT on fuel was an important factor in this result.

## AMANDA LANE AND STEVE GOLDFINCH

The other side of the picture of late 1993 was the victimisation of stewards and workers in industry, highlighted by the sacking of Amanda Lane and Steve Goldfinch, members of the CPSA branch at Bedminster in the Bristol area. There was enormous sympathy for these two sacked workers given the fact that the Bedminster Job Centre civil servants had acted in solidarity with Arrowsmith printworkers in Bristol who had been locked out for three months at that time. Steve Goldfinch and Amanda Lane were sacked for taking action in defence of the printworkers. Their sacking was not an isolated event but part of a wider strategy to undermine the trade unions by making workers who were union representatives feel vulnerable. The CPSA at national level, albeit under right-wing control, had been forced to give official backing to a two-day strike call of civil servants in Bristol. This in turn sent shock waves through management and served as a warning that the trade unions were not prepared to see workers victimised. Nevertheless, as subsequent events demonstrated, decisive action was not forthcoming from the top of the union. If the union leaders had been prepared to give a lead then there would have been no question of sackings such as those of Amanda Lane and Steve Goldfinch standing. This was the lesson which workers were absorbing as 1993 drew to an end.

## IN MEMORY: JANICE GLENNON

The year, however, had brought the lose of some valued and dear comrades. Janice Glennon died suddenly and tragically on Friday 17 September at the age of 30. Janice had played a key role in the LPYS National Committee at its height in the Eastern region. She had organised the 1987 LPYS anti-Tory demonstration in which 8,000 people had participated. She had also become vice-chair of the LPYS and had led 100 people to the International Union of Socialist Youth camp in Spain. In Britain she had spoken alongside Peter Taaffe at the 1988 Labour Party conference with a paper bag over her head in order to avoid Labour's witch-hunters. When she was expelled one of the main charges against her was that she organised a jumble sale for the *Militant* fighting fund! The day before she died she was out campaigning against domestic violence in her area.

There was enormous sympathy for her son Sean and partner Steve Glennon who plays an important role in Militant Labour. Over 200 people attended her funeral on 14 October; it was a funeral but also a celebration of her life which had been dedicated to the cause of the labour movement, the working class and of socialism. Her death was felt so keenly because she was so young and had always expressed the most optimistic face of *Militant* and Militant Labour. Her memory, Militant Labour members insisted, would endure, above all by building a powerful organisation for socialism in Britain.

## UNSHAKEABLE FAITH IN A SOCIALIST FUTURE

*Militant* had remained firm in its commitment to socialism and Marxism in the teeth of a huge ideological offensive conducted by the bourgeoisie in the early 1990s. Many of the older generation discouraged by the difficulties and what appeared to be the postponement of socialist change succumbed either to pessimism or lapsed into inactivity, waiting for "better days". Such moods are not uncommon when history either takes a more circuitous and complicated route or the class struggle appears to be stalled. Not just revolution itself but the struggle for revolution is a mighty devourer of human energy, both individual and collective. As Leon

Trotsky commented, "the nerves give way. Consciousness is shaken and characters are worn out. Events unfold too swiftly for the flow of fresh forces to replace the loss."[3]

While nursing and encouraging the older layers who did such sterling work for the cause of Marxism and *Militant* in the past, the major task which the leadership of Militant Labour had set itself was to win, steel and educate those new layers of youth and workers who could become the yeast for the rise of a new powerful workers' and Marxist movement.

From 1989 onwards, first *Militant* and then Militant Labour had argued that despite the new triumphalism of capitalism it would be incapable of solving the problems of the working class. This was underlined by the world recession of 1990-92. Nevertheless, this did not appear to coincide with a resurgence of the mass movement of the workers, particularly one with an overtly socialist character. On the contrary, even where there were movements to overthrow dictatorships, as in Africa, this led invariably to the coming to power of pro-bourgeois regimes, such as in Zambia. In the colonial and semi-colonial world an unprecedented privatisation programme unfolded. This was an attempt to imitate in the most vulgar and catastrophic fashion the embracing of the market by the advanced countries in the 1980s. Socialism, according to a whole swathe of commentators from the right to the so-called 'left', was a distant memory. Militant Labour argued the opposite case. Long before Marx and Engels came onto the scene the working class had created its own organisations in the form of trade unions and even incipient 'parties', eg the Chartists. Socialism had also developed spontaneously within the ranks of the working class of Germany, Britain and above all France. The great historic merit of Marx and Engels was to generalise the experience of the working class to develop the ideas of scientific socialism and a clear programme related to the concrete experience of the working class at that stage. A swing of the pendulum back towards class struggle and socialism was inevitable.

## VIVA MARCOS!

1994 was to see the vindication of this prognosis in Europe and on a world scale. Indeed the year began with the Zapatistas' uprising in Mexico. This was the first movement since the collapse of Stalinism which was overtly socialist. Its spokesmen declared that they wanted a society "like Cuba only better."[4]

This undoubtedly represented a clear demand for a planned economy but perhaps in a confused fashion opposition to the bureaucratic regime. This, moreover, was in the least developed state in Mexico, in a movement largely in the countryside amongst the indigenous peoples who had been robbed by the rich landlords (caciques)of their land, much of which was held communally. Mexico was a tinderbox which the Chiapas uprising ignited in the course of 1994. Even in the state of Morelos, the home state of Zapata, brutal police activity had provoked several semi-spontaneous uprisings. Initially the working class had been inspired and moved into action by the example of the Zapatistas. Before the year was out elections had been held which were won by the PRI (Institutional Revolutionary Party). But the underlying situation remains potentially explosive.

## SKREWDRIVER

Events in 1994 underlined the character of Militant Labour as a fighting organisation involved in all the major battles of the working class. This was illustrated in the continuing struggle against racism and fascism in Britain. As soon as the year had opened anti-fascists led by the YRE had mobilised 400 people to march against a gig organised at a "Skrewdriver" (a fascist band) memorial concert in Dagenham, east London. When the fascists arrived, 150 anti-fascists had reached the venue in Dagenham with a police helicopter circling overhead and 20 vans of riot police in attendance. The anti-fascists marched to the 'Blood and Honour' venue but as they were on the way the fascists ran out of the pub and scattered. The anti-fascists arrived for a victory rally outside the deserted pub. Twenty local people signed up to join the YRE. One anti-fascist commented:

> The police obviously hoped to steam in there and then. One blurted out: "We're going to have a ruck with a load of left-wing types"; but we formed stewards' lines and they held back.[5]

## WINDOW OF OPPORTUNITY

Organisers informed the police that they had achieved their aims and if the tube stations were opened they would disperse. Surrounded by riot police and miles from anywhere, the anti-racists decided under police supervision to board a train. Everyone was in a buoyant mood, celebrating the stopping of the Nazi gig. But the police effectively hijacked the train and took the anti-fascists through crowded tube station platforms from east London all the way over to west London without stopping. They eventually stopped the train at Earl's Court. A correspondent reported:

> When we stopped at stations we told people through the air vents that we were anti-Nazis who had seen off a 200-strong gang of fascists. A woman knocked on the window and asked me for a *Militant*. I sold it for 50p through the air vent - it was my window of opportunity.[6]

Most 'passengers' were joking until the train pulled into Victoria. Once more the police refused to allow demonstrators to get off the train. But when they emerged at Earl's Court, suddenly, without provocation or warning, the police charged screaming abuse and truncheoning anyone they could. They truncheoned Lois Austin across the head, who was attempting to shield a younger demonstrator from the police attack. This attempt to intimidate the YRE supporters completely failed and in fact is now the subject of legal action against the police.

## ITALY

The opposition to racism and fascism was also heightened by the victory of the right in the Italian general elections. *Militant* conceded that in the short term the neo-Nazis could gain: "In Italy in this month's general election the National Alliance (formerly the fascist MSI) could get significant support in the south."[7]

Part of the explanation for this was the fact that Fini the leader of the MSI had distanced himself from his and his party's fascist past. This was the only way that the National Alliance could attract middle-class voters who in the past supported the Christian Democrats. This prediction was borne out in the elections in Italy on 27

March. Led by Forza Italia (Come on Italy) a hodge-podge right-wing coalition had been put together including the Northern League and the neo-fascist National Alliance. The main reason for the victory of the right was the complete failure of the left parties, particularly the PDS, the former Communist Party, to put forward a viable alternative. Prior to the elections there had been explosive school occupations, massive demonstrations of 500,000 in Rome, a rail strike and even journalists going on strike during the elections. In the south there had been big demonstrations against the Mafia. The "Progressive Bloc", dominated by the PDS was for the continuation of the policies of the outgoing caretaker government which had been led by Ciampi, (ex-head of the Bank of Italy) and it promised privatisation. Berlusconi never hesitated to engage in the grossest demagogy promising at least a million jobs and a cut in taxes. From a capitalist point of view this programme was irresponsible. Hence the decision of the Confindustria, the bosses' union in Italy, to support the Progressive Bloc against Berlusconi. It was not possible, as he was soon to learn, to increase employment as well as cutting taxes. On the contrary the ruling class of Italy were demanding massive cuts in state expenditure. But the coming to power of the Berlusconi government would inevitably whip up a movement of opposition amongst the working class. Again this prognostication was to be borne out before the year was out.

## MILITANT LABOUR'S CONFERENCE

Meanwhile Militant Labour held its first annual conference as an independent organisation. This was one of the most successful conferences in the history of the organisation. The strike committee of the Timex plant in Dundee greeted the conference:

> We send our warmest greetings to your conference. Our nine-month struggle against the Timex multinational was a major event... There were times when we were down, that your comrades boosted our morale with your enthusiasm and ideas, not just about the Timex strike but about socialism. We wish you every success in the future.[8]

The most striking feature of the conference was the participation of those heavily involved in the major struggles of the British working class Amanda Lane, sacked for the solidarity support she gave to the locked-out Arrowsmith workers, detailed the battle for her re-instatement. The high point of the conference was, however, the session dealing with youth work and particularly the YRE.

And the conference was the launch for Militant Labour members to stand 32 candidates throughout Britain in the upcoming local elections. This campaign, despite the paucity of resources, was extremely successful. We achieved 18,300 votes.

As a new force, Militant Labour did not expect to make significant electoral inroads. Nevertheless, in many areas, the vote was impressive. We commented:

> Opponents poked fun at us: We wouldn't get enough voters to fill a telephone box. Pretty big phone boxes then because in every area we got a creditable vote. Not only that, but we recruited to our branches, sold thousands of extra papers and most importantly spread our influence in the communities. In these elections Militant Labour came second in 12 seats, beating the Tories, Liberals and Scottish National Party. In 20 seats we received 10-34 per cent of the vote, spread out across the country from Inverness to Swansea - an average of 17 per cent.[9]

In Scotland, SML received an average of 23 per cent of the vote in the seats we contested, while the Tories received a mere seven per cent. Unfortunately, two outstanding SML councillors, Willie Griffin and Christine McVicar lost their seats, but as the *Glasgow Herald* recognised:

> A heartening aspect of Thursday's losses from a *Militant* perspective was that the party maintained its level of votes which secured the seats in the first place.[10]

In fact, more people voted SML in these seats that in the stunning by-election victories in 1992. This demonstrated that SML had built up in a very short time a solid electoral base upon which to build.

In England and Wales, however, with no electoral experience of this character before, there were some quite exceptional results. In Sheffield, Ken Douglas, for Militant Labour, got a tremendous 682 votes, while in Waltham Forest in London, Louise Thompson, came from nowhere to achieve 423 votes, two votes behind the Liberals.

Over 400 copies of *Militant* were sold and five different leaflets, including one in Urdu, were distributed throughout the ward. In Swansea, 300-plus voted for Militant Labour, while 21 per cent voted for Militant Labour in Lambeth. *Militant* supporters were elected not just under the banner of Militant Labour but also as Labour candidates. For instance, in Hillingdon, Wally Kennedy, expelled by Labour at a national level, was elected as a Labour councillor against an imposed candidate. He actually increased his vote from 1,188 to 1,223.

However, one of the most satisfying aspects of the local elections was the defeat of the fascists in Tower Hamlets and the defeat of its lone standard bearer, Derek Beackon. The sudden death of the Labour leader, John Smith, came as a shock and immediately opened up a new leadership contest. In the emotional outpouring which greeted John Smith's death, most commentators ignored the fact that he had continued where Kinnock had left off, in attempting to show big business that Labour was better at managing capitalism than the Tories. His strategy was to rely on the Tories to tear themselves apart and dramatically narrow the gap between the two parties to such a degree that many people could see no real difference. However, the reason why he struck a certain chord with workers was that unlike Kinnock, he did not appear to be constantly at war with his own party. Nevertheless, he was part of Kinnock's team which wished to abandon socialism and cut the link with the unions. The Labour Party conference before his death, had seen him linking up with Prescott to dramatically, and significantly, undermine trade union influence at conference, by abandoning the "block vote". The contest for a new leader was temporarily held in abeyance as the European elections loomed.

## EURO-ELECTIONS

Militant Labour and Scottish Militant Labour decided to nominate Tommy Sheridan as a candidate for the European elections in Glasgow. In a very hastily organised campaign, with only two weeks in which to get out the vote, he secured a magnificent 12,113 votes, 7.6 per cent of the total votes cast. He beat the Tories, Liberal Democrats, Greens, Socialist Party, Natural Law Party and the Communist Party of Great Britain. Only Labour, with 83,000 and the SNP with 40,000 polled more.

Thus in one of the major cities of Britain, the governing party of the British ruling class received less support than the candidate of an avowedly socialist and Marxist organisation. No wonder that the *Daily Record* could say:

> To complete a night of misery for the Tories, Scottish *Militant* Tommy Sheridan polled over 12,000 votes in Glasgow, forcing the Tories into a humiliating fourth place.[11]

And this tremendous result had been achieved despite a virtual media blackout of Tommy Sheridan's campaign. For instance, the *Glasgow Evening News* carried a half-page profile of the Glasgow Euro seat, alongside photographs of the Labour, SNP, Tory and Liberal candidates. But there was not a word about Tommy Sheridan or Scottish Militant Labour while the same paper gave greater coverage during the campaign to the Natural Law Party and the International Communist Party. An indication of the affect of SML's campaign both on Labour and the SNP is shown by their dismal results in Glasgow in comparison to the rest of Scotland. While the Nationalist vote increased across Scotland, their support in Glasgow slumped by over 8,000. Once more, the critics had been confounded, particularly those who had dogmatically argued that SML could neither cut across the swing towards nationalism or dent the "loyal and solid Labour vote". This achievement of Tommy Sheridan, SML and Militant Labour is all the greater given the fact that not a single door was knocked on by canvassers because of time. It was street and factory meetings as well as literature, which carried the message to the Glasgow working class.

## A TIME TO RAGE

The Glasgow Euro-election campaign coincided with the launch of Tommy Sheridan's book *Time to Rage*, co-authored with Joan McAlpine. This was a very graphic description of the struggle against the poll tax, particularly in Scotland. A very laudatory introduction by John Pilger underlined the impact which both the author, *Militant* and Scottish Militant Labour has made on the labour movement:

I am honoured to write these words at the beginning of Tommy's book. He exemplifies the kind of political opposition that the Labour Party has abandoned and he is a source of inspiration for young people, and the rest of us, who are sometimes consumed by a sense of political impotence. This is not meant to elevate a single personality; Tommy Sheridan speaks for many like him, who have fought the ruthlessness of the British establishment in a variety of ways, such as the legions of working-class people, including the old and the alone, the disabled and the unemployed, who gathered their courage and refused to pay the poll tax.[12]

## RAILTRACK

And the message of uncompromising class struggle, of the inevitability of workers moving into action, was soon demonstrated in June as signal workers began a titanic struggle with British Rail. There had been a massive increase in the workload of signal workers, while their numbers had been halved since 1980. At the same time, they were incensed that Bob Horton, Railtrack chairman, was receiving £120,000 a year for a three-day week, while a signalman's basic weekly pay was £183. In an 80 per cent turnout, signal workers voted by four to one for strike action. It was quite clear from the outset of the strike that the government's hand was behind the intransigence of the Railtrack management.

Like Reagan in the early 1980s with the air traffic controllers, the Tories were seeking to make an example of Railtrack workers as a means of cowering public-sector workers generally. The signalworkers' dispute was to have considerable significance for the whole labour movement. The situation had begun to change in Britain compared to Thatcher's days which resulted in a colossal miscalculation by Major and Railtrack management. Despite the media barrage alleging at each stage that the strike had been broken, it was in fact solid. Uniquely for recent industrial disputes, the press and TV could hardly find any passengers against it. The government had stored up such opposition that even those affected by the strike seemed to automatically sympathise with Railtrack workers. Moreover, the attempt to unload responsibility for any undermining of safety conditions onto the workers completely rebounded on management. The overwhelming majority of travellers blamed them and accepted the arguments of Railtrack workers, that the management were risking the lives and safety of passengers. This in turn resulted in the boycott of trains on strike days, even where they were available. Railtrack management itself claimed that only seven per cent of trains were running.

Despite the relative success of this struggle, Militant Labour, whose members had thrown themselves wholeheartedly into supporting the railworkers, both politically and materially, called for decisive action by railworkers. The pretence of Frank Dobson, Labour's transport spokesman, that the dispute was not "political" cut no ice. Railworkers instinctively understood that it was a political dispute, with the Tories wanting to smash the rail unions and clear the way for private companies to step in. Militant Labour, particularly its supporters and members in the industry, urged that the union "must be prepared to call all-out strike action of the signalworkers if Railtrack continue to refuse to budge."[13] It also called for a joint meeting with ASLEF, the train drivers' union, to discuss the crucial issue of rail safety and advocated that the drivers be instructed not to work during the strike on the grounds of health and saftey: "A one-day strike of all railworkers should be prepared."

*Militant* believed that the relationship of class forces were decisively against the government and in favour of railworkers. This was likely to lead not to a defeat, but at worse to "a draw". However, the possibility of a complete victory was not ruled out. After an epic 16-week struggle, the longest dispute in the history of the rail industry, Railtrack workers were victorious. British Rail, backed up by the government, attempted to present the settlement as a victory of the bosses. In fact the total offer was worth £10.8 million - more than twice what the original 5.7 per cent offer made by Railtrack in June was worth. *Militant* commented:

> Had the Tory government not intervened to stop Railtrack making a 5.7 per cent offer for restructuring in June then it's unlikely the rail strike would have ever taken place. The right wing of the union's national executive and the full-time negotiators would have most likely accepted such a deal... But now they have a deal worth twice as much, which sees substantial increases for all grades of signalworkers.[14]

The lengths to which the ruling class were prepared to go was shown by the cost of the rail strike, £200 million to the rail industry and a minimum of £500 million for the capitalists as a whole. We commented:

> Overall, this was a victory and, will be perceived as such by the wider layers of the working class, who will draw confidence from seeing successful strike action. It will be seen as a turning point which tilted things in favour of workers in the rail industry and workers generally... The idea that militancy doesn't pay, which the right wing in the labour movement fostered, has finally been turned back. This strike has shown above all else that workers' solidarity and determination can force the bosses on to the retreat.[15]

The left on the national executive of the **RMT** sent us a letter congratulating the paper, the members of Militant Labour and supporters for the support they had given to the signal workers during the dispute.

All the indications were that the most likely outcome of any general election would be a Labour victory. However, given the relentless move to the right of the Labour leadership, this was not at all guaranteed. Labour's leadership contest, more of a "love in" than a real battle of ideas, unfolded immediately the Euro-elections were out of the way. There was little to choose between Blair, Prescott and Beckett. Most on the left voted for either Prescott or Beckett, largely because they weren't Blair, the candidate of the capitalist press and the right-wing Parliamentary Labour Party. Blair's victory signified a further lurch towards the right, which in turn led to increased support for Militant Labour and Scottish Militant Labour amongst disaffected Labour voters. The *Glasgow Herald* declared in July 1994:

> Scottish Militant Labour once again demonstrated their potential in deprived areas, by polling 519 votes and relegating the SNP into third place.[16]

SML's Harry Brown won 28 per cent of the vote after a ten-day campaign in the Sighthill/Possil ward of Glasgow, in an area where Scottish Militant Labour did not have a branch six weeks previously. Labour won the seat with 997 votes, but the success of SML, not just electorally but also with the addition of 30 new people joining it ranks, was the most decisive feature of this by-election.

## US TOUR

Fittingly, in the last months of the first 30 years of *Militant*, first-hand international accounts were a feature of the paper. I had been invited by *Militant*'s co-thinkers in the USA and Canada, supporters of *Labor Militant*, to make a tour in mid-1994. I spoke at meetings and discussed with workers in New York, Philadelphia, Boston, Chicago, San Francisco, Oakland and Seattle in the USA; as well as Toronto in the east and Vancouver in the west of Canada.

One indication of the radicalisation which looms in the USA are the developments inside the prisons. Over a million people are incarcerated in US prisons today. One of these was "Jack" convicted for murder involving a dispute over drugs and now on Death Row in one of the USA prisons. I interviewed this young man who was quite typical of a layer of poor, uneducated, Americans trapped in the spiral of violence, drugs, mass unemployment and a road leading nowhere except to the scrapheap of poverty or jail. At first hand I saw the horrific conditions of prisoners on Death Row. The most striking feature of the discussion with Jack was

> despite his surroundings, this powerfully built young man shows a thirst for knowledge and a keen intellect about working-class struggles which had me in awe.

He had followed the Youth Against Racism in Europe campaign and had convinced other prisoners of the need for racial solidarity in fighting racism and fascism. In the past a layer of black youth were changed by prison life by the "universities of the revolution".

> Something similar has happened in the US prisons. But here prison has fashioned socialists and revolutionaries out of 'criminals', who normally are not open to socialist ideas. A wave of black prisoners, influenced by the black revolt of the late 60s and 70s, have become fervent opponents of capitalism. Now this is happening to a small but significant layer of white prisoners like Jack.[25]

These prisoners see the barbarous prison system, suffer at the hands of the ruthless authoritarian regime, and have the time to read and explore the causes. This leads them to question the basis of capitalist society, to search for socialist conclusions. This in itself is an annihilating condemnation of American capitalism. Amongst what Marx called the "lumpen proletariat", who normally support reaction, are some like Jack searching for Marxist ideas. He commented:

> It's a tragedy for me that I became a socialist only in prison.[26]

In fact he had evolved on Death Row to become a very articulate advocate of socialist ideas. In searching for the truth he had read everything of a socialist and "communist" character he could find. This led him to *Labor Militant*, the journal produced by the US co-thinkers of Militant Labour in Britain. The USA, Leon Trotsky once said:

> is the anvil upon which the fate of humankind will be forged.[27]

In August a representative of Militant Labour's co-thinkers internationally in the Committee for a Workers' International (CWI) was present at the Zapatista National Liberation Army's (EZLN) National Convention. Thus in all the important international developments in 1994 Militant Labour or its co-thinkers were present and this was reflected in the pages of *Militant*, which had an unrivalled international coverage.

Not just comment but action is the hallmark of Militant Labour in the changed conditions of the 1990s. This was exemplified by the magnificent 1,000-strong camp organised in southern Germany in August by Youth Against Racism in Europe. Young people from 16 countries flocked to attend this event. A total of 800 people attended from Germany alone. This indicated the tremendous success of the YRE in Germany. Also present were representatives from Holland, Belgium, Sweden, Italy, Spain, Portugal, Britain, the Czech Republic, Poland, Northern Ireland, Southern Ireland, France, Austria, Finland, the Ukraine and Germany. So effective was the camp that the music channel MTV gave extensive coverage, which in turn generated increased inquiries about the YRE and a boost in membership.

In October and November Tommy Sheridan and I did an extensive nationwide tour taking in a number of cities to celebrate our 30th anniversary. Two things stood out from the very successful, celebratory meetings. Firstly, that the organised labour and trade union movement was at its lowest ebb, with little activity and very low attendances, perhaps the lowest for 20 or even 30 years. On the other hand, Militant Labour had built a strong national organisation with a tremendous potential to grow and develop in the changed situation which is begining to take shape in Britain. Towards the end of1994 Militant Labour successfully intervened in the struggle against the Criminal Justice Bill. The tide against the government was more pronounced as it was defeated on three key issues, of Post Office privatisation, the RMT dispute, and VAT on fuel. Despite the heroic achievements of Militant Labour over 30 years, even greater opportunities, perhaps the greatest this century, now loom for the forces of Marxism. But on one condition: that the same intransigence in defence of the basic ideas of Marxism combined with tactical flexibility in slogans and organisation continues to be the hallmark of Militant Labour.

# CONCLUSION

FROM A very small force at the beginning, *Militant* has risen, to become a significant factor in the politics of Britain and the labour movement. What guarantees are there, however, that this success can be repeated and enlarged on, in the vastly changed economic, social and political landscape, of the late 1990s and the beginning of the 21st century? Certainly, bourgeois commentators have already drawn the conclusion that Marxism is historically obsolete.

The collapse of Stalinism and the lurch to the right of the Labour and trade union leadership, has, they maintain, realised Thatcher's dream of "finishing off socialism" once and for all. But the very idea of socialism came out of the life experiences of the working class. The insoluble contradictions of capitalism, its incapacity to provide even the minimum requirements of employment, shelter and food on a world scale, drove the working class to seek an alternative system. Unless the defenders of the capitalist system can now show that late 20th century capitalism has overcome these contradictions, which Karl Marx brilliantly analysed, then its antithesis, socialism - scientific socialism, Marxism - remains as relevant as ever. This remains so, despite the fact that the understanding of the working-class of the underlying reality lags far behind the objective situation.

Human thought is in general very conservative. The working class seeks the line of least resistance, will avoid facing up to harsh reality when an 'easier', less confrontational, less brutal path appears possible. But the underlying objective situation will force itself, and is forcing itself today, into the consciousness of all classes in society, above all of the working class. True, faulty leadership can play the role of a huge brake on the working class. But leaders of parties, or general secretaries of unions, are not an independent historical factor. Far more important is the underlying situation which will break through with a mighty force at a certain stage and reshape the consciousness of the working class. Even more than was the case when *Militant* was founded, capitalism is demonstrating its utter incapacity to furnish the basic requirements of humankind.

One-third of the world labour force, more than 800 million people, are either unemployed or underemployed. 34 million are still unemployed in the advanced industrial countries while there is a massive piling up of debt, particularly of government debt. This is a consequence of the profligacy of the 1980s which means that the capitalists will have to rein back on public expenditure or risk another inflationary spiral similar to the 1970s and 1980s. This in turn presupposes a general offensive against welfare and those workers employed in the public sector. This is itself a guarantee of massive social upheaval in Britain, Japan and the US. This leaves aside the convulsions which are taking place and will increase in the colonial and semi-colonial world. In Britain there is an unprecedented degree of deprivation and poverty, unimagined at the time when *Militant* set out on its journey. This has spread like a growing ink stain on blotting paper from the traditional "depressed" areas of Britain to the Tory heartlands. Almost 30 per cent of the population no longer have an income from a job. Those who do are plagued with uncertainty and worsening conditions. In 1975 about 55 per cent of the labour force were in "secure full-time employment". This had dropped to 35 per cent in 1994 with part-time working and temporary contracts now becoming the norm together with increased exploitation of labour, which is synonymous with "American practices". The average US worker, compared to 20 years ago, is now working one month longer each year. This is the future which is being mapped out for the British workers by the boss class and their political representatives.

Even now the British worker works one hour per week extra compared to the mid-1980s. On the basis of a sane economic and political system, new technology should open up the prospect of cutting the working week, The opposite is the case. More and more workers are becoming industrial helots, as the employers attempt to squeeze out more labour, and thereby profit, from them. Exhaustion, sleep deprivation, the disappearence of the "weekend" have increasingly become part of British life. Fully 44 per cent of workers in Britain now come home each day "totally exhausted". The "luxury" of even sweated labour is denied to a greater and greater proportion of the labour force. In 1995, 15 per cent of households in Britain do not have a single person working. More than a million young people under the age of 25 are unemployed, and a quarter of a million between the ages of 16 and 25 have never worked. Truly Karl Marx's description of capitalism's "reserve army of unemployed", derided by generations of capitalist economists, is an unavoidable reality. It is moreover, an effective weapon of the bourgeois against those who are "lucky" enough to have a job. Casualisation is pushing conditions, such as in the docks, back to the beginning of this century or even to the 19th century. But similar conditions will bring forth similar results. Industrial explosions of the unskilled, as in the late 19th century, will develop in the coming period, only on a higher plane. The detonation of social upheaval is also inevitable given the brutal treatment of the poor by the Tory government, which is not likely to be lessened under a Labour government.

Such are the conditions in Britain today that one accidentally dropped match can ignite a Los Angeles-type uprising. The Bradford 'riots' are a symptom of this; 38 per cent of the Asian population in Manningham, where the riots took place, are unemployed. An uprising in industry is inevitably being prepared by the impoverishment of millions of British workers. The misnamed Job Seekers Allowance which the Tory government are proposing to introduce in 1996 is reminiscent of the darkest days of British capitalism, when the bosses sought to brutally and ruthlessly drive down wages. Under a Labour government, in particular, a revolt of the low-paid is inevitable, and Militant Labour will play a role in such a movement. Insecurity is also now a feature, not just of working class life but has increasingly affected the middle class, once the pillar of the Tory Party and of Thatcherism. In the 1980s de-regulation, although "regrettable" for industrial workers, was nevertheless tolerated alongside of a booming "housing market". But now, when it begins to affect high grade civil servants, architects, engineers, etc, howls of outrage have arisen from the leafy suburbs. This is reinforced by the shattering of the housing market with 300,000 house repossessions since 1990; the highest number of dispossessions since the Highland clearances of the 17th century! These conditions are only the outward manifestation of the catastrophic decline of British capitalism.

Forty years ago the British ruling class still ruled over one-quarter of human kind. But the loss of empire, together with its rapid economic decline has left British capitalism now as a minor player on the world and European stage. A recent survey showed that Britain has sunk to 18th place in a league of the most competitive capitalist economies. This "inglorious decay" has in turn led to the fracturing of the Tory Party, which up to recently was the oldest and the most stable capitalist party in Europe. In the past the British ruling class, in particular its main political representatives, the Tory Party, went to great lengths to hide whatever divisions existed in their ranks. They invented that special brand of British hypocrisy, parliamentary cant, ("the honourable member" etc) which allowed debate within its charmed circle while at the same time seeking to distract the attention of a "third party" that is the working class. However, with the onset of the decline of British capitalism this began to evaporate. The Tory Wets, the so-called liberal wing of the Tory Party, and Thatcherite right traded insults in a semi-public fashion throughout the 1980s. These were however merely family spats compared to the public convulsions of the present Tory government and party. Major described the Thatcherites in the cabinet - Portillo, Lilley, Howard and Redwood - as "bastards" and their heroine, Thatcher, as "the grandmother of all bastards". They reciprocated by dismissing Major as a "wimp" - "nice guy but a loser". The San Andreas fault line which runs through the Tory Party - which still exists despite Major's victory over Redwood in the Tory leadership election contest - threatens ultimately to crack wide open into a gaping chasm.

There is now open speculation that the Tory Party could go the way of the Christian Democrats in Italy, which has virtually disappeared or the Liberal Democrats in Japan, riven by factions and forced into coalition. The majority of Tory MPs are no longer "the grandees" of the past, able to rely upon income from a landed estate or inherited wealth. Tory backbenchers hope that they can avoid the complete wipeout of the Tory Party. But the right-wing leadership of the Labour Party of Tony Blair is playing right into the hands of the Tories.

Each policy pronouncement of Labour's shadow cabinet members makes Labour more and more indistinguishable from the Tories. Jack Straw, like any right wing Tory backwoodsman, has recently expressed the wish to see the streets cleared of the homeless beggars, "squeegie" windscreen washers and "winos", all of whom are the product of collapsing British capitalism. By painting Labour in the same colours as the Tories, Blair threatens to demobilise sections of potential Labour voters. Already a huge layer of youth are disenchanted, believing "all politicians are the same", and may not vote in the general election. What will probably save Blair and the right wing leadership of the Labour Party is the bitter anti-Tory mood. This is still likely, although not certain, to carry Labour to victory in a general election. But what kind of Labour government will the British workers get, given the increasingly right wing stand of Blair?

The underlying crisis of British capitalism remains and is bound to become worse. What is happening in Sweden is a warning to the British labour movement and the working class. The biggest Labour vote in a general election was recorded in September 1994, carrying the Social Democrats to power. However, they have dashed the hopes of the Swedish labour movement with the adoption of a savage austerity programme. Trapped by the crisis of British capitalism a Blair-led Labour government would be compelled to act in a similar fashion. The only way out of this impasse would be in a socialist direction, which the Blair leadership has specifically ruled out. The inaction of a Blair government, indeed the attacks on the living standards of workers, inevitable on the basis of capitalism, could prepare the ground for ferocious Tory reaction which would make Major and Heseltine appear as liberals by comparison.

Recent events in 1995 in Ontario in Canada are a warning to the British working class. After being wiped out in national elections, with their representation reduced to two seats, the Canadian Tories are back in power in the province of Ontario. They were allowed to do this because the previous National Democratic Party (NDP) dominated government in Ontario was incapable of solving the problems of the working class. This led to a right wing recoil which brought to power the Tory leader Harris, with his so-called "commonsense revolution". He promises to introduce workfare, slash welfare, and inflict further attacks on the trade unions together with the undermining of the right of minorities.

In the words of William Keegan, economic correspondent of *The Observer*, "The madness of the 1980s are alive and well and living in Ontario."[1]

Only by the mighty British labour movement adopting socialist policies, as consistently outlined and argued for by *Militant*, can future nightmares like this for the British working class be avoided. As we have seen above the bourgeoisification of the "traditional organisations" of the working class could be reflected in Britain with a serious split from the Labour Party under a right wing Blair-led Labour government.

The outline of such a split is reflected even in the *Tribune* newspaper, which has played the role of 'Left' apologists for the right-wing Labour leadership. Its columns are full of denunciations of Blair and his acolytes. Hugh Macpherson, its political correspondent, now implicitly concedes what Militant Labour has been arguing for some time; the working class base of the Labour Party is being systematically dismantled by the Blair leadership. He writes:

> There is now no doubt whatsoever that a new party is being constructed within the Labour Party that has no connection with the old, save that it provided a structure that could be used to create the new party. Tony Blair said so as he traded with Rupert Murdoch and his editors in their island paradise. By the next election he said with breathtaking sophistry it would literally be a new party, as those who joined it after he became leader will outnumber the previous members.[2]

Macpherson, referring to the creation of a new right wing party within Labour, also writes: "But were not the *Militants* expelled for being just that - a party within a party?"[3]

But what the writer does not say is how long the "two parties" - one openly bourgeois, grouped around Blair - can co-exist within the framework of the Labour Party. The increasing separation which is evident now is likely to result in a very acrimonious divorce if a Blair-led Labour government comes to power.

We support the creation of a new mass socialist party. *Militant*'s success in the past arose from a correct understanding of the objective situation of British capitalism and of the working class. But this alone was not sufficient to guarantee success. We were also able to identify the key issues at each stage, to then formulate a clear programme and through bold organisation to carry the struggle through to a conclusion. Flair and initiative matched to a careful assessment of the situation led to spectacular results in the Liverpool battle, the poll tax struggle and in the battle against the fascists in the 1990s. An equal if not greater tactical adroitness will be demanded of Marxists in the next period. The political terrain is now much more complicated, demanding a flexibility in approach together with an intransigence and implacability in defence of the Marxist programme and perspectives. Militant Labour will energetically pursue the task of building its own organisation.

But in the words of Marx, socialists "have no interests separate and opposed to those of the proletariat".[4]

At the same time as building a powerful Marxist, force Militant Labour will do all in its power to help those workers, who do not yet fully agree or are not yet prepared to join our ranks, to build the widest possible working class force to resist the bosses in industry but also to politically enhance the power and the position of the working class. Therefore, while building Militant Labour we would be prepared to join with other socialist forces to create the basis of a genuine mass socialist party in Britain. One thing is clear, the ground has been prepared for colossal social and political upheavals in Britain and throughout world capitalism before this decade is out. Militant Labour has demonstrated in the past its ability to link its programme with mass movements of the working class. However, the dramas in which it has participated will be as nothing to the mighty unfolding of events which looms. Marxism will once more arise with such force that it will astound bourgeois sceptics and socialist "fainthearts" alike. Enriched by the experience of the last 30 years, in the tumultuous events which historically impend the ideas of Militant Labour will be embraced by tens of thousands, then by hundreds of thousands and millions. This is the indispensible precondition for the labour movement to begin to refashion the world, to replace outmoded, decrepit capitalism - threatening to drag humankind into an historical abyss - with a society of human solidarity, a socialist society.

# REFERENCE NOTES

## PREFACE
1 Trotsky "On Optimism and Pessimism; on the 20th Century and on many other issues" in "The Age of Permanent Revolution" p41

## CHAPTER 1 MILITANT: ROOTS & EARLY YEARS
1 Militant 1 October 1964
2 Ibid
3 Ibid
4 Ibid
5 Militant 2 November 1964
6 Militant 4 March 1965

## CHAPTER 2 AN INTERNATIONAL OUTLOOK
1 Militant 2 November 1964
2 Militant 23 February 1967
3 Ibid
4 Militant 38 June 1968
5 Ibid
6 Ibid
7 Ibid
8 The Economist 22.6.68
9 Quoted in Doyle, "Month of Revolution", p60
10 Ibid
11 Militant 38 June 1968

## CHAPTER 3 MILITANT AND WILSON'S GOVERNMENT
1 Militant 43 November 1968
2 Militant 49 May 1969
3 Militant 45 January 1969
4 Ibid

## CHAPTER 4 NORTHERN IRELAND: THE TROUBLES
1 Militant 53 September 1969
2 Ibid
3 Ibid
4 Ibid
5 Ibid
6 Ibid
7 Ibid
8 Extract from "Barricades Bulletin", Daily newssheet of Derry labour Party, quoted ibid
9 Ibid
10 Militant 53 September 1969

## CHAPTER 5 TORY GOVERNMENT: 1970-74
1 Militant 52 August 1969
2 Militant 60 January 1970 There is an error in the numbering in some of the issues in 1970.
3 Militant 65 July 1970
4 Ibid
5 Ibid
6 Militant 69 November 1970
7 The Times 20.10.70
8 Militant 71 January 1971
9 Militant 72 February 1971
10 Militant 77 July 1971
11 Militant 79 3.9.71 This was the first fortnightly issue of Militant.
12 Ibid
13 Ibid
14 Militant 71 January 1971
15 Militant 68 October 1970
16 Militant 72 February 1971
17 Ibid
18 Militant 79 3.9.71
19 Militant 87 31.12.71
20 Militant 89 28.1.72 This was the first weekly edition of the paper.
21 Militant 97 23.3.72
22 Ibid
23 Militant 134 8.12.72
24 Militant 92 18.2.72
25 Ibid
26 Militant 101 21.4.72
27 Militant 102 28.4.72
28 Militant 110 23.6.72
29 Militant 105 19.5.72
30 Militant 110 23.6.72

## CHAPTER 6 INTERNATIONAL EVENTS: 1970-74
1 Militant 90 4.2.72
2 Ibid
3 Ibid
4 Ibid
5 Ibid
6 Ibid
7 Ibid
8 Militant 92 18.2.72
9 Ibid
10 Ibid
11 Ibid
12 Ibid
13 Militant 131 17.11.72
14 Ibid

15 Ibid
16 Militant 169 17.8.73
17 Ibid
18 Ibid
19 Militant 173 21.9.73

## CHAPTER 7 THE RISE OF MILITANT
1 Militant 125 6.10.72
2 Militant 124 29.9.72
3 Militant 136 29.12.72
4 Ibid
5 Militant 138 12.1.73
6 Ibid
7 Militant 154 4.5.73
8 Militant 159 8.6.73
9 Ibid
10 Ibid
11 Militant 168 10.8.73
12 Militant 163 6.7.73
13 Ibid
14 Militant 176 12.10.73
15 Ibid
16 Militant 183 30.11.73
17 Ibid
18 Militant 187 4.1.74
19 Evening Standard 31.12.73
20 Morning Star 28.1.74
21 Evening Standard 1.2.74
22 Militant 195 2.3.74
23 The Times 19.2.74
24 Militant 194 22.2.74

## CHAPTER 8 THE WORKING CLASS ON THE MOVE: INTERNATIONAL EVENTS 1974-75
1 Militant 205 3.5.74
2 Ibid
3 Ibid

## CHAPTER 9 A LABOUR GOVERNMENT: BUT WHERE'S THE SOCIALISM?
1 Militant 202 19.4.74
2 Militant 214 12.7.74
3 Ibid
4 Militant 219 16.8.74
5 Militant 225 4.10.74
6 Ibid
7 Militant 226 11.10.74
8 Militant 232 22.11.74
9 Militant 233 29.11.74
10 Ibid
11 Militant 222 13.9.74
12 Militant 235 13.12.74

## CHAPTER 10 ENTER MILITANT STAGE LEFT
1 Militant 264 25.7.75
2 Militant 269 5.9.75
3 Tribune 18.10.74
4 Militant 255 9.5.75
5 Ibid
6 Militant 257 6.6.75
7 'The Director' June 1975
8 Ibid
9 Militant 259 20.6.75
10 Militant 262 11.7.75

## CHAPTER 11 SPAIN, PORTUGAL AND ETHIOPIA
1 Militant 251 11.4.75
2 Militant 248 21.3.75
3 Quoted in Militant 278 7.11.75

## CHAPTER 12 THE SOCIALIST OPPOSITION GROWS
1 Militant 273 3.10.75
2 Militant 282 5.12.75
3 Observer 27.7.75
4 Daily Telegraph, "Lunatic Left and Legitimate Left", date unknown
5 From the notes of Nick Bradley
6 Ibid
7 Ibid
8 Militant 290 6.2.76
9 Ibid
10 Militant 297 26.3.76
11 Militant 308 11.6.76
12 Militant 330 12.11.76
13 Ibid
14 Militant 319 27.8.76

## CHAPTER 13 THE CRITICAL POINT
1 Militant 294 5.3.76
2 Militant 325 8.10.76
3 The Guardian 1.10.76
4 Militant 325 8.10.76
5 Militant 327 22.10.76
6 Militant 324 1.10.76
7 Militant 329 5.11.76
8 Militant 325 8.10.76
9 Ibid
10 Daily Express 10.12.76
11 The Times carried three "special articles": on 1st, 3rd and 4th Decem-

ber 1976. An editorial followed on 8th December.
12 The Times 8.12.76
13 Daily Express 27.11.76
14 The Observer, 19.12.76
15 Militant 335 10.12.76
16 Ibid
17 Ibid
18 Militant 340 28.1.77
19 The Guardian 22.1.77
20 Militant 342 11.2.77
21 Militant 358 3.6.77
22 Militant 351 15.4.77

## CHAPTER 14 THE WINTER OF DISCONTENT: BEGINNINGS
1 Militant 350 8.4.77
2 Militant 358 3.6.77
3 Militant 360 17.6.77
4 Militant 361 24.6.77
5 Ibid
6 Ibid
7 Militant 364 15.7.77
8 Ibid
9 Militant 381 11.11.77
10 Ibid
11 Militant 374 23.9.77
12 Militant 383 25.11.77
13 Militant 369 19.8.77
14 Militant 380 4.11.77
15 Militant 377 14.10.77
16 Militant 395 3.3.78
17 Ibid
18 Ibid
19 Militant 394 24.2.78
20 Militant 415 21.7.78
21 Militant 414 14.7.78

## CHAPTER 15 THE WINTER OF DISCONTENT: HIGH TIDE
1 Militant 406 19.5.78
2 Militant 426 6.10.78
3 Militant 427 13.10.78
4 Ibid
5 Militant 426 6.10.78
6 Ibid
7 Militant 428 20.10.78
8 Militant 429 27.10.78
9 Militant 432 17.11.78
10 Militant 434 1.12.78
11 Militant 426 6.10.78
12 Militant 414 14.7.78
13 Ibid
14 Militant 439 19.1.79
15 Militant 440 26.1.79
16 Militant 441 2.2.79
17 Militant 442 9.2.79
18 Militant 449 30.3.79
19 Militant 450 6.4.79

## CHAPTER 16 GENERAL ELECTION: THATCHER TO POWER
1 Militant 451 13.4.79
2 Militant 449 30.3.79
3 Ibid
4 Militant 460 15.6.79
5 Militant 454 4.5.79
6 Militant 455 11.5.79 o7 3
7 Ibid
8 Militant 454 4.5.79
9 From the election material of Terry Harrison, quoted by Peter Taaffe and Tony Mulhearn in, "Liverpool a City that Dared to Fight", p61.
10 Militant 478 9.11.79
11 Ibid
12 Militant 473 5.10.79
13 Ibid
14 Militant 474 12.10.79
15 Ibid
16 News of the World 9.9.79
17 Militant 471 21.9.79
18 Militant 474 12.10.79
19 Ibid
20 Militant 482 7.12.79
21 Ibid
22 Militant 479 16.11.79
23 Militant 493 7.3.80
24 Militant 495 21.3.80

## CHAPTER 17 THATCHER'S CHALLENGE TO THE LABOUR MOVEMENT
1 Militant 494 14.3.80
2 Militant 496 28.3.80
3 Ibid
4 Militant 541 27.2.81
5 Ibid
6 Militant 500 25.4.80
7 The Times 15.1.80
8 Ibid
9 The Sun 7.3.80
10 Militant 487 25.1.80
11 Militant 523 10.10.80
12 LPYS statement on St Paul's riots, printed in Militant 498 11.4.80
13 Militant 548 17.4.81
14 Ibid

15 Ibid
16 Ibid
17 Militant 561 17.7.81
18 Ibid
19 Ibid
20 Ibid
21 Militant 563 31.7.81
22 Financial Times 3.11.80
23 Militant 532 12.12.80
24 Ibid
25 Tribune 28.3.80
26 Militant 497 4.4.80
27 Ibid
28 Militant 543 13.3.81

## CHAPTER 18 H-BLOCKS AND SOLIDARNOSC
1 Militant 504 23.5.80
2 Ibid
3 Ibid
4 Militant 546 3.4.81
5 The Times 20.6.81
6 Militant 561 17.7.81
7 Militant 575 30.10.81
8 Ibid

## CHAPTER 19 MILITANT SURGES
1 Militant 518 5.9.80
2 Ibid
3 Militant 547 10.4.81
4 Militant 551 8.5.81
5 Militant 581 11.12.81
6 Today programme, BBC Radio 4, 15.9.81
7 Sunday Mirror 20.9.81
8 Militant 570 25.9.81
9 Militant 582 18.12.81
10 Daily Mirror 10.12.81
11 Militant 587 5.2.82
12 Militant 590 26.2.82
13 Ibid
14 Militant 591 5.3.82
15 Sunday Times 7.3.82
16 Militant 592 12.3.82
17 Ibid
18 Militant 595 2.4.82
19 Ibid

## CHAPTER 20 THE FALKLANDS/ MALVINAS WAR
1 Militant 596 9.4.82
2 Ibid
3 Ibid
4 Militant International Review 22 June 1982
5 Militant 596 9.4.82
6 Trotsky, Writings of Leon Trotsky, 1938-39, p34

## CHAPTER 21 TOWARDS EXPULSIONS
1 Liverpool Echo, 7.5.82
2 Militant 606 18.6.82
3 South Wales Evening Post 26.1.82
4 Ham and High 6.8.82
5 East End News October 1982
6 Financial Times 18.6.82
7 Militant 608 2.7.82
8 Daily Mail 24.6.82
9. Militant 608 2.7.82
10 Militant 612 30.7.82
11 Militant 609 9.7.82
12 Militant 611 23.7.82
13 Ibid
14 Mail on Sunday 12.9.82
15 News of the World 12.9.82
16 Labour Weekly 17.9.82
17 Militant 618 17.9.82
18 Ibid
19 Militant 619 24.9.82
20 Militant 621 8.10.82
21 Ibid
22 Ibid
23 Militant 623 22.10.82
24 Ibid
25 Ibid
26 Ibid
27 Ibid
28 Ibid
29 Militant 628 26.11.82

## CHAPTER 22 EXPELLED... INTO THE MOVEMENT
1 Militant 640 4.3.83

## CHAPTER 23 A WORKER'S MP ON A WORKER'S WAGE
1 Militant 650 13.5.83
2 Ibid
3 Militant 568 8.7.83
4 Daily Post 18.5.83
5 Militant 655 17.6.83
6 Militant 656 24.6.83
7 Ibid
8 Hansard, 8 July, 1983, reprinted in Militant 659 15.7.83
9 Militant 667 16.9.83

## CHAPTER 24 DARING TO FIGHT
1 Militant 677 25.11.83
2 Militant Special Issue 25.11.83
3 Militant 679 9.12.83
4 Militant 680 16.12.83
5 Ibid
6 Jeffrey Archer, First Among Equals, p283
7 The Journalist January 1984
8 Quote from a Radio One DJ, printed in Militant 692 23.3.84
9 Daily Telegraph 26.1.84
10 Mail on Sunday 13.5.84
11 Joint Matriculation Board GCE 'A' Level British Government and Politics Paper II, June 1984
12 Hansard 27.6.84
13 Militant 693 30.3.84

## CHAPTER 25 THE MINERS' STRIKE 1984-85
1 Militant 692 23.3.84
2 Ibid
3 Ibid
4 Ibid
5 Ibid
6 Militant 690 9.3.84
7 Militant 691 16.3.84
8 Ibid
9 Militant 696 20.4.84
10 Ibid
11 The Guardian, quoted in Militant 696
12 Militant 697 27.4.84
13 Militant 705 22.6.84
14 Ibid
15 Militant 702 1.6.84
16 Ibid
17 Ibid
18 Ibid
19 Militant 705 22.6.84
20 Militant 702 1.6.84
21 Ibid
22 Militant 708 13.7.84
23 Ibid
24 Militant 709 20.7.84
25 Ibid
26 Militant 710 27.7.84
27 Militant 712 10.8.84
28 Militant 717 21.9.84
29 Ibid
30 Militant 719 5.10.84
31 Ibid
32 Militant 720 12.10.84
33 Militant 728 7.12.84
34 Ibid
35 Militant 730 4.1.85
36 Militant 731 11.1.85
37 Militant 736 15.2.85
38 Militant 739 8.3.85
39 Ibid
40 Ibid
41 Ibid
42 Ibid
43 Ibid
44 Ibid
45 Ibid
46 Ibid
47 Ibid

## CHAPTER 26 INTO ILLEGALITY IN LIVERPOOL
1 Militant 694 6.4.84
2 Militant 709 20.7.84
3 The Times 11.7.84
4 Michael Crick, Militant, p209
5 Ibid, p212
6 Militant 722 26.10.84
7 Ibid

## CHAPTER 27 SCHOOL STUDENTS' STRIKE
1 Militant 741 22.3.85
2 Militant 742 29.3.85
3 Ibid
4 Ibid
5 Militant 747 3.5.85
6 Ibid
7 Ibid
8 Ibid
9 Ibid
10 Ibid

## CHAPTER 28 LIVERPOOL: ROUND TWO
1 Michael Parkinson, "Liverpool on the Brink", p124
2 Militant 741 22.3.85
3 Militant 752 7.6.85
4 Taaffe and Mulhearn, op. cit., p227
5 Liverpool Echo, quoted in Taaffe and Mulhearn, op. cit., p237
6 Militant 766 20.9.85
7 Ibid
8 Daily Mail 16.9.85
9 Militant 767b 27.9.85 A second edition of the paper was published after the one-day strike.
10 Ibid

11 The Independent 7.1.87
12 Taaffe and Mulhearn, op. cit., p300
13 Quoted ibid
14 Ibid
15 Militant 768 4.10.85
16 The Guardian 13.12.85
17 Militant 773 8.11.85
18 Ibid
19 Ibid

## CHAPTER 29 WINSTON, WESTLANDS AND WAPPING
1 Militant 768 4.10.85
2 Militant 769 11.10.85
3 Militant 782 24.1.86
4 Militant 783 31.1.86
5 Ibid
6 Ibid
7 Ibid
8 Militant 786 21.2.86
9 Ibid
10 Militant 787 28.2.86
11 Ibid
12 Militant 807 18.7.86

## CHAPTER 30 THE FIGHT AGAINST THE WITCH-HUNT
1 Sunday Times 22.12.85
2 Taaffe and Mulhearn, op. cit., p337
3 Granada Television, quoted in Taaffe and Mulhearn, op. cit., p346
4 Militant 778 13.12.85
5 Inquiry Majority Report, quoted in Militant 787 28.2.86
6 Taaffe and Mulhearn, op.cit., p377
7 Financial Times 3.3.86
8 Militant 800 30.5.86
9 Ibid
10 Sunday Sun 13.7.86
11 Daily Telegraph 3.3.86
12 Militant 798 16.5.86
13 Liverpool Echo 9.5.86
14 Militant 798 16.5.86
15 Militant 792 4.4.86
16 Taaffe and Mulhearn, op. cit., p399
17 Daily Mirror 30.9.86
18 Militant 788 7.3.86

## CHAPTER 31 MILITANT AT HIGH TIDE
1 Militant 797 9.5.86
2 Militant 811 15.8.86
3 Ibid
4 Militant 834 13.2.87
5 Militant 806 11.7.86
6 Ibid
7 Ibid
8 Militant 829 9.1.87
9 Militant 865 18.9.87
10 Militant 824 21.11.86 o7 3
11 The Guardian 16.11.86
12 Daily Telegraph 16.11.86
13 Daily Mail 16.11.86
14 Financial Times 16.11.86
15 Daily Mail 19.11.86
16 Financial Times 16.11.86
17 Ibid

## CHAPTER 32 1987 GENERAL ELECTION
1 Militant 833 6.2.87
2 Ibid
3 Ibid
4 Militant 845 1.5.87
5 Militant 838 13.3.87
6 Ibid
7 Militant 847 15.5.87
8 Liverpool Echo 8.5.87
9 Militant 847 15.5.87
10 Newsnight 7.5.87
11 The Economist 15.5.87
12 The Independent 15.5.87
13 Militant 851 4.6.87
14 Militant 853 19.6.87
15 Ibid
16 Hansard 1 July, 1987, reprinted in Militant 856 10.7.87
17 Ibid
18 Militant 867 2.10.87
19 Ibid
20 Militant 853 19.6.87
21 Ibid

## CHAPTER 33 THE POLL TAX: EARLY DAYS
1 Militant 857 17.7.87
2 Militant 864 11.9.87
3 Ibid
4 Militant 884 19.2.88
5 Militant 883 12.2.88
6 Militant 907 29.7.88
7 Ibid
8 Militant 888 18.3.88
9 Quoted ibid
10 Militant 893 22.4.88
11 "How to fight the Poll Tax", 1988, was reviewed in Militant 898 27.5.88
12 Militant 898 27.5.88
13 Militant 916 7.10.88

14 Ibid
15 Militant 913 16.9.88
16 Sunday Times, quoted in Militant 922 18.11.88
17 Militant 922 18.11.88
18 Ibid
19 Ibid
20 Militant 914 23.9.88
21 Militant 886 4.3.88
22 Quoted in Militant 880 22.1.88
23 Militant 880 22.1.88
24 Militant 882 5.2.88
25 Ibid
26 Militant 886 4.3.88
27 Ibid
28 Ibid
29 Ibid
30 Ibid
31 Militant 887 11.3.88

## CHAPTER 34 RUSSIA, TROTSKY AND THE COLLAPSE OF STALINISM
1 Militant 889 25.3.89
2 Mikhail Gorbachev, "Perestroika", p118
3 Militant 889 25.3.89
4 Militant 897 20.5.88
5 Militant 902 24.6.88
6 Ibid
7 Militant 935 10.3.89
8 Militant 938 31.3.89
9 Ibid
10 Militant 954 21.7.89
11 Ibid
12 Militant 958 1.9.89
13 Militant 940 14.4.89
14 Ibid
15 Militant 944 12.5.89
16 Ibid
17 Militant 946 26.5.89
18 Militant 948 9.6.89
19 Ibid
20 Ibid
21 Ibid
22 Ibid
23 Militant 931 10.2.89
24 Ibid

## CHAPTER 35 MILITANT IN TRANSITION
1 Quoted in Militant 897 20.5.88
2 Quoted in Militant 891 8.4.88
3 Ibid
4 Militant 910 26.8.88

5 Militant 912 16.9.88

## CHAPTER 36 INTO TOP GEAR
1 Militant 974 5.1.90
2 Militant 928 20.1.89
3 Militant 937 24.3.89
4 Ibid
5 Ibid
6 Militant 934 3.3.89
7 Militant 951 30.6.89
8 Militant 952 7.7.89
9 Militant 953 14.7.89
10 Militant 956 11.8.89
11 Militant 958 1.9.89
12 Militant 959 8.9.89
13 Militant 971 1.12.89
14 Militant 946 26.5.89
15 Militant 941 21.4.89
16 Militant 939 7.4.89
17 Liverpool Echo, quoted in Militant 939
18 Militant 939 7.4.89
19 Militant 973 15.12.89
20 Militant 978 2.2.90

## CHAPTER 37 THE GATHERING STORM
1 Militant 967 3.11.89
2 Militant 944 12.5.89
3 Militant 964 13.10.89
4 Ibid
5 The Independent 8.1.90
6 Militant 976 19.1.90
7 Militant International Review Summer No 41 1989
8 Financial Times 14.10.89
9 Militant 976 19.1.90
10 Ibid
11 Ibid

## CHAPTER 38 31 MARCH 1990
1 Militant 976 19.1.90
2 Quoted in Militant 976 19.1.90
3 Militant 976 19.1.90
4 Quoted in Militant 981 23.2.90
5 Militant 982 2.3.90
6 Militant 983 9.3.90
7 Militant 982 2.3.90
8 Militant 984 16.3.90
9 Quoted in Militant 984 16.3.90
10 Tony Benn "The End of an Era - Diaries 1980-1990 pp585-6
11 Militant 983 9.3.90
12 Ibid

13 Militant 983 9.3.90
14 Militant 984 16.3.90
15 The Times 9.3.90
16 The Times 10.3.90
17 Sunday Times 11.3.90
18 Militant 984 16.3.90
19 Ibid
20 Militant 984 16.3.90
21 Ibid
22 Militant 985 23.3.90
23 Militant 988 13.4.90
24 Ibid
25 Socialist Worker 24.3.90
26 Victor Keegan in The Guardian, quoted in Militant 986 30.3.90
27 Militant 986 30.3.90
28 Militant 987 6.4.90
29 Ibid
30 Ibid

## CHAPTER 39 THE RIOT
1 Militant 987 6.4.90
2 Ibid
3 Ibid
4 Ibid
5 Ibid
6 Margaret Thatcher, "The Downing Street Years" p661
7 Militant 987 6.4.90
8 Ibid
9 Militant 988 13.4.90
10 Ibid
11 Militant 987 6.4.90
12 Ibid
13 Militant 992 11.5.90
14 Militant 994 25.5.90
15 Ibid

## CHAPTER 40 DEFENDING NON-PAYERS
1 Militant 994 25.5.90
2 Militant 993 18.5.90
3 Militant 996 8.6.90
4 Ibid
5 Militant 997 15.6.90
6 Ibid
7 Ibid
8 Militant 999 29.6.90
9 Militant 998 22.6.90
10 Militant 1004 10.8.90
11 Militant 1005 17.8.90

## CHAPTER 41 INTERNATIONAL CHALLENGES AND A HISTORICAL SETBACK
1 Militant 979 9.2.90
2 Ibid
3 Ibid
4 Militant 980 16.2.90
5 Militant 977 19.1.90
6 Militant 981 23.2.90
7 Ibid
8 Ibid
9 Ibid
10 Militant 996 8.6.90
11 Ibid
12 Militant 979 9.2.90
13 I.Klyamkin, quoted ibid
14 Ibid
15 Ibid
16 Militant 980 16.2.90
17 Militant 993 18.5.90
18 Ibid
19 Ibid
20 Militant 995 1.6.90
21 Militant 998 22.6.90
22 Ibid
23 Militant 1000 6.7.90
24 Militant 999 29.6.90
25 Militant 1000 6.7.90
26 Militant 1002 20.7.90
27 Ibid
28 Militant 989 20.4.90
29 Ibid
30 Ibid
31 Militant 1021 14.12.90
32 Militant 999 29.6.90
33 Ibid
34 Ibid

## CHAPTER 42 THE GULF WAR
1 Militant 1004 10.8.90
2 Ibid
3 Ibid
4 Ibid
5 Militant 1006 31.8.90
6 Ibid
7 Militant 1010 28.9.90
8 Ibid
9 Ibid
10 Ibid
11 Ibid
12 Militant 1023 11.1.91
13 Militant 1024 18.1.91
14 Ibid
15 Militant 1025 25.1.91
16 Ibid
17 Spanish "Thesis on the Gulf Crisis", September 1990

18 Militant Rally against the Gulf War, 26.1.91
19 Militant 1031 8.3.91
20 Militant 1032 15.3.91
21 Militant 1031 8.3.91
22 Militant 1026 1.2.91

## CHAPTER 43 THE POLL TAX IS BEATEN
1 Militant 1013 19.10.90
2 Militant 1014 26.10.90
3 Ibid
4 Ibid
5 Ibid
6 Ibid
7 Ibid
8 Militant 1018 23.11.90
9 Thatcher, op. cit., pp848-9
10 Militant 1021 14.12.90
11 Militant 1018 23.11.90

## CHAPTER 44 MILITANT FACES A BREAKAWAY
1 Militant 1039 3.5.91
2 Militant 1044 7.6.91
3 Militant 1046 21.6.91
4 Quoted in Militant, ibid
5 Quoted in Militant 1048 5.7.91
6 Ibid
7 Socialist Worker 13.7.91
8 Minority Document - "The New Turn - A Threat to 40 Years Work", para 96
9 Ibid, para 32
10 Militant 1050 19.7.91
11 Ibid
12 Daily Mail 13.7.91
13 Militant 1052 9.8.91
14 Ibid
15 Militant 1059 4.10.91
16 Ibid
17 Militant 1068 6.12.91
18 Ibid
19 Ibid

## CHAPTER 45 TWO TRENDS IN MILITANT
1 Militant 870 23.10.87
2 Ibid
3 Minority Document "The Truth about the coup", p16
4 Alan Woods addressing an International meeting of Militant, quoted in "The Collapse of Stalinism", part 2, para 50.
5 Jarulzelski, in the 1991 Polish election campaign, quoted in "The Collapse of Stalinism, part 2, para 134.
6 Minority Document op.cit., p11
7 Militant 1054 30.8.91
8 The Times 21.8.91
9 Militant 1072 24.1.92
10 Ibid

## CHAPTER 46 SCOTTISH MILITANT LABOUR
1 Militant 1057 20.9.91
2 Militant 1059 4.10.91
3 Ibid
4 Militant 1069 13.12.91
5 Glasgow Herald, quoted ibid
6 Militant 1069 13.12.91
7 Militant 1059 4.10.91
8 Militant 1070 10.1.92
9 Militant 1073 31.1.92
10 Militant 1075 14.2.92
11 Militant 1079 13.3.92
12 Ibid
13 Ibid
14 Ibid
15 Ibid
16 Ibid
17 Ibid

## CHAPTER 47 1992 GENERAL ELECTION
1 Militant 1080 20.3.92
2 Quoted ibid.
3 Militant 1081 27.3.92
4 Ibid
5 Ibid
6 Militant 1082 3.4.92
7 Militant 1084 17.4.92
8 Ibid
9 Quoted ibid
10 Ibid
11 Ibid
12 Militant 1083 10.4.92
13 Quoted in Militant 1084 17.4 .92
14 Quoted ibid
15 Militant 1084 17.4.92
16 Quoted ibid
17 Quoted ibid
18 Militant 1085 24.4.92
19 Militant 1083 10.4.92
20 Militant 1088 15.5.92
21 Glasgow Herald 9.5.92

22 Daily Record 8.5.92
23 Scotsman 8.5.92
24 Sunday Times 10.5.92
25 Ibid

## CHAPTER 48 NEW WORLD DISORDER
1 Militant 1077 28.2.92
2 Ibid
3 Ibid
4 Ibid
5 Militant 1081 27.3.92
6 Ibid
7 Quoted ibid
8 Militant 1087 8.5.92
9 Ibid
10 Militant 1107 16.10.92

## CHAPTER 49 FIGHTING FOR SOCIALISM
1 Militant 1091 5.6.92
2 Militant 1093 19.6.92
3 Militant 1109 30.10.92
4 Militant 1095 3.7.92
5 Militant 1100 21.8.92
6 Glasgow Evening Times 4.9.92
7 The Scotsman 4.9.92
8 Glasgow Herald 4.9.92
9 Scotland on Sunday 6.9.92
10 Militant 1102 11.9.92
11 Scottish Television 4.9.92, quoted in Militant ibid
12 Radio Clyde 4.9.92, quoted ibid
13 Militant 1102 11.9.92
14 Radio Clyde 4.9.92, quoted ibid
15 Militant 1106 9.10.92
16 Ibid
17 Militant 1107 16.10.92
18 Militant 1108a 24.10.92 A special edition of 1108 was produced for the Sunday demonstration.
19 Militant 1109 30.10.92
20 Militant International Review 48 Summer 1992
21 Militant 1111 13.11.92
22 Daily Record 30.10.92
23 Glasgow Evening Times 30.10.92
24 The Herald 26.10.92
25 Sunday Times 1.11.92
26 Militant 1116 8.1.93
27 Militant 1121 12.2.93
28 Militant 1119 29.1.93
29 Militant 1126 19.3.93
30 Ibid
31 Ibid
32 Militant 1128 2.4.93
33 Militant 1125 12.3.93
34 Militant 1126 19.3.93
35 The Independent 13.3.93
36 Militant 1126 19.3.93
37 Ibid
38 Sunday Times, quoted in Militant, ibid
39 Sunday Times, ibid

## CHAPTER 50 MILITANT LABOUR
1 Militant 1128 2.4.93
2 Ibid
3 The Herald, 2.2.93
4 Militant 1128 2.4.93
5 Militant 1123 26.2.93
6 Ibid
7 Militant 1130 16.4.93
8 Militant 1133 7.5.93
9 Daily Record 18.5.93
10 Militant 1135 21.5.93
11 Ibid

## CHAPTER 51 FIGHTING FASCISM
1 Militant 1146 20.8.93
2 Militant 1149 17.9.93
3 Militant 1150 24.9.93
4 Militant 1154 22.10.93
5 Ibid
6 Ibid
7 Militant 1155 29.10.93

## CHAPTER 52 THE BALKANS
1 Militant 1131 23.4.93
2 Militant 1136 28.5.93
3 Ibid
4 The Independent 13.4.93
5 Militant 1136 28.5.93
6 Militant 1130 16.4.93
7 Militant 1152 8.10.93
8 Militant 1159 26.11.93
9 Ibid
10 Ibid

## CHAPTER 53 ON OUR WAY TO WEMBLEY
1 Militant 1134 14.5.93
2 Militant 1138 11.6.93
3 Ibid
4 Ibid
5 Ibid
6 Ibid
7 Green Left 21.7.93

8 New Statesman/Society 11.6.93
9 Militant 1138 11.6.93
10 Militant 1140 25.6.93
11 Sunday Times 20.6.93
12 Scotland on Sunday 20.6.93
13 Sunday Times 20.6.93
14 Militant International Revies 54 Nov/Dec 1993
15 Militant 1137 4.6.93
16 Militant 1145 6.8.93
17 Ibid
18 Ibid
19 Ibid

## CHAPTER 54 - STRUGGLE, SOLIDARITY, SOCIALISM
1 Militant 1151 1.10.93
2 Militant 1155 29.10.93
3 Trotsky, Revolution Betrayed, p88
4 Militant 1164 14.1.94
5 Militant 1165 21.1.94
6 Ibid
7 Militant 1173 18.3.94
8 Militant 1176 8.4.94
9 Militant 1181 13.5.94
10 The Herald 7.5.94
11 Daily Record 6.6.94
12 Tommy Sheridan with Joan McAlpine, "A Time to Rage", foreword by John Pilger pvii
13 Militant 1189 8.7.94
14 Militant 1200 7.10.94
15 Ibid
16 The Herald 1.7.94

## CONCLUSION
1 The Observer 18.6.95
2 Tribune 21.7.95
3 Tribune 28.7./4.8.95
4 Marx and Engels, The Communist Manifesto, Foreign Languages Press 1975, p49

# BIBLIOGRAPHY

Archer, Jeffrey, First Among Equals, Hodder and Stoughton, 1984.

Baker, Blake The Far Left, Weidenfeld and Nicholson, 1981.

Benn, Tony, Diaries, Hutchinson.

Branson, Noreen, Poplarism, 1919-25 - George lansbury and the Councillors' Revolt, Lawrence and Wishart, 1979.

Brown, Sally, Diary of a Poll Tax Marcher.

Callaghan, John, The Far Left in British Politics, Basil Blackwell, 1987.

Cannon, James P, America's Road to Socialism, Pioneer Publishers 1953.

Clarke, Elizabeth, and Peters, Richard, Towards a New Revolution - Workers of the Soviet Union Speak, Fortress, 1990.

Crick, Michael, Militant, Faber and Faber, 1984.

Crick, Michael, March of Militant, Faber and Faber, 1986.

Crozier, Brian, Free Agent, Harper Collins, 1993.

Doyle, Clare, Month of Revolution, Fortress, 1988.

Gilmour, Sir Ian, Inside Right, Quartet, 1979.

Gorbachev, Mikhail, Perestroika, Collins, 1987.

Grant, Ted, Taaffe, Peter and Walsh, Lynn, The State - a Warning Militant Publications.

Hadden, Peter, Divide and Rule,

Harris, Robert, The Making of Neil Kinnock, Faber and Faber, 1984.

Jolly, Steve, Eyewitness in China,

Kilroy-Silk, Robert, Hard Labour, Chatto and Windus, 1986.

Kogan, David and Maurice, The Battle for the Labour Party, Fontana Paperbacks, 1982.

Lane, Tony, Liverpool, Gateway of Empire, Lawrence and Wishart, 1987.

Leapman, Michael, Kinnock, Unwin Hyman, 1987.

Liverpool City Council, Success Against the Odds, Liverpool City Council Public Relations and Information Unit, 1986.

McCormick, Paul, Enemies of Democracy, Temple Smith, 1979.

Militant, China, Tradition of Struggle,

Militant, Import Controls
Militant, Iranian Revolution,
Militant, It's Your Paper
Militant, Liverpool Fights the Tories, Militant Publications, 1984.
Militant, Marxism on Trial,
Militant, NHS in Crisis,
Militant, Our Stand for Socialism,
Militant, Out, Proud and Militant,
Militant, A Socialist Education Programme,
Militant, Towards Political Revolution,
Militant, Way Forward for Women,
Militant, We beat the Poll Tax,
Militant, We Won't Pay!
Parkinson, Michael, Liverpool on the Brink, Policy Journals, 1985.
Reid, John, Reclaim the Game,
Seyd, Patrick, The Rise and Fall of the Labour Left, MacMillan Education, 1987.
Sheridan, Tommy (Joan McAlpine) A Time to Rage Polygon 1994
Shipley, Peter, The Militant Tendency, Foreign Affairs Publishing,
Steffen Jens-Peter, Militant Tendency Trotzkismus I.D. Labour, Peter Lang AG, Berne, Switzerland (in German) 1994
Taaffe, Peter, Cuba, Analysis of a Revolution,
Taaffe, Peter, and Mulhearn, Tony, Liverpool, A City That Dared to Fight, Fortress, 1988.
Thatcher, Margaret, The Downing Street Years, Harper Collins, 1993.
Trotsky, Leon, The Age of Permanent Revolution, Dell Publishing New York, 1974.
Trotsky, Leon, Marxism in our Time,
Trotsky, Leon, The Revolution Betrayed,
Trotsky, Leon, Writings of Leon Trotsky, Pathfinder Press, 1974.
Venton, Richard, and Hadden, Peter, Socialism, Not Sectarianism,
Walker, Denver, Quite Right, Mr Trotsky! Harvey and Jones, 1985.

# INDEX

Abbott, Diane 280, 374
Adams, Terry 142
Ahluwalia, Kiranjit 489, 490
Airlie, Jimmy 296
Aitken, Ian 379
Aitman, Tony 287
Alksnis, Colonel 411
Allaun, Frank 153, 208
Allende, Salvador 65-70, 78
Alton, David 268, 468
Anderson, Frank 435
Apps, Ray 71,80,93, 139, 153, 434
Arafat, Yasser 525, 526
Archer, Jeffrey 226, 392
Ashdown, Paddy 388, 465, 492
Ashton, Joe 140
Ashworth, Bob 96
Austin, Lois 530, 541

Baird, Colin 254
Baker James 447
Baker, Kenneth 265, 301, 302, 372
Bannister, Roger 287
Barnes, Harry 374, 375
Barratt, Lezli-Ann 217, 218
Bates, Jim 457
Beackon, Derek 514, 544
Beckett, Margaret 281, 548
Beckingham, Sue 205
Beishon, Judy 531
Bell, Ronald 143
Beloff, Nora 100, 101
Benn, Tony 37, 50, 78-80, 83, 96, 101, 103, 115, 125-127, 149, 152-155, 177-179, 181, 183, 186, 192, 198, 205, 208, 212, 223, 227, 251, 282, 283, 303, 336, 344, 345, 370, 374, 378, 428, 436, 444
Berlusconi, Silvio 542
Bevan, Andy 123-126
Bevan, Nye 126, 158, 200, 209, 440
Bevins, Anthony 267
Bickerstaffe, Rodney 318
Bidwell, Sid 136
Biffen, John 377
Biles, Hilda 368, 372
Birch, Jeremy 153
Bithell, Glenys 114
Blackhall, Shareen 186

Blair, Tony 361, 437, 440, 441, 488, 548, 555-557
Blakelock, PC Keith 273
Blunkett, David 257, 264, 352
Bolton, George 371
Boston, Razina 463
Bottomley, Henry 226
Bowman, Chief Constable Jack 510
Boyle, Pete 457
Boyson, Rhodes 416
Bradford, Andre 426
Bradley, Frances 277
Bradley, Nick 75, 89, 100, 112, 123, 126, 127, 135
Bradley, Tom 126
Brandt, Willy 91
Brittan, Leon 228, 274
Brown, Alan 536
Brown, George 15
Brown, Harry 548
Brown, Hugh 262
Brown, Ron 325, 349, 456
Brown, Sally 427
Browning, Muriel 199
Bruinvels, Peter 293
Bryan, John 300, 302, 304
Bulaitis, John 512
Bulger, Jamie 507
Burge, Ian 90
Burgess, Graham 266
Bush, George 330, 414, 423, 479
Buthelezi, Gatsha 479
Byrne, John 153

Caetano, Marcello 85
Callaghan, James 37, 41, 100, 118, 120, 123-127, 139, 152, 154, 184, 205, 216
Callaghan, Martin 393
Cameron, Jim 262
Campbell, Alistair 437
Campbell, Oliver 513
Carr, Mike 368
Carr, Robert 72
Cartwright, John 126
Castle, Barbara 37, 89, 176
Castro, Fidel 26, 109, 338
Ceausescu, Nicolai 403, 407
Chapple, Frank 219, 294

Chesterman, Doctor Patrick 144
Christie, Campbell 345, 387
Ciampi, Carlo 542
Clark, Debbie 367, 457
Clarke, Elizabeth 424
Clarke, Eric 283
Clarke, Kenneth 537
Clarke, Margi 378
Clarke, Neil 491
Clarke, Tom 505
Clements, Richard 169
Cliff, Tony 493
Coady, Detective Superintendent Bill 503
Coates, Ken 35
Coates, Laurence 75, 183, 208
Collins, Jack 272
Cook, Peter 123
Coombes, Keva 388
Cooper, Rosemary 465
Cornea, Doina 407
Cotterill, Dave 340, 434
Craven, Pat 53, 71
Creear, Margaret 180, 230
Creswell, Peter 266
Crick, Michael 250, 531
Crozier, Brian 358
Cunningham, Jim 464, 467
Cunningham, Walter 137
Curran, Frances 75, 251, 254, 283, 433, 504
Currie, Edwina 319

Daly, Lawrence 36, 101
Davie, Michael 124
Davies, Larlan 530
Davies, Roy 199
Davis, Martin 381
Davis, Paul 356
De Boer, Harry 271
De Bord, Raymond 530
De Freitas, Colin 138
De Gaulle 30, 396
De Klerk, F.W. 340, 341, 395-398, 479-481, 527
Deane, Arthur 8, 9
Deane, Brian 9
Deane, Gertie 9
Deane, Jimmy 9
Delany, Michael 291
Deng Xiao Ping 331-336
Derby-Lewis, Clive 481

Desai, Jayaben 130
Devenay, Joe 269
Devlin, Bernadette 39, 41
Dewar, Donald 315, 316, 345
Dick, Davy 22
Dick, Margaret 286
Dickinson, Anita 393
Dickinson, Keith 8, 10, 22, 208, 433
Digiorgio, Rose 89
Ditta, Anwar 180
Dobson, Frank 547
Docherty, Brian 63
Donaldson, Sir John 60, 61
Donne, Eleanor 426
Donovan, Julie 462, 500, 507, 530
Douglas, Dick 312, 351
Douglas, Ken 543
Douglas, Linda 75, 254
Douglas-Home, Alec 18
Dowling, Felicity 286, 306
Dowling, Harry 20
Doyle, Clare 8, 18, 165, 208, 328, 394, 531
Doyle, Peter 74, 75
Duffy, Micky 220
Duffy, Terry (AUEW president) 198, 225
Duffy, Terry (Wavertree) 140
Duggal, Rohit 512
Duke, Harvey 509
Dunn, John 75
Dunn, Kath 375
Dunnachie, James 346
Dyer, Michael 505

Edwardes, Michael 156
Edwards, Bob 18
Ellis, John 292, 293
Ellis, Keith 528
Engels, Friedrich 31, 100, 334, 445, 529, 539
Evans, John 208
Ewers, John 22, 367

Fanon, Frantz 26
Feather, Vic 72
Ferguson, Jim 265
Fields, Terry 133, 184, 185, 215-217, 219, 240, 250, 259, 272, 285, 300, 303, 304, 331, 349, 353, 356, 358, 394, 405, 442-444, 456, 464-466, 468, 485, 497
Fisher, Alan 116, 140
Fitch, Rod 170, 181

Foot, Michael 80, 120, 126, 163, 169, 170, 183, 184, 193, 198-200, 203, 208, 209, 215, 394
Foot, Paul 438
Ford, Ben 187
Foster, Joan 317
Fox, Colin 254, 380
Franco, General 105
Freeman, Gary 528

Galashan, Dave 20
Galbraith, Jackie 254
Gallacher, Willie 469
Galloway, George 351
Gapes, Mike 114, 115
Gibson, Janet 457, 530
Gierek, Edward 172
Gillispie, Bob 316
Gilmour, Ian 187
Gladden, Roy 269
Glaspie, April 415
Glennon, Jannice 325, 538
Glennon, Steve 381, 538
Goldfinch, Steve 537
Gonzalez, Felipe 105, 106
Gorbachev, Mikhail 323, 324, 330, 333, 336, 338, 340, 397, 402, 403, 411, 412, 414, 448, 451, 476
Gorst, John 131
Gould, Bryan 305, 489
Gould, Joyce 377
Goulding, Cathal 44
Gow, Ian 371
Gqozo, Brigadier Oupa 480
Graham, Patrick 528
Grant, Bernie 269, 280
Grant, Ted 8, 9, 21, 100, 106, 123, 127, 208, 220, 240, 249, 271, 325, 328, 338-341, 397, 420-422, 433-435, 437, 439-441, 445-447, 449, 450, 452
Grantham, Roy 131, 213
Gray, Charlie 461
Griffin, Willie 495, 543
Grimond, Jo 103
Groce, Cherry 273
Gwala, Harry 481

Hadden, Peter 328, 465, 466
Haddow, Jimmy 457
Haddow, Ruby 457
Haile Selassie 108
Hain, Peter 440

Hall, Peter 532, 533
Hamilton, John 260
Hammond, Eric 231
Haney, Geoff 297
Hanford, Paula 393
Hani, Chris 480, 481
Hardman, Alan 53, 301
Harris, Mike 556
Harris, Robert 239, 372, 471
Harrison, Terry 20, 151, 152, 185, 287
Hart, David 231
Hart, Judith 178, 208
Hattersley, Roy 75, 185, 187, 198, 220, 221, 502
Hatton, Derek 139, 153, 184, 223, 247-250, 269, 270, 279, 280, 282-285, 287, 288, 294, 430, 501-503
Havers, Sir Michael 229
Haynes, Sue 426
Hayward, Ron 93, 123, 124, 153, 210
Healey, Denis 75, 79, 93, 118, 119, 181, 183, 184, 187, 200, 205, 216
Heath, Edward 48, 81, 99, 118, 274, 336
Heemskirk, Clive 12
Heffer, Doris 437
Heffer, Eric 112-114, 120, 137, 185, 223, 268, 282, 283, 305, 306, 309, 344, 345, 368, 436
Hemson, David 256
Heseltine, Michael 166, 167, 274, 388, 430, 459, 490, 491, 494, 556
Higgins, Joe 438, 439
Hill, Alison 391
Hill, Paddy 347
Hillman, Ellis 8
Hjelm, Anders 86
Ho Chi Minh 25, 26
Hobsbawn, Eric 205
Hodge, Margaret 259
Hollifield, Anne 388, 499, 500, 534
Horton, Bob 546
Howard, Michael 555
Howe, Geoffrey 430
Howells, Denis 213
Huckfield, Les 203
Huddlestone, Archbishop Trevor 320
Hughes, Don 10
Hughes, John 456
Hughes, Simon 211, 302
Hume, John 39
Hurd, Douglas 453
Huxtable, Chris 153

Iliescu, Ion 407
Ingham, Brian 135, 236, 238, 433
Isaac, Ian 238
Izetbegovic, Alija 523

"Jack" 549, 550
Jacques, Martin 470
Jarrett, Cynthia 273
Jarulzelski, General 173-175, 450
Jarvis, Peter 290, 434
Jenkin, Patrick 249, 260, 265
Jenkins, Roy 94, 97, 99, 113, 155, 156, 169, 187
Johansson, Arne 86
Johnson, Lyndon 25
Jolly, Steve 335
Jones, Clive 416
Jones, Doreen 298
Jones, Jack 36, 46, 47, 60, 77-79, 101, 102, 120, 320
Jones, Kathleen 409
Jones, Paul 39, 63
Jones, Roy 240
Jones, Trevor 214, 249, 298
Jordan, Bill 296
Joseph, Sir Keith 99, 131

Karadzic, Radovan 523
Kaufman, Gerald 185, 227, 336, 415
Keegan, Victor 376, 556
Kelly, Lynne 534
Kennedy, Gavin 127, 128
Kennedy, Jane 266, 468, 502
Kennedy, Wally 388, 544
Khasbulatov, Ruslan 525
Khrushchev, Nikita 24
Kidd, Frances 435
Kilfoyle, Peter 368, 369, 377, 435-437, 502
Kilroy-Silk, Robert 437
King, Anthony 299, 468
King, Cecil 37, 38
King, Rodney 478
King-Murray, Lord 461
Kinnock, Neil 149, 154, 170, 181, 200, 204, 205, 208, 220, 221, 226, 239, 240, 246, 254, 267-271, 274, 275, 279, 283-285, 288, 296, 298, 303, 312, 345, 346, 360, 361, 370, 373, 374, 415, 432, 436, 440, 442, 453, 458, 466, 471-473, 488, 491, 502, 544

Kissinger, Henry 336
Kitson, Alex 178, 200
Knibb, George 284, 475
Knights, Richie 156
Kohl, Helmut 400
Krupskaya, Natalya 425
Kydd, John 508, 533

Labi, Bob 112, 145-147, 328, 420, 447
Lamont, Norman 458
Landells, David 537
Lane, Amanda 537, 542
Lang, Ian 465
Lawrence, Stephen 512
Lawson, Nigel 274, 360
Lee, Bob 139
Lenin, Vladimir Ilyich 31, 100, 194, 323, 329, 335, 403, 413, 424, 425, 445, 450, 529
Lennard, Brian 278
Lennard, Peter 266
Lester, Joan 200, 205
Lewis, Graham 391
Lewis, Julian 135, 136
Lewis, Reg 10
Lewtas, Geoff 293
Li Peng 332-336
Lilley, Peter 555
Livingstone, Ken 203, 257, 258, 466
Lloyd, Jacquie 499
Lloyd, John 363
Loach, Ken 496
Lowes, Ian 284, 287
Loyden, Eddie 103, 111, 185
Lynch, Gerry 40

M25 Three 513
MacDonald, John 10, 11
MacGregor, Ian 228, 238, 305
MacGregor, John 431
MacMahon, Thomas 260, 288
Macpherson, Hugh 557
Macreadie, John 292, 293, 318, 325, 482
Maddox, Sam 142
Maguire, Manus 40
Mahmood, Lesley 368, 437, 438, 475
Mahmoud Masarwa 346
Major, John 470, 490, 491, 493, 521, 533, 555, 556
Makarios, Archbishop 86
Mandel, Ernest 27, 28
Mandela, Nelson 395, 397, 398, 479, 481

Mandelson, Peter 282
Mao Zedong 26, 108
Marino, Joe 133
Marlow, Tony 371
Marnoch, Lord 461
Martin, Michael 536
Marx, Karl 31, 67, 100, 306, 363, 445, 529, 539, 550, 552, 554, 557
Massie, Alan 455
Massu, General 30
Mauku, Philemon 479
Maxwell, Phil 378, 515
Maxwell, Robert 225, 371
Mayhew, Sir Patrick 274
Maynard, Joan 205, 206, 283
McAlpine, Joan 545
McAvoy, Doug 392, 393
McBain, Liz 498
McCallan, Colm 277, 278
McCartney, George 10
McCluskie, Sam 210, 322
McCombes, Alan 314, 434, 461, 495
McCormick, Paul 135, 136
McGahey, Mick 82, 83
McGinn, Janette 353
McGuire, Ann 316, 487
McKay, John 426, 457
McKenzie, Hector 317
McLaughlin, Tommy 359
McNeilage, George 460
McRoy, Rachel 375
McShane, Harry 314
McVicar, Christine 361, 485, 486, 498, 543
McVicar, Jim 314
Meacher, Michael 120
Mellish, Bob 211
Mikardo, Ian 113, 114, 199
Mikhel, Doros 86
Miles, Kevin 355
Mitchell, Austin 204
Modrow, Hanse 400
Mooney, Ted 17, 20, 136
Moore, John 319
Mordecai, John 128
Morgan, Steve 75
Morris, Bill 491, 514
Morris, Mike 437
Mortimer, Jim 204, 205, 207, 210
Mountbatten, Lord 37
Mugabe, Robert 116, 256
Mulhearn, Tony 149, 153, 204, 215, 223, 240, 248, 250, 257, 258, 270, 282-284, 287, 288, 294, 309, 322, 530
Mullen, John 459
Mullins, Bill 95, 96, 434
Mulvey, John 354
Mundin, Cyril 427
Murdie, Alan 390
Murdoch, Rupert 275, 276, 290-292, 557
Murray, Dave 426
Murray, Len 161, 225

Nally, Steve 355, 367, 373, 384, 390, 391, 428, 498-500, 534, 535
Nellist, Dave 215, 216, 218, 219, 259, 274, 285, 300, 301, 303, 331, 336, 347, 353, 419, 442-444, 456, 459, 460, 464-468, 485, 497, 504, 530
Nilson, Anton 219
Nixon, Richard 87, 88, 420
Nkomo, Joshua 116
Norman, David 185
Nourse, Mr Justice 209

O'Connell, Mike 457
O'Grady, John 211
O'Loughlin, Fiona 463
O'Neill, Terry 203
Onslow, Cranley 431
Owen, David 163, 169, 521

Paisley, Ian 39
Papandreou, Andreas 87
Parkinson, Michael 257
Parry, Alan 362
Parry, Bob 185, 269
Patten, Chris 366, 388
Peace, Chris 260
Peach, Blair 149, 150
Pearce, Terry 153
Pentonville Five 60, 61, 99
Pilger, John 484, 497, 545
Pine, Richard 300
Pinochet, General 66, 70
Plekhanov, Georgii 445
Ponting, Clive 274
Poole, Roger 359
Portillo, Michael 555
Powell, Ray 443
Pozsgay, Imre 329
Prentice, Reg 99, 100, 112, 113, 119, 120, 135, 136
Prescott, John 33, 345, 528, 544, 548

Price, Andrew 100, 199, 472
Prior, James 182
Pyatsos, Andros 86

Quddus Ali 514
Quinn, Mick 457

Rabin, Yitzhak 526
Rayner, Clare 320
Raynsford, Nick 303
Reamsbottom, Barry 482
Redwood, Helen 434
Redwood, John 555
Rees, Merlyn 131, 150
Reid, Dave 199
Reid, John 357
Remoundos, Nicos 86
Reynolds, Maureen 355
Richardson, Jo 208, 283
Ridley, Nicholas 143, 162, 228
Rimmer, Harry 435
Roberts, Michael 447
Robertson, George 282
Robinson, Derek 156, 157
Roddy, Kevin 198
Rodgers, George 96
Rodgers, William 155, 156, 169
Rodriguez, Luis (Rati) 106
Rose, Paul 84, 113
Ross, Lord 461
Rule, Bert 20
Rutskoi, Alexander 525

Saddam Hussein 363, 414-418, 423, 424
Sadler, Hayley 361
Salmond, Alex 453, 496
Sandelson, Neville 136
Sarll, Mark 285
Saunois, Tony 75, 155, 172, 328, 420, 480
Sawyer, Tom 208, 279, 306, 318
Scanlon, Hugh 36, 47, 101
Scargill, Arthur 58, 128, 133, 179, 188, 212, 224, 228, 234, 239, 240, 247, 269, 303, 318, 370, 371, 394, 443, 492, 494, 509, 510
Schlesinger, Arthur 25
Seale, Bobby 489
Sedgemore, Brian 374
Segal, Eric 426
Segal, Robbie 426
Sell, Hannah 75, 349, 361, 362, 504

Sewell, Rob 433-435, 437
Shah, Eddie 224
Sheridan, Tommy 7, 313, 344, 345, 349, 352, 354, 355, 366, 384, 389, 434, 454, 455, 458, 460, 461, 464-466, 468, 469, 474, 484-486, 498, 504, 529, 533, 544-546, 550
Shore, Cyril 121
Shore, Peter 79
Short, Clare 444
Shrewsbury Two 83, 97, 99
Shriver, Sergent 30
Silcott, George 273, 530
Silcott, Winston 273, 513, 530
Silkin, Sam 131
Sillars, Jim 315
Silverman, Roger 18, 87, 123
Sirs, Bill 225
Sisulu, Walter 397
Skinner, David 76, 80
Skinner, Denis 56, 179, 186, 208, 210, 212, 259, 283, 394, 489
Skinner, Graham 56, 57
Smith, Harry 284
Smith, John 361, 440, 488, 489, 504, 544
Smith, Joss 242
Smith, Ned 243
Soares, Mario 86, 107
Spellar, John 204, 206
Spinola, General 85, 107
Stalin, Josef 424, 425
Steel, David 128
Stephanescu, Radu 385
Stevenson, Chic 348
Stevenson, Ronnie 262, 434, 464
Stokes, John 227
Stone, Norman 403
Stowell, Ian 153
Straw, Jack 555
Sullivan, Steve 250
Symes, Jimmy 60

Taaffe, Linda 12
Taaffe, Nancy 254
Taaffe, Peter 8, 20, 21, 36, 64, 65, 100, 103, 106, 112, 123, 124, 127, 154, 186, 203, 204, 208, 219, 235, 236, 240, 249, 250, 254, 271, 294, 309, 311, 325, 328, 338, 340, 374, 420, 433, 434, 447, 448, 506, 526, 529, 538, 550
Tami, Alexander 424, 425
Tatchell, Peter 183, 211

Tebbit, Norman 182, 186, 225, 271, 299
Thatcher, Margaret 37, 72, 99, 143, 144, 151, 160, 162, 165, 175, 191, 193, 196, 224, 228, 237, 243, 244, 273-275, 306, 307, 310, 311, 319, 330, 358, 360, 383, 388, 414, 430-432, 456, 468, 521, 546, 552
Thompson, Ian 457
Thompson, Louise 543
Thomson, Roy 38
Thorne, Stan 103
Thornton, Sara 461
Thraves, Alec 199, 314
Throne, John 40
Tice, Alistair 227
Tisdall, Sarah 274
Tito, Josef 26
Tocher, John 280
Todd, Ron 298
Tomlinson, Ricky 83
Tomney, Frank 13, 119, 124
Trotsky, Leon 9, 12, 24, 87, 100, 109, 169, 194, 195, 271, 324, 325, 327, 329, 330, 362, 403, 421, 424, 445, 449, 451, 452, 460, 476, 478, 529, 539
Tudjman, Franjo 523

Underhill, Reg 112-114, 127
Ursell, Anne 457

Varley, Cheryl 287
Venton, Richie 156, 287, 434
Viner, John 373
Volkov, Esteban, 325
Volkov, Veronika 325

Waddington, Mike 433
Waldegrave, William 407
Walden, Brian 360
Walesa, Lech 174
Walker, Harold 227
Walker, Sandra 529
Wall, Pat 10, 71, 127, 185-187, 198, 203, 205, 215, 284, 285, 300, 301, 304, 305, 331, 393, 426
Wall, Pauline (née Knight) 10, 187
Walsh, Andy 457
Walsh, Daniel 226
Walsh, Lynn 12, 18, 85, 208, 210, 226, 249, 328, 338, 340, 420, 424, 433, 447, 448, 480
Ward, George 130

Wareing, Bob 185
Warren, Des 83
Waterson, Julie 518
Webb, Dave 356
Webster, Bill 40, 172
Webster, Martin 73
Wedlake, Tony 260
Weighell, Sidney 198
White, Audrey 217, 218
White, David 149
White, James 212
Whitty, Larry 284, 504
Williams, Emlyn 115
Williams, Shirley 99, 122, 127, 152, 169
Willis, Norman 320, 352, 386
Wilsman, Pete 149
Wilson, Brian 316
Wilson, Cathy 149
Wilson, Harold 18, 33, 37, 75, 92, 103, 111, 116, 118, 123, 124
Winders, Fiona 153
Windsor, Rob 528
Winter, Mark 457
Wise, Audrey 208, 281
Woods, Alan 18, 106, 328, 338, 339, 341, 422, 435, 447, 449, 450
Wrack, Nick 433, 531
Wray, Jimmy 262
Wright, Bob 203
Wright, Bryan 432
Wyatt, Woodrow 10

Yanayev, Gennady 450
Yeltsin, Boris 330, 411, 450, 451, 524

Zhao Ziyang 332, 333

MILITANT LABOUR (ML) is organised in all towns in Britain. We also have groups in the trade unions. Additionally there are Militant Student societies, the ML lesbian, gay and bi-sexual group and the ML disabled persons action group. If interested in any of these phone us on 0181-533 3311.

Militant Labour is affiliated to the Committee for a Workers International who can be contacted on the same number or on e-mail: inter@ital.demon.co.uk.